Clinical Research in Communication Disorders

PRINCIPLES AND STRATEGIES

Fourth Edition

Clinical Research in Communication Disorders

PRINCIPLES AND STRATEGIES

Fourth Edition

M. N. Hegde, PhD
Anthony P. Salvatore, PhD

5521 Ruffin Road
San Diego, CA 92123

e-mail: information@pluralpublishing.com
Website: http://www.pluralpublishing.com

Library of Congress Cataloging-in-Publication Data:
Names: Hegde, M. N. (Mahabalagiri N.), 1941- author. | Salvatore, Anthony P., author.
Title: Clinical research in communication disorders: principles and strategies / M.N.
    Hegde, Anthony P. Salvatore.
Other titles: Clinical research in communicative disorders
Description: Fourth edition. | San Diego, CA : Plural Publishing, [2021] | Preceded by
    Clinical research in communicative disorders : principles and strategies / M.N. Hegde.
    3rd ed. c2003. | Includes bibliographical references and index.
Identifiers: LCCN 2019000565| ISBN 9781635501872 (alk. paper) | ISBN 1635501873
    (alk. paper)
Subjects: | MESH: Communication Disorders | Research Design | Medical Writing
Classification: LCC RC428 | NLM WM 475 | DDC 616.85/50072--dc23
LC record available at https://lccn.loc.gov/2019000565

Contents

Preface to the First Edition   *xi*
Preface to the Fourth Edition   *xiii*

PART I. Science and the Scientific Methods   1

1 Why Study Science and Research Methods?   3

Evaluation of Research   4
The Need to Study Scientific Methods   5
The Need to Produce In-House Knowledge   8
Why Research by Clinicians Is Limited   9
Problems Associated With Certain Research Practices   10
Problems Associated With the Education and Training Models   13
Summary   16
References   16
Study Guide   16

2 An Introduction to Research: The Formal and Formative Approaches   19

What Is Research?   21
Why Do Scientists Do Research?   21
How Is Research Done?   28
Serendipity in Research   34
Planning Is Still Important   37
Summary   37
References   38
Study Guide   38

3 Science and Its Basic Concepts   39

What Is Science?   40
Outcome of Scientific Activity   44
Variables and Their Types   45
Causality and Functional Analysis   50
Experiment and Experimental Control   53
Hypotheses in Scientific Research   54
Theories and Hypotheses   57
Inductive and Deductive Reasoning   58
Theories and Scientific Laws   61
Data and Evidence   62

v

Summary   63
References   64
Study Guide   65

4 Treatment Research   67
Evidence-Based Practice   68
What Is Treatment Research?   68
Consequences of Treatment   69
Treatment Research: Logical and Empirical Constraints   74
Group Treatment Research: Randomized Clinical Trials   77
Single-Subject Treatment Research: Multiple Control Conditions   87
Randomized Clinical Trials Versus Single-Subject Treatment Research   106
Classification of Treatment Research   113
Summary   119
References   120
Study Guide   122

5 Other Types of Research   123
Ex Post Facto Research   124
Normative Research   127
Standard-Group Comparisons   131
Experimental Research   133
Clinical and Applied Research   138
Translational Research   142
Sample Surveys   144
Qualitative Research   146
Mixed-Methods Research   150
The Relation Between Research Types and Questions   151
Summary   152
References   153
Study Guide   154

6 Observation and Measurement   157
Observation and Measurement   158
Philosophies of Measurement   158
Scales of Measurement   160
Measures of Communicative Behaviors   162
Client-Assisted Measurement   169
Indirect Measures: Self-Reports   170
The Observer in the Measurement Process   171
Mechanically Assisted Observation and Measurement   174
Reliability of Measurement   175
Summary   178
References   179
Study Guide   180

PART II. Clinical Research Designs

PART II. Clinical Research Designs   **183**

7 Research Designs: An Introduction   **185**
What Are Research Designs?   186
The Structure and Logic of Experimental Designs   187
Variability: Philosophical Considerations   188
Experimental Designs: Means of Controlling Variability   192
Validity of Experimental Operations   193
Generality (External Validity)   201
Factors That Affect Generality   210
Concluding Remarks   212
Summary   213
References   214
Study Guide   215

8 The Group Design Strategy   **217**
Common Characteristics of Group Designs   218
Preexperimental Designs   219
True Experimental Designs   223
Designs to Evaluate Multiple Treatments   228
Factorial Designs   231
Quasi-Experimental Designs   236
Time-Series Designs   240
Counterbalanced Within-Subjects Designs   246
Correlational Analysis   253
Group Designs in Clinical Research   255
Summary   259
References   261
Study Guide   262

9 Single-Subject Designs   **265**
Historical Background to Single-Subject Designs   266
Characteristics of Single-Subject Designs   270
Experimental Control in Single-Subject Designs   274
Preexperimental Single-Subject Design   275
Designs for Single Treatment Evaluation   276
Designs for Multiple Treatment Comparison   290
Designs for Interactional Studies   299
N-of-1 Randomized Clinical Trials   302
Single-Subject Designs in Clinical Research   303
Summary   304
References   306
Study Guide   308

10 Statistical Analysis of Research Data — 311

Historical Introduction to Statistical Analysis of Research Data — 312
Statistical Significance — 316
Hypothesis Testing — 317
Statistical Analysis of Group Design Data — 318
Systematic Reviews and Meta-Analyses — 323
Visual Analysis of Single-Subject Data — 326
Statistical Analysis of Single-Subject Data — 328
Statistical Significance Versus Clinical Significance — 333
Summary — 338
References — 339
Study Guide — 342

11 Generality Through Replications — 343

Direct Replication — 344
Systematic Replication — 347
Sample Size and Generality — 351
Failed Replications: Sources of Treatment Modifications — 353
Homogeneity and Heterogeneity of Participants — 355
Summary — 357
References — 358
Study Guide — 359

12 Comparative Evaluation of Design Strategies — 361

Research Questions and Investigative Strategies — 362
Advantages and Disadvantages of Design Strategies — 369
Problems Common to Design Strategies — 371
Philosophical Considerations in Evaluation — 372
The Investigator in Design Selection — 373
The Final Criterion: Soundness of Data — 373
Summary — 374
References — 377
Study Guide — 377

13 Designs Versus Paradigms in Research — 379

Limitations of Exclusively Methodological Approaches — 380
Research Methods and Subject Matters — 380
Philosophy as Methodology — 382
Philosophy of Subject Matters — 382
Philosophy of the Science of Speech and Language — 384
Philosophical Ways of Handling Methodological Problems — 393
The Interplay Between Philosophy and Methodology — 396
Summary — 397
References — 397
Study Guide — 398

PART III. Doing, Reporting, and Evaluating Research 399

14 How to Formulate Research Questions 401

How to Formulate Research Questions 402
Preparation of Theses and Dissertations 413
Summary 414
References 415
Study Guide 415

15 How to Write Research Reports 417

General Format of Scientific Reports 418
Structure and Content of Research Papers 419
Writing Without Bias 427
Good Writing: Some Principles 428
Writing Style 446
Writing and Revising 447
Summary 448
References 448
Study Guide 449

16 How to Evaluate Research Reports 451

Professionals as Consumers of Research 452
Understanding and Evaluating Research 452
Evaluation of Research 453
Evaluation of Research Reports: An Outline 458
A Hierarchy of Treatment Research Evidence 463
Evaluation and Appreciation of Research 467
Summary 468
References 468
Study Guide 469

17 Ethics of Research 471

Fraud in Scientific Research 472
Ethical Justification for Treatment Evaluation 476
The Protection of Human Participants in Research 479
Ethical Issues With Treatment Research 485
Consequences of Ethical Constraints 492
Protection of Animal Subjects 495
Dissemination of Research Findings 496
Summary 497
References 497
Study Guide 500

Index *503*

Preface to the First Edition

I am a student and an instructor of philosophy and methodology of science and research. In my teaching of science and research, I have found it necessary to supplement information from a variety of sources. I knew that several of my colleagues who taught courses on research and science were doing the same to make their courses more relevant and useful to graduate students. To me, this meant that we did not have a comprehensive textbook on science and research. This book is an effort to fulfill that need.

My own teaching experience and discussions with many of my colleagues suggested that a book on science and research should address the following concerns. The first deals with the basic concepts of science and scientific methods. That is, the book should point out the need to study science and research methods and summarize the basic concepts of science and research. It should describe the true and lively process of research, not an idealized and frighteningly formalized process that typically discourages the beginning student from a further study of science and research. The book should give an adequate description of the different kinds of research that are conducted in communication disorders. A discussion of observation and measurement, which are the basic tools of science, must be provided.

The second concern is clinical research designs. Most books on research designs tend to be statistically oriented. The enormously prestigious analysis of variance is constantly confused with experimental designs. A book on designs should present experimental designs, not methods of data analysis under the guise of research designs. Furthermore, the book should address both group and single-subject designs. Generally speaking, most books that offer information on research designs focus almost exclusively on group designs. Clinically more relevant single-subject designs are not well represented in those books. On the other hand, there are some books that focus exclusively on single-subject designs. There are not many books that present adequate information on both design strategies. Regardless of one's own methodologic preference and practice, a critical user and producer of research must have a knowledge of group as well as single-subject design approaches. It was thought that a single source that offered descriptions and comparative evaluations of both strategies would be useful to students and researchers alike.

The third concern is the discussion of some important philosophic issues that are an inexorable part of science and research. Research is based on methodology as well as philosophy. There is a tremendous lack of appreciation of the philosophic bases of research. Therefore, it was thought that this book should at least raise the issue of philosophy of research to stimulate further discussion in the discipline.

The fourth concern is the practical aspect of performing, writing, reporting, and evaluating research. Students need suggestions on where to find research questions, how to find current research trends, how to search the literature, how to refine research questions, and how to select designs that help answer those questions. They also need information on how to get started on theses and dissertations. A major problem instructors and students alike face is writing style and writing skills. It was thought that this book should offer basic information on principles of good writing.

The fifth concern is the ethics of research. Science and research are an ethical activity. From the beginning, science and research must be taught with due regard for the ethical principles that restrain research. A textbook on research should summarize ethical principles that govern research activities.

I have written this book with those five concerns as the guiding principles. An overall concern was to make a book on science and research especially relevant to clinical research in communication disorders and write it in a less formal, and I would hope, more readable style. It is thought that such a style would also reflect the process of research more accurately than the typical style that formalizes research to an unnatural extent.

My wife Prema and my son Manu have been a part of all of my writings. This book, which I began to write soon after completing *Treatment Procedures in Communicative Disorders,* would not have been finished without their full support.

I thank all of my former students at both the undergraduate and graduate levels who have been generous in their support and encouragement. My students have always tolerated and often appreciated my unlimited passion to teach science and research anytime and anywhere. Many students in my graduate seminar on research methods have offered excellent comments on earlier versions of several chapters in this book.

Preface to the Fourth Edition

Since its first publication in 1987, many instructors have adopted this book as the main text in various courses on research methods and designs in communication disorders. Most of these instructors have offered their gracious and positive comments on the book. The instructors have suggested that the comprehensive treatment of issues and methods of research is a strength of this book. The new fourth edition retains that strength.

I am glad to have Dr. Anthony Salvatore of the University of Louisiana at Lafayette as my coauthor of this fourth edition, published after 30 years of its first edition. Together we have extensively revised and updated each chapter. In the chapter on research ethics, we have included web-based sources that monitor research fraud and recalled studies.

The chapter on writing and reporting research papers includes the reporting standards for experimental studies, qualitative research, and meta-analyses published by various organizations.

The chapter on types of research includes new sections on translational research, qualitative research, and mixed-methods research. A critical and comparative analysis of these types of research has been included.

The new edition contains a new chapter on statistical analysis of research data. This chapter covers quantitative analysis of both group- and single-subject study results. We have outlined both parametric and nonparametric tests for analyzing research data. In addition, the chapter covers such contemporary topics as narrative reviews, systematic reviews, and meta-analyses of both group- and single-subject design data.

The sections on single-subject research analysis includes guidelines on visual analysis and assessment of quality indicators. We have reviewed the effect size statistics for single-subject data and have included nonoverlap techniques and d-statics.

Finally, the new chapter contains a discussion of statistical versus clinical significance of treatment research evidence. We have given an overview of quantitative and qualitative measures of clinical significance.

The widespread use of this book as a text in classrooms over 30 years across the country and beyond has strengthened our belief that instructors of research designs in communication disorders would welcome a text that represents both the single-subject and group design strategies along with issues of measurement; philosophy of science; ethics of research; and planning, conducting, and reporting research. We wish to express our appreciation to all those instructors who have found this book an effective teaching device and have taken time to offer their thoughtful comments.

—M. N. H.

PART I

Science and the Scientific Methods

1

Why Study Science and Research Methods?

Chapter Outline

◆ Evaluation of Research

◆ The Need to Study Scientific Methods

◆ The Need to Produce In-House Knowledge

◆ Why Research by Clinicians Is Limited

◆ Problems Associated With Certain Research Practices

◆ Problems Associated With the Education and Training Models

◆ Summary

◆ References

◆ Study Guide

Communication disorders is both an academic discipline and a clinical profession. As an academic discipline, communication disorders seeks to study and understand normal and disordered communication. As a clinical profession, it is concerned with the methods of assessing and treating various disorders of hearing, speech, language, voice, and fluency. An academic discipline can research practical problems without applying the information it generates. For example, a biochemist who develops a new drug that can be used in treating a particular disease may not treat patients with that disease. In communication disorders, researchers who develop new information or technology also may apply that information in the treatment of disordered communication. In this sense, communication disorders is simultaneously concerned with both scientific and professional matters.

As the discipline of communication disorders emerged and developed, the professional aspects, rather than the scientific bases, received greater attention. This is understandable because the starting point of the discipline was a professional concern to understand and treat speech problems, especially stuttering and speech sound disorders. The profession had to begin providing clinical services without the benefit of a history of controlled experimental research to support clinical practice. Borrowing from several basic and applied disciplines, the speech-language pathologist of earlier days began to treat communication disorders. Historically, the emphasis has been on expanding clinical services rather than conducting experimental research to produce a scientific basis for those clinical services.

An unfortunate historical lesson of many human service professions, includ-ing that of communication disorders, is that clinical services can continue to be offered without a strong experimental database. Such services may be supported by subjectively solidified clinical experience, uncontrolled observations, anecdotes widely circulated by "authorities" in the field, descriptive research, and speculative theories. Systematic experimental evaluation of treatment techniques may be lacking. As a result, clinical services the profession offers may not be based on controlled research evidence. However, this may not deter a profession from offering services, partly because of practical exigencies and partly because something better is not available.

The problem with such a history is that the clinical practice does not change quickly when experimental research information begins to flow. The clinical practice of established clinicians may continue to be based on old and unverified assumptions. Typically, it takes several years to affect clinical practice on a wide scale because the research information must be incorporated into the training of new clinicians.

Evaluation of Research

Evaluation of old and new research is about as important as the creation of new in-house knowledge. Professionals who cannot evaluate research data and theories also cannot make effective use of information. Critical evaluation of research should be a part of the clinician's repertoire, and such an evaluation requires the same knowledge needed to do meaningful research.

The process of evaluating research data follows the same logical steps as the process of designing experiments. Therefore, evaluation of research is possible only when clinicians understand how research is done. Clinicians who are not knowledgeable in science and methods of investigation in their field of study are likely to have difficulty in judging the relevance of the questions their colleagues research, the validity and reliability of observations, the relation between results and conclusions, the transition from evidence to theory, and the distinction between theory and speculation.

Furthermore, clinicians who are not sophisticated in the philosophy of science may not see logical and empirical mistakes in study designs. In such cases, clinicians who read research uncritically accept the author's interpretations. However, bad interpretations are about as prevalent as bad designs, and clinicians who cannot detect inconsistent relations between interpretations and results cannot separate data from conclusions. Data that are based on sound methods are always more valuable and durable than the author's interpretations imposed on them. Future clinicians and researchers may keep the sound data while rejecting faulty interpretations.

Even when many practitioners do treatment-related research, a majority of clinicians will read research papers mostly to improve their practice. The popular phrase "clinicians are consumers of research" has a ring of validity in that most clinicians will be users, not producers, of research. It is well known that naive consumers are victims of bad products. Similarly, clinicians who are naive in the methods and philosophy of science are likely victims of bad research; unfortunately, in a clinical science such as communicative disorders, individuals who receive services also become victims.

It is thus clear that clinicians who do not do research still need to understand science and research methods. Even if there is much research that cannot be applied, clinicians will have to keep reading and evaluating research because that is the only way they can find out what is useful and what is not. Those who avoid reading the research literature because some of it is irrelevant to clinical practice are sure also to miss what is relevant to them. Meanwhile, when research practices improve, and clinically relevant studies begin to be routinely published, clinicians will be unaware of them and unprepared to apply them in their practice. For detailed information on evaluating research, see Chapter 15.

The Need to Study Scientific Methods

It is now widely recognized that communication disorders needs to strengthen the scientific bases of its clinical practice. The need to place our clinical practice on an experimental foundation is growing because of many legal, social, professional, and scientific reasons.

Legal and Social Considerations

An increasing number of federal and state laws influence professional practices in communication disorders. A major source of influence is a set of federal laws related to the education of children with disabilities. The original Education for all Handicapped Children Act of 1977 (P.L. 94-142) had a significant effect on public school special education services, including those of communication disorders. The law was amended in 1986, retitled Individuals With Disabilities Education Act (P.L. 101-476) in 1990 and reauthorized periodically. The latest reauthorization was in 2004 and ammended in 2015. (Many federal laws are periodically reauthorized and amended to address new concerns; therefore, the reader should consult the latest versions of the laws of interest.)

Some of the most significant requirements under these laws are that special education services must be oriented to the individual child and his or her family and the service programs must have specific procedures, objectives, and evaluative criteria. The laws place considerable emphasis on clinician accountability in that the effects of treatment programs must be documented objectively so that they can be verified by independent observers. Such documentation requires that changes in student (client) behaviors be measured systematically and continuously. As we shall see shortly, these and other mandates of the laws are in harmony with the principles of scientific clinical practice.

Other kinds of legal concerns necessitate a more objective and scientific clinical practice. Third-party payment for clinical speech, language, and hearing services is common now. Various government agencies and private insurance firms that pay for the services demand more and more systematic documentation of the need, the procedures, and the outcome of such services. Uniform and objective means of evaluating treatment effects are being encouraged by agencies that pay for services.

Many social concerns are also leading us in the direction of clinical practice based on scientific methods. The profession continues to take steps to increase public awareness of speech and language problems and the services that are available to individuals with those problems. Consequently, an increasing number of individuals and families are seeking and paying for services in private clinics and hospitals. At the same time, many people who are seeking services are also inclined to question the effectiveness of those services. Inevitably, widespread social awareness of speech, language, and hearing problems combined with higher demands for services and increasing cost of service delivery will result in a thorough scrutiny of professional practices.

Professional and Scientific Considerations

Regardless of the legal and social requirements, there are professional reasons for developing a scientifically sound clinical discipline. Much concern surrounds the professional standing of communication disorders in the community of clinical professions and scientific disciplines. There is a growing concern that the profession of communication disorders does not have high social visibility. The profession may not be well recognized by other established or recently developed professions, such as medicine or clinical psychology.

A profession can try to draw attention to itself by various means. It may seek better legal recognition and protection by more effective lobbying efforts. Extensive public relations and public awareness campaigns may be launched. Services may be more aggressively publicized through advertisements in local and national media. Since all professions have a business side, most of these efforts are fiscally necessary. Indeed, all professions find it necessary to market their services ethically. Such efforts may yield somewhat quick results; however, to build a lasting and more solid reputation, the profession, in addition to taking all those steps, must put its practice on a scientific footing. In the long run, no amount of public relations campaign can compensate for questionable and subjectively evaluated clinical practice. In fact, public awareness—which is generally beneficial—can expose the inherent and widespread weaknesses of a profession.

Scientifically based and technologically competent professions enjoy good reputations and higher visibility. A profession can make significant progress when its concepts are scientific and its methods are evaluated objectively. The ideal to strive for is a solid scientific discipline and a clinical profession with a single identity. This ideal, when achieved, will help ensure the quality of speech and hearing services offered to persons with communication disorders.

The typical argument supporting a more scientific orientation is made on the basis of the legal, social, and professional requirements described so far. Such requirements are compelling, and anything that forces a more scientific orientation is welcome. However, a profession need not be driven entirely by such requirements. Professionals need not face legal, social, and professional image-oriented reasons and requirements to strive to be more scientific. Although the statement may sound tautological, science itself is a good reason to be scientific. The logical beauty, methodological elegance, and practical benefits of science antecede legal, social, and professional pressures.

Had the profession heeded the call of science from its inception, it is possible that most of the legal and social pressures would have become superflu-

ous. Clinicians who by training and practice follow the methods of science do not need a push from public laws to write treatment targets in measurable terms. For such clinicians, the requirement that changes in client behaviors must be documented objectively will not come as news or as a legal nuisance. Their personal history of training and education will suffice for such purposes. Surely, social and legal demands can force clinicians to be systematic and objective in their clinical work, but those with a strong scientific background are inclined to be so regardless of such demands. Concerns regarding bad professional image may not necessarily drive clinicians to conduct or evaluate controlled treatment research. Well-trained clinicians have better reasons, including science itself. Scientifically competent clinicians are unlikely to be overly concerned with image; nevertheless, they are probably better for the profession's image than those who are concerned with public reactions but continue to offer questionable services.

These comments should not be construed as a negative evaluation of legal, social, and professional reasons to be more scientific. In fact, governments, social groups, and professional bodies have an obligation to protect the rights of people who seek and then financially support professional services. Societal and regulatory forces are necessary for smooth and socially beneficial operations of professions as well as sciences. Such regulatory forces have helped all professions and sciences move in the right direction, as we shall see in Chapter 17. The comments are meant to underscore an additional and often neglected reason to be more systematic, responsible, and objective in clinical work: the philosophy and methodology of science that are capable of providing unsurpassed safeguards for both the profession and the public. Besides, science provides an unlimited and exciting opportunity to make significant advances in all areas of professional endeavor.

The Need to Produce In-House Knowledge

During the time when service delivery, not scientific research, is the urgent business, the profession is dependent on other disciplines for a knowledge base. Communication disorders historically has depended on some nonclinical disciplines such as linguistics, experimental psychology, and child psychology. It also has depended on clinical professions such as medicine and basic sciences such as physiology and physics.

Communication disorders has been a borrower for a long time, perhaps too much of a borrower and too little of an innovator. It borrowed not only basic or applied information but also conceptual frameworks, theories, paradigms, models, and methods of investigation and data analysis. Therefore, the slowly developing traditions of research in communication disorders have been extensively influenced by other disciplines that have offered methods and theories of varying degrees of validity, reliability, relevancy, and applicability.

It is true that certain scientific approaches, concepts, and methods are common to many scientific disciplines and professions. Nonetheless, unless a discipline quickly begins to produce its own experimental database, it will continue to borrow theories and methods that may or may not be appropriate for studying its subject matter. The only way some pro-

fessions can begin to generate their own databases is to train their practitioners to do research. Professions such as medicine have the luxury of receiving a large and varied amount of custom-produced research information from outside their professions. Medicine has chemists, biochemists, physiologists, anatomists, biologists, geneticists, bioengineers, and a variety of technologists and technical product manufacturers (including global pharmaceutical companies) who do research dedicated to medicine and supply theoretical information and practical technology. There are not comparable bands of researchers and technicians supplying information and technology to communication disorders. Much of the information and technology the discipline borrows is not produced for it; its relevance may be incidental and, in some unfortunate cases, mistaken.

Specialists in communication disorders should produce their own knowledge base and technology, but this does not mean that they should not selectively borrow from other disciplines. Like other professions, communication disorders will continue to borrow what is relevant and useful. Many fields of knowledge are interrelated. Therefore, the fields benefit from each other's research. Nonetheless, what is urgently needed is a systematic effort to increase the in-house knowledge base and technology. A discipline cannot always expect other specialists to produce the basic scientific information necessary to understand its subject matter. A profession cannot always expect others to produce a relevant and effective technology.

The most significant problem with increasing the amount of in-house knowledge is the scarcity of research institutions and sustained research programs in communication disorders. Many university programs in communication disorders are not research oriented, and large institutions that specialize in research are few or nonexistent. Producing a systematic body of reliable and valid scientific information is a slow process even under the best possible conditions. Therefore, under the existing conditions, the accumulation of valid knowledge in communication disorders will be a prolonged process. There seems to be no easy or quick solution to this problem. Several steps are necessary to increase the amount of research; for example, the discipline can seek more government and private research funds, increase the number of theses produced by master's degree candidates, accelerate research efforts at existing research and teaching institutions, and establish new programmatic research.

Another tactic is to recruit practitioners into the kind of research that does not detract from clinical activities. That is, the field can make an effort to increase research by practicing clinicians. Since the majority of persons in the field are clinicians, even a slight increase in the number of clinicians doing research may have an appreciable effect. This is the kind of in-house knowledge base that can have immediate and simultaneous clinical and theoretical significance.

Why Research by Clinicians Is Limited

It is well known that a majority of clinicians do not do research. After all, they are busy serving their clients. There are many reasons why clinicians typically do not engage in research. For example, most clinicians do not have the needed extra time for research. Besides, when research

is thought of as something unrelated to clinical service, the clinicians obviously cannot do research. Also, the client scheduling may be good for clinical work but bad for research; when clients are seen twice weekly for a few minutes each time, collecting in-depth data may be difficult.

Most clinical settings do not support or encourage research. Many public schools and hospitals do not require research from clinicians and may not encourage it. Much research, both good and bad, is done when research is required or valued in a given setting. It also may be noted that bad research can be done even when someone "wanted" to do research while it was not required to achieve promotions or pay raises. In many settings, research often is done over and above one's regular duties. When it is not required for professional advancement, the administration is unlikely to support research to any great extent.

It also is possible that clinicians themselves assume that: (a) they are not well prepared to do research and (b) research does not necessarily help them, their colleagues, or their clients. Both of these assumptions may be valid to a degree. The first assumption may be due to many practitioners' limited training and experience in research methods. To do research, one should also maintain currency in the slowly-but-surely changing field of knowledge in the discipline. The pressures of day-to-day professional practice may not be conducive to spending the needed amount of time and energy on reading the literature. Though significant advances in communication disorders have been few and far between, there has been an information explosion in recent years. It takes time just to keep up with published research. Because they do not have this time, many clinicians may think that they lack the technical knowledge of scientific procedures and current information needed to do research.

The second assumption—that research does not necessarily help clinical practice —may be based on experience. There is some question regarding the extent to which research affects day- to-day clinical practice. Douglas, Campbell, and Hinckley (2015) stated that a treatment procedure that has support based on 20 years of research may still remain unused by the clinicians. With all the emphasis on evidence-based practice, there is no evidence to support that a majority of clinicians use treatment procedures that are known to be effective. In treating clients, clinicians are likely to depend upon their past training and clinical experience. Practitioners across professional settings do not automatically apply experimentally but unsupported theories, and recent trends without substance have a greater influence on clinical practice than do technical research reports.

Workshops, presentations, discussions with colleagues, and lectures on the "latest" techniques and "hot topics" may affect clinical practice more than experimental evidence does. However, even those who give frequent workshops often think that clinicians rarely apply exactly what the workshops offered. For example, some individuals who frequently attend workshops agree equally well with totally contradictory approaches, and clinicians assimilate what they hear (or read) with their past experience and apply new techniques in modified ways. Such modifications are not necessarily bad. The only problem is that unspecified and varied modifications of published techniques make it difficult to identify successful techniques. In any case, the disturbing situation remains: Controlled and techni-

cal research does not affect clinical practice to the extent it should.

The belief that research does not necessarily help clinical practice is partially true. We are *not* just referring to basic research, which is not expected to give immediate solutions to practical problems; we are referring to the kinds of research that are expected to solve clinical problems. Purported clinical research on assessment or treatment of communication disorders also may frustrate clinicians. Clinicians who read and evaluate such research to sharpen their clinical skills may be disillusioned about the usefulness of all kinds of clinical research. In essence, certain research practices may generate a justifiable skepticism regarding the relevance of research to clinical practice.

Problems Associated With Certain Research Practices

There are multiple modes of clinical research, and not all of them are equally helpful to the clinician in solving current practical problems. In Chapters 4 and 5, we will describe different types of research in some detail. Here it may be noted that clinical-experimental research is likely to produce results that help solve immediate practical problems clinicians face. Many other types of research, although essential, may lead to solutions to practical problems but only in the future.

Clinical usefulness is not the only criterion by which the value of research is determined. Basic research often does not have immediate practical significance. However, it is valuable because it might help explain a phenomenon, put unrelated observations in a single perspective, suggest new lines of experimental analysis, or produce a discovery with powerful applied potential. Thus, in the long run, basic research may produce data that can help solve practical problems. Every discipline needs basic research: Communication disorders simply does not have enough of it.

The main problem with current research practices is that much of the research is neither basic nor experimentally clinical. Basic research can help secure the future of a discipline while experimental-clinical research can help solve current practical problems. Basic research creates a strong scientific base for a profession and experimental-clinical research helps develop treatment techniques. When these two kinds of research are sparse, the profession can neither solve its clinical problems nor generate confidence that the problems will be solved in the near future. In such a situation, skepticism regarding research is inevitable.

The clinical irrelevancy of *clinical research* is not the only reason why some clinicians have a negative approach to research in general; other factors contribute. First, if clinicians do not appreciate basic research, they may have received inadequate education and training in the philosophy and methodology of science. Second, if clinicians do not appreciate experimental-clinical research that shows better methods of treating disorders of communication, their education, again, may be to blame. A majority of clinicians neither use experimentally verified techniques nor demand such techniques from researchers. Third, if clinicians do not find a significant body of clinical research that can be applied in clinical work, then the research practices within the field must take the blame.

Education and training programs must address the first two factors, and research

scientists and clinicians must address the third. To assess these problems, we must consider the type and quality of clinical research and the education and training of clinicians.

Possibly, clinicians who can evaluate current clinical research find very little that is applicable. This is because much research in the field is not concerned with experimental evaluation and development of treatment procedures. Even clinical journals, expected to publish treatment research, may disappoint clinicians. A majority of papers published in journals in speech and hearing relate to disorder description, normative comparison, and assessment, not treatment. There is plenty of speculative theoretical writing in the discipline, and much of the research is concerned with finding differences between *normal* and *disordered* groups of subjects. For example, many studies attempt to establish norms of various communicative behaviors. In addition, classifying speech and language behaviors with no regard to their causal variables (structural analysis of language and speech) is very popular. This kind of research is typically justified because of its presumed clinical implications, but the research does not necessarily provide for more effective treatment procedures. Some clinicians who begin to read research reports of this kind may eventually stop reading them. Such clinicians decide to wait until the presumed implications are translated into procedures they can use.

A dominant research trend in communication disorders is that many who suggest clinical implications of their nonclinical research do not take time to test those implications with individuals with disorders. Many research specialists in communication disorders seem to imply that to hypothesize is their job, but to verify is someone else's. Many researchers betray a striking lack of curiosity about the clinical validity of their own hypotheses. Consequently, they have created a new division of labor: Some researchers generate hypotheses and other researchers verify them. Unfortunately, this division of labor has not worked well because many researchers are more interested in generating hypotheses than in verifying their own or anybody else's.

If studies of a different kind were to be frequently published in journals devoted to clinical practice, clinicians may find research to be valuable. This kind of research is experimental *and* clinical. Applied behavior analysis offers a clear model for this kind of research. Most of the articles published in the *Journal of Applied Behavior Analysis* are both experimental and clinical in that they report on behavioral treatment efects. Research of this kind addresses issues of immediate practical significance. The strategy involves current clinical action, not a promise of some future clinical possibility. For example, research may be concerned with topics such as different target behaviors and their clinical relevance, experimental evaluation of treatment techniques, relative effects of multiple treatments, interaction between different treatment procedures, generality of treatment effects to clients of different ethnocultural backgrounds, different tactics of response maintenance after treatment, issues in the measurement or assessment of disorders and behaviors, and independent variables that may maintain normal as well as disordered speech and language behaviors, just to sample a few. These kinds of research topics generate data of immediate clinical significance. More important, efforts to investigate these topics are identical with clinical services.

The type of research in which the relevance of alternate target communicative behaviors and the techniques of teaching them are evaluated under controlled conditions will help illustrate how research and clinical practice may be integrated. Research on the relevance of targeted behaviors for clinical intervention is barely begun. This is the question of dependent variables; it often is thought that the only significant question is that of the independent variable. In other words, professionals may think that they know what the targets are, but they do not know how to teach them. Both are important questions, however. For example, the following terms relative to language disorders are not operational in nature and thus they do not refer to measurable behaviors, which is necessay to change them: communicative competence, knowledge of the universal transformational grammar, grammatical features, grammatical rules, semantic notions, semantic rules, pragmatic notions, or pragmatic rules. Empirical response classes, on the other hand, are observable, measurable, and experimentally manipulable. Similarly, what is (are) the dependent variable(s) in the treatment of stuttering: self-confidence, self-image, approach-avoidance conflict, anxiety reduction, correction of feedback problems, appropriate airflow, correct phonatory behaviors, fluent stuttering, negative attitudes, excessive parental concern for fluency, reduction in speech rate, or reduction in the dysfluency rates? Again, what are the dependent variables in the treatment of speech sound disorders: phonological processes or patterns, phonological knowledge, or phonemic awareness? These terms do not describe the behavior that index speech sound production or the potential controlling variables. A more transparent term, speech sound production, describes empirical treatment targets.

Specification of a valid dependent variable is crucial to the development of a science. If biologists were as confused about their dependent variables as communication disorders specialists are about theirs, biology's progress to date would be unthinkable. Because communication disorders is a clinical science, it needs clearly defined dependent variables (communicative behaviors) that may be changed through manipulation of independent variables (treatment techniques). Therefore, it is essential to conduct research on the valid dependent variables that can be successfully taught to individuals with communication problems. Besides, in the course of this kind of research, the clinician simultaneously provides clinical services.

Research on the effects of various treatment strategies also is synchronous with clinical service. The value of treatment research in communication disorders is obvious but often is taken for granted. When a clinical researcher evaluates a given treatment in a controlled experiment, the clients who serve as subjects are exposed to one possible treatment. If the treatment is not effective, the clinician may evaluate another technique that may prove to be more successful. In more advanced stages of research, the clinician may evaluate the relative and interactive effects of more than one treatment technique or component. The participants of treatment research studies are the clients who receive treatment during the course of research.

The paucity of treatment-related research in communication disorders supports the notion that research and clinical services are unrelated and that training in research methods and philosophy of science is a waste of time. Contrary to this notion, research and clinical activities are more similar than different. Although done under routine conditions, each successful clinical session involves a manipulation of an independent variable (treatment) just like it is done in an experiment. Basically, treatments are a manipulation of cause-effect relations. In treating clients, clinicians produce changes in communicative behaviors by rearranging certain variables (Hegde, 1998).

What is suggested here is that treatment-related research should make research immediately attractive to the practitioners, so that the practitioners may more likely read, evaluate, and appreciate research. It is *not* suggested that basic research unrelated to immediate clinical concerns is less valuable or that there is no reason for clinicians to study basic research reports. Clinicians who do not understand or appreciate treatment research are less likely to understand or appreciate basic laboratory research. Therefore, one way of attracting clinicians to research of all kinds is to offer them treatment-related research that can make a difference in their day-to-day professional activities. Skills necessary to understand and evaluate treatment-related research, once mastered by clinicians, can help them understand basic research as well. In any case, the task of attracting clinicians to research is that of the clinical researcher, not that of the basic researcher.

Problems Associated With the Education and Training Models

As noted before, if at least a certain number of clinicians are involved in research, the amount of in-house knowledge can be increased in a fairly short time. However, when other conditions are favorable, clinicians can do research only if they are trained to do research that is synchronous with clinical services. It is impractical to expect a majority of clinicians to do basic research. It also is impractical for clinicians to engage in clinical research that does not involve direct assessment, treatment, or maintenance strategies. Even the clinical research of *implications* cannot fulfill the service requirements; that is, clinicians must investigate questions that can be answered while providing services to their clients. To accomplish this, communication disorders must adopt an integrated model of education, training, and research.

If specialists in communication disorders see their field as a clinical profession based on scientific knowledge and research, several much-debated pseudoissues—such as "Do we need to know scientific methods?" or "Are courses on research methods necessary for practitioners?"—dissipate. The education of clinicians must include an understanding of existing knowledge and technology, methods of producing new knowledge and technology, and methods of evaluating all knowledge and technology.

An educational program cannot be limited to just imparting existing knowledge and training in extant technology to future practitioners. Future clinicians also need to know how new knowledge is produced and how any knowledge is critically evaluated before it is accepted or rejected. The methods of science and research are the methods of producing and evaluating empirical knowledge. Therefore, imparting knowledge of science and research is a part of training future practitioners who evaluate new information

and contribute new information to their chosen discipline. Such a training model ensures scientific status and professional strength.

It is sometimes thought that education in the philosophy and methods of science takes time away from clinical training. Some may argue that training of professionals requires spending all the available time on clinical methods and service delivery models. That students in clinical programs should receive the best possible training in clinical methods is not controversial. Indeed, during their education and training, future clinicians should not spend time studying science and research if that study is not expected to be useful. However, time spent on science and research in the training of practitioners is a waste only if clinical service and scientific work are conceptually and methodologically divorced (Sidman, 2011). The argument that the study of science and research is a waste is irrelevant when communication disorders is viewed as a scientific discipline and a clinical profession that adopts an integrated model of research and clinical service.

Unless clinicians are educated within an integrated model of research and clinical service, time spent training clinicians in research may not be as productive as it could be. Again, applied behavior analysis has been practicing such an integrated model of training clinicians for decades. Without the integrated model, even researchers are not likely to make a significant effect on the clinical issues of the profession. Therefore, the existing models of research in communication disorders may need to be revised. If the same model is used to give more information on research at the master's level or at the doctoral level, there is no assurance that in-house treatment-related knowledge will increase. What is needed is an emphasis on, and training in, the concepts and methods of science as applied to clinical work. The clinician must have a thorough understanding of the experimental methodology used to develop and evaluate treatment techniques as well as scientific theories.

Historically, educators in the university departments of communication disorders seem to have had the dual objectives of producing researchers and therapists, instead of developing a *clinical science.* Neither objective seems to have been achieved to a satisfactory degree because of a misunderstanding of the roles of clinicians and researchers. A productive interaction between clinicians, clinical researchers, and basic researchers is possible when the education and training model combines the logic and methods of science with the concerns of clinical description, assessment, and treatment evaluation. Such an education and training model for speech-language pathologists during their graduate training will more successfully produce a clinical science.

Such a training model needs to be implemented from the very beginning. At increasing levels of complexity, students should learn various aspects of this model at appropriate levels of their education. This new model of training is needed in the training of clinicians as well as researchers at the undergraduate, master's, and doctoral levels.

Possibly, what little training most graduates receive in science and research may not be consistent with clinical work, and therefore, clinicians are not prepared to do research. Most courses on research methods may offer only statistics. Concepts of science and designs of research may be presented inadequately or not at all. Information presented on research

designs may be restricted to the traditional group designs. Clinicians quickly find that to do any clinical research, they should be thorough in statistics, have access to a large population of clients who are willing to participate in a study, select a sample large enough to be justified statistically, select it randomly, assign participants to treatment groups randomly, and deny treatment to a control group.

Clinicians find that the research process as they understood it from an introductory course on statistics and group research designs is clinically formidable, unacceptable, or both when the immediate concern is professional service. First, most clinicians do not receive the depth of training in research methods needed to design clinically significant research. Second, in their everyday work, clinicians typically deal with a small number of clients, so they cannot find a population (a large group of persons with defined characteristics) of accessible, willing persons with specific communication disorders; therefore, they cannot draw random samples as the theory says they should. Third, even if the clinicians did draw random samples, they find it ethically unattractive to have a control group to which treatment must be denied or postponed. In essence, what clinicians learn about research in most graduate schools is not easily applied in professional settings where the immediate concerns are assessment, treatment, maintenance, parent counseling, case conference, and such other clinical activities. The popularity of traditional research philosophy and methodology based on statistics and probability theory is at least partly responsible for the paucity of treatment-related research, whether by practitioners or by clinical researchers. Inadequately prepared or not at all prepared in single-subject designs, clinicians are unaware of the tactics of clinical research that provides services while evaluating treatment procedures.

Summary

- Communication disorders is both an academic discipline and a clinical profession.
- Initially, communication disorders developed more as a profession than as a scientific discipline.
- The need to study scientific methods has been created by legal, social, professional, and scientific factors.
- Various state and federal legislation and agencies that pay for clinical services require the profession to be scientific and evidence based.
- A scientific professional gains better recognition and accountability.
- In the business of generating knowledge, communication disorders needs to be as self-sufficient as possible.
- Many clinicians may be inadequately trained to do research.

- Assessment- and treatment-oriented research may better attract clinicians than theoretical, normative, and descriptive research.
- Future practitioners should be trained in a model of science and research that is consistent with clinical service delivery.
- Nonresearcher clinicians still need to understand the concepts and methods of science so they can critically evaluate technical information offered to them.

References

Douglas, N. F., Campbell, W. N., & Hinckley, J. J. (2015). Implementation science: Buzzword or game changer? *Journal of Speech, Language, and Hearing Research, 58*(6), S1827–S1836.

Hegde, M. N. (1998). *Treatment procedures in communicative disorders* (3rd ed.). Austin, TX: Pro-Ed.

Sidman, M. (2011). Can understanding of basic research facilitate the effectiveness of practitioners? Reflections and personal perspectives. *Journal of Applied Behavior Analysis, 44*(4), 973–991.

Study Guide

1. What were some of the early concerns of the discipline of communication disorders? Did those concerns include experimental evaluation of treatment procedures ?

2. What legal and social considerations are prompting the profession to be more scientific in its orientation and activities?

3. What are some of the reasons to develop a scientifically sound clinical practice?

4. How can a profession draw attention to itself? What is the most

desirable method of drawing such attention?

5. What kinds of professions generally have better reputations and higher social visibility?

6. What are some of the problems of wholesale borrowing of knowledge and methods from other subjects and professions?

7. What is meant by custom-produced information from outside a profession?

8. Why should specialists in communication disorders produce their own database?

9. What are some of the reasons many clinicians do not do research?

10. What are the two assumptions made by some clinicians regarding research?

11. What are some of the popular sources of influence on clinical practice?

12. What is the main problem with current research practice?

13. How is basic research distinguished from experimental-clinical research?

14. What are some of the reasons that many clinicians have a negative view of research?

15. What are the strengths of the experimental-clinical research strategy? What are the strengths of the applied behavior analysis strategy?

16. What are some of the problems associated with the education and training of clinicians?

17. Why were the questions "Do clinicians need to know research methods?" or "Why should clinicians do research?" described as "pseudo"?

18. What is the significance of single-subject designs in creating a science of clinical practice?

19. What is an integrated model of research and professional service?

20. From a clinician's standpoint, what are the problems of not being able to evaluate research?

2

An Introduction to Research: The Formal and Formative Approaches

Chapter Outline

- ◆ What Is Research?
- ◆ Why Do Scientists Do Research?
- ◆ How Is Research Done?
- ◆ Serendipity in Research
- ◆ Planning Is Still Important
- ◆ Summary
- ◆ References
- ◆ Study Guide

The terms *science* and *research* have an air of extreme formality. Many students and professionals alike think that research is formidable, mechanistic, difficult, and somewhat boring. Some practitioners also think that research is an esoteric activity, irrelevant to clinical service. Graduate students who are not involved in research may look upon those who are doing theses or dissertations with admiration totally devoid of envy. Undergraduate students may consider research a mysterious activity, which they will understand better in graduate school. In time, the mysterious activity may reveal itself to be both arduous and uninteresting.

To a certain extent, most of these stereotypic reactions to science and research are understandable. Textbooks on research methods are written in a formal and somewhat dull style. The books often are full of statistics in which many students and clinicians do not find much joy. Statistics are only one of several and by no means inevitable methods of analyzing data. Statistics is not the same as research, but many textbooks give an impression that it is. Typical textbooks also describe research as a highly organized, thoroughly planned, and mechanistically efficient activity. Most clinicians think they are not prepared for it. Clinicians and students may have heard or known of graduate students who have worked so hard on their theses or dissertations that those budding researchers "stopped living" until their project was completed. They may have seen professors and scientists who also seemed to have no fun doing research but went on with the drudgery for apparently no good reason. Finally, there is the reality of science and research itself: Science is restrictive and research can be hard work. There are formal aspects to science, and there is no way of getting around them.

These stereotypes and hard facts not withstanding, science can be provocative, even refreshing. The logic and the framework of science constitute one of the most elegant of the abstract structures human beings have ever built. Persons who understand the logic and structure of science will not find it too difficult to organize their work within the scope of science. The logic of science can prompt the most stimulating intellectual pursuits. Much of scientific creativity, though difficult, can be highly reinforcing. A scientist's immense reward comes when his or her work throws new light on a perplexing problem that suddenly becomes a little bit more understandable.

In our effort to gain a more favorable view of research, we can find encouragement in Bachrach's (1969) comment that "people don't usually do research the way people who write books about research say that people do research" (Preface, p. x). Though research can be hard work, it need not be a drudgery. Doing research can actually be fun; there are rewards even when it is not much fun. As we shall see later, research is not as formal an activity as most textbooks make it appear. Research scientists are people, too, and they make mistakes like anyone else. Granted, there are people who do research not because they are especially good at it, but because they are required to. There are also people who love to do research—required or not. They may not be good researchers in the beginning, but soon they learn from their mistakes and improve the quality of their work. In this process, they have frustrations and pleasures.

A more balanced view describes both the pleasures and the hard work associated with research. When the research process is described the way it is typically implemented, a more realistic picture emerges. In a later section, we shall examine two ways of describing research activity.

What Is Research?

Sometimes the terms *science* and *research* are used synonymously. The two terms have overlapping meanings but different connotations. Science is inclusive of research, but the term *research* may not capture all the nuances of science. In the next chapter, we shall consider in detail the different meanings of science.

Science is a certain philosophy, a viewpoint about natural phenomena, and how such phenomena are interrelated. Science is also a set of methods designed to investigate research questions and thereby produce reliable and valid knowledge. Finally, science refers to the actions and behaviors of scientists.

Research is the process of investigating scientific questions. Research is what scientists do in practicing science. While science is a description of certain philosophies, viewpoints, and activities, research mostly includes steps taken by scientists in their quest to more fully understand the order and uniformity of nature. Research is science in action. According to various human subject (participant) protection guidelines, any systematic investigation designed to develop or contribute to generalizable knowledge is research. See Chapter 16 for legal and ethical implications of this definition.

It is only in the sense that science includes certain methods of investigations and actions of scientists that it is synonymous with research. Therefore, research refers to those activities by which science achieves its goals. Even as

a set of methods, science is conceptual, whereas research is methodological. Science is the unifying theme and philosophy of research. It permeates all empirical research. Science gives the scientist both the conceptual and methodological means of doing research, but research refers to the behaviors of scientists in action.

It is probably not very useful to expand upon the various definitions of research. Within the realm of science, different strategies of research have been devised. The full range of meaning of the term can be appreciated only when different types, strategies, and designs of research are understood along with the major reasons for doing research. In this sense, this entire book is about research. Therefore, we shall now turn to a discussion of some of the major reasons why research is done.

Why Do Scientists Do Research?

Research is done for many reasons. For example, there are bureaucratic reasons for doing research, although these reasons are not as important as other reasons. **Bureaucratic reasons** are those that require research from scientists as a matter of employment policy. For example, research is required of faculty members in many universities. Their tenure and promotion may depend upon the amount and quality of research they publish. When scientists are paid to do research for an organizations, research becomes their duty. These are intermediate reasons for doing research, however. Even those who do research for bureaucratic reasons need to consider the more basic and universal reasons why research is done.

Curiosity About Natural Phenomena

Philosophers of science have long recognized that one of the classical reasons for doing research is people's **curiosity about natural phenomena**. Scientists tend to be curious, and once questions arise, they seek to satisfy that curiosity. In fact, Sidman (1960) has defined a scientist as a "person whose indulgence of his curiosity is also the means by which he earns his living" (p. 7).

Curiosity is not an exclusive characteristic of scientists, however. Most people are curious about various natural and social phenomena. People are curious about things they do not understand, causes that are hidden, and effects that are unknown. Often, everyday curiosity is satisfied when people find out why someone behaved in a certain way or why a certain event happened. Scientific curiosity is not that easily satisfied. **Scientific curiosity** is satisfied only when special methods find answers to specific questions. Therefore, it often takes a long time to satisfy scientific curiosity because it seeks special answers to complex questions.

While everyday curiosity may be concerned with private events, scientific curiosity is almost always concerned with objective events. Even when subjective experiences such as feelings or emotions become its object, scientific curiosity treats them as objective events. Answers produced by scientific curiosity must be verified publicly, whereas those produced by private or personal curiosity need not be.

Private curiosity tends to produce answers with private implications, but scientific curiosity compels answers with public implications. Everyday curiosity may not necessarily lead to answers that have great social effect, but the answers sought by scientific curiosity can have significant social consequences. In this sense, the scope of scientific curiosity is larger than that of private curiosity. Also, scientific curiosity is always concerned with explaining natural phenomena, whereas private curiosity may be concerned with phenomena that cannot be investigated by scientific methods at all. For example, curiosity about why people have speech disorders can lead to empirical investigations using acceptable methods of science, whereas curiosity about supernatural phenomena may not lead to such investigations. However, interest in supernatural phenomena can itself be an object of scientific curiosity; a behavioral scientist may wonder why so many people exhibit certain kinds of behaviors toward supernatural phenomena and then proceed to investigate.

In many respects, scientific curiosity is insatiable. An answer to one question may contain the seeds of several more questions that need to be investigated. A curious scientist can go from one research activity to another because every piece of work satisfies some curiosity while arousing some other curiosity. In fact, good research typically raises important questions for further empirical investigations. Some investigations may not produce any answers at all; instead, they may raise important questions for research. Such investigations keep the proverbially curious scientist busy for a long time. It is this type of insatiable curiosity that sustains a chain of investigations and a lifetime of scientific research.

Research driven by curiosity is often not designed to test formal scientific hypothesis (Sidman, 1960). Scientists who wonder what causes an event may begin to arrange conditions under which that event can be systematically observed.

A **hypothesis** is a tentative answer to a research question, but one may not have a tentative answer, only a desire to find out. After some observations, the scientist may manipulate some aspect of the situation under which the phenomenon occurs reliably. This is the stage of experimentation, which also can be devoid of formal hypotheses. The history of both natural and behavioral sciences is full of examples of research that was done to see what happens when some specific variable is introduced, increased, decreased, or withdrawn.

The contrasting features of everyday curiosity and scientific curiosity should not suggest that the two are unrelated. Everyday curiosity can be cultivated and modified into scientific curiosity. Furthermore, that science is a human activity is illustrated by all research, but it is best illustrated by research done to satisfy one's own curiosity.

Explain Events

A well-recognized reason for doing research is to explain events and effects. Scientists wish to explain why certain events take place and why variables not yet identified seem to produce certain effects. It is often said that one of the goals of science is to explain natural phenomena. Therefore, a need to explain events is a significant reason for doing scientific research.

An **explanation** of an event specifies its causes. An event is scientifically explained when its cause or causes are experimentally demonstrated. For instance, when a clinical scientist shows that a certain treatment procedure can cause an increase in specific language behaviors in a client previously with limited language, we understand how language behaviors

can be modified. Similarly, when animal experiments produce a certain disease by introducing a chemical into the animal's body, that disease is explained at some level of generality and confidence. Procedurally, experiments arrange certain conditions to see if a variable produces a measurable effect. If certain steps are taken, the influence of other potential variables is ruled out or controlled. In this manner, a cause-effect relation between two events is established.

Research aimed at explaining events can follow one of two approaches. In one approach, the scientist first offers a comprehensive theory of an event and then tests it in a series of experiments. In other words, first the event is explained and then that explanation is verified; this explain-first-and-verify-later approach is called the **deductive method**. In the second approach, the investigator first conducts a series of experiments and then proposes a theory based on the results; this experiment-first-and-explain-later approach is known as the **inductive method**. These two approaches and their advantages and disadvantages are discussed in Chapter 3.

In science, a valid explanation of an event is worthwhile in and of itself. However, in many branches of science, a well-supported explanation suggests other possibilities. In most empirical sciences, a scientifically explained event may be changed. This means that scientists can gain some control over the events they explain. Typically, events not yet explained are difficult if not impossible to control or alter; that is, to change an event, we need to manipulate the causes of that event. Only a valid explanation gives us the access to causes of events. The applied implications of a valid explanation, then, are self-evident: Valid explanations make it possible to control diseases, disorders, and undesirable social and personal conditions.

Research done to explain events poses several risks to scientists. Scientists who use the inductive method must constantly control their tendency to offer an explanation too soon. Scientists have to judge whether sufficient evidence has been gathered so that a reasonably valid explanation may be offered. On the other hand, those who use the deductive method must promptly initiate a program of research to verify their explanations. Furthermore, scientists should modify the initial explanation to suit the data gathered through systematic experimentation.

It should be noted that the validity of scientific explanations is a matter of degree and that no explanation is 100% valid. This is because no scientist can claim to have made all possible observations of a phenomenon. There is always a possibility that some new observations will produce new data that may question the old explanation. Therefore, science treats all explanations as more or less tentative. Explanations with adequate support are sustained only until new data indicate otherwise.

Solve Practical Problems

Another reason to do research is to **solve practical problems**. There are many varieties of practical problems that scientists try to solve, but they can be grouped into two broad kinds. The first kind of problems scientists try to solve is found in the physical, chemical, social, and behavioral realm of the scientists' milieu. These are the problems that people, including scientists, face in their day-to-day living. Much of applied research is designed to solve practical problems of

this kind—for example, researching better ways of constructing houses, developing more effective fertilizers to improve crops; developing new types of energy, reducing highway accidents, and treating cancer and communication disorders. Obviously, this kind of research has the most immediate and highly visible social effect; therefore, it is the better known of the two kinds of research designed to solve practical problems.

Research done to solve practical problems is crucial for clinical sciences because this type of research includes efforts to evaluate treatment procedures. The systematic experimental evaluation and modification of existing treatment procedures and the development of new and more effective procedures are important for any clinical profession. One would think that a significant part of research in communication disorders is of this kind. Unfortunately, this is not the case. Other kinds of research dominate the field. Some of the reasons why treatment evaluation research is not commonly done were discussed in Chapter 1.

When research done to solve practical problems is successful, it gives rise to technology. **Technology** is the application of the results of scientific research in further solving problems, improving living and working conditions, saving natural resources, enhancing the behavioral potential of people, treating various disorders and diseases, and so on.

The second kind of practical problems that scientists address are **in-house problems**. Scientists face many practical problems that impede or even prevent a scientific analysis of a problem under investigation. Most scientists cannot continue their research if effective methods of **observation** and **measurement** are not available. Before conducting a conditioning experiment involving rats, for example, early experimental psychologists had to build the needed experimental chambers themselves. When available methods of measuring a phenomenon are inadequate, new methods must be developed. When a phenomenon of interest cannot be directly observed, the scientists first have to work on a means of observation. For example, the inventions of the microscope, the telescope, the physiograph, the audiometer, and the flexible fiberscope were in response to the need to solve the practical problems of observation. Such instruments extend the range, the power, or the precision of scientists' observations. New devices make it possible to observe events that were never directly observed before. For example, the laryngeal behaviors during stuttering were a matter of speculation for a long time, but the behaviors themselves were not directly observed until the fiberscope and cineradiography were developed and used.

Besides developing new instruments of observation and measurement, scientists also develop new methods of **controlling phenomena**. New experimental designs often are tried to see if they afford better control over the variables under study. When existing methods of arranging experimental conditions prove inefficient or in some ways unsatisfactory, new arrangements may be tested to find out if they help overcome the problems with the existing arrangements. Behavioral research contains many examples of new experimental arrangements developed to overcome some of the problems of the statistical approach to research. Skinner (1953), for example, found that the traditional method of superficially studying a large number of participants was not suitable for an experimental analysis of behavior. He therefore devised the

method of intensive study of individual participants. When methods of averaging group performance to impose order on diverse behavior patterns were given up in favor of controlling conditions under which an individual organism could be studied, a true order and behavior patterning emerged. In essence, Skinner was able to gain better control over the behavior because he could then alter patterns of behavior by changing the conditions under which the organisms behaved.

The emergence of new experimental designs illustrates how scientists solve their methodological problems. Applied behavioral research has developed many new experimental designs. For example, when it became evident that the single-subject *ABA* design (see Chapter 8) was undesirable for clinical research, the multiple baseline design was developed as an alternative (Baer, Wolf, & Risley, 1968). In the *ABA* design, a behavior is first base rated, and then a variable that will change that behavior is introduced, and finally that variable is withdrawn. With these operations, the investigator hopes to show that the behavior changed from the baseline when the variable was introduced and that the change was nullified when the variable was withdrawn. However, the design that served well in laboratory experiments proved undesirable in treatment evaluation because the experiment would end with a no-treatment condition and the participant-clients would be where they were before the treatment was started.

The multiple baseline, which was designed to overcome the problems of the *ABA* design, afforded an opportunity to demonstrate the effect of treatment without neutralizing it. In this design, several behaviors of a client are baserated, and the behaviors are treated in sequence. Every time a behavior is treated, the remaining untreated behaviors are base rated to make sure that only the treated behaviors changed while the untreated behaviors did not. This strategy has been used extensively in clinical treatment research.

An experimentally active discipline is constantly seeking new ways of observing, measuring, and controlling the phenomena of interest. Efforts to extend the control techniques to a new range of phenomena are also made continuously. The amount of research done to solve practical problems and bring new range of phenomena under experimental control is often an indication of a discipline's degree of scientific progress.

Demonstrate Certain Effects

Finally, research may be done to **demonstrate the effects** of newly discovered variables. Research of this kind often results in the observation of new phenomena. Generally speaking, scientists start with a certain effect and then proceed to find out what caused it. The experimental search for the cause of an event involves the active manipulation of selected variables. If the event changes following such manipulation, then the manipulated variable may be the cause; if it does not, then some other factor may be the cause. In this manner, and with appropriate control procedures, the scientist determines what caused an event. It must be noted that in all such cases, the scientist has a clear understanding of the event but is not sure of the cause.

In contrast, the research study designed to demonstrate the effects of a certain variable starts with a causal variable. What is not clear in this case is the effect of that variable. This kind of research situ-

ation arises frequently, although it takes a keen observer to notice new variables whose effects are yet undetermined.

A new variable that may produce new effects is often discovered accidentally. Lee (1950, 1951), for example, accidentally found that a speaker's speech becomes disturbed when a delay is introduced in the auditory feedback of one's own speech. Lee, an engineer, was working on some audiotaping systems that accidentally introduced a delay in feedback and found himself "stuttering" under this condition. He and other researchers then began to investigate the effects of delayed auditory feedback more thoroughly to determine the full range of its effects on speech. It must be noted that in the beginning, Lee was not at all studying the effects of delayed auditory feedback on speech. The variable emerged accidentally, and its effects were then evaluated.

The literature on behavioral research contains many such examples of accidental discovery of certain variables whose effects were later investigated. Skinner (1956) documented several of these examples in his own research; the now well-documented effects of intermittent reinforcement on behavior were discovered entirely accidentally. At a time when Skinner was reinforcing rats with custom-made food pellets, he had to manufacture his own supply of pellets with a hand-operated machine that he had constructed. He was also reinforcing every lever press response (continuous reinforcement). As Skinner told the story:

> One pleasant Saturday afternoon I surveyed my supply of dry pellets and [found] that unless I spent the rest of the afternoon and evening at the pill machine, the supply would be exhausted by ten-thirty Monday morn-

ing . . . [This] led me to . . . ask myself why *every* press of the lever had to be reinforced. . . . I decided to reinforce a response once every minute and allow all other responses to go unreinforced. There were two results: (a) my supply of pellets lasted almost indefinitely; and (b) each rat stabilized at a fairly constant rate of responding. (p. 111)

The above story points out several interesting aspects of the research process. Skinner did not *hypothesize* that intermittent reinforcement causes a more constant response rate than continuous reinforcement. Initially, he did not *design* a study to evaluate the effects of not reinforcing every response. Of course, he knew well that on that Saturday afternoon, he had changed the way the rats were reinforced. But he had no clear idea of what it would do to the response rate; he probably thought that it would make no big difference in response rates. But the data he saw on Monday morning were different. This led him to start a series of studies on the many different ways in which a response could be reinforced. These studies by Skinner and others (Ferster & Skinner, 1957) showed that different reinforcement schedules have characteristic effects on response rates and patterns. This area of research contains some of the most well-controlled and replicated evidence in behavioral research. More important, it showed how a variable discovered accidentally can suggest a new line of investigation to more fully assess its effects.

Physical and biological sciences also are full of examples of accidental discoveries of certain variables whose effects were studied subsequently. It is well known that penicillin was discovered accidentally (Batten, 1968; Wilson, 1976).

In the process of culturing bacteria for other research purposes, Sir Alexander Fleming repeatedly found that a green mold that developed in the dish routinely killed his colony of bacteria. Some other scientist might have ignored the green mold, considered the death of the bacteria an accident, and perhaps proceeded to develop a fresh colony of bacteria. Although Fleming did this to a certain extent, the repeated deaths of bacteria forced him to take a closer look at the effects of the green mold. Eventually, the presence of the unexpected green mold led to the discovery of penicillin, whose effects were studied extensively in later experiments.

The four kinds of reasons for doing research described in previous sections are not exhaustive, but they include the major factors that typically lead scientists to research and experimentation. Also, the reasons are by no means mutually exclusive; in fact, they are interrelated. Research done to satisfy one's curiosity may explain an event. Often, curiosity compels one to ask why a certain event is happening, and an answer to that question also may isolate the cause of the event. Curiosity can initially draw a scientist to a field of investigation. But soon, the scientist may be doing research to explain events (develop theories), solve practical problems, or demonstrate certain effects. It should also be clear that research done for any other reason will also satisfy the scientist's curiosity and serve the other goals of science.

Research done to explain events can lead to additional research that may help solve practical problems. For example, an experimentally based explanation of language disorders should also suggest ways of treating or preventing them. Because an explanation always points to at least one cause of an event, additional research on the methods of manipulating that cause should provide a means of controlling that effect. Controlling a cause to produce an effect is a treatment procedure.

In a similar manner, research done to solve practical problems can eventually lead to an explanation of certain phenomena. For example, successful treatment of language disorders through certain environmental manipulations may suggest that certain variables facilitate language learning. The absence of those variables may contribute to language disorders. Unfortunately, a widely held assumption is that applied research cannot explain phenomena but can only manipulate them with the knowledge derived from basic research. However, well-controlled experimental treatment research can offer excellent suggestions on the controlling variables of successfully treated phenomena. This is because in solving practical problems, often the independent variables (causes) of the phenomenon of interest must be found. Obviously, the same causal variables can explain the phenomenon.

How Is Research Done?

In this section, we present two approaches to describing research activity. The actual mechanics of doing research are not addressed here, for that is the running theme of this book. Different ways of conceptualizing and describing research activity may impede or facilitate a more complete understanding of it.

It was noted earlier that the traditional view of research is that it is an extremely well-organized, formal activity; it was further noted that this view may be largely mistaken. A more accurate view of research is that it is always a formative, not necessarily formalized, activity. We shall take a closer look at the research process and contrast these views to emphasize that research is what some *people* do. Research is a human activity that includes initial groping despite methodological planning, subsequent methodological refinement, and, with some luck, taking leaps of imagination.

The Formal View

It is *not* proposed here that there are two ways of *doing* research, one more formal and organized than the other. What is proposed is that research is *described* in two ways, and that *all* research is less formal and organized than published articles and textbook descriptions suggest.

The popular and standard view of research is that it is a formal process with clear-cut steps and linear progression. Accordingly, research involves an invariable, systematic, and step-by-step progression from the literature review to the problem, methods, results, and conclusions. However, this view of research is probably due to the format of published research. Those who write textbooks on research tend to support that view by omitting the *process* of research while describing the mechanics of organizing research already done.

A student of research methods who reads a published journal article to understand the process of research may gain the impression that the researcher knew everything from the beginning. It might appear that all that the researcher had to do was simply take the predetermined and incredibly clear steps of conducting the research. The student is apt to think that the experimenter had read everything about the past research well before the research problem was given its final form. Existing research being clear, the imagined brilliant researcher suddenly and inevitably generated the question that needed to be researched. The question as originally conceived must have been clear-cut and well formulated, for there is no indication in the article that the question was modified, was rewritten, or was not at all the original question considered for investigation. There is certainly no hint that the question investigated was one of several considered or that it was initially quite fuzzy.

The student might then think that as soon as the problem was posed, the researcher knew what kind of results would be obtained, so a hypothesis was formulated. However, to avoid giving the impression that the investigator had a personal stake in supporting his or her guesses, a **null hypothesis**, which is essentially a prediction that the events investigated are not related, was proposed (see Chapter 3 for more on null hypothesis). The investigator then knew exactly what to do to test the hypothesis. It might appear to the student that there was no question as to what kind of design to use in the study. The design used must have been the only one available. If alternatives were available, the choice must have been easy and clear. The procedure of participant selection must also have been clear from the very beginning, since there is no indication of troubled decisions on this matter. All participants must have been readily available, and all the experimenter had to do was ask them to participate in the study. Furthermore, it may appear that the investigator was sure of the best method of measuring and manipulating the variables. In

this manner, the student is likely to imagine that the scientist simply moved through a series of well-defined steps, which resulted in the conclusion of the study.

The student may further assume that once the data were collected, the predetermined method of analysis was applied to the results. Apparently, the meaning of the results was also unambiguously clear to the scientist; after all, the article talked about a definite number of implications that seem to have emerged full-blown in the order in which they were presented. With great ease, the scientist must have seen the relation between the study's findings and those of other investigations.

In essence, a typical journal article gives the student the impression that research is possible only when everything is brilliantly clear to the scientist. Because the student has not heretofore seen anything so complex and yet so clearly and beautifully organized, research seems to be both a unique and formidable task.

That a student gains such an impression of the research process is not a fault either of the student who reads research reports or of the scientist who writes them; doing research and organizing it for publication are simply two separate activities. In writing a research article, the scientist describes the research question, the methods of investigation, the results, and the implications of those results. In this description, it is most efficient to omit the details of the research process. The process of doing research is full of various personal, practical, ideational, emotional, and organizational details that may not be entirely relevant to an understanding of what was done and what results were obtained. Furthermore, these factors, if chronicled in an article, may confuse readers. Besides, no journal will have space to print the *story* of research in addition to the research itself, no matter how interesting the story might be. Therefore, the preceding characterization of the research process that can be gleaned from journal articles is not meant to suggest that research reporting should reflect the complexity of research process.

One would expect, however, that when research scientists talk about how they did their research or when authors write books on how to do research, the empirical research process would be reflected. Unfortunately, many authors who talk or write about research paint an unreal picture of how they do it. The textbooks on research procedures, especially those based on statistics, are particularly vulnerable to this criticism. Textbooks typically reinforce the questionable notion of the clear-cut, step-by-step research process that the students gain from reading journal articles.

The Formative View

A research report documents: (a) several decisions made by the investigator, (b) how those decisions were implemented, (c) what results followed that implementation, and (d) what the author thinks of those results. Authors decide on the problem of investigation, the meaning of previous research, the method of investigation, and the manner of interpretation. However, these decisions should not be confused with the actual process of arriving at those decisions. Students who wish to know how to do research should gain an understanding of how such decisions are made. When this process is considered, a different view of how research is done emerges. Scientists who describe the process by which they made their own

discoveries tend to create a synthetic vision of formality, clarity, logical precision, and inevitable movement through specific steps. In an article entitled "A Plea for Freeing the History of Scientific Discoveries From Myth," Grmek (1981) expressed skepticism about the validity of many famous scientists' autobiographical accounts of the *process* of scientific discovery. Grmek stated that in describing their own past discoveries, many scientists resort to "rationalizing readjustment, whereby the actual sequence of events is transmuted in favor of logical rigor and coherence" (p. 15).

Many authors who consider themselves competent researchers may be somewhat reluctant to talk about the typically uncertain, sometimes confusing, and generally groping nature of doing research. There may be an implicit assumption that "science" cannot be anything but utter clarity, beautiful organization, and superb efficiency. Scientific research may be thought of as entirely official, proper, prim, and uncompromising. However, when science is viewed as something people do, the emerging picture of the research process may be less magnificent, but it will be more real. Science is a formative enterprise. Scientists learn as they go. Among others, Sidman (1994) gives an outstanding example of a formative research story.

The formative view suggests that research is an evolving process. It is a process in which concepts, ideas, procedures, and skills emerge and develop gradually, sometimes slowly. A formative research process changes and improves. The formative view of research implies that even with much planning, research is an evolving process, not a process whose sequence and progression are fixed at the beginning. The movement from *problem* to *discussion* is not as certain, neat, and linear as a published article might imply. There is a beginning and an end to a particular study, but the boundaries are not always clear. More important, everything in between may involve many back-and-forth movements. Grmek (1981) believed that the typical textbook depiction of the linear ascent toward truth is a myth. He also stated that "neither the meanderings of individual thought, nor the advances of scientific knowledge within a community, proceed by successive approximations, always in the right direction, towards truth. The path to discovery is a winding one" (p. 20).

Research activity has patterns but they are broad, general, and flexible. There are broad conceptual and methodological patterns. There are patterns pertaining to theory and practice. Unfortunately, most textbooks turn those broad and flexible patterns into specific and rigid steps of doing research.

The formal and clearly stated research question as it finally appears in a published article may barely resemble the early troubling but uncertain, vague yet haunting sensations that often are a coalescence of thoughts, images, and feelings about the phenomenon of interest. If questioned as to what he or she is doing at this stage, the scientist's answer might be more confusing than illuminating. The scientist's thoughts may appear not well organized at all. In all likelihood, at this stage, some phenomenon is bothering the scientist, but there is no fully articulated research problem that can be investigated. At such a time, the scientist's speech, if he or she is willing to talk about the problem at all, will certainly not resemble the convention lecture given on the completed research a year later.

There may be a few exceptional scientists who, without much effort and time,

can formulate significant research questions that, when investigated, yield meaningful data. In most cases, however, the emergence of research questions is a slow and formative process. Generally speaking, the beginnings of a research question may be felt after much reading on the issue. Some researchers may think of questions while talking about an issue or a topic. Others may sense potential questions while engaged in some practical work, such as working with a client.

Research itself is probably the most productive locus of additional research questions. Tentative research questions may emerge when the scientist observes something or while investigating a related problem. The results of an experiment might suggest additional questions for future investigation. The researcher may have found out that the method selected was not effective and that a different tactic might prove more useful. Thus, both effective and ineffective research can suggest valid questions to be investigated. Descriptive research might suggest questions for experimental research. Similarly, a basic analysis of a phenomenon might suggest applied research questions.

A clinician who is a keen observer may think of many questions during treatment sessions or simply while watching client behaviors. An inefficient treatment should be an excellent source for treatment-related research questions. The clinician who has carefully broken down the treatment into separately manipulated components may be able to observe differential effects of certain components. The clinician may pursue such differential effects in a research study.

In most cases, extensive or intensive reading, keen observation, critical analysis of research literature, some experience in research, an understanding of logic and the philosophy of science, and critical thinking are all necessary to formulate significant research questions.

As noted before, most research questions are not very clear in the early stages. Furthermore, upon further thinking and reading, those that were clear to begin with may be judged the wrong kind of questions. The refinement of the question takes much thinking, and most questions undergo several revisions before they are ready for investigation. The relative emphasis on the variables within a question may be changed when the investigator thinks of a strategy to implement the experiment.

Once the question becomes reasonably clear, the scientist begins to think about the ways of answering it. Different methods can be used to answer the same research question. For example, the effects of a new dysarthria treatment program can be tested within a single-subject design or a group design. In the former, all participants receive the experimental treatment. In the latter strategy, participants in one group receive treatment and the members of the other group do not, thereby serving as a control group. The investigator selects what he or she considers the best strategy to answer the particular research question; the scientist's own investigative history probably plays a key role in that selection. Here too, the investigator is likely to go through a period of vacillation. Finally, a design may be selected for certain practical reasons. A group design, for example, may be selected simply because a certain number of participants happen to be available.

Various other aspects of the procedures of a study are decided one way or the other, often without any clear-cut guidelines or requirements. When there are no stringent guidelines, the investigator judges whether the selected procedure can be justified on some grounds. Also, a given course of action may be taken because no other option is available. For example, how many participants should be selected for the study? A group design would require more participants than a single-subject design, but in many cases, the answer depends simply on the availability of participants, especially in clinical fields. If 10 people who have dysarthria are available for a study, the investigator decides to go with that number. It may happen that only 6 individuals with dysarthria are willing to participate, and the study has to be completed with them. When the report is written, however, it seems to indicate that the planned and well-considered number of participants was 6. Indeed, planning may have nothing to do with the number of individuals who participated in a study.

Answers to many other questions may be similarly determined. What kinds of equipment will be used? In what facility will the experiment be conducted? Investigators construct new mechanical devices and buy new instruments when funds are available; ideally, the best available instrumentation must be used for the study, but in practice, most investigators use what is available. Sometimes, a problem already defined may have to be redefined or modified to accommodate the only available instrument. For example, an investigator who wanted to monitor different physiologic variables such as heart rate, muscle potential, cortical electrical potential, blood volume, and breathing patterns in people who stutter during treatment sessions might drop one or more of those variables simply because a multichannel polygraph that measured all of them was not available. More than planning, practical exigencies would have determined the variables selected for the study, but the written report is unlikely to reflect this.

Many times, research problems literally sit on the shelves collecting dust because the investigator does not have the time, participants, money, or all of these to complete the studies. Other problems may not be investigated because of methodological difficulties; an investigator may not see how a problem can be researched or how a dependent variable could be measured. In other situations, a problem that has been forgotten or neglected may suddenly be revived because a certain number of clients or type of clients suitable for the study becomes available. The investigator will somehow make time and convince himself or herself that the existing equipment, although not ideal, will do. During an incidental and entirely informal conversation with a colleague, a method to study a perplexing problem may emerge. Or, a recently published article may suggest an innovative method. Not infrequently, the investigator may think of a procedure while taking a walk or while just sitting and thinking about the problem. Suddenly, the problem lying on the shelf is picked up and dusted off, and the investigator drops everything else and becomes immersed in the new study. Meanwhile, other research ideas may be neglected.

In any discipline, there are probably countless studies that remain half-finished or that were abandoned soon after they were begun. But the number cannot be too small. Many investigators are likely to have a few studies that were implemented to varying degrees and discontinued for any of a number of reasons. Maybe the investigator found out that it was not a great study (meaning it was bad) after all. Maybe the researcher came across a more interesting study or obtained some grant

monies that forced attention into some other area of investigation. Perhaps the investigator got sick during the course of the study and never again had time to finish it. Furthermore, participants may drop out, equipment may break down, or the investigator may move to another position. All of these not-so-formal reasons for discontinuing research are real and more common than the books on research methods lead us to believe.

A certain number of research studies that are completed may never be published. Again, objective data on the number of such studies are lacking, but editors of journals can testify to the number of rejected articles. An article rejected by one journal may be published in another journal, but still, many articles prepared for publication may never be published. Besides, a completed research study may never be written up for publication. A study may have been completed without its flaws having been realized, but one look at the data may convince the investigator that the study is not worth publishing.

The sequence of research found in published articles gives an impression of an orderly progression through an invariable sequence. Most empirical research articles have a rigid sequence because scientific journals require it. An article starts with an untitled Introduction or the Review of Literature, proceeds to the Method, then to the Results, and finally to the Discussion or Conclusion. The article ends with References, Appendixes, or both. But this rigid sequence is rarely a reflection of how the research itself was conducted. In some cases, investigators have sufficient reason to do a study with only a minimal survey of literature. This is especially true when an investigator knows that no study of the kind being considered has been completed. After the study has been completed, a more thorough search of the literature may be conducted to determine if the new findings can be related to any of the published findings. Often, methodological considerations precede a more thorough analysis of the research problem itself. One may have a general idea of the research problem, such as an evaluation of two language treatment programs, but the more critical factor to be assessed at the very beginning may be the number of participants available for the study. This may then determine the design of the study. A researcher may not wish to use statistical methods of analysis, in which case considerations of data analysis may determine the design to be used. In this manner, the investigator considers factors sometimes in the sequence in which the paper is written but many times in a sequence dictated by the practical contingencies that affect the researcher.

It must be recognized, though, that some research practices are more rigid than others. The statistically based group research designs are relatively more rigid in their strategies than are the single-subject designs. Typically, in the group research designs, the study is completed the way it was planned even if it becomes evident that something is wrong with the study. The design itself is rarely, if ever, modified in the middle of an investigation. To the contrary, a study with a single-subject design may be modified when the data warrant a change. For example, if found ineffective, a treatment procedure in experimental clinical research may be changed in a single-subject strategy but usually not in the group strategy. The number of days for which the experimental treatment is applied may be predetermined in the group approach but not within the single-subject approach. For instance, people who stutter may be treated for a fixed duration in a group design study. In a single-subject study, the same treatment may be continued until stuttering is reduced markedly or until it becomes evident to the researcher that it is no use to continue the experimental treatment. Such judgments, made *during* the course of the study, are considered undesirable in the group research strategy. However, the same judgment or similar judgments made *prior* to the implementation of the study are considered a part of good planning.

Serendipity in Research

We noted earlier that accidental events have often helped scientists discover new phenomena. That "accidents" lead to significant scientific findings also suggests that all research is not totally planned. By definition, accidental discoveries are unplanned, but they are scientific discoveries nonetheless. Some accidental discoveries have proved more valuable than the planned research during which such accidents happened.

Walpole's story *The Three Princes of Serendip* has given rise to the term *serendipity* in research (Cannon, 1945). The story goes that three princes, while looking for something that they never found, nevertheless found many interesting things that they had not thought of finding. Often, when looking for something, scientists may find something else. Such accidental discoveries may help scientists begin new lines of productive investigations. We noted earlier that Fleming's discovery of penicillin was accidental, as was Skinner's discovery of the effects of intermittent reinforcement on response patterns.

A particularly fascinating story of accidental discovery in medical sciences is that of Ignaz Semmelweis, a Hungarian physician who worked in a maternity ward of the Vienna General Hospital from 1844 to 1848 (Sinclair, 1901). The hospital had two maternity wards, and Semmelweis worked in the first. An anguishing puzzle he faced was that in his ward, the death rate due to childbed (puerperal) fever among women after delivery was as high as 11%, but in the other, identical ward, the death rate was around 2%.

Like most investigators, Semmelweis began to test various logical possibilities and opinions about the causation of the unusually high mortality rate. Unfortunately, none of the possibilities proved to be the cause of the death rate. He found that such variables as overcrowding, unexplained "epidemic influences," rough examination by medical students, the posture women assumed during delivery, and a variety of psychological factors all proved to be inconsistent with facts or specific manipulations. For instance, overcrowding was common to both the wards and hence could not explain a differential death rate. Reducing the number of examinations by medical students did not reduce the death rate. Semmelweis reasoned that unexplained epidemic factors must be common to both the wards.

The puzzle was eventually solved in 1847, but the solution did not come from any of Semmelweis's rigorous hypothesis testing. It came from an unfortunate accident. While performing an autopsy, a student's scalpel punctured a wound in the finger of his instructor, Kolletschka. Soon Kolletschka became violently ill with the same symptoms of childbed fever. He died, just like many women with childbed fever. This led Semmelweis to think that perhaps the "cadaveric matter" the student's scalpel had introduced into Kolletschka's bloodstream must be the cause of the disease. The medical students were not trained in the other ward that had the low death rate. In that ward, midwives who did not dissect cadavers delivered babies. It then dawned on Semmelweis that he, his colleagues, and the medical students regularly came to examine the women in labor soon after completing dissections. Possibly because they did not wash their hands thoroughly, the physicians and medical students themselves were the carriers of the deadly microorganisms that were introduced into the bloodstream of women in labor.

Semmelweis solved the problem when he ordered that before examining the women in the ward, all physicians and medical students wash their hands thoroughly with a solution of chlorinated lime. Consequently, the death rate in Semmelweis's ward declined to the level found in the other ward. As the Semmelweis story suggests, a problem is not always solved by a planned test of a formal hypothesis. An accident that reveals an unsuspected relation between events can solve a problem that had proved frustrating.

A source of accidental discovery that is not widely recognized is apparatus failure. All scientists know that instruments break down and that in most such cases, they create problems for the scientist. Most scientists dread apparatus failure in the course of an experiment. Nevertheless, important discoveries have been made when apparatuses broke down in the middle of experiments. Two examples from behavioral research illustrate this.

First, the discovery of operant extinction was aided immensely by a breakdown in the equipment Skinner was using to reinforce responses. In fact, one of Skinner's (1956) unformalized principles of scientific practice is that "apparatuses sometimes break down" (p. 109). As it happened, one day the food magazine, which was a part of the mechanical device used to automatically reinforce the bar press responses in rats, became jammed. Consequently and against the plan of the experiment in progress, the rat's responses went unreinforced. The result was an extinction curve, which led to a series of experiments on the properties of extinction and on the functional relations between the prior reinforcement contingencies and later patterns of extinction.

The second example also comes from experimental research on conditioning and is provided by Sidman (1960):

An experiment on avoidance behavior was in progress in which an animal was scheduled to receive only 20 percent of all the shocks that became due when it failed to make the avoidance response in time. A relay failure in the automatic programming circuit altered the procedure one day in such a way that every *fifth* shock was delivered *regardless* of whether or not the animal had made an avoidance response. The apparatus failure was discovered when the animal's usually stable rate of lever pressing began to accelerate, and continued to increase throughout the experimental period. The increased rate of avoidance responding in the face of unavoidable shock was so unexpected that a new research program was immediately launched, a program which has been productive for three years and is still continuing. (p. 9)

The phenomenon Sidman discovered because of an accidental failure of apparatus has come to be known as the Sidman avoidance, in which an organism has no prior signal of an impending aversive stimulus, and there is no escape, but each response postpones the aversive stimulus for a fixed period of time. It is known that the Sidman procedure produces a high and consistent rate of response, which is unusually resistant to extinction. Sidman's original finding has been replicated widely, and its human behavioral and clinical implications are extensive. But, the point to be made here is that the discovery of this important phenomenon of aversive conditioning was entirely due to a breakdown in instrumentation.

When experimental apparatuses break down, many scientists may be tempted to discard the data collected up to that point because of the "contamination caused by equipment failure." Usually, after having cried on the shoulder of a friendly colleague, the scientist will rebuild the apparatus and start all over again. In many cases, equipment failure can be a cause of worry, especially when all the data are lost and there is nothing to discover. However, the results produced by failures are always worth a serious examination. The investigator may find new problems for exciting research in those unexpected results.

Serendipity in research not only shows that not all research is thoroughly planned but also that research need not necessarily test hypotheses. If research is done only to test hypotheses, then the chances for accidental discoveries are eliminated. In hypothesis testing, the scientist asks a question and then formulates a tentative answer, which is then put to experimental test. The results of such research studies are always evaluated in terms of their relation to the hypothesis. Anything not relevant to the hypothesis is not of interest. Because "accidental confirmation of a hypothesis" is a contradiction of terms, accidental discoveries must be necessarily useless. But we know that this is not the case.

Planning Is Still Important

The view that research is more formative than formal does not imply that research is casual or that there is no need for planning or preparation. It must be noted that most accidental discoveries happen in the process of well-planned investigations. The scientist needs to be an intellectually prepared person. A thorough knowledge of existing research is usually necessary, if only to avoid the same conceptual or methodologic mistakes committed by other scientists. In the research process, evidence accumulates slowly and is built by the continuous collective efforts of scientists. The building blocks of scientific knowledge are the little pieces of research done by a variety of researchers past and present. Therefore, researchers must be able to see interrelations among research findings, and this takes painstakingly achieved scholarship.

Good research also requires a working knowledge of the methods of manipulating and measuring variables. Some skill and experience in looking at data and thinking about their importance are also necessary. Undoubtedly, many questionable investigations are due to poor scholarship, inadequate technical skills, and lack of sufficient planning on the part of researchers.

The formative view of research is that it is a flexible, open, human, sensitive, and practical activity. At the conceptual and methodological levels, research is forma-

tive in the sense that different contingencies continuously affect the process. A good research scientist is always willing to go back and forth and to change ideas or the plan of an experiment. A scientist is not necessarily bound by rigid sequences that may not promote creativity. Such a scientist is sensitive to unplanned events that happen during the course of research and does not have the great investment in his or her own guesses (hypotheses) that seems to create a scientist's affliction called *hypothesis myopia* (Bachrach, 1969). Though he or she is knowledgeable regarding previous research findings, the scientist's thinking is not limited by those findings. The scientist knows that nature is likely to display events not suggested by previous research and not predicted by hypotheses and theories. Such a scientist is fully prepared to seize an unplanned and unexpected moment of creativity.

Summary

- Science is a certain philosophy, a set of methods, and a certain behavioral disposition. Research is science in action.
- Scientists do research to satisfy their curiosity about natural phenomena, explain events, solve practical problems, and demonstrate certain effects.
- In the formal view, researchers follow rigid, clear, and linearly sequenced steps from thinking about a problem to completing the study. In the formative view, research is an evolving, changing, and improving process.
- Accidental discoveries (serendipity) are of great importance in science.

- Good planning for research is still needed because accidental discoveries often are a part of well-planned research.

References

Bachrach, A. J. (1969). *Psychological research: An introduction.* New York, NY: Random House.

Baer, D. M., Wolf, M. M., & Risley, T. R. (1968). Some current dimensions of applied behavior analysis. *Journal of Applied Behavior Analysis, 10,* 117–119.

Batten, M. (1968). *Discovery by chance: Science and the unexpected.* New York, NY: Funk & Wagnalls.

Cannon, W. (1945). *The way of an investigator.* New York, NY: W. W. Norton.

Ferster, C. B., & Skinner, B. F. (1957). *Schedules of reinforcement.* New York, NY: Appleton-Century-Crofts.

Grmek, M. D. (1981). A plea for freeing the history of scientific discoveries from myth. In M. D. Grinek, R. S. Cohen, & G. Cymino (Eds.), *On scientific discovery* (pp. 9–42). London, UK: D. Reidel.

Lee, B. S. (1950). Effects of delayed speech feedback. *Journal of the Acoustical Society of America, 22,* 824–826.

Lee, B. S. (1951). Artificial stutter. *Journal of Speech and Hearing Disorders, 16,* 53–55.

Sidman, M. (1960). *Tactics of scientific research.* New York, NY: Basic Books.

Sidman, M. (1994). *Equivalence relations and behavior: A research story.* Boston, MA: Authors Cooperative.

Sinclair, W. J. (1901). *Semmelweis: His life and his doctrine.* Manchester, UK: Manchester University Press.

Skinner, B. F. (1953). *Science and human behavior.* New York, NY: Free Press.

Skinner, B. F. (1956). A case history in scientific method. *American Psychologist, 11*(22), 1–233.

Wilson, D. (1976). *In search of penicillin.* New York, NY: Knopf.

Study Guide

1. Define and distinguish research and science.

2. Describe the various reasons for doing research.

3. Explain why research done to satisfy one's own curiosity may not involve hypothesis testing.

4. What is a scientific explanation?

5. Write a (hypothetical) statement of explanation of a selected communicative disorder.

6. What are the two kinds of practical problems scientists try to solve?

7. What kind of research results in the observation of new phenomena?

8. What are the two approaches to describing research activity? Compare and contrast the approaches.

9. What is meant by the statement that "research is more formative than formal"?

10. Give an example of accidental discovery in scientific research. Find an example not given in this text.

3

Science and Its Basic Concepts

Chapter Outline

◆ What Is Science?

◆ Outcome of Scientific Activity

◆ Variables and Their Types

◆ Causality and Functional Analysis

◆ Experiment and Experimental Control

◆ Hypotheses in Scientific Research

◆ Theories and Hypotheses

◆ Inductive and Deductive Reasoning

◆ Theories and Scientific Laws

◆ Data and Evidence

◆ Summary

◆ References

◆ Study Guide

We all seem to know what science is, but "What is science?" is not an easy question to answer. Scientists have given different answers, each describing some aspect of science. A comprehensive description of science applies to all disciplines that seek knowledge in a certain scientific manner.

There are also many popular misconceptions about science, and it is instructive to know what science is not. Some of these misconceptions may be entertained by persons who are otherwise educated but have not formally studied the philosophy and methods of science.

What Is Science?

Let us first clear up some popular misconceptions about science. Science is not any particular subject matter. It is not the same as physics or biology. Science is not a *body of knowledge* because there are plenty of nonscientific bodies of knowledge. Science is not necessarily a laboratory-based activity, although much scientific activity happens there. Scientific research in many fields is done outside laboratories. Science is not necessarily tied to complex instruments, although such instruments are used in many branches of science. Finally, science and technology are not the same. Technology is the application of science to solve practical problems.

Instead of trying to define science, it may be more appropriate to describe the three major aspects of it. Accordingly, **science** is: (1) a philosophy, (2) a certain kind of behavior, and (3) a set of methods. We shall briefly describe each of these views. All three are necessary to obtain a comprehensive view of science.

Science as a Philosophy

Science is a certain philosophical position regarding nature and the nature of events. A philosophy, simply put, is a certain view point, a foundation for some activity. The philosophic foundations of science include *determinism* and *empiricism.*

Determinism states that events are caused by other events. Events do not happen haphazardly; they are determined by their causes. Therefore, science is a search for the causes of events.

The early history of science shows that laity as well as learned people had difficulty accepting the philosophy of determinism. People in most societies believed that events happened because of a divine design beyond the scope of human observation and investigation. Science, on the other hand, insists that events are caused by other events and that the causes can be observed, studied, and, in many cases, controlled. Before the advent of science, theology and a closely affiliated branch of philosophy called *scholasticism* ruled the world of knowledge, understanding, and explanation. Both scholasticism and theology had their explanations of the physical, chemical, biological, and human world. Often, science found itself in conflict with traditional religious wisdom. Both science and scientists have faced negative consequences because of this.

It is well known that physical, chemical, and biological phenomena were among the very first to come under the scope of the philosophy and methods of science. Science replaced the notion that the earth is flat and that it is the center of universe. Science challenged the notion that human beings suddenly emerged because of divine creation. It showed that physical, chemical, and biological phenomena are lawful and that those laws can be discovered. The progress in such basic scientific analyses eventually led to technology, which helped solve many problems of living. Technology began to make life a little easier and thus reduced some of the resistance to science. Nevertheless, new inventions and discoveries provoked and continue to provoke social resistance (Johnston & Pennypacker, 2009).

Generally speaking, resistance to the philosophy of science is less marked in the case of physical and chemical phenomena. As applied to biological phenomena, however, scientific philosophy still provokes considerable resistance. The continuous controversies over teaching science versus creationism in U.S. public schools testify to this persistent resistance to the philosophy of science.

The resistance to the concept that human behavior is determined is even more vocal. Human behavior has been the last stronghold of antiscientific ideology. Asserting that human beings are created and not evolved, theology tends to discredit the possibility that human behavior is determined. Human actions are supposed to be due to inner forces such as free will. Many people who readily accept the philosophy that natural events are caused by other events vehemently oppose the notion that human behavior has its causes that can be studied and controlled by the methods of science. The science of human behavior has been one of the most attacked of the sciences.

Within the domain of human behavior, language, thinking, and such higher human activities have been a particular stronghold for the traditional, nonscientific philosophies of rationalism, mentalism, and scholasticism. For example, when the evidence that most forms of human behaviors can be analyzed by the methods of science became overwhelming, traditional thinkers insisted upon exceptions. Language and creativity seemed like an urgently needed exception if traditional concepts of human behavior were to be maintained. The nativists' strong rejection of the behavioral analysis of language is but one indication of this tendency.

The history of science shows that it is easier to objectively analyze the physical world. But looking at ourselves and analyzing our own actions has been a difficult scientific activity. The historical resistance to the concept of determinism as applied to human behavior may be part of this difficulty.

Empiricism, another philosophical cornerstone of science, asserts that sensory experience is the basis of knowledge. Traditional (nonscientific) thinking would suggest that knowledge may be derived from rational thinking and intuition, or by mystical, religious, and divine revelations. To the contrary, science insists that valid knowledge is based on sensory experience. This experience must be socially and objectively verifiable; after all, even divine revelation can be an "experience." The methods of empiricism make experience acceptable to science.

Science as Behavior

The term *science* includes the actions and behaviors of scientists. Obviously, science is the result of what *scientists* do. The view that science is a **certain kind of behavior** is not well known because of the emphasis on objective methods, procedures, and philosophies in descriptions of science. While such an emphasis is entirely valid, we need to understand the behavior of scientists to appreciate the full meaning of science. Viewing science as the product of scientists' behaviors may have the best pedagogical value. Young people may understand science better when told how accomplished scientists tend to behave.

The view that science is a certain kind of behavior is relatively new. Behavioral scientists such as Skinner (1953, 1974) have insisted that the behavior of scientists is a subject of the science of behavior. Systematic analysis of the behavior of scientists has barely begun, partly because of the belief that scientific as well as literary creativity is mysterious and unique and thus beyond the scope of scientific analysis. There is some fear that an objective analysis of the process of writing a poem, painting a picture, or discovering some lawful relations in nature will adversely affect such valuable (but poorly understood) activities. Possibly, the resistance to a scientific analysis of the behavior of scientists and artists may simply be a part of the historical skepticism regarding determinism of human behavior.

Consistent with some of the misconceptions of science, there also are several misconceptions about scientists as people. Scientists are popularly depicted as impractical, fanciful, and unsociable. They may be considered maniacs who wish to control the world and all humanity. Scientists are often thought to be absentminded and slovenly. They may be described as cold, mechanical, and lacking in feelings and warmth.

As Bachrach (1969) put it, such a stereotypical notion of scientists is "arrant nonsense" (p. 111). More sensibly, scientists are described as curious people who often are dissatisfied with the existing "explanations" of events they wish to study. Skinner (1953) stated that scientists are disposed to "deal with facts rather than what someone has said about them" (p. 12). Curiosity, dissatisfaction with existing "explanations," and a tendency to deal with facts all lead to a disposition to reject authority. The history of science shows that science "rejects its own authorities when they interfere with the observation of nature" (Skinner, 1953, p. 12).

A scientist is more willing than other people to set aside his or her wishes and expectations and let the facts and results of experiments speak for themselves. The scientist is interested in replacing subjective opinions and convictions with objectively demonstrated relations. As pointed out by Skinner (1953), intellectual honesty —the opposite of wishful thinking—is an important characteristic of scientists. A scientist may find that the results of an experiment are not as expected and predicted or that they contradict his or her own well-known theory. In such cases, an honest scientist would report the findings as they were observed, because "the facts must stand and the expectations fall. The subject matter, not the scientist, knows best" (Skinner, 1953, p. 13).

Another characteristic of scientists, according to Skinner (1953), is that they are willing to remain "without an answer until a satisfactory one can be found" (p. 13). Beginning students in many fields often are surprised when told that there is no satisfactory answer to certain questions. When students are told that we do not know precisely how language is acquired or how stuttering is caused, they find it hard to believe that "all those experts do not have any idea" and that the experts can live with such uncertainties. Scientists can tolerate such uncertainties because they are trained to reject premature explanations and theories.

That something cannot be explained at a given time is generally less bothersome to scientists than it is to nonscientists. Instead of accepting whatever explanations that may be available, scientists tend to investigate.

Sometimes people think that when there is no good explanation, the knowledge that is available can be, or even must be, accepted. Such acceptance would be dangerous, however. Unfortunately, this practice often is encouraged by investigators who, after having advanced their own explanations, challenge others to either accept those explanations or offer better ones. Good scientists do not pay much attention to such challenges. A scientist need not propose a better explanation to reject a bad one. Explanations stand on their evidence, and if there is no acceptable evidence, they just do not stand. A scientist can examine alternative explanations and reject one in favor of the other. But an explanation also can be rejected in favor of none (Hegde, 1980).

The debate over the Chomskyan innate hypotheses in the explanation of language acquisition illustrates this issue. During the 1960s, many linguists and psycholinguists who had proposed a variety of innate hypotheses to explain language acquisition had also repeatedly challenged empiricists to either accept those hypotheses or offer better explanations. Addressing this kind of challenge, and referring to Chomsky's nativist theory, Goodman (1967), a philosopher of science, stated that although one may not have an alternative explanation for a phenomenon, "that alone does not dictate acceptance of whatever theory may be offered; for the theory may be worse than none. Inability to explain a fact does not condemn me to accept an intrinsically repugnant and incomprehensible theory"

(p. 27). This again underscores the view that scientists are people who can go without an explanation.

Science as a Set of Methods

In addition to certain philosophies and behavioral dispositions, science is a set of methods. The definition of science as methods is generally better understood than either the philosophy of science or the behavioral dispositions of scientists. This is understandable because in the teaching of science and research, tangible methods receive greater attention than philosophies and behavioral dispositions.

Science can be defined as a publicly verifiable method of studying events and solving problems. Science is a set of methods designed to investigate research questions in a verifiable manner that is acceptable to scientists. The methods of science can also be described as rules that dictate scientists' conduct in carrying out a piece of research. Violation of these rules produces questionable results. Therefore, scientists are trained in those methods so that they can engage in activities that produce valid knowledge.

The most important aspect of the methods of science is that they help answer research questions. The methods are structural and conceptual means of investigating research problems. The selection, formulation, and definition of research problems; selection of participants; specification of variables or factors to be analyzed; the manner in which the variables are measured and manipulated; and the techniques of data analysis are all a part of the scientific method.

Objective procedures are those that are publicly verifiable. Public verification simply means that other scientists can reproduce both the procedures and the results. Similar scientific procedures should produce similar results. Of all the aspects of scientific methods, observation, measurement, and experimentation are the most fundamental.

Observation is systematic study of phenomena to note its characteristics. **Measurement** is assigning numbers to properties of events. Objective and precise measurement is necessary to make a scientific analysis of a phenomenon. In Chapter 6, observation and measurement are described in greater detail.

Experiments are means of establishing cause-effect relationships between events. Once a phenomenon comes under systematic observation and measurement, experimentation becomes possible. The concept of experiment is described later in this chapter.

To summarize, a comprehensive view of science includes the philosophical, behavioral, and methodological considerations just described. Throughout this book, these aspects of science are addressed in different practical and theoretical contexts.

Outcome of Scientific Activity

Science is said to have certain *goals*. However, when we talk about the goals of science, we are actually talking about the eventual outcome of scientific activity. *Goals* are future events that cannot affect scientists' or anyone else's behavior. Scientists do what they do because of their past and present contingencies, not because of some future events called *goals*. Therefore, consideration of the typical outcome of scientific activity is more meaningful.

Description of natural events (phenomena) is a basic outcome of scientific activity. After having observed an event, scientists describe its characteristics. Therefore, describing a phenomenon is usually the first step in scientific analysis. An adequate description of the characteristics of an event often is useful in taking additional steps such as experimentation and prediction. At this stage, mostly the observable properties of the event under study are described. A researcher observing the language behaviors of a 2-year-old child may note the conditions under which specified language behaviors are produced. The observation might answer questions about the number and types of language behaviors a 2-year-old child produces under specified conditions of stimulation.

Some disciplines rely heavily on naturalistic observations. Ethology, for example, is a study of the behavior of animals in their natural habitat. Ethologists typically do not manipulate the animal's natural environment to see what effects follow. Rather, the goal is to understand the relation between animal behavior and its habitat, including the animal's social milieu. Similarly, astronomy is mostly observational, not because of choice but because of necessity. Nonexperimental, observational sciences do not seek to effect changes in the phenomena they study. However, in many branches of science, mere description of a phenomenon is not sufficient for a complete scientific analysis. This is because in the case of many complex events, descriptions tell us what is happening, but not necessarily why. Therefore, whenever practical and ethical, a description should lead to experimentation designed to find out why the event is taking place.

In communication disorders, descriptive studies and models are emphasized.

This is partly understandable because other kinds of studies, especially those designed to develop theories or find the instigating causes of speech-language disorders, have been few, mostly inadequate, and therefore frustrating. This does not mean, however, that we should stop at the level of descriptive analysis. As we shall see in later chapters, experimental analysis of the causal variables of speech-language behaviors is much needed. Such an analysis makes it possible to effect changes in disorders of communication.

Understanding natural phenomena is another significant outcome of science. We do not understand an event when we do not know what causes it. No amount of description is sufficient to achieve an understanding of a given event. Therefore, discovery of cause-effect relations through experimentation is one of the most desirable outcomes of scientific activity.

Explanation is another outcome of science that is closely related to understanding an event. Science seeks to explain events. In a technical sense, an explanation is the specification of a cause-effect relation. Scientists explain events by pointing to their causes. Therefore, the two outcomes—understanding and explanation—are realized simultaneously.

Prediction follows a valid explanation. In most cases, a demonstrated cause of an event will help predict the occurrence of that event. Scientific predictions are reliable to the extent the explanations are valid.

Control of natural phenomena is the final outcome of science. In most sciences, scientists can control an event when they understand its cause and predict its occurrence. Events are controlled when they are changed in some manner. An extreme change is achieved when an event's occurrence is prevented or greatly increased. Other kinds of changes are obtained when some properties of the event are altered. The event may still take place but at a reduced magnitude, duration, or intensity.

Control may be an optional outcome of science. One might understand, explain, and predict an event but be unwilling to change it. To a certain extent, an option to control an event may be a matter of social policy. For example, experimental genetics might show that it is possible to create new forms of life, but society may not wish to exert that control. On the other hand, some sciences cannot exert significant control on most of the phenomena they study even though the scientists understand them and reliably predict their occurrence. Astronomy is a significant example. The movements of planets and resulting events such as eclipses are well understood and reliably predicted, but no control is exerted on these events.

Most of the outcomes of science depend upon one thing: the specification of cause-effect relations. Much of the methodological activity in advanced sciences seeks to isolate cause-effect relations among natural phenomena. Disciplines that do not focus upon this kind of activity usually cannot achieve other outcomes such as explanation or prediction. They also are less likely to be regarded as sciences.

Variables and Their Types

The basic method of scientific investigation is empirical analysis. This means that in many cases, the phenomenon to be studied is broken down into smaller components that can be observed more easily, measured more precisely, and manipulated more successfully. Very broadly defined phenomena often are not suitable for scientific investigation, especially during the early stages. In the analysis of a phenomenon, scientists first identify some specific aspect that can be defined in a narrow and precise manner. Variables are narrowly defined aspects of an event that can be measured and manipulated. In this sense, a phenomenon refers to a broad event, and variables are certain aspects of it.

Variables are specific aspects of events that *change* (vary). Everything that exists varies across time and conditions. In fact, much of the methodology of science has been designed to isolate and (when appropriate and feasible) to control the sources of variability in naturally occurring events. Science seeks to analyze variables; they are what the scientist observes, measures, changes, and manipulates in some way.

Natural events—physical, chemical, biological, behavioral, and other kinds— are a bundle of variables. Articulation (speech sound production), language, fluency, and voice are the four large classes of phenomena scientists in communication disorders investigate. The typical as well as the clinical aspects of these phenomena create a host of specific variables that must be measured and manipulated. The phenomenon of language is a collection of such specific variables as the production of *plural s* or *two-word phrases*. The phenomenon of articulation contains specific variables relating to the production of various phonemes at different levels of response topography. Similar specific variables can be identified for other aspects of communicative behaviors and communication disorders.

A discussion of different types of variables can be helpful in gaining a better understanding of this important concept in scientific research, especially experimentation, and theories. The most important variables include the following: dependent, independent, active, assigned, and intervening.

Dependent Variables

Dependent variable is the effect that scientists study. In many cases, scientific analyses start with some dependent variables, which may be the effects of suspected or unknown causes. Confronting an effect, the scientist may try to find its cause. In other words, the dependent variable is an event or an aspect of some event that needs to be researched and explained.

Dependent variables are carved out of broader constructs or concepts. *Language*, for example, is a construct and cannot be a dependent variable unless it is broken down into specific, narrowly defined, and thus measurable aspect of it. For example, a researcher might ask, how do children acquire *the production of plural morpheme?* The *production of a plural morpheme* is a narrowly defined dependent variable. Other dependent variables are specified in such questions as the following: What are the causes of *naming errors* in *aphasia?* What are *speech dysfluencies?* Why do some children fail to learn the correct production of *speech sounds?* What is the best way of teaching the *manual sign for mother* to children who are deaf? What causes high-frequency *hearing loss?* These are some of the many questions the communication disorders specialist typically asks and tries to answer. Thus, all aspects of speech and language, when specified in measurable terms in a research study, and treated as an effect of some causal factor, are dependent variables.

As the term suggests, the existence of dependent variables is contingent upon some other variables. Dependent variables are said to be a *function* of causal variables. In other words, effects depend upon causes; therefore, no causes, no effects.

Dependent variables are typically measured and monitored by the scientist, but they are not directly manipulated. They can be manipulated only indirectly and only when their causes are known. For instance, we cannot directly enhance correct phoneme production. We can enhance it only when we have access to a treatment method that increases it. We treat disorders and teach communicative skills only by manipulating teaching or treatment methods. This is what is meant by *indirect manipulation of dependent variables*. Throughout a scientific study, scientists measure the dependent variables while they manipulate other variables expected to change the dependent variables. Such measures tell the scientists whether the manipulations are affecting the dependent variables. An educator, for example, may continuously measure specific, operationally defined language behaviors in children who are exposed to a teaching method.

To be useful in research, dependent variables must be defined in precise terms. They must be defined **operationally**, which means that the definition must specify how the variable will be measured. In communicative disorders, *language, stuttering, dysarthria, or speech sound disorders*, for example, are constructs that are too broad to be dependent variables in clinical or basic research studies. As mentioned before, specific dependent variables may be carved out of those broad constructs.

Independent Variables

Independent variables are the causes of the observed effects. Independent variables often are unknown, many times presumed or hypothesized, and sometimes accidentally stumbled upon. When a research question aimed at discovering a cause-effect relation is effectively answered, an independent variable will have been identified. For example, when data show that language disorders are due to some form of environmental deprivation, we have both a dependent variable (language disorder) and an independent variable (environmental deprivation). Similarly, when audiological research shows that prolonged exposure to high-frequency noise (cause) produces a type of hearing loss (effect), we have a dependent and an independent variable. Therefore, the specification of independent variables is crucial to any type of causal analysis. In many cases, the effect (i.e., the goal or objective) of successful scientific research is the description of an independent variable. Independent variables **explain** dependent variables because an explanation of an event is nothing but a specification of its cause.

Scientists directly measure and manipulate their independent variables. Such manipulations can induce systematic changes in a dependent variable. When there is no access to the independent variable of an event, the scientist cannot induce changes in that event. In communication disorders, all teaching and treatment methods are independent variables. We can effect changes in communicative behaviors only by manipulating those methods.

There are three important kinds of independent variables in communication disorders. The first kind of independent variables *explains normal communicative behaviors in general.* The potential causal variables of oral and sign language, speech, voice, and fluency fall into this category. For example, one can ask what causes fluency or what causes language or phonological acquisition. Answers to such questions explain communicative behaviors in general.

The second kind of independent variables *explains disorders of communication.* Why do children fail to acquire language, phonological responses, or fluent speech? The same questions can be rephrased in terms of the causes of disorders of language, articulation, fluency, or voice. Such questions address the causes of disorders and diseases in a clinical science. The first and second kinds of independent variables can be counterparts of each other. For example, if language acquisition is made possible by parental stimulation (whatever that means), then a disorder of language may be due to deficiencies in such stimulation.

The third kind of independent variables is the *treatment techniques.* Treatment variables are the causes of positive changes in the disorder being treated. They can help change undesirable effects (diseases or disorders). To effect changes in a disorder, the clinician must gain access to a treatment (independent) variable. The treatment variable is systematically manipulated so that the effects are eliminated or modified.

Most variables do not have a fixed position of being dependent or independent. They can be either, depending on the frame of reference of particular studies. A given variable may be independent in one study and dependent in another. For example, in one study, a clinician may try to show that speech-related anxiety increases stuttering, defined and measured in some specific way. In this case, anxiety is the independent variable and stuttering is the dependent variable. The investigator may hope to show that systematic increases or decreases in experimentally manipulated anxiety produce corresponding changes in the frequency of stuttering. In another study, the investigator might try to show that when stuttering is reduced, speech-related anxiety also is reduced and that when stuttering increases, anxiety in speaking situations also increases. In this case, stuttering is the independent variable and anxiety is the dependent variable. Similarly, hearing loss is a dependent variable when its cause is investigated, but it is an independent variable when its effect on communication or academic performance is assessed.

Active and Assigned Variables

An **active variable** is a controlled (manipulated) independent variable. Typically, research studies involve many variables, only some of which the researcher controls. In experimental research, the investigator controls at least one independent variable. But the investigator might suspect the existence of other potential independent variables, some of which are not manipulable or simply not manipulated.

An **assigned variable** is a presumed or potential independent variable the investigator does not or cannot manipulate. Assigned variables may influence the dependent variable under study. Assigned variables that cannot be manipulated that may still have an effect include the characteristics of participants used in research.

In research involving biological organisms (including human participants), assigned variables are thought to play an important role. The typical assigned variables include such factors as age, gender, intelligence, socioeconomic status, occupation, education, ethnic and cultural background, physical and mental health, behavioral (personality) characteristics, and genetic predispositions. One or several of these assigned variables may influence (reduce or increase) the actual effect of an active (manipulated) independent variable. For example, an investigator may study the effects of a parent stimulation program on the rate of normal language acquisition. In this case, the parent stimulation program is the active, manipulated, independent variable. At the same time, the rate of language acquisition may be partly determined by assigned variables such as the child's intelligence, gender, age, and undetermined genetic predispositions. Obviously, the investigator cannot control such participant characteristics. They are treated as assigned independent variables whose contribution often is inferred.

In experimental research, it is possible to rule out the influence of most assigned variables. For example, an investigator can show that the parent stimulation program works regardless of children's intelligence, gender, and socioeconomic status.

Assigned variables are most troublesome in nonexperimental research, in which investigators do not manipulate independent variables and do not control the potential assigned or other variables. In certain kinds of research, participants are grouped on the basis of assigned variables. Subsequently, the groups may be shown to be different on some dependent variable. Then the investigator may conclude that the differences in the dependent variable are due to the difference in the assigned variables. For instance, a sample of children may be grouped according to

their social class while measuring their language performance. Any difference in the performance of the groups may then be attributed to the participants' social classes. In this type of research, there is no control of potential independent variables, and therefore there is no assurance that the conclusions are valid. In Chapter 4, different types of research are described and compared in greater detail.

Intervening Variables

Intervening variables are events or processes that are supposed to be active inside a person's body. Of all the kinds of variables researched by social, behavioral, and biological scientists, these are the most controversial. They are informally described as "in-the-head" variables. They may also be called *hypothetical constructs*. *Mind, nervous system,* and *cognition* are among the major intervening variables. These variables are thought to provide a link between observed dependent and independent variables. Such a link is considered missing when only the observed cause-effect relations are described.

The study of human behavior and particularly that of language is replete with intervening variables. Such presumed variables as language processing, linguistic competence, internalized rules of grammar, the theory of mind, and knowledge of phonologic rules in the current linguistic analyses are intervening variables. The term *cognition,* for example, is an enormous collection of a variety of intervening variables. The observable, productive language behavior is thought to be impossible without cognitive inputs and information-processing strategies.

Mentalism, the source of all intervening variables, asserts that observable behaviors are a product of internal, mental (psychological) processes that are not observable. According to mentalism, the unobservable mind is the source of observable actions. In due course, the nervous system, especially the brain, became more attractive as a source of action. Various kinds of processes are supposed to underlie observable actions. A popular source of action in general, and language in particular, is cognition.

Intervening variables are attractive to theorists who believe that an explanation of observable behaviors lies in unobservable events taking place in presumed entities or processes. The main problem with intervening variables is that they are simply inferred from observable behaviors, often in the absence of any kind of experimental manipulations or evidence. The most questionable practice relative to intervening variables is that processes inferred from observable behaviors are immediately offered as explanations of those behaviors. For instance, the presence of cognitive processes is inferred from certain language behaviors; in turn, cognitive processes are offered as explanations of those language behaviors. Because they are not directly measured, observed, or experimentally manipulated, the explanatory status of cognitive processes is highly questionable. What is inferred from an action cannot explain that action.

Causality and Functional Analysis

As noted earlier, science is essentially a search for cause-effect relations in natural events. Basic and applied scientists as well as clinicians need to gain access to causes of effects that need to be modified, controlled, or eliminated. Diseases and disorders can be treated more effectively when their causes are known. Also, as noted before, when causes are specified, events are explained.

A problem in scientific analysis of causality is that a dynamic set of complex events causes other events. Because this has been demonstrated repeatedly, a basic assumption of science is that events typically have multiple causes. Multiple causation generates methodological and analytical consequences.

Multiple Causation and Levels of Causality

Multiple causation is an empirical assumption that each event has several causes. Because of their multiple causality and attending complexity, most events cannot be analyzed in total or all at once. Therefore, scientists analyze them at different levels of observation. At each level of observation, a cause may be found. This results in different causes at different levels of analysis. In many cases, it also is possible to identify multiple causes at the same level of analysis. This means that causes and effects are nothing but a string of events. Depending on the temporospatial locus of analysis, an event is a cause of the succeeding effect, which is in turn a cause of the next event in the string. For instance, in a given individual, a stroke is an immediate cause of aphasia, a ruptured blood vessel in the brain may have caused that stroke, high blood pressure may have caused the rupture, and eating habits and genetic predisposition may have caused the high blood pressure. At a given level of analysis, only one causal variable may be found (e.g., stroke as a cause of aphasia).

Although experimental demonstrations are rare, it often is thought that most communication disorders are caused by a combination of genetic, neurophysiological, behavioral, and environmental factors. Therefore, speech and language disorders can be analyzed at the levels of genetic, neurophysiological, behavioral, and environmental events. At each of these levels, there may be multiple causes. Theoretically, many genetic conditions, some of which may be active simultaneously, can be causally related to a given disorder. Cleft palate, for example, can be a result of several genetic, teratogenic, and toxic factors. Neurophysiological variables may be genetically determined to a certain extent, but some of them may not have a clear-cut pattern of inheritance, thus making it difficult to identify potential genetic factors in given cases. Nevertheless, at the level of neurophysiologic functioning, multiple factors may cause a given disorder. The neurophysiologic mechanism may show an inherited weakness, an injury-based (environmentally induced) deficiency, or a disease-based problem. Similarly, an environmental analysis may show deficiencies in stimulation, reinforcing contingencies, or educational practices.

When different causes of a disorder are identified at different levels of observation, the causal analysis may be shifted to a more complex level. The investigator may now analyze potential interactions between different types of causes. For instance, an initial analysis at the genetic level may show that stuttering is partly determined by a genetic predisposition. Next, an analysis at the neurophysiological level might reveal neural and muscu-lar aberrations in persons who stutter. A further analysis at the learning and conditioning level might show that certain types of conditioning or environmental variables also are important in the etiology of stuttering. Eventually, the investigator might analyze how these three types of causal variables interact to produce the final effect (stuttering).

It must be understood that a tentative determination of a cause at a given level may not necessarily negate the importance of causes at other levels of analysis. For example, the strong possibility that there are some genetic factors in the etiology of stuttering does not rule out the presence of environmental factors. Similarly, experimental demonstration of environmental factors does not negate the importance of genetic influence. It often is believed that genetic and neurophysiological explanations of behavioral phenomena will automatically discredit explanations based on environmental or conditioning variables. However, the philosophy of multiple causation does not support this belief. For example, the evidence that stuttering is associated with a genetic predisposition does not negate the experimentally demonstrated effects of a conditioning contingency. Neurological investigations may find that when someone stutters, blood flow to motor speech areas increases, but such findings do not minimize the importance of *experimentally demonstrated* effects of reinforcement of fluency or the reduction in stuttering due to time-out contingency. Similarly, future neurologic research may be better able to describe what happens in the nervous system when a child learns the alphabet or produces the very first word. Such a description, however, cannot negate the influence of teaching and other environmental variables. The parents and teachers still provide certain stimulus conditions and arrange certain response consequences for the learning to take place.

Instigating Causes Versus Maintaining Causes

Instigating causes create an effect and **maintaining causes** sustain that effect over time. Many disorders, including those of communication, may have been caused by one set of causes and maintained by an entirely different set of causes. Possibly, an event may be caused and maintained by the same multiple causes. However, in many cases, instigating and maintaining causes may be different. Also, instigating causes might still be working while new maintaining causes may have been added. Alternatively, regardless of how it was started, an event may be maintained by different causes at different times.

In physical and medical sciences, the maintaining causes may not always be radically different from the original or instigating causes. The same infection, tumor, or injury can be the original (instigating) as well as the maintaining cause of a given disease. This is not to say that either the cause or the effect is static. Both are in fact dynamic. They change and produce additional effects, which become new causes of new effects. Nevertheless, physical, chemical, or topographical similarities between the instigating and maintaining causes can often be identified. In disorders of human performance or behavior, however, the instigating and the maintaining causes could be entirely different.

Several hypotheses in communication disorders illustrate this point. For example, it may be hypothesized that parental punishment of dysfluencies causes stuttering in young children. Thus, the instigating cause of stuttering may be parental punishment. However, if stuttering continues into adult life in the absence of parental punishment, the maintaining causes are clearly different from the instigating causes. One might hypothesize that the maintaining causes are negatively reinforcing events stemming from avoidance of difficult speaking situations. In this case, the maintaining causes may be diametrically opposed to the original causes (punishment vs. reinforcement). To take another example, the speech and voice disorders of a child with cleft palate might persist even after adequate surgical repair of the cleft. This persisting disorder cannot be attributed to the nonexistent cleft. In such cases, the disorder has a different set of maintaining causes.

It is well known that searches for the causes of communication disorders have often been frustrating. At best, such searches have led only to speculative reasoning. When parents ask such questions as, "What caused my child's stuttering?" or "What is the cause of my child's language delay?" we often go into a discussion of possibilities and conjectures that may have only a general relevance to groups of persons with the disorder. But such discussions are dissatisfying to the parents, who expect an answer relevant to *their* child. It also is equally well known that in the "diagnostics" of communication disorders, clinicians do not diagnose anything in the medical sense, because within the medical model, diagnosis means finding a cause or causes of a given disease. Often, this failure to find causes of communication disorders has led to a belief that clinicians should simply be descriptive and not be concerned with causes.

Description is only the beginning stage of scientific analysis. There is no substitute for a causal analysis in basic or applied sciences. The frustrating searches in the field have been concerned mostly with original causes of communication disorders, be they organic or environmental. Such causes of communication disorders have not been understood, perhaps for several reasons. One possibility is that the original causes may be physical or chemical conditions that are unavailable for examination as long as the disorder persists. Another possibility is that even if physical or chemical conditions do cause communication disorders, such conditions may not be enduring. Therefore, those conditions may not be present at the time of examination, which is typically done some time after the manifestation of the disorder. Still another possibility is that the causal, physical, or chemical conditions are as yet unobservable because of technical limitations. Furthermore, there may be temporary environmental causes, which also are not detected upon later examination.

We know more about the maintaining causes of communication disorders than we do about the instigating causes. The search for environmental maintaining causes has generally been more productive and less speculative than searches for original causes. It is known that in treating many disorders of communication, clinicians alter possible maintaining causes and teach behaviors that are incompatible with the existing faulty behaviors. For example, a clinician who ignores misarticulations while reinforcing correct productions tries to alter the factors that may have been maintaining those misarticulations. Similarly, a language clinician who withholds all attention to gestures and grunts while reinforcing meaningful vocal productions is eliminating potential maintaining factors of inappropriate behaviors. Though the instigating causes of many

communication disorders are unknown, clinicians can still treat several disorders successfully. This suggests that clinicians generally manipulate maintaining causes of appropriate and inappropriate behaviors in their clients.

It is desirable to find the original causes of diseases and disorders. A knowledge of the original causes can be useful in preventing a disorder. To reap the applied advantages of original causes, they must be experimentally demonstrated, not just inferred from the effects. However, most presumed original causes are difficult to manipulate experimentally. Johnson's hypothesis that stuttering is a result of parental negative reaction to the child's normal "nonfluency" is a case in point (Johnson & Associates, 1959). For ethical reasons, negative parental reactions are not experimentally manipulable. For example, we cannot ask parents to react negatively to dysfluencies of fluently speaking children to see if stuttering develops.

Experiment and Experimental Control

As noted earlier, establishing cause-effect relations is the key to understanding, explaining, predicting, and controlling natural phenomena. To establish cause-effect relations, scientists engage in various activities, including observation, measurement, and data analysis. However, the most important of these activities is an experiment because it is the most powerful of the strategies available to scientists to establish cause-effect relations.

An **experiment** can be technically defined as the manipulation of an independent variable or variables under controlled conditions to produce systematic changes in a dependent variable or variables. Not every kind of research is an experiment. There is no experiment unless the researcher has clearly identified at least one causal factor whose influence on a dependent variable is assessed while other potential causes are controlled.

Manipulation of an independent variable is accomplished by introducing or altering that variable. It is the most important feature of an experiment. The typical question that prompts an experiment is, "What happens when I do this?" and in this sense, the researcher is already clear about the potential independent variable.

In clinical treatment research, an independent variable is **manipulated** whenever a treatment technique is introduced, withdrawn, reversed, or varied in some systematic manner. A treatment is **introduced** when it is first applied, **withdrawn** when it is simply discontinued, **reversed** when it is applied to some other behavior or disorder, and **varied** when its frequency or intensity is altered. When the number of treatment sessions is increased or decreased, the strength of the independent variable is altered. Within given sessions, the frequency of applications of an independent variable may be changed. The frequency of reinforcer delivery, for example, can be changed within or across treatment sessions. Manipulations of an independent variable include these and other alterations introduced by the researcher.

Another important feature of an experiment is that the independent variable is manipulated under controlled conditions. **Controlled conditions** exist when extraneous independent variables are systematically ruled out. In other words, when establishing a cause-effect relation, the researcher must ensure that other potential causes were not also involved in the experiment. When several potential causes are present, it becomes impossible to determine the cause or the causes of the effect being analyzed. Thus, the essence of an experiment is the manipulation of a single independent variable that produces an effect on the dependent variable under controlled conditions.

In clinical research, experiments are the means to demonstrate that certain treatment variables were indeed effective. Through experimental manipulations, clinicians can demonstrate that changes in disorders were brought about by particular treatment variables and that those changes were unrelated to other potential treatment variables. We shall return to this type of research in Chapter 4.

The cause-effect relation isolated by an experiment is known also as a **controlling relation**. Well-designed experiments help isolate a controlling relation between two variables: The cause controls the effects. Controlled conditions, however, should not be confused with controlling relations. **Controlled conditions** are various procedures designed to rule out the potential causes other than the one the researcher is interested in. In essence, controlled conditions are structures of experiments, whereas controlling relations include a manipulated cause and an effect, observed in temporal proximity.

Hypotheses in Scientific Research

Hypotheses are predicted relations between two or more variables selected for an investigation. A good hypothesis specifies a dependent variable and at least one independent variable. Therefore, all hypotheses are statements of cause-effect relations between certain variables.

Because hypotheses are typically formulated prior to the actual experimentation, they are predictive statements. A hypothesis predicts that when a certain event is present, a certain other event will follow as a consequence.

Scientific hypotheses contrast with everyday guesses, predictions, and assumptions about cause-effect relations. For the most part, hypotheses of everyday life are informal, sometimes vague, and rarely expressed in measurable terms. As a result, popular hypotheses are difficult to verify. Scientific hypotheses, on the other hand, are more formal, specific, and expressed in operational (i.e., measurable) terms. For those reasons, scientific hypotheses are testable. Furthermore, unlike everyday guesses, good scientific hypotheses are based on systematic observations. Ideally, scientific hypotheses tend to be verified, whereas everyday hypotheses may lead to untested beliefs.

Although hypotheses bearing no particular relation to a theory are sometimes formulated and tested, most hypotheses are derived from a theory. In fact, hypotheses are the means by which theories are tested. A complex theory may give rise to a number of hypotheses, each of which is tested independently. If most of the hypotheses are verified with positive results, then the theory is said to have received experimental support.

Need for Hypotheses: Two Views

Whether hypotheses are essential in the conduct of meaningful empirical research depends upon the investigator's research style and philosophy. Traditionally, research is equated with hypothesis testing. It often is said that scientific research starts with a hypothesis. The statistical approach to research asserts that hypotheses are essential in empirical research (Kerlinger, 1973). It is argued that hypotheses give direction to research because they suggest what to look for. It is believed that without a hypothesis, there may be nothing to investigate. It also is believed that hypothesis testing is the most important —if not the only—means of verifying scientific theories. Moreover, the hypothesis is described as "the most powerful tool man has invented to achieve dependable knowledge" (Kerlinger, 1973, p. 25).

Advocates of the usefulness of hypotheses suggest that scientists should first formulate a hypothesis and then design an experiment to test that hypothesis. Depending on the results of the experiment, the hypothesis is either retained or rejected. When a substantial number of hypotheses derived from a theory are verified and accepted, the theory is validated.

An alternative view on the usefulness of hypotheses has been suggested by the experimental analysis of behavior (Bachrach, 1969; Sidman, 1960; Skinner, 1974). This view questions the need for, and the importance of, formal hypotheses in the conduct of research. Proponents of this view suggest that it is possible to investigate important research problems without the directive of formal hypotheses (Sidman, 1960; Skinner, 1956). One of Newton's famous statements is *Hypotheses non fingo* ("I do not make hypotheses"). Skinner (1972) has also stated that he has "never attacked a problem by constructing a Hypothesis" (p. 112).

Hypotheses, as noted earlier, are proposed after a research question has been formulated. In this sense, a hypothesis is nothing but the prediction of results of a planned experiment. Skinner (1972) wrote that one can ask a question and immediately proceed to answer it through an experiment. He saw the intermediate step of hypothesis formulation as an unnecessary exercise. Whether predicted or not, a well-designed experiment may produce results that throw light on the relation between the variables investigated. Because the experimental results are the final test of a relation between variables, the need to predict those results beforehand is not clear. Because it is the evidence that stands, not necessarily the hypothesis, it is best to ask a question and produce results through experimentation. The results then help shape a valid statement of a cause-effect relation.

There are other problems with the formulation of hypotheses prior to experimentation. If one insists that all meaningful research should start out with a well-formulated hypothesis, it is hard to imagine how unsuspected relations between variables could ever come to light. Hypothesis testing minimizes the importance of accidental discoveries. And yet, as we noted in Chapter 1, many important scientific discoveries were made accidentally. By nature, accidental discoveries are unsuspected and hence unformulated in terms of an a priori hypothesis. Often, accidental findings are noted during the course of research designed to test formal hypotheses. The history of natural sciences is replete with examples of accidental discoveries that proved to be more important than the planned research during which such "accidents" occurred (Bachrach, 1969).

Another problem with formal hypotheses is that they can bias the investigator. A researcher who hypothesizes that *A* is the cause of *B* fully expects to support that hypothesis by the results of his or her experiment. If not, there would be no point in proposing that hypothesis. Theo-

retically, negative results should lead to a prompt rejection of the hypothesis. In practice, however, some investigators may show a tendency to explain away negative results in an effort to breathe life into their dying hypotheses. There is always the possibility that a hypothesis was true but the results did not support it because of methodological problems, but in the absence of convincing evidence of such problems, the hypothesis must be at least temporarily rejected. This may not happen because of the researcher's belief and investment in the hypothesis.

Those who use formal hypotheses recognize their biasing effects. Because the need for hypotheses is taken for granted, statisticians have offered a unique solution to the problem of bias: the null hypothesis (Fisher, 1956). The term *null* means zero, and a **null hypothesis** is a statement of no relation between two variables. It also is known as a *statistical hypothesis*. If using a null hypothesis, an investigator who believes that *A* is the cause of *B* would actually propose that *A* and *B* are unrelated. For example, an investigator who thinks that the parental punishment of dysfluencies in speech causes stuttering would actually state that parental punishment and stuttering are unrelated. The investigator then hopes to show that this null hypothesis is not true and that parental punishment and stuttering are indeed causally related. When a hypothesis is stated in positive terms, the investigator expects to support it, and when it is stated in the null form, the investigator expects to reject it. Nonetheless, it is presumed that an investigator who proposes a null hypothesis *instead* of a positive one would not be biased in the interpretation of results.

It is highly questionable whether the null is an answer to the biasing effects of hypotheses. The null is no more than a surrogate for a positive hypothesis the investigator believes in. All knowledgeable readers of research papers know that a null hypothesis really means the opposite of what is stated. An investigator's efforts are directed toward *rejecting* a null hypothesis just as much as *supporting* a positive one. Therefore, when the results fail to reject a null, the investigator may try to explain the results away—the null was not what was really believed. The null is a façade and a transparent one at that. It is hard to imagine how it can help remove or reduce the investigator's bias. For these reasons, those who do not believe in the value of formal hypotheses do not take the null seriously. Skinner (1969) has stated that in his research, "the null hypothesis finds itself in the null class" (p. 81).

The biases of an investigator are a fundamental problem that cannot be eliminated by statistical devices and null hypotheses. Investigators who do not state a hypothesis may still exert biases in interpreting their results. Therefore, not stating a hypothesis is not effective as a means of overcoming one's own biases regarding the outcome of research. On the other hand, an explicit statement of a hypothesis commits an investigator to a public position. It can thus create an additional pressure on the investigator to support the stated position. Typically, hypotheses are derived from already published theories for which the investigator may be well known. In such contexts, formation of hypotheses can have an especially biasing effect on the interpretation of results.

Objective interpretation of experimental results requires a rigorous high level of intellectual discipline. This discipline is a part of the scientist's disposition to value evidence more highly than his or her opinions and expectations. Artificial

devices such as the null hypothesis do not solve the difficult problem of investigator bias. The solution is to train scientists who are objective and who continue to be so because of their personal history, shaped mostly by education and experience.

Theories and Hypotheses

It is common knowledge that scientists build theories. Probably it is no exaggeration to say that most people equate theory building with scientific research. Many philosophers of science believe that the aim of scientific research is to develop theories. Theories help us understand events around us. Theories are valued products of scientific investigations.

A **theory** can be defined as a set of statements concerning a functional relation between a class of independent variables and a class of dependent variables. Therefore, a theory *explains* an event. In the technical sense, a clearly specified functional relation between variables is the heart of a theory.

In a more general sense, a theory can be described as a systematic body of evidence-based information concerning a phenomenon. A theory begins with a thorough description of the event or the effect to be explained. It states the conditions under which the occurrence of that event is probable. The properties of the event, such as the topography (form), frequency, magnitude, intensity, and levels of complexity, also are specified. Variations in the properties and the conditions associated with specified variations are described.

After having described the event, the theory explains the event by specifying why it occurs. In other words, the causal variable or variables are specified. In essence, a theory states that *Y* exists because of X. Furthermore, the theory may describe limitations of the discovered causal relation. It might specify any exceptions noted during the systematic, experimental observations. Finally, a good theory clearly specifies how it can be verified; in other words, a theory specifies conditions under which the proposed cause-effect relations can be accepted or rejected by other investigators.

A hypothesis can be contrasted with a theory. A theory is a more comprehensive description and explanation of a total phenomenon. A hypothesis, on the other hand, is concerned with a more specific prediction stemming from a theory. Hypotheses are testable propositions derived from a theory. It is possible, however, to propose hypotheses that are not a part of theories. In either case, the scope of a hypothesis is more limited than that of a theory. For example, a theory of language disorders might explain all kinds of language disorders found in all age groups, whereas a hypothesis might be concerned with the specific language problems of a particular group such as people with intellectual disabilities or autism spectrum disorder.

Inductive and Deductive Reasoning

Logic and reasoning play an important role in designing and conducting research studies and in the formulation of theories. As a part of philosophy, logic describes formal rules of correct reasoning. Because incorrect reasoning may lead to faulty experiments as well as faulty interpretation of results, it is necessary to understand the logical basis of science and scientific

experiments. The early development of the scientific method was due to philosophers' interest in logic and reasoning. In fact, many early scientists were also the philosophers, logicians, physicists, and psychologists of their times.

The philosophers recognized two important modes of logical reasoning: deductive and inductive. Deduction and induction are a part of everyday reasoning as well, but they are used in a more formal manner in scientific thinking. These modes of reasoning are especially involved in the process of constructing scientific theories. Therefore, theories themselves often are described as either inductive or deductive.

Induction is reasoning from the particular to the general. Inductive reasoning starts from an observation of particular instances of an event and eventually arrives at some general conclusions regarding the nature and causation of that event. Every time an event is observed, such factors as the precipitating conditions, intensity, magnitude, and so on are carefully recorded. Observations of this kind are made until several individual instances of the event have been observed and described.

The observed individual instances are categorized to see if some common patterns emerge. It may be determined that whenever the event occurred, certain common conditions were also present, and whenever the event failed to occur, the common conditions were absent. For example, an audiologist might observe that whenever some patients took a certain prescription drug, their hearing thresholds were temporarily elevated, and whenever they were free from the drug, the thresholds were lower. It also may be observed that when certain conditions systematically vary across instances, the magnitude of the event also varies. In our example, whenever the dosage increased, the hearing thresholds were lower and vice versa. Such observations could result in a collection of reliable facts about the event.

The facts gathered through observation lead to certain conclusions regarding the nature and causation of the observed event. The scientist may tentatively conclude that the events that reliably precede an effect are the cause of the effect. A simple logical rule scientists follow is that *causes precede effects.*

In the inductive reasoning used in modern science, observation is not limited to describing the observed event or effect. Observation also includes experimentation, without which a valid theory cannot be built. Instead of waiting for the event to occur, a scientist may create it by manipulating what is believed to be the causal factor and then withdraw the factor to see if the event disappears. The cause-effect relations receive their maximum support when such experimental manipulations are successfully carried out. When such experiments are repeated with comparable outcome, a theory may emerge out of the data.

Inductive reasoning is the very method by which we draw conclusions based on our personal experiences. We know that it is not prudent to draw conclusions based on isolated experiences regarding an event or an individual. When similar experiences accumulate, certain conclusions may be considered more appropriate. For example, a person who knows nothing about the education of speech-language pathologists might come in contact with one of them and find out that the pathologist is a college graduate. The same person may later come in contact with another clinician who also is a college graduate. In this manner, the person may meet many

clinicians, each with a college degree. That person may then conclude that all speech-language pathologists are college graduates. Inductive reasoning used in theory building is a more systematic use of this process with the added feature of controlled experimentation.

Deduction is reasoning from a general rule or set of rules to particular instances. Deductive reasoning starts with what are known as logical premises that are assumed to be valid. Premises are general statements, which suggest that given their validity, certain specific statements also are true. In other words, conclusions are deduced from valid propositions. A set of assumed and deduced statements is known as a **syllogism**, which is a logical device described by the ancient philosopher Aristotle. A syllogism starts with two general statements whose validity is assumed. For example, one may state that "all speech-language pathologists have a college degree" and "Jane is a speech-language pathologist." These two statements will then serve as the basis for the deduction, or conclusion, that "Jane has a college degree." Syllogisms, as described by Aristotle, are used in modern deductive logic with very little modification. Thus, deductive reasoning begins with generalities and ends with relevant specific instances.

In building a deductive theory, a scientist first makes a series of proposals. Of course, these proposals are based on observations that suggest the existence of certain cause-effect relations. In essence, a theory may be proposed on the basis of observations. From this theory, specific predictions may be derived. Predictions suggest that if the theory is valid, certain specific results must be observed. For example, an audiologist might make a theoretical statement that noise exposure is a cause of certain type of hearing loss. If this theory is valid, a prediction that the frequency of that kind of hearing loss in people living in quiet, remote mountain communities is lower than that in people living in noisy environments should be true. When feasible, predictions of this kind are then put to experimental test. If the results of the experiment confirm the prediction, the theory is supported. If repeated experiments confirm various predictions of the theory, then that theory is accepted as valid.

Deductive theories are more commonly proposed in physical sciences than in behavioral sciences. In behavioral sciences, many have tried to develop such theories, but few have succeeded. This is because a large body of well-established facts is needed to attempt the formulation of even a rudimentary deductive theory. Compared to social and psychological sciences, physical sciences have an impressive body of accepted facts and methods of observation; that is, physical sciences have a long tradition of experimentation, which has produced a more solid database. Because of this, better deductive theories can be proposed in physical sciences than in psychological and social sciences.

An investigator who uses the deductive method proposes a theory without having conducted certain crucial experiments. Therefore, the investigator takes some risk in proposing a deductive theory. The ensuing experiments may support all, some, or none of the predictions made by the theory. The investigator is then expected to revise the theory in light of the evidence gathered or abandon it altogether. Further predictions of the revised theory are then tested experimentally. Thus, continued experimentation

may appropriately modify and eventually validate a deductive theory.

Deductive and Inductive Theories Compared

It is useful to compare inductive and deductive theories. Both types of theories start with certain systematic observations of a given phenomenon. Questions are then raised regarding such aspects as the nature, frequency, and magnitude of the phenomenon under investigation. The two approaches immediately diverge, however.

The investigator using the deductive approach will propose a theory, whereas the one using the inductive method will proceed to experiment. In other words, within the deductive framework, questions lead to answers that need to be verified, whereas within the inductive method, questions lead to experiments, which may supply the answers. The deductive method is quick in providing an explanation but slow in verifying it. The inductive method is slow in offering an explanation, but the offered explanation tends to be based on better evidence. Significant amount of experimental work lies *ahead* of a deductive theory but *behind* an inductive theory. The inductive theorist must resist the temptation to offer a theory without evidence, and a deductive theorist must resist the tendency to avoid the difficult course of experimentation after having proposed an explanation.

Most, if not all, of the differences between the two approaches lie in the process of theory construction, not necessarily in the final product, which is a validated theory in either case. Validated deductive theories are no different from validated inductive theories. Whether one builds a deductive or an inductive theory depends upon the state of the art of the scientist's subject matter and his or her personal dispositions shaped by the history of training, education, and experience.

Generally, the inductive method is somewhat safe in disciplines that do not have widely accepted dependent variables, methods of observations and measurements, or a relatively long tradition of experimentation that has produced data of some generality. Communication disorders is such a discipline. Therefore, the inductive approach may be the more desirable of the two strategies. Deductive theories in communication disorders tend to be based on meager evidence and hence more speculative than they ought to be. Besides, it takes a substantial amount of time to verify a deductive theory, and in the meantime, many persons may prematurely accept it as valid.

Other dangers of deductive theories are personal. Some of those who propose deductive theories may find it harder to face negative evidence that refutes their well-known position. In such cases, instead of revising or rejecting the theory, some investigators may be more inclined to find faults with the data. A much worse situation arises when investigators propose deductive theories but fail to launch a program of research to verify their theories. This type of mistake is quite common in many fields, including communication disorders. Some deductive theorists seem to imply that their theories are already validated, because some evidence suggested them. Such a tendency betrays a misunderstanding of the deductive process. Initial observations help develop a deductive theory, but they do not validate it. The theory is validated only when

experimental tests of specific propositions deduced from that theory produce positive results. When this difficult validation process is neglected, the deductive approach becomes an excellent refuge for armchair theorists whose easy victims are colleagues who lack a sophisticated understanding of logic and science.

Theories and Scientific Laws

Validated theories allow scientists to move on to the next stage of scientific activity: formulation of scientific laws. **Scientific laws** are relatively brief statements of replicated or repeatedly confirmed relations between events; they are mostly predictive in nature. Compared with scientific laws, which apply to narrowly defined set of events, theories are broader in scope. Theories may still have portions that need to be verified or evidence that needs to be replicated. Scientific laws, on the other hand, are statements that have received maximum experimental support. Scientific laws are tersely written summaries of replicated evidence. Therefore, scientists are more confident in scientific laws than they are in theories.

It takes a long tradition of experimental research for a discipline to state its laws. Laws cannot be based on controversial evidence. Therefore, what is needed is agreement among scientists that similar observations lead to the same or similar results. Therefore, whether a set of statements (theories or laws) is accepted as valid depends largely on the opinion of scientists in the field. Scientific evidence is always relative because no scientist can claim that all possible observations of the phenomenon under investigation have been exhausted. Though several scientists may have repeatedly observed the same cause for a given event, there is no assurance that some other cause of the same event will not emerge in later observations.

The relativity of scientific evidence also means that evidence suggests probabilities and not certainties. Observed cause-effect relations may be more or less probable. When different investigators repeatedly observe the same empirical relationships between certain events, the probability that the relationships are valid is increased. In essence, continued accumulation of positive evidence increases the probability that a cause of the event investigated has been isolated. The continued efforts to gather more evidence may also help identify exceptions to the commonly observed relations. Special conditions under which the generally valid cause-effect relations do not hold may become evident. This will also help the scientist refine his or her statement of the cause-effect relations. When the evidence reaches a certain point of accumulation, scientists begin to think that a theory has been validated or that a more specific statement of a scientific law can be made.

Data and Evidence

It is clear from our previous discussions that theories are validated by scientific evidence. At this point, it is necessary to consider the process of developing scientific evidence. The process typically starts with the observation and collection of data.

Data are defined as the results of systematic observation. When a scientist observes an event and records some measured value of that event, data begin to accumulate. Scientific data are empirical in the sense that they are based upon actual happenings that resulted in some form of sensory contact. This then may lead to a more systematic measurement of the phenomenon. Such measured values constitute empirical data.

As noted earlier, a phenomenon may be observed at different levels. As a result, the data generated by observations may vary in validity and power to support theories. At the first and the lowest level of observation, an event is witnessed and described. This results in **descriptive data**, which are data in the minimal sense of the term. Descriptive data are useful in identifying the properties of an event but not in supporting a theory. Generally, descriptive data pertain to dependent variables. Although they might suggest potential independent variables, descriptive data cannot isolate such variables.

At the second level of observation, an event may be witnessed and thoroughly described, and some aspect of that event may be systematically measured. For example, one might describe *and* measure the frequency of stutterings, misarticulations, and so on. This level of observation provides the investigator with more than mere descriptive data. It generates **quantitative data**. This is an improvement over the first level of observation, but these data still cannot explain the event or support a theory.

At the third level of observation, the event is not only described and measured but also systematically manipulated. At this level, the event is brought under *experimental control*. To manipulate the event, the experimenter may select and apply a potential independent variable. This level of observation is comparable to clinical treatment in applied settings.

A disorder, for example, is described, measured, and *treated* to modify it. However, such treatment or the manipulation of an independent variable may have been done with no controls; that is, the experimenter may not have taken steps to rule out other potential causes. This level of uncontrolled experimentation yields **uncontrolled data**. In such cases, the resulting data may be suggestive of a cause-effect relation, but they still cannot support a theory.

The fourth level of observation includes everything specified under the third level, plus adequate controls to rule out the influence of extraneous independent variables. For example, the investigator may show that a clinical group that received treatment improved while a second comparable group, untreated, showed no improvement. This level of controlled experimentation produces **controlled data**, which are essential for supporting a theory. Controlled data can explain an event because the cause of the event will have been isolated through controlled experimentation. For the scientific community to accept the theory, however, an additional set of observations is necessary.

The fifth and the last level of observation is probably the most time-consuming and complex because it seeks to establish the *generality* of controlled experimental data. Experimental data established in one setting (laboratory or clinic), with one set of participants, by a given investigator, may or may not have generality. In other words, whether the same data can be obtained by other investigators in other settings with different participants is not known. **Generality** is the wider applicability of data and methods. A theory begins to gain a wider recognition only when its generality across settings, participants, and investigators is established.

Replication is the method of establishing generality of experimental findings; it is the repetition of an experiment in different settings, by different investigators, and with different participants. Replication yields **controlled replicated data**. Replicated data are obtained at different stages. Therefore, at any one time, there may be a greater or lesser degree of replicated data supporting a theory. We shall consider replication in greater detail in Chapter 11.

Scientific data obtained at any level of observation are objective in the sense that they are publicly verifiable. To establish the reliability of some data, different observers observing the same event must report similar values of measurement. Verified and replicated data also are known as **scientific evidence**. In essence, *evidence*, not mere observation, supports a theory.

Summary

- Science is a certain philosophy, behavioral dispositions, and a set of methods.
- Determinism means that all events have causes. Empiricism insists that all forms of knowledge are derived through sensory experience.
- As behavioral dispositions, science is what scientists do. Scientists tend to be objective, curious, nonauthoritarian, and skeptical of explanations not supported by data.
- Science is a set of objective methods used in investigating research questions.
- The outcome of scientific activity includes description, understanding, explanation, prediction, and control of natural phenomena.

- Scientists study variables that are narrowly defined aspects of events. The types of variables include dependent, independent, active, assigned, and intervening.
  - Dependent variables are the effects under study.
  - Independent variables are the causes.
  - Active variables are manipulated independent variables.
  - Assigned variables are presumed but not manipulated independent variables.
  - Intervening variables are presumed, unobservable, "in-the-head" independent variables.
- Science believes that events have multiple causes and that different levels of analysis reveal different causes. Instigating causes start an event and maintaining causes keep it going.
- Experiment, a central concept of science, is the manipulation of independent variables under controlled conditions to produce some effects or change some independent variables.
- Hypotheses are statements about yet-to-be-verified cause-effect relations. Some researchers believe that they are essential to research and others believe that they are unnecessary.
- A theory also is a statement of cause-effect relations, but it has a larger scope than a hypothesis. Many hypotheses may be derived from a single theory.
- Theories are built either through deductive or inductive reasoning. Using deductive reasoning, a scientist first proposes a theory and then verifies it. Using inductive reasoning, the scientist first experiments and then proposes a theory based on the results.
- Scientific laws are based on replicated evidence; hence, they are more credible than hypotheses or theories.
- Data are the results of systematic observation. Data may be descriptive, quantitative, uncontrolled, controlled, and replicated. Controlled and replicated data are evidence that supports a theory.

References

Bachrach, A. J. (1969). *Psychological research: An introduction.* New York, NY: Random House.

Fisher, R. A. (1956). *Statistical methods and scientific inference.* London, UK: Oliver & Boyd.

Goodman, N. (1967). The epistemological argument. *Synthese, 17,* 23–28.

Hegde, M. N. (1980). Issues in the study and explanation of language behavior. *Journal of Psycholinguistic Research, 9,* 1–22.

Johnson, W., & Associates. (1959). *The onset of stuttering.* Minneapolis, MN: University of Minnesota.

Johnston, J. M., & Pennypacker, H. S. (2009). *Strategies and tactics of behavioral research* (3rd ed.). London, UK: Routledge.

Kerlinger, F. N. (1973). *Foundations of behavioral research* (3rd ed.). New York, NY: Holt, Rinehart, & Winston.

Sidman, M. (1960). *Tactics of scientific research.* New York, NY: Basic Books.

Skinner, B. F. (1953). *Science and human behavior.* New York, NY: Free Press.

Skinner, B. F. (1956). A case history in scientific method. *American Psychologist, 11*(22), 1–233.

Skinner, B. F. (1969). *Contingencies of reinforcement: A theoretical analysis.* New York, NY: Appleton-Century-Crofts.

Skinner, B. F. (1972). *Cumulative record: A selection of papers* (3rd ed.). New York, NY: Appleton-Century-Crofts.

Skinner, B. F. (1974). *About behaviorism.* New York, NY: Knopf.

Study Guide

1. What is science? Write a descriptive and critical essay.

2. Define determinism. Illustrate your definition with an example from communication disorders.

3. Distinguish science from technology.

4. What is empiricism? What is its importance to science?

5. Define *objectivity.*

6. What are the outcomes of scientific activity? What is an optional outcome of science?

7. Give an example for each kind of variable: dependent, independent, active, assigned, and intervening.

8. Name all the variables in the following statement: *Five-year-old children belonging to the upper middle class are more likely to produce grammatic morphemes at 90% accuracy than are children coming from lower socioeconomic strata. Mothers of the upper middle class read more to their children, and this may be the reason why the children are advanced in their language production.*

9. What are the limitations of intervening variables?

10. Select a communicative disorder and illustrate the concept of multiple causation and levels of causality.

11. Give an example of an instigating cause and a maintaining cause of a particular disorder.

12. Describe the elements of an experiment. Illustrate your description with a hypothetical experiment.

13. Discuss the two views on the need for hypotheses in scientific research.

14. Describe a theory. Find a theory in your reading of the scientific literature. Identify the elements of that theory.

15. Give your own examples of inductive and deductive reasoning in everyday life.

16. How are inductive and deductive theories built?

17. Distinguish between theories and scientific laws.

18. Distinguish between data and evidence. Describe the different levels of observation that produce different kinds of data.

4

Treatment
Research

Chapter Outline

- ◆ Evidence-Based Practice
- ◆ What Is Treatment Research?
- ◆ Consequences of Treatment
- ◆ Treatment Research: Logical and Empirical Constraints
- ◆ Group Treatment Research: Randomized Clinical Trials
- ◆ Single-Subject Treatment Research: Multiple Control Conditions
- ◆ Randomized Clinical Trials Versus Single-Subject Treatment Research
- ◆ Classification of Treatment Research
- ◆ Summary
- ◆ References
- ◆ Study Guide

Treatment research, a variety of clinical research, holds special relevance for clinicians and clinical researchers. Because of its importance in speech-language pathology and all clinical disciplines, this separate chapter is devoted to treatment research.

Treatment research is contrasted with basic research, laboratory research, survey research, and other kinds of research. Chapter 5 describes and contrasts several types of research. Essentially, treatment research is done to establish the effects of treatment to support evidence-based practice.

Evidence-Based Practice

Treatment research affects professional practice more than any other form of research. Without treatment research evidence, there is no evidence-based practice. The evidence in evidence-based practice comes from controlled treatment research that shows that treatment is better than no treatment.

Clinicians' selection of treatment procedures depends on available treatment evidence. Clinicians are expected to select only those treatment procedures that have been subjected to experimental evaluation and found to be effective. Consumer satisfaction with services received also depends on receiving interventions known to be effective.

In private practice and hospital settings, third-party payment for services also may depend on available evidence to support treatment techniques offered to clients. To receive reimbursement, clinicians may have to justify the treatment procedures offered to clients. Such justifi-cations may be acceptable only when they are based on treatment research evidence.

Finally, it is an ethical responsibility of clinical researchers to evaluate treatment procedures experimentally before recommending them to professionals. Therefore, it is important to understand both the conceptual and methodological issues involved in conducting and evaluating treatment research.

What Is Treatment Research?

Treatment research is a variety of clinical research designed to measure the consequences of treatment applications. Some varieties of treatment demonstrate that treatment is better than no treatment. Other varieties of treatment research may establish the cause-effect relation between treatment and the changes that follow in those who receive it. Treatment research is a precursor to evidence-based practice.

The goals of treatment research are to: (a) describe improvement due to treatment, (b) establish effects of specific treatment procedures, (c) measure generalization of clinically established behaviors and their expansions, (d) record maintenance of clinically established behaviors and their expansions, (e) describe functional outcomes of treatment, (f) document generality through direct replication of previous findings on treatment techniques, and (g) document generality through systematic replication of previous findings.

Treatment research may be uncontrolled or controlled. Uncontrolled research shows that the individuals who received treatment improved or not. There is no demonstration of cause-effect relation between treatment and improvement if present. Controlled research shows that treatment is or is not better than no treatment. That is, controlled research ensures that treatment was responsible for observed improvement.

Treatment research may be original or replications. Replications are studies that repeat the original studies to establish reliability of findings. Replications, in turn, may be direct or systematic. Direct replications are often done by the original investigator, whereas the systematic replications are done by other investigators in different settings. The latter help establish generality of findings.

Each variety helps establish certain kind of data that the clinicians may use in evaluating and selecting treatment procedures. In a final section of this chapter, we describe the different varieties of research and the kinds of data they generate.

Consequences of Treatment

A treatment is offered with the expectation that it will produce certain measurable and favorable changes in the participants. An ineffective treatment will produce no consequences. When changes are observed, they may be the consequences of treatment and may be described as *improvement, effects, effectiveness, efficacy, efficiency,* or *outcomes.* As we will describe later, distinction among some of these concepts is appropriate but distinctions among others may be questionable.

Conceptual clarity helps scientists design treatment studies and evaluate evidence stemming from such studies. In making valid conceptual distinctions, the conditions under which a treatment was offered and the purpose for which the changes were measured must be considered.

Improvement

A common consequence of treatment offered in routine clinical settings is improvement in clinical conditions or skills targeted for enhancement. *Improvement* contrasts with *effectiveness.* **Improvement** is documented positive changes in client behaviors while they receive treatment within routine professional settings or in uncontrolled case studies. Improvement in clinical conditions that follows routine treatment does not necessarily mean that the treatment was effective, necessary, or that the client would not have improved without the treatment. Treatment that was offered and improvement that followed are correlated events with no assurance of causation. Therefore, improvement should never be misinterpreted as effectiveness.

Under routine clinical conditions, professionals are expected to document improvement that follows treatment, not treatment effectiveness. Positive changes that document improvement will justify treatment from a clinical and social standpoint; it will enhance clinician accountability. Improvement data will convince other clinicians that the clients who receive a treatment benefited from it.

Improvement is a direct consequence of treatment offered under uncontrolled clinical conditions. **Direct consequences** are immediate and constitute positive changes in the skills to which the treatment has been applied. They may be contrasted with such **indirect or delayed consequences** as generalization and maintenance. Frequency of target skills are the most common direct measures, but the measures may be of intensity, amplitude, duration, intertrial interval, and so forth.

Treatment Effects

Treatment effects are documented positive changes in the health status, behaviors, or skills of individuals who receive intervention under controlled experimental conditions designed to demonstrate that the documented positive changes are due to the treatment itself. Controlled experimental conditions help assert that variables that could produce the same effect but were not manipulated in the experiment did not contribute to the observed effects. For instance, to show that a certain treatment is effective in teaching language skills to children, the researcher needs to demonstrate that neither the child's teachers nor parents could take credit for the positive changes in the child's language skills. In essence, then, to claim effects for a treatment, one should show a cause-effect relation between the treatment and the changes that follow.

To demonstrate a cause-effect relation between a treatment and the changes that follow, one should show that there would be no such change when the treatment is absent and that changes do appear when the treatment is present. Several experimental methods are available to demonstrate the effects of treatment and their absence. These methods are classified as group designs or single-subject designs, described respectively in Chapters 8 and 9.

Treatment effects are immediate and direct consequences of applying a treat-ment procedure. Direct effects should be first demonstrated before measuring such indirect consequences as generalization and maintenance. In group designs, such effects are measured in pretests and posttests (see Chapter 8). In single-subject designs, direct effects are measured continuously (see Chapter 9). In either case, direct effects of treatments are typically measured objectively. Quantitative increases in the skills taught are more easily documented than indirect changes that follow in natural environments as in the case of generalized responses. Direct effects are temporally close to the treatment offered under controlled conditions. Therefore, such effects help establish a cause-effect relation between treatment and the changes in skill levels.

Clinically Significant Effects

Treatment research may produce effects that are statistically significant. That is, the effects observed in the experimental group could not be due to chance and could only be attributed to treatment. However, such an effect may or may not be meaningful from some other standpoint. The question raised is this: Is the statistically significant effect also clinically significant?

Clinical significance is the degree to which the consequences of a treatment are socially and personally meaningful. To be meaningful, the consequences of a treatment should enhance the quality of life, which may mean changes in different aspects of life, depending on the nature of treatment and the condition for which the treatment was offered. Clinically significant medical treatments should reduce the death rate, enhance the overall quality of life, improve the health status, instill a sense of well-being, or increase the level of physical activity. Just a statistically significant reduction in symptoms may not ensure clinical significance of treatments. In communication disorders, clinical validity is ensured when the clients who receive treatment show significant gains in social interaction, personal and occupational communication, improved academic performance in the case of children, and so forth. Here too, just a reduction of symptoms, for instance, a reduction in stuttering in the clinical situation, may not ensure clinical significance of a stuttering treatment. In Chapter 10, we return to clinical significance, further contrast it with statistical significance, and describe how it may be assessed.

Generalized Consequences

Generalized consequences of treatment are additional and indirect changes in the target behaviors or related skills (Hegde, 1998). Clinicians hope that a client who learns certain limited skills under treatment will topographically expand them within and outside the clinic with no additional treatment. For instance, a child might expand a phrase learned in clinic into sentences and produce them at home. A child who learns to correctly name pictures in the clinic may then name the corresponding objects at home and school. An individual with aphasia may produce the clinically acquired naming skills in his or her home and other natural communicative situations.

Measurement of generalized consequences is more difficult than measurement of direct consequences observed in the clinic. Limited expansions observed in the clinic are more readily measured than complex changes that take place in natural communicative situations. Such complex changes are not always obtained without additional clinical effort. For instance, the parents of a child with language disorders may have to be trained in evoking and reinforcing the clinically established skills and their expanded versions at home.

Generalized consequences, though highly desirable from a clinical standpoint, are not necessary to claim that a treatment was effective. Direct consequences observed under controlled conditions are sufficient to claim treatment effectiveness. However, generalized consequences enhance the meaningfulness of clinical services or treatment research results. Because they are more natural, more useful, and more socially recognizable, generalized consequences of treatment help establish clinical validity of treatments.

It is generally difficult to claim that generalized consequences were indeed produced by an experimental treatment because of the time that typically separates them and the possibility of extraneous variables affecting generalized consequences. Such consequences are at best correlated with treatment with no assurance of a cause-effect relation between the two sets of events. In essence, generalized consequences are neither necessary nor sufficient to claim treatment effectiveness.

Maintained Consequences

Maintained treatment consequences are clinically established skills that are sustained over time. Only the direct consequences of treatment (treatment effects or improved skills), generalized indirect consequences, or both may be maintained across time and situations. When only the direct consequences are maintained, the client will have derived somewhat limited benefit from treatment. When both the direct and generalized consequences are maintained, the treatment will have produced more meaningful, long-term, and presumably more satisfying results for the clients. Maintained consequences imply that the treatment offered was socially and personally meaningful, and therefore, they establish the clinical validity of treatments offered.

Although important and highly desirable, durability of direct effects of treatment does not mean that the treatment was indeed effective. Maintained skills are no basis to claim a cause-effect relation between treatment and the skills maintained. Whether the treatment was offered under controlled conditions or in routine clinical situations is of no consequence. At best, maintained consequences, along with generalized consequences, may be correlated with treatment with no assurance of causation. One will have to assume that if treatment consequences were maintained, some lasting independent variables in the natural environment have gained control over the dependent variables (skills and behaviors). In other words, the time that lapses between treatment and maintained consequences will offer plenty of opportunities for other variables to come into play. Only additional experimental analysis, if successful, can help establish that maintained consequences are due to treatment. Unfortunately, it is impractical to sustain an extended experimental analysis in the natural environment. In essence, then, maintained consequences, like generalized consequences, are neither necessary nor sufficient to claim effects for a treatment procedure.

Treatment Outcomes

In recent years, treatment outcomes have gained much professional attention in education and health care. Currently popular and often market-driven outcomes research in health care professions raises important issues of both scientific and professional value. Treatment outcomes are currently of great concern to service providers and those who financially support those services. Unfortunately, there is a danger that outcomes will be confused with effects of treatments. Should there be such confusion, outcomes research will replace or diminish the treatment efficacy research. Several sources do not make a distinction between the methods of efficacy research and those of outcomes research (Kendall, Flannnery-Schroeder, & Ford, 1999; Smith & Sechrest, 1998). A clear distinction between treatment effects and treatment outcomes is necessary to maintain the integrity of both kinds of research.

Treatment outcomes are generalized, maintained, indirect, and clinically valid consequences of treatment with no assurance that treatment caused them. Outcomes are essentially an extended notion of improvement because they are not established through controlled experiments. Careful documentation of outcomes will help justify treatment and its cost to the society. Professionals gain credibility when outcomes of their services are socially acceptable. The goals of outcomes research are often described as: (a) finding out what works and what does not, (b) documenting functional status of clients, (c) general health perceptions, (d) overall quality of life, (e) assessing service quality with a view to improve it, (f) assessing consumer satisfaction with services, and so forth (Frattali, 1998; Hicks,

1998; Robertson & Colburn, 1997). Most of these goals are addressed through clinical measurement of dependent variables, not through experimentation.

Unfortunately, outcomes research rarely finds out what works and what does not. Outcomes research is not treatment effects research. That there might be a confusion between experimentally established treatment effects and nonexperimentally (clinically) measured outcomes is evident in certain definitions and descriptions of outcomes. For instance, Donabedian (1980) defined outcome as "a *change* in the current and future health status *that can be attributed* to antecedent health care" (p. 82, italics added). The phrase *attributed to antecedent health care* suggests that outcomes are the effects of treatment. Outcomes, however, are not the same as effects for two reasons. First, only an experimentally demonstrated effect can be attributed to its manipulated antecedent. Second, outcomes are clinical measures of extended improvement with no experimental manipulations. So far, outcomes research has not used experimental methods, and it is unlikely that it will to any great extent. Like generalized and maintained consequences, outcomes may at best be *correlated* with treatment. Therefore, outcomes and effects should be defined differently.

Systematic documentation of socially and personally meaningful changes in clients' health status, functional communication or other skills, satisfaction with services, general well-being, and so forth are highly desirable. Nonetheless, outcomes research rarely has asked: What techniques produce acceptable outcomes under controlled conditions? It typically asks: Are acceptable outcomes of routine clinical services documented? Outcomes research data are meaningful only if it is first established that the treatments used are effective. Outcomes in the absence of such controlled efficacy data are ambiguous and may be unrelated to treatment.

An important aspect of good treatment outcomes is that to obtain them, one should select personally and socially meaningful targets for intervention. A child with a language disorder, for example, may be taught either language skills unrelated to academic success or those that are closely related. Carefully selecting language skills that increase the child's chances of academic success is likely to produce functional outcomes of treatment for that child. Similarly, an individual with aphasia who experiences naming problems may be taught the names of family members, pets, and medications, or some names of objects not relevant to his or her living environment. The two sets of target behaviors will produce different outcomes for the individual.

In essence, then, outcomes are a composite notion of expanded improvement that includes meaningful target behaviors selected for intervention, generalized and expanded production of clinically established target behaviors, and maintenance of those behaviors over time. All aspects of outcomes are measured under uncontrolled conditions.

Treatment Efficacy Versus Effectiveness

There is a distinction sometimes made between treatment efficacy and effectiveness. Those who make this distinction define *efficacy* as the effect realized under ideal conditions of a treatment given in controlled experiments and *effectiveness* as the actual effect realized in the real-world experiments that are not as well controlled (Agency for Health Care Policy and Research, 1994; Hoagwood, Hibbs, Brent, & Jensen, 1995; Kendall & Norton-Ford, 1982). The distinction implies that when a treatment study's controls are good, the result is efficacy, and when they are poor, the result is effectiveness. This is an artificial distinction that does not have conceptual or methodological consequences. If real-world experiments do not produce as good an effect as those observed in better controlled and perhaps laboratory-based treatments, then the difference is due to methodological deficiencies of the real-world experiments. It is better to analyze reasons for failure to obtain the same results as those found in better controlled results. Giving the results of poorly controlled studies a euphemistic name (such as *effectiveness*) will not help clarify the problems and will not encourage efforts to solve them.

The term *effectiveness* has always meant that a cause-effect relation is established with reasonable degree of certainty. Furthermore, experimental control is not categorical; it is a matter of degree. Few if any laboratory studies are so perfect as to deserve a different term for the effects they document. If the real-world clinical experiments are so poorly designed as to require a new name for their effects, then their effects probably are not trustworthy. Therefore, in this book, the terms *effectiveness* and *efficacy* are used synonymously.

Treatment Research: Logical and Empirical Constraints

Of the various goals of treatment research, the one that seeks to establish the effects of a given treatment is perhaps the most important. If a treatment's effects are unknown, then other goals, when real-

ized, remain ambiguous. For instance, when a treatment whose effects have not been experimentally established is associated with improvement, generalization, maintenance, or functional outcomes, one would not know whether to attribute such consequences to treatment or to some other variable that could also produce those consequences. Therefore, while other goals are clinically important and socially valuable, treatment effects need to be first established.

Treatment's effects may be established only through controlled experimentation. Controlled experiments show that the treatment caused the changes that followed it. Clinically, a controlled treatment experiment demonstrates that the participants needed the treatment and that without treatment, they would not have improved. This demonstration justifies treatment, its cost, and the effort involved in offering it and getting it.

There are two major approaches to conducting controlled experimentation in treatment research: the group design approach (described in Chapter 8) and the single-subject approach (described in Chapter 9). Both design strategies ensure that: (a) treatment was the cause of changes in the clients, (b) no other variable was responsible for the changes, and (c) the clients would not have improved without it. In establishing treatment effects, researchers in both design approaches adhere to certain logical constraints and create certain empirical conditions.

Logical Constraints and Empirical Conditions Necessary to Claim Treatment Effects

While a researcher is busy showing that a treatment is the cause of changes in the study participants, many other factors may quietly contribute to the change. When this happens, the claim that treatment is the sole cause of the effects is invalid. To convince others that the treatment alone produced the changes, the researcher must arrange experimental conditions such that other potential factors cannot account for the changes documented in the study participants. This action is typically referred to as *ruling-out extraneous variables.*

Extraneous variables are potent variables that could produce the same effect the treatment could or did produce. *Extraneous* in this context does not mean irrelevant or ineffective. They are extraneous only for the purpose of the experiment, which was to show that a treatment alone produced the effect.

A researcher, for example, may use a new technique to teach language skills to children with autism spectrum disorder. The researcher may establish initial baselines or pretest scores to show that the children did not produce the language behavior targeted for intervention. The researcher may then teach the new language behavior with the treatment. After a period of teaching, the researcher may measure the targeted language behavior in probes or posttests. Observing that the probe or posttest scores are higher than the baselines or pretest scores of the children, the researcher concludes that the treatment was effective. A critic may point out that the study did not produce evidence for the treatment's effectiveness because the researcher did not rule out extraneous variables. What are some of the extraneous variables in this example?

The critic may point out that the study only showed that the children's language skills improved under the teaching method, but why they improved is not clear. The documented improvement may

or may not be due to the treatment. The language skills of the children may have improved without treatment. Children's language skills naturally improve as they grow older. (This is known as the *maturation* factor, discussed in Chapter 7.) The language skills probably improved because the parents began a home language stimulation program after the child was assessed and the parents were counseled. The language skills may have improved because of the special education teacher's efforts in the classroom. Perhaps the siblings, too, may have played some role in stimulating language skills in their family member with autism. These are the examples of extraneous variables; they could produce the same effect as the language treatment procedure. But the researcher's claim concerned only the language treatment he or she was investigating, not these other extraneous variables. Therefore, the critic will contend that the study did not produce evidence for the treatment's effectiveness. More technically, the critic may contend that the researcher's study did not have *internal validity;* the researcher did not rule out extraneous variables and hence did not convince others that the treatment alone produced the language changes. The critic will remind the researcher that the study was an uncontrolled case study and did not have the power to establish a cause-effect relationship between the treatment and the language changes in children.

Ruling out extraneous variables is a logical, not exclusively a methodological, matter. Methodologically, the researcher cannot: (a) prevent maturation in children, (b) convince parents not to stimulate language in their children, (c) ask teachers not to do anything with language skills, and (d) refrain siblings from engaging in social communication. Therefore, ruling out extraneous variables does not mean that the variables were removed or minimized. Instead, the researcher arranges some empirical conditions such that the extraneous variables play their usual role, but nonetheless the changes are demonstrated to be the effect of a treatment. Once the correct empirical conditions of an experiment are created, the conclusion that the treatment alone was effective is a logical exercise.

Empirical conditions of an experiment that are necessary to make a logical claim of causation may be illustrated with an example of experimental group research design. In a group design, for instance, the investigator may draw a random sample (a smaller number) of clients or students form a defined population (e.g., all children with autism spectrum disorder living in a certain geographic area). The children may then be randomly assigned to either the experimental group or the control group. The treatment to be evaluated will then be offered to only the children in the experimental group. If the positive changes occur only in the experimental group children, the researcher may claim that the treatment was effective because the extraneous variables were ruled out. Once again, this is done on a logical basis, by pointing out that: (a) if maturation were to be responsible, the language skills of children in the control group, too, would also have improved, but they did not; (b) if the parents' language stimulation were to be responsible, randomly selected parents in the two groups would have stimulated language equally in their children, but again, children in the control group did not gain in their language skills; (c) if teachers' work were to be responsible for improved language skills in the experimental group, those in the control group children should have also improved because the children in the two groups

attended similar or similarly diverse schools; and finally, (d) if improvement in language skills of the experimental group was due to the siblings' language interactions, then the skills in the control group should have improved, because they had similar sibling interactions. A single-subject design study may rule out extraneous variables just as effectively, albeit with different experimental conditions (see Chapter 9). Note again that these are logically based conclusions that the treatment was the cause of the effect (improved language skills) even though the extraneous variables were not methodologically removed or diminished.

Although there are many complications, the basic logic of causation is simple. To claim a cause-effect relationship, certain conditions must be met. For instance, (a) causes precede effects, and effects follow causes; (b) causes and effects cannot be the same events, and they have to be different; (c) causes and effects are temporally separated, so they cannot co-occur in such a way as to be confused; (d) causes are typically multiple, which means that most events have several causes; (e) among multiple causes, some may be sufficient to produce an effect, which means that when they are present, effects are present and no other factor needs to render a helping hand; and (f) causes may be necessary but not sufficient, which means that without them, the effects will not appear, but unless some other factors also are present, their presence will not automatically result in the effect (Clatterbaugh, 1999; Rothman & Greenland, 1998; Ruben, 1990; Wilson, 1985).

In scientific experiments, a cause is called an **independent variable**. It is the same as treatment in clinical research. The effect is known as a **dependent variable**. It is the same as the disorders and diseases that are changed by intervention. An **experiment** is a means to show that an independent variable (e.g., treatment) is the cause of changes noted in a dependent variable (e.g., changes in the skill level, health status, symptom reduction). An independent variable is experimentally manipulated to show corresponding changes in the dependent variable. In clinical terms, a treatment is introduced, withheld, withdrawn, reintroduced, and so forth to show changes in the skill or health status. Depending on the results of such experimental manipulations, an investigator may conclude that an independent variable is indeed a cause if: (a) the effect appears when the independent variable is introduced, and (b) the effect disappears when the independent variable is withdrawn or withheld (Clatterbaugh, 1999; Ruben, 1990). When systematic manipulations of treatment in a controlled experiment are followed by predictable changes in the dependent variable, extraneous variables will have been ruled out.

Group Treatment Research: Randomized Clinical Trials

Controlled experiments may include an experimental group that receives treatment, and as a consequence, changes, and a control group that does not receive treatment and does not change significantly. The experimental group designs help demonstrate such changes or lack thereof.

This section gives an overview of some methodological aspects of treatment research involving groups of participants. Chapter 8 describes specific designs this approach offers.

Random Selection of Participants for Clinical Trials

The group design approach offers several specific designs to evaluate treatment effects (see Chapter 8 for details). Among these designs, the classic pretest-posttest control group design is the most frequently used experimental design to establish treatment effects. In clinical literature, especially in medicine, studies that purport to use the pretest-posttest control group design are typically called *randomized clinical trials* (RCTs). However, RCTs do not precisely adhere to the requirements of the pretest-posttest control group design; therefore, it is more appropriate to say that RCTs are loosely based on the pretest-posttest control group design.

Randomized clinical trials are experimental studies of treatment effects in which randomly selected individuals of similar characteristics are randomly assigned to two or more groups, one of which may receive a new treatment to be evaluated and the other may receive no treatment or a placebo, or all of which may receive a different treatment. The purpose of RCTs is to establish the absolute effect of a treatment offered to one group compared with a control group (which receives a placebo or does not receive any treatment) or to determine the relative effects of multiple treatments when all groups receive a specific treatment. A *clinical trial* is the same as a controlled treatment experiment. The term *randomized* refers to the procedure an investigator uses to select participants and form different groups to evaluate one or more treatments.

It is generally believed that in 1948, Sir Austin Bradford Hill reported the first prototype of an RCT in *The British Medical Journal* (Randal, 1998; Silverman &

Altman, 1996). Hill assessed the effects of streptomycin on pulmonary tuberculosis in patients randomly selected across several hospitals in England. This was also the first study in which the investigators (who read chest X-rays to evaluate the effects of treatment) were blinded; that is, they did not know who had received the treatment and who had not. In subsequent decades, RCTs became the established method to experimentally assess medical treatment effects.

In RCTs, the concept and the technique of randomization are important and related to participant selection. There are two issues in participant selection. First, when a treatment is compared with a no-treatment control group (or placebo) or one treatment is compared against other treatments, the individuals in the two or more groups should be similar; if not, the conclusions will not be valid. Second, when a treatment study is completed, the group design researcher's aim is to extend the results to the population (i.e., claim statistical generality). To accomplish these two goals, the researchers wish to draw random samples that represent their population.

A **sample** is a smaller number of individuals who represent a larger population of individuals with defined characteristics relevant to a study. The results of a study can be extended to the larger population only when the sample represents the population. A **population** is a large number of individuals with defined characteristics from which a representative sample is drawn. For instance, a population may be defined as *all children who stutter in Grades K–12 in California public schools.* Another population may be defined as all those who have experienced a stroke in a given calendar year in the United States. Populations may be defined more or less narrowly. Researchers may define limited regional populations and large national populations (e.g., all voting-age persons in the United States). It should be noted that random selection is not haphazard. It is a method of selecting participants without bias. The different methods of random selection that are available vary from the ideal to the most compromised. The ideal may be difficult to achieve, but the most compromised will not serve any purpose.

Probability Sampling

The most ideal random method of participant selection is called **probability sampling**, which is a method in which the participant selection is unbiased, all members of the defined population are available and willing to participate in the study, and each member of the population has an equal chance of being included in the sample. There are several variations of probability sampling. The very best of the probability sampling methods is known as the **simple random sampling**, in which a required number of participants are selected from the population by such methods as a lottery. Unfortunately, it is rarely, if ever, achieved in experimental research.

In clinical treatment research, simple random sampling is particularly impractical because entire populations of clients and patients are rarely identified. Even when practical, simple random sampling does not begin with a defined population but with only an accessible population. For instance, in an aphasia treatment study, not all patients with aphasia living in a state or even a city may be accessible. Only those who have sought clinical services may be accessible. This already represents a compromise in probability sampling because those who are not seeking services are excluded. Nevertheless, once the accessible population is identified, the required number of participants may be drawn randomly by using published tables of random numbers or by the common lottery method.

Systematic sampling is another probability random selection procedure in which the selection is made with a specified *sampling interval*. In this method, 1 in K (K standing for a specific number) will be selected to achieve the total sample. For instance, in selecting 200 clients from a list of 2,000 in an accessible population, one might select every 10th person on the list. Systematic sampling is more convenient than simple random sampling in which the subjects are selected entirely randomly (e.g., with the lottery method). It might serve the purpose of obtaining a representative sample well if the list of accessible persons in the population is complete, unbiased, and all selected clients participate in the study.

Stratified random sampling, yet another practical method of probability sampling, is a method in which the population is first divided into groups of unique characteristics, and the required number of participants is selected from each group. Groups that contain homogeneous individuals with common characteristics are called **strata**. Typical strata that are used in clinical research include participants from different socioeconomic classes, educational backgrounds, disorder or disease severity levels, and so forth. Essentially, any factor that might influence the treatment outcome may be a stratum. Populations typically contain several of these strata, and just as typically, the proportion of individuals within a given strata varies. For instance, people living in a given geographic area may be more

rich than poor, more highly educated than less educated, more single than married, or more belonging to one ethnic group than the other. When this is the case, the researcher will draw a **proportional stratified sample**, in which the number of selected individuals from a given stratum will reflect the size of that stratum. The larger the stratum, the greater the number of participants selected. Within each stratum, participants are selected randomly.

Cluster sampling, a variation of probability sampling, is a method in which the required number of participants is sampled in stages, each stage being identified as a cluster and serving as a sampling unit. Cluster sampling is sometimes referred to as *multistage sampling* because the sampling units are drawn from successive stages. For example, an investigator may wish to draw a national random sample of children with language disorders in the elementary grades. The investigator might initially decide that she will draw a sample of students from 10 U.S. states that roughly represents children in all the states. In Stage 1 cluster sampling, the investigator will randomly draw 10 U.S. states from the list of 50 states. The randomly drawn states form the *initial cluster*. In Stage 2, she will randomly draw a certain number of school districts, say 10, to form the second cluster. In Stage 3, she will draw a random sample of five schools from each district, resulting in the third cluster. She will then select children with language disorders in each of the five schools. The children are the final sampling unit, and the investigator reached them by successive and progressively smaller clusters.

Cluster sampling is more manageable than simple probability sampling, especially when dealing with a large population with defined characteristics. Unfortunately, the more manageable the sample, the less accurate it might be in representing the total population.

Nonprobability Sampling

Even more practical than some of the variations of simple random (probability) sampling is nonprobability sampling. Strictly speaking, **nonprobability sampling** is a compromised nonrandom sampling, with no assurance that the sample represents the population. By definition, nonrandom samples cannot fulfill the mathematical requirement of the probability theory on which random samples are based. In nonprobability sampling, all individuals of specified characteristics in the population are not identified and all do not have the same chance of being included in the sample. As with probability sampling, nonprobability sampling allows various techniques, some better than others.

Convenience sampling is a variety of nonprobability sampling in which participants are selected simply because they were available. Also known as *accidental sampling,* convenience sampling is often used in clinical treatment research. Patients who are seeking clinical services, students in regular or special education classes, and college students enrolled in courses are all groups of typical participants in many kinds of experiments. Such groups are selected because they are available, not because they represent a population.

Consecutive sampling, a variety of convenience sampling often used in clinical research, is recruitment of participants as they become available over time. For example, patients as they seek treatment in a medical facility may be recruited to participate in a new drug treatment evaluation study. The required number of patients may be recruited, not all at once as in probability sampling. This type of sampling is frequently used in medical treatment research. Researchers may continue to sample patients for a treatment study over a period of months or even years. Patients who seek clinical services during such extended times may be screened and those who meet the selection criteria may be included in the study.

Note that the participants selected because of convenience are self-selected, not randomly or objectively selected. **Self-selection** means that the participants select themselves to a study, not by the investigator using some unbiased method such as the simple random selection. The results of a study that involved self-selection cannot be extended to others who did not participate in the study. Self-selection, however, may be a factor in all samples, including simple random samples drawn for clinical treatment research. Even in simple random sampling, all those randomly selected do not agree to participate; those randomly assigned to control groups may drop out or demand treatment; and those in the treatment group also may drop out. The study is then completed only with self-selected samples (Hegde, 2007).

Quota sampling, a method similar to stratified sampling, requires the investigator to select a fixed number of people belonging to different categories in the population. For instance, an aphasia treatment researcher may select 5 persons in their 50s, 10 persons in their 60s, and 20 in their 70s to reflect the increasing number of older individuals who suffer strokes and other conditions that cause aphasia. This method is an improvement over purely convenient sampling in which selected individuals may not be as diverse and may be much less representative of the population; in the example of aphasia, a convenient sample may consist mostly of 70-year-old patients because of the possibility that relatively more from this age group seek treatment.

Snowball sampling—a nonprobability sampling common in clinical treatment research—is a practical method in which participants themselves find other participants in a chain referral manner. Each or most of a small number of persons initially selected may find other participants in a snowballing fashion until the required number of participants is found and recruited. Also known as *reputational sampling,* this method is useful when the researcher cannot find individuals with specified characteristics and depends on participants to spread the word among their friends, colleagues, and relatives and make referrals to the investigator. The investigator will screen the referred persons to see if they meet the study's selection criteria. This technique may not be productive in clinical research involving diseases or disorders of low frequency, but the method may be effective in recruiting individuals from some hidden populations (e.g., drug addicts, gay or lesbian people in certain communities or countries). This method also may be used in some genetic research, where an initially selected participant helps recruit a family member who has the same disorder who then starts a snowball effect to recruit others.

Purposive sampling is a nonprobability method of handpicking individuals because they have special characteristics that are necessary for the study. Note that in all sampling techniques, including probability sampling (simple

random sampling), participants meet certain criteria because the population itself is defined in terms of those criteria (e.g., all 70-year-old individuals who have had a stroke in the past 3 months). Still, the individuals are not handpicked, not even in the convenient sampling method (although convenient and purposive sampling techniques are similar). Purposive sampling, in some of its applications, may be similar to snowball sampling, too. But the hallmark of purposive sampling is an effort to find individuals with narrowly defined characteristics.

Purposive sampling is useful in general clinical and treatment research. For instance, a clinician may design a child language stimulation program that parents conduct at home. In this case, the clinician's goal is to find out if: (a) the parents may be adequately trained to implement the program at home and (b) when implemented, whether the children's language skills increase. The clinician may reason that for the initial study, she needs mothers or fathers with college degrees who can devote the required amount of time to get trained and then implement the program at home. A convenient sample of parents whose children attend the clinic may not identify the kinds of parents the researcher is recruiting. A simple random sample, even if practical, may yield too many parents who do not qualify. Therefore, purposive sampling may be the best choice. To hand-pick parents for the study, the clinician may check the case histories of children with language disorders and interview available parents; obtain information on their education, occupation, and available free time; and judge their level of sophistication, motivation, commitment, and so forth.

Purposive sampling typically sacrifices generality while gaining specificity.

A researcher who wishes to generalize results to others in the population will not use purposive sampling. Once a study shows an effect for a procedure with a purposive sample, subsequent studies can use more representative samples to establish the generality of findings.

Random Assignment of Participants

Within the group design approach, participants who were randomly selected from a population are randomly assigned to either the experimental group (or groups) or the control group. **Random assignment** is a method of forming the experimental and control groups without bias and based on the mathematical assumption that each participant has the same probability of being included in any of the groups to be formed for a study. For instance, in a study that involves two groups—a control group and an experimental group—all randomly selected participants have the same chance of being selected to the control group or the experimental group. If two treatments are offered in a study, all participants have the same chance of getting either Treatment 1 or Treatment 2. If the participants were matched, one in each matched pair will be randomly assigned to the experimental group and the other will be assigned to the control group. Random assignment of participants eliminates any investigator bias that might influence who gets treatment, who gets which treatment, or who does not get any treatment.

Random assignment ensures **sampling equivalency**, which is the similarity of participants across groups formed for a study. Sampling equivalency is impor-

tant because the group design approach is based on the assumptions that: (a) the people in the groups were similar to begin with; (b) the presence of treatment in the experimental group was the only difference the investigator created; and therefore, (c) any difference in the group performance observed at the end of the experiment must be due only to the treatment offered to one group. Random assignment helps validate these assumptions.

It is important to note that random selection and assignment serve different purposes. Random selection ensures that the sample is representative of the population from which it was drawn. Therefore, the investigator can extend the conclusion of the study to the population. Random assignment, on the other hand, ensures that the two or more groups of a study are similar. Therefore, the investigator can conclude that any changes observed in the experimental group should be due to the independent variable that was absent in the control group.

In most studies on medical, behavioral, or educational methods of treatment or teaching, random assignment is possible, although true random selection is not. Nonetheless, random assignment may not always eliminate biases, even when the investigator's bias has been eliminated. There are several other sources of biases that may negatively affect the results of a study. First, randomly assigned participants may or may not stay in their assigned groups until the end of the experiment. Different kinds of participants may differentially drop out of the experimental and control groups; that is, those who dropped out may be different kinds of participants than those who stayed in the study. For instance, participants with greater severity of the problem under investigation may drop out of the experimental group, creating the possibility that the treatment will look better than it is. Second, some participants assigned to a traditional treatment may refuse that treatment and demand that they receive the new treatment being offered to others. Consequently, those who remain in the traditional treatment group may not be comparable to the ad hoc group that evolves for the new treatment. Third, some participants who were assigned to the control group with no treatment may demand that they receive treatment. Again, as a consequence, the two groups that are eventually formed may be different from those originally formed. Fourth, when a new treatment whose effects are completely unknown is being evaluated or when a treatment that poses known risks is being evaluated, only very sick or terminally ill patients may volunteer for that study. Patients with better prognosis may necessarily be included in the traditional treatment or no-treatment control groups, creating group disparities. These and perhaps other factors essentially nullify randomization in randomized clinical trials (Hegde, 2007).

Matching: An Alternative to Randomization

An alternative to randomization is called **matching**, a procedure in which selected characteristics of one participant are matched with the characteristics of another. When it is not possible to gain access to a large population of participants, all of whom are willing to participate, the investigator may recruit available participants and then match individuals to achieve sampling equivalency.

Matching **pairs of participants** is one such method, in which the investigator matches pairs of participants on known (relevant) variables and then randomly assigns one member of each pair to the experimental group and the other to the control group. For example, suppose that an investigator knows that in the treatment of speech sound disorders, the severity of misarticulations is a significant variable influencing the treatment outcome. In this case, the investigator may find pairs of participants who are equal in severity of misarticulation. One member of each pair will be assigned to the control group and the other to the experimental group. Another pair of participants may have a different level of severity. Matched pairs can be created on multiple variables. For example, pairs of participants can be matched on age, gender, socioeconomic status, intelligence, occupational background, and so forth.

When matching pairs of participants is impractical, one might use **equivalent frequency distribution matching** in which the two groups are matched not on individual characteristics but on group averages. If age, severity, and intelligence of participants are considered relevant variables in a particular investigation, a comparable distribution of these variables in the two groups may be obtained. For example, the mean IQ of the experimental and control group participants may be 110 and 108, respectively, with a standard deviation of 4.5 and 5.2. The distribution of the variables is considered comparable when the mean and the standard deviation of the measured values of those variables for the two groups are comparable. This equivalent frequency distribution matching is less precise than the paired-participants procedure, but it is practical.

Individuals are not matched one-to-one, but the groups are matched on a statistical basis.

The most serious limitation of matching is that, under the best possible circumstances, it can create two groups that are comparable on **known variables only**. Investigators match participants on characteristics considered important because of available information. The groups may still differ on variables that have an effect but were unknown and hence were not considered in matching the participants. In our example, it is possible that a family history of speech sound errors or the presence of other communication problems may be important variables, but because of no prior research on them, they are not considered in matching the participants.

Matching participants in clinical research poses serious practical problems. It is difficult to find pairs of clients who are similar on one or more relevant variables. Many clients will have to be rejected because another client who shares the same characteristics selected for matching is not available. The clinical researcher often cannot afford this luxury of rejecting available and willing participants. Equivalent distribution of variables in the two groups may be more feasible, but it still requires a large pool of participants. Furthermore, individuals across two groups formed by equivalent frequency distribution may still be very different because comparable means may not ensure comparable individuals.

Theoretically, random selection and assignment ensure equivalence on all of the relevant variables, known and unknown. Therefore, randomization is preferred to matching. In most clinical trials, randomization, not matching, is used to form the two or more groups for experimentation, although as noted, there is no assurance that the groups remain equal.

Treatment Administration

Once the groups are formed and before the treatment is offered, all participants are assessed to establish the pretreatment measures that will be compared against the posttreatment measures. Such pretreatment assessments are called **pretests** in the group design approach. In medical research, diagnostic protocols and laboratory measurements of relevant aspects of health and disease (e.g., blood tests or radiological tests) constitute pretests. In behavioral and educational research, various skills and behaviors may be measured during pretests. Pretests may be standardized test scores (e.g., scores on a language performance scale or a test of articulation) or specific measures obtained on each participant (e.g., a speech or language sample from each child participant or the frequency of self-injurious behaviors in a child with autism).

Completion of pretests sets the stage for experimentation. One or more treatment groups receive their respective treatments and a no-treatment control group goes without any treatment. In such treatment studies, additional opportunities for biased observations arise. Participants who receive treatments and the investigators who make systematic observations of people during the study may all introduce some biases into the results. Procedures have been designed to control for these biases.

Single or Double Blinding

Biases that participants introduce may be significant in certain studies. For instance, patients who receive a new drug for arthritis may feel better simply because they know that they have been receiving the new drug, not because the drug is doing any good. They may report reduced pain to the measurement team, but there may be no objective basis for this. Experts who measure the various effects of a new drug, depending on positive or negative—but always subjective—evaluation of the drug, may record greater or lesser effect of the drug, again with no objective basis.

To eliminate or reduce the participant and researcher biases in reporting or recording the treatment effects, investigators in medicine use a technique known as *blinding*. **Blinding** is a method in which the information about who gets what treatment or no treatment is withheld from the participants, investigators who measure the effects, or both the parties. In **single blinding**, only those investigators who measure the treatment effects are unaware of their patients' treatment or no-treatment status. In **double blinding**, both the measurement team and the patients are unaware of the participant status. In other words, neither the patient nor the medical personnel in charge of measuring the effect of the treatment under investigation know the group membership.

In medicine, administering a placebo to the participants in the control group is a standard method of blinding the participants. Originally, a **placebo** (meaning *to please* in Latin) was a dummy treatment given to patients just to please them. Placebos were thought to be especially useful with intellectually unsophisticated or generally uninformed patients. In 1807, Thomas Jefferson, who found out that his physician friend had prescribed more fake medicines than real ones to his patients, is reported to have called it a *pious fraud*

(Kaptchuk, 1998). In the past, physicians used them in routine practice. Currently, placebos are offered to control group participants in medical treatment evaluation studies.

The notion of placebo has been extended to many forms of treatment evaluation. The typical pharmacological placebo in drug evaluation studies is a lactose tablet. A typical physical placebo (such as those used in physical therapy research) may be a sham movement or exercise regimen, often administered with the help of a mechanical devices to enhance the placebo effect. When different forms of psychotherapy and counseling are evaluated for their effects, placebo may be a neutral discussion or conversation with a therapist (Hrobjartsson & Gotzsche, 2001).

In 1955, Beecher first claimed that dummy treatments (placebo) can produce an effect. Analyzing 15 medical treatment studies, Beecher asserted that 35% of 1,082 patients receiving a placebo experienced relief from symptoms. In subsequent years, the placebo effect was generally accepted, and a need to control for it in treatment research was widely recognized (Kienle & Kiene, 1997). When evaluating the effects of a treatment, investigators were expected to have a control group that received only a placebo to distinguish the true effects of medication given to the experimental group. To claim effects for a new treatment, the experimental group that receives the real treatment should show an improvement that is over and beyond any placebo effect observed in the control group. When a placebo is used, the treatments and patients are coded and those who administer the treatment and placebo, as well as those who measure the effects (and maybe patients as well), are unaware of the meaning of patient codes. Only after the study is completed are the codes revealed. The patients and their treatments are identified only after all data have been collected and before the data are analyzed.

The placebo is not a practical method of blinding the participants in some kind of treatments. It is most effective in drug evaluations where the control participants swallow a dummy pill on the same schedule as those in the experimental group who receive the medication. It is impractical to blind participants to surgical procedures, although some ethically questionable sham surgeries have been performed on control group participants (see Chapter 16 for details). Most behavioral treatment and educational teaching methods cannot be blinded, although in some cases, dummy activity that looks like treatment may be offered to the control group. However, it is hard to conceal teaching sign language to deaf children and offering positive reinforcement for fluency to persons who stutter.

Several medical researchers have questioned the very existence of the placebo effect (Hrobjartsson & Gotzsche, 2001; Kaptchuk, 1998; Kienle & Kiene, 1997). Making a reanalysis of the studies Beecher (1955) used to claim the placebo effect, Kienle and Kiene (1997) have concluded that none of the studies have shown any placebo effect. Their general conclusion is that placebo effects have not been documented in any of the studies, before or since Beecher's publication. Apparently, some placebo-group members will have received other treatments whose effects were ignored. In some studies, recipients of placebo may have deteriorated, a fact also typically ignored. Studies that have compared placebo with no treatment have generally failed to show a placebo effect, which is typi-

cally (and perhaps erroneously) claimed when a placebo is compared against a new or established treatment. It makes sense to say that placebo effect is possibly due to some other variables because the term *placebo effect* is an oxymoron that claims that nothing produces something (Kaptchuk, 1998).

On the other hand, Hrobjartsson and Gotzsche (2001) have suggested that in RCTs in medicine, a small placebo effect may be seen only when the dependent variable measured is pain felt by patients. That is, the sensation of pain, more than any other symptom, may be subject to the placebo effect. The placebo effect is more likely to be documented when it is measured or reported subjectively. Again, pain is subjectively reported and evaluated, and hence the possibility of a placebo effect in pain management. Objective measures of treatment effects are less likely to be affected by the placebo. For instance, laboratory measurements of the dependent variable (e.g., blood analysis or radiological findings) are unlikely to be affected by placebo (Hrobjartsson & Gotzsche, 2001). Even subjective reports of improvement in pain may not be a placebo effect. The improvement may be due to several factors that Kienle and Kiene (1977) describe as the more valid reasons for reported improvements attributed to placebo: spontaneous recovery from symptoms, regression to the mean, natural fluctuation of symptoms, patients' tendency to please physicians, concurrent treatments the placebo group members may have received, and so forth (Kaptchuk, 1998).

The role of placebo effect in speech and language treatment is unclear and perhaps highly questionable. Objectively measured production of grammatical morphemes or phonemes by children with language delay, rates of stuttering in adults who stutter, swallowing skills in patients with dysphagia, and communication skills in persons with aphasia, to name a few, are unlikely to be affected by sham treatment.

Once the groups are formed and decisions are made about blinding, pretests are administered to members of both the groups to establish the pretreatment measures of the dependent variables. Ideally, the pretreatment measures of the dependent variable should be comparable across the two groups. If they are not, the groups are different. Investigators then may recruit additional participants and assign them to the groups to make them more equal.

Control and Experimental Groups

Treatment administration may begin after obtaining acceptable pretest measures. In most behavioral and educational research, blinding is uncommon, and the new treatment or teaching method is applied to the experimental group and withheld from the control group. Although the classic notion of a control group is that it does not receive treatment, there are studies in which a control group may receive a treatment. As noted before, placebo-control groups in medical research receive a dummy treatment. Offering dummy treatment is not typical of behavioral and educational research and is full of ethical complications in medical research.

In some medical, behavioral, and educational research, a control group may receive a standard treatment while the experimental group receives the new treatment being evaluated. For instance, a medical research team may administer an established medicine for patients with arthritis in the control group and a new drug for those in the experimental group. A special educator may offer standard reading instruction to children with hearing loss in the control group and offer a new method of teaching reading to the experimental group. This strategy helps avoid the ethical dilemma of not offering treatment to individuals who need it. It also helps evaluate whether the new treatment produces better outcomes than a standard (common, established) treatment.

At the end of the treatment or teaching period, the investigator administers the posttests to both the groups. Posttests may take a variety of forms, depending on what was initially measured on the pretests and what was treated. In medicine, symptoms may be subjectively evaluated, along with objective laboratory measures of various disease and health status of patients. In behavioral and educational settings, pretests may include measures of target skills that were initially pretested and later taught. The pretest-posttest scores are used to make a variety of statistical analyses of the treatment effects, mentioned briefly in the context of specific group designs described in Chapter 8 and more fully addressed in Chapter 10.

Single-Subject Treatment Research: Multiple Control Conditions

A second experimental approach to evaluating treatment effects is the single-subject approach. This approach, too, uses the same logic of experimental control and establishment of cause-effect relations.

Its methods and certain conceptual bases, however, are different from those of the group design approach. While the group designs use a control group to demonstrate that a treatment is effective, single-subject designs use control conditions to do the same. Just like the control groups, control conditions help rule out the influence of extraneous variables.

Instead of control groups, single-subject designs use multiple control mechanisms to rule out the influence of extraneous variables. Together, they provide a comprehensive tactic of isolating the effects of independent variables on dependent variables. The control mechanisms variously employed in the single-subject strategy include replication, withdrawal, reversal, reinstatement, criterion-referenced change, rapid alternations, baselines, and simultaneous multiple baselines.

A description of these control mechanisms follows. The major single-subject designs themselves are described in Chapter 9.

Replication

One of the important characteristics that distinguish the single-subject strategy from the group strategy is the **replication** of experimental conditions, and hence the treatment effects within individual participants. In most group designs, treatment is introduced once, and when it is discontinued, it is not reintroduced. Therefore, within the group design strategy, there is no replication of the treatment effect in the experimental group or the lack of it in the control group. The experimental group that shows change remains changed, and the control group that does not show change remains unchanged.

In the single-subject strategy, the treatment condition, the control condition, or both is changed from one state to the other. During an experiment, one or more of the earlier states are recaptured. In other words, the effects of the independent variable are shown once by introducing it and thereby changing the dependent variable; the effects are shown a second time by removing the independent variable, thereby changing the dependent variable a second time. A pre-experimental state or an approximation of it is recaptured. The simplest of the single-subject designs, the *ABA* design—which involves a baseline *A,* treatment *B,* and withdrawal of treatment *A*—replicates the original steady state (baseline).

In the *ABAB* design, a baseline is first established *A,* a treatment is then introduced *B,* subsequently withdrawn *A,* and finally reintroduced *B*. This design replicates the pretreatment steady state or baseline once (the two *A* conditions). In addition, the design replicates the treatment effects as well (the two *B* conditions).

When the relative effects of two or more treatments are evaluated, the single-subject designs repeatedly present and withdraw treatment variables. A series of replications may thus be achieved to observe different patterns of responses under the two treatment procedures. When the interactive effects of two treatments are evaluated, one treatment is withdrawn and reintroduced against the background of a constant treatment variable. In this manner, target response rates under treatment and no treatment are established repeatedly.

Replication of treatment or no-treatment condition in the same participant is called the **intrasubject replication**, and by itself, it is not the strongest of the control procedures. However, when an effect is repeatedly demonstrated and repeatedly neutralized, the experimental operations gain credibility. When intrasubject replication is combined with other control procedures, it can be effective in ruling out extraneous variables.

Intrasubject replication must be distinguished from **intersubject replication** in which a treatment effect is replicated across individuals. Most single-subject designs involve both intrasubject and intersubject replication of treatment effects. When multiple participants are used in a single-subject study involving a design such as the *ABAB,* the same treatment effects are demonstrated repeatedly both within and across participants.

Withdrawal of Treatment

In using **withdrawal** as a control mechanism, the treatment that was in effect for a certain duration is discontinued. The measurement of the dependent variables is continued to document their gradual reduction in frequency. Such a withdrawal can also demonstrate control of the independent variable over the dependent variable.

In a clinical research study, for example, the clinician may wish to find out whether production of morphological features can be reinforced by verbal praise. After establishing the baseline production levels of selected morphologic features, verbal praise may be made contingent on the production of those features in phrases or sentences. When an increase in the production of these behaviors becomes evident, the clinician may withdraw verbal praise. The selected stimuli are presented continuously to evoke relevant verbal responses to see if the production of the morphemes decreases. If

they do, the clinician may conclude that the treatment variable was responsible for the initial increase and the subsequent decrease in the morpheme productions. Figure 4–1 shows the visual effects of the withdrawal procedure in which a target behavior increases under treatment and decreases under withdrawal.

Withdrawal of treatment in single-subject designs is not the same as the termination of the treatment followed by the posttest in a group design. The withdrawal of treatment is a sensitive operation in that it is supposed to demonstrate the presence and the absence of the effects corresponding to the presence and the absence of the independent variable. In the group strategy, the treatment is not terminated to show that the effects are reduced or eliminated. Also, researchers in the group strategy do not need to have the treatment effect neutralized; they have the control group to show that when there was no treatment, there was no effect.

Withdrawal of treatment and the resulting decrease in the response rate help rule out the effects of history and maturation, two important extraneous variables (see Chapter 9 for details). If events in the life of the participants are responsible for the changes observed during treatment, then the withdrawal of treatment should not affect the response rate. If the behavior increases when the treatment is applied and decreases when it is withdrawn, then the probability that events in the life of the participants are responsible for the changes is reduced greatly. Similarly, if biological or other internal changes taking place in the participants are responsible for the increase in the behavior during the treatment condition, then such an increase should at least be maintained, if not continued, when the treatment is discontinued.

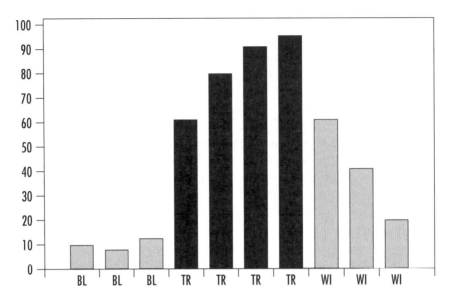

Figure 4–1. The controlling effects of the withdrawal procedure. A target behavior that is stable under baseline (BL) increases when treated (TR) and decreases when the treatment is withdrawn (WI).

As a control procedure, withdrawal has its disadvantages. It can be clinically undesirable because the treatment effects are neutralized even if only temporarily. Withdrawal poses no serious problem in basic laboratory research in which various independent variables are introduced and withdrawn to create and remove their effects. For example, in animal research, some response such as bar pressing can be increased by reinforcing it and decreased by withholding the reinforcer. This way, the experimenter can bring the bar-pressing response under experimental control and rule out the influence of other variables. In clinical situations, however, withdrawal of treatment and the resulting decrease in the target behavior may not be appropriate. Withdrawal serves an experimental purpose, but it damages the clinical purpose of keeping and enhancing the behavioral change the treatment produces. Therefore, it is not a control method of choice in clinical research. However, withdrawal can be used in combination with other control procedures in which the treatment is reestablished (as in the *ABAB* design, for example).

The other problem associated with withdrawal is that the investigator needs to judge when to withdraw treatment. There are no objective rules to do this, but certain patterns of responses dictate the decision. Before it is withdrawn, the researcher must see a pattern of change in the dependent variable that can be objectively related to the treatment. Once the change reaches a convincing level, the treatment should not be continued. In other words, it should be withdrawn as early as possible so that the baseline or an approximation of it can be recaptured. However, when the response rate under treatment is highly variable, withdrawal may be delayed to find out if a continuation of treatment will stabilize it at a level higher than the baseline.

A more troublesome phenomenon could occur when the behavior initially increases under treatment but slowly or abruptly begins to decrease in later treatment sessions. While this is happening, withdrawal is inappropriate because it will only show a continuation of the trend already established during the treatment phase. The investigator once again may wish to continue treatment for a period of time to determine if the declining rate of response can be checked or even reversed. A point may still come, however, when the treatment is withdrawn despite a persistent declining rate of response. Although the results cannot be interpreted clearly in this case, the suggestion is that the treatment perhaps has had only a temporary effect or no effect at all. The problem must be addressed in additional research.

Finally, if the response rate does not approximate the baseline rate when the treatment is withdrawn, the results cannot be interpreted. The possibility that some extraneous variable is responsible for the change observed during the treatment condition cannot be ruled out.

Reversal of Treatment

Reversal of treatment is an alternative to withdrawal. Sometimes, the terms *withdrawal* and *reversal* are used interchangeably. However, this practice is avoided here because of the procedural differences between them. In withdrawal, the treatment is simply discontinued. In **reversal**, the treatment is applied to an alternative, incompatible behavior. That is, the treatment is not withdrawn altogether; it is withdrawn from the particular behavior for which it was applied only to apply it on some other behavior.

Another way of looking at the distinction between withdrawal and reversal may be helpful. While withdrawal is a short- or long-term termination of treatment, reversal involves an intrasubject but interbehavior replication of treatment. Initially, the investigator hopes to show that the application of the treatment to behavior A resulted in an increase in that behavior. The treatment of behavior A is then discontinued. Next, the investigator demonstrates that an application of the same treatment to behavior B (reversal) increased behavior B while decreasing behavior A. This documents experimental control on both the behaviors, resulting in interbehavior-intrasubject replication. In essence, withdrawal is a singular procedure, but reversal is a dual procedure that includes withdrawal of treatment from the original behavior and its application to an incompatible behavior.

A hypothetical example will clarify this dual process. Suppose a clinician treats a client who stutters by reinforcing durations of fluency in conversational speech. A stable baseline of fluency and stuttering is established before the initiation of treatment. Reinforcement of speech fluency durations results in a marked increase in overall fluency. At this time, the clinician cannot conclude that the reinforcement is responsible for the change, since the factors such as history and maturation have not been ruled out. At this point, the clinician stops reinforcing fluency and starts to reinforce stuttering, a response that is incompatible with fluency. As a result of the reversal of the treatment contingency, fluency decreases and stuttering increases. This then demonstrates that the reinforcing contingency is indeed responsible for the changes in fluency as well as stuttering.

Reversal has some of the same problems as withdrawal. Initially, the investigator must decide when to withdraw treatment from the first behavior according to the suggestions offered earlier. Then the investigator must select a behavior that is incompatible with the first behavior. Unless the behavior to be reinforced next is incompatible with the original behavior, a partial replication of the treatment effect may be all that can be achieved. The original behavior may or may not show a swift and concomitant change when the treatment is applied to a compatible behavior.

For example, in the treatment of an individual with a language disorder, the clinician may first apply the treatment to the production of regular plural allomorph *s* in words. After having seen a substantial increase in the production of this allomorph, the clinician may decide to reverse the treatment. Now, the clinician must make sure that the behavior to be treated next is incompatible with the plural allomorph. The best strategy is to reinforce the production of the same words used in training the plural allomorph but in their singular form while showing the plural stimulus items. When the plural responses to plural stimulus items decrease, the singular responses to the same stimulus items increase. Should the clinician reinforce the present progressive *-ing* or some other behavior that is not incompatible with the plural allomorph, the production of the latter may not show a concomitant change under the reversal condition.

Reversal presents special problems in clinical research. Therefore, other control procedures are preferred. The procedure requires that the clinician increase the frequency of an undesirable behavior after having increased its counterpart—a desirable behavior. Whenever it is used, the treatment for the original, desirable target behavior is reinstated in the next phase. Reinstatement then shows that the undesirable behavior decreased, and its counterpart increased a second time. Thus, the treatment achieved its clinical goal.

When it takes several sessions to increase an incompatible, undesirable behavior, reversal is inefficient and perhaps unacceptable as well as unethical. The parents or other members of the client family may react negatively to the clinician who first teaches a correct response and then spends an extended duration and considerable energy teaching the incorrect response. In institutional research, staff members who are asked to reverse the treatment may be reluctant to do so (Barlow, Nock, & Hersen, 2009). For example, in a reversal design, aides in agencies for individuals with intellectual disability who are asked to reinforce gestures instead of the word responses that had been reinforced in therapy sessions may not be willing to follow this reversal procedure.

In a more conservative use of the reversal strategy, the clinician can make sure that both the reversal and reinstatement of treatment are achieved in a single session. If the clinician is not sure of this possibility, the reversal strategy may be avoided. In our example of language treatment research, if the clinician is not confident of increasing the production of the singular morpheme in relation to plural stimulus items (reversal) and then an increase in the correct production of the plural allomorph in relation to plural items (reinstatement)—all in a single session—reversal may be avoided.

In many cases, it is possible to reverse and reinstate treatment in a single, perhaps a little extended, session. In child language treatment research, grammatical features established in the previous treatment condition have been reversed and reinstated in the same session (Hegde & McConn, 1981). Also, the wrong responses need not be increased to the 100% level and stabilized there. Though there are not quantitative guidelines on this, an increase from a low, 10% to 15%, error rate to a moderately high, 40% to 50% error rate may be adequate for the purposes of control. The clinician can then reinstate treatment for the correct response. The correct response rate under reinstatement can also be achieved quickly. When reversal and reinstatement are thus achieved in a single session, the client is not sent home with an increased or increasing rate of wrong responses.

Reinstatement of Treatment

Reinstatement of treatment is yet another control strategy within single-subject designs. **Reinstatement** is reintroduction of treatment that was either withdrawn or reversed. Thus, it is a contingent control condition that has a cumulative control effect within a design. It is contingent upon withdrawal or reversal that will already have demonstrated significant control over the dependent variable. The reinstatement of treatment then adds additional control.

Reinstatement may be an optional control strategy in basic research. In non-clinical settings, a behavior shaped or taught can be eliminated by withdrawal.

Along with this, another behavior may be increased with reversal. However, in clinical research, reinstatement of effective treatment is almost mandatory when the control procedures of withdrawal or reinstatement are used.

The concepts and procedures of withdrawal, reversal, and reinstatement, though separate, are closely related. They also converge on the concept of replication. A single withdrawal replicates the baseline condition by showing an initial increase from, and then a decrease to, the baseline response rate. A single reversal replicates the treatment effect twice, first by showing that the initial target behavior increases and then by showing that the incompatible behavior increases under reversed contingencies.

When a treatment is *withdrawn* and then *reinstated* once, the effects of treatment are demonstrated three times: first when the treatment is initially applied, second when the treatment is withdrawn, and third when the treatment is reinstated. In the first and third cases, an increase in the frequency of the target behavior is demonstrated. In the second case, a decrease in the frequency is demonstrated. Together, the three demonstrations strengthen the possibility that the extraneous variables were ruled out. Figure 4–2 shows the effects of a single withdrawal and reinstatement of a treatment.

When a treatment is *reversed* and then *reinstated* once, the treatment effects are demonstrated six times. The first demonstration occurs when the treatment is first applied to the target behavior that shows an increase; the second occurs when the treatment is withdrawn and the target behavior decreases; the third occurs when the treatment is reinstated for the

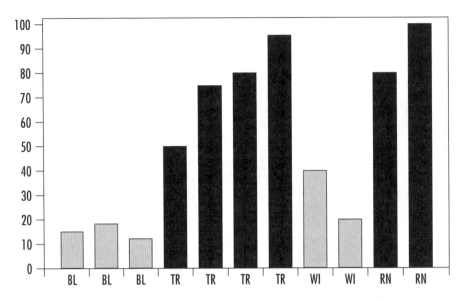

Figure 4–2. The controlling effects of a single withdrawal and reinstatement of treatment. A stable and low rate of a target behavior during the baseline (BL) increases during treatment (TR), decreases during withdrawal (WI), and increases again during reinstatement of treatment (RN).

target behavior, which shows an increase again; the fourth occurs when the incompatible behavior decreases when the target behavior is treated; the fifth involves an increase in the incompatible behavior when the treatment is applied to it; and the sixth is evident when the incompatible behavior decreases under reinstatement of treatment for the target behavior. Figure 4–3 shows these demonstrations with the hypothetical target example of fluency (target, 1) and stuttering (incompatible behavior, 2).

A combination of reversal or withdrawal with the reinstatement procedure can provide a convincing demonstration of the treatment effect by making it difficult to explain the results based on extraneous variables. When systematic changes are associated with the experimental manipulations of withdrawal or reversal on one hand and reinstatement on the other, the probability that the changes are due to those manipulations increases.

Criterion-Referenced Change

In one of the single-subject designs, some level of control of extraneous variables is achieved by showing that the dependent variable changes in relation to a criterion, and the criterion is changed several times in subsequent stages of the experiment. Thus, the **criterion-referenced change** is reliable, and multiple changes in target behaviors are consistent with changing treatment criteria.

The criterion-referenced change has not been used frequently in demonstrating the experimental control of independent variables (Barlow et al., 2009). The basic idea is that if changes in a dependent variable approximate a preset criterion, and

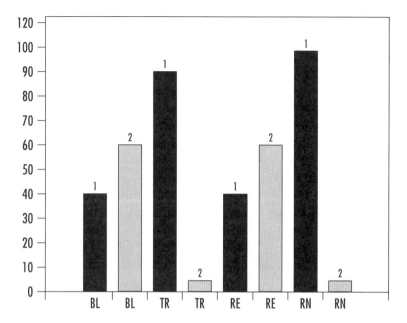

Figure 4–3. Six demonstrations of a treatment effect with a reversal and reinstatement. Fluency (1) and stuttering (2) are base rated (BL) and then fluency is treated (TR). The treatment is reversed (RE) and finally reinstated (RN) for fluency. Note the corresponding changes in the two incompatible behaviors.

if whenever the criterion is changed the dependent variable also changes in accordance with the new criterion in force, then the experimental control is demonstrated. In this case, the changes in the dependent variable follow a more predictable pattern that corresponds to the changing criteria.

A hypothetical example can illustrate the criterion-referenced change. An investigator may wish to find out if the amount of homework done by a child is a function of the reinforcement contingency. To rule out the influence of factors other than the reinforcement contingency, the investigator may devise a series of changing criteria that the dependent variables may track. For example, initially the child may be asked to complete five academic tasks in a given time. This is the initial criterion to which the dependent variable

is held. The investigator will continue to measure the number of tasks completed. Reinforcement is provided for task completion. Suppose that in due course, the child stabilizes at the five completed tasks required by the criterion. After this, the investigator changes the criterion to eight tasks, and the child's behavior reaches and stabilizes at this level. In subsequent stages, the criterion is changed to 10, 14, 16, and 18 tasks. If the number of tasks completed by the child reaches and stabilizes at each new criterion in force, a certain degree of control over the dependent variable becomes evident.

If the dependent variable does not reach the criterion or stabilize at that level, then the control is not evident. Capricious changes unrelated to the criterion in force will also invalidate the data. The dependent variable should closely parallel the criterion in force to demonstrate an acceptable degree of control.

The criterion-referenced change is probably the weakest of the control procedures available within the single-subject strategy. By itself, it does not provide for such no-treatment control conditions as withdrawal and reversal. However, such control procedures can be incorporated into the criterion-referenced change. Treatment may be withdrawn at some stage to determine if the behavior returns to at least one of the previous levels. Or, by periodically switching back and forth to a higher and a lower criterion, bidirectional control over behavior may be demonstrated. This also provides replication at the repeated criterion levels. The control function demonstrated by criterion-referenced change is illustrated in Figure 4–4. The criterion-referenced change is involved in a design known as the changing criterion design, described in Chapter 9.

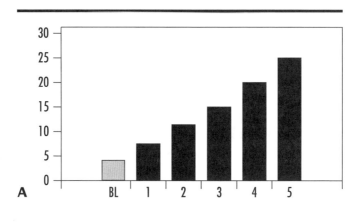

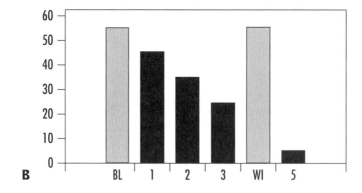

Figure 4–4. Criterion-referenced change showing control over a desirable behavior with an initial baseline and five changing criteria that increase the behavior (**A**). The lower portion (**B**) shows changing criteria decreasing an undesirable behavior with an added withdrawal (WI) feature that shows a temporary increase.

Rapid Alternations

Another form of control used in some of the single-subject designs is the rapid alternation of two or more conditions. The conditions may include treatment and no treatment, or two or more treatments. Of course, two or more treatments may be alternated along with no-treatment conditions as well. Quick changes in experimental conditions and corresponding changes in target behaviors define **rapid alternations** as a control mechanism.

Rapid alternation of conditions serves the control function when the changes in the dependent variable are equally rapid and consistent with the alternations of conditions. For example, when treatment and no treatment are alternated, the dependent variable may show appropriate increases and decreases. When the treatment is repeatedly introduced and withdrawn with results showing appropriate changes, the investigator increases the probability that the changes are due to the rapidly changing conditions of the experiment.

Rapid alternation of treatment and no-treatment conditions is not the same as treatment conditions interspersed with baseline conditions. In the latter strategy, one can initially baseline a behavior and introduce a treatment that will be continued for a certain length of time. After the behavior shows a convincing change, the treatment may be withdrawn until the client returns to the baseline. This second baseline may also be continued until the behavior shows a change toward the baseline. Then once again the same or even a different treatment may be introduced and maintained for an extended time. This strategy attempts to expose the participants to treatment and baseline conditions for a duration needed to produce changes that do differentiate the conditions.

On the other hand, in rapid alternation of treatment and no treatment, there is no attempt to continue either the treatment or the no-treatment condition until some change is judged to have occurred. Each session involves a different condition, and the treatment and no-treatment conditions may be alternated even within sessions. In rapid alternations, the investigator expects to show a data trend over a time involving several alternations.

In the rapid alternation of two or more treatments, an initial baseline may be established, although it is not always required. The purpose of such a strategy is to determine the relative effects of two or more treatments, not the absolute effect of either of them. Therefore, baseline or any other form of control procedure is not necessary, though it is desirable. The control function of rapid alternations involving two treatments (X_1 and X_2) is illustrated in Figure 4–5. Note that Treatment 1 was more effective than Treatment 2 in increasing the target behavior from its baseline level.

A clinician, for example, may wish to evaluate the relative effects of two kinds of stimulus items in teaching vocabulary items to a child with language disorders. The stimulus variables to be evaluated in the study may be actual objects and pictures that represent the words to be taught. During the training, objects and pictures may be rapidly alternated. However, through such alternations, training trials on a given word will have a constant type of stimulus. Each stimulus type may involve several target words. Over several rapid alternations, several words may be taught with each of the two types of

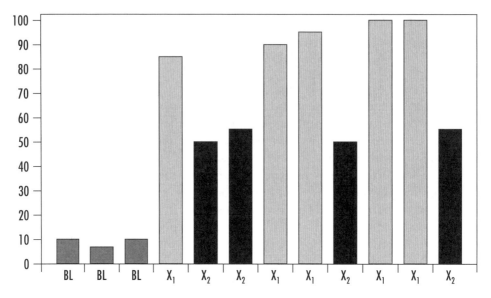

Figure 4–5. The demonstration of experimental control with rapid alternations of two treatments (X_1 and X_2). Note that in increasing the frequency of the target behavior, Treatment 1 was more effective than Treatment 2.

stimulus materials preceding specific targets. The data may be analyzed in terms of the number of training trials (or sessions, or both) needed to achieve an operationally defined training criterion for the set of words taught with objects versus pictures as stimulus antecedents. Or when the number of sessions is held constant, the number of words learned within the two procedures can also be analyzed. Such analyses can reveal the differential effects of the two stimulus variables.

Rapid alternation of two or more treatments, by itself, does not provide for strong controls within the design. That is why it is more suitable for evaluating relative, not absolute, effects of two or more treatment variables. When the alternations involve treatment and no-treatment conditions, appropriate controls exist to rule out extraneous variables. Lacking such a control condition, the multitreatment alternations can only identify which one

had a greater effect on the dependent variable. However, control conditions such as a withdrawal of all treatments can be built into the alternating sequence. In that case, questions regarding whether treatments had any effect when compared to no treatment can also be answered.

Baselines

An important and almost invariably used control strategy within single-subject designs is the baselines or baserates of responses. **Baselines** are response rates in the absence of the independent variable whose effects are being experimentally analyzed. They also are described as *natural rates* of responses and the *operant level* of responses. Baselines document the frequency of the dependent variable before the independent variable is introduced. The absence of treatment during the baseline condition makes it the control condition within single-subject designs. The dependent variable measures obtained in the treatment and baseline conditions are compared to assess the treatment effects.

It is important to note that a mere baseline at the beginning of the experimental manipulation does not rule out extraneous variables. If a study includes only the baseline and treatment conditions, it is an *AB* **case study**, not an experiment, comparable to the one-group pretest-posttest design. Neither can rule out the influence of history or maturation. Therefore, what is needed in addition to a baseline is either withdrawal of treatment, reversal of treatment, rapid alternation, or criterion-referenced change. Baselines serve a control purpose only in conjunction with one of these procedures. Most frequently, baselines and either withdrawal or reversal are used to demonstrate the internal validity of experimental operations.

There is an exception to the rule that baselines must be combined with other control procedures to eliminate or minimize the influence of extraneous variables. The exception constitutes *simultaneous multiple baselines* described in a later section.

Baselines established before the introduction of treatment must fulfill certain standards of acceptability, which are called **baseline criteria**. Reliability through multiple observations, stability of the measures, and the potential for contrast are the three acceptable baseline criteria.

Reliability through multiple observations is the first baseline criterion. Unlike pretests in a group design, which normally involves a single observation of the dependent variable, baselines are held to an initial criterion of multiple observations. A single measurement of the dependent variable is inadequate because of its unknown reliability. By definition, **reliability** is consistency across measures, and therefore, multiple measures are needed to ensure reliable measurement of the dependent variable as it naturally occurs. It has been suggested that at least three separate observations are needed before the adequacy of a baseline can be evaluated (Barlow et al., 2009). In fact, three observations may suggest that either additional measures are needed or the behavior has stabilized so that the treatment can be introduced.

Stability of the measures is the second baseline criterion. A highly variable baseline does not permit a valid comparison with the response rate under the treatment condition. If the rate of response is constantly fluctuating from observation to observation, then the treatment effects may be buried in this variability. However, variability itself can have some patterns, and it is important to note them.

If the response rate is variable in a predictable fashion, it has a pattern, which is better than variability with no pattern whatsoever. For example, the behavior may show a consistent increase in one session and decrease in the other session, and the overall data may show this duplicating pattern. Or the measures may show no pattern in the first few observations, and then a pattern either of stability or alternating increases and decreases may emerge. Another possibility is that the variability may be too high in the beginning, but gradually its extent may be reduced though no pattern emerges. Baselines with no pattern and unpredictable variability are not acceptable. Treatment should not be introduced.

A stable response rate is the one **without a trend** and unpredictable variability. A trend is evident when the rate of responses either increases or decreases over time. A stable response without a trend is considered the ideal baseline. When the pretreatment baseline is stable, it is relatively easy to detect the effects of the independent variable.

A stable baseline is difficult to obtain in many cases, and fortunately it is not the only acceptable baseline. A **deteriorating baseline** (Barlow et al., 2009), with a clear trend in which the problem to be treated is getting worse across sessions, is acceptable. For example, in a study designed to evaluate the effects of time-out on stuttering, the clinician observes the rate of dysfluencies in conversational speech over several sessions to establish baselines. The measures of dysfluencies may show an increasing trend over the baseline sessions, showing a deterioration in the fluency problem. Deteriorating baselines are acceptable from a scientific as well as ethical standpoint. Scientifically, treatment is expected to produce an opposite trend in the data. If time-out is effective, it will not only check the deterioration in stuttering but will also reverse the trend. Indeed, a treatment that reverses a deteriorating baseline can be considered a strong one. Ethically, deteriorating baselines require that the researcher intervene immediately. If the participant's problem is getting worse by the day, the researcher will have to place the client's welfare ahead of any research demands.

An **improving baseline**, on the other hand, is trend that is clearly not acceptable, both scientifically and ethically. For example, a clinician who base rates fluency and stuttering may find that there is a clear trend toward increased fluency and decreased stuttering across base rate sessions. In such cases, treatment cannot be instituted simply because the positive effects of the treatment, if any, will be confounded with the baseline trend of improvement in fluency. With such a trend, one will have to assume that fluency would have improved in the absence of treatment. Furthermore, it would be ethically unjustified to offer treatment for a problem from which people are recovering without professional help.

The best course of action to take when baselines are unstable without a pattern is to continue measurement until an acceptable pattern or trend emerges. Basic research has repeatedly shown that when the conditions are well controlled and the observations are repeated, variability eventually dissipates. It is easier to take this course of action in basic research than in clinical research, however. In clinical settings, baselines cannot be extended indefinitely. The clients who serve as participants also are seeking treatment for their problem, and because one of the strengths of the single-subject designs is an integration of research and clinical service, the treatment must be introduced as soon as possible. Possibly, the person whose baselines do not stabilize is no longer a candidate for research. He or she may be offered treatment outside the scope of the study.

Another way of handling the variability, which has proved successful in basic behavioral research, is to make variability itself the subject of experimental analysis. For instance, when dysfluency rates do not stabilize despite repeated observations, the clinician may begin to wonder why and think of strategies to find out. It is possible that the conditions of observation are not constant. The time of making observations, the method of evoking speech, or the topics discussed may have been variable. If the observational conditions have been constant, then perhaps factors in the life of the individual are affecting the dysfluency rates. Are there patterns of events that are related to the changes in the dysfluency rates? Such an inquiry also is relatively easily conducted in basic research, where the entire life and genetic history of an experimental animal is under the control of the investigator. However, a serious attempt to find out the sources of variability may be fruitful, though difficult, in applied settings. Possibly, it may be found that variability in stuttering in a woman is related to premenstrual and menstrual conditions. Another person's stuttering variability may be due to the frequency with which he or she has meetings with the boss before coming to the baseline sessions. Still another person's stuttering variability may be due to fluctuating marital problems at home.

Although tracking the variability of behaviors is worthwhile because it can lead to new information, it does involve taking a step back from the immediate clinical task at hand. The treatment will have to be postponed until the question of baseline variability is resolved. Obviously, this is not always desirable in clinical situations.

Potential for contrast is the third baseline criterion. Baseline and treatment response rates should contrast with each other to convincingly show that a treatment was effective. **Contrast** is obvious differences in base rate and experimental conditions. A very high or very low baseline can be either acceptable or not acceptable, depending upon the direction in which the dependent variable is expected to be changed by the treatment variable. For example, a high rate of stuttering is acceptable, because the treatment is supposed to lower it. However, a high rate of fluency (with a negligible rate of stuttering) may be unacceptable because there is not much room to show the effects of treatment on fluency.

The best baseline provides a good contrast to the treatment condition. The behavior that is very low in the baseline condition may be shown to be very high in the treatment condition. When the reversal procedure is used in the later part of an experiment, the rates of manipulated behaviors may contrast with each other. An incompatible behavior the experimenter manipulates will be high, and the other will be low.

In some cases, the potential for contrast may make it possible to accept a highly variable response rate after all. Once again, a hypothetical example from stuttering may help. Assume that the stuttering is highly variable with no clear pattern. But the clinician may find out that although there is a wide range to the variability, the lowest level of stuttering, replicated a minimum of three times, is still considerably high. Let us say that over repeated observations, the least amount of dysfluency ever recorded is 15%, with a variability range of 15% to 37%. In this case, the clinician may decide to introduce treatment despite the variability, on the assumption that the treatment will bring stuttering to such a low frequency that there would still be a contrast against the minimum, 15%. When a large effect of treatment is expected, then the resulting contrast will have justified the introduction of treatment at a time when it would normally be considered undesirable. However, if only a small degree of change is expected of the treatment, the clinician should continue baseline observations or seek an analysis of the reasons for variability. If either of these options is precluded, for whatever reason, the study may be abandoned, and the client may be treated.

The basic strategy of analysis used in the single-subject designs requires contrasting levels of response rates in the adjacent conditions of experiments. A contrastive shift in the rate of response must be evident in the treatment condition compared with the baseline condition. When the treatment is withdrawn, the declining (and decreased) response rate should provide a contrast with the increasing (and increased) response rate found in the treatment condition. Or, when the reversal follows treatment, the behaviors that changed in the opposite directions should contrast.

Although contrast helps demonstrate experimental control, a lack of contrast between certain conditions also is part of the analysis in single-subject designs. The baseline and the withdrawal conditions are expected to show a lack of contrast. In the reversal design, the behavior from which the treatment is withdrawn is expected to show the same lack of contrast, although its counterpart would provide increased contrast. The various baseline patterns that illustrate stability, pattern, and the presence and the absence of contrast are illustrated in Figure 4–6.

Simultaneous Multiple Baselines

The final form of control used in the single-subject strategy involves simultaneous multiple baselines. Normally, a single, stable baseline of a single target behavior is established before the treatment is started. This is the kind of baseline that was discussed in the previous section. In **simultaneous multiple baselines**, several behaviors are observed before the introduction of treatment, and baselines are established on all of them. The base-lines are repeated throughout the course of the experiment.

In the simultaneous multiple baselines, experimental control is demonstrated by stability of untreated behaviors (baselines). For example, an investigator may obtain baselines of four grammatical features in an effort to establish the effectiveness of a language treatment program. Suppose that each of the behaviors is at the 0% baseline. The clinician then treats one of the grammatical features, increasing its production to 90% accuracy. Then, the other three morphemes are baserated again to show that their frequency did not change since they were not treated. The second morpheme is trained next, and the remaining two morphemes are baserated to document their unchanged status in the absence of treatment. In this manner, every time a behavior is brought under control, the baselines of unchanged behaviors help document the effects of treatment.

The visual effects of the control feature of the simultaneous multiple baselines on four target behaviors are illustrated in Figure 4–7.

The multiple baselines can be behaviors of the same or different participants. The baselines may also be situations where a particular behavior of a given individual is measured. When different participants constitute simultaneous multiple baselines, participants are treated in sequence and baselines are repeatedly established on untreated participants. Unchanged behaviors of untreated participants help rule out the influence of extraneous variables. When different situations are the multiple baselines, the same behavior is treated in sequence in different situations, and the rate of that behavior in untreated situations helps demonstrate the effects of the treatment.

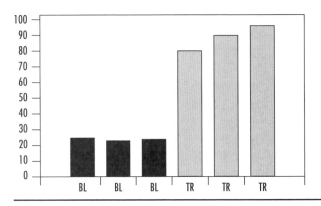

A. A stable baseline with an obvious increase in the response rate under treatment providing good contrast.

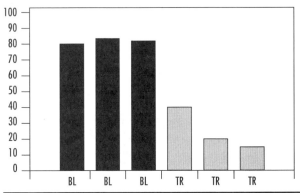

B. A high but stable baseline with a notable decrease in the response rate under treatment providing good contrast.

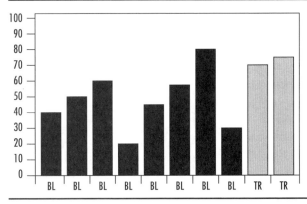

C. A variable baseline with an unclear treatment effect due to poor contrast.

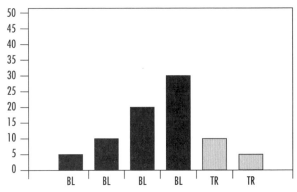

D. A deteriorating baseline (increasing frequency of an undesirable behavior) with a reversed trend under treatment with good contrast.

Figure 4–6. Seven patterns of baselines showing variability, stability, low and high floors, and good and poor contrast. *continues*

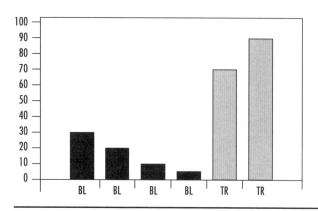

E. A decreasing baseline (increasing frequency of a desirable behavior) with a reversed trend under treatment with good contrast.

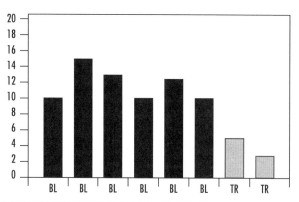

F. A variable but acceptable baseline of a high floor (10%) that provides good contrast with the treatment effect.

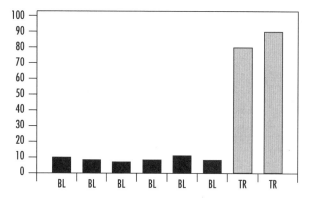

G. A variable desirable behavior providing a low floor for a high contrast when the behavior increases significantly when treated.

Figure 4–6. *continued*

These three versions of the simultaneous multiple baselines correspond to the three versions of the *multiple baseline designs* described in Chapter 9.

The logic of the simultaneous multiple baselines comes close to that of the group design strategy. In group experimental designs, untreated participants serve the control function. In simultaneous multiple baseline strategy, untreated behaviors, participants, or situations serve the same function. Unlike in the group

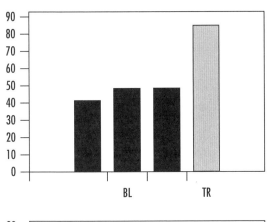

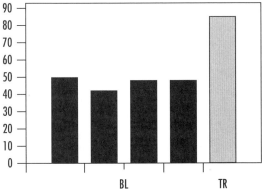

Figure 4-7. Simultaneous multi-baselines (BL) and treatment (TR). Baselines are longer for behaviors that are treated later in the sequence. Each behavior increases only when treated.

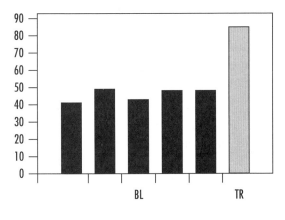

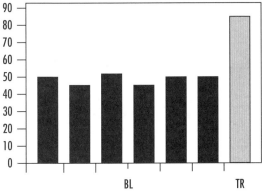

105

design strategy, all participants eventually receive treatment in simultaneous multiple baseline designs.

Randomized Clinical Trials Versus Single-Subject Treatment Research

Randomized group designs are well established in medical and surgical treatment research. Many medical researchers promote the RCTs as the gold standard of treatment research and conduct a large number of them. Annually and globally, several hundred RCTs are typically in progress. Many treatment researchers in communication disorders, too, tend to favor RCTs of communication treatment procedures, although such trials are few and methodologically questionable (Hegde, 2007).

Single-subject treatment approaches and RCTs are based on the same logic of causes and effects. They both use the experimental method to show that the treatment was the cause of improvement in people who receive it. Nonetheless, there are some important conceptual as well as methodological differences between the two approaches. Therefore, it is necessary to consider the following in understanding the differences between the two approaches: experimental control and internal validity, statistical and clinical generality, self-selection in randomized clinical trials, ethical issues with control groups, and treatment research in medicine versus communication disorders.

Experimental Control and Internal Validity

The first concern of any treatment researcher is to establish good experimental control and achieve internal validity by ruling out extraneous variables. Under acceptable conditions, both RCTs and single-subject treatment research can achieve good experimental control and internal validity for the results. It should be noted that no experimental treatment evaluation is ideal or perfect. All treatment researchers are forced to make certain compromises because of practical exigencies. Too many and too serious compromises in methods of a study, however, will invalidate the results. For instance, a researcher using the randomized group design usually cannot select participants randomly from a defined clinical population. The researcher may recruit available people for participation. This may be an acceptable compromise assuming that the researcher will not claim external validity or statistical generality for the results. (Unfortunately, the researchers usually do.) On the other hand, the researcher who fails to randomly assign participants to different groups will have made an unacceptable compromise. In that case, the researcher cannot claim internal validity for the results because there is no assurance that the two groups were equal at the beginning of the study. Furthermore, if there is differential attrition in the experimental and control groups, internal validity cannot be claimed. (Unfortunately, researchers continue to claim.) (Hegde, 2007).

Single-subject researchers, too, may make acceptable and unacceptable compromises. For instance, before introducing the treatment to be evaluated, single-subject treatment research requires stable baselines of target behaviors with little variation across baseline sessions. In some cases, such stability of target behaviors may be difficult to obtain. The investigator then may make an acceptable compromise and introduce treatment if the variability is within a certain range and the treatment produces large effects that override the variability. On the other hand, an investigator who introduces treatment when the target behaviors are highly unstable and the treatment effects are unclear against the background variability will have made an unacceptable compromise.

Statistical Generality Versus Clinical Validity

As defined previously, **statistical generality** refers to the degree to which the conclusions of a study based on a randomly selected and assigned sample may be extended to the population and **logical generality** is the extent to which the conclusions of a treatment study may be extended to individual clients who are similar to those who have served in a single-subject treatment study. **Clinical validity**, also called **clinical significance**, on the other hand, refers to the degree to which the treatment effects are personally and socially meaningful to those who experience it. Group and single-subject designs differ much on statistical generality, logical generality, and clinical validity or significance.

The typical assertion has been the results of group experimental designs have statistical generality, whereas those of single-subject designs do not have it because of their small number of nonrepresentative participants (Campbell & Stanley, 1966; Shadish, Cook, & Campbell, 2002). However, because the participants are not randomly selected from the population, the claim of statistical generality for group designs in questionable. Whether group or single-subject designs, generality is achieved only by direct and systematic replications. Randomization provides no shortcut to generality. The

issue, however, is whether statistical generality, even when it does exist, can imply clinically significant results.

We address this issue in some detail in Chapter 10. Therefore, we might just note here that statistically significant results of a treatment study may or may not have clinical significance. Small changes in the treated groups may be statistically significant, especially when the sample size is large. But such small changes may not make a difference in the daily living of individuals treated in randomized clinical trials. And at other times, small changes may make big difference for clients. Therefore, it may be more meaningful to seek clinically significance results (clinical validity) rather than mere statistical significance and the elusive inferential generality.

Self-Selection in Randomized Clinical Trials

Before 1974, there were no laws in the United States to prevent abuse of human participants in experimental or nonexperimental research. Human participants were often not told about the purpose and methods of the experiment in which they were about to participate. In many cases, researchers have actively misled the research participants about the purposes and procedures of experiments. While testing new and dangerous drugs, for instance, the patients were led to believe that they were getting some safe and effective treatment. Such instances as not treating patients with syphilis to see what happens to them or injecting healthy patients with tumor cells have been documented (Beecher, 1966). When these and many other abusive practices in biomedical research came to light, the U.S. Congress passed the National Research Act of 1974 (P.L. 93-348) to prevent such abusive and dangerous research. See Chapter 17 for a short history and review of human participant protection measures.

Currently, in most countries where biomedical and behavioral research is conducted, potential human participants should give informed consent to participate. The research protocol and the human participant protection procedures should be reviewed and approved by an independent committee, formally known as the *institutional review boards* and more popularly called the *human participants protection committees* (see Chapter 17 for details). Of all the procedures involved in protecting human participants, the informed consent has serious consequences for initial selection of participants and their eventual and complete participation until the end of a treatment study. These consequences negate randomization and, therefore, eliminate any possibility of statistical generality. Obviously, it is more important to protect human participants than it is to achieve statistical generality. Nonetheless, the inevitable consequences of informed consent on participant selection process must be clearly understood.

Aspects of informed consent that affect the participant selection process include the following. First, potential participants must be fully told about the purpose and methods of the study. Second, the potential participants must fully understand the potential risks and benefits of treatments they will receive. Third, after fully understanding the objectives, methods, benefits, and risks of a study, individuals may decline to participate or give free and voluntary consent to participate. Fourth, all participants who initially give voluntary consent to participate are totally free to withdraw any time during the study. Fifth, all participants retain a

right to demand alternative treatments to which they are not assigned, demand or reject the experimental treatment, refuse to be a part of a control group that does not receive treatment, and simply drop out of a study without giving any reason. When these conditions are fulfilled—all researchers are legally required to fulfill them, and most if not all participants fully exercise their rights—there is no random selection or assignment of participants in so-called RCTs.

Treatment researchers *recruit* participants for RCTs. Researchers may randomly select patients among available patients; however, this is not random selection from a population of patients. It is now well established that a large number of potential participants who have been recruited for a study refuse to participate. In medical research, many primary care physicians do not refer their patients to RCTs because their patients who need urgent treatment may be assigned to a risky new treatment, to a no-treatment control group, or to a fake treatment placebo group (Taylor, 1985). Consequently, those who eventually *agree to participate* do not constitute a randomly selected sample. In fact, investigators no longer can select and keep patients in a study; it is the patients who select an investigator and then continue only if they so choose.

The self-selection process continues throughout the study period. After obtaining informed consent, researchers randomly assign recruited (not randomly selected) participants to experimental and control groups. An individual's assignment to new treatment, an established treatment, or a placebo control group may or may not be revealed, depending on the blinding procedure. The self-selection tendency begins to exert its greatest influence when patients find out or suspect their group assignment. Patients who are assigned to a risky new treatment (the treatment being evaluated in the study) may demand a well-established older treatment. To the contrary, when it is suspected that the new treatment involves fewer risks than the older treatment, patients may refuse to receive the older treatment. Many who are assigned to the placebo control group may demand treatment, the new or the old, depending on what they learn about them. Some who are assigned to placebo group may simply drop out of the study to seek treatment outside the scope of the study. Those who find either treatment unattractive also may drop out of the study. Furthermore, those who have received one or the other treatment but are disappointed with its effects may drop out as well. Finally, some individuals who reluctantly accept an undesirable treatment may not comply with the treatment protocol, inducing data distortions. A consequence of such patient action is that those who complete the new treatment regimen are even more self-selected than the initial, already self-selected volunteers. As a result, the new treatment will have been evaluated on a special group of individuals. Therefore, there is nothing random about their selection or assignment.

Biases introduced by self-selection of participants make it difficult to extend the conclusions of a study to the population. This is because self-selected individuals may not represent the unselected individuals in the population. There is now plenty of evidence that volunteers and those who stay with a study until its completion have different characteristics than those who do not volunteer or drop out after volunteering (see the review of evidence in Hegde, 2007). Evidence suggests that those who volunteer to participate in RCTs tend to be poorer, less educated, and more seriously ill than those who refuse participation. A majority of those who volunteer for new treatment studies lack health insurance and have a poor health status. On the other hand, those who volunteer to participate in a study designed to enhance health status or prevent diseases are more affluent and better educated than those who refuse participation in such studies (Gorkin et al., 1996; McKee et al., 1999). In any case, those who initially volunteer to participate and those who eventually complete the study do not represent the population to which they presumably belong. Therefore, the typical claim that RCTs or group experimental designs that use large numbers of participants have statistical generality is an unacceptable claim.

Because of the human subject protection procedures, participants in single-subject research also are self-selected. Self-selection does not pose a serious problem when statistical generality based on a single study is not claimed. It poses a problem only when the mistaken claim of statistical generality is made based on a single RCT. Single-subject researchers typically avoid this mistake.

It is true that eventually, researchers want to establish treatment procedures that work with a larger number of individuals with given diseases or disorders. That is, statistical generality is a worthy goal. Unfortunately, it cannot be achieved by a single study of any kind. It can be achieved only by systematically replicating a treatment study in different settings, by different investigators, and by recruiting a variety of patients or clients. Multiple replications that repeatedly sample a small number of participants to study them intensively are more likely than RCTs to contribute more to statistical generality.

Ethical Issues With Control Groups

All participants in single-subject designs experience treatment even if the treatment offered initially is withdrawn for a short duration of time in certain of the designs. When a no-treatment control group is used in group designs, the treatment is denied to members of that group. When a placebo control group is used, a fake treatment is offered to members of that group. The placebo-control group is the same as the no-treatment control group except that the members of the former group are misled to believe that they may be getting the real treatment. Treatment denial and placebo controls raise much more serious ethical concerns than temporary withdrawal of treatment found in some single-subject designs (e.g., the *ABAB* design and its variations; see Chapter 9; also see Chapter 17).

The ethical issues related to no-treatment or placebo-controlled RCTs are addressed in greater detail in Chapter 17. In medicine, placebo control is more often used than no-treatment control. Here we will note that treatment denial or sham treatment may be unethical and socially unacceptable, except in certain highly circumscribed situations (e.g., a total absence of a treatment for a disease except for the one being evaluated). Unfortunately, far too many medical treatment studies are still conducted with no treatment or placebo controls.

Placebo procedures in surgical treatment research raise the most serious ethical questions. In some studies, placebo-control group patients in heart surgery research have had their chest cavity cut, opened, and then closed without taking any remedial steps, to give the patient an impression that the intended surgical procedure has been carried out on them. In studies on Parkinson's disease, holes were drilled in the skulls of placebo-control group patients to simulate intracerebral transplantation of fetal mesencephalic tissue (Brody, 1998; Dekkers & Boer, 2001; Morris, Zaritsky, & LeFever, 2000; Verdu-Pascal & Castello-Ponce, 2001). Instead of offering some benefit or even no benefit, performing such invasive surgeries on control group participants to expose them to significant risk, pain, and suffering is hard to justify ethically or to reconcile with the medical goal of doing no harm.

Those who believe that RCTs are the only means of establishing treatment effects accept the ethical problems as inevitable. In most behavioral research, control conditions (e.g., baselines, treatment withdrawal, treatment reinstatement, multiple baselines) will satisfactorily establish treatment effects with no control groups. In most medical research, too, control conditions will work fine. The same patients' symptoms or health status may be measured under baseline, under administration of new medicine, and under temporary withdrawal of medicine, which is reinstated as quickly as possible. All patients will be treated in this arrangement. Single-subject designs are quite effective in disease prevention studies. For instance, multiple baseline designs will work well in studies on weight loss, smoking cessation, cholesterol reduction, exercise programs, and so forth. Other single-subject designs will work just as well. While all treatment studies raise some ethical issues, single-subject designs minimize the ethical dilemmas more satisfactorily than the RCTs. Several medical researchers dissatisfied with the limitations of RCTs have been advocating and performing *N* of 1 clinical trials (single-subject design studies). See Chapters 8 and 9 for more on the use of single-subject designs in medical research.

Treatment Research in Medicine Versus Communication Disorders

Although the basic logic of establishing cause-effect relationships is the same in all sciences, there are some important structural and practical differences between treatment research in medicine and speech-language pathology. In fact, all behavioral (nonmedical) treatment or teaching procedures, including those used in counseling, clinical psychology, social work, physical therapy, health science, occupational therapy, special and regular education, and so forth, contrast with medical procedures in certain important respects. Therefore, it is necessary to understand the nature of treatment in these disciplines to evaluate objectively the different options available for treatment research.

In medicine, treatment research (RCT) is typically conducted in three phases. In Phase I trials, new drugs are tested to evaluate their safety, not effectiveness. Whether a drug produces a toxic effect is the main concern in Phase I trials. A small number of individuals (typically 10 to 30), mostly healthy volunteers, are tested. There is no random selection or random assignment of participants in Phase I trials. There are no control groups either. Treatment that passes the Phase I trial is advanced to Phase II trials in which 50 to 100 patients with the target disease may be tested. A few Phase II trials may use randomization and a control group, but most do not (Finn, 1999; Meinert, 1986; Pocock, 1983). Phase II trials involve homogeneous participants selected with clearly specified criteria, as against RCTs that use heterogeneous participants.

Treatments that pass the first two phases are advanced to Phase III trials in which the new procedure is experimentally evaluated. Experimental and control groups are involved only in Phase III trials. Large numbers of patients in multiple centers and multiple countries may be selected for participation. Trials involving multiple centers and countries also involve hundreds of medical personnel helping collect data.

Randomization in Phase III RCTs is limited to an initial random assignment of available patients to the experimental and control groups. As noted before, randomization is negated by self-selection of participants and the participants' right to withdraw or demand other treatments. In any case, the effects of a new treatment are often evaluated in an experimental group compared against control groups that receive either a standard treatment, no treatment, or a placebo.

Important differences emerge when RCTs in medicine are compared with treatment research in speech-language pathology and many other health professions. Institutional, economic, and scientific distinctions need to be considered. Nationally and internationally, many medical hospitals are large institutions that house great numbers of patients who may at least initially consider participation in treatment research. Such a large subject pool is typically not available in speech-language pathology. Limited subject pool also characterizes clinical psychology and several other health-related professions. Within the medical discipline, such specialties as surgery and psychiatry also face a dearth of subject populations for treatment research. For instance, RCTs are fewer and use few participants in surgery and psychiatry. While in medicine, some large-scale studies have used a few thousand to 40,000 or more patients in multiple centers, psychotherapy research has used an average of 12 to 13 patients (Pocock, 1983; Shapiro & Shapiro, 1983). In speech-language pathology, large-scale studies are few, and the number of participants used rarely exceeds a few dozen.

Economic factors that distinguish treatment research in medicine from that of speech-language pathology may be even more powerful than the institutional differences in service delivery. Most RCTs in medicine, simultaneously conducted in multiple centers in several countries, are fully supported by global pharmaceutical companies that are highly motivated to bring their product to market. Legally, drugs cannot be marketed without extensive experimental evaluations. Therefore, the pressure to conduct treatment research in medicine is much higher than that in such disciplines as communication disorders, education, clinical psychology, counseling, and so forth. The legal requirement to evaluate new procedures and the enormous financial stakes involved in developing and marketing new treatment products in medicine force drug and other treatment product manufacturers to support global RCTs. Additionally, government and private agencies, too, offer a significant amount of financial support for medical treatment research. Compared to this, the amount of financial support available for conducting large-scale treatment research in speech-language pathology is minuscule. Small-scale studies on behavioral techniques, such as those done with single-subject designs, are more practical and hence more often performed and reported.

Scientific distinctions include the nature of independent and dependent variables in speech-language pathology and medicine. Treatment (independent variables) in medicine is relatively easily administered by a large number of well-trained individuals in multiple centers. New drugs being evaluated have clear prescriptions on how much, when, and how to administer to selected patients. A large number of medical technicians or nurses in different countries can relatively quickly administer treatment with little variation in procedures.

For several reasons, treatment in speech-language pathology, compared to that in medicine, is difficult to administer to a large number of individuals. First, being behavioral in nature, treatment in speech-language pathology is not as standardized as drug administration. Even though many procedures are clearly described (e.g., the discrete trial procedure in language treatment, syllable prolongation in stuttering treatment, or cueing hierarchy in treating naming deficits in individuals with aphasia), their administration may be as varied as the number of clinicians who use them. Speech-language pathologists do not follow strict treatment protocols, although it is possible to train them to do so. Such training will be necessary in any treatment research. If the treatment research is an RCT, multiple clinicians will have to be trained to follow a strict treatment protocol. The required training expense may be prohibitive to most treatment researchers.

Second, compared to medical treatment, treatment in speech-language pathology is more labor intensive. Stuttering treatment for a child or an adult might take 9 months of individual therapy, offered twice weekly, in sessions lasting 45 to 60 minutes. Similarly, treatment of language and speech sound disorders takes months of regular therapy. Treatment of aphasia or dysarthria may last a year or more. RCTs on such speech and language treatments with a large enough number of participants to be meaningfully randomized will involve an incredible number of clinician-client contact hours. Such treatments cannot be administered by technicians or aides. On the other hand, the administration of most drugs in RCTs may require a few minutes of daily patient contact, is likely to be over in a few days or weeks, and is typically accomplished with the help of large numbers of readily available nurses, medical technicians, and other aides.

Third, training a large number of speech-language pathologists to administer treatment uniformly in a large RCT will pose significant practical and economic hurdles. The task of training medical personnel in following a drug administration protocol for a randomized study would involve much less effort, training time, and research funds than training a large number of speech-language pathologists to administer a treatment for stuttering, speech sound disorder, or aphasia. Until funds for treatment research in speech-language pathology are increased geometrically, this kind of clinician training will be impractical. Without such training, data generated by RCTs in speech-language pathology and related disciplines will be uninterpretable.

Fourth, the nature of dependent variables or skills taught to clients with communication disorders also poses problems for speech-language pathologists conducting RCTs. Similar to treatment administration in speech-language pathology, documenting changes in communication skills due to treatment is more labor-intensive, is riddled with controversies, and takes more time than documenting changes due to medical treatment. This problem can get compounded beyond practicality in a large RCT, which may require multiple measures of the dependent variable to achieve reliability. Although unreliable dependent variable measurement is a problem in medicine as well (e.g., questionable results of a single laboratory test for blood cholesterol), reliability can be more easily achieved with multiple measures that are less time-consuming than in speech-language pathology (e.g., recording, transcribing, and analyzing multiple language samples for each of hundreds of children in a randomized language treatment study).

The differences between treatment research in medicine and communication disorders suggest that small groups of participants, studied intensively, will produce more practical and valid treatment efficacy data. Relatively small number of homogeneous individuals may be studied either with group designs or single-subject designs. Participants may be randomly assigned to groups, but no statistical generality will then be claimed. Both the single-subject and group design studies will eventually claim generality only on the basis of successful direct and systematic replications.

Classification of Treatment Research

Treatment research is done at various levels. As noted before, treatment research may document improvement, generalized consequences, and functional outcomes or may establish a cause-effect relationship between treatment and its effects. Therefore, the first criterion in classifying treatment research is **causality**, or the degree of experimental control used in studies that evaluate different treatment procedures (Hegde, 2004, 2010).

The second criterion to be used in classifying treatment research is **generality**, or the presence, absence, and degree of replication; generality is the extent to which the conclusions of a treatment study may be extended to all those who need or could benefit from the same or similar treatment. When the results of a treatment study are replicated, professionals may use the technique with greater degree of confidence.

The first criterion of causality produces treatment research at two major levels: uncontrolled and controlled. The second criterion of generality results in three major levels: unreplicated, directly replicated, and systematically replicated treatment studies. The two criteria interact with each other to produce six levels of treatment research: (1) uncontrolled unreplicated, (2) uncontrolled directly replicated, (3) uncontrolled systematically replicated, (4) controlled unreplicated, (5) controlled directly replicated, and (6) controlled and systematically replicated (Hegde, 2004, 2010). We shall now address these six levels of treatment research and the evidence they create.

Uncontrolled Unreplicated Treatment Research

Treatment research is uncontrolled when it does not use an experimental design and, therefore, lacks internal validity. A study is unreplicated when it is the first in a series on a given technique. Therefore, **uncontrolled unreplicated treatment research** is an original **case study** on a new treatment technique. Because case studies use no control groups or control conditions, there is assurance that the clients would *not* have improved without the treatment under investigation. Chapters 8 and 9 describe methods of uncontrolled case studies. In the group design strategy, it is the typical single-group design that receives treatment preceded by a pretest and followed by a posttest. In single-subject designs, it is the *AB* design in which the target behavior is base rated (*A* condition) and then the treatment is offered (*B* condition). Neither design rules out the extraneous variables.

An unreplicated study does not test the reliability of already reported findings on a treatment technique. It reports new findings, even if they are uncontrolled. Therefore, an uncontrolled unreplicated study is the first case study on a treatment technique. The goal of such a study is to demonstrate improvement in clients who receive a treatment.

Among the different consequences of treatment described earlier, case studies may measure improvement generalized and maintained consequences, and functional treatment outcomes, but not effects or effectiveness.

Case studies make a significant contribution to treatment research literature. Kazdin (1998) recommends several steps to increase the chances that the reported improvement may be due to treatment in a case study. First, case studies should offer objective data gathered from direct observations; they should not depend on anecdotal accounts to document improvement. Second, assessment of improvement should be frequent, not limited to just a pretest and a posttest. Pretreatment measures should show that the problem was stable and was unlikely to disappear without treatment. Continuous measurement of improvement during treatment sessions will show the course of treatment and the correlated improvement. Third, the improvement demonstrated should be large enough to be clinically significant and immediately follow the application of treatment. Delayed and limited improvements are not as credible as improvements of greater magnitude that appear soon after the application of the technique. Fourth, improvement should be demonstrated in multiple cases. Credibility of improvement demonstrated in multiple *and* heterogeneous cases will inspire greater confidence.

Results of carefully done case studies on treatment can help both professionals and treatment researchers. Professionals can discard treatment techniques that do not produce improvement in case studies. A technique that did not produce improvement in case studies is unlikely to be found effective in experimental studies, and such experimental studies are unlikely to be conducted. If the results of case studies, especially replicated results, are positive, there is a good chance that an experimental study will establish the effect of that treatment.

Uncontrolled Directly Replicated Treatment Research

The reliability of improvement that results from a treatment when first evaluated in a case study is unknown. The clinically significant improvement initially obtained may not be sustained in subsequent case studies. Therefore, clinicians who first reported improvement with a technique need to replicate their case study.

Uncontrolled directly replicated treatment research is a repetition of the original case study by the same investigators in their original setting with new clients who exhibit the same disorder. If the results are similar to those reported in the original study, a successful replication will have been accomplished. A successful replication increases the probability that the results of the original study were reliable. Repeated direct replications will generate more confidence in the results and the technique's ability to produce improvement.

As with the original case studies, successful but uncontrolled direct replications cannot claim treatment effects or a cause-effect relation between treatment and positive changes in clients, although the technique may be considered a good candidate for an experimental evaluation. Besides improvement, uncontrolled direct replications also may document treatment outcomes, generalized consequences of treatment, and maintenance of clinically acquired skills and their expansions. Such replications may suggest that the technique may have generality to new clients, as each direct replication uses new clients.

Uncontrolled Systematically Replicated Treatment Research

Successful direct replications show that a treatment reliably produces improvement in the original setting, when the original clinicians used the technique with new clients. Such replications do not show that other clinicians in other settings may obtain improvement in their clients with the same technique. In other words, the technique's generality to clients served in other clinics by other clinicians remains unknown.

Uncontrolled systematically replicated treatment research is the repetition of a case study by other clinicians, in new settings, using new clients to establish the generality of improvement. Generally, new clinicians in new settings will use the treatment procedure as described in the original case studies. In such cases, the new clinicians will not change the treatment procedure. If the clinicians are successful in systematically replicating the results of the original case studies, the generality of improvement data begins to emerge.

In some systematic replications, the new clinicians may modify the procedure in light of their clinical experience, theory, or their client characteristics. Such modifications are a part of systematic replications. For instance, clinicians who systematically replicate a case study may offer the treatment more or less frequently than in the original studies. They may change the reinforcement schedule, amount of modeling, feedback for error responses, and so forth. In fact, even the original investigators, after having directly replicated their findings on a treatment, may make systematic modifications in treatment to obtain greater improvement in their clients. When such modifications are made, the replications are *systematic* even if done by the original investigators.

Besides improvement, uncontrolled systematic replications also may document other types of consequences that follow a treatment's application, including treatment outcomes, generalized consequences of treatment, and maintenance of clinically acquired skills and expansion of

those skills. Once again, there would be no justification for drawing a cause-effect relation between these consequences and the treatment.

Systematic replications of treatment in case study formats will greatly enhance the possibility that the treatment will be found effective in experimental studies. In the absence of controlled experimental data on treating certain disorders, clinicians should at least look for a technique that is associated with systematically replicated improvement in case studies.

Controlled Unreplicated Treatment Research

When a treatment is shown to produce improvement in direct or systematic replications, the next logical step is to evaluate it in an experimental study to find out if it is effective. An initial controlled treatment study is the beginning of treatment efficacy research. Therefore, **controlled unreplicated treatment research** is the first experimental study on a new treatment procedure. Although it is preferable to design a controlled study on a technique that is shown to reliably produce improvement, in practice it may not always happen that way. Treatment researchers may design a controlled experimental study to evaluate the effectiveness of a technique even when there are no case studies on it.

A group or a single-subject experimental design may be used to establish a cause-effect relation between a treatment and the consequences that follow. To demonstrate that it was the treatment and no other variable that produced the consequences, researchers may use the pretest-posttest control group design, described in Chapter 8. This design will effectively rule out extraneous variables and establish a treatment's effects by showing that only those who received the treatment, and not those in the control group, showed positive changes. Significant changes in the posttest scores observed only for the experimental group will help demonstrate the treatment effectiveness. Because randomization is likely to be deficient, the researcher will refrain from claiming inferential generality.

Similarly, the single-subject *ABAB* design or the multiple baseline design, described in Chapter 9, will help accomplish the same goals as the experimental group design. While these designs avoid a control group that does not receive treatment, they use multiple control conditions to show that when the treatment was absent, the consequences, too, were absent in the same individuals. All participants receive treatment in single-subject experiments, although in multiple baseline designs, participants may receive it in a staggered fashion. In other designs, treatment may be withdrawn, reversed, and reinstated.

In addition to treatment effects, controlled unreplicated studies also may measure treatment outcomes, generalized consequences of treatment, and maintenance of clinically acquired skills and their expansions. Of all these measures, only the effects observed during the treatment sessions may be causally linked with the treatment. The other measures may or may not be due to treatment because other variables may be responsible for them.

When an experimental design is used to evaluate a treatment, the researcher can conclude that the treatment was or was not effective, depending on the data. But in no case can a researcher claim that the results of an initial (unreplicated) study apply to other clients, served in other settings, by other clinicians. In fact, the researchers cannot claim that their future clients will react the same to the treatment. This is because the reliability of the results of a single experiment is unknown, regardless of the sample size. That reliability is established only through replications. Only the replications will tell whether the treatment will apply to other clients in the same or different setting.

Controlled treatment evaluation may involve single treatments or multiple treatments. In the group design strategy, multiple treatment evaluation requires multiple groups, one group for each treatment. The effect a single treatment produces is known as the **independent effect** or **absolute effect**. This effect is studied within several group and single-subject designs as described in Chapters 8 and 9.

Controlled evaluation of multiple treatments requires complex designs. Multiple treatment evaluations seek to assess the relative effects of two or more treatment procedures. **Relative effects** refer to lesser or greater effects of two or more treatments. Whether one treatment is more effective than the other is the main research question to be investigated. Group and single-subject designs to study the relative effects of multiple treatments are described in Chapters 8 and 9.

Controlled treatment evaluation also may involve treatment interactions. When two or more treatments are combined, one might expect an effect that is larger than just the additive effects of those combined. Combined treatment effects that are larger than what might be expected by just adding each treatment's independent effects are known as **interactional effects**. This is an important area of treatment research because clinicians hope to increase the effectiveness of their treatments by combining procedures that enhance the overall effect. As described in Chapters 8 and 9, both group and single-subject designs are available to investigate treatment interactions.

Controlled Directly Replicated Treatment Research

The first step in evaluating the general applicability of a treatment procedure that was shown to be effective in an initial experimental study is to conduct controlled direct replications. **Controlled directly replicated treatment research** is the repetition of an original experimental study by the same investigators in their setting with new participants (clients). The original investigators will apply the experimental treatment in the same manner as before to see if the results of the initial experiment can be recaptured. The investigators may use the same experimental design as before, but some investigators may use a different design. For instance, a researcher who had shown a treatment's effectiveness within an *ABAB* design may replicate it within a multiple baseline design. It is important to note that what is replicated is the experimental treatment and its results, not necessarily the experimental design.

Controlled directly replicated studies also may measure additional treatment consequences, including treatment outcomes, generalized consequences of treatment, and maintenance of clinically acquired skills and their expansions. As with the original controlled studies, such replications cannot claim that these additional consequences were the effects of treatment.

Controlled directly replicated experiments that show that the treatment effects are replicable begin to establish the generality of that treatment's effects. Although more replications are needed, a successful direct replication of a treatment effect might suggest that other replications, too, may be successful. Direct replications only show that the treatment effects are reliable in the original setting, with the original investigators. There is no assurance that the treatment will produce the same positive results in other settings, in the hands of other clinicians. Systematic replications are needed to find out if the treatment will produce the same or similar results in other settings.

Controlled direct replications may involve a single treatment, multiple treatments, or interaction between treatments. Either group or single-subject designs may be used. See Chapter 11 for achieving generality through replications.

Controlled Systematically Replicated Treatment Research

The highest level of treatment research evidence is produced by controlled systematic replication of treatment effects. **Controlled systematically replicated treatment research** is the repetition of an experimental treatment study, typically conducted by other investigators in new settings recruiting new clients. Although the highest form of systematic replications will be performed by investigators other than the original researchers in different settings, the original researchers themselves may begin such replications. Selecting new participants, the investigators who have completed direct replications of their prior controlled studies on a treatment may begin to fine-tune the technique to produce better results. Wondering if the technique will be effective with clients who are older or younger than those in the original and direct replication series, the researchers may apply the technique to clients with different age levels to find out. The investigators may sample clients of different genders, ethnocultural groups, and even those with a different disorder. For instance, an intervention found to be effective with speech sound disorders may be effective with language disorders. All such efforts of the original investigators of a treatment procedure constitute systematic replications, although they are done in the original setting. Replications of this kind show that the treatment is or is not effective with clients who differ from those in the original study on some defined dimension. In essence, such replications help establish generality or the limits of generality of the treatment procedure.

Investigators who replicate studies published by other researchers help expand the scope or define additional limits of generality. When other investigators' replications in new settings are successful, the technique's generality across settings, clients, and clinicians begins to emerge. When multiple investigators in varied settings obtain similar results in controlled studies, the technique's generality is well established. See Chapter 11 for details on treatment research replications.

In addition to treatment effects, controlled systematically replicated studies may measure outcomes, generalized consequences, and maintenance of clinically acquired skills and their expansions. As with all forms of controlled research, only the effects observed in the treatment sessions may be causally linked with the treatment. Outcomes, generalized productions, and maintained skills may or may not be due to treatment because other variables may be responsible for them.

The previous section emphasizes that generality is not only not achieved by a single study; it is not achieved even by a few replications. Only multiple replications in varied settings with varied clients and clinicians will eventually establish generality as well as its limits. Establishing generality of treatment procedures requires systematic replications conducted over several years. See Chapter 10 for more on generality and replications. Controlled systematic replications may address a single treatment, multiple treatments, or interaction between treatments.

Summary

- Treatment research is conducted to establish the consequences of treatments; only controlled research can establish treatment effects; uncontrolled research only can establish improvement; generality requires replicated treatment research.
- Consequences of treatment include: (a) improvement, (b) effects, (c) generalized consequences, (d) maintained consequences, and (e) outcomes.
- Experimental treatment research should demonstrate: (a) internal validity, (b) clinical validity, (c) external validity or generality, (d) statistical generality, and (e) logical generality.
- Group designs help demonstrate treatment effects with an experimental group and a control group; such studies in medicine are called randomized clinical trials in which the participants are expected to be randomly selected and assigned to

the groups; matching is an alternative to randomization.

- Single-subject treatment research demonstrates treatment effects by intensively studying a small number of participants, all of whom receive treatment; single-subject designs use multiple control conditions that include baselines, withdrawal, reinstatement of treatment, and multiple baselines.
- Generality is a matter of replications, not experimental designs.
- All participants in randomized clinical trials and single-subject designs are self-selected.
- Denial of treatment to control groups and placebo controls in group designs is ethically questionable.
- Treatment research in medicine and treatment research in communication disorders differ on institutional, economic, and scientific grounds.
- Treatment research may be classified according to the degree of experimental control (causality) and generality.

References

Agency for Health Care Policy and Research. (1994). *Distinguishing between efficacy and effectiveness.* Rockville, MD: Author.

Barlow, D. H., Nock, M. K., & Hersen, M. (2009). *Single-case experimental designs: Strategies for studying behavior* (3rd ed.). Boston, MA: Pearson.

Beecher, H. K. (1955). The powerful placebo. *Journal of the American Medical Association, 159,* 1602–1606.

Beecher, H. K. (1966). Ethics and clinical research. *New England Journal of Medicine, 274,* 1354–1360.

Brody, B. A. (1998). *The ethics of biomedical research: An international perspective.* New York, NY: Oxford University Press.

Campbell, D. T., & Stanley, J. C. (1966). *Experimental and quasi-experimental designs for research.* Chicago, IL: Rand McNally.

Clatterbaugh, K. (1999). *The causation debate in modern philosophy 1637–1739.* New York, NY: Routledge.

Dekkers, W., & Boer, G. (2001). Sham neurosurgery in patients with Parkinson's disease: Is it morally acceptable? *Journal of Medical Ethics, 27*(3), 151–156.

Donabedian, A. (1980). *Explorations in quality assessment and monitoring: Vol. I. The definition of quality and approaches to assessment.* Ann Arbor, MI: Health Administration Press.

Finn, R. (1999). *Cancer clinical trials.* Sebastopol, CA: O'Reilly.

Frattali, C. (Ed.). (1998). *Measuring outcomes in speech-language pathology.* New York, NY: Thieme.

Gorkin, L., Schron, E. B., Handshaw, K., Shea, S., Kinney, M. R., Branyon, M., . . . Follick, M. J. (1996). Clinical trial enrollers vs. nonenrollers: The Cardiac Arrhythmia Suppression Trial (CAST) Recruitment and Enrollment Assessment in Clinical Trials (REACT) project. *Controlled Clinical Trials, 17*(1), 46–59.

Hegde, M. N. (1998). *Treatment procedures in communicative disorders* (3rd ed.). Austin, TX: Pro-Ed.

Hegde, M. N. (2004, July). *Levels of evidence: A design-neutral hierarchy.* Paper presented at the ASHA SID4 Leadership Conference, Portland, OR.

Hegde, M. N. (2007). A methodological review of randomized clinical trials. *Communicative Disorders Review, 1*(1), 17–38.

Hegde, M. N. (2010). New levels of treatment research evidence. *Journal of the Indian Speech and Hearing Association, 24*(2), 73–83.

Hegde, M. N., & McConn, J. (1981). Language training: Some data on response classes and generalization to an occupational setting. *Journal of Speech and Hearing Disorders, 46,* 353–358.

Hicks, P. L. (1998). Outcomes measurements requirements. In C. Frattali (Ed.), *Measuring outcomes in speech-language pathology* (pp. 28–49). New York, NY: Thieme.

Hoagwood, K., Hibbs, E., Brent, D., & Jensen, P. J. (1995). Efficacy and effectiveness in studies of child and adolescent psychotherapy. *Journal of Consulting and Clinical Psychology, 63,* 683–687.

Hrobjartsson, A., & Gotzsche, P. C. (2001). Is the placebo powerless? An analysis of clinical trials comparing placebo with no treatment. *New England Journal of Medicine, 344,* 1594–1602.

Kaptchuk, T. J. (1998). Powerful placebo: The dark side of the randomized controlled trial. *Lancet, 451,* 1722–1725.

Kazdin, A. E. (1998). Drawing valid inferences from case studies. In A. E. Kazdin (Ed.), *Methodological issues and strategies in clinical research* (2nd ed., pp. 403–417). Washington, DC: American Psychological Association.

Kendall, P., Flannery-Schroeder, E. C., & Norton-Ford, J. (1999). Therapy outcome research methods. In P. C. Kendall, J. N. Butcher, & G. N. Holmbeck (Eds.), *Research methods in clinical psychology* (2nd ed., pp. 330–363). New York, NY: Wiley.

Kendall, P., & Norton-Ford, J. (1982). Therapy outcome research methods. In P. Kendall & J. Butcher (Eds.), *Handbook of research methods in clinical psychology* (pp. 429–460). Hoboken, NJ: Wiley.

Kienle, G. S., & Kiene, H. (1997). The powerful placebo effect: Fact or fiction? *Journal of Clinical Epidemiology, 50,* 1311–1318.

McKee, M., Gritton, A., Black, N., McPherson, K., Sanderson, C., & Bain, C. (1999). Interpreting the evidence: Choosing between randomized and non-randomized studies. *British Medical Journal, 319,* 312–315.

Meinert, C. L. (1986). *Clinical trials: Design, conduct, and analysis.* New York, NY: Oxford University Press.

Morris, A. D., Zaritsky, A. L., & LeFever, G. (2000). Evaluation of ethical conflicts associated with randomized, controlled trials in critically ill children. *Critical Care Medicine, 28*(4), 1152–1156.

Pocock, S. J. (1983). *Clinical trials: A practical approach.* New York, NY: Wiley.

Randal, J. (1998). How RCTs came to their own. *Journal of the National Cancer Research Institute, 90,* 1257–1258.

Robertson, S. C., & Colburn, A. P. (1997). Outcomes research for rehabilitation: Issues and solutions. *Journal of Rehabilitation Outcomes Measurement, 1*(5), 15–23.

Rothman, K. J., & Greenland, S. (1998). Causation and causal inference. In K. J. Rothman & S. Greenland (Eds.), *Modern epidemiology* (2nd ed., pp. 7–28). Philadelphia, PA: Lippincott Williams & Wilkins.

Ruben, D. (1990). *Explaining explanation.* New York, NY: Routledge.

Shadish, W. R., Cook, T. D., & Campbell, D. T. (2002). *Experimental and quasi-experimental designs for generalized causal inference* (2nd ed.). Boston, MA: Houghton, Mifflin, and Company.

Shapiro, D. A., & Shapiro, D. (1983). Comparative therapy outcome research: Methodological implications of meta-analysis. *Journal of Consulting and Clinical Psychology, 51,* 42–53.

Silverman, W. A., & Altman, D. G. (1996). Patients' preferences and randomized trials. *Lancet, 347,* 171–174.

Smith, B., & Sechrest, L. (1998). Treatment of Aptitude × Treatment interactions. In A. E. Kazdin (Ed.), *Methodological issues and strategies in clinical research* (2nd ed., pp. 495–520). Washington, DC: American Psychological Association.

Taylor, K. M. (1985). The doctor's dilemma: Physician participation in randomized clinical trials. *Cancer Treatment Report, 69,* 1095–1100.

Verdu-Pascal, F., & Castello-Ponce, A. (2001). Randomized clinical trials: A source of ethical dilemmas. *Medical Ethics, 27*(3), 177–178.

Wilson, F. (1985). *Explanation, causation, and deduction.* Boston, MA: Reidel.

Study Guide

1. Define treatment research.

2. What can be claimed through uncontrolled treatment research? What cannot be claimed?

3. What is the method of controlled treatment research?

4. What is *replication?* Define and distinguish direct and systematic replications.

5. Define and distinguish all consequences of treatment.

6. Define and describe internal and external validity of experimental results.

7. Distinguish the different forms of generality.

8. What are *extraneous variables?* How are they ruled out?

9. How are causes and effects related? What conditions must be met to claim that *A* is the cause of *B*?

10. What are *randomized clinical trials?* What kinds of designs are used in them?

11. Describe the various kinds of sampling techniques and point out their strengths and limitations.

12. Describe the two kinds of matching techniques. Which one is better? Which one is more practical?

13. Describe the procedures and purposes of blinding in treatment research.

14. What is a *placebo?* Why is it used in some medical research?

15. Describe the various control mechanism used in single-subject treatment research. How do they help rule out the influence of extraneous variables?

16. Distinguish *withdrawal* from *reversal.* Critically evaluate the usefulness of these two control mechanisms.

17. What are *baselines?* What are the *baseline criteria?*

18. Compare RCTs with single-subject treatment research. Point out their strengths and limitations.

19. Do RCTs and single-subject designs differ in terms of internal validity? Why or why not?

20. Why is the claim of statistical generality for RCTs questionable?

21. Describe how participants in randomized clinical trials are essentially self-selected.

22. What is the effect of self-selection of participants of treatment research?

23. Give an overview of ethical issues involved in having a no-treatment control group in treatment research.

24. Describe the differences and similarities of treatment research in medicine versus that in communication disorders.

25. How is treatment research classified? Describe the different types of treatment research.

5

Other Types of Research

Chapter Outline

◆ Ex Post Facto Research

◆ Normative Research

◆ Standard-Group Comparisons

◆ Experimental Research

◆ Clinical and Applied Research

◆ Translational Research

◆ Sample Surveys

◆ Qualitative Research

◆ Mixed-Methods Research

◆ The Relation Between Research Types and Questions

◆ Summary

◆ References

◆ Study Guide

Research in everyday usage includes a variety of activities. A student wishing to apply to a graduate program may research various universities, the faculty, tuition and other costs, and social life on the campus and compare such information across selected universities. A couple planning to buy a house may research the housing market, interest rates, and lending institutions. The term *research* in these contexts refers to relatively well-planned and systematic activity to produce helpful information.

Scientific research, on the other hand, requires more formal planning because more technical activities are needed to answer research questions. Nevertheless, scientific research can also be more or less formal and may include a variety of activities designed to obtain different kinds of information or answer different kinds of questions. For example, a speech-language clinician may research the number of children with speech sound disorders in a school district. A second clinician may research the typical language behaviors of a group of 5-year-old children. A third clinician may research the conditions under which stuttering began in a group of children. A fourth clinician may research the effects of a treatment procedure on the language skills of persons with aphasia.

Each of the research activities just described has a different question behind it. Different research questions need different methods to answer them. Methods have unique strengths and limitations that determine the kinds of conclusions one can draw from the results. Therefore, it is necessary to understand different types of scientific research so that questions are researched with appropriate methods and the results are interpreted within the scope of those methods.

There are different ways of classifying research, and several classic types are common across classifications. The following types of research may be found to varying extents in many basic and applied sciences and professions, including communication disorders: ex post facto research, normative research, standard-group comparison, experimental research, clinical research, translational research, qualitative research, mixed-methods research, and sample surveys. These research types are neither exhaustive nor mutually exclusive. There are research styles that combine different types or their specific (selected) elements. In Chapter 4, we have considered treatment research, a form of experimental clinical research because of its special relevance to communication disorders and all health care professions. In this chapter, we discuss the other types of research.

Ex Post Facto Research

Ex post facto research is a type of research in which a retrospective search of the causes of events is made without manipulating an independent variable. As the term suggests, it is an "after the fact" type of research in that the independent variables have occurred in the past and the investigator starts with the effect.

Ex post facto is a nonexperimental type of research because it does not create phenomena. Existing phenomena are analyzed to find their potential causes. Many research studies published in communication disorders are of this type.

Procedures of Ex Post Facto Research

The case study (history) method used in clinical sciences is an excellent example of ex post facto research. Case studies help describe many disorders or diseases. In fact, the causes of most human disorders and diseases are not experimentally manipulable. Some experimental research on certain diseases and disorders may be possible only at the subhuman level. However, the results of subhuman experiments may or may not be applicable to human beings. Therefore, much of the research in clinical disciplines, including medicine, uses the ex post facto method.

In the case study method, the starting point of an investigation is a disease or a disorder. The investigator then proceeds to find out what may have caused the problem. The onset of the disorder has occurred in the past; therefore, the investigator begins by taking a detailed case history—a chronology of events that are relevant to the disorder under investigation. The client and other informants (such as family members and professional caregivers) may be interviewed. Information on the conditions under which the disorder was first noted is gathered. If events that may be potential causes of the disorder are reported to have occurred, the investigator may conclude that a potential cause-effect relation has been identified.

The retrospective search for causes often is guided by past research and theoretical expectations. The past research may provide some clues to the potential causes of the problem under study, and the investigator may search the case history for those causes. The investigator may look for causes suggested by deductive theories. Should the case history provide evidence of events suggested as causes by either past research or a current theory, the investigator may conclude that those events may have caused the disorder.

Many currently accepted likely cause-effect relations are based only on ex post

facto research at the human level. For example, the relation between smoking and lung cancer is based entirely upon ex post facto research. Repeatedly, case studies have reported that smokers have a higher chance of developing lung cancer than nonsmokers, leading to the conclusion that smoking and lung cancer may be causally related. Such conclusions have formed a basis for medical practice and social and legal policies such as those requiring warnings on cigarette packages. Examples of ex post facto studies in medicine suggesting potential cause-effect relations include the association between obesity and diabetes, various kinds of foods and heart diseases, and lifestyle changes and health status (e.g., exercise and heart health).

In communication disorders, Johnson's extensive research on the onset of stuttering in young children illustrates the ex post facto variety (Johnson & Associates, 1959). Johnson and associates interviewed the parents of stuttering children about such factors as family conditions, the child's health, the child's speech and language development, amounts and types of dysfluencies, and so on. They gathered similar interview data from parents of nonstuttering children.

Johnson's interview data revealed that children who stuttered and those who did not exhibit the same kinds of dysfluencies (e.g., repetitions, interjections, prolongations, incomplete phrases, etc.), suggesting to Johnson that some parents get alarmed by normal nonfluencies in their children and diagnose stuttering. This became the well-known diagnosogenic theory of stuttering. Johnson theorized that the origin of stuttering was the parental negative evaluation of normal nonfluencies and the mistaken diagnosis of stuttering. This unjustified diagnosis would soon start the real problem—apprehension, anxiety, struggle, and avoidance reactions developed by the children. For Johnson, dysfluencies themselves were not the major problems. The problems were the events that followed the diagnosis of stuttering based on normal nonfluencies.

Johnson's research and the resulting theory illustrate both the method and the problems of the ex post facto research. Obviously, Johnson's method was retrospective (ex post facto). The identified independent variable (potential cause) was the parental diagnosis of stuttering in the absence of stuttering. The presumed independent variable had occurred in the past. He did not (of course, could not) observe or experimentally manipulate the parental diagnosis that, in his judgment, caused stuttering. Therefore, the cause-effect relation between the parental diagnosis and stuttering was based upon an *interpretation* of interview information, not upon experimental evidence. In other words, Johnson did not show that no other factor was responsible for stuttering.

Strengths and Weaknesses of Ex Post Facto Research

Ex post facto research: (a) is not experimental, because a causal variable is not introduced or withdrawn and (b) lacks control in that extraneous independent variables are not ruled out. Consequently, the suggested causal relation remains an inference and not convincingly established.

Carefully done case histories may reveal that children with language disorders did not receive enough language stimulation, or that they had limited intelligence, or that they experienced certain emotional problems, or that they came from lower socioeconomic strata. However, the case history method cannot demonstrate that such variables actually caused the language disorder.

The ex post facto method cannot assert cause-effect relations for both empirical and logical reasons. As pointed out earlier, the empirical reasons are a lack of experimental manipulations and an absence of controls to rule out competing hypotheses. The logical reason is that either the causes have occurred in the past and not observed at all (e.g., the parental diagnosis as the cause of stuttering), or in many other cases, both the effect and the presumed cause are measured at the same time. For instance, unhealthy eating habits and heart diseases may be observed simultaneously. Thus, the minimum requirement of a causal relation—causes precede effects—is not fulfilled in ex post facto research.

In the ex post facto method, inferences are made based on correlations between events (e.g., smoking and lung cancer). However, statisticians often warn that correlations suggest that events tend to coexist or covary, but the cause of one or both of the variables may be some other unobserved factor.

The ex post facto research is justified because many significant problems are amenable only to that method. It is true that investigators in the past did conduct experimental studies on human diseases (see Chapter 16 on ethics of research), but such efforts are now proscribed by ethical principles. The only way, then, is to explore the history of patients with given diseases and disorders for possible causal factors. In such situations, however, one should be clear about the distinction between the social and scientific implications of ex post facto research. From the standpoint of good evidence, the impracticality of experimentation is beside the point. Weak scientific evidence does not become stronger because better evidence cannot be produced.

Similarly, from the standpoint of social policies designed to protect human lives, the limitations of scientific evidence may be recognized but considered unimportant. In such cases, each society evaluates the available evidence to support social policies that are judged best for its people. Scientists would support those policies as long as social and scientific evaluations of research data are not confused. People may justifiably accept the social implications of weak scientific evidence because such a course of action serves their best interests. Relative to questions such as smoking and lung cancer, eating habits and heart diseases, members of a society may be more willing to take the risk of being scientifically wrong than being prematurely dead. The life of R. A. Fisher, the great statistician, inventor of many group experimental designs, is a sobering story about ex post facto research. Fisher was a heavy pipe smoker. When the association between smoking and lung cancer was brought to his attention, Fisher, a paid consultant to a tobacco company, pointed out that *correlation is not causation*, now a famous and often repeated but generally ignored statement. Fisher died of colon cancer, a disease also correlationally linked to smoking and a high rate of mortality.

The scientific evaluation of ex post facto research may be done independent of social policies. The main limitation of ex post facto studies is that it is not possible to explain an event on the basis of their results. The social or personal significance of the results is beside the point. If possible, the exploratory ex post facto research should lead to experimental research. In practice, however, many investigators who use the ex post facto method move on to theorize, instead of

verifying their suggestions with better methods. Such weak theories have enjoyed a certain degree of incongruous acceptance in communication disorders.

In many cases, the difficulty in conducting better-controlled research is somewhat exaggerated. Certainly, Johnson could not have asked parents of fluently speaking children to diagnose stuttering to see what happens; however, it is possible to design large-scale preventive studies in which parents of high-risk children are asked not to diagnose stuttering and see if imminent stuttering is avoided. Or, by selecting children in the very early stage of stuttering, one can modify the punitive parental behaviors to see what effects follow. With appropriate control measures (such as a control group whose parents are not asked to change their behaviors), it is possible to gather more convincing evidence than that produced by interviews and questionnaires. In the case of human diseases, similar preventive experimental studies are possible. For example, cholesterol intake of individuals may be differentially monitored and modified to see what health benefits and risks follow. Such naturalistic experiments have been conducted. In addition, when appropriate, animal experimental research might strengthen ex post facto data.

Normative Research

An extremely popular form of research in communication disorders as well as in psychology and medicine can be called *normative research*. Traditionally, it is not recognized as a separate type of research, but the enormous amount of effort that goes into this kind of research makes it necessary to consider it separately.

Normative research is the type of research in which the distribution of selected dependent variables across age groups is observed and recorded. For example, the number of phonemes correctly produced (dependent variable) by 2-, 3-, and 4-year-old children may be observed and recorded. The major purpose of normative research is to arrive at *norms* that are the averaged performance levels of presumably typical reference groups. Normative research, also known as developmental research, seeks to establish behavioral differences across age groups. It provides descriptive data on typical behaviors of different age groups.

It is generally believed that for clinical disciplines, norms are much needed. It is argued that norms tell us how children's behaviors change as they grow older and that such information will help us judge whether a given child's behavior is normal or disordered. It is further suggested that unless the clinician knows age-based norms, target behaviors for clinical intervention cannot be determined. For example, the clinician should know the typical language behaviors of 4-year-olds to judge whether a child of that age has a language disorder. Also, once it is judged that the child has a language disorder (because, perhaps, the child's language approximates that of a 2-year-old), norms are needed to establish the treatment targets. Assuming that the child in our example has all the behaviors of average 2-year-old children, initial target behaviors may be that of average 3-year-olds and eventually that of average 4-year-olds.

The bulk of research in morphology, syntax, phonology, semantics, and pragmatics is normative (as well as theoretical). It is thought that lack of norms in certain aspects of speech and language creates problems for making clinical judg-ments relative to evaluation and treatment. Therefore, it is considered a high-priority research.

Procedures of Normative Research

Normative research typically uses the participant and response sampling procedure to establish the statistically averaged response patterns across age groups. Theoretically, norms are established on cross-sectional randomly selected participants who are representative of the population. Unless the sample is representative, conclusions cannot be extended to all the children in the population. Because the goal of normative research is to determine the typical behaviors of children in the population, not merely that of selected children, normative research must use adequate statistical sampling procedures.

Chapter 4 contains a discussion of random (probability) sampling. In essence, to draw a representative sample, the investigator must have access to the entire (defined) population, such as all school-age children with language disorders. Every member of that population must be willing to participate in the study, and to avoid the investigator bias in selecting participants, all members must have an equal chance of being selected.

In a normative study, the speech and language skills of the sampled children may be observed and recorded. Each participant may be administered a brief test designed to sample the behaviors of interest. Various tests of speech and language skills may be used to sample behaviors in normative research.

The researcher calculates the mean performance levels and standard deviations for each age group sampled in the study. The mean scores may be statistically transformed into other types of scores (e.g., percentiles and standard scores) to reduce variability across participants and to facilitate comparisons among participants. The means and other kinds of scores typical of the age group are considered the norm for that age group. Children in the population at large are expected to show the same kinds of behaviors as those of the sampled children at specific age levels. In evaluating individual clients, the clinician is expected to use such norms to judge whether a child deviates from the expected (typical) performance levels. The presence of deviation suggests a clinical problem, whereas the degree of deviation determines the severity of the problem.

Strengths and Weaknesses of Normative Research

The strength of normative research is its logical appeal and not its empirical validity. It is useful to know the typical language behaviors of children of different ages and sex, and of people in different socioeconomic and occupational levels; the availability of such knowledge makes the diagnosis of a disorder or deviation less demanding.

It is also useful to know how the dependent variables are distributed in the population. Science starts with the observation of some effects (dependent variables). Before other kinds of research manipulations can be attempted, one must be clear about the dependent variables. Therefore, a good description of speech, language, fluency, vocal, and auditory behaviors across variables that do make a difference in these behaviors would be essential for further empirical research and sound clinical practice.

Most of the serious problems of normative research are empirical. The procedures and assumptions of this type of research often lack empirical validity, a problem that has received surprisingly little critical attention in communication disorders.

The problems inherent in normative research are common to most research studies based on the statistical theory of probability and random sampling from the population. These problems are discussed in Chapters 7 and 9 and, therefore, will be mentioned only briefly here.

The first empirical problem is that true random samples that permit the nationwide use of the resulting normative information are rarely, if ever, drawn. Most normative studies draw local samples based upon varying degrees of randomization. Therefore, the behavior patterns found across age groups may or may not be representative of the children in the target population. As a result, the major goal of normative research is rarely achieved in practice.

The second empirical problem is also related to the sampling procedure. Normative researchers sample not only participants but also responses under investigation. Because groups of participants are examined at different age levels, most often the investigators can collect only a small sampling of responses. Whether it is language or speech sound production, the opportunities to produce specific behaviors are extremely limited. For example, children may be given two or three chances to produce a given phoneme or a grammatical morpheme. The reliability of age-based norms based on such limited sampling of responses is doubtful. Unfortunately, the only kind of sampling the normative researcher typically thinks of is participant sampling, which is done inadequately anyway.

The third empirical problem is a more serious one and involves a logical problem as well. Any population is heterogeneous, not homogeneous; that means that among a large number of persons, there is much variability. This is nothing but the popular notion of individual differences and uniqueness. A good sample, therefore, must be as heterogeneous as the population it seeks to represent. Consequently, the more heterogeneous the sample, the more variable the participants' performance. Unfortunately, the more variable the performance, the less meaningful the average (the norm). In other words, even when an investigator achieves a representative random sample, the resulting norms will be highly variable, a contradiction of terms. Therefore, it is likely that the notion of norms is a logical and empirical fallacy.

The fourth empirical problem is probably due to a misapplication of the statistical theory of probability and the random procedure to questions of individual performance. The theory and procedure are designed to extend the results from the sample to the population and not from the sample to an individual. An average performance of a smaller group is supposed to help predict the average performance of the larger group. Within the theory, there is no empirical basis to predict an individual's performance based upon a sample study. Disregarding this, clinicians routinely assume that what is true of an averaged sample performance of a group is also true of an individual client's specific (unaveraged) performance.

The fifth empirical problem of normative research is also a matter of practice. Normative research asks how the behaviors are distributed across certain arbitrarily selected variables such as age or socioeconomic status; it was never intended to answer the question of why those behaviors are distributed the way they are. In other words, normative research can only describe the events observed; it cannot explain those events. Investigators of normative research do not exert any kind of control on potential independent variables. As such, no matter how extensive, normative research cannot support a theory. It seems that this limitation is also mostly ignored in practice, for most of the theories on how and why children acquire language, semantic notions, pragmatic rules, or phonological systems are based upon normative research.

Normative research assumes that the arbitrarily selected variables across which the behaviors seem to show different patterns are indeed the independent variables. For example, most investigators of language acquisition explicitly or implicitly assume that age is an independent variable. This commonly held assumption needs a careful look.

Age is a measure of the passage of time relative to the beginnings of some living or nonliving entity. While time is impersonal and physical, age is personal and biological. We observe that as age changes, certain behaviors also change. Most people then assume that age is the cause of those changes. Age is an implicitly or explicitly offered explanation of any kind of behavioral development in most normative research.

It is hard to think that age, which is a personal measure of the passage of time, is an independent variable of anything. If it is, it is a discouraging variable for clinicians who wish to remediate disorders because the only course of action open to them would be to let the time pass for the child with communicative disability to show improvement. Of course, the disturbing question of why the time did not help the child would have to be stoically ignored. Fortunately, *in practice,* most clinicians believe that treatment is a more important variable than the mere passage of time.

Age is a convenient term for known and unknown variables that influence observable behaviors as time passes. Some of these variables include biological changes that take place within organisms; others include events in the environment. A better explanation of behaviors might emerge if manipulable independent variables are taken seriously. More important, a better technology of treatment would simultaneously become available. There is some evidence to show that "developmental milestones" of language are susceptible to environmental contingencies that can be experimentally manipulated (Capelli, 1985; De Cesari, 1985). In other words, experimental research on language acquisition is possible, and it offers a more valid means of explaining the language-learning process than the age of children.

If normative research is applied strictly to observe and describe dependent variables, it can serve a meaningful purpose. However, to generate clinically useful data, the normative researchers may have to curtail the overuse of the cross-sectional method, in which the individual behaviors are sampled inadequately. Repeated and more intensive observation of small numbers of children may produce data that are more applicable to individual cases (Brown, 1973). When behaviors are observed more intensively, patterns that may not become apparent under the cursory cross-sectional method may be observed. Such observations would still not explain the behavioral changes but can possibly suggest potential independent variables for further experimental inquiry.

Standard-Group Comparisons

Another type of research not traditionally recognized as a distinct variety, but quite popular in communication disorders, can be called standard-group comparison. The standard-group comparison method is a cross between the ex post facto and the normative types of research. A great deal of research of this kind is done in clinical sciences. In communication disorders, standard-group comparisons are almost as popular as normative research.

Standard-group comparison is a type of research in which groups formed on the basis of one dependent variable are compared on the basis of the same or other dependent variables. Typical group comparisons involve two groups that are different on an initial a priori variable. On the subsequent measured dependent variables, the group may or may not be different, though the expectation is that they will be. In many clinical disciplines, including communication disorders, "clinical" groups are compared with "normal" groups on measures of one or more dependent variables.

Standard-group comparisons are not the same as the two (or more) group experimental research. The latter type of research is experimental and is described in the next section. In the standard-group comparison, there is no manipulation of an independent variable. Only the dependent variables are measured and compared.

Procedures of the Standard-Group Comparison

For the most part, the standard-group comparison is an extension of the logic and methodology of normative research.

After having discovered the distribution of certain dependent variables in certain general samples of participants, some clinical researchers move on to find out if the distribution of those variables is in some way different across *selected* samples of participants. The general sample is the "normal" group, and the special samples selected for comparison are the "clinical" groups.

The clinical groups are formed on the basis of a clinical diagnosis. For example, children with language disorders, persons with aphasia, or persons who stutter can be identified through clinical assessment. Once a clinical group has been formed, the researcher proceeds to form a normal group with no communicative problems. Certain screening procedures may be used to rule out the existence of a communication disorder. The two groups are then compared on selected dependent variables. There are two strategies for comparing the two groups.

In the first strategy, the groups are compared further on the same criterion variable that separated the groups in the first place. In the second strategy, the groups are compared on variables that did not serve as explicit criteria for the initial separation of the groups.

The first strategy is illustrated by studies in which children who have language disorders are compared with typical-language children on the age at which they master selected grammatic morphemes or other language skills. It must be noted that comparisons in such instances are made on the same criterion variable that separated the two groups. Language skills separated the two groups to begin with, and it is on the same variable that the two groups are further compared.

This kind of comparative analysis may lead to a description of further language differences between those who are typically acquiring language skills and those who are not. For example, an investigator might find out that, compared with normally speaking children, children with language disorders do not produce cohesive narratives or passive sentences.

In the second strategy, the criterion and the comparison measures are different. Groups are formed based on one variable, and they are compared on the basis of different variables. For example, an investigator may assess the difference between stuttering and nonstuttering persons on motor performance. The criterion variable in this case is stuttering (and its absence), which is the basis for forming the two groups. The variable on which they are compared, on the other hand, is entirely different. It is a measure of motor proficiency, which is not the same as stuttering. Later, stuttering and motor proficiency measures may be linked theoretically, but they are different kinds of responses. There are many examples of this kind of comparison. Persons with and without aphasia may be compared on the basis of memory skills or on a test of intelligence. The performance of children with speech sound disorders on a motor proficiency test may be compared with that of normally speaking children. A measure of intelligence of normal children may be compared with that of children who have language problems.

Strengths and Weaknesses of Standard-Group Comparisons

The standard-group comparison can yield useful information regarding the differences between typical ("normal") and clinical populations. It is necessary to understand the differences between those who have a communicative disorder and those who do not. Furthermore, it is also necessary to understand the difference between particular disorder groups and typical groups. The standard-group comparison studies can describe, for instance, the dependent variables on which individuals with and without voice disorder or those with and without dysarthria differ in some specified domain. The method is useful in identifying and describing dependent variables. Because it is necessary to have clear descriptions of the dependent variables we study, the standard-group comparisons serve a useful purpose.

The standard-group comparison method poses no significant problems when the investigator stops after describing observed group differences. Problems arise when the method is misapplied, and the investigator begins to speculate, but none recognize that it is only a speculation. Many investigators show a problematic tendency to *explain* disorders on the basis of standard-group comparisons. For example, finding that cerebral blood flow patterns are different across people who speak fluently and those who stutter, stuttering has been explained as a problem of cerebral blood flow variations. In other words, cerebral blood flow variations are suggested as the cause of stuttering. However, in a standard-group comparison, there is no independent variable at all. As observed and measured in the studies, the cerebral blood flow variations are a dependent variable, not an independent variable. Therefore, there is no reason to suggest that such variations cause stuttering; in fact, they may be the effects or covariables of stuttering. In fact, no causal relation of any kind would be clear in a standard-group comparison, because it is not an experimental procedure. There

is no assurance that an unidentified and unobserved variable is the cause of the effects under study. As such, standard-group comparison cannot support theories or explanations.

Some investigators designate the normal group as the *control group* and the clinical group as the *experimental group* in a standard-group comparison research. This practice is misleading, because the method is not experimental. Clinical groups are not to be automatically considered experimental groups. Unless a group receives a treatment variable under controlled conditions, it is not an experimental group.

Experimental Research

The most powerful strategy available to discover functional relations among events is experimental research. For more on the basic characteristics of this type of research, the reader is referred to "Experiment and Experimental Control" in Chapter 3 as well as "Experimental Designs: Means of Controlling Variability" in Chapter 7.

Experimental research has its distinguishing feature the *experiment,* which is not a part of other kinds of research. Nonetheless, experimental research shares many characteristics with other types of research. The formulation of a research question, the task of finding a suitable method, systematic observation of the phenomenon under investigation, and analysis and interpretation of data are all common across research types.

An **experiment** can be defined as a series of controlled conditions of dynamic arrangement in which one or more independent variables are manipulated and the effects of such manipulations on the dependent variable are measured. Alternatively, an experiment is a method of arranging conditions in such a way that a functional (cause-effect) relation between events may be revealed.

In an experiment, the investigator manipulates an independent variable to: (a) produce a dependent variable (effect), (b) increase the magnitude of a dependent variable, (c) reduce the magnitude of a dependent variable, or (d) eliminate the dependent variable. Logically, any one of those successful manipulations is evidence of a functional relation between the independent variable and the effect (dependent variable). A combination of such manipulations will further strengthen that evidence. Replications of those functional arrangements and comparable results will enhance the generality of the evidence.

Procedures of Experimental Research

The effect (i.e., the purpose) of an experiment is to reveal a functional relation between two or more events. Descriptive research asks, what is it? Experimental research asks, what causes it? In other words, experimental research seeks to explain an event by discovering its causal variables. Therefore, experimental research is essential for constructing deductive and inductive theories.

To find out what causes a phenomenon, the researcher must gain control over its potential cause or causes (independent variable or variables). Gaining control means manipulating it in some way to change the dependent variable. This is true of applied situations as well. A physician, for example, cannot directly manipulate a disease (the dependent variable).

The disease is brought under control only through effective treatment (independent variable). A speech-language pathologist cannot directly affect aphasia; it can be affected only through certain treatment techniques.

An independent variable is manipulated in many ways. An independent variable is manipulated when it is introduced, increased or decreased in magnitude, withdrawn, or reintroduced. For example, in assessing the effect of white noise on stuttering, the experimenter may first establish the baseline of stuttering and then introduce noise through headphones while the participant who stutters is talking. The experimenter will continue to measure the rate of stuttering. The level of noise may be increased or decreased within appropriate experimental conditions. In subsequent conditions, the noise may be withdrawn to observe the effects on stuttering. Finally, the noise may be reintroduced to find out if the original effects can be replicated. Alternatively, the investigator may introduce the noise to one group of persons who stutter and withhold it from another group of persons who do not.

A critical aspect of experimental manipulations is that they must be done under controlled conditions. **Controlled experimental conditions** exist when it is possible to rule out the influence of potential independent variables not under investigation. This means that most events (including improvement in a clinical condition) have multiple causes, and in any given experiment, the investigators are interested in only one or a few of them. Therefore, the investigators need to demonstrate that the other potential causes, typically called **extraneous variables**, did not produce the effect. When the extraneous variables are ruled out, the effects observed on the dependent variable can be attributed to the manipulated independent variable because no other variables were present. In effect, under controlled conditions, the experimenter isolates a cause-effect relation.

Physically isolated and specially constructed laboratories often are used in creating controlled conditions. The need for such physical control measures varies across disciplines and with the nature of the problems under investigation. Generally speaking, a certain degree of control over the physical setup is necessary in all types of experimental research. But the setup can be more or less structured depending upon the nature and phase of research. For example, an experiment on auditory perception might need a highly controlled experimental setup (a sound-proof booth). A clinical experiment in which a certain language treatment procedure is evaluated may initially need a controlled physical setup, but in the later stages—in which generalization to the natural environment is evaluated—the setup must be more natural. In all cases, the extraneous independent variables must be controlled.

It is somewhat difficult to control independent variables in natural settings, but it can be done. Experiments on the effects of teaching methods evaluated in regular classrooms, those on child social behaviors conducted in playgrounds, or those on different modes of teaching sign language in special education classrooms illustrate naturalistic experiments. Experiments conducted in naturalistic settings are also called **field experiments**.

In addition to physical control measures, an experiment should also include control measures designed to minimize the influence of other variables related to the participants themselves. An inves-

tigator must make sure that other events in the lives of the participants were not responsible for the changes observed in the dependent variable. In many cases, biological events such as those included under the term *maturation* must also be ruled out. For example, a clinician who evaluates the effects of a language treatment program must show that no other treatment was simultaneously applied and that maturational factors were not responsible for the eventual gains in the participants' language skills. There are two basic approaches to rule out such extraneous variables: the between-groups strategy, in which the experimental group or groups receive treatment and a control group does not, and the single-subject strategy, in which treatment and no-treatment conditions are arranged for comparison. Chapters 8 and 9 describe these two strategies and Chapter 12 offers their comparative evaluation.

Basic and Applied Experimental Research

Experimental research has two varieties: basic and applied. **Basic research** may be theoretical, and the problems addressed may not have immediate practical applications, although potential for such applications in the future may exist. **Applied research** is practical, designed to solve immediate problems.

It is sometimes assumed that experimental research is always basic and laboratory oriented whereas applied research does not use experimental methods. This notion is strengthened by the view that basic research finds out answers to important questions and applied research simply exploits those answers in solving practical problems. This is a mistaken notion. Both basic and applied research can use the same experimental methods. When related applied and basic research are equally experimental, a useful interaction results. Such an interaction can speed up the process of finding solutions to practical problems.

In some cases, it may take a long time for the basic researcher to give answers to applied questions. In other cases, there may be no basic science that would ask and answer the same questions that have to be answered by the applied scientist. To a certain extent, this seems to be the case with communication disorders. There are no scientists other than speech-language pathologists who do basic treatment-related research on language, fluency, or speech sound disorders. Speech-language pathologists have often looked to linguistics for answers. But by its very nature, linguistics is not likely to ask such questions as whether language treatment procedure *A* is more effective than procedure *B*. Linguistics and other nonclinical disciplines may describe potential dependent variables (effects) but may not give any clues as to what independent variables may be necessary to change those dependent variables. That is the task of specialists in communication disorders. See Chapter 4 for more on using experimental research to evaluate clinical treatment methods and educational teaching methods.

Prudent applied or clinical scientists learn to do at least some of the basic research to take care of their own business. Experiment is the most needed operation in an applied science. Based on whatever information is made available by basic researchers, an applied scientist may begin to experiment to find out answers to practical questions. Interestingly enough, applied or clinical experimental research not only can help solve practical problems but also can generate new knowledge that can influence basic sciences. In essence, an experiment is a method to answer certain types of questions, and those types of questions must be answered in applied sciences as well.

We shall return to the question of applied experimental research in the section on applied or clinical research.

Strengths and Weaknesses of Experimental Research

There is an argument that in behavioral sciences, experimental research is artificial, too mechanistic, and, therefore, limited in its usefulness (Creswell & Poth, 2017). Specially created and fully controlled experimental situations are so far removed from the social settings in which behaviors naturally occur that the results may not have much validity. In a single study, the experimental investigator often isolates one cause for an effect, but under natural conditions, single variables may not be responsible for specific effects. Behaviors are multiply caused (determined). For these and other reasons, the experimental results may not be relevant to the behavioral events taking place in the natural world.

The argument that experimental research is too mechanistic for human behavioral sciences is an old one. There is a long-held belief that the scientific approach may be appropriate for physical phenomena and animals but not for humans and their behaviors. It is further believed that the mechanistic approach of science will dehumanize the human species. The origin of such beliefs is in the ancient philosophical position that human beings are unique in the scheme of the universe. Although Darwin did much to dispel this cherished sense of self-importance, some of the prejudices against the science of human behavior have persisted and have appeared and reappeared in various disguises.

Another weakness of experimental research is that the effects of independent variables manipulated in human experiments may be weak. Many times, controlled experiments manage to demonstrate only small changes in the dependent variables, whereas the same variables in real-life situations may produce much larger effects. For example, expansion of children's utterances in a laboratory study may result in only small increases in language complexity, but the same variable in real life may produce larger effects.

None of the criticisms of experimental research are strong and valid enough to discourage its practice. The fact that independent variables are isolated is a strength, not a weakness, of experimental research. Only by isolating the effects of a variable can an experimenter observe functional relations between variables. Real-life situations are typically confounded, making it difficult to determine specific cause-effect relations. That in natural situations variables are multitude and the relations complex is not contradicted by technical isolation of specific causes. After having analyzed the isolated effects of major factors, the scientist proceeds to analyze the interactive effects of those multiple factors. Such analytical steps are taken to eventually obtain an integrated picture of the phenomenon under investigation. In this way, a better approximation of the reality is achieved through laboratory research than through rational arguments.

The critics of the experimental method do not suggest an effective alternative to an analytical approach to determining functional relations. If isolated functional relations are unreal, then the complex, real, but hopelessly confounded relations do not permit any conclusions. In addition, many events cannot be held for observation in their totality. Often, there is no technological means of experimentally manipulating a complex pattern. Besides, some apparently complex situations may hold only a few causal factors while the rest of the multitude may be a collection of covariables with very little functional significance.

The objection that the experimental approach is too mechanistic may be consistent with certain scholastic traditions but not with any empirical evidence. Science neither glorifies nor degrades its subject matter. Human behavior will not be transformed into mechanical events because the methods of science have been used in studying it. For example, when we gain a better understanding of the language-learning process through application of the experimental procedure, human language will not turn into machine language. Behaviors or feelings called *love* or *cooperation* will remain the same even after scientists have experimentally analyzed them.

The final criticism—that compared to situations in real life, experiments tend to produce relatively weak effects of independent variables—probably applies to some research traditions and some specific studies. However, this problem is not inherent in the experimental approach itself. Not producing large enough effects is a technical problem that can be improved upon. Just because a treatment produced weak effects, the experimental treatment evaluations may not be abandoned. Experiments can and have produced large effects significant in natural settings, but the traditional statistical approaches to experimentation have asserted that large effects are not necessary to draw valid conclusions. *Statistically significant* small effects are considered sufficient to permit statements of cause-effect relations. The experimental tradition can be completely divorced from this statistical philosophy. There is nothing in the logic or the tactics of the experimental method that would prevent the production of larger effects of independent variables.

The strengths of experimental research are the strengths of science itself. Experimental research is the most appropriate method to isolate a cause-effect relation. Clinically and educationally, it is the only method to firmly establish the effects of treatment and teaching methods. Many other types of research can suggest possibilities of causal relations, but only the experimental approach can confirm them. Therefore, in developing theories and testing empirical hypotheses, no other research type matches the power of experimental research. Because a theory is both a description and an explanation of some natural phenomenon, investigators need the experimental procedure to rule out alternative explanations. Types of research such as the ex post facto and the normative may suggest hypotheses and theories, but typically, the same piece of research may suggest several rival hypotheses without testing their relative validity. Only experimental research can examine alternative hypotheses and theories, supporting one while ruling out the others.

Clinical and Applied Research

Clinical and applied research often are contrasted with basic or experimental research. Clinical and applied research are thought to be qualitatively different from experimental research. However, only a few contrasts are valid because basic/experimental and applied/clinical research have much in common.

Clinical and applied research both address questions of immediate practical significance. They are designed to solve pressing physical, social, or personal problems. While basic research may yield data that may be used in the future to solve some practical problems, clinical and applied research seek solutions to current problems. Basic experimental research may be theoretical or may be designed to find order and uniformity in natural events; it may seek to explain events, understand their causes, and predict their occurrences. Clinical and applied research, on the other hand, may seek to modify undesirable effects that have already taken place, improve certain existing conditions, or prevent certain unfavorable consequences. Research aimed at treating language disorders, improving an articulation treatment program, or developing better ways of teaching arithmetic skills to people with intellectual disabilities illustrate these kinds of applied or clinical efforts.

Clinical research is an investigation of diseases and disorders of living organisms. Therefore, as in medicine, many research studies in communication disorders are clinical. Research aimed at understanding and treating various disorders of communication is necessarily clinical.

The distinction between applied research and clinical research is not crucial except that in many cases, **applied research** may be nonclinical as defined here. For example, research aimed at reducing energy conservation in homes is applied but not clinical. Similarly, research aimed at building better bridges or safer highways is applied without being clinical. However, both clinical and applied research try to solve problems, and in this overriding sense, they are the same. Therefore, in this book, the terms *clinical research* and *applied research* are used interchangeably and will be distinguished only when necessary.

Clinical research uses the same basic procedures as the other types of research; its procedures are not necessarily unique. Depending upon the particular clinical study, the method may be descriptive or experimental.

Descriptive clinical (applied) research is nonexperimental and seeks to describe a phenomenon. Definition of disorders and descriptions of their symptoms are good examples. All case studies and investigations of onset and development of disorders, attitudes and feelings of clients and their family members, and "personality" characteristics of people with different disorders are descriptive.

Experimental clinical research is typically treatment research in all clinical sciences, including communication disorders. Once a disorder and its characteristics are known, researchers move to find out how it may be reduced or eliminated with treatment procedures. Such a move requires the manipulation of an independent variable (a new treatment procedure) to see what effects follow on the dependent variable (the disorder).

In communication disorders, even routine clinical treatment is like an informal experiment. Treatment, by definition, is the application of a variable that will change the disorder. The only and significant difference between routine clinical treatment and experimental research is that the former may lack controls for extraneous variables. Such controls are essential in experimental research so the question

whether a given treatment procedure is effective may be answered. See Chapter 4 for more on treatment evaluation.

Epidemiological Research

The variety of clinical research, known as *epidemiological research,* is mostly nonexperimental. **Epidemiology** is the science of the frequency and distribution of diseases, injury, and health-related behaviors and events. It seeks to determine the potential causes of diseases and unhealthy behaviors and conditions with the goal of designing programs to control and prevent their spread in human populations. The term is derived from *epidemics,* the outbreak of deadly diseases or other health-related events. Epidemiological research has greatly improved human health and community sanitary standards. Through this kind of research on diseases and their distribution, modern societies have developed means of transporting clean drinking water, mechanisms of sewage treatment, and refrigeration of food and beverage.

Studying incidence and prevalence of diseases, disorders, and other health-affecting events is a major effort of epidemiologists. **Incidence** refers to the events that happen over time or the occurrence of an event in a specified duration of time. For instance, to say that the incidence of stuttering in most societies is 1% means that 1% of any nonstuttering population may develop stuttering. The **prevalence** of a diseases refers to the proportion of a population that already has a disease or a disorder. To say that there are 500 children who stutter in a given school district is to make a statement of prevalence. Through the study of incidence and prevalence, epidemiologists establish patterns of distribution of specified diseases and disorders in human populations.

A pattern of distribution of a disease may suggest or hint at conditions under which the disease appears and develops. Such conditions are of great interest to epidemiologists. In the past, they were concerned with conditions under which epidemic diseases such as plague and cholera would occur. Modern-day epidemiologists are concerned with the distribution of a wider variety of factors such as heart diseases, various forms of cancer, criminal behavior of youths, child abuse, domestic violence, sexual harassment, drug abuse, teen smoking, exercise behavior, and dietary habits. Once the distribution is known, epidemiologists search for potential causes that may be controlled or eliminated to reduce the frequency of the disease or disorder. Even controlled experimental evaluation of various treatment and public health programs is epidemiological in nature.

Epidemiology is now a vast field of research with varied research topics and methods (Carneiro, 2018; Rothman, 2012). Only a few epidemiological research methods are highlighted here.

Epidemiological research may be experimental or nonexperimental. *Experimental research* in epidemiology includes controlled treatment evaluations, field studies, or community intervention. **Controlled treatment evaluations** are the same as *randomized clinical trials* described in Chapter 4. As noted in that chapter, experimental and control groups are used to evaluate the effects of various treatment procedures on patients with specific diseases or disorders. **Field trials**, on the other hand, are conducted on healthy persons to evaluate the effectiveness of health promotion or disease prevention programs. Such programs often are conducted in natural settings because healthy people do not seek treatment in clinics and hospitals. For example, there have been large-scale field trials to evaluate the effects of vitamins and diet in reducing mortality due to heart disease or cancer or in reducing the frequency of common colds. Experimental evaluations of various vaccines or cholesterol-lowering drugs (sometimes controlled with placebo) also are field studies. Both randomized clinical trials and field studies use the group design strategy described in Chapter 8.

Community intervention is a type of experimental epidemiological research in which the participants are not individuals (as they are in clinical and field trials) but whole communities of people living in a certain geographic area. For instance, as part of a program to reduce the incidence of dental caries in a community, the community's water supply may be treated with fluoride. Note that the treatment is aimed not at a particular individual but the entire community. Another community whose water is not fluoridated may be selected as a control. Police may institute a program to reduce the number of red-light runners or drunk drivers; the program is exposed to all in the community simultaneously.

Nonexperimental research in epidemiology includes several methods, but we shall highlight only cohort studies and case-control studies (Rothman, 2012). Most nonexperimental epidemiological studies may be retrospective or prospective. **Retrospective studies** are those in which a disease or a condition is already evident and perhaps has been for some time. In **prospective studies**, some participants are known to have been exposed to the risk factor, but the clinical condition has not yet appeared. For instance, children who have had early traumatic brain injury and those without a history of such injury may be two groups of cohorts. In this case, traumatic brain injury is the risk factor for developing learning disabilities later in school. In a retrospective study, children who are already in grade schools and who already have learning disabilities may be compared with those who do not have the history and are doing well in the schools. In a prospective cohort study, observation of both groups will start before any evidence of learning disability emerges; the investigators observe its emergence.

Cohort studies involve a group of people who have a common characteristic or face a similar risk for developing a disease. For example, children who have a family history of language disorders constitute a cohort. They share a family history and possibly are at risk for developing language disorders. All adults with a parental history of premature death due to heart disease are another cohort.

A study may involve more than one cohort. Two groups, one exposed to a risk factor (e.g., family history of learning disabilities) and the other unexposed to the same risk factor (e.g., no family history of learning disabilities), constitute two cohorts. One or more cohorts may be observed for a relatively long duration to determine the incidence of a disorder, disease, or health-related event. For instance, two cohorts, one with and one without a family history of learning disabilities, may be followed for several years of schooling to determine the effect of the exposure (family history) on the incidence of learning disabilities in children.

Case-control studies involve a clinical group (cases) that has a disorder and a control group that does not. These studies are similar to standard-group comparisons described earlier. Case-control studies also are similar to cohort studies in that the cases and controls are cohort groups. The main difference between the two types of studies is this: In the cohort method, none of the cohorts yet exhibit the clinical condition, although some may be at risk; in the case-control method, one group already exhibits the clinical condition and is being compared with another that does not.

Typically, retrospective, case-control studies compare the history of the two groups and any other current information that might contribute to an understanding of why the cases manifest the diseases while the controls do not. The investigator may collect data from interviews, case histories (cases), biographical information (controls), questionnaires, and previously recorded laboratory measures, clinical findings, and diagnostic and treatment data to see if the cases and controls differ systematically on some variable or variables. The difference found may be hypothetically linked to the clinical condition.

Case-control is a commonly used clinical research method. An investigator, for instance, might select people who have had a recent stroke and compare them with healthy individuals with no history of strokes. The case-control research methods may reveal that there were systematic differences between the two groups on two variables: diet and exercise. These two variables then might be related to the incidence of strokes in the cases and presumably in the population. Johnson's diagnosogenic theory of stuttering may be described as a case-control epidemiological study (Johnson & Associates, 1959). After studying parental attitudes toward fluency and stuttering in parents of stuttering (case) and nonstuttering (control) children, he concluded that parents who are excessively concerned with fluency and who diagnose stuttering on the basis of normal nonfluencies in their children actually cause stuttering.

Strengths and Limitations of Clinical and Applied Research

Clinical and applied research offers many advantages to individuals and society. These two types of research are the main means by which science helps solve practical problems, improve individual living conditions and general social conditions, reduce disease frequencies, promote health and fitness, and find new treatment procedures for illnesses and disorders. Clinical and applied research studies always address socially and personally significant problems. The best kinds of research studies in this category build on basic research and thus help extend its usefulness. Experimental clinical research, as noted before, is indispensable in evaluating treatments for their effectiveness.

Compared to nonclinical basic research, clinical research has its limitations. Clinical research is sometimes more difficult to implement than nonclinical research. Clinical research raises many ethical concerns. Sampling a sufficient number of participants for clinical research can be difficult. Some kinds of clinical variables are more easily investigated through experimental procedures than are others. For example, environmental variables are more easily built into experimental designs than genetic or neurophysiological variables. Almost all genetic and most neurophysiologic variables typically tend to be described and not manipulated, although genetic modifications to reduce the risk of diseases or eliminate the diseases are a possibility.

In group experimental designs, achieving sampling equivalence between the experimental and control groups also may be difficult. In nonexperimental clinical or applied research, it is difficult to draw firm conclusions about cause-effect relations. Many of the strengths and limitations of clinical and applied research are discussed and elaborated in Chapters 4, 8, and 9.

Translational Research

Translational research is the application of the findings of basic scientific and laboratory research. Basic research findings are *translated* into solutions to practical problems (e.g., diseases and disorders) in clinical settings. Translational research has many definitions, none clearly distinguished from applied (clinical) research and randomized clinical trials (DeMaria, 2013; Forth, Herr, Shaw, Gutzman, & Starren, 2017; Unger, 2007). Much of the literature is in medicine where the investigators try to apply the findings of genome and other kinds of basic laboratory research to improve human health conditions. For instance, when a gene responsible for a disease is identified, translational research may begin to find ways in which the gene and the associated disease may be modified (Khoury et al., 2007). Translational research is also known as *translational science*. A related term that emphasizes a wider application (extension) of effective treatments into community settings is *implementation science*. All these terms have come into vogue in speech-language pathology (Douglas, Campbell, & Hinckley, 2015; Klein & Jones, 2008; Raymer et al., 2008).

In medicine and pharmacology, there are several steps in conducting translational research. In the first phase of translational research, some basic research finding is tested at the human level. For instance, in clinical trials, a new drug may be initially tested for their safety (Phase I clinical trials) and subsequently tested for their effectiveness (Phase II clinical trials). These phases may be common to translation research. In the next phase of translational research, the findings are disseminated so the method may be more broadly applied. There is no agreement on the different levels, steps, or phases of translational research or how it relates to better defined clinical trial research. Translational research may be described as either an attempt to bridge the gap between basic and applied research or as a continuum between the two types. More researchers view the two types on a continuum.

In speech-language pathology, translational research is most frequently discussed in the context of communication disorders with neurological bases. Aphasia and disorders of communication associated with traumatic brain injury and other neurological conditions are thought to be good areas for translational research. Here, the basic or laboratory-based research often comes from animal research where the effects of, and recovery from, experimentally induced brain injury is studied, often in rats and monkeys. For example, rat research has shown that if a paralyzed (surgically induced) limb is not forced to be used through rehabilitation, the eventual recovery will be adversely affected (the *use it or lose it* principle of neuroplasticity). This means that impaired functions should be taught and practiced. Other principles translated or translatable from animal research include intensity of training, repetition (repeated trials), timing of treatment initiation, directly target-ing specific skills instead of some general or presumed underlying skills, salience (meaningfulness) of treatment targets, and so forth. To understand how these principles are discussed in the context of aphasia treatment, see Klein and Jones (2008) and Raymer et al. (2008).

Implementation science is the science of extending or "translating" effective treatment procedures to community clinics. As such, it may be considered a part of translational research. It begins with training clinicians in correctly applying the newly translated treatment procedure to a larger number of clients. The treatment procedure may be modified as found appropriate. Finally, clinicians' continued use of the procedure (maintenance) is assessed (Douglas et al., 2015). Unfortunately, there are no good examples of a full-scale implementation research in communication disorders. Its emphasis on extending effective treatments to practical clinical settings and assessment of their maintenence in those settings is a worthy aspect of this kind of research. Nonetheless, even without a model of "implementation research," treatment researchers may move on to train other clinicians and assess the effects in natural settings. Clinicians, too, take steps to extend the treatment benefits to their clients' natural settings. Is *implementation research* a *buzzword*? Some have asked and answered it in the negative (Douglas et al., 2015). But *implementation research* is most likely a buzzword, because better accountability and quality control, improved clinician satisfaction, and more effective outcomes for clients—all considered hallmarks of implementation research, have always been a part of good treatment (applied) research. The new term adds nothing new to research methods or concepts.

Strengths and Limitations of Translational Research

Translational research emphasizes clinical application of basic research findings. While this is highly desirable, whether we need this new term is questionable. Clinical and applied researches, from their very inception centuries ago in medicine, have always been defined as application of basis research findings in solving practical problems, including unfavorable health conditions. When there is no basic research to apply, and there is very little in speech-language pathology, clinical researchers do treatment research to reduce or eliminate diseases and disorders.

In treating communication disorders associated with brain injury or diseases, one might assess the effects of behavioral treatment on brain functions. For example, brain imaging and cerebral blood flow studies may help document changes in brain function as a result of behavioral treatment of aphasia or traumatic brain injury. Such attempts help understand what treatment does at the cerebral level, no doubt an important outcome. However, documenting cerebral changes due to or associated with behavioral treatment is not *translation* of anything. It is measuring another dependent variable (changes in the brain), which may not have been measured before.

Whether they are called treatment research, clinical research, or applied research, they have done and are still doing what translational research is now advocating. Therefore, it is neither a new type of research nor a new research design. It is not an innovative research method or a research philosophy. Translational research has failed to produce new insights in treating aphasia, a disorder on which the topic has been discussed extensively (e.g., Raymer et al., 2008). For instance, such clinical principles as repetition of treatment trials, treatment intensity, age of the individual receiving intervention, treatment timing postonset, specificity of treatment, and practically all other principles that have been swept under the new "principles of neuroplasticity" have been discovered independent of a translational framework and are unrelated to the principles of neuroplasticity. In fact, most of those "principles" have been known to be important considerations in treating any disease or disorder long before the term *translational research* appeared in PubMed in 1993 (DeMaria, 2013); they are important also in treating communication disorders not associated with brain pathology.

Sample Surveys

Surveys assess some characteristics of a group of people or a particular society. Like normative research, surveys try to understand specific behaviors of a set of individuals. For example, a survey researcher might be interested in finding out the attitudes of teachers toward hearing-impaired students in certain elementary schools. Another investigator might be interested in the most frequently used aphasia therapy procedure in university clinics. Yet another researcher may wish to assess the opinions of school administrators regarding the necessity of speech-language services in schools under their administration. Research concerns such as these require the survey method.

Technically, surveys try to find out how the variables such as attitudes, opinions, and certain social or personal practices are distributed in the population. However, rarely can a surveyor assess the entire population. The typical strategy is to draw a representative sample of the population and find out its members' reactions to a set of questions designed to evoke answers of interest. Therefore, scientific surveys often are called *sample surveys.*

Surveys are routinely used in assessing public opinions and attitudes on issues, trends, and events. Some of the well-known surveys include the Gallup polls, the Harris polls, the Pew Research Center, and those that are conducted by television networks, national newspapers, and candidates for public offices. Most of the attitudes and opinions assessed in these polls are related in some way to political, social, or economic issues. Predicting voter behavior, for example, is a regular form of survey research. Surveys frequently assess people's attitudes toward contemplated legislation and economic policies. The need for such sample surveys is so great that many commercial firms specialize in conducting them and selling their results to media and political candidates.

In academic and clinical fields, surveys might address questions regarding the distribution of certain variables either in the population at large or in specific groups. A professional organization may wish to find out the percentage of people who know about speech-language pathologists. In this case, knowledge, defined in some operational way, is the dependent variable whose distribution in the general population is measured in a survey. Similarly, a speech-language pathologist may conduct a survey to find out how many families, among those with a person who has dementia, access community rehabilitation services.

The results of surveys are only as valid as the sampling technique used in them.

Technically, a random sample is needed to accurately assess the dependent variable. A nonrepresentative sample will lead to invalid conclusions. The issues surrounding the random theory are discussed elsewhere in the book. It is sufficient to note here that all sampling techniques have a margin of error. Currently, the typical national sampling of citizens of voting age in the United States involves about 1,500 individuals. It may carry a sampling error of 4 to 6 percentage points. For example, assuming a 5% sampling error, when a survey reports that 34% of the voting-age population favor a tax reform package, the actual percentage in the population may be anywhere between 29 and 39.

Strengths and Limitations of Sample Surveys

It is necessary to understand what surveys can and cannot do. Surveys can help formulate certain professional and social policies. They let us know what people are thinking on certain issues or what kind of actions the people think they might take in certain situations. For example, it may be important to know whether school administrators might support more speech-language pathology positions in the schools.

Surveys, however, cannot answer questions of causality because of lack of experimental manipulation. For example, a survey might show that a certain procedure is widely used in the treatment of persons with laryngectomy, but it cannot determine whether the technique is indeed effective. Such a survey reflects a current practice, not its effectiveness or validity. As in normative research, when the question concerns the distribution of the dependent variables, surveys are useful, but when the questions concern functional relations between events, they are not.

The best surveys with adequate random samples can help predict group behaviors but not the behaviors of an individual. One might find out, for example, that a certain number of speech-language pathologists in the United States believe that childhood apraxia of speech (CAS) is a valid diagnostic category. However, from this survey information, one cannot answer the question of whether a specific clinician also believes in the existence of CAS. Similarly, an opinion survey may show that a given candidate is likely to be elected by a majority of voters, but this is of no help in predicting the voting behavior of an individual citizen.

An additional limitation of surveys is that they tend to focus on *soft* dependent variables. Attitudes and opinions are the most frequently sampled dependent variables in a survey research. However, in most cases, attitudes and opinions themselves are of little interest to the survey researcher, who in fact tries to predict actions or behaviors of individuals in the populations. The researcher infers certain imminent actions from the people to whom the conclusions of the sample survey are extended. However, there is very little assurance that presumed attitudes and opinions always translate into actions. In some limited instances, opinions and attitudes may more accurately reflect a group behavior. For example, exit polls may reflect voting preferences better than polls taken months before the election. In such cases, a television network may be able to declare a winner a few minutes or a few hours ahead of the official announcement. Such accurate but competitive predictions may have commercial advantages, but their scientific utility is limited.

Qualitative Research

Qualitative research describes dependent variables (effects) and may try to categorize them. It is an effort to describe the properties of a phenomenon. A typically made distinction, questioned later, is that qualitative research is a separate type of research, standing in contrast to the quantitative variety. This type of research is done in all basic and applied disciplines, including communication disorders, psychology, medicine, and health professions (Creswell & Poth, 2017; Silverman, 2016). Of the several varieties of qualitative research, we briefly review a few major ones.

Qualitative research is not easy to define. The name suggests that it is not quantitative because it eschews traditional measurement of the dependent variables under study. Damico and Simmons-Mackie (2003) define qualitative research as "a variety of analytic procedures designed to systematically collect and describe authentic, contextualized social phenomena with the goal of interpretive adequacy" (p. 132). But qualitative research can also include not just social phenomena but also personal experiences (biography and idiographic research). It is claimed that qualitative research not only describes behavior patterns under study but also seeks to explain them (Damico & Simmons-Mackie, 2003). But as we will see later, it is questionable whether nonexperimental qualitative research can explain the events it describes. Furthermore, quantitative research, too, uses analytic procedures and systematically collects authentic (valid) data. Interpretation and its adequacy are not unique to qualitative research. Therefore, except saying that qualitative research deemphasizes quantitative measures of the dependent variables, there is hardly anything specific that defines it. But even this is problematic because qualitative researchers do use quantitative measures, especially so in empirical clinical sciences.

Common qualitative methods of data collection include observation of behaviors under natural settings, interviews that avoid the investigator biases (ethnographic methods), conversation and discourse analysis, biography, case study, grounded theory, and the investigator's intuition and introspection. We have noted in previous chapters that case study is one of the nonexperimental research methods used in all clinical sciences, including speech-language pathology. Conversational analysis is commonly performed in understanding such language skills as turn taking and conversational repair in clinical and nonclinical populations (see Damico & Simmons-Mackie, 2003, for a review). Related to conversational analysis, narrative and discourse analyses are common in speech-language pathology (Nippold, 2014). Language sampling in naturalistic and family-oriented contexts and analyzing the data with no particular emphasis on numbers is qualitative. (But it is only predominantly qualitative because quantification of observations in cross-sectional or longitudinal language development studies is common.) It is generally argued that because of its complexity, human communication is more adequately studied by qualitative, descriptive methods than quantitative methods (Simmons-Mackie & Damico, 2003).

Behaviors are observed in their natural and authentic contexts, not in contrived laboratory settings. This feature is thought to contrast the most with the quantitative experimental research. To observe the behavior patterns in naturalistic settings, the investigator may be a **participant-observer**. In practical terms, the investigator may spend some time as an observing member of the community under study. In some anthropological research, investigators have lived in the community they studied for months or years.

Qualitative research is systematic and well organized, but it is also thought to be more flexible than the quantitative method. Earlier observations may force changes in the later observational methods. Qualitative research does not avoid measuring the frequency of behaviors, but it goes beyond those numerical values. For instance, in analyzing the effect of stuttering on a person's social life, not only the frequency of dysfluencies and avoidance of social interactions are measured but also the person's feelings and verbal descriptions (qualitative indexes). In aphasia research, perspectives of family members on living with a person with aphasia may be explored and described. People's experiences may be categorized but not necessarily quantified.

Ethnographic research is a type of qualitative research method. Originated in anthropology, ethnography is a method of studying cultural and behavioral patterns in different societies. Understanding different cultures is its goal. Because ethnographic research avoids the formation of hypotheses at the outset of research, it is described as discovery driven in that new and surprising observations may be made (Damico & Simmons-Mackie, 2003; Schensul, 2013). It may use all methods of qualitative research, including traditional direct observation, participant observation, questionnaires, and interviews.

The participants in typical ethnographic research in communication disorders have been clients with speech-language disorders and their families. Participants belonging to minority populations have been studied especially with ethnographic methods. Studies often have addressed such issues as beliefs and attitudes toward communication disorders, treatment expectations, mother-child interactions, culturally sensitive methods of interviewing clients and their families, and so forth. Frequently studied cultural groups include Hispanic Americans and African Americans. Much of the research on multicultural issues in speech-language pathology may be construed as ethnographic. Speech and language sampling, various kinds of questionnaires designed with cultural sensitivity, and structured interview formats designed to obtain information on cultural and linguistic diversity have been the predominant methods of ethnographic enquiry in speech-language pathology. Both the questionnaires and interviews seek responses to more open-ended and broad questions. During the interview, the researcher may minimize questions that require yes/no responses, frequently restate the interviewees' responses, encourage statements that reflect their own feelings and opinions, and refrain from making critical judgments. Empathy and respect for differences and diversity are important principles of ethnographic interviews and questionnaires.

Grounded theory, oddly named for a *method* of research, is a variety of qualitative research in which collected data are allowed to suggest a theory. It is an inductive method of developing theories with no preconceived hypotheses (Birks & Mills, 2011; Glasser & Strauss, 1967). There is an interplay between data collection and theory building; as the data of a study are analyzed, a theory may be generated, but this theory may be continuously modified or elaborated as new observations are made and new data

demand changes in the theory. A rigorous effort is made to match the data with the theory. The grounded theory was probably a reaction to the common practice of theory building in social sciences with loose, little, or no connection to solid data, even if they were observational.

All methods of qualitative research, including direct observations, participant observations, diaries, letters, autobiographies, biographies, historical accounts, media materials, and interviews, may be used to collect data. Although grounded theory is considered a qualitative method of research, quantitative data are acceptable and are combined with qualitative data. In many instances, quantitative data may be necessary in developing grounded theories.

As the name suggests, developing a theory is the main goal of the grounded theory research method. Interpretation of data is considered a theory in grounded theory research; it makes no claim to absolute reality out there. It is an interpretation of patterns found in the behaviors of groups of people, and therefore, the perspectives (feelings, thoughts, opinions, comments, reactions) of people who are studied is the main concern in data analysis. People's perspectives are analyzed along with the researcher's perspectives (interpretations). This may contrast with some other types of qualitative research in which description of personal and group behavior patterns may be the main outcome with little or no emphasis on theory building. This method has tackled a variety of research topics, including dying in a hospital, chronic illness experiences, divorce and remarriage, the work of scientists, and so forth. Beyond sociology, the method has been used in psychology and health sciences and professions.

Strengths and Limitations of Qualitative Research

Qualitative research is useful, is essential, and may be the only kind possible in understanding many human problems where the experimental method is ethically precluded. Even when experimentation is possible, a descriptive account of the event (the dependent variable) is necessary. Descriptive understanding of the problem or the phenomenon precedes experimentation. In clinical sciences, no disorder can be effectively treated unless there is a clear description of it. Many exploratory studies in speech-language pathology tend to be qualitative and highly informative. Longitudinal studies of speech and language learning in children have been valuable. Qualitative studies on cultural and verbal behavior across different ethnic groups have given us new perspective with which to view what is "normal" (typical) and what is disordered in need of clinical or educational intervention. Qualitative research has also expanded our understanding of treatment research effects by including an assessment of satisfaction with the treatment received and improved quality of life of individuals receiving services.

Qualitative research is highly desirable as long as it is done with an understanding of its limitations and it is justified for good reasons. *Quality* and *quantity* are typically contrasted in qualitative research. There is even a *Journal of Quality and Quantity*. Historically, qualitative research was a response to what were thought of as the limitations of quantitative methods, especially in social sciences, particularly in sociology.

Qualitative research, as practiced in most cases, can offer rich and meaningful descriptions, but not explanations. Whether a study is typically descriptive, is particularly ethnographic in its character, or uses the grounded theory method, it cannot explain the event studied because it cannot effectively rule out alternative explanations. Well-designed and executed qualitative research may suggest possible explanations, may hint at the ones that are more likely than the others, but it cannot confirm any one of them. It may also fail to reveal other possible explanations. But not being able to offer explanations is not a negative comment on qualitative research. It is understood that descriptive research is needed and valuable and often precedes quantitative research as stated before. Problems emerge when its limitations are unappreciated or violated.

Critics object only when the qualitative researchers cross their boundaries and begin to build theories and explanations based on observations, interviews, normative descriptions, case studies, ethnographic observations, and studies based on grounded theory. Very few qualitative researchers refrain from making theoretical or explanatory statements at the end of their study. Fewer still follow up on verifying their statements through another, more suitable method that happens to be experimental, which is not necessarily entirely quantitative. Grounded theory avows to build theories based on observational data, which may be both qualitative and quantitative, but this is a difficult goal for any nonexperimental research method to achieve.

Critics also may object when qualitative research is presented as a more desirable alternative to quantitative methods. No method is more desirable than the other; none replaces others. Each method is good for answering questions it can handle well. When questions posed are scientifically valid and are likely to produce useful data when investigated, the method is an important but secondary consideration.

Sometimes, qualitative methods are justified for invalid reasons. One such invalid justification is the claim that speech and language behaviors, conversations, narratives and discourse, stuttering, aphasia, or dysarthria are such multilayered complexities that they cannot be adequately analyzed with quantitative methods. Numbers are trivia; words are profound. One of the spectacular achievements of science is that it has brought progressively more complex phenomena under quantitatively experimental control. Excluding certain subject matters or specific problems from quantitative methods will only perpetuate the fallacy that complex behaviors cannot be studied quantitatively, more specifically, experimentally. And there is yet another problem.

That problem is the artificial and categorical distinction between the qualitative and quantitative research. The distinction many not be valid at all (Allwood, 2012). No quantitative research avoids qualitative observations and descriptions. Statements of hypotheses (when made) and observations that led to those hypotheses, the literature review, participant descriptions, data interpretation, relating findings to previous research, and discussion of theoretical or clinical implications are all words, not numbers. If "words are data," as one qualitative researcher declared (Tesch, 1990), quantitative studies have plenty of them. Furthermore, numbers in quantitative research do stand for meaningful, qualitative behaviors. A significant reduction in stuttering frequency under treatment is not an empty numerical symbol; it may also mean that a young man can

now order in a restaurant, propose to his girlfriend, enjoy a satisfying job, and have extended conversations with his friends. He might say that his quality of life has improved. Documenting such beyond-the-numbers outcomes is important, however.

There may be pure qualitative studies that have not measured the variables studied, but they are few and the researchers who had to do that tend to be apologetic about it. The majority of good qualitative studies do quantify their dependent variables to varying extents. Even the interview data, child development and speech-language learning data, ethnographic multicultural difference studies—all quantify their observations. Classifying the results of observations, coding categories, ranking observations, reporting frequencies, and counting other features are typical aspects of qualitative research. Qualitative researchers are aware that it is good to know what exists, but it is better to know how much of it does. In fact, the history of qualitative research is a relentless movement toward greater quantification. Validity and reliability of observations are qualitative researchers' concern, too (Sale, Lohfeld, & Brazil, 2002). It is to their credit that they can do that without losing sight of the "quality." Nonetheless, there is no resolution here. As described in the next section, however, the debate continues in a research method that purports to mix *quality* and *quantity*, highlighting, if not widening, the chasm again.

Mixed-Methods Research

Mixed-methods research (MMR) is a mixture of qualitative and quantitative methods in a single study. It has been promoted as a new research method, presumably highly desirable because it incorporates the two most important methods of investigation (Creswell & Plano Clark, 2018). There is a journal devoted to MMR (*Journal of Mixed Methods Research*). Books and articles on the topic are so astonishingly numerous that one critic called it a growth industry and noted that MMR is akin to an independent nation because the researchers claim "dual citizenship" in the qualitative and quantitative research nations (Sandelowski, 2013).

All experimental designs described in Chapters 8 and 9 help generate quantitative as well as qualitative data; predominantly qualitative research has just been discussed. Therefore, we need not go into greater details about the MMR that includes the two methods that are familiar to the reader. A few salient features may be noted, however.

In MMR, any single or a combination of qualitative methods may be used along with any single or a combination of quantitative methods. A study is *not* MMR if it combines several elements of only the qualitative (QL) or only the quantitative (QN) research traditions. Authentic MMR should have at least one qualitative and one quantitative procedure in it. Furthermore, the two elements from the two traditions should be mixed in the same aspect of the study (e.g., sampling, data collection, or data analysis). MMR proponents believe that QL and QN are categorically different methods but it is useful to combine them in a single study (Sandelowski, 2013). Either QL or QN is considered a monomethod with limited value in studying complex behaviors. As we saw in the context of qualitative research, complex behaviors are a hallowed research territory. Historically, access to such behaviors was claimed by QL researchers, denied to QN researchers. The new MMR shuts both QL and QN researchers off from complex behaviors. Only MMR researchers have the special key to complex, significant, and higher-order behaviors.

Strengths and Limitations of Mixed Methods

Methodological flexibility is MMR's greatest asset and offers a relaxing lesson to tensed monomethodologists. MMR investigator may borrow methods appropriate to answer their research questions from both QL and QN approaches. Consequently, MMR researchers must have competence in multiple methods of empirical investigation. That one should select the procedures that are best suited to answer a particular research question, regardless of particular research traditions, is good advice.

Mixing methods of research may be a mixed-up concept, however (Sandelowski, 2013). The mixed-methods concept rests on the validity of a distinction between qualitative and quantitative research. As noted in the previous section, the distinction may not be valid as most studies in most disciplines use a combination of qualitative descriptions and quantitative measurements. Mixing descriptions and numerical values in a single study has been a well-established tradition long before the mixed-method research was proposed. In fact, it is nearly as old as research itself. Therefore, there is nothing new in MMR approach.

The Relation Between Research Types and Questions

The different research types described so far are not mutually exclusive. There may be other ways of classifying them.

A research type or strategy is a methodological response to a research question. Each method handles a unique research question. The nature of the question determines the type of method used.

Research types are not entirely matters of methods, however. They reflect both methodological and philosophical stances. With some experience, most researchers tend to investigate certain types of questions. A majority of those who are typically interested in normative research in language development, for example, may not be inclined to ask questions that require experimental analysis. Those who wish to find cause-effect relations rarely indulge in normative research or sample surveys.

Broadly speaking, the different research types can be grouped into three categories. The first category contains the ex post facto research, which can answer questions regarding potential relations between events that have passed. The investigator infers a cause of an effect from knowledge of past events.

The second category contains the normative, standard-group comparisons, survey, and qualitative research, which are capable of answering questions concerning "the way things are." These four types of research tend to be descriptive and nonexperimental. They are generally concerned with the distribution of dependent variables in the population. There are philosophical and other differences between the four types within this category. Normative research is based on the philosophy of developmentalism and seeks to establish typical performances of defined groups. Standard-group comparisons are made to find differences between identified groups. Both normative and standard-group comparisons are thought to help determine boundaries of normal and disordered or deviant behaviors. Qualitative research may be predominantly descriptive, but as noted, the distinction between that and quantitative is not entirely valid.

The third category contains experimental research of all varieties: laboratory, clinical, nonclinical, and translational. Experimental research does not search for causal relations in the past, nor does it simply ask a question about the way things are. The way things are is known before an experimental research is conducted, however. It creates conditions under which expected or unexpected things may happen. What happens when an independent variable is manipulated under controlled conditions is the concern of experimental research. Therefore, research questions about cause-effect relations in which the experimenter has a reasonable degree of confidence dictate the use of the experimental method.

Many beginning researchers often wonder what type of research they should do. Instead, they should wonder about the types of questions they would like answered. Within their limitations, all types of research contribute something to the knowledge base. Some types of research, however, do more than others in helping us understand the events we study. The experimental method does the most in helping us both understand the events and gain control over those events. Understanding and controlling events are the essence of *science,* regardless of such qualifications as applied, clinical, and basic.

Summary

- **Ex post facto research** describes an effect and searches for its potential causes that have occurred in the past; case studies are ex post facto.

- **Normative research** helps find out how certain dependent variables are distributed in the population by establishing norms.
- **Standard-group comparisons** compare and contrast clinical and nonclinical and other types of groups to understand their differential characteristics.
- **Clinical and applied research** seek to solve a practical problem; clinical research is applied, but applied research need not be clinical.
- **Translational research** is a new term for applied research; it is research in which basic research findings are applied ("translated") to solve practical, often clinical problems.
- **Sample surveys** describe opinion and attitudes through representative random samples; it is nonexperimental and cannot explain opinions and attitudes.
- **Qualitative research** emphasizes description and categorization as against measurement and quantification; has several varieties that include the ethnographic method; but the distinction between qualitative and quantitative research is questionable.
- **Mixed methods** is a blend of quantitative and qualitative research approaches; it probably is not a unique research method because most if not all studies have always done that.

References

Allwood, C. M. (2012). The distinction between qualitative and quantitative research methods is problematic. *Quality and Quantity: An International Journal of Methodology,* *46*(5), 1417–1429.

Birks, M., & Mills, J. (2011). *Grounded theory: A practical guide.* London, UK: Sage.

Brown, R. (1973). *A first language: The early stages.* Cambridge, MA: Harvard University Press.

Capelli, R. (1985). *An experimental analysis of morphologic acquisition* (Unpublished master's thesis). California State University, Fresno, CA.

Carneiro, I. (2018). *Introduction to epidemiology* (3rd ed.). London, UK: McGraw-Hill Education.

Creswell, J. W., & Plano Clark, V. L. (2018). *Designing and conducting mixed methods research* (3rd ed.). London, UK: Sage.

Creswell, J. W., & Poth, C. N. (2017). *Qualitative inquiry and research design: Choosing among five approaches* (4th ed.). Washington, DC: Sage

Damico, J. S., & Simmons-Mackie, N. N. (2003). Qualitative research in speech-language pathology: A tutorial for the clinical realm. *American Journal of Speech-Language Pathology, 12,* 131–143.

De Cesari, R. (1985). *Experimental training of grammatic morphemes: Effects on the order of acquisition* (Unpublished master's thesis). California State University, Fresno, CA.

DeMaria, A. (2013). Translational research? *Journal of the American College of Cardiology, 62*(24), 2342–2343.

Douglas, N. F., Campbell, W. N., & Hinckley, J. J. (2015). Implementation science: Buzzword or game changer? *Journal of Speech-Language-Hearing Research, 58,* S1827–S1836.

Forth, D. G., Herr, T. M., Shaw, P. L., Gutzman, K. G., & Starren, J. B. (2017). Mapping the evolving definitions of translational research. *Journal of Clinical and Translational Research, 1*(1), 60–66.

Glasser, B., & Strauss, A. L. (1967). *The discovery of grounded theory: Strategies for qualitative research.* Chicago, IL: Aldine.

Johnson, W., & Associates. (1959). *The onset of stuttering.* Minneapolis: University of Minnesota.

Khoury, M. J., Gwin, M., Yoo, P. W., Dowling, N., Moore, C. A., & Bradley, L. (2007). The continuum of translational research in genomic medicine: How can we accelerate the appropriate integration of human genome discoveries into health care and disease prevention? *Genetics in Medicine, 9*(10), 665–674.

Klein, J., & Jones, T. A. (2008). Principles of experience-dependent neural plasticity: Implications for rehabilitation after brain damage. *Journal of Speech-Language-Hearing Research, 51*, S225–S239.

Nippold, M. A. (2014). *Language sampling with adolescents* (2nd ed.). San Diego, CA: Plural.

Raymer, A. M., Beeson, P., Holland, A., Kendall, D., Maher, L. M., Martin, N., . . . Gonzalez, L. J. (2008). Translational research in aphasia: From neuroscience to neurorehabilitation. *Journal of Speech-Language-Hearing Research, 51*, S259–S275.

Rothman, K. J. (2012). *Epidemiology: An introduction* (2nd ed.). Oxford, UK: Oxford University Press.

Sale, J. E. M., Lohfeld, L. H., & Brazil, K. (2002). Revisiting the quantitative-qualitative debate: Implications for mixed-methods research. *Quality and Quantity, 36*(1), 43–53.

Sandelowski, M. (2013). Unmixing mixed-methods research. *Research in Nursing and Health, 37*, 3–8.

Schensul, S. L. (2013). *Initiating ethnographic research: A mixed methods approach.* Lanham, MD: AltaMira Press.

Silverman, D. (Ed.). (2016). *Qualitative research.* London, UK: Sage.

Tesch, R. (1990). *Qualitative research analysis types and software tools.* New York, NY: Falmer Press.

Unger, E. F. (2007). All is not well in the world of translational research. *Journal of the American College of Cardiology, 50*(8), 738–740.

Study Guide

1. Define *ex post facto research*. Describe its procedures. Justify the need for this kind of research.

2. You are seeing a client with a sensorineural hearing loss. Design an ex post facto study to identify some of the potential causal variables. Describe possible independent variables and the procedures of uncovering them. Specify the limitations of this kind of study.

3. What are the logic and the procedures of normative research?

4. Suppose you wish to establish the stages by which children learn to produce the regular and irregular plural forms with 80% accuracy. You also wish to have a local representative sample. Design a study to accomplish your objectives.

5. Summarize the strengths and limitations of normative research.

6. Is chronological age an independent variable? Why or why not?

7. Describe the method of standard-group comparison. It is similar to what other type of research?

8. Justify the statement that standard-group comparisons cannot establish cause-effect relations.

9. Define experimental research. Describe its procedures.

10. Suppose you wish to experimentally evaluate the effects of an articulation treatment procedure. Describe a hypothetical treatment procedure and design an experimental study to evaluate its effects.

11. Specify the criticisms of experimental research. How would you refute those criticisms?

12. Define and describe epidemiology.

13. Compare the cohort study method with the case-control method. Define both and give examples.

14. What is the purpose of sample surveys? Write two research questions that can be answered by the survey research.

15. Critically examine the issues related to the distinction between qualitative and quantitative research.

6

Observation and Measurement

Chapter Outline

- Observation and Measurement
- Philosophies of Measurement
- Scales of Measurement
- Measures of Communicative Behaviors
- Client-Assisted Measurement
- Indirect Measures: Self-Reports
- The Observer in the Measurement Process
- Mechanically Assisted Observation and Measurement
- Reliability of Measurement
- Summary
- References
- Study Guide

Observation and measurement are two basic scientific activities. The beginnings of observation are in the sensory experiences generated by some natural phenomena. When people see, hear, touch, and smell things and events, they also may wonder about their characteristics and causes. They may then take a closer, more systematic look at the event. Observation is, at the simplest level, looking at something and describing what is seen. Other senses, including hearing, touch, smell, and taste, also may be involved in observation. In essence, observation is establishing a sensory contact with an event and then making a report on that experience. In this sense, observation is an everyday activity.

Compared with everyday observation, **scientific observation** is more systematic, thorough, and objective. Scientific observation is *systematic* because it is structured, and the results of observations are carefully recorded. The observation is *thorough* in that the scientist attempts to observe as many instances and as many aspects of a phenomenon as possible. It is *objective* in that the results of observation may be publicly verifiable because different observers can try to achieve the same or similar results.

Scientific observation is rooted in empiricism. Normally, scientists do not take seriously events that do not generate sensory consequences. Exceptions emerge when indirect evidence and theory suggest the existence of a phenomenon, though there are not yet direct sensory consequences. The existence of a phenomenon that cannot be measured may be temporarily postulated when many strong empirical reasons support it. In many cases, instruments allow for the observation of events that do not generate sensory stimulation. The issue of mechanical aids to observation will be addressed in a later section.

Observation and Measurement

Scientific observation is essential for measuring a phenomenon. Without systematic measurement, a scientist cannot go much beyond observation. For example, to experiment, the event should be measured before, during, and after the introduction of the independent variable. Changes in events should be documented through measurement.

Measurement has been defined as "assignment of numbers to represent properties" (Campbell, 1952, p. 110) and as "assignment of numerals to objects or events according to rules" (Stevens, 1951, p. 1). In essence, **measurement** quantifies observed objects, events, and their mathematical properties. This is done according to a standard set of rules that define units of measurement (Johnston & Pennypacker, 2009).

Quantified observations are the measured value of an event, object, or its property. Technically, what is measured is not the event, object, or its property but some *dimensional quantity*. Frequency of an event, for example, is a **dimensional quantity** of an event because standard number units can be assigned to that frequency; other dimensional quantities of behavioral events include duration, latency, and interresponse time.

Philosophies of Measurement

Social and psychological sciences have evolved a philosophy of measurement that is different from that of natural sciences (Johnston & Pennypacker, 2009). Natural sciences have found that absolute and standard units of measurement are essential to objective quantification of observations. Johnston and Pennypacker (2009) have called this kind of measurement **idemnotic**, that is, the units of measurement have a standard and absolute meaning. Idemnotic units of measurement are independent of the measured phenomenon. Without idemnotic measurement, natural scientists would not have achieved the level of precision and objectivity for which they are well known.

To the contrary, social and psychological sciences often do not measure the dimensional quantities of events using absolute and standard units of measurements. Instead, they measure those quantities in relative standards that are defined within the confines of the variability of the phenomenon under investigation. Johnston and Pennypacker (2009) have called this type of measurement **vaganotic**, meaning the units of measurement vary.

In vaganotic measurement, standards of measurement keep changing depending upon the amount by which a phenomenon varies. For example, a rating scale developed to measure the severity of stuttering typically yields different values depending upon the amount of variability found in different groups of people who stutter. Different rating scales designed to measure the same stuttering severity yield different values when used on the same clients. Similarly, rating scales developed to measure different disorders will result in vastly different values.

Social and psychological sciences often measure dimensional quantities indirectly. Instead of directly observing behaviors, social or psychological scientists may sample participants' verbal statements (or those of others who are supposed to know). For example, a supervisor may fill out a questionnaire on the productivity of his or her employee. The investigator will use the questionnaire responses as though they were direct observational values of productive behaviors themselves. However, the investigator will not have directly observed and counted productive behavior with a standard and absolute system of numbers.

The proverbially derogative statement, "By taking a new job, he raised the IQ of the people he left and the people he joined," illustrates this philosophy of relative and indirect measurement defined in terms of the variability of the phenomenon being measured. Nobody's intelligence was increased or decreased by a person's move, but because the variability changed, the assumption is that the measured value also changed. If one were to assume that a given student on a university campus is as intelligent as the "average student" on that campus, then that student's intelligence will continuously change depending upon which university he or she attends. Compared to a group of clinically anxious groups, I may have less anxiety, but compared to someone who is unusually calm, I may have more anxiety. All along, my level of anxiety may not have changed, but the relative scale used to measure it assumes that it has.

Johnston and Pennypacker (2009) have traced the history of vaganotic and idemnotic measurement. In the 17th and 18th centuries, mathematicians and scientists were concerned with the variability in measured values of a given phenomenon. When a natural phenomenon is measured repeatedly, the values are typically not constant. The question, then, was what is the "true" value of the phenomenon? This concern eventually led to the development of modern statistics in the works of Adolphe Quetelet (1796–1874). Quetelet proposed that such human characteristics as height vary only because nature missed the ideal. What nature missed could be calculated by measuring the heights of many individuals. In effect, when repeated measures are plotted, the result is a normal curve, which to many suggests the ideal in the form of a mean. Thus, the nonexistent average person, created to neutralize the measures of variability in people, gave not only a stable measure of persons but also the concept of an ideal person.

It was Francis Galton (1822–1911) who believed that mental abilities are also distributed normally and that the distribution of measured values across a vast number of participants would suggest the ideal (the average). Soon, Binet (1857–1911) and Cattell (1860–1944) developed tests of intelligence, and the tradition of vaganotic measurement based on the variability of the phenomenon measured became firmly established in psychology and social sciences. The tradition was strengthened by the development of statistical techniques designed to infer the true value of a population from the measured sample values.

Although psychology and social sciences use indirect and relative systems of measurement, the radical behaviorism of Skinner has shown that the use of absolute and standard units of measurement is possible in the study of human behavior. Skinner (1953) avoided indirect and statistically based measurement of behavior by defining his dependent variable as the rate (frequency) of observable and directly measurable responses of an organism. When the occurrence of a given response of a class of responses is counted, a direct and absolute number system is used. For example, when a clinician counts the number of times a child produces the regular plural morpheme *s* in a segment of conversational speech, an absolute value of frequency is established. The value would not be relative to the variability found in the phenom-

enon of plural *s* usage. To the contrary, the normative statement, "On the average, 5-year-olds produce the plural *s* with X percent accuracy," is relative to the variability found in that phenomenon.

The measurement philosophy and the nature of a subject matter interact in a curious manner. A measurement philosophy can influence the way a subject matter is conceptualized and researched. To a certain extent, intelligence and personality were conceptualized as they were because of the measurement philosophy and technique adopted by those interested in mental measurement. In turn, the way a phenomenon is conceptualized determines to some extent how it can be measured. If variability is believed to be intrinsic to the behaving organism—as with the statistical approach—then group designs and statistical methods of neutralizing variability are necessary techniques of research. On the other hand, if it is believed that variability is extrinsic to the behaving organism, it becomes a subject of experimental analysis. The measurement procedure adopted in this case would not be solely determined by the variability of behaviors.

Scales of Measurement

Psychologist Stevens (1946) originally proposed the *scales of measurement,* also known as the *levels of measurement.* Those scales are now commonly used in social and psychological research. By rating and ranking phenomena of interest, scales or levels offer indirect measurements. The levels are closely related to statistical scaling techniques. Stevens (1946, 1951) described four scales of measurement: nominal, ordinal, interval, and ratio.

Nominal Scale

Nominal scale simply helps distinguish one event or object from the other. The numbers assigned to an event or object have no mathematical meaning. Therefore, the numbers are much like proper names; hence, the term *nominal*. Nominal scales yield categorical data: 1 may stand for the female participant and 0 for the male participant. What is "measured" is simply given a parallel symbol system, which may consist of numbers without their mathematical meanings. Questionnaires that evoke *yes* or *no* responses illustrate nominal measurement, as do telephone numbers and numbers assigned to football players. Diagnostic categories such as stuttering, apraxia of speech, and aphasia are clinical examples of nominal measurement.

Nominal measurement is described as the crudest or the simplest of the measurement levels. It is probably no measurement at all. It does not measure a dimensional quantity, and it does not serve any purpose other than distinguishing one set of observations from another. It does not accomplish anything that a name would not, and naming a thing is not the same as measuring it.

Ordinal Scale

Ordinal scale applies to properties that are continuous, not categorical; relative concepts such as *greater than* and *less than* are used in ordinal measurement. Rank-ordering of events, objects, or properties because of their graded increases or decreases helps establish relative values. For example, a school that graduates the most straight-A students may be assigned the rank number 1, and the school that graduates the lowest number of straight-A students is assigned the last rank. The rank-ordering of students on the basis of their Graduate Record Examination (GRE) scores is ordinal measurement. Ranks only tell that one student has scored more or less on the GRE in relation to students with higher or lower ranks. Ranked values do not tell how much more they scored, nor do they indicate an absence of the quality measured. In other words, there are no absolute numbers and there is no zero that indicates the total absence of the measured property.

The frequently used 5-point Likert-type rating scale consists of ordinal measurement. When a person expresses *strong disagreement, disagreement, neutral, agreement,* or *strong agreement,* the opinion on the issue in question is measured on an ordinal scale. The categories of judgments can be given numbers to derive numerical values. For instance, *strong agreement* may be given a scale value of 1 and *strong disagreement* a scale value of 5. However, such numbers and their corresponding categories do not have mathematical meaning. Also, the intervals between numbers or categories are unknown and probably not equal. For example, one cannot assume that *strong agreement* is twice as strong as *agreement.* Therefore, numbers assigned to ordinal categories cannot be added or subtracted.

Ordinal scales at best provide indirect and subjective measures of properties measured. They are greatly influenced by the uncontrolled, momentary, and subjective judgments of the observer. There is no standard unit of measurement. This type of measurement is commonly used in the assessment of such subjective and highly variable intervening variables as attitudes and opinions.

Interval Scale

Interval scale is an improvement over ordinal scale in that the numerical distinctions of the scale do suggest similar distinctions in the measured property; that is, the difference between 1 and 2 on an interval scale would be the same as that between 3 and 4. As noted before, there is no such assurance in an ordinal scale. The interval scale has a zero, but it is arbitrary. The zero does not mean the absence of the measured property. Therefore, the scale values of an interval scale, though of known equal intervals, cannot be added or subtracted.

Measurements of temperature and calendar time are examples of interval scales. On either the centigrade or Fahrenheit scales, zero does not mean an absence of temperature. The beginning of the Christian calendar is also arbitrary. If four clients' stuttering is measured on an interval scale, the client who is assigned a score of 4 stutters twice as severely as the client who receives a 2. Again, because of a lack of zero, the numbers are not additive or subtractive.

Ratio Scale

Ratio scale, the final level of measurement in Steven's (1946) classification, has all the properties of the earlier levels and also has a zero that represents an absence of the property being measured. Ratio measurement uses the number system in its mathematical sense. It is possible to count, add, and subtract the values of a ratio scale. Most measures in the natural sciences are on this scale; most of those in the social sciences are not.

Behavior science usually uses the ratio scales. The dependent variable in behav- ior science is the frequency of responses. In communication sciences and disorders, too, frequencies of speech-language behaviors measured are on the ratio scale. Such measures as attitude scales and severity ratings of disorders are on the ordinal scale. The frequency of discrete target response in treatment sessions is also measured in real numbers, hence on the ratio scale. A zero-response rate means that the organism did not respond.

Measures of Communicative Behaviors

Speech and language behaviors can be observed, measured, and recorded in different ways. The kinds of measures used depend on the definition of the communicative behavior targeted for measurement. Some definitions allow direct measurement whereas others permit only indirect and inferential measurement. For example, language may be defined either as linguistic competence or as the production of various verbal responses. Linguistic competence cannot be measured directly; it is inferred from other kinds of data. The production of particular responses, on the other hand, is directly measurable on the ratio scale. Generally speaking, a phenomenon can be measured more directly if it is defined operationally. **Operational definitions** are descriptions of procedures involved in measuring an event; for example, the term *articulatory proficiency* does not define anything operationally, but the statement *production of /s/ in initial positions of 10 words at 90% accuracy* does.

We describe seven types of measures that are relevant for most clinical research in communication sciences and disorders: frequency, duration, interresponse time, latency, time sampling, momentary time sampling, and verbal interaction sampling.

Frequency Measures

The **frequency** with which a behavior is exhibited under specified stimulus conditions is one of the most useful and objective of the measured values of verbal behaviors. This measure often is used in clinical research.

Frequency measures can be used in counting the number of times a client produces language responses of particular classes, the number of sounds misarticulated, the number and types of dysfluencies, the number of pitch breaks, and other such communicative behaviors. To establish frequency measures of various speech and language behaviors, the observer often should count also the number of **contextually correlated behaviors**—behaviors that typically occur only in certain contexts. These are typically the number of syllables or words spoken; speech sounds, dysfluencies, and so forth normally occur only in the context of syllable and word productions.

The measurement of the frequency of speech and language behaviors poses a special problem. Communicative behaviors are discriminated. In other words, their production is not reflexive and automatic but context dependent. Therefore, in measuring the frequency of verbal and nonverbal (but communicative) behaviors, the investigator should first arrange the discriminative stimulus conditions that set the stage for the particular kinds of behaviors targeted for observation and measurement. Various kinds of stimulus pictures, objects, topic cards, and conversational devices help evoke verbal and nonverbal responses.

In establishing the frequency measure of specific speech-language behaviors, the investigator should take into consideration the number of opportunities afforded those behaviors in a given period of observation. For example, in the measurement of the frequency of grammatical features, the number of discriminated opportunities to produce those features should be considered. Brown (1973) has described such opportunities as **obligatory contexts**, which are the structural contexts of phrases and sentences in which the use of a particular grammatical feature is dictated by the rules of a given language. For example, the regular plural inflection would be obligatory in the context of "I see two frog*s* here." The concept of obligatory contexts can be used in measuring other kinds of speech-language behaviors.

The productions of specific sounds also have their discriminated opportunities. An omission is suggested when a child does not produce the /s/ at the beginning of the word *soup* because of the obligatory context for that production. The number of syllables or words spoken may be the discriminated opportunities for the production of dysfluencies. Speech itself is the discriminated opportunity for various voice qualities.

When the discriminated opportunities and the number of opportunities in which the behavior under observation appears are both measured, a percent-correct response rate can be derived. This measure can be calculated for most of the communicative behaviors whose frequency can be measured. The percentage of (correct) articulation of a given speech sound in a given word position and that of dysfluencies are among the commonly reported frequency-based measures in research studies. Studies on language have also frequently reported percent-correct measures of productions of various grammatical features and vocabulary items.

Frequency measure, though simple, direct, and objective, may not be practical in measuring all kinds of speech-language behaviors. Frequency measure is most appropriate for behaviors that are of relatively low rate and have a clear beginning and end. In other words, the behaviors should be discrete and should be a part of other behaviors. Many speech and language behaviors fulfill these two criteria. Grammatical features, for example, are used in the context of other behaviors and are therefore of relatively low rate. They also are discrete behaviors in the sense that their onset and termination can be easily determined.

Frequency counts may not be appropriate for some nondiscrete communicative behaviors of high rate. For example, such voice qualities as hoarseness or harshness cannot be efficiently counted according to their rate. A pervasive hoarseness of voice (high rate) that does not have a discernible beginning or end (except for speech-silence dichotomy) should be measured some other way.

Another limitation of frequency count is that it may not be a comprehensive measure of certain behaviors. Mere frequency count may miss other equally significant dimensional quantities of a behavior. Other important dimensional qualities, such the duration of certain behaviors, may be missed in the frequency count. For instance, a frequency measure of dysfluencies may not necessarily reflect their durational quantity. Theoretically, dysfluencies of low frequency may be of relatively long duration, and those of high frequency may be of short duration. This theoretical pos-

sibility has not been observed in a majority of stutterers, however. In most cases, low frequency of dysfluencies is associated with relatively shorter duration and vice versa. But in those exceptional cases where frequency and duration are unrelated or opposite to each other, both measures should be obtained.

Procedures of counting the frequency of a behavior may be simple or complex. Many speech-language behaviors can be counted with the help of various kinds of counters. In most clinical sessions, behavioral frequency can be counted with certain kinds of marks on a piece of paper. Speech-language behaviors, because of their transitory nature, require some form of recording before they can be reliably counted. Audio or video recordings often are necessary to count speech-language behaviors. In most cases, the recorded behaviors should be reviewed repeatedly to obtain accurate measures.

Durational Measures

The **duration** over which a specified behavior is sustained can be a useful measure. It is especially useful in the case of continuous behaviors. The total number of seconds or minutes for which the behavior is sustained is usually measured and compared against the total duration of time for which the observation was made. For example, a clinician may record the duration for which a client maintains an inappropriately high pitch within a 30-minute conversational speech. In this case, the percentage of time spent exhibiting the appropriate pitch can be calculated.

Duration, being a temporal measure of behavior, gives a different kind of information than does frequency. Frequency, which shows the number of times a behavior is exhibited, gives no clues to the length of behavioral episodes. As pointed out earlier, duration of dysfluencies is an important dimensional quantity. It can be of both empirical and theoretical significance in a research study. In communication disorders, most vocal qualities are better measured for their duration. If talking behavior (a global measure of language use) is the subject of experimental manipulation, the time spent talking (instead of specific language behaviors) may be a more appropriate measure.

The durational measure can be impractical with many behaviors. Duration is a valid measure of behaviors that have an appreciable temporal dimension. It is true that all behaviors have a temporal dimension, but depending upon the purposes of a study, measurement of duration may or may not be essential or practical. For example, in the measurement of grammatical features or semantic notions, the interest may be in frequency and not duration. How many times a child produces the present progressive *-ing* in a conversational sample may be of greater interest than the duration of *-ing* productions.

In clinical research, duration measures are less frequently used than frequency measures because extremely brief durations of behaviors are hard to measure without sophisticated instrumentation. The duration should be noticeable for durational measures to be used in routine clinical research. For example, sound or silent prolongations of stuttering persons have a noticeable durational dimension, whereas *schwa* interjections do not. Therefore, measurement of duration is relatively easy in the case of prolongations and difficult in the case of interjections.

In clinical research, durations that can be measured with a stopwatch may be reported more frequently than those that require complex instrumentation. Clinical target responses of extremely brief durations are better measured for their frequency. Generally speaking, without instrumentation, durational measures are harder to record than are frequency measures.

Whenever possible, durational measures should be combined with frequency measures. Together, they give a better measure of behaviors. In some cases, a pure duration measure can be meaningless unless the frequency measure is also reported. For example, it may be misleading to report the mean duration of sound prolongations of a person who stutters. For this observation to be meaningful, the frequency of such prolongations also should be reported.

Interresponse Time Measures

Interrersponse time measure, another durational measure, is the duration that lapses between any two discrete responses or other events. Interresponse time can be a useful measure in some kinds of research. For example, in clinical studies that are concerned with too sparse response rates, the clinician might be interested in decreasing the interresponse time.

Clinically, interresponse time may be a function of the rate at which the clinician presents the training stimuli. For example, a clinician may present language or articulation stimulus cards at a faster or slower rate, generating a shorter or longer interresponse time. When the rate of stimulus presentation is changed, the interresponse time also may change. Other treatment variables may affect interresponse time. One can investigate such variables with a view to increasing the response rate and decreasing the time spent not giving the target response.

It is obvious that interresponse time is closely related to the frequency of responses. A high response frequency is likely to be associated with short interresponse durations; a low response frequency is likely to generate long interresponse durations. Therefore, it is meaningful to report the frequency measure along with the interresponse durations.

Latency Measures

Latency, another temporal measure, is the time that lapses between the termination of an environmental event (often a stimulus) and the onset of a response. It is the traditional *reaction time*. Latency measure differs from duration measure in that it is not a measure of time for which a response was sustained. The time it takes for an organism to respond after stimulation is sometimes taken as a reflection of learning: the faster the reaction time, the stronger the learning. Whether this is valid or not, reaction time can be an indirect measure of frequency; other things being equal, the greater the latency, the lower the frequency of responses per unit of time.

Latency is an important aspect of communicative behavior. In conversational speech, the listener and the speaker alternate their roles. Each provides certain verbal and nonverbal signals to the other person to switch the role (initiate or terminate responses). Therefore, latency measures may be necessary in an analysis of conversational speech. In clinical research, a client's response latency can be a useful dependent variable in that shorter latencies often are one of the targets of treatment. A delayed response

may be as good as no response, and often it is scored as such. Decreasing the latency, then, becomes a primary target of treatment.

A few seconds of reaction time is considered typical in clinical situations. Most clinicians allow up to 5 seconds for the client to respond. If the response latency is too long, the clinician tends to shape progressively shorter latencies.

Latency has been a dependent variable in several studies on the vocal behaviors of people who stutter. Two latency measures have been researched extensively: the *voice initiation time* (VIT) and the *voice termination time* (VTT). Several kinds of stimuli can be used to initiate or terminate a vocal response, although auditory stimuli have been used most frequently. In using an auditory tone as the stimulus, the experimenter may instruct the participants to initiate a vocal response such as /a/ as soon as the tone is heard and terminate the response as soon as the tone ceases. The actual time that elapses between the onset of the tone and the onset of the vocal response is the VIT. The time that elapses between termination of the tone and that of the response is the VTT. Studies of this kind have generally shown that the reaction time of people who stutter is somewhat slower than that of people who do not stutter and that reaction time tends to improve with practice (Bloodstein & Ratner, 2008).

Time Sampling Measures

Time sampling gauges time intervals during which behaviors selected for observation occurred. Time sampling should not be confused with the response duration measure, which is also based on time. The *time* in time sampling refers to periods during which the occurrence of a behavior is observed and recorded; in duration measurement, the length of a response is recorded.

In time sampling, the investigator observes a behavior during selected intervals of time. The intervals may be of short durations: a few seconds to a few minutes. An entire treatment session of 45 minutes may be subdivided into 5-minute blocks. During each block, whether or not a specified behavior occurred is recorded. During the observational interval, multiple occurrences of the same behavior are not distinguished; the behavior is scored only once during the interval. The duration of the response is also ignored.

The observational periods may be consecutive or may be interspersed with nonobservational periods. This method requires intensive observation because during the interval or period of observation, the investigator should pay continuous attention to the participant being observed. For example, a special educator might observe a child for 10 minutes, divided into 10-second intervals. During the interval, whether the child exhibits a given target behavior such as quiet sitting or reading is noted. At the end of the interval, the presence or the absence of the behavior is recorded. Similarly, in an assessment of mother-child interactions, an investigator may use time sampling to observe specific communicative behaviors (such as conversational turn taking) during selected intervals.

Because it generates categorical data (presence or absence), time sampling may not accurately reflect the frequency of measured behaviors. It is most useful in measuring behaviors that do not have a clear beginning or end. The results of time sampling are analyzed in terms of the number of intervals during which the behavior occurred against the number of intervals in which the behavior was absent.

Momentary Time Sampling

Momentary time sampling, also called **spot checking**, is a method of periodically observing and recording the occurrence of a behavior. When it is known that a behavior is somewhat constant or of high frequency, continuous observation and measurement may not be necessary. It may be sufficient to observe the behavior periodically and record its occurrence.

In momentary time sampling of behaviors, the investigator predetermines the times at which the behavior will be checked. Some kind of signaling device, such as a timer or a wrist-alarm, may set the occasion to observe the behavior. As soon as the timer goes off, the investigator looks at the participant and determines whether he or she is exhibiting the target behavior. The behavior is scored as present or absent at *the moment of observation.* A percentage is then calculated by dividing the number of momentary samples during which the behavior was present by the total number of samples and multiplying the quotient by 100. For example, at 30-minute intervals that are set off by a wrist-alarm, a special educator may observe a child to see if he or she is sitting quietly. Assuming that over a few days the specialist had 38 total spot checks and the behavior was scored as present in 24 of them, the percentage of time-sampled value would be 63 (24/38 × 100 = 63).

One advantage of momentary time sampling is that it does not require continuous observation of the target behavior. Clinicians and classroom teachers working with groups are not able to observe a particular client or child constantly. And yet, clinicians and teachers need to measure and monitor various behaviors of the individuals in the group. In such cases, momentary sampling can be useful. Momentary time sampling can be appropriate to measure various noncooperative behaviors of specific children in a group therapy session. At predetermined times, the clinician can check a particular client to see if the client is exhibiting nonattending, off-seat, or any other undesirable behavior.

Verbal Interaction Sampling

Verbal interaction sampling is measuring the typical or atypical communicative exchanges between individuals. Most of the measures considered so far are suitable for measuring behaviors that are relatively independent, discrete, and exhibited by one or a few individuals. The various language productions of one or a few individuals may be measured for their frequency, duration, and interresponse time. Many of these measures may be obtained through either time sampling or momentary time sampling. However, verbal behavior presents the need for another kind of measure—verbal interaction sampling.

Ethologists and animal psychologists have observed social interactions between members of groups of animals either in natural habitats or laboratories. In this method of observation, sometimes called **sequence sampling**, a sequence of behaviors of multiple individuals is recorded (Altman, 1974). In some respects, the problem faced by the speech-language pathologist is similar to that of the ethologist and the animal psychologist interested

in patterns of social behaviors. Verbal behaviors are social interactions. Studied in natural settings, speech-language responses involve an interaction in which multiple sequences of verbal behaviors can be simultaneously active.

The term **dyadic interaction** refers to communicative exchanges between two persons. This kind of interaction often is used to describe the kind of behavior that is sampled in what we have called here *verbal interaction*. In many cases, verbal interaction is dyadic. Much of the current research in normal and disordered communication is concerned with interaction between two individuals, often a child and his or her mother or other caregiver. Nonetheless, verbal behaviors are not always dyadic. An analysis of verbal interaction between three or more individuals has barely begun, but it can be expected to be an important part of language analysis. Therefore, the term *verbal interaction sampling* may be more suitable to describe a method of observation designed to measure interactive verbal behaviors of multiple individuals. The term does not restrict, on a priori grounds, the number of individuals involved in verbal interactions.

In verbal interaction sampling, two or more individuals' verbal behaviors are sampled. Interactions are usually arranged for the specific purpose of observation, and in this sense, they may not be as naturalistic as everyday conversations. However, every attempt is made to make the interaction as natural as possible. A mother and a child, for example, may be asked to talk to each other in their usual manner. A variety of play materials, pictures, and other stimulus items may be provided to stimulate verbal interaction. This kind of observation may be made at the participants' home or in a research laboratory.

The actual measures obtained through verbal interaction sampling depend upon the research questions and theoretical orientations of the researcher. For the most part, the frequency of a variety of types of verbal responses is noted. For example, the number of requests, comments, and topic initiations the child and the mother make may be observed and recorded. Verbal interaction sampling also may be used to observe other conversational skills, including turn taking and topic maintenance.

The frequency, duration, interresponse time, latency, time sampling, momentary time sampling, and verbal interaction sampling measures all require direct observation of the behavior to be measured. When necessary, the conditions of behavioral occurrence should be carefully arranged, and the observer or a mechanical device should be present to record the dimensional quantity of the measured behavior. Any of these measures can be obtained in experimental or nonexperimental research conducted in naturalistic settings or laboratories.

Measures obtained by investigators are preferable to those obtained by participants themselves. However, in clinical research, it is sometimes necessary to obtain the measures of behaviors in the client's natural environment in the absence of the clinical investigator. In such cases, client-assisted measurement may be used.

Client-Assisted Measurement

In **client-assisted measurement**, the client performs some important task necessary to document the occurrence of his or her own behavior being measured. The clinical investigator is not present while the behavior of interest is naturally occurring. The client can record his or her own behavior with audio- or video-recording devices and submit the records to the clinician. It is the clinician who measures the frequency or other dimensional quantity of the target behavior from the submitted recordings.

This kind of measurement is especially important in establishing a reliable frequency of the target behaviors in the natural environment before, during, and after treatment. Direct measurement in the clinic or laboratory may not fully and accurately reflect the communicative behaviors of clients in the home, school, office, and supermarket. When the concern is the assessment of treatment effects sustained in such natural environments, client-assisted measurement is necessary.

Client-assisted measures may be preferred even when the clinical investigator can be present in a client's everyday situation to measure the target behaviors, because the presence of the clinician may affect the frequency of measured behaviors. Usually, the effect is positive; the clinician is a discriminative stimulus for the treated behaviors. Because the clinician is not a permanent part of the client's natural environment, a more valid measure of the target behavior can be recorded only when the clinician is absent.

The client should be trained to record his or her behavior in natural settings. Most clients should be trained in the correct use of a digital recorder or a video-recording machine. In communicative disorders, clients often are asked to record their conversational speech at home or in other situations. They should be given detailed instructions on how to arrange the conversational situations. The conversational speech should be natural (habitual) and should be long enough to permit reliable measures of the dependent variables targeted for treatment. Possibly, the conversations with different individuals may have to be recorded at different times of the day. Typically, repeated recordings are needed.

When both are obtained, direct and client-assisted measures can give a more comprehensive and reliable picture of the dependent variables. However, some investigators also may use another kind of measurement in which the dependent variable is neither observed as it occurs nor measured through client-submitted recordings. This is the indirect measurement of behaviors.

Indirect Measures: Self-Reports

Indirect measures are those obtained without the experimenter coming into contact with the dependent variable in vivo or after the fact. There is no direct observation of the event being measured. Individuals may self-report. The investigator may ask participants to describe their behaviors. The participant can report orally or in writing, and the format of the report may be more or less standardized.

The most commonly used self-reports are questionnaires of various kinds. Questionnaires of personality, attitudes, interests, fears, anxieties, and avoidance reactions are frequently used in clinical research. In assessing behavior disorders, clinical psychologists and psychiatrists use most of these questionnaires. In communication disorders, attitudinal scales to measure the reactions of people who stutter to various speech situations are used by some researchers and clinicians. Also

available are various rating scales that seek information from persons who stutter regarding their fluency and dysfluency levels in many speaking situations. Other questionnaires may measure attitudes and reactions of parents, teachers, or employers toward various speech-language disorders. Speech and hearing centers may seek the reaction of its patrons regarding the services offered.

The validity of questionnaire measures depends upon the correspondence between what the participants report and the actual behavior that is being reported upon. If there is a good correspondence, self-reports may be valid. However, the approach assumes that the participants themselves are reliable and keen observers of their own behaviors, a questionable assumption at best.

A distinction should be made between those self-reports that seek information from the client on specific behaviors exhibited in situations that are not easily accessible to direct observation and those that seek to assess internal states such as attitudes and personality traits. A person who stutters, for example, may be asked to compare the extent of his or her dysfluencies in home and at work. When this client reports more dysfluency at home than at work, one might take it as a reasonably valid statement. However, if the investigator then assumes that the person has a negative attitude toward the workplace, he or she is going beyond reported observations. Therefore, self-reports that simply supply additional information on behaviors exhibited in extraclinical situations are more useful than those that seek to measure internal states or inferred entities.

Accepting even those self-reports that simply describe behaviors exhibited in extraclinical situations can be problematic, however. One cannot be sure that a participant's reports are reliable. Therefore, self-reports of clients are an inadequate substitute for direct observation. Client-assisted observation is preferable to self-reports.

Self-reports are an indispensable method in the case of some dependent variables, however. When an investigator is concerned with what the client thinks and feels, verbal or written reports are the only means of assessment. For example, in communication disorders, it is possible that a clinician is interested in the feelings and thoughts associated with a speech or language disorder. In such cases, self-reports provide the only means of assessment. The clinician then should exercise caution in interpreting self-reports because the dependent variables may not have been quantified objectively.

The Observer in the Measurement Process

The process of observation has two important components: the phenomenon being observed and the individual who observes it. The scientist-observer is supposed to record the events impartially, without injecting his or her own prejudices and biases. Sometimes the mere fact of observation may change the phenomenon. Such phenomena are called reactive, described in Chapter 8. However, the reactivity of dependent variables is not as major a problem in communication disorders as it is in such fields as social psychology.

Two issues often are raised in the discussion of the human observer: observer bias and the training of the observer. The first, **observer bias**, refers to a potential tendency on the part of the observer to produce data that might support his or her

preconceived ideas or formal hypotheses about the phenomenon being observed. Subtle changes in the method, duration, and intensity of observation can distort data. For example, if a child is known to talk more at home but less at school, the investigator who spends more time observing the behavior at home may introduce subtle biases into the data. In another example, short-term effects of treatment may be more impressive than the long-term effects, and an observation may be terminated before the data show a decline. The percentage of dysfluencies calculated on the basis of the number of syllables spoken may give a different picture than that based on the number of words spoken.

Faulty analysis of results and improper conclusions drawn from data also may be due to observer biases. However, this is not a significant problem when the data resulting from the observations are clearly separated from the inferences and conclusions. It is only when the observer records inferences instead of the dimensional quantities of events that this problem becomes serious. For example, when a clinician records that "the client was aggressive on five occasions during the treatment session," independent observers have no data to judge the client behaviors. On the other hand, if the clinician records the observable actions (five times the client hit another person) instead of inferring what the actions mean, then the independent observers can come to their own conclusions.

Observer bias is not a problem restricted to the person doing the observing. It is also a matter of the way the dependent variables are conceptualized. Biases are inevitable when the dependent variables are poorly conceptualized, and methods of observing them should of necessity be indirect. In essence, indirect measurements and vague dependent variables create opportunities for observer bias. When discrete responses are dependent variables, observer bias can be minimal or, at the least, when it does occur, external observers can rectify it.

The second issue, **observer training**, is much more important because proper training can help generate reliable and valid data with minimal or no observer bias. As pointed out by Johnston and Pennypacker (2009), observation is a response of the scientist, and objective (bias-free) observation is strictly under the control of the event being observed, not the preconceived ideas of the investigator. Like any other complex response, the act of observation is a learned skill and improves with experience.

In communication disorders, the training of observers has received little systematic attention. Many investigators hire research assistants who may be only minimally trained in observational skills. Some of these assistants are graduate students who at best receive some instructions on what to look for and how to record what is being measured. Graduate students may consider themselves "experienced" if they have had an opportunity to watch a senior investigator make some scientific observations.

To make scientific observations, the observer: (a) should be clear about the topographical aspects of the event, (b) should know the dimensional quantity selected for observation, (c) should be aware of the rough limits of variability of the phenomenon, (d) should have observed and recorded along with an experienced (reliable) observer before working on his or her own, (e) should have mastered the technical aspects of observing and mea-

suring, and (f) should have the disposition of a scientist. These conditions will not guarantee reliable and objective observations, but in their absence, measurement is questionable.

First, the observer should have a thorough knowledge of the form of the response targeted for observation. The observer should know what the behavior looks and sounds like. A person who is unsure of the topography of the response under observation is not likely to record its occurrence consistently, if at all. For example, a student who is not sure of the structure of a verb phrase will not be able to observe and record its occurrence in a language sample. Observers who do not know the form of various dysfluencies cannot be expected to count their frequency. Students who do not know how a vocal fry sounds will not be able to indicate its presence or frequency.

One can be relatively sure of the response topography when it is conceptualized directly and defined operationally. In the self-or-other training process, dependent variables that are unobservable internal events ("cognitive reorganization," for example) often are inferred, not directly observed. Inference is not observation, and if the act of observation itself requires inference, then training objective observational skills is especially difficult.

Second, a clear understanding of the dimensional quantity selected for observation is essential, and observer training should be specific to that. What aspect of the event should be observed and measured? Is it the duration, the frequency, or some other dimensional quantity? Are there multiple dimensions, such as duration *and* frequency, that should be measured simultaneously? How should repetitions of the same response topography be recorded? For example, when a person who stutters says, "I stu-stustu-stutter," the same response topography is repeated three times. Is this scored as one instance of syllable repetition or three? (Most researchers would count this as one instance of part-word repetition.)

Third, the observer should have some idea about the limits within which the phenomenon under observation can vary. Repeated events do show some variability in their topography. Sound prolongations may be relatively long or short, or they may be produced with greater or less muscular effort (force). But they are all still counted as sound prolongations only. The same morphological feature may be used in inflecting a word, or it may be a part of a phrase or a sentence. The hypernasality of a client may be more pronounced on certain speech sounds and less on others. But such variations may not be considered significant in measuring the *presence* of hypernasality.

Fourth, an observer should first observe and record the same event along with an experienced observer. This is probably the most important aspect of actual training in observation. It is not sufficient for the awestruck student to merely watch the senior scientist's smooth observational skills. The student observer should observe and record the behavior along with the more experienced observer. The two (or more) persons should measure the same event simultaneously but independently of each other.

Contingent feedback is an essential part of this phase of training. The student and the scientist should compare their measured values and discuss the differences. It often is necessary to talk about the differences as soon as an instance of

observational act is completed. This is more efficient when the behaviors to be observed are recorded. While measuring behaviors from audio- or videotapes, the scientist and the student observer can freeze the event to discuss the behavior and its dimensional quantity being measured. The student in this process should receive contingent corrective and informative feedback on all aspects of measurement.

Fifth, when instruments are used in observing and measuring a behavior, the observer should have the necessary technical skills to operate the instruments. The use of relatively simple instruments such as audio or video recorders necessitates some training and skill. Complex instruments require much more training time, and the student observer should be sure of operating them correctly. The observer should also be able to recognize malfunctions of instruments.

Sixth, the observer should have the behavioral disposition of a scientist. The observer should separate observations from opinions, data from inferences. During the act of observation, the observer should not be interpreting the phenomenon. The sole purpose during observation and measurement is to record the selected dimensional quantity of the event under study. Interpretations and inferences come later. They are offered in such clear distinction with measured values that other observers can make their own interpretations and inferences.

The training of observers is difficult and tedious, but it is the first step in the training of scientists. I have had the experience of training undergraduate and graduate students in measuring stuttering, defined as specific dysfluencies whose measured dimensional quantity is frequency. Instructors who have done this know that teaching students to observe and measure behaviors reliably takes several sessions. Accurate observational behavior should be shaped with contingent feedback in a series of small steps.

Mechanically Assisted Observation and Measurement

Mechanical devices are instruments that extend, sharpen, or otherwise enhance the power of human sensory observation. Objects or events that are too small can be enlarged so that they can be seen, measured, and recorded. Objects or events that are too far away to be seen may be visually brought closer for more detailed observation. Events or processes that do not normally generate sensory consequences also can be tracked and recorded by machines or instruments. Instruments also can magnify processes that are too subtle to be measured by human observers. All of these instruments are valuable tools in scientific observation and measurement.

Mechanical instruments can be simple or complex. A *handheld counter* may be useful in recording the frequency of many communicative behaviors. An *audio recorder* or a *video-recording machine* can give scientists a somewhat permanent record of fleeting and temporary behavioral processes. Such records can be used to observe a phenomenon repeatedly in training observers and obtaining more accurate measures. Various electronic response-monitoring devices, such as operant programming devices, can help record responses mechanically and deliver response consequences contingently and automatically.

A variety of mechanical devices simply give the scientist access to what should be measured. For example, a **fiber-optic scope** can be used to view the laryngeal area directly; it does not measure or record any of the laryngeal behaviors. However, a fiber-optic scope can be a part of a video-recording system. In this case, the video camera and the recording and monitoring system can make it possible to see the generally inaccessible laryngeal mechanism and record different laryngeal behaviors under different conditions of stimulation and experimentation.

Several other instruments help measure various neurobehavioral processes. **Electromyography**, for example, measures electrical activity in muscles. It can be used in basic research designed to analyze muscle activities in speech production. Electromyography also can be used in evaluating the effects of treatments on the muscles of speech with corresponding changes in some perceived aspect of speech. They are useful in biofeedback research with persons with stuttering, cerebral palsy, and voice disorders. A **kymograph** measures specific muscle activity (nonelectrical) involved in breathing.

Various instruments directly track the electrical impulses of muscles and nerves. With suitable recording devices, one can obtain a permanent recording of the electrical activities of different neuromuscular systems. **Electroencephalography** measures the electrical activity of the brain, picked up by surface electrodes placed on the scalp. Different patterns of discharge are indicative of different kinds of neurobehavioral activity, including linguistic and nonlinguistic activities. Equipment to measure the **galvanic skin reflex** or response (GSR) can help measure the resistance the skin normally offers to the electrical conductance. This resistance is reduced under conditions of emotional arousal. Therefore, GSR is typically taken as a physiological measure of emotion.

Cineradiography is one of the techniques used in recent years to measure various parameters of the movement-related variables involved in speech production. The technique helps measure the movements of the muscles of the jaw, tongue, and larynx in the production of speech. Such movements cannot be measured precisely without cineradiography, which films the entire sequence of action with X-rays.

The parameters of airflow involved in speech production can be measured by a **pneumotachograph. Oscilloscopes** make speech visible by displaying various wave patterns associated with differential speech forms on a television-like screen.

A variety of other instruments are available for the researcher in speech-language pathology. Advances in computer technology have provided additional mechanical capabilities in the measurement, monitoring, and modification of speech-language behaviors that cannot otherwise be measured precisely. This section is not intended as an introduction to instrumentation used in normal speech and speech pathology. When a particular research investigation requires the mechanical tracking of an independent variable, the investigator should use the instrument that will permit an accurate and reliable measurement of the variable (Behrman, 2018; Speaks, 2018).

Instruments are devices that help observe and record phenomena. However, in most cases, the human observer should also exercise his or her judgment in the use of instruments and in the evaluation of observations recorded by instruments. An adequate level of technical training in the use of instruments is necessary. The instruments themselves should be reliable so that they are not a source of internal invalidity of research data.

Reliability of Measurement

In research studies, measured values are useful only to the extent that they are adequate for the purposes of a scientific investigation. Measured values of phenomena are evaluated mainly for their reliability.

The concept of reliability can be understood in different ways. In everyday language, a person is said to be reliable if his or her behavior is consistent across situations and time. Therefore, **consistency** with which something occurs or something is measured suggests reliability. **Stability** also means reliability—if a person's behavior is unstable, it is not reliable. In a restricted sense, **predictability** also suggests reliability—you can predict an event if it is known to be reliable. Unpredictable events are also unreliable. **Dependability** is yet another term that implies reliability —dependable phenomena are stable, predictable, and reliable.

Reliability refers to consistency among repeated observations of the same phenomenon. When the measurement of an event is repeated, the measured values should be comparable. If they differ widely, then the measurement is not reliable. When events are measured repeatedly, values are unlikely to be the same. Chance fluctuations in the phenomenon and subtle variations in the measurement procedures can cause different values. Nevertheless, to be considered reliable, the divergence in the values of repeated measures should remain within certain limits. These limits are usually arbitrarily defined.

Reliability should not be confused with the term *accuracy*. While reliability refers to the consistency of repeated observations of the same event, **accuracy** refers to the extent to which the measured values reflect the event being measured. For example, if the measurement of language behaviors in a group of children reflects the "true" performance of those children, one can say that the measurement was accurate. An unreliable measurement may still be accurate in the sense that it reflects the truly fluctuating response of some participants. A reliable measure may not be accurate in that its repeated values are comparable, but the values do not reflect the actual performance of the participants studied.

Repeated observation is the key to establishing reliability. The same event is observed more than once either by the same individual or by different individuals. We have a measure of **intraobserver reliability** when the same person measures the same phenomenon repeatedly and a measure of **interobserver reliability** when the same phenomenon is measured by different observers.

In most cases, intraobserver reliability does not pose serious problems. Generally speaking, an observer, even while not measuring something accurately, can be consistent with himself or herself. The same constant mistakes made in the measurement process can result in acceptable reliability of measures. Therefore, intraobserver reliability is typically not reported in research studies. However, it often is required in theses and dissertations. When the research question itself concerns the reliability of measurement of some specific phenomenon, both kinds of reliability may be important.

Interobserver reliability is a crucial element of scientific measurement. With-

out an acceptable level of interobserver reliability, the results of a study cannot be accepted. Interobserver reliability is one means of convincing the audience that the data are objective. Objectivity in science is realized only by an agreement among different observers regarding the measured values (not opinions) of a given phenomenon. Therefore, interobserver reliability is one of the criteria used in the evaluation of scientific data.

Assessing Interobserver Reliability

There are three general methods of estimating the reliability of research data. The first method, sometimes referred to as the **unit-by-unit agreement ratio**, requires that two observers agree on the individual instances of the response being measured. For example, if two observers measure the frequency of the correct production of /s/ in a speech sample, they both should agree on the particular instance of /s/ production to score agreement. In measuring stuttering, the two observers should agree on specific instances of stuttering and their loci in speech.

Compared to agreement based on total scores of two observers, the unit-by-unit agreement ratio is a much more stringent method of scoring agreement. Research has shown that in the measurement of stuttering, two observers can more easily agree on the total number of instances of stuttering in a sample while disagreeing widely on specific instances of stuttering.

The procedure for estimating the unit-by-unit agreement ratio is as follows. First, the number of units (e.g., responses and events) on which both the observers agreed is determined (*A*). Next, the total number of units on which the observers disagreed is obtained (*D*). Finally, the following formula is applied to obtain the agreement index. It is usually expressed in percentages:

$$\text{Unit-by-unit agreement index} = \frac{A}{A + D} \times 100$$

Suppose the two observers scored 37 responses as correct and 22 responses as incorrect. The agreement index in this case would be 62% (37 + 22 = 59; 37 ÷ 59 × 100 = 62%). This index has been used extensively in clinical research involving various kinds of communicative behaviors.

The unit-by-unit agreement index is most useful when responses are scored on discrete trials or time intervals. In the measurement of stuttering, Young's work (1969a, 1969b, 1975) pointed out the importance of the unit-by-unit analysis. He also developed the following formula to calculate the unit-by-unit agreement index when three or more observers are involved:

$$\text{Agreement index} = [1/(n - 1)] [(T/T_d) - 1]$$

n = number of observers

T = total number of words marked as stuttered

Td = total number of different words marked as stuttered

Young's (1975) formula has been frequently used in assessing interobserver agreement involving more than two observers. It is especially useful in assessing the effects of technical training programs designed to enhance reliable measurement

skills in student clinicians (Gittleman-Foster, 1983).

The second method uses statistical correlations to calculate interobserver agreement. A **correlation**, such as the Pearson product-moment coefficient, indexes the degree of covariation between any two sets of measures. In calculating interobserver reliability with this method, scores or measures of one observer are correlated with those of another observer. In calculating correlation coefficients of reliability, each observer should supply several measures. That is, each observer should observe the responses on different occasions, trials, sessions, and so on. For example, the observers may score the correct productions of /s/ in a total of seven sessions. Each observer supplies a *total* score for each session. This yields seven pairs of scores. These pairs can be correlated to obtain a measure of reliability.

The method of scoring a unit-by-unit agreement ratio can be contrasted with the correlational method of scoring agreement. The correlational method gives only a global notion of reliability; in this method, the two observers may score comparable numbers of correctly produced /s/, but they may have disagreed on many individual instances. In other words, there may have been many /s/ productions scored as wrong by one observer and correct as another observer, but because both scored about the same total number of correct and incorrect responses, the resulting reliability index may be spuriously high. Generally speaking, a high correlation results as long as the total scores of the two observers are not too divergent. Such high correlations can mask the fact that the two observers agreed only on very few individual instances of responses. It is known that the unit-by-unit method of scoring agreement is a more accurate method of estimating reliability than the correlational method.

The third method, infrequently used, is called a *frequency ratio*. In this method, the smaller of the two observations is divided by the larger and the resulting quotient is multiplied by 100 to express the ratio in percentages. Each observer's total number of observations is used in this calculation. Suppose that one observer scored 22 correct productions of /s/ and the other observer scored 16. The frequency ratio for this would be 72% (16 ÷ 22 × 100 = 72%). Because of its global nature of assessment of reliability, the method is less preferable to the unit-by-unit procedure.

If desired, the original unit-by-unit interobserver agreement formula can be used to calculate the intraobserver agreement as well. In this case, the units (response instances) on which the investigator agreed on both the occasions of measurement are first determined. Then the instances on which the two measurements of the investigator disagreed are determined. The same formula is then applied to derive the intraobserver agreement index. The Young formula should not be used to measure intraobserver agreement because it is meant only for multiple observers.

Reliability of Standardized Tests Versus That of Research Data

The reliability of a standardized test should be distinguished from that of research data. Different procedural details are involved in establishing the reliability of standardized tests. These procedures will not be discussed here and the student is referred to other sources (Anastasi & Urbina, 1997; Roseberry-McKibbin, Hegde, & Tellis, 2019).

The reliability of a standardized test may show that when the original sample of participants is tested and retested, the scores are comparable. This is generally taken to mean that any time the test is used to measure other individuals' behaviors, the resulting measures are automatically reliable. This is one of the most questionable assumptions associated with the popular practice of using standardized tests to measure behaviors. From the standpoint of scientific data, reliability is established for the particular measures; it is not inferred from the reliability established elsewhere, by someone else, and in measuring other individuals' behaviors.

The reliability in research is data specific, whereas the reliability of standardized tests is instrument specific. Like a well-calibrated audiometer, the test may be said to be reliable. But the reliability of hearing thresholds reported in a research study may be questionable. That is, even when an audiometer is reliable, certain measured hearing thresholds may not be. Therefore, in scientific research, regardless of the previously demonstrated reliability of measuring instruments, the reliability of specific observations across the experimental conditions should be evaluated and reported.

Summary

- In **observation**, an observer makes a systematic report on some sensory experience. In **measurement**, an observer assigns numbers to properties of events.
- **Idemnotic** measurement has absolute and standard units. **Vaganotic** measurement uses relative standards based on variability in the measured units.

- There are four traditional scales of measurement:
  1. **Nominal:** Events are given names or numbers without mathematical properties.
  2. **Ordinal:** Events categorized relatively and may assign ranks.
  3. **Interval:** The difference between units is constant, but there is no zero.
  4. **Ratio:** All numbers have mathematical properties and there is a zero.
- Communicative behaviors may be measured in terms of their **frequency, duration, interpersonal response time, latency, time sampling, momentary time sampling**, and **verbal interaction sampling**.
- In **client-assisted measurement**, the client records behaviors in natural settings and the clinician scores them.
- **Self-reports** are indirect measures of behaviors supplied by the participants themselves.
- **Subjective biases** of an observer may influence the results of observation. To minimize bias and make appropriate scientific observations, the observer should
  1. be clear about the **topographical aspects** of the event,
  2. know the **dimensional quantity** selected for observation,
  3. be aware of the rough **limits of variability** of the phenomenon,
  4. shave **observed and recorded** along with an experienced (reliable) observer,
  5. have mastered the **technical aspects** of observing and measuring, and
  6. have the **disposition** of a scientist.

- **Mechanical aids** of observation extend, sharpen, or otherwise enhance the power of human sensory observation.
- The **reliability** or consistency of repeated measurement is essential in scientific observation.

References

Altman, J. (1974). Observational study of behavior: Sampling methods. *Behavior, 7*, 227–267.

Anastasi, A., & Urbina, S. (1997). *Psychological testing* (7th ed.). Upper Saddle River, NJ: Prentice-Hall.

Behrman, A. (2018). *Speech and voice science* (3rd ed.). San Diego, CA: Plural.

Bloodstein, O., & Ratner, N. B. (2008). *Handbook on stuttering* (6th ed.). Clifton Park, NY: Thomson Delmar Learning.

Brown, R. (1973). *A first language: The early stages.* Cambridge, MA: Harvard University Press.

Campbell, N. (1952). *What is science?* New York, NY: Dover.

Gittleman-Foster, N. (1983). *Observer reliability in the measurement of dysfluencies with trained and untrained observers* (Unpublished master's thesis). California State University, Fresno, CA.

Johnston, J. M., & Pennypacker, H. S. (2009*). Strategies and tactics of behavioral research* (3rd ed.). London, UK: Routledge.

Roseberry-McKibbin, C., Hegde, M. N., & Tellis, G. (2019). *An advanced review of speech-language pathology* (5th ed.). Austin, TX: Pro-Ed.

Skinner, B. F. (1953). *Science and human behavior.* New York, NY: Free Press.

Speaks, C. E. (2018). *Introduction to sound* (4th ed.). San Diego, CA: Plural.

Stevens, S. S. (1946). On the theory of scales of measurement. *Science, 103*(2684), 677–680.

Stevens, S. S. (1951). Mathematics, measurement, and psychophysics. In S. Stevens (Ed.), *Handbook of experimental psychology* (pp. 1–49). New York, NY: Wiley.

Young, M. A. (1969a). Observer agreement: Cumulative effects of rating many samples. *Journal of Speech and Hearing Research, 12*, 135–143.

Young, M. A. (1969b). Observer agreement: Cumulative effects of repeated ratings of the same samples and knowledge of results. *Journal of Speech and Hearing Research, 12*, 144–155.

Young, M. A. (1975). Observer agreement for marking moments of stuttering. *Journal of Speech and Hearing Research, 18*, 530–540.

Study Guide

1. As described in this chapter, what are the two basic activities of science?

2. Describe the characteristics of scientific observation.

3. Describe the relation between empiricism and observation.

4. How did Campbell define measurement? How did Johnston and Pennypacker define it?

5. What is another name for quantified observations?

6. Describe briefly the idemnotic and vaganotic measurement philosophies. Compare and contrast them.

7. A clinician rates the severity of speech-language disorders on a 3-point scale as follows: mild, moderate, and severe. Is this idemnotic or vaganotic measurement? Why?

8. In his study of behavior, what is the absolute and standard unit of measurement adopted by B. F. Skinner?

9. Are the norms of speech-language behaviors based on absolute or relative measurement? Why?

10. A research clinician assigns a number to each of the 10 aphasic participants in an experiment. What kind of measurement is this (nominal, ordinal, interval, or ratio)?

11. Roger Brown has rank-ordered 14 grammatical morphemes according to the order in which the children he studied mastered them. What kind of measurement is this?

12. A researcher sent out a questionnaire to measure the attitudes of people who stutter toward speaking situations. The questionnaire asked participants to respond to items such as "my wife (or husband) makes telephone calls on my behalf" with such response options as "always, usually, infrequently, rarely, or never." What kind of measurement is this? What are its limitations?

13. In what sense is the interval measurement an improvement over the ordinal measurement?

14. Give an example of a frequency measure in speech, language, or hearing. Describe how you obtain the measure.

15. Taking the example of dysfluencies in conversational speech, show how a given measure of dysfluencies can be converted into a percentage value.

16. What are some of the difficulties faced in obtaining reliable and valid frequency measures of most communicative behaviors?

17. What are the general limitations of the frequency measure?

18. Define a durational measure and give an example. What kinds of behaviors are best measured with this procedure?

19. In routine clinical sessions, how would you measure hypernasality in conversational speech? What kind of scores or values would you derive from your measurement procedure?

20. When would you use the inter-response time measure in clinical research? Give an example.

21. What are latency measures? In one of the *ASHA* journals, find a study that measured the latency of a particular behavior. How was it done?

22. How would you use time sampling in measuring specified language responses produced in conversational speech?

23. How do you score the multiple occurrences of nonattending behavior of a child within blocks of time scheduled to measure that behavior? Are they counted once or as many times as the behavior occurs?

24. Give an example to illustrate the statement that time sampling generates categorical data.

25. Describe the momentary time-sampling technique. Is this procedure suitable for high- or low-frequency behavior? Give an example from a group therapy situation.

26. Describe the potential of verbal interaction sampling procedure in conducting experimental studies of mother-child interaction and interaction between three or more individuals.

27. Specify the need for, and the importance of, client-assisted measurement in clinical research.

28. What are indirect measures? What are some of the frequently used indirect measurement tools?

29. What are the indirect measurement tools that focus on internal states? What are some of the problems associated with them?

30. What are some of the sources of observer bias?

31. What are the requirements of objective scientific observation? Summarize the six conditions that were described in the text.

32. What is the function of mechanical aids to observation? Do they negate the need for human observation and judgment? Justify your answer.

33. Define reliability. Distinguish it from accuracy of measurement.

34. Describe interobserver and intraobserver reliability. Which one is generally more important in research?

35. What is the unit-by-unit agreement index? Why is it better than a global measure of reliability?

36. Two clinicians, measuring the number of correct and incorrect articulations of selected phonemes by a child, have scored the following: 63 correct and 45 incorrect. Calculate the unit-by-unit interobserver agreement index for these scores.

37. Specify Young's formula for calculating the agreement index when three or more observers are involved.

38. Describe how a statistical correlation can be used to assess reliability. What is its most significant limitation? Illustrate your answer with an example.

39. What is the difference between the reliability of standardized tests and that of research data?

PART II

Clinical Research Designs

7

Research Designs: An Introduction

Chapter Outline

- What Are Research Designs?
- The Structure and Logic of Experimental Designs
- Variability: Philosophical Considerations
- Experimental Designs: Means of Controlling Variability
- Validity of Experimental Operations
- Generality (External Validity)
- Factors That Affect Generality
- Concluding Remarks
- Summary
- References
- Study Guide

Whether the investigator will produce reliable and valid data on the researched question will depend mostly on the design used in the study. Before we consider the two major kinds of research designs in the following chapters, we review the definitions, descriptions, structures, and logic of research designs along with why they are needed and what purposes they serve.

What Are Research Designs?

In a general sense, **research design** refers to the methods and procedures of an investigation, an *overall plan of an investigation*. The plan describes the research question or questions, the methods of observation and measurement, the different conditions of observation, procedures of collecting data, and the method of data analysis. Many investigators use the term *research design* in this general sense. This general definition applies to both nonexperimental and experimental studies.

A more technical definition of a research design applies only to experimental research. Technically, an **experimental research design** may be defined as a structure of temporospatial arrangements within which the selected variables are controlled, manipulated, and measured. An alternative technical definition is that research designs are a *scientist's arrangement to reveal a cause-effect relation*. To reveal such a cause-effect relation between events selected for investigation within an experimental design, the researcher controls, manipulates, and measures variables.

The various elements of our technical definition of an experimental research design may be elaborated. A design is basically a *structure* within which certain operations are performed to see what happens. It is an arrangement of conditions for observation, manipulation, and measurement of variables selected for investigation. For example, a design structure may arrange conditions of pretests or baselines, experimental manipulations, withdrawal of those manipulations, and posttests or probes of the dependent variables. Thus, each arrangement within the structure serves a particular purpose while making it possible to observe and measure the dependent variable. This is what is meant by the structure or the arrangement of conditions of a study.

A design structure is *more or less flexible* depending upon the philosophy on which it is based. Some research designs are less flexible; once selected, design changes during the implementation of the study are considered undesirable. Other research designs allow changes in the course of a study if data warrant them. Typically, group designs of research, described in Chapter 8, have more rigid structures than the single-subject designs described in Chapter 9.

The arrangement of a design allows the researcher to *control variables*. A significant part of experimental research is controlling variables. Variables need to be controlled to establish a functional (cause-effect) relation between events. The researcher should demonstrate that the independent variables not under observation do not influence the dependent variable. A good research design makes it possible for the experimenter to rule out the influence of such extraneous variables. This is generally what *controlling the variables* means.

A design also is a *framework* within which to manipulate the independent variable selected for the study. An independent variable is manipulated when it is introduced, withheld, varied in magnitude, withdrawn, or reintroduced to see if corresponding changes occur in the dependent variable. For example, in the initial stage of a study, an independent variable—say, a new form of treatment for a speech disorder—is typically held back while taking pretest or baseline measures of the disorder (dependent variable). In the next condition, the treatment is introduced. There may be a group of participants who do not receive treatment. Alternatively, the same participants who receive treatment in one condition may be observed in a no-treatment condition. Such manipulations can demonstrate the effects of an independent variable on a dependent variable.

Finally, a design is a condition that allows *systematic observation and measurement* of the variables of interest. Both the dependent and independent variables need to be measured. The variables may be measured for their frequency, duration, latency, amplitude, intensity, and so forth. For example, the number of times an independent variable, such as a reinforcer, is delivered in a treatment condition may be measured. The frequency of treatment sessions and the length of each session may be measured as indexes of treatment intensity. In a drug evaluation experiment, the dosage and its frequency are measured throughout the study. Dependent variables such as the production of a plural morpheme or a phoneme may be measured for their frequency. Dysfluencies in speech may be measured for their frequency, duration, or both. Most responses given in relation to a specific stimulus may be measured for latency. Acoustic signals may be measured for their amplitude and intensity.

The Structure and Logic of Experimental Designs

As we noted in Chapter 2, the scientist's task is to find order in, and functional relations between, natural phenomena. However, order and causal relations tend to be concealed rather than revealed in nature. Therefore, science is a *search* for something that is not so readily seen. Nature is a complex flux of multitudinous events that are in a constant state of change, variability, and transformation. Events in nature may be independent, correlated, causally related, or interactive.

Science seeks to determine whether certain events are **independent** or related and, if related, what exactly the type of relation is. Events are **independent** when they are not causally related. Independent events do have their causes, but the observations made have not captured them. Events are **correlated** when they vary together. Two correlated events may increase or decrease at the same time or vary in opposite directions. They may be doing this because of an unobserved third factor that is the cause of both the events; in such cases, because the cause is not observed, one might erroneously think that the correlated events also are causally connected. Two correlated events may indeed be **causally related** in that one is the effect of the other, but a correlation itself does not establish this fact. Finally, there may be **multiple causation** in that several events may produce the same effect, and all of them may be simultaneously present. When multiple variables are simultaneously active, they may interact with each other. **Interactive** variables are those that come together and produce an effect that is larger than the added effect of those events: The whole is greater than the sum of the parts.

A scientist who discovers that certain events are independent, are correlated, are causally related, or have multiple causes that are interactive is said to have found *order* in nature. Order may be discovered in a small part of nature, but no part of nature is insignificant. The process of such a discovery is called an *experiment*, and how that experiment is temporospatially arranged is its *design*.

An experimental design should be arranged in such a way that if there is a relation between the two events, it will be revealed as clearly as methodologically possible because such a relation is anything but clear in the natural flux. In fact, the typically concealing nature can also be misleading, suggesting relations that are not real. Of course, nature does nothing of this sort, but it may certainly seem so for those studying natural phenomena. An experimental design is the scientist's method of uncovering relations against a background of events that vary. The challenge the scientist faces is that a systematic relation lies in the process of what may appear to be chaotic and confusing variability. In some cases, the logic and the structure of a design permit the scientist to observe a relation between events despite their variability and the variability of surrounding and correlated events. In other cases, designs make it possible to reduce the variability and thus see the effects of manipulated independent variables on selected dependent variables. In this sense, variability and how to control it are important aspects of experiments and their designs. Therefore, we should take a closer look at the issue of variability and how it is handled in experimental designs.

Variability: Philosophical Considerations

Variability characterizes practically everything we experience. Physical and chemical events vary constantly, and natural scientists have always tried to analyze the sources of this variability. When biological events began to be studied more closely with the methods of science, the same variability seen in physical and chemical phenomena became apparent. Eventually, it became evident that animal and human behaviors also are highly variable under natural conditions.

The fact of variability, however, is not purely a scientific discovery. Philosophers, poets, and theologians as well as ordinary persons have been aware of variability in physical, biological, and behavioral phenomena. While the statement that natural phenomena, including biological and behavioral phenomena, are variable has never been especially controversial, how to explain it and technically handle it have been controversial. The controversy has been most intense with respect to *human behavioral* variability. The variability of physical events may create methodological problems for the scientist who wishes to control such variability, but it does not seem to raise many philosophical concerns in people who are not natural scientists. Variability may be viewed more as a technical problem the scientists should handle. However, the fact of human behavioral variability has been a matter of philosophical, theological, and scientific controversy.

Historically, there have been two distinct approaches to the question of variability in general and of human behavior in particular (Barlow, Nock, & Hersen,

2009; Johnston & Pennypacker, 2009; Sidman, 1960). One view, the older of the two, holds that variability is intrinsic to the events that vary. The other, more recent view is that behavioral variability is due to external factors that can be controlled.

Intrinsic Variability

The concept of **intrinsic variability** holds that internal or inherent factors, not external, cause variability. Assumptions of intrinsic variability have played an important role in the extrascientific understanding of human behavior. Certain traditions of philosophy and theology have asserted that behavior springs from within the individual and, therefore, is not controlled by external events. Internal causes have taken many shapes, the most famous of which is probably the concept of *free will*. Behaviors vary across time, situations, and individuals. A given individual's behavior also varies across time and situations as well as within them. Traditionally, this is explained by pointing out that people behave differently because of their free will. The popular notion of free will accepts external causes for physical events, but such a notion, extended to human behavior, violates the idea of freedom of action. In essence, the view of intrinsic variability holds that behavioral variability has unique sources and, therefore, is not the same as the variability of physical phenomena.

The concept of intrinsic variability has played a significant role in the purportedly "scientific" study of human behavior as well. In this context, *mind* has been an important internal source of behavior. This theory proposes that people behave differently because each person has his or her own unique mind. Some speculative neurological theorizing has also buttressed this notion, but these theories have replaced *mind* with *brain* as the intrinsic source of action and behavior. Psychoanalysis and other kinds of psychological theories also are full of intrinsic causes of behavior and its variability. Unconscious forces of motivation, such as the id, ego, superego, self-image, and self-confidence, have been considered intrinsic sources of behavior. It has been hypothesized that the acquisition of language has been made possible by innate ideas and innate knowledge of universal grammar. Anything innate is intrinsic to the organism.

The question of variability and the hypothesis of intrinsic causes of behavior may seem separate, but they are closely related. If behavior varies because of intrinsic factors, then that variability is inaccessible to experimental investigation. Most hypothesized intrinsic causes of behavior are indeed inaccessible. The mind, soul, free will, unconscious forces, and innate knowledge that are thought to cause behaviors and their variability cannot be observed, measured, or experimentally manipulated.

The concepts of intrinsic causes and intrinsic variability of behavior converge to produce a significant effect on the experimental strategy. Obviously, variability that is intrinsic to the behaving organisms cannot be controlled. Therefore, experimental attempts at reducing or eliminating variability would be futile. Consequently, the experimenter has no choice but to accept variability as inevitable and uncontrollable. Nonetheless, the scientist should reduce variability to find out cause-effect relations between variables. It is hard to identify the causes of events that vary randomly. Therefore, when the assumption of uncontrollable intrinsic variability is made, researchers should find ways of working around it.

The traditional answer to the problem of behavioral variability in social and behavioral research has been to use large numbers of participants and determine the average performance of the group. Statisticians recommend that the greater the variability, the larger the number of participants needed to show the effect of an independent variable. Obviously, the mean performance of a large number of participants does not fluctuate, simply because it is a single measure. It is the behavior of individuals in the group that fluctuates, but a mean is no reflection of this fact. When this mean is used as the primary measure of the dependent variable in the inferential statistical analysis, it is supposed that somehow the problem of variability has been handled satisfactorily.

The amount of deviation from the mean shown by individuals (standard deviation) does affect the eventual inferential statistical analysis of the data. However, when a large sample is drawn to overcome the problem of variability, one also is sampling a larger amount of variability. The statistical answer to this problem is to require only a greatly reduced magnitude of the effect of the independent variable before the investigator can conclude that the cause manipulated in an experiment had an effect over and beyond chance. For instance, when experimentally evaluating a new treatment program with a large number of clients, the researcher might accept favorable but small effects as significant.

In essence, the traditional research strategies based on the theory of probability and inferential statistics handle variability by ignoring it. Individual vari-

ability is minimized post hoc by the averaging method and by accepting only small effects of the independent variables. Typically, such effects are wrested by complex statistical analyses.

It is a common practice in social and psychological sciences to think of variability (the more frequently used term is *variance*) as *random* fluctuations that the investigator can handle only through averaging group performance data and analyzing them with inferential statistical techniques (Kerlinger & Lee, 2000). It is assumed that the true measured values of a variable are constant and the variability of actual measures are errors (Portney & Watkins, 2008), although it is difficult to imagine variables that are constant (do not vary). In the statistical analysis of group design studies, *error variance* includes unexplained (and uninteresting!) individual differences, fluctuations in the behaviors introduced by random variables, and errors of measurement. The kind of variability introduced by the independent variable is called **systematic variance**. Yet another kind of variance is described as **extraneous variance**, which is the amount of variability introduced by independent variables that are not being manipulated or measured by the investigator. Within this framework, an experimental design is expected to enhance systematic variance, minimize error variance, and control extraneous variance. These recommendations are not controversial except for the way the basic variability of behaviors is treated as errors of measurement.

Extrinsic Variability

The concept of **extrinsic variability** holds that behavioral variability is extrinsic to the behaving organisms (Barlow et al., 2009; Johnston & Pennypacker, 2009; Sidman, 1960). Much behavioral variability is not a property of either the behavior or the behaving organism but is imposed by external factors. Behavior varies because the factors responsible for it vary, and many of those factors are in the environment. Internal, but not intrinsic, variables do affect behavioral variability, but such variables have nothing to do with free will, soul, mind, and such other intrinsic entities. Behavior is a function of the individual's past history and the present environmental events to which he or she is exposed. Therefore, behavioral variability is not unique; it is a part of the scheme of natural events.

Extrinsic variability does not imply that variables within the organism exert no influence on behaviors. Internal physiological states (such as thirst and hunger) and changes over time (*maturation*) have certain effects on behaviors. The impairment of the neurophysiological mechanism as in diseases also is an internal factor that influences behaviors. Similarly, genetic factors set limits on the behavioral variability imposed by natural or experimentally created environmental events. Nonetheless, the assumption of extrinsic variability suggests that most of those sources of variability, when studied appropriately, lead to a better understanding of behaviors than the assumption that variability is a property of behavior itself.

It is clear that the two views of intrinsic and extrinsic variability have profound but contradictory philosophic implications. From the standpoint of experimental methodology, the ultimate truth or falsity of the two assumptions is not of immediate concern. Whether behavioral variability is intrinsic or extrinsic is an empirical question that will require

lengthy experimental research. However, whether systematic attempts to produce that answer will be made at all depends upon the assumption of extrinsic, not intrinsic, variability. This is not one of those situations in which contradictory views are both testable and either view has the same chance of producing a valid answer.

If all scientists took the position that behavioral variability is intrinsic, then there would be no reason to design experiments in which such variability is experimentally analyzed, for the assumption is inconsistent with such experimentation. The assumption of intrinsic variability precludes experimental analysis of the sources of behavioral variability. After having placed (intrinsic) variability outside the scope of experimental analysis, researchers will continue to use statistical means of handling it.

A position most valid from an empirical standpoint is to treat all variability as extrinsic at least tentatively, so that experimental analysis of variability may be attempted. Sustained experimental analysis will reduce the territory held by variability that is supposed to be intrinsic. Every time a source of behavioral variability is identified, a chance to control it presents itself. As Sidman (1960) pointed out, "Each time such control is achieved, intrinsic variability loses another prop" (p. 143).

Such an approach to variability has a chance of showing that it is difficult to control some sources of variability. This difficulty may be due to the limitations of experimental techniques. Improvements in those techniques may help control that variability. Or, the approach may show the limits beyond which individual variability cannot be controlled. In either case, only the assumption of extrinsic variability can lead us in the direction of self-corrective data. As such, the assumption of extrinsic variability has a chance of disproving itself because the assumption keeps pushing experimental manipulations that, under some circumstances, produce negative evidence. On the other hand, the assumption of intrinsic variability may not correct itself because once assumed, it does not encourage experimentation on controlling behavioral variability.

Experimental Designs: Means of Controlling Variability

The two philosophical positions on variability often are associated with two kinds of experimental designs: between-groups design and single-subject design. Generally, the group design approach assumes that behavioral variability is intrinsic and that this variability can only be handled statistically. The single-subject designs are more often based on the assumption of extrinsic variability. But it should be noted that both the approaches to designing experiments recognize the need to control variability; they differ only in terms of what kinds of variability should be controlled and in what manner.

Group designs, even with the assumption of intrinsic variability, include mechanisms to control and isolate the variability produced by independent variables. This approach recognizes the need to control variability produced by factors not under observation (extraneous variability). There is no significant conceptual difference between the group and the single-subject designs on these issues, although there are some methodological differences that will be addressed in later chapters. The difference between the two approaches lies mostly in how the background variability created by differences in the individual response rates is handled and also in how the variability produced by the experimental variable is analyzed.

The effects of all experiments are analyzed against a certain amount of background variability. Suppose, for example, that an investigator wishes to evaluate the effect of a new stuttering treatment program. If the basic two-group design is selected, the investigator forms an experimental and a control group of people who stutter using the random procedure. After taking pretest measures of stuttering in both groups, the investigator treats the participants only in the experimental group. At the completion of the treatment program, the researcher gives a posttest to both the groups. To find out if the treatment was effective, he or she statistically analyzes the pre- and posttest measures of the two groups.

The control group helps rule out the influence of extraneous independent variables. If the mean performance of the control group did not change significantly from the pretest to the posttest, but the mean performance of the experimental group did change, the researcher may conclude that extraneous variables were controlled. However, this evaluation of the effect of the treatment variable is made, of necessity, against the background of random (hence, uncontrolled) variability. In a group design, the larger the individual differences within the groups, the greater the background variability. As noted before, much of this variability is handled statistically with the help of the arithmetic mean.

The effect of the treatment also is handled statistically. The difference in the performance of the two groups is evaluated on the basis of the mean, which ignores individual differences in response to treatment. Thus, in a group design, both the background and the systematic variability are evaluated nonexperimentally.

On the other hand, the investigator who selects a single-subject design to evaluate the same stuttering treatment program will not try to draw a random sample of participants. Available people who stutter will be used in the study, but each participant will be described in detail. The stuttering behaviors will be baserated until some criterion of stability is reached. The baseline helps reduce the intrasubject variability before the introduction of treatment. The treatment is then introduced and continued until it produces an effect. Subsequently, the treatment may be withdrawn to return the rate of stuttering to its baseline. Finally, the treatment may be reapplied to replicate the treatment effects. In this procedure, no effort is made to average individual performances to show some kind of stability before, during, or after treatment. Variability is handled on an individual basis. As long as the behavior continues to be variable, baselines are extended. It is generally found that when conditions are controlled, sooner or later the behavior stabilizes. Obviously, this approach to pretreatment variability is very different from that found in group designs in which a single pretest measure (arithmetic mean) represents stability.

The treatment effect within a single-subject design is not evaluated by statistical means. The assumption is that when the effects are large enough to be evaluated by visual inspection, there is no need for statistical analysis, which typically tries to identify relatively small effects against a background of uncontrolled variability. Such large effects of the treatment variable neutralize the issue of intersubject variability found in group designs.

Within the single-subject approach, when individual behaviors vary greatly, either during baselines or during treatment, the experimenter may then proceed to find out why (Sidman, 1960). In other words, the variability itself becomes an object of experimental inquiry. Investigators may be willing to postpone their study of the original problem and begin the new task of tracking the intrasubject variability. It may be found, for example, that the variability found in the frequency of stuttering exhibited by a client during baseline sessions is due to the client's participation in rather traumatic staff meetings held every other day. Many clients' variable response rates in treatment sessions may be a reaction to various uncontrolled factors that the clinicians dump under "a good day" and "a bad day."

Regardless of philosophical and methodological differences on the issue of variability, it is clear that experimental designs should address them; after all, a design is a way of controlling some kind of variability while creating another kind of variability. It should control the variability found within and across individuals, and it should produce a large enough variability that can be attributed to the effect of the independent variable. It should be noted that a change in the behavior when treatment is introduced also is variability, but it is the type of variability the experimenter hopes to see and takes every step to create.

Validity of Experimental Operations

By allowing the researcher to control and create variability, experimental designs help identify functional relations between variables. The task of an experimental design is to isolate a cause-effect relation between events. Therefore, we should now consider issues relative to this task.

In human clinical and nonclinical research, the demonstration of a cause-effect relation is made with the help of selected individuals, whether in a few individuals as in a single-subject design or in groups of participants as in a group design. This raises two closely related questions. The first question is whether, in the individuals who served as participants in a given experiment, the cause-effect relation was demonstrated convincingly. This is the question of *internal validity.* The second question is whether the demonstrated cause-effect relations can be generalized to individuals who have not participated in the experiment. This is the question of *external validity* or *generality* of findings.

The validity of experimental operations refers to the confidence with which other scientists can accept the experimenter's claim of a cause-effect relation. In nontechnical terms, the results of an experiment are valid when the observed cause of an event is not mistaken. When the results are not valid, conclusions drawn from the study may not apply to the individuals who served in the experiment or to those who did not. In other words, there is neither internal nor external validity.

The validity of *experimental operations* should be distinguished from the validity of *measured values* of the dependent variables. The validity **of measured values** is the degree to which the measurement of the dependent variable is indeed the best possible reflection of the true value of that variable. The **validity of experimental operations**, on the other hand, is the degree to which the overall experimental arrangements, manipulations, and control procedures lead to valid conclusions. As such, the validity of measured values has a narrower scope than

the validity of experimental operations. In a sense, the validity of measures of dependent variables is a part of the validity of experimental operations.

Internal Validity

To achieve internal validity, the investigator should make sure that during the experimental operations, only the independent variable selected for the study was present and that any of the other potential independent variables were not. When the selected independent variable produced acceptable changes in the dependent variable in the absence of other potential variables that could have produced the same results, the data are said to have internal validity. Therefore, **internal validity** is the degree to which the data reflect a true cause-effect relation. Thus, the major concern is to make sure that the variables other than the one selected for study were appropriately controlled for (ruled out) in the design.

In some individual participants, factors that affect the dependent variable may require special analysis. Historically, though, several common factors that affect internal validity across experiments have been recognized (Campbell & Stanley, 1966; Shadish, Cook, & Campbell, 2002). These factors also are described as *threats* to internal validity or *sources* of internal *invalidity.*

Most of the sources of internal invalidity can be found in poor research designs. Keeping in perspective a prototype of a poor design in which those factors can easily come to play will help clarify the sources of internal invalidity. Most sources of internal invalidity come to play in the traditional case studies used frequently in clinical research. For example, a clinician may measure (pretest) language disorder (the dependent variable) in a group of children and then subject them to a new treatment program whose effect is being evaluated. After several months of treatment, the children's language behaviors may be evaluated again. This posttest may show that the children's language behaviors have improved significantly. The investigator may then conclude that the new treatment program was responsible for the changes observed in the dependent variable. However, as discussed in the next section, there are several factors that can affect internal validity in a study such as this.

History

History is the participants' life events that may be totally or partially responsible for the changes recorded in the dependent variable after the introduction of the independent variable. A design that does not rule out the influence of those events cannot demonstrate that the treatment variable had an effect on the dependent variable. In other words, history is a source of internal invalidity in such a design.

In our prototypic example of language treatment research, it is possible that the treatment was ineffective or only had a negligible effect. A variety of extraneous factors not monitored by the research clinician may have been totally or partially responsible for the results. For example, the classroom teacher *may have started a language-stimulation program for* the *same children* receiving treatment from the clinician, and this program may have been responsible for the improvement in children's language. Or the parents, after having discussed their children's language problem with the clinician, may have begun to talk more to their children

or read more stories to them at bedtime. Such changes in the parents' behavior may have caused improvement in the children's language. Because the case study method did not rule out such extraneous variables, the clinician cannot conclude that there was a functional (cause-effect) relation between the treatment variable and the changes in the language of the children.

It should be noted that the term *history,* though used to describe the effects of extraneous variables, may not be the most appropriate term. It does not refer to the events that have taken place in the past but to events that are contemporaneous with the experimental manipulations.

In the group design strategy, showing that those who do not receive treatment do not show significant changes in the dependent variable helps control the influence of history. When a control group—also is exposed to factors of history—does not show changes, then history is ruled out as a potential variable responsible for changes observed in the experimental group. In the single-subject strategy, after exposing participants to treatment, the experimenter may withdraw treatment and reintroduce it later. When the behavior changed under treatment, returned to the baseline when treatment was withdrawn, and changed again when treatment was reintroduced, the investigator may conclude that the factors of history were not responsible for the positive changes observed in the treatment sessions.

Maturation

When the course of an experiment is long, changes taking place within the participants themselves may produce some effect on the dependent variable. In some cases, such changes may account for the entire effect supposedly produced by the independent variable manipulated by the experimenter.

Maturation refers to biological and other kinds of unidentified changes that take place in participants simply as a result of the passage of time. To what extent mere passage of time can produce effects on behaviors is not always clear, however. Obviously, maturation is indexed by the age of the participants. As noted in Chapter 4 on normative research, age by itself may not be a cause of anything. Age may indirectly refer to changes that take place within the organism. Also, maturation and history may not be as distinct as they are generally thought to be. Possibly, events in the life of the participants while they are supposed to be maturing (getting older) may be responsible for the changes that are attributed to maturation.

In our prototypic example of research, during the time required to complete the experimental language treatment, maturational changes can be expected to have taken place. Those changes may have been responsible for the improved language in the children.

In both the single-subject and group design strategies, the problem of maturation is handled in the same way as the problem of history. Either a control group or a no-treatment condition that follows treatment can rule out the influence of maturation. It can be expected that the members of the control group who do not change over time experience the same amount of maturation as the members of the experimental group. Similarly, participants who change once when the treatment is introduced but change again when it is withdrawn indicate that maturation is not responsible for the changes in the dependent variable. The logic is that when maturation is given a chance

and fails to show its effects, the only effect seen is that of the independent variable manipulated by the experimenter.

Testing

As a source of internal invalidity, **testing** refers to the changes that take place in a dependent variable because it has been measured more than once. Pre- and posttests or repeated baselines may be sufficient to change the dependent variable. In such cases, the experimenter's conclusion that the treatment variable of the study was responsible for the changes observed during the experiment or recorded on a posttest may be erroneous.

Some behaviors are known to change somewhat when repeatedly tested or measured. Measures of behaviors that change as a function of repeated testing or measurement are known as **reactive measures**. Scores obtained through questionnaires designed to measure attitudes, opinions, feeling states, personal adjustment, and personality are known to be notoriously reactive. People answering a questionnaire on their attitudes toward racial minorities, for example, may show significant changes when retested even though nothing has been done to change such attitudes.

Because most experiments involve repeated measurement of the dependent variable, one should make sure that testing does not affect the behavior. One way of handling the problem of testing is not to use reactive measures at all. Opinions, attitudes, and personality are weak and inferential measures of behaviors. Whenever possible, it is better to measure behaviors directly. For example, one may either ask a person to fill out a questionnaire on moviegoing behavior or measure the frequency with which that person goes to the movies. Obviously, a score on the latter measure is difficult to obtain, but the more easily accomplished score on the questionnaire may be useless. Also, the actual behavioral measure is less reactive than the questionnaire measure. An employer who has never hired a member of a minority group is not likely to suddenly hire one simply because his or her attitudes showed reactive changes on an attitude scale.

Reactive measures are not as bothersome in single-subject designs as in group designs. Single-subject designs do involve repeated measures—in fact, more so than the group designs. For the most part, single-subject designs avoid the use of indirect and reactive measures of behaviors. Group designs have a method of handling testing effects by adding an additional group that does not receive pretests while receiving only the posttest. This design, known as the Solomon four-group design, is described in Chapter 8.

Instrumentation

Problems with measuring instruments that negatively affect internal validity are grouped under the term **instrumentation**. This factor includes not only mechanical instruments that might deteriorate or improve between pretests and posttests but also the changes that may take place in human beings who serve as judges, raters, and observers. In much social and psychological research, persons with varying degrees of expertise observe, score, and measure behaviors. Of course, human observation and measurement is basic to all sciences, but the experimenters' reliance on others to make measurements for them is more extensive in social and psychological research. Observes help collect data in communication disorders as well.

An instrument that was in normal working condition at the beginning of the study may develop problems by the time the posttest is made. Or an instrument that already had some problems from the beginning may have been corrected just before the posttest. In cases such as these, the difference between the pretest and posttest scores would not reflect the actual effects of the experimental manipulations. Suppose that in a study of the effects of some medical or surgical intervention procedure designed to improve a certain type of hearing loss, the audiologist used a defective audiometer to establish the initial hearing thresholds of the participants. Possibly, because of the mechanical defect, all participants' thresholds were 10 dB higher than their actual level of hearing. Also suppose that as a matter of routine maintenance procedures, the audiometer was serviced and calibrated just before the posttests. Unaware of the history of the instrument, the audiologist may measure the hearing in the participants after the completion of the medical or surgical treatment. Thresholds on this posttest are likely to show at least a 10-dB improvement over the pretest, but this finding is entirely invalid. In the same study, an audiometer that was working normally but had deteriorated by the posttest would have led to an opposite finding, also equally invalid.

Judges who observe and score behaviors may induce invalidity of findings in several ways. When a group of speech pathologists is used to rate the severity of stuttering before and after some form of experimental treatment, the observers in the group may change their idea as to what constitutes different levels of severity between the pre- and posttests. The criteria used by individual judges may become more or less stringent. The observers may get bored during the post-test. The judges also can become more experienced in measuring stuttering, so they may now score more stutterings than they did during the pretest observations.

Most clinical supervisors may have seen beginning clinicians who scored more and more stuttering behaviors as therapy progressed during the first few weeks. At one time, a very disconcerted student clinician came to one of the author's office and showed this kind of data. This first-time clinician had her worst fears confirmed: Her therapy was making the client stutter more, although the client's fluency seemed to have improved. Her measurement procedures were then analyzed, and it was found that she had gradually become defter at observing and measuring silent pauses, interjections, and more subtle forms of dysfluencies that she had not initially noticed.

In any type of research, the investigator should make sure that the selected instruments are carefully calibrated and found to be in good working condition. Frequently checking the integrity of mechanical devices throughout the course of an investigation is the most effective method of avoiding validity problems due to mechanical defects. In the case of human observers, adequate training in observation, scoring, and rating before the experiment is started will help avoid validity problems due to errors or changes in judgment. Both inter- and intrajudge reliability should be ensured. See Chapter 6 for a discussion of observer training and reliability.

Statistical Regression

In clinical research, individuals who happen to seek clinical services are recruited for research studies. It is known, however, that many patients and clients seek clinical services at a time when their problem hits a new peak. This is more likely to happen with those disorders that vary across time and situations and hence are somewhat cyclic. Stuttering, for example, can be a cyclic speech disorder. Many chronic medical conditions, too, may vary across time and on occasion be much worse than the usual. Such diseases and disorders may not stay at their worst level for long, however. They soon will return to their less severe and more common level. Such a return from an extreme point to an average level is known as **statistical regression** or **regression to the mean**.

Regression can pose serious problems for internal validity if the clinical condition is at its worst at the beginning of the experiment but returns to its average level as the experiment progresses. Such an improvement in the clinical condition can give the impression that the treatment was effective. Obviously, such an erroneous conclusion would not have internal validity.

Statistical regression does not mean that every client will improve without treatment. It is simply a change in the extreme scores of a group of participants; when such changes are confounded with the treatment effects, a problem of internal invalidity exists.

Theoretically, our prototypical example of language treatment research does not rule out statistical regression. Whether children with language disorders show statistical regression is a different question, however. The problem of regression to the mean is controlled for in the group design by random selection and assignment of participants to an experimental group and a control group. The amount of regression would then be the same in the two groups. Unfortunately, the random procedure is impractical where it is needed the most. In clinical research, finding a population of clients with a given disorder from which a sample can be randomly drawn is not practical.

In single-subject designs, regression is handled by establishing a stable baseline before starting an experimental treatment. For instance, if the frequency of stuttering shows an improving trend that may be due to regression, treatment would not be started until stuttering stabilized. Also, throughout the experiment, the frequency of stuttering would be measured. Furthermore, treatment typically follows a period of no treatment or treatment applied to some competing behavior. These steps help rule out regression to the mean.

Subject Selection Biases

Subjective factors that influence the selection of participants in a study, and thus introduce problems of invalidity, are grouped under **subject selection biases**. Whenever two groups of participants are used in experimental studies, it is possible that the groups were different to begin with. Therefore, the differences found on the posttest may not be due to the treatment but to the initial differences in participants.

The typical answer to the problem of subject selection biases is to use randomly selected and assigned groups or groups that have carefully matched participants. As already noted, random sampling of clinical participants is not always practical. In matching, one should find pairs of participants who are similar on important variables, but clinically, this procedure is about as impractical as the random procedure.

In single-subject designs, participant selection bias is not a major problem because the conclusions are not based upon group comparisons. Whether or not the treatment is effective in individual clients whose characteristics are well described is the question for analysis. Therefore, there is no need to make sure that the participants are similar, even when several participants are used in a single-subject design.

Attrition

Also known as *subject mortality,* **attrition** is the problem of losing participants in the course of an experiment, which in turn has an effect on the final results as interpreted by the investigator. Attrition of participants is not as uncommon as most investigators wish it to be. Graduate students, who generally secure participants for their theses and dissertations with great difficulty, dread this problem the most. Current ethical guidelines appropriately guarantee the participant's right to withdraw from research with no consequences (see Chapter 17), and some participants exercise this right freely and in the middle of a study.

In group designs, attrition can be a serious source of internal invalidity. Analysis of results based on group averages can be affected markedly by differential attrition of participants. If, in our prototypical study on language treatment, children with more severe language disorders were to drop out during the course of treatment, the mean of the posttest of language behaviors would be higher (better) than that of the pretest. This might then suggest a feigned treatment effect leading to invalid conclusions. When two groups are used, *differential* participant dropout in the experimental and control groups can create a problem of greater magnitude. More severely affected participants may drop out from the experimental group, whereas less severely affected participants may drop out of the control group. This would create major differences in the pre- and posttests of the two groups even when the treatment is totally ineffective.

Attrition is a problem only when statistical analysis based on group means is used. In the analysis of results, an investigator may take into consideration the participant attrition and also describe individual data. However, these may not be practical when the groups are large. Unfortunately, even when it is possible, such individual-specific discriminated analysis is not a typical part of the *practice* of group design strategy.

In single-subject designs, attrition is not a factor affecting internal validity. Whenever possible, new participants replace those who drop out. Because the data analysis is specific to individuals, attrition and replacement of participants in single-subject designs do not affect the final conclusions. However, the single-subject researcher may face another problem relative to attrition: The study simply may have to be postponed to a later date when additional participants become available. In the case of participant attrition, the group design strategist runs the risk of drawing invalid conclusions, whereas the single-subject strategist runs the risk of not having a study at all.

Diffusion of Treatment

Diffusion of treatment is persistence of treatment effects even when the treatment is withdrawn to show a reduction in the effects (Kazdin, 2010). In most single-subject designs, the treatment is introduced once and *then withdrawn to show* corresponding changes in the behaviors.

However, when the treatment is withdrawn, target behaviors may sometimes continue because they have come under the influence of other independent variables or even the same independent variables (treatment) administered by other persons. Parents or spouses who have observed the investigator prompt and reinforce naming responses of a person with aphasia may begin to do the same at home. The family members may do this at a time when the investigator is trying to reduce the naming to its original baseline. Consequently, the person with aphasia may sustain the naming behaviors. The investigator then cannot conclude that the treatment was effective because the effects continued when the treatment was withdrawn, and the skill was expected to decline.

Some single-subject designs involve two or more treatments whose relative (not interactive) effects are evaluated. Such designs also may have the problem of diffusion of treatment affecting internal validity. The two or more treatment conditions may not be clearly discriminated. In such cases, the effect of one treatment may influence the effect of another treatment, but such influences may remain obscured.

Because treatment withdrawal is not a typical control strategy in group designs, diffusion of treatment is not a problem in them. The participants who receive treatment and those who do not are in different groups. Therefore, the question of treatment diffusion from one condition or treatment to the other does not arise.

In summary, history, maturation, testing, instrumentation, statistical regression, participant selection biases, mortality, and diffusion of treatment are the eight sources of internal invalidity. These sources must be minimized or eliminated in a controlled experimental study. Critical consumers of research should evaluate each published treatment study for these factors that may invalidate or limit the usefulness of conclusions. It should be noted, though, that designs are not perfect and that they control for these sources with varying degrees of efficiency. Therefore, most studies are likely to have certain control problems and to varying extents, but these problems should not be serious enough to invalidate the study. A study appearing to have a single potential source of internal invalidity that may or may not have operated is judged differently from the one with multiple sources, each posing a definite and serious threat to internal validity.

Generality (External Validity)

Unlike internal validity, generality (external validity) is not always a matter of the experimental design itself. **Generality** is the extent to which the investigator can extend or generalize the results of a study to other situations, participants, experimenters, and so forth. One may have internal validity but may not be sure of generality. The investigator may be confident that external variables have been ruled out and that the demonstrated relation between the dependent variable and the independent variable is valid within the confines of the study. However, the extent to which the results can be generalized, which is of course the question of external validity, may be unclear. In a treatment research study, the investigator may be confident that treatment indeed produced the positive results, but whether other clinicians, in other settings, with other clients would realize the same results may remain doubtful.

In many books and articles, discussions of external validity, generality, or both can be confusing. Three sources have contributed to an elaboration and potential confusion of these concepts. One of the traditional sources of discussion on external validity is the group design strategy, with its emphasis on statistical inference. The second source of information is the single-subject design strategy. The third source is applied behavioral research, with its explicit clinical concerns. As a result of these converging approaches and sources, various terms and concepts are used in discussing external validity. An attempt is made here to provide an integrated view of this important concept.

Types and Limitations of Generality

The major concern of the group design approach to generality has been the extent to which the results of a study based on a sample of participants can be extended to the population from which the sample was drawn. Within the group design strategy, random sampling and assignment of participants and inferential statistical techniques help achieve population generality.

The single-subject design strategy has faced the problem of external validity from a different standpoint. Because the strategy does not draw a sample of participants from a population, extending the results of a particular study to a population is not of immediate concern. However, the strategy has faced a different kind of problem: extending the results from a single participant or a few participants to other similar individuals. When the single-subject strategy began to be used more frequently in applied research, additional concerns emerged. For example, if a behavioral technique is demonstrated to be effective in the treatment of some problem behavior, can the technique be effective with other problem behaviors? Will the technique be equally effective in other clinical or professional settings? Answers to such clinical questions have helped identify additional sources of generality.

In this chapter and elsewhere in the book, the terms *generality* and *external validity* will mean the same. In some respects, the concept of generality is more transparent than external validity and can include various forms of clinical generalities. Therefore, the term *generality* is preferred. What follows is a description of two major types of generality: statistical (inferential) and clinical. The latter includes several subtypes of generality. *Clinical validity*, a closely related concept, also will be discussed.

Statistical (Inferential) Generality

Inferential generality is the degree to which the conclusions of a group design study with a randomly drawn sample of participants from a population may be extended to others in the same population. Randomized clinical trials claim inferential generality. A **population** is any defined, relatively large group of persons in research studies. For example, all citizens of voting age in a country, all individuals in a state or region who stutter, all children in the seventh grade in a particular school district, and all children with unrepaired cleft living in a particular city illustrate research populations. A **sample** is a smaller number of participants who

represent a specific population. The sample should be randomly selected from the population and then randomly divided into two or more groups that participate in an experiment. Typically, one group receives treatment and one other does not. It is assumed that a random sample of a population is as heterogeneous as the population, and therefore, it represents the population. Studying a sample is good enough to extend conclusions to a population, which is nearly impossible to study. In clinical research, when it is shown that treatment and positive changes in a disorder are causally related in a representative sample of participants, it may be concluded that the same treatment will produce similar positive changes in the entire population with that disorder. Such a conclusion is the essence of inferential generality. This concept of inferential generality is illustrated in Figure 7–1.

Inferential generality is so called because it is based on **inferential statistical techniques** that help *infer* the values of the dependent variables in the population. *Analysis of variance* is a commonly used inferential statistic. Investigators who use random samples from the population may, with the help of inferential statistics, infer that all those in the population who might receive the same treatment might react similarly to those in the study. Because the population is not tested, generality is a matter of making a valid inference as supported by the theory and technique of statistics. See Chapter 10 for an overview of statistical techniques used in analyzing treatment research data.

Two major problems affect inferential generality: lack of random selection of participants and potential interaction between participant characteristics and treatment that is masked in group aver-

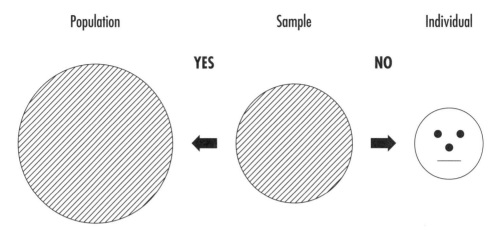

Figure 7–1. The direction of inferential generality—from a random sample to the population. Inferential generality does not permit generalization from the sample to an individual.

ages. Random sampling is very difficult to accomplish, especially in the experimental evaluation of treatment procedures. Populations of children with speech sound disorders or language disorders, or persons with aphasia or apraxia of speech, typically are not available for the researcher. Moreover, those who are initially selected randomly may not agree to participate because under the current research guidelines, all participants are self-selected (see Chapters 4 and 16 for details on *self-selection*). Also, those who initially agree to participate may not continue their participation until the end of the study. Consequently, there is no assurance that the results of a group design study can be generalized to the population. Therefore, a serious threat to inferential generality is the lack of random sampling that is so typical of group clinical research.

A randomly drawn sample should also be randomly assigned to the experimental and control groups to make sure that the two groups are equal. This, as we noted earlier, is a matter of *internal validity*. The critical factor for inferential generality is the original random sampling of the participants from the population.

The other factor that affects inferential generality, the interaction between participant characteristics and treatment, is related to the method of data analysis. Most group designs average the performance of individual participants under treatment to make inferential statistical analyses. Therefore, it is difficult to determine whether all participants benefited to the same extent from the treatment or whether individuals with certain characteristics benefited more or less than those with other characteristics. For example, an experimental study may have demonstrated that a certain treatment is effective, on the average, with a sample of children with speech sound disorders. However, it is possible that only those children with mild disorders or high levels of intelligence benefited from the treatment, whereas those with other characteristics may not have experienced any improvement. Such interactions between participant characteristics and treatment effects usually are masked in the group performance analyses. Therefore, whether there was an interaction and, if so, its type remain unknown.

The problem of unknown but possible differential response to treatment by different participants in an experimental group can pose a significant problem for the clinician who wishes to apply the treatment to her own individual clients with specific characteristics. The clinician can conclude only that, *on the average,* particular sets of clients seem to improve under treatment. It would not be possible to determine whether given individual clients would improve under that treatment. This problem is inherent in most group designs because the direction of inferential generality is from the sample to the population and not from the sample to the individual. Typically, clinicians try to generalize from small groups of clients or individuals to other small groups or individuals. In essence, inferential generality does not serve a clinical science very well.

Clinical Generality

External validity or generality is too general a term that does not do justice to all forms of generality clinicians look for in treatment research. Therefore, clinical researchers have delineated several specific forms of generality that apply most forcefully to treatment research. These forms of generality have lacked a common term; therefore, the term *clinical generality* is used here to include various forms of generality that treatment researchers typically try to establish. In Chapter 4, **clinical generality** was defined as the extent to

which the conclusions of a study may be generalized to other clinical parameters.

Logical Generality

Because of a lack of random samples, the results of single-subject designs cannot be extended to the population. In other words, the results of particular single-subject design studies do not have inferential generality. However, single-subject designs do not seek inferential generality. Instead, they seek what is known as logical generality (Barlow et al., 2009).

Logical generality is the extension of the results of a study to individuals who are *similar* to the participants of that study. Because single-subject designs use only a few individuals at a time, the investigator usually gives a thorough description of each of the participants. It should then be possible to tentatively conclude that persons who are similar to those who have served in the study may react to the experimental treatment in the same way as the participants. Logical generality may also be described as generality based on *individual profiles*. A clinician may select an experimentally evaluated treatment for her client if at least one participant's profile in the study matches that of the client. The concept of logical generality is illustrated in Figure 7–2, which also contrasts it with inferential generality.

Logical generality proceeds from a set of study participants to a single individual or a few individuals. It is generality from either a homogeneous or a heterogeneous set of experimental participants to a similar set of individuals who have not been tested yet. For example, an investigator experimentally evaluates a new treatment on five individuals with dysarthria and describes in detail the specific characteristics of each participant (partici-

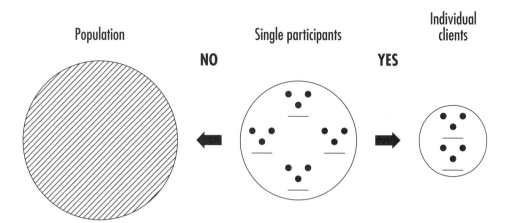

Figure 7–2. The direction of logical generality—from single participants to similar individual clients. Logical generality does not permit generalization from the participants to the population.

pant profiles). Practically, the investigator conducts five separate experiments, each involving a single participant. However, the conditions of the experiment across the participants are the same: baseline, treatment, withdrawal of treatment, and reinstatement of treatment. In the study report, each client's dysarthria and personal and behavioral characteristics (profiles) are provided in full. Their responses under the conditions of the study are presented and analyzed separately. Suppose that in the study, a participant with a college education improved much better than another with only a high school education, then the clinician can expect to obtain much better improvement if she applied the treatment to college-educated persons with dysarthria. If a participant with a certain profile did not benefit under the experimental treatment, then the clinician would not select that treatment for a client who exhibits a similar profile. Different single or multiple personal characteristics may lead to different outcomes. Note that in this type of

generality, any conclusion regarding how the population of people with dysarthria would react to the same treatment would be inappropriate.

Logical generality can eventually achieve the presumed power of inferential generality through various kinds of replications. If different experiments are performed by different clinicians in a variety of settings involving varied participants with the same disorder, the treatment in question will have been tested across different conditions of generality.

Generality Across Individuals. The extent to which the result of a study may be extended to other persons is **the generality across individuals**, and in clinical research, it is **generality across clients**. This type of generality is an important factor in all human research, especially in clinical research. Logical generality is a restricted form of generality. At least in the initial stages of a treatment evaluation, success in profile matching can be limited. The clinician might be serving many clients whose profiles do not match those of participants in single-subject experiments. Eventually, what the clinician should look for is generality across participants so that there is no compelling need to precisely match the client and the research participant profiles.

Generality across clients addresses several important questions. If a language treatment is known to be effective with 4-year-old children with language disorders, will the treatment be equally effective in the treatment of 10-year-old children with similar language problems? Will the treatment be effective with children who have other disabilities, such as intellectual disabilities? The treatment may or may not be effective with older or younger children or with those who have other disabilities in addition to language impairment. The results of a treatment study may not be generalized to clients who differ from participants in an experiment. It is precisely in these circumstances that logical generality will not help. Logical generality will support the use of a technique when the participant and a client profiles match; it stays neutral when profiles do not match. However, if replicated research with the same treatment procedure involving participants of diverse characteristics is successful, then generality across different kinds of clients may be achieved without a concern for profile matching.

Generality Across Ethnocultural Groups. In all ethnoculturally diverse societies, whether treatment efficacy data have generality across different ethnocultural groups is an important question. In fact, the concern extends to all kinds of human research, both basic and applied. In treatment research in communication disorders, this is a pressing concern.

Historically, different ethnic groups have not been balanced in most assessment or treatment research. In most countries, the United States included, treatment efficacy data have largely been collected on the ethnic majority (Battle, 2012; Payne, 2014). As the U.S. population has grown more diverse in its ethnocultural composition, the new concern has a new urgency as well. What if the assessment and treatment techniques found to be valid and effective with the majority group just do not work with people of different ethnocultural backgrounds? Obviously, this is an important question that practitioners ask before selecting procedures that suit their diverse clients.

To achieve ethnocultural generality, treatment researchers need to recruit representative samples from different ethnocultural groups. From a practical standpoint, though, such balancing is not always possible because in some settings, one or a few ethnocultural groups may be all that are available for sampling. Therefore, when studies are published on a given treatment with inadequate balancing of participants from different ethnocultural groups, the practitioner will have to be cautious in extending the conclusions to members of unrepresented ethnocultural groups. Meanwhile, other treatment researchers who do have access to certain ethnocultural groups should replicate the findings with members from those groups. Systematic replication, therefore, seems to be the best strategy to establish ethnocultural generality.

Although the issue of ethnocultural generality of treatment data deserves special attention, the other forms of generality may subsume this issue. For example, generality across participants may include generality across ethnocultural groups. Lack of generality across participants may be viewed as due to differing ethnocultural background of participants and further analysis may either support or reject this possibility. Even so, in the past, the issue of ethnocultural generality of treatment evidence has not been addressed fully or explicitly. In view of its importance, it is essential to consider it as a separate form of generality so that treatment researchers may include different ethnocultural groups in their research.

Generality Across Settings. It is important to establish that the findings of a study conducted in one setting are valid in other settings as well. Of necessity, most research studies are conducted in one or more particular settings. The results may have excellent internal validity. However, it may not be clear that the same results would be obtained if the experiment were to be repeated in other settings, especially in a multitude of settings. **Generality across settings** is the extent to which the results of a study conducted in one or more settings may be extended to many other settings not involved in the original study. Obviously, clinicians look for this important type of generality.

The extent to which a physical setting itself affects the generality of research findings is not always clear. Clinicians sometimes wonder why certain procedures, known to be effective in one professional setting, do not work well in other settings. What works best in a private speech and hearing clinic may not work equally well in a public school setting. Often, the reason why the results of a study are not replicated in another setting is a failure to use the proven procedure in its original form. In any case, if there is no setting generality, additional experimental analyses should be made to determine why. Such analyses may uncover deficiencies in the implementation of the tested technique or suggest ways of improving it so that it can produce more uniform results in different settings.

Generality Across Experimenters. Sometimes another experimenter or a clinician may not obtain an effect demonstrated by one experimenter. The results then do not have **generality across experimenters**, which is the extent to which the results obtained by one investigator may be extended to other investigators who use the same procedure. In clinical research, other clinicians may not replicate dramatic effects of certain treatment programs administered by some clinicians.

It is possible that special characteristics, training, and skills of the experimenter contribute to the effects of the experimental treatment. Effects are enhanced when those characteristics are present and downgraded when they are absent. However, when such personal factors are involved, the problem may not be one of experimental design but of who implemented it and in what manner. Designs cannot be blamed if the techniques themselves are used with varying degrees of efficiency and accuracy by different investigators or clinicians. Regardless, the effect on generality is negative.

What an experimenter expects will happen in a study also may affect the results. Those who expect to reject the null hypothesis may more often than not find evidence to reject the null. Teachers who believe that certain students are brighter than others (who are, in fact, equally bright) may find the former group perform better than the latter. Such an experimenter expectation effect is known as the **Rosenthal effect** (Rosenthal, 1966), which is well documented. It is important to note, however, that a *mental expectation* does not have any effect on the result. To affect the results, that expectation should really be certain behaviors of the experimenter. For example, teachers may offer more positive reinforcement and other forms of encouragement to those students they believe are more capable than others. In addition to expectation, the physical appearance, race, gender, personal characteristics, and such other variables associated with the investigator also may affect the results. However, the actual effects of such variables in treatment research are not well understood.

It is possible that experimenter effects are more troublesome when the independent variable manipulated in a study is relatively weak and the dependent variable measured in the study is an unstable, reactive behavior. Also, when an investigator describes the treatment procedures poorly or incompletely, others who try to replicate the study may, of necessity, modify it in unknown ways. If the results are negative, the investigator may conclude that some personal characteristic of the original investigator was an important variable. But, in fact, the problem might have been that the method itself was not applied as it was in the original study, perhaps because of inadequate descriptions in the original study. When the procedures are clear, variables are strong and nonreactive, and the experimenter is well trained in the methods of the study, these effects should not pose significant problems for experimenter generality. Eventually, all clinical sciences strive to develop treatment techniques whose effects override any personal quality differences except for training and skill.

Generality Within and Across Response Classes. In human and clinical research,

a certain independent variable may be demonstrated to have an effect on certain responses. The responses manipulated may belong to a single class, for example, the production of the present progressive -*ing* in sentences. The results may demonstrate that the treatment program was effective in teaching the production of -*ing*. A clinician then may wonder whether the same treatment technique may be used in teaching plural morphemes, passive forms of sentences, correct articulation of phonemes, or a manual sign. Each of these clinical targets belongs to a separate response class.

A **response class** is a group of responses that share the same causal variables and have similar effects on others, listeners in the case of verbal behaviors. From a practical standpoint, response classes are groups of responses, all of which may be learned on the basis of generalization when only some of them are taught. For instance, in teaching the present progressive -*ing*, one need not use all different forms of sentences in which that structure is used. Teaching a few correct exemplars of -*ing* may result in the generalized production of many different forms of sentences in which the morpheme is correctly included. A different class of response, for instance, the regular plural morpheme, is not affected by the training of the present progressive. The plural morpheme belongs to a separate response class and needs separate training.

The same treatment that was effective in teaching the present progressive may also be effective in teaching other response classes (e.g., the plural morpheme or the passive sentence form), however. Therefore, the question of **generality across response classes**—the extent to which the results of one treatment investigation may be extended to response classes not investigated—is clinically (as well as theoretically) important (Hegde, 1998). More often, researchers ask whether a proven technique is useful in treating a disorder that is similar to the one treated in the original investigation. However, one may ask whether the treatment will be effective in treating a very different response class—whether, for example, the technique known to be effective in teaching specific language behaviors (one response class) can be used to train mathematical or musical skills (very different response classes).

Generality across response classes is important in clinical research and treatment. Clinicians sometimes assume that a method demonstrated to be successful in the treatment of one disorder of communication may not be effective in the treatment of another disorder. However, clinical evidence shows a considerable degree of generality of treatment variables (Hegde, 1998). It is important to establish such generality through systematic research because it reduces unnecessary diversity in therapeutic practices.

Clinical Validity

A concept closely related to clinical generality is **clinical validity**, which is the degree to which the treatment effects are socially and personally meaningful. This type of validity is also known as *clinical significance, clinical relevance,* and *social validity* of behavioral and medical interventions (Kazdin, 1999; Ogles, Lunnen, & Bonesteel, 2001). All are contrasted with the concept of *statistical significance,* described and evaluated in Chapter 10. Statistical analysis of a treatment study's results may show that the

technique was effective. The procedure may reduce symptoms in clinical settings (e.g., reduced dysfluency rates), but if the effects do not generalize to everyday situations, the clinical reduction will not be of social or personal significance. A child with a language disorder might learn to produce a few morphological structures in the clinic but may still lack language skills necessary to succeed in the classroom. Medically, symptoms of a diseases may be reduced, but the patient's general well-being may still be poor. These examples underscore the need to go beyond narrowly defined clinical goals of treatment as well as statistically found significance of treatment research results.

To be socially and personally meaningful, treatment in communication disorders should achieve broader, lasting, and generalized goals that improve a person's social and personal communication. Furthermore, in the case of children, treatment should enhance academic performance. In the case of working adults, treatment effects should lead to better occupational performance and efficiency. Persons who receive treatment should be *satisfied* with the results, measured in some objective way. The persons should report a higher quality of life that they attribute to treatment. Such broader effects realized through treatment should also last and be sustained across varied circumstances. That a treatment is effective may only mean that certain changes were reliably associated with treatment and that, without treatment such changes, would not have taken place. But an effective treatment may not have been personally and socially significant. Especially in group designs of research, treatment effects may be statistically significant, but the actual effects may be small. (See

Chapters 9 and 10 for more on statistical vs. clinical significance.) Ideally, clinical researchers should strive to achieve both effectiveness (internal validity) and clinical validity (clinical significance).

Clinical validity has consequences for generality. If an effective treatment's clinical validity is in doubt, then other clinicians would be unsure as to its application. Therefore, lack of clinical validity will limit wider application of a technique known to be effective.

Factors That Affect Generality

The types of generality described so far have their limitations, but they are not by themselves negative or positive factors. All are desirable types of generality that may be achieved to various degrees. However, there are some factors that affect generality in general or generality of a specific kind. What follows is a discussion of factors that negatively affect generality.

Pretest and Posttest Sensitization to Treatment

The pretest, or the initial assessment of the dependent variable, may sensitize participants to the treatment in such a way as to enhance its effect. For example, smokers may become sensitized to the magnitude of their problem when the number of cigarettes smoked is measured prior to implementation of a treatment program. The treatment may have a larger effect in these participants compared with participants who were not pretested and thus were not sensitized to their problem and hence to the treatment. Therefore, the

results may not be generalized to participants who will not be given the same or a similar pretest.

In some research studies, the posttest may also act as a sensitizer of treatment variables. While the pretest may sensitize participants to treatment, the posttest may help demonstrate the effect that would otherwise not have appeared. This can happen because the posttest can help participants recall the information presented in the treatment sessions. For example, questionnaires and interviews designed to find out the effects of a film on attitude change can help the participants simply recall some of the information presented in the film, which may be interpreted as an effect of the film. The posttest of an academic teaching program may have similar effects on the dependent variable.

Sensitization is a more serious problem with reactive variables such as attitudes and opinions. After they are measured, they tend to become more sensitive to strategies designed to change them. The reactive variables then show additional changes simply as a function of the posttest. Rates of actual responses, on the other hand, are less reactive than a participant's verbal statements about those responses.

Sensitization to treatment that limits external validity should not be confused with testing that affects internal validity. Internal validity is threatened when testing directly changes the dependent variable to any extent. In this case, the independent variable may not be responsible for some or all of the changes observed on the posttest. Sensitization, on the other hand, affects the external validity or generality of findings by making the results less relevant to the participants who are not given a pretest. Testing can directly affect the dependent variable, whereas sensitization can make the participants react more favorably to the treatment. What is common to both factors is the reactive dependent variable.

Hawthorne Effect

The knowledge on the part of the participants that they are participating in an experiment may produce an effect in addition to that of the independent variable. The results then may not be extended to participants who lack such knowledge. Being observed and getting attention from a research team may affect the behavior or symptoms of a disease. This effect may be a part of the overall treatment effect reported in a study. The participants may be aware of the purposes of an experiment and, besides, may know what kinds of responses are expected of them under the different conditions of the study. As a result, they may be more inclined to respond in expected directions. Furthermore, experimental participants may be apprehensive about being evaluated in some way. Such apprehension may also affect the results either positively or negatively. The extent to which the participants' knowledge of being in an experiment affects the results is called the **Hawthorne effect**. It is named after the city of Hawthorne (a suburb of Chicago) where the original experiment was conducted at a Western Electric Factory.

The well-known *placebo effect* is part of the Hawthorne effect. This effect is evident when participants react to a treatment favorably simply because it is presented as a treatment by experts. The treatment may be totally ineffective, but the participants report otherwise. In drug evaluation experiments, a placebo, which looks like the drug being tested but is actually an inert material, is routinely used to rule

out this effect. An effective drug should produce effects over and beyond the placebo effect. The placebo effect can also be troublesome in behavioral treatment programs. When self-report data on the effects of treatments are sought, the clients may report a magnitude of improvement that is greater than that of the actual improvement.

The existence and the extent of the Hawthorne and placebo effects have come under close scrutiny. Some researchers doubt the existence of both, and the Hawthorne effect has been dubbed a myth (Rice, 1982). Medical treatment researchers, on the other hand, contend that a knowledge of research participation itself has some effect on the results, but the conditions under which they appear, their mechanisms, or their magnitude are unclear, and therefore, new concepts are needed to replace the Hawthorne effect (McCambridge, Wilton, & Elbourne, 2014). Please see Chapter 4 for a discussion of the issues associated with placebo-controlled randomized clinical trials in medicine and surgery.

Multiple Treatment Interference

In most research studies, the effects of a single independent variable are assessed. However, in some experiments, the effects of multiple independent variables may be investigated. Clinical research of this kind is especially valuable. For example, a clinician may wish to find out if, in the treatment of speech sound disorders, immediate feedback on the accuracy of a client's response is more effective than delayed feedback. The two different methods of providing the feedback would be the two treatment variables in the study.

When such experiments are conducted, a potential problem is that of **multiple treatment interference**, which is the positive or negative effect of one treatment over the other.

When two or more treatments are applied in sequence to the same participants, effects of the first treatment may confound those of the second. Also, the overall effect observed in the participants may be at least partly determined by the order in which the multiple treatments were applied. If the same treatments are applied in a different order, the same results may or may not be obtained. This affects the generality of findings. The results may be valid only in terms of the sequence in which the treatments were administered. The generality of the findings with regard to individual treatments would also be unknown.

Multiple treatment interference is a serious problem when the same participants are exposed to different treatments within a single study. Therefore, it often is a problem with certain single-subject and within-subjects group designs. However, this problem can exist within other group designs when the same participants are repeatedly recruited in several experiments. It is known that often the same college students serve in a multitude of experiments, especially when the students are paid for their participation. The same clients of speech and hearing centers may also be repeatedly recruited in certain experiments, including treatment evaluations. In such cases, the participants' performance on subsequent experiments may be partly determined by their participation in earlier experiments. Therefore, the results of subsequent studies may not have much relevance to participants who do not have the cumulative experience of having participated in many experiments.

Multiple treatment interference is further discussed in Chapters 8 and 9.

Concluding Remarks

Researchers and consumers of research information should be concerned with internal and external validity. Whether the demonstrated relation between variables is valid and whether the same relation would hold in other circumstances are the two most important judgments that investigators and consumers of research should make.

Although researchers may be able to control for some of the factors that threaten external validity in a study, it should be realized that no single study could demonstrate all kinds of generality. Generality of research findings is a matter of replication. Eventual generality of experimental findings is established only when other experimenters in different settings using new participants repeat studies. There are different procedures for establishing the generality of research data, and all are described in Chapter 10.

Before we conclude this chapter, a note on the distinction between *generality* and *generalization* is in order. Some investigators use the terms interchangeably. However, this practice is confusing because they are not the same. Our discussion so far makes it clear that *generality* refers to the applicability of research data to participants, responses, settings, experimenters, and so on that were not involved in the original study. The process of repeating the experiments under varied conditions achieves it. Generality, therefore, is a result of certain actions, but it is not in itself a behavioral process in the sense that generalization is. **Generalization** refers to a temporary response rate when the process of conditioning is discontinued, and the response is allowed to be made. On the other hand, generality does not refer to any response rate; it refers to functional relations between events under new conditions of experimentation.

The act of establishing generality of research findings is a behavioral process, but that is true of the original experiment as well. In this sense, all research activity is behavior, as we noted in Chapter 3. There is one sense in which generality and generalization are similar, however. When experiments are repeated, and the same functional relation is seen again and again, the scientists are said to have demonstrated generality. It means that as long as the same functional relation is encountered, scientists behave as though the differences in settings, conditions, participants, and other such factors do not matter. The scientists' behavior, then, shows the same properties that characterize generalization. In essence, we can view generality as a functional relation that repeats itself in nature and we can view generalization (in this particular context) as the behavior of scientists toward generality. A scientist would generalize only when the generality of findings has been demonstrated.

Summary

- **Research designs** generally are methods of a study and, more technically, as structures of temporospatial arrangements within which the selected variables are controlled, manipulated, and measured.
- Research designs help detect independent, related, correlated, and interactive relation between events and help control variability.
- The **intrinsic view** of variability in human behavior holds that variability found in behavior is inherent (intrinsic) to human beings and therefore controlled mostly statistically, not experimentally.
- The **extrinsic view** holds that much of the variability is due to external factors that may be controlled experimentally, not statistically.
- The results of an experiment are subject to an evaluation of their internal validity, generality, and clinical validity.
- **Internal validity** is the degree to which a design rules out the influence of such extraneous variables as *history, maturation, testing, instrumentation, statistical regression, subject selection bias, attrition*, and *diffusion of treatment*.
- **Generality**, also called *external validity*, is the extent to which the conclusions of a study may be extended to new settings, persons (participants), response classes, and investigators.
- **Statistical (inferential) generality** is the extent to which the conclusions of a study based on a sample of participants may be extended to the population from which the sample was drawn.

- **Clinical generality** is the extent to which the results of a treatment study may be extended to other relevant conditions; forms of clinical validity include *logical generality, generality across participants, generality across settings, generality across experimenters,* and *generality across response classes.*
- **Clinical validity** is the extent to which the treatment effects are socially and personally meaningful.
- **Generality** may be affected by pretest-posttest sensitization to treatment, (possibly) the Hawthorne effect, and multiple treatment interference.

References

Barlow, D. H., Nock, M. K., & Hersen, M. (2009). *Single-case experimental designs: Strategies for studying behavior* (3rd ed.). Boston, MA: Pearson.

Battle, D. (Ed.). (2012). *Communication disorders in multicultural and international populations* (4th ed.). New York, NY: Elsevier.

Campbell, D. T., & Stanley, J. C. (1966). *Experimental and quasi-experimental designs for research*. Chicago, IL: Rand McNally.

Hegde, M. N. (1998). *Treatment procedures in communicative disorders* (3rd ed.). Austin, TX: Pro-Ed.

Johnston, J. M., & Pennypacker, H. S. (2009). *Strategies and tactics of behavioral research* (3rd ed.). London, UK: Routledge.

Kazdin, A. E. (1999). The meaning and measurement of clinical significance. *Journal of Consulting and Clinical Psychology, 67*(3), 332–339.

Kazdin, A. E. (2010). *Single-case experimental designs: Methods for clinical and applied settings* (2nd ed.). New York, NY: Oxford University Press.

Kerlinger, F. N., & Lee, H. B. (2000). *Foundations of behavioral research* (4th ed.). Fort Worth, TX: Harcourt College.

McCambridge, J., Wilton, J., & Elbourne, D. R. (2014). Systematic review of the Hawthorne effect: New concepts are needed to study research participation effects. *Journal of Clinical Epidemiology, 67*(3), 267–277.

Ogles, B. M., Lunnen, K. M., & Bonesteel, K. (2001). Clinical significance: History, application, and current practice. *Clinical Psychology Review, 21*(3), 421–446.

Payne, J. C. (2014). *Adult neurogenic language disorders: A comprehensive ethnobiological approach* (2nd ed.). San Diego, CA: Plural.

Portney, L. G., & Watkins, M. P. (2008). *Foundations of clinical research: Applications to practice* (3rd ed.). Boston, MA: Pearson.

Rice, B. (1982). The Hawthorne defect: Persistence of a flawed theory. *Psychology Today, 16*(2), 7074.

Rosenthal, R. (1966). *Experimenter effects in behavior research*. New York, NY: Appleton-Century-Crofts.

Shadish, W. R., Cook, T. D., & Campbell, D. T. (2002). *Experimental and quasi-experimental designs for generalized causal inference* (2nd ed.). Boston, MA: Houghton, Mifflin, and Company.

Sidman, M. (1960). *Tactics of scientific research*. New York, NY: Basic Books.

Study Guide

1. Distinguish between the general and technical definition of research designs.

2. How does a researcher manipulate an independent variable?

3. Define and distinguish intrinsic and extrinsic variability. Describe how they affect experimental designs.

4. What is the name for the variability induced by the independent variable?

5. What is error variance?

6. A clinician wishes to find out why persons who stutter seem to exhibit varying amounts of stuttering on different occasions. How would you try to answer this question on the basis of (a) intrinsic variability and (b) extrinsic variability? What kinds of research will these two assumptions lead to?

7. How is variability handled in the group design and the single-subject design strategies?

8. Distinguish between internal validity and generality.

9. What is clinical validity? How is it related to generality?

10. What kind of validity is demonstrated by a clinician who convincingly shows that a particular treatment procedure was indeed responsible for changes in the participant's communicative behaviors?

11. What is internal validity? How is it achieved?

12. What are the factors that adversely affect internal validity?

13. How is maturation controlled for in the group design strategy and in the single-subject design strategy?

14. What are reactive measures? What kinds of dependent variables are most likely to be reactive?

15. What is statistical regression? What kinds of disorders are likely to show this phenomenon?

16. A clinical investigator had 10 participants in each of two groups (experimental and control). The 20 participants had a speech sound disorder whose severity varied across individuals. With this example, show how differential participant attrition could invalidate the conclusions based on the group means.

17. Is external validity strictly and always a matter of research designs themselves? Why or why not?

18. Distinguish between inferential and logical generality. Point out the limitations of each.

19. What is pretest/posttest sensitization to treatment? What kind of validity is affected by this?

20. What research strategy is especially vulnerable to multiple treatment interference?

8

The Group Design Strategy

Chapter Outline

- Common Characteristics of Group Designs
- Preexperimental Designs
- True Experimental Designs
- Designs to Evaluate Multiple Treatments
- Factorial Designs
- Quasi-Experimental Designs
- Time-Series Designs
- Counterbalanced Within-Subjects Designs
- Correlational Analysis
- Group Designs in Clinical Research
- Summary
- References
- Study Guide

It was noted in Chapters 4 and 7 that there are two basic approaches to designing experiments: the group designs and the single-subject designs. They are the means by which treatment effects are established. Therefore, we describe the group design strategy in this chapter and the single-subject strategy in the next chapter.

The group design strategy is well established in psychology, education, drug evaluations in medicine, and social sciences. The strategy is controversially advocated as the standard of treatment evaluation for all clinical disciplines.

Common Characteristics of Group Designs

Ronald A. Fisher, the famed British biostatistician, developed many of the currently used group designs of research during the first half of the 20th century. Fisher's experimental designs and statistical analysis of their results were originally developed on an agricultural research station (Fisher, 1925, 1942, 1951, 1956). See Chapter 10 for a historical introduction to Fisher's influential work and the growth of statistics in the analysis of group experimental designs.

Our description of group designs of research is based on a classic in the field of experimental designs as they are applied in psychology, education, and medicine: Campbell and Stanley's (1966) *Experimental and Quasi-Experimental Designs for Research*. This slim volume describes all of the designs Fisher developed but puts them in the context of behavioral and medical research. Campbell and Stanley helped standardize various design terminology and the overall schemes of describing them.

The group design strategy, also known as the *between-groups strategy,* as well as the *parallel-groups strategy*, requires the formation of groups on the basis of randomization, although not all group designs are formed randomly. **Randomization** is a method of selecting study participants in an unbiased manner. Theoretically and ideally, the investigator first identifies a population of potential participants, all of whom are accessible and willing to participate in the study, although this situation usually is not realized with human participants. The required number of participants is then randomly drawn from the population—meaning that each potential participant had an equal chance of being selected for the study and each selected participant agreed to participate. Once the participants are randomly selected, they are then randomly assigned to the different groups of the study (Shadish, Cook, & Campbell, 2002).

Individuals randomly selected from the population are said to represent the population; they are a **representative sample**. Therefore, how they respond to treatment is an indication of how the population with the same disease or disorder will respond. The investigator may generalize the results of the sample study to the population; this is known as **inferential generality**; how the population performs if treated is *inferred* from the sample data.

The logic of the group design requires that the groups formed for the study be equal on all relevant variables at the beginning of an experiment. This is sometimes referred to as the *sampling equivalence* of groups. The groups are presumed equal if they are truly randomly selected from the population, randomly assigned to treatment and control groups, and the randomization held until the end of the study. The treatment to be evaluated is applied to the experimental group and withheld from the control group. If, as a result of this experimental operation, the groups differ in their performance, the difference is attributed to the independent variable because that was, presumably, the only difference between the groups.

Well-controlled group designs have at least two equivalent groups: the experimental and the control groups. However, an uncontrolled (preexperimental) design may have only one group that receives treatment. Some advanced and complex designs can have more than two groups, and a specially defined control group can receive an established treatment whose effects are not being evaluated. As noted in Chapter 4, randomized clinical trials in medicine often include control groups that receive a standard treatment or a placebo compared against experimental group or groups that receive one or more new treatments.

In a majority of group designs, investigators measure the dependent variable only on two occasions: once before the independent variable is introduced (pretest) and once after (posttest). The difference between the pretest and posttest scores is an important element of a statistical analysis as further described in Chapter 10.

As noted earlier, group designs that have representative samples attempt to establish inferential generality. Whether this is justified is somewhat controversial, and we will address this issue in a later section. In any case, group designs are not expected to help extend the conclusions from a random sample to a single or a few specific individuals. In other words, they do not have logical generality.

Since the publication of Campbell and Stanley (1966), it is customary to use diagrams with abbreviations to represent group research designs. For the sake of consistency and clarity, the same system will be used in this chapter in representing various group designs. In these diagrams, the experimental and control groups are represented with E and C, respectively. The measurement of the dependent variable is represented by O, which stands for observation. Pretests and posttests may be indicated by O_1 and O_2, assuming that there were only those two measures in a study. The treatment variable is indicated by X and the random participant selection by R. In some textbooks, Y may represent the dependent variable. In science and mathematics, X is the cause and Y is the effect. The Y is said to be a function of X, which means that X is the cause of Y.

It also is an accepted practice to describe group designs as *preexperimental designs*, *true experimental designs*, *quasi-experimental designs*, and *correlational analysis*. In different books and articles, however, the reader will find differing and sometimes confusing terms in the description of the same research designs. When appropriate, multiple names of the same design will be pointed out.

Preexperimental Designs

Preexperimental designs are commonly used in clinical, educational, social, and psychological research. Although these designs have serious limitations, they are eminently practical and useful in applied settings. They often precede experimental research on a treatment.

Several preexperimental group designs are available. Three most commonly used preexperimental designs are the *one-shot case study*, the *one-group pretest-posttest design*, and the *statistic-group design*.

The One-Shot Case Study

The one-shot case study is a design in which the treatment is applied to a known clinical group with only a posttest. For instance, to find out the effects of a new treatment for apraxia of speech (AOS), a clinician may select some adults diagnosed with the disorder and apply the selected treatment procedure. The clinician in this case does not have pretest results and simply assumes that the diagnosis of AOS provides a sufficient basis to evaluate the results of treatment. Also missing is a control group. The design is shown in Figure 8–1.

The posttest may contain a measure of the participants' speech production skills obtained either through a standardized test or a speech sample. If the posttest shows no evidence of AOS in the group, the clinician may conclude that the treatment was effective.

The greatest weakness of this design is its total lack of control. The absence of a control group makes it difficult to rule out the influence of factors other than the treatment. There is no valid basis to evaluate the changes documented by the posttest because there was no pretest. In fact, the absence of a pretest makes it impossible to say whether there were any changes due to treatment at all. Not

knowing to what extent the participants had difficulty producing speech sounds, the researcher is unable to judge the degree of improvement, unless the treatment completely eliminated the disorder, an unlikely event.

The one-shot case study is not useful in making valid judgments regarding the effectiveness of treatments. Despite the logical appeal of the treatment program and thoroughness of the posttest, investigators cannot demonstrate a functional relation between the treatment and the possible changes in target behaviors. Of the factors that affect internal validity described in Chapter 7, history, maturation, and statistical regression typically invalidate the results of one-shot case studies. Depending on the particular study, other sources of internal invalidity may also be involved.

The One-Group Pretest-Posttest Design

The one-group pretest-posttest design is similar to the one-shot case study in that there is no control group. However, unlike the previous design, this one includes a pretest of the dependent variables. Typical case studies in clinical sciences are of this kind. The treatment is introduced

X	O
Treatment	Posttest

Figure 8–1. One-shot case study. Note that the design lacks a control group and pretests.

after the pretest, and a posttest is conducted to evaluate the effects of the treatment. Positive changes from the pretest to the posttest are interpreted as the treatment effect. The design is illustrated in Figure 8–2.

To continue with our hypothetical example of AOS treatment research given under the previous design, the clinician using the one-group pretest-posttest design measures the speech production skills of the participants both before and after the treatment. These measures help document the changes in speech production skills that may have taken place during the course of the study.

The results of the one-group pretest-posttest design can be analyzed through statistical methods. The most frequently used technique is the parametric t test for correlated samples. Nonparametric tests may also be used in analyzing the results. Two such tests are the sign test and the Wilcoxon matched-pairs signed-ranks test (Gravetter & Walnau, 2017; Huck, 2012).

Although the design is an improvement over the one-shot case study, it still is not able to generate data that can support a functional relation between the changes in the dependent variable and the independent variable. The clinician in our example can be reasonably sure that the speech production skills of individuals with AOS studied did (or did not) change over the course of the experiment. However, he or she will not be able to conclude that the observed positive changes (the differences between O_1 and O_2) are due to the AOS treatment program. The design cannot rule out the influence of history, maturation, testing, instrumentation, statistical regression, and differential participant attrition. In essence, the design lacks internal validity.

There is no assurance that something the participant's family members did, unspecified biological change taking place within the participants, or a combination of these and other unknown factors was not responsible for improved speech production skills. Similarly, the pretest itself may have introduced some changes in the speech production skills or the testing instruments may have been unreliable. Although statistical regression may not be a characteristic of AOS, the design itself cannot rule it out. Differential participant attrition can certainly be an additional problem. The posttest scores may be better than the pretest scores simply because more severely affected participants may have dropped out during the course of the experiment. However, because the design uses only one group, participant selection bias is not a factor.

O_1	X	O_2
Pretest	Treatment	Posttest

Figure 8–2. The one-group pretest-posttest design. Note that the design lacks a control group.

The Static-Group Comparison

Another frequently used preexperimental design is known as the static-group comparison. This design uses two existing groups: one that has already received treatment and another that has not. It is called the static-group comparison method simply because no new groups are formed. The design is diagrammed in Figure 8–3.

The static-group comparison design does not have pretests of the dependent variables. The difference in the dependent variable between the group that has received treatment and the group that has not is attributed to the treatment. For example, a clinician may evaluate a stuttering treatment program offered by a large clinic. The persons with stuttering who just completed the treatment program may be compared with those who are yet to receive the same treatment. No pretest measures are obtained for the "control" group because none are available for the experimental group, which has already received the treatment. The static-group comparison also is involved when children with repaired cleft palate who have had speech therapy may be compared with those who have not. Speech intelligibility measures may be the dependent variable. Then the better speech intelligibility found in the experimental group may be attributed to their past speech therapy.

The results of the static-group comparison are analyzed through a parametric *t* test. Such nonparametric tests as the Mann-Whitney *U* test and the median test also may be used. A chi-square test also is appropriate (Huck, 2012).

In static-group comparisons, the group that does not receive treatment does not help control extraneous variables. The first major problem of internal validity faced by this design is that of participant selection bias. There is no assurance of random sampling of the two groups before the treatment because the design does not require it. For example, people with mild stuttering may have gone through the treatment program, whereas those in the control group may have had more severe stuttering. The experimental group of children with repaired cleft may have had good speech intelligibility all along. The second major problem is that of differential participant attrition. Even when the two groups are identical to begin with, they may become different not because of treatment but because of participant attrition. As such, the static-group comparison cannot rule out the influence of extraneous variables and, therefore, cannot help establish functional relations between variables.

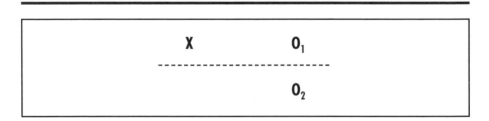

Figure 8–3. The static-group comparison design. Note that the design uses existing groups (not randomly formed) and lacks pretests.

True Experimental Designs

As noted in Chapter 7, an experimental design should help establish a functional relation between an independent and a dependent variable. Among group designs, true experimental designs rule out the influence of extraneous variables, mainly through the use of experimental and control groups. The two or more groups in a study are formed on the basis of the preferred randomization or its alternative, matching. Therefore, true experimental designs are those that reveal a reasonably clear cause-effect relation between the manipulated independent variable and the measured dependent variable. Therefore, the designs have internal validity.

True experimental designs may involve either a single or multiple treatment (independent) variables. The pretest-posttest control group design, the posttest-only control group design, and the Solomon four-group design involve a single treatment variable. On the other hand, the multigroup pretest-posttest design, multigroup posttest-only design, and several types of factorial designs make it possible to evaluate the effects of multiple treatments. Because all true experimental designs are expected to use randomization

to achieve sampling equivalence between groups, the diagrams of each design show R for randomization, but it may be substituted with M for matching.

The Pretest-Posttest Control Group Design

The pretest-posttest control group design is prototypical of the true experimental group designs. It also is the simplest. This design elegantly illustrates the logic and the strategy of the group designs. It requires two groups: an experimental group, which receives treatment, and a control group, which does not.

To assess the effects of an independent variable with two groups, the only difference between them shall be that variable. Therefore, the investigator should start with two groups that are similar on relevant variables. If the groups are different on some known or unknown variables other than the treatment, then the observed effect of that treatment may be due to those unknown variables. This critical task of achieving group similarity may be accomplished with randomization or matching.

The pretest-posttest control group design is illustrated in Figure 8–4. The diagram shows that the participants were

E	R	0_1	X	0_2
C	R	0_1		0_2

Figure 8–4. The pretest-posttest control group design. Note that this is the prototype of group experimental designs, with randomly selected and assigned groups.

randomly selected (R) from a population and were randomly assigned to the two groups. The experimental group (E) is exposed to the treatment variable (X), whereas the control group (C) is not. The dependent variable is measured (O) twice in each group, once before and once after the experimental group has received the treatment. This basic arrangement permits a relatively unambiguous evaluation of the effects of most independent variables.

The typical pretest-posttest control group design has only one treatment variable and a true control group that does not receive treatment. However, randomized clinical trials in medicine use variations of this design. In one such variation, both the groups receive treatment, but the experimental group receives a new treatment being investigated, and the control group receives a well-established, and already evaluated, treatment. The research question is whether the new treatment is at least as good as the older treatment.

In yet another variation of the basic pretest-posttest control group design, the investigator may have three groups. One may receive the new treatment being evaluated, the other may receive a placebo (see Chapter 4 for details), and the third may receive a standard treatment whose effects are known. All these design variations seek to establish the effectiveness of the new treatment. Therefore, the group that receives a standard treatment may technically be called control groups (along with, of course, the placebo group).

In the analysis of the results of the basic version of the design, it is important to avoid some common mistakes. In one of the mistaken analyses, the pretest and posttest scores of the experimental group may be compared with one t test, and the scores of the two tests of the control group may be compared with a different t test. These two comparisons are based on the assumption that if the experimental group's posttest mean is significantly higher than the pretest mean and the control group's pretest and posttest means are comparable, then the effect of the independent variable has been demonstrated. Actually, this analysis does not involve a direct comparison of the performance of the two groups. Sometimes investigators compare the two pretest scores with a t test and the two posttest scores with another t test. This also is an inappropriate analysis of the results because it does not adequately reflect changes in the dependent variable across the conditions of an experiment.

The correct method of analysis involves either a gain score procedure or an analysis of covariance. In the former, each participant's pretest scores are subtracted from the posttest scores to obtain the gain scores. The individual gain scores are then averaged to obtain two mean scores, one for each of the two groups. The two means are then compared with either the parametric independent samples t test or the nonparametric Mann-Whitney U test. A median test may also be used to compare the two means. A preferred and more complex statistic is the analysis of covariance (Mertler & Reinhart, 2016).

The basic version of the design, which has a control group that does not receive treatment, is able to rule out extraneous factors relative to history and maturation. Events in the life of the participants (history) or maturational changes that may affect the dependent variable are assumed to be common to the two groups. Therefore, significant changes in the dependent variable, if shown by the experimental group, cannot be attributed to history or maturation.

Regression to the mean can occur, but to the extent that the groups were equal to begin with, this phenomenon will be held constant across the two groups. For example, if stuttering rate returns to the mean level in the experimental group some time after the pretest, the same thing can be expected to happen in the control group also. Similarly ruled out is the factor of participant selection as long as the samples were drawn, or at least assigned, randomly. However, if participants are matched, then none of the sources of participant selection biases can be ruled out (Campbell & Stanley, 1966).

Testing as a factor of internal validity is controlled for in the design because both the groups were pretested; therefore, changes due to measurement of the dependent variable should be common across the two groups. When the same instruments are used in obtaining all measures of the variables in both the groups, the effects of the instrumentation also are not of concern.

Differential participant attrition can be a problem in the pretest-posttest control group design. The experimenter, however, would know whether attrition could have affected the results. Any dropout of participants from the experimental group is suggestive of this potential problem. It is difficult to determine the nature or extent of the effect of attrition when it is known to have occurred, however. Unfortunately, the effects of participant attrition are "commonly swept under the rug" (Campbell & Stanley, 1966, p. 15). The loss of participants during the course of the experiment may be reported but not handled in the data analysis. This mistake is easy to commit in a group design in which, despite some participant loss, the investigator seems to have some data to be analyzed.

The *external validity* of this, or in fact any design, is a different matter. Most textbooks tend to advise that as long as a random sample has been drawn from the population, the results should have generality. As noted in Chapter 4, clinical treatment studies—including randomized clinical trials—typically do not select participants randomly. Because of the requirement of informed consent, all participants in treatment research are self-selected. In the absence of random selection, there is no generality without replication.

The pretest-posttest control group design may demonstrate inferential generality, but not necessarily other kinds of generality. Even the best random sample does not help demonstrate generality across responses, settings, and experimenters until different investigators replicate the experiment with different responses in varied settings. The position advocated here, and expanded in Chapters 4 and 10, is that generality is a function of replication; therefore, a single study using even the best of the experimental designs of either the group or the single-subject strategy does not ensure it.

Posttest-Only Control Group Design

In the posttest-only control group design, neither the experimental nor the control group participants are given a pretest. After randomly selecting and assigning participants into the two groups, the treatment variable is applied to the experimental group. At the completion of the experimental treatment, the two groups are given a posttest. The design is illustrated in Figure 8–5.

A pretest is considered indispensable by many investigators. Therefore, this

E	R	X	0
C	R		0

Figure 8–5. The posttest-only control group design. Note that the design lacks pretests, which are assumed to be similar to the posttest scores of the control group.

design is not used very frequently. However, Campbell and Stanley (1966) argue that pretests are not at all necessary when the participants are selected randomly. Therefore, they strongly recommend this design and consider it superior to the pretest-posttest control group design. It certainly avoids the pretest-posttest sensitization to treatment because there is no pretest. The design can also control for other sources that affect internal validity, except for differential participant attrition.

The justification for this design rests heavily on the adequacy of randomization. The argument is that when participants are selected and assigned randomly, the groups are equal at the beginning. The pretest is only a confirmation of this fact. However, if pretests are expected to create problems, or for some reason are not practical, then they can be avoided without loss of scientific rigor, because the groups are comparable anyway. A statistically significant difference in the posttest scores of the two groups should be due to the experimental variable only. An analysis of such a difference usually involves a *t* test.

If the probability theory and random procedures were as practical as they are elegant, there would be no problem with this design. However, in most clinical sciences that need to evaluate the effects

of treatments in persons with various diseases and disorders, random selection of participants from the population is not possible; in most cases, not even attempted. In other designs, the pretest will at least let the investigator know that the groups are or are not equal. When there is no pretest, the experimenter has no way of checking sampling equivalence of the two groups. The design places too heavy a burden on the theory of random samples and too great a confidence in its practicality. Unfortunately, the probability theory promises much at the level of theory but delivers less at the level of clinical research.

The Solomon Four-Group Design

A four-group experimental design that Solomon proposed in 1949 quickly became one of the most prestigious of the group designs used in social and psychological research. Solomon was the first to formally recognize the interaction of pretest sensitization and treatment as a potential threat to external validity. However, previous investigators must have implicitly acknowledged this problem, because the design without a pretest was already available. Solomon proposed a design that provided not only an opportunity for the interaction to take place but also a method to measure its magnitude.

The four-group design is considered the most appropriate strategy for investigation when the pretest sensitization is expected to interact with the independent variable (Figure 8–6). It is clear from the diagram that the design is actually a combination of two previously described designs: the pretest-posttest control group and the posttest-only control group. The design has two experimental and two control groups. One of the experimental groups receives both the pretest and the posttest. The second experimental group is not pretested; it receives only the posttest. One of the two control groups receives both tests, whereas the second control group receives only the posttest.

The design controls for all the factors that affect internal validity. Therefore, the design can evaluate treatment effects. In addition, it also demonstrates the presence and the extent of pretest sensiti-

zation as a threat to external validity. A difference between the means of the pretested groups and an absence of such a difference between the means of groups not pretested reveals the effects of sensitization. Also, from a descriptive standpoint, if the pretest sensitizes the participants, the treatment effects are larger in the first experimental group than in the second. Because the first experimental group receives both tests whereas the second receives only the posttest, the performance of the second group is free of pretest sensitization. The two control groups also indicate any effects of the pretest on the dependent variable (a factor of internal validity). If the pretest has a direct effect on the dependent variable, the control group receiving both tests behaves differently than the one receiving only the posttest.

It has been recognized that analysis of the results of the Solomon design is difficult. A single statistical technique that can simultaneously analyze all the observations of the design is not available. Therefore,

E	R	O_1	X	O_2
C	R	O_1		O_2
E	R		X	O
C	R			O

Figure 8–6. The Solomon four-group design. Note that the design has two experimental groups and two control groups; an experimental and a control group receive no pretests.

the pretest scores are ignored and a two-way analysis of variance is performed. This analysis is arranged in terms of the scores of participants who have been pretested/not pretested and treated/untreated.

The design, though considered ideal in many respects, is of limited practical and paradigmatic value. It presents the immense practical problem of finding a population from which four groups of participants can be drawn randomly. Because it is a combination of two designs, it is about twice as hard to implement as any of the basic group designs. Therefore, there are hardly any clinical treatment studies in which the four-group design was used. The design is simply not used often even in nonclinical social research where it is more practical.

It can also be argued, in an admittedly controversial manner, that the design offers a methodological solution for the problem of paradigm. Obviously, the design is needed only when the pretest sensitization is a consideration. It is a consideration mostly in research that addresses reactive measures such as attitudes and opinions. In other words, the design is needed when the dependent variables are weak and at best offer indirect measures of whatever is measured. For example, we can measure the attitude of a group of speech-language pathologists toward people who stutter in public schools, as several researchers have done. One would assume that this type of research is done to determine whether the clinicians are unlikely to treat people who stutter because of their negative attitudes or whether, when they do treat people who stutter, the outcome may not be favorable, again because of negative attitudes. Or the researcher may wish to change the clinicians' negative attitudes with an informational package (the treatment variable). In this second instance, the researcher would need the four-group

design. Incidentally, much of the research on attitudes in communicative disorders is done only to uncover negative attitudes; hardly anything is done about them. A conceptually different approach to the issue is to find out how many people who stutter are not receiving treatment in a given setting and then proceed to find out why.

The finding that some clinicians have a negative attitude toward stuttering is hardly illuminating. It is likely that clinicians have negative attitudes toward stuttering because of their deficient training in treating the disorder. Therefore, it may be more meaningful to study and improve the clinicians' expertise in treating stuttering than to go on analyzing their negative attitudes. In essence, a solution to the problem of reactive measures is to try to avoid such dependent variables in favor of those that are less reactive, more stable, and perhaps more meaningful. Obviously, those who think that attitudes and opinions are important variables would disagree with this suggestion.

Designs to Evaluate Multiple Treatments

So far, we have discussed group designs to evaluate the effects of a single treatment. In many cases, though, the effects of more than one treatment may be of interest. In clinical sciences, it often is necessary to determine whether one treatment is more effective than the other. This generally is the question of *relative effects* (as opposed to absolute or independent effects) of treatments.

Group design strategy offers some excellent options to study the relative effects of two or more treatments. We describe two designs that are an extension of the designs presented earlier: multigroup pretest-posttest design and multigroup posttest-only design. We also will describe a separate class of designs, known as *factorial designs*, which help evaluate multiple treatment effects and their interactions.

Multigroup Pretest-Posttest Design

In the evaluation of two or more treatment techniques, the basic pretest-posttest control group design may be extended to include the needed number of additional groups. Extensions are limited by the ease with which the groups can be formed; each treatment built into the study will need an additional group. Also, data analysis will become increasingly complex with the addition of groups. Even an extension of the basic design by a single additional treatment can introduce a considerable amount of complexity.

The multigroup pretest-posttest designs can evaluate the relative effects of selected treatment techniques. In other words, the design can answer the question of whether one treatment is more effective than the other, and in the case of three or more treatments, the design can help evaluate their progressively increasing or decreasing effects.

Control group is optional in evaluating the relative effects of multiple treatments because each treatment's absolute effects will have been demonstrated. Each treatment will have been compared with the no-treatment control group. However, in randomized clinical trials, questions of relative effects may be researched without having completed research on absolute effects. An added control group will help evaluate both the relative and the absolute effects of the treatment techniques and will improve the study's internal validity as well.

A multigroup design that can evaluate the relative effects of three treatments is illustrated in Figure 8–7. The control group is placed in parentheses to suggest it is optional. The design affords a chance to determine the most and the

E	R	0_1	X_1	0_2
E	R	0_1	X_2	0_2
E	R	0_1	X_3	0_2
(C	R	0_1		0_2)

Figure 8–7. The multigroup pretest-posttest design. Note that the design can evaluate the relative effects of multiple treatments and may include an optional control group.

least effective of the three techniques. Research involving this kind of design is highly desirable in areas where multiple treatment techniques are recommended by different clinicians to treat the same disorder. Such therapeutic diversity exists in the treatment of most disorders of communication.

In medicine, randomized clinical trials often employ this design. In such trials, one of the experimental groups may receive a new drug whose effect is being evaluated for the first time. The other experimental groups may receive more established treatments to see which one produces greater benefits for the patients. More often, the control group will receive a placebo, in which case, the study is called a *placebo-controlled randomized clinical trial*. Placebo-controls are relatively uncommon in behavioral and educational research, although a new method can always be compared against an established treatment or teaching method.

The results of the design can be analyzed with a variety of statistical techniques, including analysis of covariance, analysis of variance based on gain scores for each participant (see pretest-posttest control group design), or a Lindquist Type I repeated-measures analysis of variance (Mertler & Reinhart, 2016). Most of these techniques of analysis simply indicate whether there is a significant difference in the performances of the groups. Therefore, when a significant difference between the groups is evident, additional analysis involving pairwise group comparisons is necessary.

Multigroup Posttest-Only Design

This is an extension of the posttest-only control group design presented earlier. In this design, two or more treatments are evaluated for their relative effects in the absence of a pretest. A diagram of the design with three treatments and an optional control group is presented in Figure 8–8. As in the original design, the

E	R	X_1	0
E	R	X_2	0
E	R	X_3	0
(C	R		0)

Figure 8–8. The multigroup posttest-only design. Note that the design lacks pretest scores, which are assumed to be similar across groups because of randomly drawn and assigned samples.

participants are selected and assigned to the groups randomly, resulting in equivalent groups that need to be retested. Each group is exposed to a different treatment.

The results of the multigroup posttest-only design can be analyzed with a one-way analysis of variance or with nonparametric statistics such as the Kruskal-Wallis and chi-square tests.

The design shares the same strengths and weaknesses as the posttest-only control group design. It is needed when the pretest sensitization is expected to interact with the treatment variable. Unless the investigator is sure that the groups were equal to begin with, there is no assurance of internal validity. The design is as good as the random procedure in practice.

Factorial Designs

Factorial designs also are true experimental designs, originally described by Fisher (1925, 1942). They are an excellent example of research strategies based mostly on the method of analysis of variance that Fisher developed in his agricultural research. Fisher discovered that instead of applying multiple treatments (e.g., different levels of fertilization or watering) to multiple agricultural plots in a systematic manner, applying treatments across randomly selected plots reduced errors of observation. This discovery has led to factorial designs that are now used in educational, medical, social, and behavioral research.

Analysis of variance is a collection of related techniques, the complex forms of which can be used in the simultaneous analysis of two or more variables and their interactions. In the terminology of factorial designs as applied to research

with human participants, a **factor** is the same as an independent variable (teaching or treatment).

Factorial designs have two or more independent variables that may be either active, assigned, or a combination of the two. It may be recalled that an experimenter can manipulate active independent variables, but cannot manipulate such assigned variables as the age, gender, education, intelligence, socioeconomic status of the participants, and the severity of disorders even though they may affect the results (see Chapter 3 for details on variables). A factorial design that includes only assigned variables is not an experimental study but belongs to the ex post facto category, described in Chapter 5. Therefore, we shall not be concerned with that type of design here. An experimental factorial design will have at least one active independent variable. Most factorial designs have a combination of active and assigned variables.

An independent variable used in a factorial design has a minimum of two levels. For this reason, certain factorial designs are referred to as **treatment-by-levels** designs. The levels of an active (manipulated) independent variable may be the presence or the absence of it (treatment versus no treatment). Two treatment techniques will be two levels. Furthermore, a technique whose intensity is varied can create different levels. For instance, in randomized clinical trials in medicine, different dosages of the same medicine will create levels.

As a further example from special education, an investigator may wish to evaluate the manual and oral methods of teaching individuals with hearing loss. In this case, the treatment variable has two levels, which are actually two separate treatments. Having a control group that is not exposed to either of the two teaching methods creates a third level. Another clinician may wish to test regular (twice a week) versus intensive (five times a week) scheduling of clients while using a single treatment procedure. The two schedules create two levels.

An assigned variable also typically has two or more levels. For example, individuals with hearing loss selected for a certain treatment evaluation may be grouped according to the degree of hearing loss: mild, moderate, and severe. These three categories are the three levels of the assigned variable. Most other assigned variables such as age, gender, socioeconomic class, and intelligence have two or more levels.

Within the group design strategy, factorial designs are the primary techniques of assessing the interaction of two or more variables. An **interaction** is an effect that emerges when two or more independent variables are combined to produce an effect that is different from the separate or independent effect of each variable combined. For instance, Drug A may effect a 20% reduction in some symptoms whereas Drug B may effect a 30% reduction. But when the two are administered in combination, a 90% reduction in symptoms (not merely the additive 50%) may be observed. The increased magnitude of the effect that goes beyond the mere additive effect is known as *interaction*.

Interaction may be positive or negative. The example just given illustrates **positive interaction** in which the combination of treatments enhances each other's effects. **Negative interaction** is the antagonistic effects of one treatment on the other when the two are combined. In negative interaction, one variable may suppress the positive effects of another

variable or may even induce harmful effects as in certain drug combinations that produce toxicity.

It is believed that most phenomena we study are multiply determined in an interactive fashion. In other words, most events have several causes, which in various combinations produce the effects we normally see. The designs that manipulate single variables at a time actually simplify the phenomenon for the sake of clearer analysis. Designs that permit the manipulation of multiple variables are more powerful. They also better approximate reality.

The factorial design also is based on the random procedure. The participants should be selected and assigned to the groups randomly. Once the participants are selected randomly, however, only the active variables permit random assignment. In our example, the clinician may be able to assign participants to the treatment and control conditions but not to any of the categories of hearing loss (e.g., mild, moderate, or severe). Each participant's hearing loss, not the power of randomization, determines whether he or she is assigned to one or the other category of severity.

There are several factorial designs; some are simpler than the others. The complexity of a factorial design is directly related to the number of independent variables (assigned and active) and the number of levels of each of those variables.

Randomized Blocks Design

A 1920s invention of Fisher (1942), a randomized blocks design has at least one active variable and one assigned variable. It can have more than two variables, but one of the variables should be assigned.

If each variable has two levels, then we have the basic randomized design, which often is represented as the 2 × 2 (two-by-two) design. Such a design also may be referred to as a *two-way* factorial design. Teaching or treatment methods are examples of active variables. The clinician or the educator can directly manipulate those methods. The participants' level of intelligence or the severity of a disorder, when categorized into levels, creates non-manipulable assigned variables.

A 2 × 2 randomized blocks design would have four cells or conditions; a 2 × 3 design would have 6. A 2 × 3 randomized blocks design is illustrated in Figure 8–9. The design has two independent variables, one manipulated treatment variable with two levels (manual and oral teaching methods) and one assigned variable with three levels (mild, moderate, and severe hearing loss). To conduct such a study, a population of individuals who have mild, moderate, and severe hearing loss (defined in some operational manner) is

first identified. Next, a certain number of individuals are randomly drawn from each level of hearing loss in what is known as a stratified random sample (see Chapter 4). The samples are then assigned to the teaching methods, as shown in Figure 8–9.

Each level of the assigned variable is considered a *block* from which a random sample is drawn. The design may include a control group that does not receive treatment, and if it does, the participants should also represent the levels of the assigned variable. Other research examples for which the randomized blocks design is appropriate include the effects of two aphasia treatment programs administered to persons who have had a stroke during the past month versus those who had a stroke 6 months ago (a 2 × 2 design). In medicine, the effects of two new drugs may be evaluated for their effects in women whose breast cancer was diagnosed early compared to those whose cancer was diagnosed late, defined in some operational manner.

| Treatment | Levels of Hearing Loss | | |
	Mild	Moderate	Severe
Manual			
Oral			

Figure 8–9. A 2 × 3 randomized blocks design. Note that the design includes two active (treatment) variables and three levels of participant characteristics; each cell represents a certain number of participants with defined characteristics.

Factorial designs can help determine the separate (independent) effects of the treatment methods as well as their interactions. The *main effects* in an analysis of variance of the results of a factorial design are the effects of the separate treatment variables (Mertler & Reinhart, 2016). In our example, the oral and the manual methods of teaching produce two main effects in the study.

The other important effect the analysis can reveal is the interaction of treatment with participant characteristics. It is possible that the oral method of instruction is most effective with participants who have only a mild hearing loss and that the manual method is more effective for those with severe hearing loss. Individuals with a moderate level of hearing loss may benefit equally from the two procedures. This kind of relation is what is implied in an *interaction*. Obviously, discovery of such relations is important in offering effective services. When such interactions exist, simpler questions that address the effects of single variables in isolation do not reflect the complexity of the phenomenon under investigation. For example, the question of whether the oral or the manual method of teaching is more effective may not be answerable unless the levels of hearing loss are taken into consideration.

When the number of variables and their levels are increased, the complexity of the design increases. The need for participants is directly proportional to the number of variables and levels in a factorial study. In the design illustrated in Figure 8–9, there are six cells, and assuming that at least 15 participants to a cell are needed, the investigator will have to find 90 participants to complete the study. A control group, when used, creates a need for additional participants.

Completely Randomized Factorial Design

In the previous design, one of the two factors is active (teaching) and the other assigned (levels of hearing loss). It is possible to design a factorial study in which all the factors are active, however. Such a design is known as the *completely randomized factorial design*. Because no assigned variable is included, there is no *blocking* in a completely randomized factorial design.

It is evident that complete randomization of participants is possible only when all the factors are active. An experimenter cannot assign participants randomly to gender or intelligence. Participants can be assigned randomly only to treatment conditions that are under the experimenter's control. Another invention of Fisher (1942), the completely randomized factorial designs use only active variables and do not address issues relative to potential interactions between treatment variables and participant characteristics.

A completely randomized factorial design is illustrated in Figure 8–10. It shows a 2 × 2 design in which two independent variables, both active, are studied. The research question of the example is whether the airflow or the syllable prolongation component of stuttering therapy is more effective and whether the effects depend upon the presence or absence of contingent feedback on the participants' performance during treatment sessions. Both the forms of treatment and feedback are active; the experimenter controls all of them. The participants are randomly assigned to the conditions of the study. In other words, who receives airflow or prolongation treatment and who receives either of these with or without contingent feedback are decided randomly.

	Contingent Feedback	
	Present	**Absent**
Airflow		
Prolongation		

Figure 8–10. A 2 × 2 completely randomized factorial design. Note that the design includes only active treatment variables; each cell may contain 10 to 15 participants.

The 2 × 2 design just described would probably need at least 60 persons who stutter, 15 to each condition (the four empty boxes in the diagram). A control group, when used, would require an additional 15 participants. The design can be extended to include other active independent variables. For example, in an educational research study, two methods of teaching mathematical skills to children may be implemented with and without the help of computers, creating a 2 × 2 factorial design.

In a randomized clinical trial in medicine, two drugs may be evaluated at two levels of dosage, creating a 2 × 2 design (Machin & Fayers, 2010). In medicine, often a variation of this design involves a combination of two treatments and a placebo: Group 1 (cell 1) receiving treatment *A*, Group 2 (cell 2) receiving treatment B, Group 3 (cell 3) receiving both *A* and *B*, and Group 4 (cell 4) receiving placebo (Sedgwick, 2012). Although useful in studying the effects of multiple drugs and their interactions, factorial designs are not appropriate when combinations of drugs produce increased toxicity or negative interaction (Lee, Lieberman, Sloand, Piantadosi, & Lipman, 2001).

Factorial designs are among the most powerful of the group designs. They can help answer complex and clinically significant questions. It is a common clinical observation that most treatment procedures do not seem to work equally effectively with all types of participants. Clinicians suspect that to a certain extent, the effects of treatment procedures depend upon several participant characteristics, which often reflect other variables. Some of those variables may be related to the client's learning history, the precise nature of the disorder, unsuccessful treatment in the past, and so on. Even such characteristics as gender and socioeconomic class may be a mixture of variables, some of which are external factors in the life of the individual. It is important to know how different variables, including those the clinician calls "treatment," come together to produce the final, desirable effect in different clients. Factorial designs can help answer such important clinical questions.

The problems with factorial designs are mostly practical. Randomization, which is required at some or all levels, creates problems that have been discussed before. Although a factorial design can theoretically handle several variables, the complexity and the need for participants increase in proportion to the number of variables. It is difficult to find sufficient numbers of persons who have dysarthria or aphasia and are willing to participate in an experimental study to permit random assignment to the various cells of a factorial design. Clinical conditions that are relatively rare present the same problem with a much greater magnitude. The analysis of results also becomes more and more difficult with increases in the number of variables or their levels. As a result, firm and clear conclusions regarding the interaction between several variables and levels are difficult to offer.

Quasi-Experimental Designs

Quasi-experimental designs are those in which the investigator is not able to exert full control over all the relevant variables and operations. Originally, they were suggested as a means of conducting experiments in natural settings rather than in the well-controlled laboratories (Campbell & Stanley, 1966; Shadish et al., 2002). In practice, quasi-experimental designs are used whenever practical considerations prevent the use of better (more controlled) designs of research.

Quasi-experimental designs are weaker than true experimental designs because certain control procedures are not used. When studies are conducted in natural settings, it is not always possible to use some of the control procedures, and yet the opportunity for limited experimentation may exist. For example, it may not be possible to draw a random sample of pupils in conducting an experiment on improving teaching methods in an elementary school. Similarly, when a new program of diet or physical exercise for the elderly is initiated in a nursing home, the investigator may not have a chance to select or assign participants randomly. Experimental evaluation of programs in various institutions necessarily uses existing participants and living arrangements. Therefore, some of the quasi-experimental designs do not have groups that are formed especially for the purposes of research. In such cases, the investigators often use already existing natural groups, called *intact groups,* of participants.

Field studies are quasi experimental and are conducted in natural or less artificial conditions than the laboratory studies. Because they use intact groups, field studies lack randomization. Consequently, they lose control over some of the factors that affect internal validity.

Nonequivalent Control Group Designs

The quasi-experimental nonequivalent control group design is similar to the pretest-posttest control group design with one major difference: There is no random selection or assignment of participants in the former. It has two groups: one experimental and one control. Both are pretested. The experimental group receives the treatment. The posttests of the two groups follow. The design is presented in Figure 8–11. Note the absence of R for randomization in the diagram. A line of

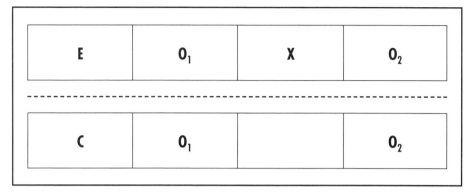

Figure 8–11. The nonequivalent control group design. Note that the design lacks random selection and assignment of participants, indicated by the dashed line.

dashes separates the two groups to suggest that there is no assurance of equivalence based on the random sampling procedure.

The design can have more than two groups. Also, both the groups in a two-group nonequivalent design can receive treatment when the purpose is to evaluate the relative effects of two treatments.

The design often is necessary in settings such as schools, general and mental hospitals, nursing and extended care homes, and rehabilitation institutions for people with intellectual, physical, and other kinds of disabilities. The same-grade children in different sections, groups of patients, or residents in different wards or housing units may serve as the different groups of the study. For example, all persons on the first floor of a residential facility may serve as the experimental group, while those on the second floor may serve as the control group. This results in intact experimental and control groups. Which group receives a treatment and which serves as the control is determined randomly.

Some nonequivalent control group designs may have participants who volunteer for the study. In this case, the sample is self-selected. The investigator then has a self-selected experimental group. A control group may be created from those who do not volunteer for the study.

Intact experimental and control groups are better than the self-selected experimental groups. Possibly, those who volunteer for a study are quite different from those who do not. When the investigator forms a control group, he or she may have no knowledge about the differences between those who wish to participate and those who do not. As a result, the experimenter is likely to have two groups that are so different as to make them unacceptable even within a quasi-experimental design.

It is important to realize that the design does not recommend dispensing with the notion of preexperimental equivalence of groups. It permits an experiment under conditions of no assurance of equivalence based on randomization. The investigator is still expected to take every feasible step to make the groups as similar as possible. For example, an investigator may be interested in the evaluation of a treatment program designed to increase verbal behaviors in institutionalized children with autism spectrum disorder. It is possible that the residents of one ward are more verbal than the residents of another ward. In this case, the investigator should not select the ward with more verbal autistic children for the experimental group and the ward with less verbal children for the control group. The investigator cannot use these two intact groups. If it is possible to move children around to balance the verbal skills of children across the two wards, then the investigator can go ahead with the research.

The same statistical techniques used in the analysis of the results of pretest-posttest control group design are applicable to the nonequivalent control group design. However, the use of analysis of covariance, which is based on a strong assumption of preexperimental sampling equivalence of groups, is questionable.

The most critical problem with the nonequivalent control group design is the selection biases that threaten internal validity. Other threats include statistical regression and differential participant attrition. The participants (either selected or volunteered) may have had unusually high pretest scores to begin with that might regress to the mean during the course of an experiment. This may lead to an erroneous conclusion that the independent variable was responsible for the change. For example, in a study designed to evaluate a new exercise program for senior citizens, residents who are not making progress under the treatment program may withdraw from the study, leaving only those participants who do show improvement.

The design was originally recommended for experiments in natural settings where a better design is not suitable. However, in practice, many investigators in social and psychological research have used the design in laboratory-oriented research, partly because the requirement of randomization poses significant practical problems for all kinds of research, not just for field experiments. Nevertheless, when one of the true experimental designs can be used, the nonequivalent control group design is a poor choice.

Separate Sample Pretest-Posttest Design

Sometimes investigators wish to study certain behaviors or practices of very large natural groups such as workers in a factory, children in large schools or school districts, people living in various parts of a city, or speech-language clinicians in a large school district. In such cases, it often is not possible to randomly select individual participants to form experimental and control groups. However, the investigators usually can randomly select groups of people who will be observed before and after treatment. The separate sample pretest-posttest design is applicable in situations such as these.

This design is represented in Figure 8–12. Note that, unlike the nonequivalent control group design, this design uses the random procedure in selecting groups (not individuals). The two groups, therefore, are assumed to have sampling equivalence, although this might often be a questionable assumption because the individuals are not randomly selected. Only one sample is pretested, and then this sample is presented with a treatment variable not relevant to the study: the X in parentheses. It is the second group, the one not receiving the pretest, which is the true experimental group in the design. The treatment variable is applied to this group, and a posttest follows.

C	R	O	(X)	
E	R		X	O

Figure 8–12. The separate sample pretest-posttest design. Note that the groups, not individuals, are randomly selected; the effects of one of the two treatments—the *X* in parentheses—are ignored.

The design can be illustrated with a hypothetical example. Suppose a coordinator of speech-language services in a large school district wishes to find out the most frequently used therapy technique for speech sound disorders before a new technique is presented to the clinicians in a workshop. The coordinator also wishes to find out if the clinicians would be likely to change their techniques after the presentation. However, he or she needs to avoid the problem of pretest sensitization to treatment, a problem of external validity. Therefore, the investigator randomly selects two subgroups of clinicians in the district and randomly assigns the groups to the experimental and control conditions. A subgroup may consist of all clinicians in a certain number of schools in the district. One of the groups is pretested on the speech sound therapies they use. Then they receive a presentation on the new therapy whose effects are ignored. The other group, in the absence of the pretest, receives the same information. The posttest evaluates the effects of the presentation in terms of any change in the clinicians' inclination to use the new technique.

The results of a separate-sample pretest-posttest design can be analyzed with the parametric independent sample *t* test or nonparametric Mann-Whitney *U* or median test (Gravetter & Walnau, 2017; Huck, 2012).

The separate-sample pretest-posttest design is one of the weaker group designs as it does not control for the effects of history, maturation, and differential participant attrition. Once again, like all of the quasi-experimental designs, it is used when a more appropriate design is not feasible.

Regression Discontinuity Design

A quasi-experimental design that was originally proposed by Campbell and Stanley (1966), expounded by Shadish et al. (2002), has had a checkered history (Cook, 2008). It gained no attention for decades, was used in some studies later, promptly faded, and staged a comeback, mostly in education and economics. Its application in other disciplines has been limited. The design has some interesting features that are suitable to certain treatment evaluations in communication disorders.

The **regression discontinuity design** (RDD) uses a cutoff score on a *continuous dependent variable* to assign participants to different groups in a quasi-experiment in which the participants are not randomly assigned to the groups. The treatment and control group participants are presumed to be the same or similar except for their score on the assignment dependent variable. For instance, in a certain clinical setting where the demand for treatment is very high but the resources are limited, the clinicians might limit treatment to more severely affected individuals, arbitrarily defined. In a VA hospital, for example, persons with aphasia may be administered a test that rates the severity of aphasia on a 7-point scale on which the higher the number, the greater the severity. The clinicians might decide that only those who scored 5 and above will be treated for aphasia. In this case, a severity rating of 5 is a *cutoff score*. On this basis, two groups of individuals are formed: those with a score of 4 and below who are not treated and those with a score of 5 and above who are. Note that the severity is a continuous variable, despite categorical numbers assigned to it. An RDD with an experimental group (E, receiving treatment X), a control group (C), to which the participants are assigned on the basis of a cutoff score (Co), who take a pretest (O_1) and a posttest (O_2), is illustrated in Figure 8–13.

Expected results of a study with RDD is that the linear regression line that shows continuity of scores will break into *dis-continuity* at the cutoff score, hence the name of the design. That is, if the treatment is effective, the severity rating for those in the experimental group will be much lower than that for those who did not receive treatment. What was a straight regression line of severity is no longer continuous because the more severely affected individuals improved with treatment whereas the less severely affected remained at the same level on the regression line because they were controls. In simpler terms, the groups that were similar before treatment become dissimilar after one group is treated.

Because there is no random assignment of participants to the experimental and control groups, RDD is thought to be weaker than the pretest-posttest control group design with randomization. However, in clinical research, random assignment of individuals with diseases and disorders rarely holds, and therefore, the weakness of RDD may not be as critical as generally thought.

Time-Series Designs

The designs described so far, including the true experimental designs, involve at the most only two measures of the

E	Co	O_1	X	O_2
C	Co	O_1		O_2

Figure 8–13. The regression discontinuity design. Note that the distinguishing feature of the design is the assignment of participants to the two groups on the basis of a cutoff score (*Co*, a dependent variable).

dependent variable: the pre- and the posttests. From a statistical standpoint, the two measures may be sufficient to demonstrate the effect of the independent variable. However, those measures do not give a total picture of the initial stability of the phenomenon and the subsequent systematic changes the dependent variables cause. Time-series designs are an alternative strategy that tracks the dependent variable more often than the pretests and posttests. These designs are quasi-experimental.

Time-series designs are those in which a series of repeated measures are taken on the dependent variable and then an intervention is introduced. After the intervention, another series of observations are made on the dependent variable. Because the intervention interrupts the series of measures, the design is also called **interrupted time-series designs** (Glass, 1997). These flexible designs may be used with single participants or groups of participants and with one or more independent variables. They can be used with interventions that have relatively temporary or permanent effects. They are especially suited for studying changes in social behaviors that are a result of new social or legal policies.

There are many time-series designs, and it is not possible to review them all here. Interested readers should consult other sources (Cook & Campbell, 1979; Glass, 1997; Glass, Wilson, & Gottman, 1974). A few of the typical time-series designs are presented here.

Single-Group Time-Series Designs

In the basic **single-group time-series design**, one group of participants is observed several times before and after the introduction of an independent variable. The design has several variations. In the simplest form of the design, there is a single temporary treatment before and after which the dependent variable is measured several times.

The design is illustrated in Figure 8–14. The diagram shows that the treatment was applied once to a single group of participants. The dependent variable was measured four times before and four times after the introduction of the treatment. This is the simplest of the interrupted time-series designs (Cook & Campbell, 1979). The multiple measures before the treatment provide a better picture of the variability, if any, in the dependent variable before the application of treatment. Repeated observations after the treatment can help evaluate the maintenance of the treated behaviors over time.

A temporary treatment of the kind suggested in the design is used frequently in clinical sciences. A group of individuals with aphasia may be observed repeatedly by obtaining several conversational

| O_1 | O_2 | O_3 | O_4 | X | O_5 | O_6 | O_7 | O_8 |

Figure 8–14. A single-group time-series design with temporary single treatment. Note that the dependent variable is measured four times before and four times after the introduction of treatment.

language samples before introducing a treatment program. The treatment may be continued for several days before it is terminated. Then the language samples may be resumed for the next several days or weeks in an effort to monitor the maintenance of the treatment effect.

The basic time-series design shown in Figure 8–14 has several variations. The first involves the continuation of treatment during some of the posttreatment measures of the dependent variable. This design is illustrated in Figure 8–15, which shows that the first four measures were taken before treatment and only the last two were truly the posttreatment measures. Measures 5 and 6 were made while the participants were still receiving the treatment, suggested by the dashed lines under X and the respective O measures. In our earlier example of research on the treatment of aphasia, the treatment may be continued until two measures of the dependent variable have been recorded before it is withdrawn.

In a second variation of the single-group time-series design, treatment is continued while the dependent variable is measured. This design is illustrated in Figure 8–16. The measurement of the dependent variable is continuous in the design as suggested by the dashed lines under X and all of the subsequent measures of the dependent variables.

The design is better able to track the effects of the treatment, because it measures the dependent variable during the course of the treatment. In a daycare facility for people with intellectual disabilities, for example, a group language treatment program may be initiated after several measures of the individuals' language have been taken. The periodic language sampling is then continued throughout the course of the treatment to track the changes in language skills. In contrast, the traditional pretests and posttests are inadequate for the purposes of documenting the course of therapeutic changes that take place over an extended period of time.

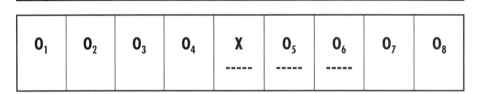

Figure 8–15. A single-group time-series design with continuous treatment and withdrawal. Note that the treatment is continued during Observations 5 and 6.

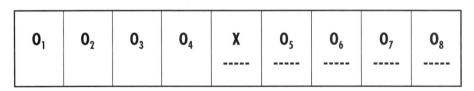

Figure 8–16. A single-group time-series design with single continuous treatment. Note that once initiated, the treatment is continued during all periods of observation.

The design often is used in social research. In many cases, the repeated measures of a dependent variable before treatment may have already been recorded simply as a matter of routine organizational policy. For example, a state department of motor vehicles may keep the records of bodily injuries sustained by people in traffic accidents. An investigator may gain access to such information recorded over a period of time. Incidentally, information of this kind is called **archival data,** which can be used as the repeated pretreatment measures. Then the state legislature may pass a mandatory seatbelt law that requires all drivers and passengers to wear seatbelts. The frequency of accidents involving bodily injury will continue to be recorded, providing the necessary repeated posttests. The treatment (the new law) continues to be applied while the dependent variable is measured. A significant reduction in the frequency of injury reports in the absence of a significant change in the accident rates may be interpreted as a favorable effect of the seatbelt law.

In the example just given, it should be noted that the repeated measurements of the dependent variable do not necessarily involve the same group of participants. The persons who had accidents before the seatbelt law went into effect may not be the same as those who had them after the law went into effect. In other words, people who get into accidents do not constitute a single static group, although some individuals may have a longer membership in that group. In all probability, it is a group whose membership keeps changing. Therefore, in such situations, the measurements of the dependent variable are taken on **replicated groups**, which are groups with changing membership but a defined characteristic (such as those who have accidents). A replicated group contrasts with a **repeated group**, which is a group whose membership is constant. In this latter case, participants in the same group are measured repeatedly. In a majority of time-series designs, measures are taken on repeated groups.

A third variation of the single-group time-series design consists of repeated measures and two or more treatments. The design is illustrated in Figure 8–17. The diagram shows that after obtaining three measures of the dependent variable, the first treatment (X_1) was introduced. After the first treatment was terminated, three more measures were obtained. Then, a second treatment was introduced (X_2), followed by three more observations of the dependent variables. The design can be extended to include additional treatments.

This design may be used in the evaluation of the temporary effects of two or more treatments on the same behavior. A program to teach speech production skills to a group of children with childhood apraxia of speech (CAS) may contain two different treatment procedures

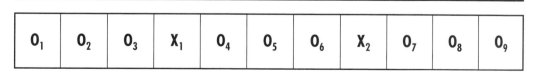

Figure 8–17. A single-group time-series design with multiple temporary treatments. Note that there are two treatments that are separated by observations without treatment.

(X_1 and X_2). Repeated measurement of the dependent variable is interrupted by the two treatments. In implementing a study such as this, it is necessary to have measures of dependent variables (measures of CAS in our example) that are independent of each other. Also, the selected target behaviors should be equally easy or hard to learn.

The single-group time-series design with multiple treatments can be implemented with continuous treatment. After the initial set of observations, the first treatment is initiated and the measurement of the effects is continued until the treatment is terminated. The second treatment is then introduced and the measurement continued until the conclusion of the experiment.

All the single-group time-series designs described so far may be used with single participants as well. In fact, multiple observations before, during, and after treatment are one of the most important characteristics of single-subject designs. There are, however, some important differences between the single-subject and the time-series designs. In single-subject designs, the pretreatment observations are continued until the dependent variable shows an operational degree of stability. There is no such requirement in the time-series designs. Therefore, the pretreatment measurements are made a certain number of predetermined times. Furthermore, single-subject designs typically do not use archival data unless supported by independent observations. More important, single-subject designs differ in terms of how control is achieved. For instance, after a treatment is withdrawn, it is rarely reintroduced in a time-series design, but such reintroductions of treatment are typical of some single-subject designs (see Chapter 8 for details).

The analysis of the time-series designs involves complex statistical procedures, most of them designed especially for the kind of data generated by the strategy. The techniques are unique and involved. A set of statistical techniques often employed uses an **integrated moving average model**, which takes into account the change in the level of the repeated measures and change in the slope. Whether or not there was a slope also may be considered in the analysis.

A serious limitation of single-group time-series designs is the lack of control over extraneous variables, especially those included in the history. The changes recorded at the time the independent variable was introduced into a time series may have been due to some other variables in the life of the participants. The design is not able to rule out directly the influence of extraneous variables. However, when the repeated measures are reasonably stable before the introduction of the treatment and an abrupt and dramatic change is recorded soon after the introduction, the data may strongly suggest a relation that can be confirmed with additional research using designs that permit greater control.

The investigator has less confidence in the results of a single-group time-series design if the changes are small and gradual or highly variable or when a clear trend in the data was evident in the predicted direction from the very beginning of the study. With regard to this last point, the pretreatment measures of language in a language treatment study may show an increasing trend from the beginnings of observation. When this trend continues with the introduction of treatment, the results cannot be interpreted to mean that the treatment was effective. The researcher cannot be sure that language measures would have continued to increase without treatment. One also could suspect an interaction between treatment and other unidentified variables that created the increasing trend in the first place. But the nature and extent of this interaction will not be clear.

Multiple-Group Time-Series Designs

The single-group time-series designs can be extended to include two or more groups. However, the groups in a time-series design are not randomly drawn from a population, and therefore they do not have sampling equivalence. Usually, intact (available) groups are used in these designs.

There are several variations of the multiple-group time-series design, and it is not possible to describe them all here. A basic **multiple-group time-series design** has two nonequivalent groups, one of which is exposed to the treatment variable. Both the groups are repeatedly measured for the dependent variable before and after the experimental manipulation in one of the groups. This design is illus-

trated in Figure 8–18. The figure separates the two groups with dashed lines to suggest lack of sampling equivalence. It also shows four measures before and four measures after the introduction of the independent variable in the experimental group. The dependent variable in the control group also is measured to the same extent.

The design is similar to the nonequivalent control group design (see Figure 8–11) except that the dependent variable is measured repeatedly. The suggestions offered earlier on how to form the two nonequivalent groups are relevant here also.

Compared with the single-group design, the two-group design—even without sampling equivalence—is better because the investigator has a chance to compare treatment with a no-treatment control group. If the repeated measures of the dependent variable do not show significant change although such a change was evident soon after the independent variable was introduced into the experimental group, the possibility of a cause-effect relation is increased.

All the designs illustrated in Figures 8–14 through 8–18 can be modified into

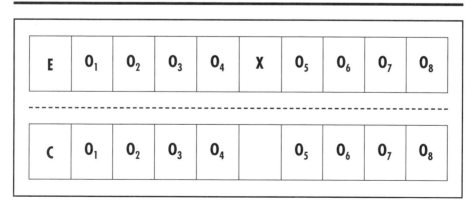

Figure 8–18. A nonequivalent two-group time-series design. Note that the dashed lines suggest nonrandom formation of the groups.

two-group or multiple-group time-series designs by adding one or more groups. An added group can receive treatment when the purpose is to evaluate the relative effects of two treatments. When people in institutions or cities serve as experimental groups, people in other comparable institutions or cities may serve as the control groups.

An interesting multiple-group time-series design involves two staggered treatments. The design, illustrated in Figure 8–19, shows two groups that each receive a different treatment but in a staggered sequence. Possibly, treating both the groups simultaneously may be impractical for reasons of money or personnel. In such cases, one group is treated first and the second group next. In clinical research, one group of clients may be treated first and clients on the waiting list treated next. When measures are repeated before, after, and possibly during the treatment, a staggered multi-group time-series design is in effect.

Counterbalanced Within-Subjects Designs

The common method of establishing cause-effect relations within the group design strategy involves two or more groups, but each group is exposed to at least one different condition of the design. Differences between the groups after one or more groups have been treated are the main data for analysis. For this reason, the group designs discussed so far also are appropriately called the *between-groups strategy* or *parallel-groups strategy*.

There are, however, designs within the group strategy that do not compare the performance of different groups exposed to different conditions of an experiment. Such designs, known as **within-subjects designs** or **counterbalanced designs**, expose participants of all the groups to all the conditions of an experiment. Other names for these designs include *rotation experiments, crossover designs*, and *switch-over designs*. Of these, the term *crossover design* also refers to a particular type of counterbalanced within-subjects design.

The term *within-subjects design* has been occasionally used to refer to single-subject designs. This usage is avoided here. For a long time, the term *within-subjects design* has been a part of the group design terminology, and some of the group within-subject designs have been known since the early 1920s (Edwards, 1960; McCall, 1923). Therefore, in this book, the within-subjects design refers

O_1	O_2	O_3	X_1	O_4	O_5	O_6							
							O_1	O_2	O_3	X_2	O_4	O_5	O_6

Figure 8–19. A two-group time-series design with two staggered treatments. Note that the second group's observation and treatment begin only after the first group's observation was completed.

only to a variety of group designs with counterbalancing as their major feature.

There are some similarities between counterbalanced within-subjects designs and single-subject designs, however. In either strategy, there is no control group that does not receive treatment. Also, in both the strategies, each participant is said to serve as his or her own control. When a controlled condition is a part of an experiment, all participants are assigned to it. Each participant experiences all the experimental conditions in both the strategies. These may be the reasons why some refer to single-subject designs as within-subjects designs. Nevertheless, there are important philosophical and methodological differences between the two approaches. Being a group design, the counterbalanced within-subjects designs use two or more groups of participants. It uses the random procedure in participant selection and the assignment process. The results of counterbalanced within-subjects designs are analyzed through inferential statistics. Most single-subject designs do not share these characteristics. Therefore, single-subject designs are not within-subjects designs.

One-Group Single-Treatment Counterbalanced Design

The simplest form of a counterbalanced within-subjects design, which helps evaluate a single treatment, is the **one-group single-treatment counterbalanced design** in which an investigator has only one group of participants who are all exposed to all conditions of an experiment. The design is sometimes described as *ABBA* counterbalanced design, which should not be confused with the single-subject *ABAB* design.

The one-group single-treatment counterbalanced design has two conditions that are exposed to all of the participants in the group: a no-treatment and a treatment condition. (In the *ABBA* terminology, the two conditions are designated *A* and *B*.) In exposing the participants to the two conditions of the study, the investigator divides participants into two subgroups: One of the subgroups goes through the no-treatment and treatment sequence and the other goes through the treatment and no-treatment sequence.

Note that the two subgroups do not make it a two-group design. There is only one treatment, and the formation of two subgroups is a means of counterbalancing the experimental and control conditions.

Suppose an investigator wishes to study the temporary effects of masking noise on stuttering with a single group of people who stutter. After having selected the participants, preferably on a random basis, the investigator randomly forms two subgroups with an equal number of participants. When the number of participants is small, and typically it is in a counterbalanced design, the random procedure accomplishes very little. In any case, the two subgroups are then exposed to the noise and no-noise conditions in the counterbalanced order. One possible sequence of the design is represented in Figure 8–20. Of course, the sequence shown can be switched across the groups.

Whether the first subgroup should go through the noise and no-noise sequence or vice versa may also be determined randomly. A toss of a coin may determine the initial sequence. If it is determined that the first subgroup will experience the treatment condition (noise) first and the control condition (no noise) next, the second subgroup will automatically follow the opposite sequence. Thus, each half of

	Sequence of Conditions	
	First Condition	**Second Condition**
Subgroup 1	Treatment ➡	**No Treatment**
Subgroup 2	No Treatment ➡	**Treatment**

Figure 8–20. One-group single-treatment counterbalanced design. Note that the treatment and no-treatment conditions are counterbalanced across the subgroups.

the participants will have been exposed to one of the two possible sequences.

The results of each of the conditions are pooled and averaged from the two groups. That is, the mean number of stutterings exhibited by all the participants in the control condition is compared with the mean number of stutterings in the treatment condition. (This is yet another reason why the design is considered to have only one group.) A significant difference between the two means as evaluated by a statistical test of significance suggests the possibility of an effect of the treatment variable.

Counterbalancing is a method to eliminate the *order* as a factor that influences treatment effects. It is possible that when all the participants experience the noise condition first and then the control condition, their stuttering in the second condition may be higher or lower simply because of the previous condition. Counterbalancing—by having half the participants experience one condition first and the other half experience the other condition first—seeks to balance

the order effects across the groups. In this sense, counterbalancing can be seen as a method of equating the order and sequence effects in the groups.

Counterbalancing also can be done on an individual basis. Using the random procedure, the sequence with which each participant experiences the two experimental conditions may be determined. In this method of **intrasubject counterbalancing**, the first participant may go through the control-treatment sequence and the second participant may go through the treatment-control sequence. Care must be taken to ensure that there are equal numbers of participants in both the sequences. The more typical counterbalancing of subgroups, shown in Figure 8–20, is called **intragroup counterbalancing**.

The one-group single-treatment counterbalanced design does not control for extraneous variables of history, maturation, testing, differential participant attrition, and so on. Though it includes a control condition, it does not fully control all or even most of the factors that affect internal validity. The control over the extraneous factors is increased if the same participants, after having experienced no-treatment and treatment conditions, again experience a no-treatment condition. The investigator can then show that changes in the dependent variables follow both the introduction and the removal of an independent variable. Such designs are typical within the single-subject strategy.

Crossover Design

Another counterbalanced within-subjects design is known as the **crossover design** in which two treatments are evaluated with two groups, both of which are exposed to the two treatments in a crossover fashion. It is also known as the *repeated-measures design* (Cozby & Bates, 2018). That is, halfway through an experiment, the participants switch over to another treatment. The design is represented in Figure 8–21. The diagram shows that the groups are formed on a random basis and both the groups receive the two treatments selected for evaluation. Therefore, there is no control group that does not receive treatment.

A hypothetical example can clarify the design arrangement. Suppose a clinician wishes to evaluate the effects of two treatment approaches in remediating speech sound disorders in school-age children. The clinician selects a random sample of children with multiple speech sound errors and divides the sample into two randomly formed groups. The children who have specific speech-sound errors may be selected, which would necessitate an access to a large number of children with those specific speech-sound errors. The participants are pretested (O_1), for example, by standardized tests and conversational speech samples, to determine the specific speech sounds misarticulated by the children. Next, the order in which the groups will receive treatment is determined randomly. Each group then receives the two speech sound treatments in a different order. The design requires an assessment in the middle of the study when the participants are crossed over to the other treatment. A final assessment at the end of the study also is required of both the groups.

Treatment crossover is also a feature of some single-subject designs that evaluate more than one variable. For example, in the *ABACA/ACABA* design described in the next chapter, the same individuals experience one treatment first and then cross over to another. Such single-subject crossover designs are also used in *N*-of-1 clinical trials mentioned later in the chapter and described in Chapter 9.

R	E	O_1	X_1	O_2	X_2	O_3
R	E	O_1	X_2	O_2	X_1	O_3

Figure 8–21. A crossover design with two treatment and two groups. Note that each group receives both the treatments in a counterbalanced order.

Complex Counterbalanced Designs

When only one or two treatments are evaluated, the counterbalanced designs are somewhat simple because each treatment may be offered in the first and the second position in the sequence. However, experiments involving three or more treatments require complex counterbalanced arrangements. The basic requirement of counterbalancing is that each treatment appear at least once in each of all possible positions. To achieve this, the investigator should initially identify all possible sequences of the selected number of treatments.

A counterbalanced design involving only three treatments is already fairly complex. The three treatments, X_1, X_2, and X_3, combine into six sequences: $X_1X_2X_3$, $X_1X_3X_2$, $X_2X_1X_3$, $X_2X_3X_1$, $X_3X_1X_2$, and $X_3X_2X_1$. Each treatment appears twice in each of the initial, medial, and final positions. If the investigator were to use intrasubject counterbalancing, each participant would be randomly assigned to one of the six sequences. However, one should make sure that each order has a comparable number of participants. This often results in ad hoc modifications in the random procedure. In intragroup counterbalancing, six comparable groups are initially formed, and each group is randomly assigned to one of the sequences.

A counterbalanced design with four treatments would have 24 sequences ($1 \times 2 \times 3 \times 4 = 24$). However, when the number of treatments is increased by just one to a total of five, the number of sequences increases to a formidable 120 ($1 \times 2 \times 3 \times 4 \times 5 = 120$). Obviously, numerical increases in the number of treatments result in factorial increases in the num-ber of sequences that need to be counterbalanced. As a result, the need for participants, the number of groups, or both increases dramatically. This can be a serious problem in clinical research where the required number of comparable clients with specific disorders may not be found. For these reasons, completely counterbalanced designs are generally limited to fewer than four treatment variables. Even then, the designs are used infrequently in clinical treatment research.

The practical difficulties involved in achieving complete counterbalancing of multiple treatment variables have led to a compromised procedure of incomplete counterbalancing. Some of the designs that use incomplete counterbalancing also are known as Latin square designs. In a **Latin square design**, each treatment in each position appears only once in each group. Therefore, conditions do not precede or follow each other in all sequences or in equal numbers. Consequently, not all combinations of multiple treatment variables are implemented in a Latin square design.

A Latin square arrangement is represented in Table 8–1. The numbers of groups, treatments, and positions (sequences) are all equal when a Latin square design is represented in the form of a table. Such a table has the same number of rows, columns, and cells in relation to any one group. The same four treatments ($X_1X_2X_3X_4$) in the table shown permit other combinations. A given set of treatments can be represented by different Latin squares. It must be emphasized that the arrangements of treatment sequences in a Latin square are limited. As noted before, complete counterbalancing of the four treatments shown in Table 8–1 would have required not 4 but 24 groups.

Table 8–1. One of the Latin Square Arrangements for Four Treatments, X_1 Through X_4

Groups	Order of Treatment			
	1	2	3	4
I	X_1	X_2	X_3	X_4
II	X_2	X_1	X_4	X_3
III	X_3	X_4	X_1	X_2
IV	X_4	X_3	X_2	X_1

Note. This counterbalanced design requires four groups (I–IV). Each group receives the four treatments in a different order.

Limitations of Counterbalanced Within-Subjects Designs

When several treatments are administered to the same individual or the same group of participants, several potential problems may make it difficult to interpret the results. One should take these limitations into consideration in designing and interpreting the studies of counterbalanced within-subjects designs. Some of these problems can be seen in a few single-subject designs as well.

Order Effects

The influence a particular sequence with which multiple treatments are offered to the same individual is known as the **order effects**. In this case, some or all of the effects of two or more treatments can be explained on the basis of the specific order in which they were administered. Obviously, designs with multiple treatments that are administered to the same

participants necessarily have an order. Therefore, order as a factor cannot be ruled out on a priori grounds.

The problem of the order effect can be understood clearly when two treatments are administered in a single, fixed order to all participants. Suppose that an investigator wished to evaluate the relative (and interactive) effects of a new and an established therapy for reducing vocally abusive behaviors in a voice client. If the investigator were first to apply the established therapy to all the study participants and then to follow it with the new therapy, the results—especially of the new therapy—would be mostly uninterpretable. The effects observed during the administration of the new therapy may be due to the order in which it was administered. The investigator would not know whether the same results would be obtained if the treatments were to be administered in a different order.

The order effect is sometimes described as *practice effect*. The second treatment may be more effective simply because of the increased familiarity with the experimental tasks, arrangements, and repeated practice of some of the skills measured in the sessions. In other words, the treatment itself may not have contributed much to the changes observed in the dependent variable under treatment.

Theoretically, order effects are neutralized in a completely counterbalanced design, which provides for all possible orders in which the selected set of multiple treatments is administered. However, when the orders included in a study do not exhaust all possible positions for all treatments, then the order effects cannot be ruled out. Generally, the greater the number of treatments, the harder it is to present each of them in every possible order, and therefore, the higher the chances of order effects.

Carryover Effects

The second problem associated with the administration of multiple treatments to the same participants is known as *multiple-treatment interference* or *carryover effects,* also referred to as *sequential confounding* or *sequential effects.* While the order effect is due simply to the position in which a given treatment appears, the **carryover effect** is due to the influence of the previous treatment on the succeeding treatment. The prior treatment may have a positive or a negative effect on the succeeding treatment.

When the carryover effect is **positive**, the second treatment will appear stronger than it really is. When the carryover effect is negative, the second treatment will appear weaker than it is. When administered alone, they may produce effects that are different from those observed in a sequential arrangement. The carryover effects may be cumulative over repeated phases, or they may be limited to adjacent phases. Cumulative carryover effects show increasingly larger magnitude across experimental conditions.

Whether the carryover effects have occurred or not can be assessed in a completely counterbalanced design in which each treatment precedes and follows every other treatment more than once. The presence of a positive carryover effect is suggested when the effect of a treatment is typically larger when it follows a given treatment and smaller when it precedes the same given treatment. This relationship between two treatments is illustrated in Figure 8–22. A negative carryover effect is suggested when the effect of a treatment is typically smaller when it follows a given treatment and larger when it precedes the same treatment. This relationship is illustrated in Figure 8–23.

Ceiling and Floor Effects

Two other problems associated with counterbalanced multiple-treatment designs are the ceiling and floor effects. The **ceiling effect** refers to the maximum extent of change produced by a prior treatment, leaving the next treatment no room to show its effect. In a study done to evaluate the effects of two treatments on stuttering, the first method may reduce stuttering to a very low level, perhaps less than 1%. When the second treatment is applied, only a minimal reduction in stuttering may be evident. This small change associated with the second treatment may be due to the ceiling effect created by the first treatment.

As long as the first treatment has any effect at all, the second treatment in a sequence starts with a different *floor* created by the first. The **floor effect**, or the base level of performance, may be high or low, depending upon the effect of the previous treatment. This can also limit the extent of change that a variable can produce. The floor effect is actually a counterpart of the ceiling effect.

The ceiling and floor effects are striking when one treatment is stronger than the other. However, the effect can be seen when both are equally strong. In this case, the first treatment creates a ceiling effect on the second treatment, and the effect is mutual. Automatically, a new floor is created for the next treatment.

Most of the problems associated with counterbalanced designs discussed so far do not exist when all the treatments being evaluated are equally ineffective. Also, the problems are not serious when the treatments have only a temporary effect. That

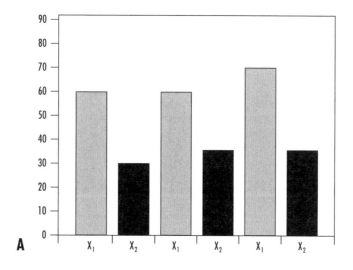

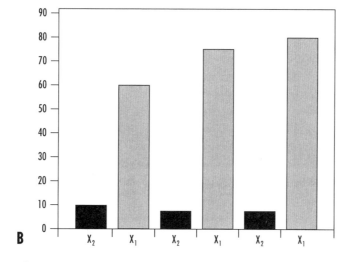

Figure 8–22. Positive carryover from Treatment 1 (X_1) to Treatment 2 (X_2). Note that Treatment 2 had a larger effect when it followed Treatment 1 (**A**) than when it preceded Treatment 1 (**B**).

is, when the effects of a treatment disappear as soon as the treatment is stopped, the carryover, ceiling, or floor effects are not serious considerations. Therefore, the designs are more applicable to behaviors that take a relatively long time to change permanently but can show temporary but clear-cut changes in the short term.

Correlational Analysis

The final type of group research strategy to be considered is variously called *correlational analysis design, correlational design,* or *correlational studies.* Whatever the name, it is not a research design and

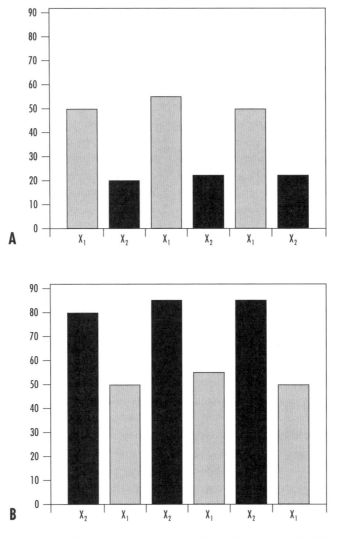

Figure 8–23. Negative carryover from Treatment 1 (X_1) to Treatment 2 (X_2). Note that Treatment 2 had a smaller effect when it followed Treatment 1 (**A**) than when it preceded Treatment 1 (**B**).

certainly not an experimental design. It is a method of data analysis. In a **correlational analysis**, relation between events is studied, but there is no possibility of experimental manipulation of an independent variable. Many of the studies using correlational analysis are of the ex post facto variety described in Chapter 4.

A **correlation** is a statistical procedure that suggests that two events are somehow related. The relation may be positive or negative. Possibly, no relation may be revealed when a suspected relation is tested. A correlation is positive when the measured values of two variables are equally high or low; the variables seem to change in the same direction. When one increases, the other also increases and vice versa. The negative correlation is evident when one variable is high and the other is low and vice versa. A negative correlation suggests that when one event increases, the other decreases. Two events are not related (neutral) when their measured values do not correspond in any particular way.

Such measured values of two variables may be subjected to certain statistical analyses to derive a correlation coefficient that ranges between a perfect negative correlation of −1.00 to a perfect positive correlation of +1.00. Actual correlational coefficients rarely reach these perfect values. Even if the events are perfectly correlated, the measurements are not perfect, and therefore, the correlation will not reach either −1.00 or +1.00.

When an independent variable is not manipulable, one may look for natural events that seem to be related in some specific manner. Two selected variables may be measured once or repeatedly to determine if the measures reflect systematic changes in one or the other direction. A correlation coefficient is calculated for the measured values. Significant positive or negative correlations are interpreted to suggest a relation between the variables.

A correlation does not confirm a cause-effect relation. Even if two events are causally related, the correlation itself does not specify which is the cause and which is the effect. Once a significant correlation is found, causes and effects are usually sorted out on the basis of prevailing theories and empirical knowledge. For example, when it is shown that academic performance and intelligence are highly (and positively) correlated, one concludes that the intelligence is the cause of better academic performance on the basis

of available knowledge about these two variables. Such conclusions are not firm statements regarding functional relations between variables that are correlated. In many cases, causal relation inferred from correlation may be totally erroneous: Two variables may be correlated because they are both an effect of a third variable not at all observed by the investigator.

Once significant correlations between certain events have been found, experiments may be designed to manipulate one of the variables to see what effects follow. Unless this kind of experimental research is performed and the extraneous variables ruled out, it is not possible to draw firm conclusions regarding the meaning of correlations.

It is obvious that correlation is a statistical method of data analysis, not an experimental design in which variables are manipulated, controlled, and measured. As a statistical procedure, it is seen most frequently in the ex post facto type of research.

Group Designs in Clinical Research

The group design strategy described in this chapter has evolved over many years of research in several disciplines. The most significant impetus to this design strategy has come from the development of mathematical, psychological, medical, and agricultural statistics.

The statistical theory of probability, random selection and assignment of participants, inferential statistical analyses of differences in the mean performance measures of groups, evaluation of the effects of independent variables against a background of chance variability, and extension of the conclusions to the population from which the sample was drawn are all distinguishing characteristics of the group design strategy.

Strengths of Group Experimental Designs

The group design strategy, like any other strategy, has its strengths and weaknesses. It works better with certain kinds of research problems investigated in certain settings. It does not work as well with certain other kinds of problems researched in other settings. We make a comparative evaluation of group and single-subject design strategies in Chapter 11. Therefore, here we take note of the main strengths of group experimental designs.

Group experimental designs can effectively isolate cause-effect relations. Carefully designed and properly implemented group experimental designs have acceptable internal validity (probability that the treatment caused the changes in the participants). Group experiments of good quality can demonstrate treatment effects if the investigators succeed in producing clinically significant effects.

Smaller group experiments are more effective than large groups. Group designs with a smaller number of participants can produce more convincing effects and allow for an analysis of individual variability in response to treatment. Such variability may be analyzed more systematically in fewer rather than many participants. This can be done without averaging the responses across individuals. But if the groups are large, the statistical analyses become imperative, and such analyses mask individual differences in response to treatment

Nonexperimental group designs work even better than experimental group designs. Group strategy is more effectively used in such nonexperimental research as sample surveys, ex post facto studies, normative research, and standard-group comparisons. Differences and similarities between groups of people and the way certain variables (such as public opinions) are distributed in the population are studied exclusively by group designs. In such studied, inferential generality tends to be higher than that in group experimental designs.

Limitations of Group Experimental Designs

Significant problems arise when the same strategy that has worked well in large-scale social, agricultural, and certain kinds of psychological research is applied to clinical problems of treatment evaluation (Hegde, 2007). The nature of the everyday clinical business and the feasible strategies of clinical research make the widespread application of the statistical approach impractical. Medicine has been more successful than other clinical disciplines in using the group approach in evaluating drug effects. However, as noted in Chapter 4, randomized clinical trials have made significant methodologic compromises in using the group design strategy.

The required random *selection* of participants from the population is unattainable. Unlike R. A. Fisher's agricultural fields, clinical populations are not accessible for random sampling. Regional or national populations with disorders of language, speech sound, fluency, and voice and those with dysarthria, apraxia of speech, right hemisphere disorders, aphasia, or traumatic brain injury are not readily available for random sampling in which every patient or client has an equal chance of being selected for the study. Even with big budget support from pharmaceutical companies and multiple national and international research centers, RCTs in medicine are not successful in randomly selecting participants from a defined population of target patients. All participants in RCTs are recruited.

Random *assignment* of participants to groups does not work. The National Research Act of 1974 (P.L. 93-348) gives the research participants certain rights and these rights rightfully invalidate both random selection and random assignment. By implication, denying such rights is unethical. The era of forced and uninformed participation in research, one would hope, is over. Informed consent that the participants must give makes all participants *self-selected*. When potential participants are informed about the purpose of a clinical experiment, nature of the treatment to be evaluated, and the alternative treatments available to them, many patients refuse to be randomized. Those who consent select themselves to the study, those who enter the study may not stay in the study, and those who find themselves in the control group may demand treatment and, by their right, get it. The researchers have very little control over this process. Consequently, the results of a group treatment study cannot be generalized to the population of patients needing the same or similar treatment. Therefore, the claimed superiority of group designs in demonstrating statistical (inferential) generality of research findings remains elusive (Hegde, 2007).

Group designs are ill-suited to communication treatment research. In medicine, a new treatment (e.g., a new drug) and the control (a placebo) may be relatively easily administered to a large number of patients in multiple national and international centers. The amount of staff training needed to administer the new drug is negligible. To the contrary, the behavioral treatment techniques are difficult to apply to large number of participants with communication disorders (Hegde, 2007). Much clinical work in speech-language pathology is specific to the individual. In nonclinical research, the independent variables can be presented in groups. A film on attitudes or sensitivity, a set of slides that are supposed to change participants' rated moods, a training program designed to enhance sales clerks' skills, and so on can be easily presented in groups. However, in a treatment method consisting of various steps in which communication skills of individuals with dysarthria, for example, have to be shaped and enhanced to a substantial degree, group presentation of the independent variable is inefficient at best and useless at worst. Although this comment does not apply to group therapies designed to maintain and enrich social communication skills in individually treated persons, large-group treatment to establish skills in clinical populations is yet to be demonstrated effective.

Statistically significant effects may not suffice. Within the group strategy, treatment effects can be small but the study can be considered a success. Statistical techniques tease out small changes that are not clear when visually inspected and help declare that the treatment was effective. Such small changes may certainly have theoretical significance and clinical potential, but they are not of immediate clinical significance. However, in clinical sciences, the changes in stuttering or apraxia of speech induced by experimental or routine therapies should be large enough to make a difference in the lives of the clients. A statistical difference at the .001 level may or may not correspond to the magnitude of change required by real-life conditions. Therefore, practicing clinicians painstakingly shape and change individual behaviors to a point where the positive changes are evident to the client and family. When this happens, the use of statistical techniques that are especially designed to detect small changes seems unnecessary as well as unimaginative. When one can talk about individuals in a meaningful manner, the statistical mean is as irrelevant as it is mythical.

The average effect does not inform individual therapy decisions. Regardless of the medicine's insistence on the group design strategy as the "gold standard of treatment research," averaging an individual participant's measures of dependent variables to perform statistical analysis is of questionable value for medicine as well as all clinical sciences. Groups in group designs are not true biological entities; only the individuals in them are (Johnston & Pennypacker, 2009). Combining individual treatment effects to calculate a statistical mean for the group makes no empirical sense. There is no true group treatment effect; no mean (average) treatment effect is ever real; all treatment effects are experiences of individual participants. An average effect size of a treatment does not help tailor treatment to a single patient or client.

Inferential generality of group designs is overstated. Both the extent of inferential generality achieved in group designs and its relevance to clinical work are typically overestimated (Hegde, 2007). When a clinician reads a report on a new treatment technique in a professional journal, he or she is not especially worried about the population of clients to which the conclusions may be applied. Such a concern about the behavior of the population is real to a politician seeking a majority vote, but the clinician faces a different kind of problem. The clinician's immediate concern is whether the treatment is applicable to the individual client he or she is currently working with. This means that the clinician's immediate concern is logical, not inferential, generality. Group designs do not offer much help in this regard.

Technically, group designs themselves cannot be faulted for lack of inferential generality because all types of generality, including the inferential variety, are a matter of replication. It becomes a problem only when it is claimed for a single large N RCT with no replications. We address the concept and methods of replication in Chapter 10.

Medical researchers do use alternatives to RCTs. Not all medical researchers believe RCTs set the often-repeated "gold standard" for treatment research. They do not agree that the RCTs produce the highest level of treatment evidence or that they produce data useful to practicing physicians. As pointed out in greater detail in the next chapter, many medical practitioners who do treatment research on behalf of their own patients, instead of multinational pharmaceutical companies, find the results of big N RCTs inapplicable to their individual patients. They find the presumed inferential generality of RCTs unhelpful in selecting the best treatment for their patients. Since the 1980s, several medical practitioner-researchers have advocated the use of single-subject designs in evaluating treatment effects in a series of studies they called the N-of-1 randomized trials. What they randomize is multiple treatments offered to the same patients, in the manner single-subject designs do (Gabler, Duan, Vohra, & Kravitz, 2011; Guyatt et al., 1988; Guyatt, et al., 1990; see also the *Journal of Clinical Epidemiology*, Volume 76, August 2016, devoted to N-of-1 trials in medicine).

There are also a considerable number of medical researchers who use the single-subject designs without the N-of-1 nomenclature. Their motivation to use the single-subject designs is to develop individualized treatments as they believe the outcomes of RCTs cannot be generalized to their individual patients (Janosky, 2005; Logan, Slaughter, & Hickman, 2017; Schlosser, 2009; see also the *Journal of Neuropsychological Rehabilitation,* Volume 24, Issues 2–3, 2014, devoted to single-subject designs).

The reader is referred to Chapter 11 for more on the advantages and disadvantages of group experimental designs. Because the advantages and disadvantages of a given approach are better understood in a comparative context, we shall evaluate both group and single-subject design strategies after we have considered the latter in the next chapter.

Summary

Group designs may be preexperimental, true experimental, and quasi-experimental. Preexperimental design has only one group that received treatment. Experimental group designs may have two or more groups.

Experimental group designs are expected to randomly draw participants from a population and randomly assign them to the groups. Preexperimental and quasi-experimental designs lack randomization. Participants may be matched when randomization is not possible.

Group experimental designs rule out extraneous variables by comparing treatment with no treatment (control group) and thus show that treatment caused the changes in the participants. Pretests and posttests help evaluate the treatment effects.

True experimental designs may evaluate single treatments with two groups (control and experimental) or multiple treatments with multiple groups. More complex factorial designs help assess not only the effects of multiple treatments but also any interactions between those treatments and between treatments and participant characteristics (assigned variables).

When multiple treatments are evaluated in the same subjects, the treatments are counterbalanced to minimize the order and carryover effects.

Nonexperimental correlational analysis is based on statistical methods of correlation and do not permit statements on causation.

Well-done group design studies demonstrate internal validity, but external validity requires replication. Group designs that randomly draw a representative sample may permit inferential generality, but this type of generality is not useful in predicting the performance of individual clients.

Table 8–2 offers a summary of major group designs and the kinds of questions they can address (i.e., their applications).

Table 8–2. Summary of Major Group Designs and Their Applications

Design	Research Questions	Strengths and Limitations
One-shot case study	Does the history suggest a cause?	Clinically useful; results are only suggestive
One-group pretest-posttest design	Is there an apparent change due to treatment?	Clinically useful; lacks control; cannot isolate cause-effect relations
Static-group comparisons	Does a treated group differ from an untreated group?	Uses existing treated and untreated groups; lacks pretests
Pretest-posttest control group design	Is a treatment effective? Is there a cause-effect relation?	True experimental design; well controlled; can isolate cause-effect relations; often clinically impractical
Posttest-only control group design	Is a treatment effective? Is there a cause-effect relation?	Well controlled when randomization is used; clinically impractical
Solomon four-group design	Is there an interaction between pretest and treatment? If so, what is its extent?	Useful in studies on reactive variables; impractical in clinical research
Multigroup pretest-posttest design	Is one treatment more effective than the other? What are the relative effects of treatment?	Well controlled; useful to the extent practical; clinically important
Multigroup posttest-only design	Is one treatment more effective than the other? What are the relative effects of treatment?	Well controlled; useful to the extent practical; lacks pretests
Factorial designs; randomized blocks design; completely randomized factorial design	What are the effects of two or more treatments? Is there an interaction between treatments or between treatments and client characteristics?	Excellent designs to study interaction; the most effective strategy to study interaction between participant characteristics and treatment; difficult to find enough participants in clinical research
Single-group time-series design	Is there a change following treatment? Do multiple treatments seem to produce change?	Multiple measures help demonstrate changes in dependent variables; relative effects of treatment can be evaluated; lack of control
Multiple-group time-series design	Is a treatment effective? What are the relative effects of two or more treatments?	Multiple groups ensure some control; multiple measures help demonstrate reliability; no sampling equivalence

Table 8–2. *continued*

Design	Research Questions	Strengths and Limitations
One-group single-treatment counterbalanced design	Do treatment and no-treatment conditions differ significantly?	Has a control condition instead of a group; clinically useful
Crossover design	Do the same participants react differently to two different treatments?	Useful when two treatments should be exposed to the same participants; somewhat weak control
Correlational analysis	Do the selected variables covary?	Can show covariation, not causation

References

Campbell, D. T., & Stanley, J. C. (1966). *Experimental and quasi-experimental designs for research*. Chicago, IL: Rand McNally.

Cook, T. D. (2008). "Waiting for life to arrive": A history of the regression-discontinuity design in psychology, statistics, and economics. *Journal of Econometrics, 142*(2), 636–654.

Cook, T. D., & Campbell, D. T. (1979). *Quasi-experimental design: Design and analysis issues for field settings*. Chicago, IL: Rand McNally.

Cozby, P. C., & Bates, S. C. (2018). *Methods in behavioral research* (13th ed.). New York, NY: McGraw-Hill.

Edwards, A. L. (1960). *Experimental design in psychological research* (Rev. ed.). New York, NY: Holt, Rinehart, Winston.

Fisher, R. A. (1925). *Statistical methods for research workers*. London, UK: Oliver & Boyd.

Fisher, R. A. (1942). *Design of experiments*. London, UK: Oliver & Boyd.

Fisher, R. A. (1951). *The design of experiments* (6th ed.). New York, NY: Hefner.

Fisher, R. A. (1956). *Statistical methods and scientific inference*. London, UK: Oliver & Boyd.

Gabler, N. B., Duan, N., Vohra, S., & Kravitz, R. L (2011). N-of-1 trials in medical literature: A systematic review. *Medical Care, 49*(8), 761–768.

Glass, G. V. (1997). Interrupted time series quasi-experiments. In R. M. Jaeger (Ed.), *Complementary methods for research in education* (2nd ed., pp. 589–608). Washington, DC: American Educational Research Association.

Glass, G. V., Wilson, V. L., & Gottman, J. M. (1974). *Design and analysis of time-series experiments*. Boulder, CO: Colorado Associated University Press.

Gravetter, F. J., & Walnau, L. B. (2017). *Statistics for the behavioral sciences* (10th ed.). Clifton Park, NY: Cengage.

Guyatt, G., Keller, J. L., Jaeschke, R., Rosenbloom, D., Adachi, J., & Newhouse, M. T. (1990). The n-of-1 randomized controlled trial: Clinical usefulness. Our three-year experience. *Academia and Clinic, 112*, 293–299.

Guyatt, G., Sackett, D., Adachi, J., Roberts, R., Chong, J., Rosenbloom, D., & Keller, J. L. (1988). A clinician's guide for conducting randomized trials in individual patients. *Clinical Epidemiology, 139*, 497–503.

Hegde, M. N. (2007). A methodological review of randomized clinical trials. *Communication Disorders Review, 1*(1), 17–38.

Huck, S. W. (2012). *Reading statistics and research* (6th ed.). Boston, MA: Pearson.

Janosky, J. E. (2005). Use of the single subject design for practice based primary care research. *Postgraduate Medical Journal, 81*, 549–551.

Johnston, J. M., & Pennypacker, H. S. (2009). *Strategies and tactics of behavioral research* (3rd ed.). London, UK: Routledge.

Lee, J. J., Lieberman, R., Sloand, J. A., Piantadosi, S., & Lipman, S. M. (2001). Design considerations for efficient prostate cancer chemoprevention trials. *Urology, 57*(4), 2005–2012.

Logan, L. R., Slaughter, R., & Hickman, R. (2017). Single-subject research designs in pediatric rehabilitation: A valuable step towards knowledge translation. *Developmental Medicine and Child Neurology, 59*, 574–580.

Machin, D., & Fayers, P. M. (2010). *Randomized clinical trials: Design, practice, and reporting.* New York, NY: Wiley-Blackwell.

McCall, W. A. (1923). *How to experiment in education.* New York, NY: Macmillan.

Mertler, C. A., & Reinhart, R. V. (2016). *Advanced and multivariate statistical methods* (6th ed.). New York, NY: Rutledge.

Schlosser, R. W. (2009). *The role of single-subject experimental designs in evidence-based practice times* (Technical Brief No. 22). Washington, DC: National Center for the Dissemination of Disability Research.

Sedgwick, P. (2012). Randomized controlled trials with full factorial designs. *British Medical Journal, 345*. https://doi.org/10.1136/bmj.e5114

Solomon, R. L. (1949). An extension of control group design. *Psychological Bulletin, 46*, 137–150.

Shadish, W. R., Cook, T. D., & Campbell, D. T. (2002). *Experimental and quasi-experimental designs for generalized causal inference* (2nd ed.). Boston, MA: Houghton, Mifflin, and Company.

Study Guide

1. Distinguish between statistics and research designs. Specify the role of each in research.

2. What is sampling equivalence? How is it achieved in the group strategy?

3. Compare and contrast the methods of measuring the dependent variables in group and single-subject designs.

4. Can a "control" group ever receive treatment? Why would it then be called a control group?

5. Describe the essential features of preexperimental, experimental, and quasi-experimental designs.

Point out their strengths and limitations.

6. Describe how a one-group pretest-posttest control group design would not be able to demonstrate internal validity of its results.

7. How do true experimental designs rule out the influence of extraneous variables?

8. Compare and contrast random sampling and matching (of participants). Point out the strengths and limitations of each.

9. A clinician wishes to evaluate the effects of a language treatment procedure with the help of the

pretest-posttest control group design. The participants are school-age children. Design this study and justify its procedure.

10. Describe the factors of internal invalidity that affect research studies. What are some of the mechanisms of controlling those factors?

11. What specific problem is the Solomon four-group design thought to avoid?

12. Suppose you wish to evaluate the effects of three treatment techniques used in the management of childhood apraxia of speech. What would be your experimental design? Draw a diagram of the design.

13. What are factorial designs? What purposes do they serve?

14. Define and contrast randomized blocks designs and completely randomized factorial designs. Give an example of each type, complete with all the variables involved.

15. Define a *block* and a *level* in a factorial design. Give examples.

16. What are quasi-experimental designs? When do you use them?

17. In what respect does the nonequivalent control group design differ from the pretest-posttest control group design?

18. What is meant by intact experimental and control groups? Give examples.

19. Illustrate the use of a separate sample pretest-posttest design with an example of your own.

20. What is the most important characteristic of time-series designs?

21. A clinician evaluated a certain treatment procedure used in the management of language disorders. The clinician measured the language performance of the clients four times before starting treatment. The treatment was then applied for 3 months. Finally, the clinician took four more measures of language behaviors in the absence of treatment. What kind of design did the clinician use? What kinds of conclusions were justified?

22. Demonstrate how you can evaluate the effects of two or more treatments in a time-series design. Illustrate your answer.

23. What is the most distinguishing feature of the regression discontinuity design?

24. What are counterbalanced within-subjects designs? Are they the same as single-subject designs?

25. What is a crossover design? Do you evaluate a single treatment or multiple treatments in this design?

26. What is a Latin square design? What are its limitations?

27. Define order effects. Distinguish between positive and negative carryover effects. How are they minimized in counterbalanced within-subjects designs?

28. Distinguish between ceiling effects and floor effects. Under what conditions are they significant in a study?

29. What are the limitations of correlational analysis designs?

30. Evaluate the usefulness of group designs in clinical treatment research.

9

Single-Subject Designs

Chapter Outline

- Historical Background of Single-Subject Designs
- Characteristics of Single-Subject Designs
- Experimental Control in Single-Subject Designs
- Preexperimental Single-Subject Design
- Designs for Single Treatment Evaluation
- Designs for Multiple Treatment Comparison
- Designs for Interactional Studies
- *N*-of-1 Randomized Clinical Trials
- Single-Subject Designs in Clinical Research
- Summary
- References
- Study Guide

In the previous chapter, we described a research strategy in which the basic data represent differences in the performance of two or more groups of participants. In this chapter, we describe another strategy in which the data represent differences in performance of the same participants under different conditions of an experiment. The research designs of this strategy are known as single-subject designs (SSEDs) or single-case designs.

The SSED strategy is now well established. The approach is appropriate for establishing cause-effect relations in animal and human behavior. It is also as effective as the group design strategy in evaluating treatments in most disciplines, including all branches of medicine and rehabilitation, nursing, physical therapy, counseling, social work, and clinical psychology (Janosky, 2005; Janosky, Leininger, Hoerger, & Libkuman, 2009; Morgan & Morgan, 2009; Schlosser, 2009). Its usefulness is proven in regular and special education and behavioral research (Bailey & Burch, 2017; Barlow, Nock, & Hersen, 2009; Cozby & Bates, 2018; Johnston & Pennypacker, 2009; Kazdin, 2010; Sidman, 1960), which include almost all of the treatment procedures used in communication disorders.

Historical Background to Single-Subject Designs

The SSED strategy, though fully developed by behavioral scientists in the 20th century, has a historical record that includes the work of early psychologists who studied psychophysics; physiologists and neurologists who studied individual differences in anatomy, physiology, and neurology; and psychiatrists and clinical psychologists who studied behavior disorders and their unique manifestations in individual clients. Beginning with the second half of the 20th century, applied behavior analysts and speech-language pathologists have been making significant contributions to speech and language treatment research by conducting SSED experiments.

Generally speaking, the work of these diverse scientists was concerned mostly with the individual, not groups of people. Scientifically, understanding patterns of individual behaviors and their experimentally manipulable causes, and clinically, understanding the uniqueness of individual symptoms and responses to treatment were the main concerns that led to the development of single-subject approach.

Study of the Individual

Studying the behavior of single individuals, as against the behavior of groups of individuals, has a long and productive history in both clinical and basic sciences. Whereas the statistical developments in the early 20th century established the study of individuals in groups and differences between groups, certain academic and clinical developments in late 19th century and continuing into the present have helped establish a parallel trend of studying the individual.

Academic developments that led to systematic observations of individuals first took place in early psychology and physiology. We will briefly review a few major trends in early psychology, physiology, and clinical disciplines before we trace the development of experimental and applied behavior analysis that fully developed not only the study of individuals but experimental demonstration of cause-effect relations.

Psychological and Neurophysiological Study of the Individual

Much of the early descriptive and experimental psychology was concerned with single or a few individual participants. Group comparisons were uncommon in the first few decades of experimental psychology and, as noted in the next section, uncommon in the early development of most clinical sciences as well.

Experimental psychology began in 1860s in the works of German mathematicians, philosophers, physiologists, and psychologists of the time. It was in the works of Gustav Fechner (1801–1887) and Wilhelm Wundt (1832–1920) that gave birth to the basic science of psychophysics, which laid the foundation for experimental psychology in Germany (Boring, 1950). What is of interest to us is that the method used by early experimental psychologists was self-examination and examination of a few well-trained participants who were presented with precisely measured sensory stimuli of various kinds. The participants reported their experiences (sensation and perception) in a method called *introspection*. Fechner is reported to have injured his eyes because he was his own single participant in experiments on visual after-images as he gazed at the sun through colored glasses (Boring, 1950).

The tradition of self-experimentation was continued in the works of Hermann Ebbinghaus (1850–1909), the inventor of the nonsense syllable, who did the earliest experiments on memory. He, too, was his own single participant and learned various nonsense syllables and recalled them under varied conditions to find out the relationship between such variables as learning and the length of the material learned, frequency of repetition, and the strength of recall. Such experiments with few or single participants led to an understanding of fundamental processes in sensory physiology and psychology.

In learning and conditioning, most experiments have been conducted with few animal or human participants. Pavlov conducted his experiments on classical conditioning with only a few dogs. Nonetheless, the principles of conditioning that Pavlov formulated have been shown to have generality at the animal as well as human levels. Pavlov (and Skinner's as we shall soon see) produced data of such generality mainly because of the degree of experimental control he achieved in his experiments and the precision with which he measured the dependent and independent variables. Similarly, Watson and Rayner's (1920) well-known experiment on conditioning of fear in a single child to white rats eventually demonstrated that data generated from single participants may have generality.

Early physiological and neurological research, too, has been based on systematic observations of, and experimentation on, one or a few individuals. It is well known that Broca's discovery of the motor speech center in the third frontal convolution of the left cerebral hemisphere was based initially on a single case and subsequently on just a handful of cases. By carefully examining an individual with aphasia, Broca kept detailed records of his speech problems and ruled out any pathology of the larynx or paralysis of the speech muscles. When the patient died, Broca performed a brain autopsy and found a lesion in the third frontal convolution in the left cerebral hemisphere. Broca's speech area and Broca's aphasia are now generally accepted although not without some controversy. His careful observations of single patients underscored the value of intensive study of single or few individuals in making valid contributions to scientific knowledge (Hegde, 2018).

Other early neurophysiological discoveries also used single or few participants. For instance, the discovery of localization of motor functions in the brain by Fritsch and Hitzig in 1870 was based on human single case observations and few animal experiments (Boring, 1950). Similarly, Wernicke's discoveries of a sensory speech area in the posterior portion of the lcft superior temporal gyrus and a type of aphasia associated with lesions in this area were based on single case observation. Mapping of the brain functions has always been done only with a small number of participants, often single participants, who had to undergo brain surgery for such diseases as epilepsy (Hegde, 2018).

The Case Study Method

The case study method was born out of clinical case histories that clinicians take during assessment of clients with disorders and diseases. Case studies, however, go beyond the case history in the sense that they are a more scientific method of studying a phenomenon by making systematic observations and measurement (Yin, 2017). The case study method is used in studying clinical as well as nonclinical phenomena in such diverse disciplines as psychiatry, history, anthropology, medicine, psychology, linguistics, speech-language pathology, and sociology.

In both case history and case study methods, the attention is paid to the individual. The case study method has provided careful and detailed description of diseases, disorders, and their symptoms in individuals. Such descriptions are essential

to diagnose and treat disorders and diseases. In psychiatry, thorough observations of patients to describe their symptoms by such early German psychiatrists as Kraepelin (1856–1926) have been the beginnings of the case study method. Freud's psychoanalysis was founded entirely on the case study method (Freud, 1944).

Clinical psychology, which flourished after World War II, fully exploited and extended the potential of the clinical case study method to observe and record the symptoms of mental and behavioral disorders. Speech-language pathology, being a clinical discipline, also began to use the case study method to document various disorders of communication.

As noted before, the method has been widely used in the study of other issues in human and animal research. For instance, the study of language acquisition in children has been greatly advanced by the case study method involving longitudinal observations of one or a few children. Parents' systematic observation of their single child's language behaviors, recorded over an extended period of time, is a standard method of tracing language acquisition. Brown's (1973) well-known research on language acquisition had only three young children as participants. Much of Piaget's (1959) renowned work on intellectual development in children was based on extended observations of his three children.

Experimental Analysis of Behavior

Although systematic observations of individuals have been a well-established scientific method in several disciplines, such observations were often nonexperimental. For instance, most research on language acquisition in children is nonexperimental. Nonexperimental observations of individuals, while providing valuable insights and hunches, cannot establish a functional relation between the variables measured or recorded. In a systematic clinical case study, for instance, it is not possible to firmly establish the cause of the disorder. When a case study reports favorable results of a treatment, clinicians cannot be sure that the treatment actually caused those results. The typical case study is an ex post facto analysis of factors that may have been responsible for an effect, but it lacks experimental control. Case studies rely heavily on the method of correlation, not experimentation. Therefore, while systematic observations of single participants are a good start, such observations need to incorporate experimental manipulations.

Skinner (1953) was foremost among the scientists who used the SSED approach to develop an *experimental method* to create a science of behavior. To make a functional (causal) analysis of animal and human behavior, Skinner developed the method of intensely studying individual behaviors under *different experimental conditions*. He did not believe that studying the behavior of large samples of individuals randomly drawn from a population would yield strong experimental data to build a science of behavior. In his view, large samples force superficial observations under weak experimental controls, resulting in data that fail to throw light on causal relationships. To this effect, he stated that "instead of studying a thousand rats for one hour each, or a hundred rats for ten hours each, the investigator is likely to study one rat for a thousand hours" (Skinner, 1966, p. 21).

Skinner's experimental analysis of behavior has clearly shown that to achieve generality, one does not need randomized samples of large number of participants. Most of the operant conditioning principles, including positive and negative reinforcement schedules, extinction, generalization, discrimination, and punishment, were established with a few rats and later extended to human participants through various replications. Skinner's research has made it clear that replications are the best method to achieve generality. Studies using single-subject experimental designs (SSEDs) can be more easily replicated than group design studies to produce scientifically valid knowledge.

Applied Behavior Analysis

Most of the currently used SSEDs in treatment research were developed by applied behavior analysts, who extended Skinner's experimental analysis of behavior to make a functional analysis of personally and socially significant problems. For instance, multiple baseline designs were developed specifically to evaluate clinical treatment techniques and educational teaching methods. The kinds of dependent and independent variables manipulated in these designs have been influenced to a great extent by behavioral philosophy. Nevertheless, the designs have been extended to study problems in medicine, nursing, social work, education, and other disciplines with no commitment to behavioral philosophy.

Applied behavioral research has clearly demonstrated that clinical and educational problems of social and personal significance can be meaningfully analyzed with SSEDs. Unlike traditional case studies, applied behavioral analysis is typically experimental. The nonexperimental and the experimental case study methods use a single or a few participants, but the latter makes its observations under controlled conditions and induces systematic experimental manipulations to rule out the influence of extraneous variables. SSEDs have been especially useful in evaluating behavioral treatment and teaching methods.

Characteristics of Single-Subject Designs

The SSEDs also are described as *single-case designs, intrasubject replication designs,* and *designs of behavioral analysis.* As noted in Chapter 8, occasionally they also are called *within-subjects designs.* However, there exists a variety of group designs that has historically been known as within-subjects designs. Therefore, this term should not be used to describe SSEDs.

Several characteristics are common to SSEDs that are currently used in treatment research. We shall take a look at these before studying the actual designs.

Intensive Study of Small Number of Participants

To avoid large samples, SSEDs concentrate on fewer individuals. The approach places a heavy emphasis on understanding the behavior of individuals. Intensive study of individuals makes much clinical sense. Clinicians are much more interested in changing the health status or undesirable behaviors of their individual clients. Clinical work, even if it involves a large number of individuals, is essentially concerned with how individuals react to different diagnostic and treatment proce-

dures. Therefore, SSEDs use a small number of available participants who meet the selection criteria. Clinical treatment studies with just few participants generate a significant amount of data largely because of extended observations of individual behaviors under such changing experimental conditions as baserate, treatment, and treatment withdrawal.

One of the mistaken notions about SSEDs or single-case designs is that only one participant can be used in a study. Though some reported studies may have had single participants, the designs themselves are not restricted in this manner. Typically, multiple participants, perhaps six to eight, are used in most SSEDs. Obviously, the number of participants used in SSEDs is much smaller than that in group designs.

Importance of Individual Differences

The emphasis on the behavior of individuals also means that individual differences are of both scientific and clinical interest. From a statistical standpoint, individual differences are within-group variance (variability). Starting with the dawn of statistics in the 19th century, variability in the data collected on individuals has been considered *errors* of measurement in the group design strategy, which is most interested in variance between the experimental and control group. To the contrary, SSEDs do not treat behavioral variations within and across individuals as errors or anomalies. There is nothing erroneous about individual differences. Behavioral variability is worthy of experimental analysis. It is only such experimental analysis of individuals and their behavioral variability that will lead to a better understanding of individual differences and commonalities. Controlling experimental conditions tightly to see if the behavioral variability is reduced is a unique characteristic of SSEDs. If the variability is not reduced even under strict experimental conditions, efforts to understand why may then be initiated.

Because of its interest in behaviors of individuals, the SSEDs do not make group comparisons. Instead of comparing the mean performance of participants receiving treatment with the mean performance of participants not receiving treatment, the single-subject strategy compares the same individual's performance under treatment and no-treatment conditions. For this reason, SSEDs are said to use *the same person as his or her own control*. Treatment and control conditions are both experienced by each and every participant in SSEDs. In the group designs, experimental and control conditions are experienced by different individuals. It is in this sense that single-subject experiments are truly single; each experiment is complete within one individual who is exposed to both treatment and control conditions.

The problem of denying treatments to individuals who need them is avoided in SSEDs because, as noted, each participant is exposed to both treatment and no-treatment conditions. Denial of treatment to sick people in the control groups in medical research is a troublesome ethical issue (Hegde, 2007).

Repeated Measurement of the Dependent Variables

Repeated measurement of the dependent variables is required in SSEDs. There are no pre- and posttests, as in the group design approach. Both the terminology and the practice of pre- and posttests are determined mostly by educational research methods. In the SSEDs, the dependent variables are not *tested* or assessed with some standardized instrument but *measured* continuously—before, during, and after treatment.

Before the treatment is introduced, the dependent variables (behaviors that are treatment targets) are measured repeatedly. The repeated measures made before the introduction of treatment are typically known as **baselines** or **steady states** (Sidman, 1960). As noted in Chapter 4, these initial baselines are held to a criterion of stability and reliability. In some cases, baseline observations may be done over several days to stabilize the behaviors under controlled conditions. Treatment is introduced only when the behaviors, stabilized across observations, provide contrast to treatment effects.

In treatment sessions, too, the target behaviors are continuously measured. This may not be the case in group designs that depend on a posttest administered at the end of the study. Session-by-session measures of target behaviors give a better picture of the course of changes in the dependent variables than the two-point measures of pre- and posttests.

Another measure of the dependent variable taken throughout SSED studies is known as *probes*. **Probes** are measures of target behaviors in the absence of treatment. But unlike baselines, which are a *pretreatment* measure, probes are measured in treatment session while the intervention is temporarily suspended. Probes may also be taken at the end of treatment and during follow-ups. They may be taken in the treatment room or, in many cases, outside the room. Probes help assess the stability of treatment effects when the treatment is temporarily discontinued and generalized production of target skills in the natural environment. Such generalized productions in everyday situations enhance the social validity of treatment procedures.

Selection of Available Participants

In the SSEDs, no attempt is made to randomly draw a representative sample from a defined population. Because of the requirement that all participants give informed consent to take part in research studies, participants in all treatment (and nontreatment) studies, including randomized clinical trials, are self-selected (Hegde, 2007). In SSED studies, available individuals are considered appropriate for experimental analysis. As in group design studies, not all available participants are selected; only those who meet certain selection criteria thought to be relevant for the research question are chosen for participation. For instance, such variables as age, gender, severity of the disorder, prior treatment, or prior exposure to a certain technique may lead to specific selection criteria.

Because no effort is made to have a representative sample of a population, the conclusions of an SSED study are not extended to the population on the basis of a single study or a few studies. Unreplicated SSED study cannot and does not claim inferential (statistical) generality. The SSED researchers do believe that generality should be established for all treatment procedures. They take a different route to generality of treatment effects, however. These researchers believe that generality from a few individuals to many more individuals is a matter of replica-

tions and that even the most representative sample, if ever drawn, is not likely to have all kinds of generalities. All studies need to be replicated to achieve generality.

Strong on Logical Generality

Although one or few SSED studies do not claim inferential (statistical) generality, they do claim logical generality. **Logical generality** is the extension of the conclusions of a SSED study to individuals in a routine clinical setting who match the profiles of study participants. Because the reports of SSED studies give full details on individual participants, it is easier for practitioners to match their client profiles with those of study participants.

Because SSED studies describe each participant's data separately, the reader of such reports knows who improved, who did not, and who deteriorated under the experimental treatment. The reader can thus match a participant's personal characteristics with the results obtained. For instance, if only those with a more severe disorder improved under an experimental treatment, the practitioner can then apply the treatment to such clients only. Group designs, even if they do have statistical generality, and typically they do not, lack logical generality because the studies do not give individual profiles or individual data in sufficient detail to be useful to clinicians.

Visual Inspection of Data Versus Statistical Analysis

Visual inspection or **visual analysis** is the main and most frequently used method of SSED data analysis. Most behavioral scientists find a visual analysis of marked contrast in response rates across baseline, treatment, withdrawal, reversal, and multiple baselines sufficient to draw conclusions about the effects of treatment (Lane & Gast, 2014). We return to visual analysis and statistical analysis of single-subject data in Chapter 10.

For three main reasons, the results of SSEDs generally are not analyzed with statistical techniques. The first is that the experimental effects produced in SSEDs are large enough to support conclusions without statistical analyses. Most statistical techniques are designed to detect small changes in dependent variables against a background of poorly controlled natural variability. SSEDs depend upon empirical (observable) significance in differences across conditions, not statistical differences. Figure 9–1 shows the difference between the group and the SSED data of a hypothetical study.

If a certain treatment of stuttering is evaluated within a two-group study and also an SSED study, the kinds of results that are depicted in Figure 9–1 are likely. The data from the SSED, shown in the upper part of as bar graphs (A), make the effects of treatment visually obvious. There has been a systematic and clinically impressive reduction in the frequency of stuttering.

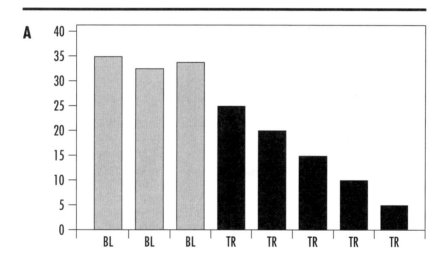

B

	Pretest Percent stuttering	Posttest Percent stuttering
Control Group	37	35
Experimental Group	36	25

Figure 9–1. Differential visual effects of single-subject (**A**) and group design studies (**B**) of a hypothetical treatment effect on stuttering. Note that the single-subject data are presented for three baseline sessions (BL) and five treatment sessions (TR). The data for the group design study are the pretest and posttest means for the two groups.

On the other hand, whether the difference in the mean frequency of stutterings of the two groups, shown in the lower portion (B), is due to the treatment or chance fluctuations is not so readily apparent. Therefore, the effects of treatment in group designs are better determined by statistical analysis.

If an SSED study did not produce visually impressive effects, the behavior scientist is less likely to go in search of a statistical technique that will tease out small effects that are unlikely to be of clinical significance. Instead, the scientist is more likely to spend his or her energy in refining the independent variable (treatment) or test another independent variable to produce relatively large and clinically significant effects.

The second reason is philosophical rather than methodological. All inferential statistical techniques designed to find significant difference between the group performances in experiments are based on averaging the scores of individuals in the groups. Significance tests cannot handle individual scores. Variability of individual performances must be reduced to a mean. The 18th-century proponent of statistics and eugenics, Francis Galton, wrote that the object of statistics "is to discover methods of epitomising a great, even an infinite, amount of variation in a compact form" (Galton, 1880, p. 306). Ironically, the founder of *differential psychology*, Galton was interested in individual differences, not compressed similarities. Behavior scientists believe that epitomized individuals and compressed variations eliminate any chance of understanding individual differences in human animal behavior.

The third reason for not making statistical analysis of SSED data is that a majority of inferential statistical techniques are based on the random theory and require

both random sampling and random assignment of participants. Although most participants in group designs and randomized clinical trials are truly self-selected and not at all randomized (Hegde, 2007), the routine use of statistical tests to find significant differences between groups is rarely questioned. However, it has always been pointed out that inferential statistical techniques may not be appropriate for evaluating unaveraged data of individual participants.

If inferential techniques are inappropriate, could the statisticians devise procedures that are uniquely appropriate to SSED results? The answer has been a resounding *yes*. Those who equate statistics with objectivity believe that SSEDs need their own statistics. There is now a plethora of statistical procedures to analyze the results of SSED studies so the conclusions, presumably, are more objective and scientific. We review them in Chapter 10 on statistical analysis of research data. Nonetheless, a majority of behavioral scientists primarily use visual analysis of SSED data.

Experimental Control in Single-Subject Designs

Group and SSEDs differ in the way they introduce experimental control to rule out the influence of extraneous variables to claim internal validity. Group designs rule out the influence of extraneous variables by the use of *control groups* that do not receive treatment and hence do not show significant change at the end of an experiment. On the other hand, SSEDs rule out extraneous variables by a combination of *control conditions*.

It was argued in Chapter 4 that control conditions and control groups are the primary and equally powerful methods of showing that a treatment, and no other variable, was responsible for the positive changes documented in an experiment. In the same chapter, we have described such control conditions as baselines, treatment withdrawal, treatment reversal, reinstatement of treatment, criterion-referenced change, rapid alternations, and simultaneous multibaselines. The designs described in the subsequent sections of this chapter illustrate those control mechanisms.

Preexperimental Single-Subject Design

Preexperimental designs do not adequately control the factors that affect the internal validity of an experiment. The *AB* **design** is a nonexperimental single-subject design that parallels the group preexperimental one-shot case study. Common in all clinical sciences, the *AB* design is similar to a traditional case study of a single patient or client who undergoes a form of treatment.

In the *AB* design, a baseline of the target behavior is first established; the treatment is then applied and the dependent variable is measured continuously. When the treatment objective is achieved, a report is made on the recorded changes in the client behaviors. The design is illustrated in Figure 9–2.

It is obvious that the *AB* design lacks experimental control of extraneous variables. Therefore, it is a case study design, not an experimental design. The observed changes in the dependent variable may or may not be due to the influence of treatment. There is no assurance that in the absence of treatment, the behaviors would not have improved because the treatment is not compared with no treatment.

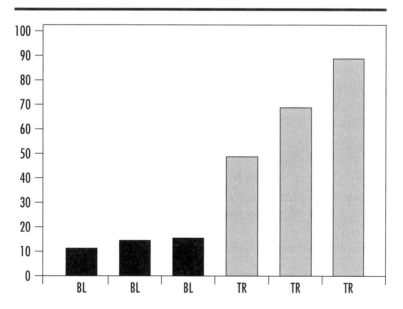

Figure 9–2. The baseline (BL) and treatment (TR) conditions of an AB (preexperimental) design.

Therefore, history and maturation, among other factors, may explain the results of case studies and *AB* studies.

The *AB* studies, though they do not permit statements on cause-effect relations, are valuable tools of clinical research. Their positive results may prompt for more controlled research. Negative results of an *AB* study, on the other hand, are a significant finding because a treatment that does not produce an effect under uncontrolled conditions is unlikely to produce an effect under controlled conditions.

The matter of experimental control is not an either-or phenomenon because different designs have varying degrees of control. The *AB* designs can also vary in terms of the degree of confidence one can place in the results. Some of them can be more trustworthy than others. Carefully designed studies with multiple observations before, during, and after treatment with stable measures and good contrast can enhance the validity of *AB* studies.

Designs for Single Treatment Evaluation

Unlike the preexperimental *AB* design, SSEDs—**single-subject experimental designs**—seek to rule out extraneous variables with appropriate control mechanisms. When adequate control mechanisms are used, the investigator may claim internal validity for the results.

Effects of single or multiple treatments and interaction between two or more treatment procedures may be evaluated with SSEDs. We shall begin with the most basic of the SSEDs: the *ABA* and *ABAB* designs. We then move on to more complex designs for evaluating rela-

tive and interactive effects of multiple treatments.

The *ABA* Withdrawal Design

The *ABA* withdrawal design, illustrated in Figure 9–3, is the original SSED. In the laboratory research involving animal behavior, subjects are typically run for an extended period of time to establish the operant level (baseline) of selected behaviors. It is not uncommon to run animal subjects for several weeks to achieve behavioral stability. Following a stable response rate, various kinds of stimulus and response-consequent contingencies are applied to assess the effects on behavior patterns.

Depending on the research question, the experimental contingencies also are applied over an extended time. A marked shift in the response rate creating a contrast between the baseline and the treatment conditions is sought by this prolonged experimental manipulation. After such a shift is observed, the independent variable is withdrawn, and the subjects or participants are allowed to respond. Normally, the response rate gradually decreases until it approximates the original baseline level. When the independent variable investigated is a reinforcer, the withdrawal condition also is known as the *extinction* condition.

In Figure 9–3, note that the baseline and treatment withdrawal conditions are more similar to each other and contrast with the treatment condition. The response rate is higher under the treatment condition, which contrasts with the baseline and extinction conditions.

The *ABA* withdrawal design is a well-controlled design. When a stable baseline

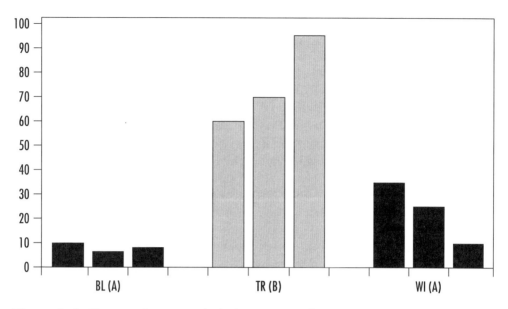

Figure 9–3. The *ABA* design in which the positive effects of a treatment are cancelled by withdrawal.

response rate changes dramatically when the treatment is introduced but returns to the baseline level when the treatment is withdrawn, a treatment effect is convincingly demonstrated. The basic logic of the design is that when a variable is present, it produces an effect, but when the variable is absent, the effect disappears. When this happens, other factors cannot account for the presence and absence of the effect.

Much of the basic information we have on the principles of learning and conditioning, including reinforcement, punishment, and the effects of various reinforcement schedules, has been generated by this *ABA* withdrawal strategy. It continues to be one of the most important experimental strategies of research in experimental behavioral analysis.

It is clear that the final phase of the *ABA* withdrawal design does not involve treatment. When it is used in clinical set-

tings, the improvement shown by the client in the treatment condition is neutralized in the final *A* condition. Therefore, it is not a clinical treatment design. However, the design has a place in clinical research. Its use in clinical research can be justified on certain discriminated grounds.

The *ABA* design is appropriate when the effects of a new technique of treatment must be evaluated and there is no evidence yet that it will be the long-term treatment for the disorder under investigation.

There is a more important reason for using the *ABA* design. Whether a variable has any effect at all on a given behavior is an important research question. The effects may be temporary, in which case they may not lead to the development of a treatment effect. They may be relatively permanent, in which case the possibility of developing a new treatment technique exists. When the initial research question is whether a particular variable has any effect at all, the *ABA* withdrawal design is appropriate. For instance, it is reasonable to ask whether verbal or other kinds of stimuli have any effects at all on dysfluencies, speech sound errors, vocal pitch breaks, or other kinds of speech-language problems.

If the answer produced by an *ABA* withdrawal design is positive, more clinically appropriate designs can be employed to develop treatment techniques. For cxample, much of the operant research on stuttering involving such aversive stimuli as shock, noise, and verbal stimuli was done with the *ABA* design. Hindsight would now justify the use of the *ABA* withdrawal strategy because stimuli such as shock and aversive noise have not led to routine clinical treatment procedures.

Whether such stimuli would increase or decrease stuttering was a worthwhile question to investigate, with important theoretical implications.

The *ABA* Reversal Design

The reversal operation described as a control mechanism in Chapter 4 can be used in the *ABA* format. It is illustrated in Figure 9–4. In terms of the baseline and treatment, the design is the same as the *ABA* withdrawal design. However, during the second *A* condition, the treatment may be reversed. Instead of simply withdrawing the treatment from the target behavior, another, incompatible behavior, may be treated. As a result, it can be shown that the first behavior returns to the baseline and the second behavior shows new and systematic changes. One can conclude

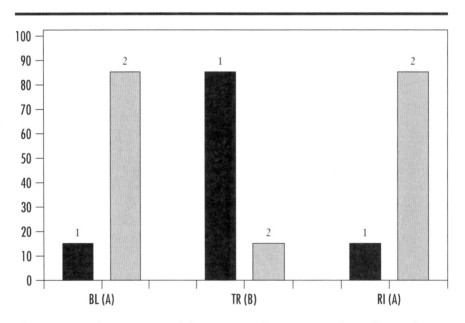

Figure 9–4. The *ABA* reversal design. Note the corresponding effects of treatment (TR) and reversal (RI) on a target (1) and its incompatible behavior (2).

that only the treatment was responsible for the changes in the two incompatible behaviors and that extraneous variables were not operative.

For example, if the design is used in evaluating a treatment procedure for speech sound disorders, the clinician first decreases the correct production of selected phonemes and then reverses the contingencies to increase the original incorrect productions of the same phonemes. In the treatment of language disorders, participants' production of selected grammatical features in words may be first increased and then decreased in the treatment reversal condition. For instance, if a child initially omits the auxiliary *is*, resulting in such responses as *boy running* and *girl writing,* the reversal involves a reinforcement of these responses. Thus, in the reversal design, as in the withdrawal version, the participants return to the baseline. Because the wrong responses are reinforced in the reversal, the baselines may be approximated sooner than in the withdrawal design that uses the slower extinction process (correct responses slowly decline and the wrong responses slowly recover).

When a reversal is used, there is no need to increase the error response to a level that is higher than that observed at the baseline. When the baseline is at zero, and the treatment increases the target behavior to 90% or higher, then the reversal need not be continued until the target behavior reaches zero. A reduction from 90% to 30% or 40% may be convincing. As such, reversal and withdrawal are both mechanisms either to recover the baselines or to force the target behaviors in that direction.

As was suggested in the context of the withdrawal design, when there is no expectation of producing lasting effects, reversal may be just as appropriate as withdrawal. Questions of effects of various stimulus conditions on communicative behaviors and disorders may be researched within the reversal strategy because they have important theoretical implications. Whether a treatment procedure will eventually be developed out of this research may be an extraneous or a later consideration.

It must be noted that when either the withdrawal or the reversal strategy is used, the client participates in an experiment that ends in a status quo of his or her problem. Taking appropriate human participant protection steps (see Chapter 12), the investigator can recruit clients for this kind of research. However, at the end of the experiment, it must be possible to offer those clients a treatment procedure that will remedy their specific clinical problem. Our next design ends in treatment, benefiting the participants.

The *ABAB* Design

To evaluate clinical treatment procedures, the *ABAB* design and its variations are better alternatives to the basic *ABA* design. It is a clinically more useful design because it ends with treatment, thus benefiting the participants. Also, the treatment effects are replicated within the design.

The *ABAB* design starts with the establishment of an acceptable baseline of the dependent variable (the first *A* condition). The treatment is then introduced in the first *B* condition and continued until the experimenter observes an unmistakable change in the dependent variable or concludes that a change is unlikely to take place. If found effective, the treatment is either withdrawn or reversed in the second *A* condition. The effects of this withdrawal or reversal are measured for an appropriate period of time. Finally, the treatment is reintroduced to replicate and continue the treatment effects in the second *B* condition. The withdrawal version of the *ABAB* design is shown in Figure 9–5.

Assuming that the treatment is effective in changing the behavior when it is first introduced, a change in the opposite direction during the withdrawal or reversal (the second *A* condition) must be evident. When the treatment is reintroduced a second time, the response rate must change again in the opposite direction.

Let us suppose that a clinician wishes to assess the effects of a behavioral intervention on the production of selected grammatical features by a child with a language disorder who is producing those targets at a low rate. The clinician initially baserates the production of the selected morpheme by presenting it in the context of several sentences to be evoked by pictorial stimuli and an appropriate question. This is the first *A* condition, which may show that the morphemes are produced with 15% accuracy. Then the clinician shows selected pictures to evoke particular responses, models the correct responses, and reinforces correctly imitated and later spontaneously produced target morpheme in sentences. This is the first treatment condition *B,* in which the production of the morpheme may increase to 86%. At this point, the clinician withdraws the verbal praise and continues to evoke the target responses on a series of trials. This is the second *A* condition, withdrawal of reinforcement, during which the response rate decreases to 21%. In the final and second *B* condition, the clinician reintroduces the verbal praise for correct production of the morpheme, which may increase to 95% or better. The treatment may be continued until generaliz-

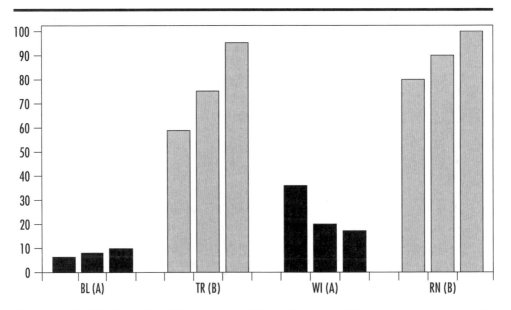

Figure 9–5. The baseline (*A*), treatment (*B*), withdrawal (*A*), and reinstatement (*B*) conditions of an *ABAB* design.

ed and maintained productions of the morpheme in conversational speech evoked in naturalistic settings are recorded.

A variation of the *ABAB* design is known as the *ABCB* design in which the target behavior is baserated and a treatment applied, as in the *ABAB* design. However, the next condition involves neither withdrawal nor reversal. Therefore, this third condition is known as *C* instead of *A*. In this *C* condition, the reinforcer may be delivered on a noncontingent basis. In other words, the reinforcer does not follow correct production of the target behavior, but it may happen to follow any of the nontarget behaviors that happen to be produced. Consequently, the target behavior that had increased in the previous condition when it was reinforced may decrease, essentially showing the controlling function of the reinforcer. The amount of reinforcer delivered noncontingently is the same as that in the previous treatment condition.

The *ABAB* (and the *ABCB*) design permits the reinstatement for the target behavior and continuation of treatment until the clients are ready to be discharged. However, the design does require the use of either withdrawal or reversal of treatment to show that no other variable is responsible for the changes in the behavior. In this respect, it shares all problems associated with withdrawal and reversal. When the treatment is withdrawn, the rate of the target behavior may not show a decline. Reversal may take an unduly long period of time, raising questions of ethical justification concerning "teaching the wrong response."

Reversal or withdrawal in any variation of the *ABAB* design is inappropriate for behaviors that are self-injurious or abusive of other persons. In such instances, reversal or withdrawal of suc-

cessful treatment leads to increased frequency of injury to the self or to other persons. However, in many cases—especially in communication disorders—withdrawal and reversal are achieved in a relatively short time so that the treatment is reinstated quickly without any negative effects on the client or other persons. When treatment is withdrawn, speech sound production errors, dysfluencies, inappropriate vocal qualities, and inappropriate language responses show a relatively prompt return to the near-baseline level, and reinstatement of treatment can result in equally prompt recovery of the appropriate target responses. The *ABAB* design has been used extensively in modifying a variety of problem behaviors in clinical and educational settings.

Despite its limitations, some clinical research questions require the *ABAB* strategy. For example, the design helps determine if certain target behaviors are independent of each other. All independent target behaviors belong to separate *response classes* and, therefore, need separate treatment whereas some target behaviors change when other targets are taught. The issue is important because a resolution of it often clarifies the number of clinical target behaviors in given treatment situations.

Take, for example, the question of subject noun phrase and object noun phrase. Are they separate clinical targets needing separate treatment or are they one and the same? If they are, teaching one would affect the other. Are verbal auxiliary and copula one and the same or are they different clinical targets? In other words, what is the effect of training subject noun phrase on object noun phrase (and vice versa), and training verbal auxiliary on copula (and vice versa)? Questions such as these are appropriately answered by the *ABAB* design. For example, the object noun can be trained, reversed, and reinstated to see if the subject noun phrase also is produced, reversed, and reinstated without a direct application of the treatment variable. Such an outcome would suggest that the two are not separate clinical targets despite the structural distinctions between them. A study of this kind has suggested that subject and object noun phrases belong to the same response class (McReynolds & Engmann, 1974). Similarly, an *ABAB* reversal study suggested that the verbal auxiliary and copula belong to the same response class (Hegde, 1980). The *ABAB* design provides an excellent means of determining whether language structural categories are independent responses that can be clinically taught.

The Multiple Baseline Designs

The multiple baseline designs (MBDs) are among the most desirable of the SSEDs because they avoid the problems of withdrawal and reversal. The structure of the MBDs includes a series of baseline and treatment conditions across different behaviors, persons, settings, and some combinations of these. The design is essentially a multiple *AB* series. It is still able to control for the extraneous variables by arranging a series of simultaneous multibaselines in such a way that the dependent variables change *only* when they come under the influence of the treatment variable.

The MBD has three standard versions: multiple baseline design across behaviors, across participants, and across settings. We shall consider these standard versions as well as some variations.

Multiple Baseline Across Behaviors

Since its formal recognition in 1968 by Baer, Wolf, and Risley, the multiple baseline across behaviors has been used extensively in clinical research involving treatment evaluation. This design requires that the investigator have several dependent variables for experimental manipulation in a single participant or client. In most clinical situations, this is easily accomplished, because clients usually need treatment for several target behaviors. For example, clients with speech sound disorders typically need treatment for multiple phonemes, and those with language disorders need treatment for multiple grammatical, semantic, pragmatic, or response class targets. Also, most clinicians are unable to treat all target behaviors simultaneously. Single behaviors or just a few behaviors may be targeted for treatment at any one time. When the training is accomplished on certain behaviors, other behaviors are targeted for further training. This typical clinical situation is well suited for multiple baseline evaluation of treatment.

In the evaluation of a given treatment procedure with multiple baseline across behaviors, the clinician selects a participant who needs treatment on several behaviors. To begin with, all of the target behaviors are baserated. When a stable response rate is established for at least one of the target behaviors, the treatment is applied to that behavior. The treatment is withheld from other behaviors that are still at baseline. The first behavior is trained to a specified criterion, say 90% accuracy on probe trials that do not involve treatment (no reinforcement, for example). Then the remaining behaviors are once again baserated to make sure that the behaviors not trained did not change relative to the original baseline.

The second behavior is then trained to the selected criterion. The other target behaviors remain in baseline, which is reestablished before the third behavior is trained. After obtaining another baseline of untrained behaviors, the fourth behavior is trained. In this manner, every time a behavior meets the training criterion, the untrained behaviors are baserated to demonstrate their lack of change in the absence of treatment. The typical results of an MBD study involving four target behaviors are illustrated in Figure 9–6.

There are two important considerations in the use of the MBD across behaviors. The first consideration is that to demonstrate the controlling effects of the experimental manipulation, a minimum of three behaviors must be included in the design (Kratochwill et al., 2010). Three (or more) behaviors give an adequate chance to show that the behaviors change only when treated and not when in baseline. In this case, the experimenter can establish a clear trend in the data that demonstrate the effect of an independent variable.

The second consideration is the independence of the behaviors selected for experimental manipulation. It is more difficult for a priori judgments. The problem is that when two behaviors in an MBD are not independent of each other, then the treatment applied to one behavior may affect the other, which is supposedly still in the baseline. Changes in untreated behaviors may be due to either uncontrolled independent variables or a dependence between the treated and changed, though untreated, behaviors.

The independence of behaviors selected for a multiple baseline design often is judged on the basis of theory, clinical experience, or empirical evidence. In given cases, these bases may or may not be valid. Untested theories and unverified

clinical experiences are especially risky. The best empirical basis is provided by past evidence. In speech-language pathology, the independence of behaviors is one of the most troublesome issues for clinical researchers because speech and language behaviors often are distinguished on the basis of response topography only. Behaviors are independent when they have different causes (independent variables), not necessarily because they are topographically (structurally) different. However, structural distinctions among behaviors that are insensitive to the independent variables may prove misleading under conditions of experimental manipulations.

The misleading nature of behavioral distinctions based on untested theoretical grounds is evident in research on language treatment. The grammatical, semantic, and pragmatic theories of language have identified an endless variety of response categories that are based solely on the basis of *form* of responses. Formally distinct responses may or may not be functionally independent.

My associates and I had an opportunity to find out the hard way that some of the grammatical categories may be unreal. An experiment on language training and contextual generalization within the MBD across behaviors included contractible auxiliary (*he's* riding), contractible copula (*she's* happy), uncontractible auxiliary (*he was* painting), and possessive morpheme s (*lady's* hat) (Hegde, Noll, & Pecora, 1978). Initially, the four behaviors were baserated in a child with a language disorder. The correct production of the behaviors on the initial baseline was 0%. After first teaching the production of contractible auxiliary, baserates repeated on the untrained behaviors showed that the correct production of the contractible

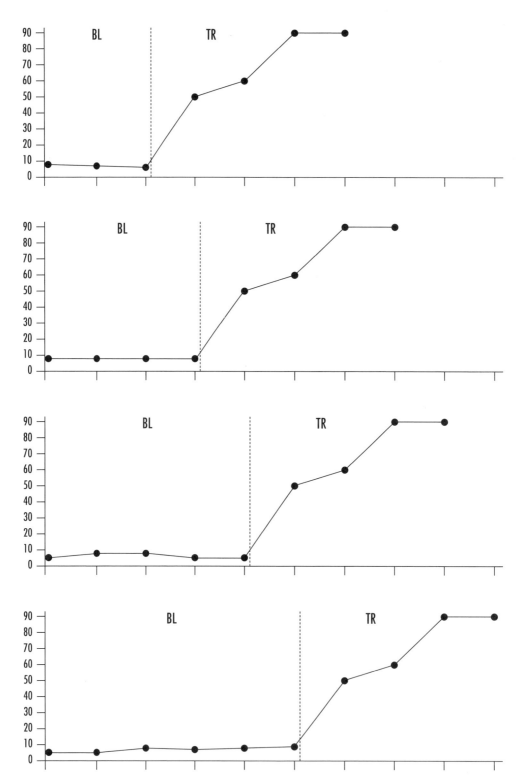

Figure 9–6. The multiple baseline design involving four target behaviors. Note the progressively increasing number of baseline observations for the second and subsequent targets. Each behavior increases only when brought under the influence of treatment. Data from multiple baselines across subjects and settings may be similarly charted.

copula was 100% accurate. This raised the possibility that either contractible auxiliary and copula were not independent of each other or some extraneous variable was responsible for changes in the first target behavior.

Fortunately, two other baselines did not show any change when measured a second time (uncontractible auxiliary and the possessive morpheme). This supported the possibility that the contractible copula changed not because of an extraneous treatment but because it is not independent of contractible auxiliary. However, we could not be sure, because within a multiple baseline design, change in an untreated behavior *must* be considered to represent weakened experimental control. We decided to see if we would get similar results by first treating contractible copula and then testing contractible auxiliary in a multiple baseline design applied to another child. This child who did not produce contractible copula, contractible auxiliary, uncontractible auxiliary, uncontractible copula, and the possessive *s* morpheme was the participant. In this case, there were five baselines.

After establishing the initial baselines on all five morphemes, we first trained the contractible copula and found that the production of the contractible auxiliary also increased to 100% on the second baseline. However, the three remaining untrained behaviors showed no change, and they continued to show no change until each of them was brought under the influence of the treatment contingency. This once again suggested that the contractible auxiliary and copula probably belong to the same response class and hence are not independent behaviors. However, switching the sequence of the two morphemes across two participants was not considered a crucial test of the independence of the auxiliary and copula, since a multiple baseline design could not provide such a test. An altered sequence was applied to another subject in the hope that some additional suggestive evidence might emerge. And it did. Eventually, an appropriate test of the independence of the two behaviors was made within the *ABAB* reversal design (Hegde, 1980).

When the design includes four or more baselines (target behaviors), a potential interdependence between two of them may not be damaging. The other baselines that do not show changes until treatment is applied to them will continue to serve the control function within the design.

Obviously, that lack of independence between behaviors, though troublesome, can provide interesting hints on responses that belong to the same class. When such hints are taken up for experimental analysis, more specific information on clinical target behaviors is likely to emerge. In this sense, interdependence of behaviors shown by a multiple baseline design, when confirmed, can be considered worthwhile accidents in research.

Multiple Baseline Across Subjects

When a given target behavior is baserated across individuals rather than across different behaviors of the same individual, we have the MBD across subjects. Thus, a speech-language clinician may baserate a single grammatical morpheme such as the plural *s* across four individuals. Then the language treatment to be evaluated may be given to the first individual while the other individuals remain in baseline. When the first participant's production of the plural morpheme reaches the training criterion, the baselines are repeated on the remaining participants. Assuming that the untreated participants are still not able to produce the morpheme, the clinician applies treatment to the second participant. The third and the fourth participants remain untreated until the second one is treated. After another set of baseline measures, the third subject receives treatment, and the fourth subject is baserated for the last time and then receives treatment.

Typically, the same behavior is baserated across different individuals. However, the basic logic of the design permits base rating *different behaviors across different individuals*. For example, four different morphemes such as the plural *z,* present progressive *-ing,* regular past tense *-ed,* and possessive *s* can be the four respective targets across four individuals. As long as the behaviors of participants who are not yet treated do not change from the baseline, the design is able to demonstrate that the treatment is effective.

Another variation of the MBD across subjects is to apply treatment sequentially to *groups of participants.* For example, three groups of children, all having language disorders, may be treated sequentially. The selected target behaviors are initially baserated in all participants in the three groups, and then the treatment is applied to the participants in the first group. After repeating the baselines on the two remaining groups, the treatment is given to participants in the second group. After an additional baseline, the third group receives treatment in the final stage of the experiment. If participants in each group change only when treated, potential external variables are ruled out.

When groups of participants are used in the multiple baseline format, it is necessary to present evidence of change in individual participants as well. For this reason, large groups are not practical in this format.

It is recommended that the participants selected for a multiple baseline across participants be similar to each other and that they be living in the same or similar environmental conditions. However, finding similar individuals living in the same or similar environments can be difficult. Moreover, "environmental similarity" is not easy to determine. However, because the individual data are analyzed separately, finding similar subjects is not crucial. Homogeneous or heterogeneous, individuals may react differently to the same treatment.

Demonstration of an experimental effect in individuals who are different from each other in terms of the clusters of problem behaviors (symptoms) or in terms of one or more of assigned variables (participant characteristics) can actually enhance the generality of experimental data. Therefore, unmatched participants can be used as long as the experimenter is aware of the potential risk involved. The risk of having a behavior change in a participant who is still in baseline must be weighed against the potential of producing data with enhanced generality. However, as noted earlier, the risk is logically justified, but it may be empirically weak enough to allow some creative risk taking on the part of the experimenter.

Multiple Baselines Across Settings

When a given behavior of a single participant is measured in different settings and when the treatment is applied sequentially in those settings, we have the MBD across settings. In the most typical version of this design, the same behavior of the same participant exhibited under different settings provides the multiple baselines. The treatment is sequentially applied in the settings, interspersed by baselines to show that the behaviors did not change in untreated settings.

The design can be illustrated in the treatment of a speech sound disorder. A child's misarticulation of a given phoneme may be measured in different settings such as the office of the clinician, the classroom, the school cafeteria, and the playground. The treatment contingency may be positive reinforcement of correct production of the phoneme in single words. After the initial baselines have been established in those settings, the treatment may be started in the clinician's office. When the treatment is successful in this setting, the behavior is baserated in the untreated settings. The treatment is then applied in the classroom setting with the cooperation of the teacher. Baselines are repeated in the cafeteria and the playground. In this manner, the clinician applies treatment sequentially in different settings, showing that in each setting, the correct production of the phoneme increases only when treated in that setting.

The correct production of the phoneme in one or some of the untreated settings creates design problems. Such a production may be due to generalization of the treatment effect or to some uncontrolled variables. Therefore, just as in the other versions of the MBD, independence of baselines is necessary for unambiguous interpretation of data. The design depends upon the discriminated responding in different settings. It assumes a lack of generalization of treatment effects across settings until treatment is applied in those settings. This assumption may or may not hold in given situations. In some cases, behaviors established in one setting may generalize to other settings although they may or may not be maintained over time.

In other cases, the production of target behaviors may be restricted to the setting in which it is supported. Speech-language clinicians typically find that, at least in the initial stages, target behaviors are situation specific. The person who stutters who has learned to speak fluently in the clinic may still be markedly dysfluent at home, in the office, or at the supermarket. In such cases, the design can demonstrate experimental control by showing that changes in the target behavior are associated with treatment in different settings.

Typically, the multiple baselines across settings involves single participants, but it can be used with a group of participants whose behavior is measured and treated in different settings. In this variation, treatment is offered to the group as a whole. For example, a special educator may apply a group token system for "quiet behavior" during the class, in the library, or in the cafeteria. When a group of participants is used, the clinician must still present data on individual participants to show that changes reported are not based on the group averages that mask individual differences. For this reason, a large group may be impractical from the standpoint of data analysis and presentation.

The Problem of Repeated Baselines

Repeated measures of target behaviors are a cumbersome aspect of the MBD. The last behavior, subject, or setting will have been measured (baserated) repeatedly. The greater the number of series in a design, the more often the baselines need to be repeated. Most behaviors studied within the designs are not reactive, that is, do not change simply because they were measured often, but some may change due to repeated baseline measures. Obviously, reactive changes make it difficult to isolate the effects of treatment.

A partial solution offered to the problem of repeated measures is to treat more than one behavior in the MBD across behaviors. For example, if six phonemes are targeted for treatment, two phonemes may be simultaneously treated, resulting in only three sets of phonemes to be baserated instead of six individual phonemes. Similarly, in the MBD across participants involving eight participants, baseline and treatment may be alternated with sets of two participants. In the MBD across multiple settings, treatment may be given in two settings while two sets of two settings each are kept in baseline.

Another solution offered to the problem of the repeated baseline measures is known as the multiple probe technique (Horner & Baer, 1978). This technique was originally described as a means of verifying the status of untreated target responses that are a part of a behavioral chain. Complex skills, such as the use of a hearing aid, for example, need to be taught in terms of specific target responses that are chained (Tucker & Berry, 1980). The child may be taught to remove the hearing aid from its box, place it behind the ear, turn the power on, adjust the volume, and so on. Each of these responses constitutes a chained element in the total behavior under training. In cases such as this, it is not necessary to spend much time measuring the subsequent behaviors of the chain when the client has still not learned the responses that need to be mastered earlier. For example, trying repeatedly to measure the response of adjusting the volume of the hearing aid when the client has not even learned how to put the aid on is a waste of time.

The probe technique, however, can be used in the treatment of independent behaviors as well. Instead of continually measuring behaviors yet to be trained, the behaviors may be probed periodically to see if they are stable. A probe is a quick test of a given response, usually used to assess generalization of treatment effects. A more detailed measure of a particular behavior just before treatment is considered the baseline. If there are additional behaviors in the baseline, they can be probed without detailed measurement. For example, in the treatment of four grammatical features, the clinician may establish baselines (more detailed measurement) on all of them. Each feature may be baserated in the context of 20 sentences, each presented on a modeled and evoked trial. The first feature is then trained. Then the second feature is baserated with the 20 sentences whereas the third and the fourth features are probed with only a few sentences. The second feature is then trained. The baseline is repeated on the third feature, but the fourth feature is only probed. Finally, the fourth feature is trained after a full baseline measure on it has been obtained. Especially in the treatment of language and speech sound disorders, periodic probes are all that are needed to retain the control function of the design. Full baseline measures must be established initially on all behaviors and on every behavior just before it is treated.

Additional Control Within the Multiple Baseline Designs

As noted previously, the MBDs arrange a series of *AB* conditions. Control is demonstrated by either the untreated behaviors, the untreated participants, or the untreated settings. Each participant, however, experiences only two conditions: the baseline and the treatment. Therefore,

MBDs are considered somewhat weaker than reversal or withdrawal designs.

An MBD can be combined with either reversal or withdrawal, however. When this is practical, the control aspect of the design is increased significantly. In the multiple baseline design across behaviors and participants, treatment can be withdrawn for a brief period of time as soon as a particular treated behavior or participant shows a considerable change from the baseline. The treatment can then be reinstated. Reversal and reinstatement can be used in the same manner. In the MBD across settings, treatment can be reversed or withdrawn in each of the treatment settings and then reinstated in each setting.

Although withdrawal (or reversal) and reinstatement can add additional control to the MBDs, they also neutralize the main advantage of these designs. The designs are more suitable for clinical purposes precisely because they do not require reversal or withdrawal to demonstrate experimental control. When an MBD includes four or more baselines (behaviors, participants, or settings) and each baseline changes only when treatment is applied, the experimental control so exhibited can be considered satisfactory.

The Changing Criterion Design

A critical element of the experimental strategy is to demonstrate that the behavior varies in accordance with a specific experimental manipulation. A design that retains this feature but does not use the control features of the previously described designs is known as the **changing criterion design** in which a behavior is forced to repeatedly approximate a preset criterion of performance (Hart-man & Hall, 1976). Whenever the clinician changes the criterion to which the behavior is held, the behavior changes and approximates that criterion. The *criterion-referenced change* discussed in Chapter 4 is the control mechanism in this design.

The best example of the design comes from the original Hartman and Hall (1976) study on controlling smoking behavior with response cost. After establishing baselines of the number of cigarettes smoked per day, the investigators set a progressively lower number of cigarettes allowed to be smoked. When a low criterion was met, a new, lower criterion was set. In this manner, they reduced the number of cigarettes smoked to near-zero levels. The study showed that every time a new (and lower) criterion was imposed, the client's rate of smoking approximated the criterion in force. The smoking behavior changed only at times when the criterion was changed. This fact helped rule out the influence of extraneous variables.

The changing criterion design may be used to either shape down an undesirable behavior with decelerating criteria as Harman and Hall did or to shape a target skill up with accelerating criteria. For example, in assessing the effect of a treatment procedure to increase the number of names recalled by a person with aphasia, the clinical researcher may set a low criterion to begin with (e.g., three names recalled in a specific period of time). Successive criteria will involve progressively greater number of names recalled when stimuli are presented. If the naming skill approximates each of the criteria set for the person, then the experimental control will have been established.

Another example is illustrated in Figure 9–7. It shows hypothetical data from a changing criterion design in which the

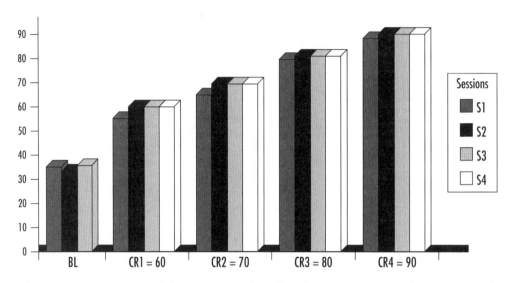

Figure 9–7. Hypothetical data generated by the changing criterion design. A child's percent correct speech sound production rate is baserated (BL) and then subjected to four changing criteria (CR1 through CR4) across sessions; the correct response rate increases to the set criteria.

percentages of correct speech sound productions are increased by escalating criteria. The data show how a behavior being shaped up comes under experimental control.

In the use of the changing criterion design, the clinician should demonstrate changes consistent with *multiple criteria* to ensure the experimental control. If additional control procedures are necessary, the treatment can be totally withdrawn in one of the phases to show that the behavior returned to the original baseline. A more practical strategy is to return the client to an earlier criterion. In this case, the target behavior would reverse and approximate the earlier criterion. Following this, new criteria may be imposed in successive stages.

The design may not have been formally used in communication disorders, but clinicians probably have used it in their uncontrolled clinical treatment of their clients. Every time a clinician says, "Last time you produced sounds correctly on 6 out of 10 attempts. Let us see if you can get 8 correct out of 10 attempts today," he or she is using changing criteria in treatment sessions.

Designs for Multiple Treatment Comparison

Within the SSED strategy, the *ABA,* the *ABAB,* and the MBDs are useful in answering whether a given treatment is effective compared to no treatment. These designs can evaluate only one treatment at a time. We have seen in Chapter 7 that within the group design strategy, factorial designs and multiple groups help evaluate multiple treatments in a single study. There are some SSEDs that permit an experimental evaluation of multiple treatments.

A study is designed to compare two treatments only when each is known to be effective. When nothing is known about the effects of a given treatment, a logical start is to find out if it is effective at all by using an *ABA, ABAB, BAB,* or MBD. In the next stage of the experiment, the two treatments that have produced favorable effects in separate studies may be evaluated within a single study. There are two methods of evaluating the effects of two or more treatments with SSEDs.

The *ABACA/ACABA* Design

A clinician may be interested in evaluating the effects of two methods of teaching alaryngeal speech, speech sound production, or language responses. The two procedures, X_1 and X_2, may be applied to the same participant or participants interspersed by baselines *A*. The resulting design is known as the *ABACA/ACABA* design. The two portions of the design are needed to counterbalance the two treatment variables. Each portion of the design (*ABACA* or *ACABA*) is applied to one or more participants. For a given participant or set of participants, either the *ABACA* or the *ACABA* design applies. In the design, B represents the first treatment, X_1 and C represents the second treatment, X_2. The design is illustrated in Figure 9–8 with its two sequences of treatment presentations, 1 and 2.

The two sequences (*ABACA* and *ACABA*) counterbalance the order of presentation of the two treatments. If only one of the two sequences is used in a study, potential order effects cannot be ruled out. If the investigator were to use four clients in a study designed to evaluate the effects of two treatment procedures, the first two participants would undergo the first sequence, and the second two participants would undergo the second sequence. This way, each treatment precedes and follows the other treatment. It may be noted that the *counterbalanced crossover group designs* are similar to this SSED.

In this design, baselines separate the treatments. Therefore, the design can incorporate withdrawal or reversal. Either version of the design can demonstrate whether one or both of the treatments are effective. Once it becomes clear that one or both of them are effective, the clinician can reinstate a treatment to achieve the clinical goals.

The results generated by the design can be suggestive of the *relative* effects of the two treatments but do not permit firm conclusions. In other words, whether one treatment is more effective than the other is a difficult question to handle within this design. Any suggestion regarding the relative effects of treatments from this design should be evaluated within other designs. In the single-subjects strategy, the relative effects of two or more treatments are compared only when they are administered in *adjacent* conditions. Interspersed baselines result in treatments that are separated in time, and data points that are separated in time are not reliable for analysis of the relative effects of two or more treatments. For this reason, the alternating treatments design, to be described shortly, is considered the most appropriate strategy to analyze the relative effects of two or more treatments.

A potential problem with the *ABACA/ACABA* design is that the first treatment may be so effective as not to leave any opportunity for the second treatment to show its effects. This is the **ceiling effect** described in Chapter 7. The clinician should know when this happens, however.

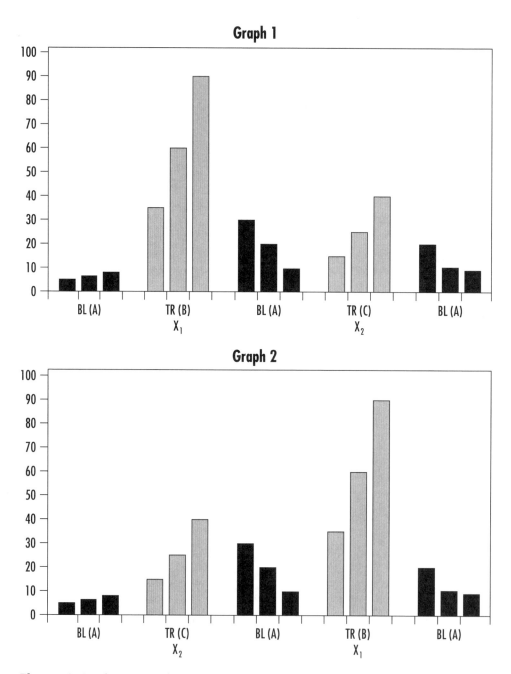

Figure 9–8. The *ABACA/ACABA* design. The first sequence (Graph 1) shows the administration of Treatment 1 (X_1) followed by Treatment 2 (X_2) with an interspersed baseline. The second sequence (Graph 2) is opposite to the first. In either case, Treatment 1 had a larger effect than Treatment 2.

When the wrong response rate is reduced dramatically to near-zero levels by the first treatment, the application of the second treatment may not serve any purpose. The design may also suffer from some carry-over effects despite the interspersed base-lines. In other words, some of the effects of the first treatment may be carried over to the second treatment. The second base-line may give some indication of a carry-over, however.

The Alternating Treatments Design

Once it has been determined that several treatment techniques are all effective with a given disorder, the clinician faces a different question. Can it be that one treatment technique is *more* effective than the other? The question, then, does not concern the absolute effects of a given treatment but the *relative* effects of two or more treatments. Alternating treatments

design (ATD) offers a strategy to answer such questions.

The design can also help answer other questions of relative effects. For example, is one therapist more effective than the other? In answering this question, a *single* treatment may be administered by two different therapists whose participation is alternated across sessions. Or both the therapists may alternately administer the two treatments. Another question an ATD can answer is whether the time of treatment can make a difference. The design can help answer this question by arranging treatments at different times of the day, while making sure that each treatment is administered in all of the selected time periods equally often. The basic arrangement of the ATD involving two treatments is illustrated in Figure 9–9.

The ATD is based on the logic that when the same participant receives two or more treatments in a rapidly alternating fashion, the relative effects of the treatments can be determined in a fairly short

A. Alternating patterns for one set of participants (starting with Treatment 1)

Session	1	2	3	4	5	6	7	8
Treatment	X_1	X_2	X_2	X_1	X_2	X_1	X_1	X_2

B. Alternating patterns for another set of participants (starting with Treatment 2)

Session	1	2	3	4	5	6	7	8
Treatment	X_2	X_1	X_1	X_2	X_1	X_2	X_2	X_1

Figure 9–9. Counterbalanced arrangements (*A* and *B*) of experimental conditions of an alternating treatments design involving two treatments and two sets of subjects.

time. The treatments may be alternated in a single day with the number of daily treatment sessions corresponding to the number of the treatments being compared. The nature of the clinical phenomenon under investigation determines how rapidly the treatments are alternated. If daily measurement of the phenomenon is not appropriate and weekly measurement is most likely to reveal changes, weekly alternations may be acceptable.

In the treatment of stuttering, for example, a clinician may examine the relative effects of stuttering-contingent aversive noise and verbal *No*. Let us assume that both the procedures have been evaluated in separate studies showing that they reduce the frequency of stuttering to varying extents. The clinician can then evaluate the relative effects of the two procedures by applying both to the same individual or individuals. Aversive noise and verbal *No* are alternated in the treatment sessions. In the analysis of the results, the rates of stuttering observed in the treatment sessions are separated according to the two

procedures. The stuttering rate under the aversive noise sessions is compared with those under the verbal stimulus.

Typical results of an ATD investigation are represented in Figure 9–10, which shows that the first treatment, X_1, was more effective than the second treatment, X_2.

Order Effects and Counterbalancing

The reader may have noticed that in Figure 9–9, the treatments were not alternated systematically. If one treatment systematically follows another treatment, treatment effects may be confounded by the **order effect**, which is the influence of sequence with which multiple treatments are presented to the same individuals. Therefore, the order of treatment presentation is semirandomized.

The two treatments also should be counterbalanced across participants so that each treatment precedes and follows every other treatment applied in the design. To accomplish this, the design

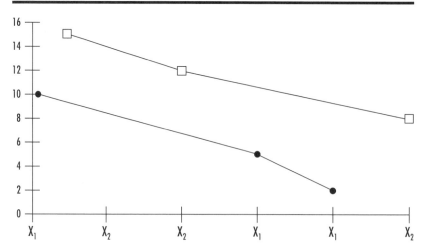

Figure 9–10. Typical graphic representation of the results of an alternating treatments design. The graph shows a larger effect for Treatment 1 than for Treatment 2.

requires two sets of participants. One can use, for example, two sets of three participants each, for a total of six participants. In the first session of the experiment, Treatment 1 will be offered to the participants in the first set and Treatment 2 will be offered to those in the second. In this arrangement, each treatment appears in the first and the second position. From then on, the order of treatment is semirandomized.

Each treatment can be made to precede and follow every other treatment *equally often,* although this is not always done, nor is it always necessary. As long as the treatments precede and follow more than once and the sequences are roughly comparable in number, the order effects can be minimized.

When two or more clinicians administer the same treatment, the order in which the two clinicians treat the client must be counterbalanced. When two clinicians administer two or more treatments, both the treatments and the clinicians must be counterbalanced. When two treatments are evaluated by the same clinician, it is possible that the sessions are held during a morning and an afternoon session; in this case, each treatment must be administered in roughly the same number of morning and afternoon sessions. Such counterbalancing avoids the potential for a given treatment to be more effective because it is administered by a particular clinician or at a certain time.

Counterbalancing requires multiple participants. For example, if the clinician counterbalances the time of treatment, he or she may apply the first treatment to the first participant in the morning session and the second treatment to the same participant in the afternoon session. From then on, the order of presentations is semirandomized and counterbalanced. In

a second participant, the second treatment may be given in the first morning session and the first treatment in the first afternoon session. As in the first participant, the treatment presentations from then on are counterbalanced. In this case, the two treatments and time periods also are counterbalanced across the two participants.

Carryover and Contrast Effects

In addition to a potential order effect, the ATD can pose two additional problems: carryover and contrast effects. Both these effects create problems for an unambiguous interpretation of data.

As described in Chapter 7, the term **carryover effects** refers to generalization of the first treatment effect to the second treatment. In this case, the observed effects of the second treatment are larger than what might be expected if the second treatment were administered alone. In terms of our earlier example of the relative effects of aversive noise and verbal *No,* a stuttering participant's fluency in the verbal punishment condition may be higher because of the carryover effects of the aversive noise condition.

Contrast is evident when the effect of a subsequent treatment is opposite to that found during the prior treatment. In other words, a behavior that increases under the first treatment condition decreases under the adjacent condition and vice versa. For instance, in a token reinforcement program for fluent durations in speech, relatively more or fewer tokens may be presented for each unit (fluent durations or fluent sentences); this is known as the response/token ratio. A large number of tokens (high token ratio) given for each unit of fluency in one experimental condition may cause an impressive increase in fluency. If in the next condition, fewer tokens (low token ratio) are given for the same units of fluency, fluency may decrease dramatically, although the same low token ratio may increase fluency if it were not contrasted with high ratios.

It is evident that contrast and carry-over are opposite effects, although both may be subsumed under the term *multiple-treatment interference* (Barlow et al., 2009). Carryover effect has also been described, quite appropriately, as *induction* or *generalization.*

In applied human research, it is thought that the carryover and contrast effects are not as great a problem as they might initially appear. Multiple-treatment interference may be a more serious problem in basic research than in applied research (Barlow et al., 2009). Nevertheless, the clinician wishing to use the alternating treatments design should take at least two steps to counteract its potential problems. First, the clinician should counterbalance the treatment conditions. This will help minimize both the order effects and the carryover effects. Second, the treatment sessions must be separated in time, and only one treatment must be administered in a given session. Originally, it was suggested that within a single session, two treatments may be alternated.

It is possible that even when there is a carryover effect from one treatment to the next, the relative effectiveness of the two treatments may still be the same as it would have been in the absence of carryover effects. In any case, should an investigator be concerned with the carryover effects in a particular study, he or she can proceed to analyze such effects by making them the object of further experimental inquiry. Procedures to analyze the carryover effects are described in Sidman (1960) and Barlow et al. (2009).

At the beginning of each session in an ATD study, investigators instruct the participants what particular procedure will be in effect during that session. The researcher tells the client, "In this session, we will be using the treatment procedure _____." No additional steps to ensure discrimination between alternating procedures may be needed.

The ATD does not require a formal baseline before the treatment variables are introduced. For this reason, it is thought that the alternating treatments design is especially useful in case of behaviors that are inherently variable. The ATD may be relatively insensitive to background variability in behaviors. True differences between treatments can emerge against a background of variability. Nonetheless, most investigators do establish baselines of target behaviors before introducing treatment so that they can analyze the effects of different treatments in relation to baselines as well.

Simultaneous Treatments Design

In the simultaneous treatments design (STD), also known as a *concurrent schedule design,* multiple treatments are concurrently made available to participants to evaluate their preference for a treatment. Although the design was developed to study client preference for treatments, it can offer some initial data on the relative effects. Whereas the ATD helps evaluate the relative effects of multiple treatments to their fullest extent, the STD may do it up to a point. In the STD, after establishing the baselines, two or more treatments are simultaneously offered to a participant in the beginning; subsequently, only the one the participant prefers is offered. From the point at which the client preference emerges in a study, administration of multiple treatments is discontinued. Only the preferred treatment is offered; however, if the preferred is not the most effective, then the most effective may be offered.

Browning's (1967) study on decreasing the frequency of grandiose bragging in a 9-year-old boy is the first in which the simultaneous treatment design was used. Six therapists, forming three teams of two each, administered the three treatments in a counterbalanced order. They either offered positive reinforcement, verbal admonishment, or extinction (ignoring) for bragging. All therapists were simultaneously available to administer the treatments. Three weeks of simultaneous treatments showed that the boy preferred verbal admonishment and sought out those who administered it. Preference in this case meant that the boy's bragging increased when verbally admonished. His least preferred treatment was extinction (fewer bragging instances); he soon began to avoid the teams that administered it. Browning then offered extinction as the only treatment available and reduced the boy's bragging.

The STD, though not used frequently, has excellent potential in communication disorders. For instance, in the treatment of adults who stutter, syllable prolongation and time-out from speaking made contingent on stuttering are both known to be effective. However, it is known whether individuals who stutter prefer one method over the other. To find out, two clinicians may both offer both the treatments and be available for the participants to seek them out, but at any given day or week, the participants would know who offers what treatment. After experiencing similar reductions in stuttering under all three treatments, the participants might prefer one of the two treatments because of personal liking, minimum aversiveness, reduced task demand, and other such factors. The participants would reject therapists who offered unattractive treatments on scheduled days or weeks. The study would generate some limited data on relative effects and convincing data on preference. Hypothetical data from such a study are presented in Figure 9–11.

The STD is not the method of choice to evaluate the relative effects of multiple treatments because the participants are not offered all treatments equally often. Once the preference or relative effectiveness emerges in the design, only one of the treatments will continue to be offered. The effect is that the frequency of different treatment administration will have been unequal. Therefore, the ATD in which treatments are not simultaneously available but all treatments are offered equally often remains the method of choice for this purpose. Similarly, because all treatments are offered equally often on a predetermined semirandomized sequence, the ATD does not help assess client preference.

It should be noted that client preference and effectiveness may be different matters. In the Browning (1967) study, the preferred technique was the least effective in reducing bragging; in fact, it increased that behavior. Young children, too, possibly prefer ineffective fun-and-play speech therapy to effective discrete trial therapy. The safer strategy in using STD is to offer two effective procedures, as in our example of stuttering treatments. Whichever the participants prefer, they will have received effective treatment.

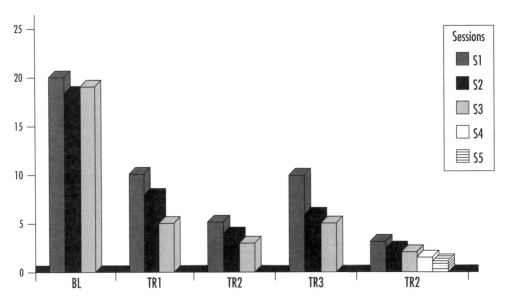

Figure 9–11. Hypothetical data generated by a simultaneous treatments design. Data show the percent stuttering rates under baseline, three stuttering treatments (TR1 through TR3) administered simultaneously for several days, and the final condition in which TR2, found to be the most effective (with the lowest frequency of stuttering) as well as the most preferred treatment (TR), was offered.

Ineffective Treatments in Multiple Treatment Evaluations

Sometimes the clinician may find that one or more of the treatments in a multiple treatment evaluation are ineffective. In an *ABACA/ACABA* design, for example, it may be found that Treatment *B* is ineffective. In such cases, there is no point in returning the participant to a period of baseline measurement. The *B* condition, for all practical purposes, is comparable to the baseline in that there were no changes in the response rate. The next treatment can then be introduced without the second, formal baseline. In such cases, the design is redesignated as an *A=BCA* design, which means that the first treatment was treated like a baseline because of lack of effect. If in the second sequence, Treat-

ment *C* is ineffective, Treatment *B* may be introduced without a preceding baseline, resulting in an *A=CBA* design.

Because ineffective treatments are functionally equivalent to baselines, SSED strategies allow modifications in treatment procedures within a single study. Such modifications typically are not done within the group design strategy. Even when the experimenter realizes that the treatment is not producing changes in the behavior, the study is completed as planned. However, within the SSED strategy, a clinician can introduce another treatment without baselines or make modifications in the original treatment. For example, if a 5-second time-out proves ineffective in reducing the frequency of stuttering, a 10-second time-out contingency may be applied. No baselines need to be interspersed between the treatment variations as long as the first treatment did not result in a changed baseline. If verbal praise does not act as a reinforcer for the correct production of target phonemes, a token system may be implemented. Of course, the treatment variable that produces changes in the baseline will have to be evaluated with such controls as untreated multiple baselines, withdrawal, or reversal.

Designs for Interactional Studies

Clinicians know that, in most cases, what is considered a single treatment for a given disorder is actually a combination of several treatment components. In treating stuttering, for example, counseling, Van Riper's pull-outs, and slower speech may all be offered in a "comprehensive" treatment package. Such therapeutic packages that combine different components, none or only some experimentally evaluated, are quite popular in speech-language pathology.

In controlled studies, the overall effectiveness of a treatment package may be demonstrated. Such a demonstration, however, is no testimony to the effectiveness of the individual components included in the package. In a package that is effective, some or several treatment elements may be ineffective. In our example of stuttering treatment package that consists of three elements (counseling, pull-out, or slower speech), one, two, or none may be effective. The degree of effectiveness may vary among the effective elements. None of this will be clear when a total package is found to be effective. When two or more treatment components within a package are effective to any degree at all, then the question of interaction, discussed in Chapter 7, emerges.

Interaction is not limited to components of a treatment package. Interaction between independent treatments that are not components of a package also is of interest. For instance, one might study potential interactions between two independent treatments for stuttering—psychological counseling and fluency shaping. In the rehabilitation of patients with traumatic brain injury, one might study the interaction between cognitive therapy and behavior therapy. In the treatment of aphasia, different strategies of prompting names may interact.

There are SSEDs to analyze such interactional effects of two or more independent treatments or components of therapeutic packages. In addition, the designs can help isolate treatment or treatment components that are effective to any extent from those that are not at all effective. The importance of such a design strategy in the task of developing a clinical science is obvious.

The SSED to study interaction has two variations. It is helpful to think of them as Type I and Type II interactional designs. In Type I interactional design, a single treatment (or component) is first applied and a second treatment (or component) is added and removed. In Type II interactional design, the combination of two treatments or the entire package is first applied and a treatment or a component is removed and added. Each type requires two experimental sequences, requiring two sets of participants. In any given study, only one of the two types need to be implemented.

The Type I interactional design, usually described as an *A-B-BC-B-BC* design in behavioral literature, is presented in Figure 9–12. However, because of the two sequences involved in it, it is more

Sequence 1 (First set of participants)	A	B	BC	B	BC
	Baseline	X_1	$X_1 + X_2$	X_1	$X_1 + X_2$
Sequence 2 (Second set of participants)	A	C	CB	C	CB
	Baseline	X_2	$X_2 + X_1$	X_2	$X_2 + X_1$

Figure 9–12. Type I interactional design in which a single treatment (X_1 or X_2) is constant and another treatment is added and removed; in the first set of participants, Treatment 1 (B) is constant (A-B-BC-B-BC); in the second set of participants, Treatment 2 (C) is constant (A-C-CB-C-CB).

complete and less confusing to refer to it as an *A-B-BC-B-BC/A-C-CB-C-CB* design. As can be seen in Figure 9–12, the first sequence of *A-B-BC-B-BC* is applied to one set of participants and the second sequence of *A-C-CB-C-CB* is applied to another set of participants. Each set may have three or more participants. These two sequences counterbalance the two single treatments and the two combinations; each single treatment appears in the first position once, followed by the combination. Furthermore, in the first sequence, only Treatment 1 is tested in isolation, and in the second sequence, Treatment 2 is tested in isolation. In each sequence, statements cannot be made about the independent effects of the treatment untested in isolation.

The Type II interactional design, usually described as an *A-BC-B-BC-B* design, is presented in Figure 9–13. This variation, too, is better represented as *A-BC-B-BC-B/A-BC-C-BC-C* because of the two necessary experimental sequences. It may be noted in Figure 9–13 that in the first sequence, the investigator offers the combined treatments to both sets of participants in the initial condition of the experiment. Subsequently, the investigator removes the second treatment, adds it, and removes it again. Thus, the first sequence has

only Treatment 2 in isolation. If only this sequence is implemented, the study cannot answer the question of independent effects of Treatment 2. On the other hand, the participant in the second sequence experiences Treatment 2 as the isolated condition. If only this sequence is implemented, the study cannot evaluate the independent effects of Treatment 1. When both the sequences are implemented in the counterbalanced fashion, the independent and interactive (combined) effects of both the treatments can be evaluated.

An example will help clarify the actual implementation of this design. Suppose that a clinician wishes to study the independent and interactive effects of two treatment components in remediating stuttering: reduced speech rate X_1 and modified airflow X_2. Let us further suppose that the clinician wishes to use the Type I interactional design with its two sequences. The clinician selects six adults who stutter and creates two sets of three participants each. In the first experimental sequence, the clinician establishes the baselines of stuttering *A* and then applies the speech rate reduction strategy (X_1) in the initial treatment *B* condition to the first set of three participants. After several sessions of rate reduction, the clinician *adds* the modified airflow component (X_2) to

Sequence 1 (First set of participants)	A	BC	B	BC	B
	Baseline	$X_1 + X_2$	X_1	$X_1 + X_2$	X_1
Sequence 2 (Second set of participants)	A	BC	C	BC	C
	Baseline	$X_1 + X_2$	X_2	$X_1 + X_2$	X_2

Figure 9–13. Type II interactional design in which a combination of two treatments (X_1 and X_2) is constant and one treatment is removed and added; in the first set of participants, Treatment 2 (*C*) is removed and added (*A-BC-B-BC-B*), and in the second set of participants, Treatment 1 is removed and added (*A-BC-C-BC-C*).

the existing speech rate reduction component. This combined treatment condition (*BC* or $X_1 + X_2$) will be in effect for a certain number of sessions. In the next condition, the clinician withdraws the modified airflow procedure, leaving only the speech rate reduction as the treatment (the second *B* or X_1 condition). Finally, the clinician adds the modified airflow a second time to the speech rate reduction component (the second *BC* or $X_1 + X_2$ condition). In this sequence, the independent effects of speech rate reduction, but not that of modified airflow, can be assessed along with the combined (interactional) effect.

In the second experimental sequence, the clinician applies the modified airflow to the second set of participants in the first treatment condition. The clinician then adds the speech rate reduction in the next condition and subtracts it in the following condition. In the final condition, the clinician once again adds the speech rate reduction to the modified airflow component. In this sequence, the clinician can evaluate the independent effects of modified airflow but not that of speech rate reduction.

Assuming that the speech rate reduction results in some decrease in stuttering frequency, the addition of airflow may show a further decrease. When the airflow is subtracted, the stuttering frequency may increase; frequency may once again decrease when the airflow is added. Similarly, addition of speech rate reduction to the airflow may enhance the treatment effect on stuttering, and the magnitude of this effect may decline when the component is withdrawn. On the other hand, it may be evident that one of the components has a greater effect than the other. Adding one component may not make a big difference, whereas adding the other component may result in a more dramatic decrease in stuttering. In essence, the results may show that both the components are equally effective or equally ineffective or that one is more effective than the other. The results may also show that each of the two components is weak by itself but that the two in combination can produce notable effects (interactional effect).

The same experiment may be conducted with Type II interactional design in which the application of both treatments is common to the first treatment condition in the two sequences. Subsequently, in the first sequence, Treatment 2 is removed, added, and removed again (*A-BC-B-BC-B*), thus testing the combination and Treatment 1 in isolation. In the second sequence, Treatment 1 is removed, added, and removed again, thus testing the combination and Treatment 2 in isolation.

The two types of interactional design differ in terms of whether in the initial stage of treatment the entire package or only one of the components is applied. If the entire package is applied, one of the components is first *subtracted* and then added in subsequent conditions. If only one of the components is applied initially, another component is *added* and then subtracted in subsequent conditions. As noted before, any one type is satisfactory when both the experimental arrangements are used. However, both types, when applied with both the sequences, can strengthen the conclusions.

In using either of the sequences, it is important that the researcher adds or subtracts the same variable. For example, if the clinician starts with the rate reduction as the first treatment condition, then the airflow is added and subtracted. One cannot add airflow in one condition and subtract rate reduction in the other. In other words, the first treatment component stays constant; the second component is added or subtracted. When the clinician starts with the airflow component, rate reduction is added and subtracted; airflow stays constant. When both the components are applied in the initial treatment condition, only one of them is subtracted and added in any one or a set of participants. The other component is subtracted and added only in another participant or set of participants.

Interactional designs have not been used frequently in communication disorders. The design deserves greater application because many untested treatment packages exist in the treatment of speech, language, voice, and fluency disorders.

Even when a total package is known to be effective, we need to determine the independent and interactive effects of each of the components of the package so that ineffective components can be discarded and more effective components can be combined.

N-of-1 Randomized Clinical Trials

Although SSEDs were fully developed in the context of behavioral research, the approach has medical and clinical roots as we noted in the first part of this chapter. As we saw in the previous chapter, drug evaluations in medicine predominantly use the parallel experimental and control groups to test the effects of new drugs. Although they are called **randomized clinical trials** (RCTs), participants are not randomly selected from a relevant population and random assignment to the study groups is continually invalidated by individuals who refuse participation, especially in control groups, resulting in self-selected participants. Nonetheless, the traditional randomized clinical trials, a clear misnomer, include hundreds and thousands of participants in multiple centers. The main problem for the practicing clinicians is that the results are not generalizable to their individual patients or clients. Being keenly aware of the pitfalls of large *N randomized clinical trials,* many medical researchers have performed what are known as *N-of-1 randomized clinical trials.* Borrowing SSEDs from behavior sciences, Guyatt and associates were the first to initiate a series of *N*-of-1 randomized trials (Guyatt et al., 1988; Guyatt et al., 1990; Vohra, 2016). The method has been extended to investigate individualized treatments for patients with a variety of stable and chronic diseases that are especially suitable for this type of research (see *Journal of Clinical Epidemiology,* August 2016, Vol. 76, a special issue on *N*-of-1 clinical trials).

The *N*-of-1 trials differ from the traditional large *N* RCTs in some important ways. The most important distinction is that the *N*-of-1 trials do away with the random selection and assignment of participants that are central to large *N* RCTs. The *N*-of-1 clinical trials recruit available patients in the medical practitioner's routine practice, just as researchers who use SSEDs do. The *N*-of-1 researchers do use randomization in one respect: They randomly assign to the same individual multiple treatments or treatment and placebo. Such randomization is also used when multiple treatments are evaluated in SSEDs. Large *N* RCT investigators do the same, but they randomly assign treatments to different groups.

Most *N*-of-1 clinical trials use the multiple baseline, *ABAB, ABACA/ACABA,* and interactional SSEDs. Although extended baselines are uncommon in these trials, the target patients are those with chronic diseases with stable symptoms or health status. Placebo and treatment conditions are randomly alternated, sometimes each offered for at least one week; if two or more treatments are evaluated, they are similarly randomly assigned across time periods to the same patient. Each treatment or treatment pairs are offered at least three times to establish a clear and reliable data trend. Because the same patient experiences both the placebo, single treatment, or multiple treatments in some random order, the designs are also described as *single-subject crossover designs,* the parallel group version of which was described in Chapter 8.

One treatment may be withdrawn for a period of time before introducing another treatment if carryover effects are suspected. The period of withdrawal will depend on the needed drug washout period. Period may be longer if the drug effects linger longer.

To avoid subjective evaluation of treatment effects, investigators and the patient are blinded to the treatment and control conditions. Visual and statistical analyses both may be performed. The results of *N*-of-1 trials and the traditional randomized trials may be combined to perform meta-analyses (Punja et al., 2016).

Single-Subject Designs in Clinical Research

In many clinical educational disciplines, including applied behavior analysis, communication disorders, medicine, surgery, and special education, the application of SSEDs is now an established practice. Despite the current emphasis on randomized clinical trials in speech-language pathology, SSEDs offer more opportunities to evaluate treatment effects. Randomized clinical trials conducted in speech-language pathology, just like in medicine, make too many methodological compromises to generate valid data. On the other hand, many SSED studies have established effective treatment procedures for most if not all disorders of communication.

In advancing treatment research in any clinical discipline, SSEDs have unparalleled advantages. If the *N*-of-1 trials in medicine can offer speech-language pathology a lesson, it is that the clinicians and educators can integrate their service delivery with experimental evaluation of their techniques. All *N*-of-1 treatment clinical trials were conducted by practicing physicians, not funded by pharmaceutical companies that support the traditional large *N* RCTs. Using SSEDs, clinicians can answer questions of practical significance while providing clinical services. Because the SSEDs do not require random sampling of a large number of participants, clinicians can collect data as they work with their clients. Because the designs avoid control groups, treatment need not be denied to anyone who needs it. Therefore, SSEDs help bridge the gap between research and clinical services.

If practicing clinicians were to use SSEDs on a large scale, the amount of in-house knowledge on the effectiveness of treatment procedures would be greatly increased. Although theoretically the group designs can offer the same opportunities for experimental-clinical research, it is the single-subject strategy than can actually make it happen.

Although traditional levels of evidence advocated by medicine did not include SSED studies, the 2011 levels of evidence proposed by Oxford University's center for evidence-based practice considers the properly done *N*-of-1 trial results as Level 1 evidence, along with the traditional randomized clinical trials (OCEBM Levels of Evidence Working Group, 2011). Other researchers, too, place the evidence generated by well-controlled SSEDs at the highest level (Logan et al., 2008). If the *N*-of-1 trials are expected to produce the highest level of evidence, there is no reason to downgrade the evidence coming from SSED studies. The *N*-of-1 design is essentially an SSED. In fact, SSED studies in behavioral research (including treatment research in communication disorders) are more robust than the *N*-of-1 trials in medicine because the former

establish reliable baselines before introducing treatment, something missing in the latter.

We address the levels of evidence again in Chapter 15 and propose a different way of looking at the levels of evidence. The levels we propose are design neutral and place emphasis on the degree of experimental control and experimental replication that ultimately determine both the effectiveness of procedures and their generalizability.

Summary

Cause-effect relations based on individual performances under different conditions of an experiment may be established with SSEDs. The designs permit extended and intensive study of individual participants and do not involve comparisons based on group performances. Instead of the pre- and posttests of the group designs, SSEDs measure the dependent variables continuously. Typically, the magnitude of effects produced within SSEDs are large enough to be appreciated via visual analysis. As described in Chapter 6, several statistical techniques are available to evaluate the significance of SSED data, however.

Each participant serves as his or her own control in SSEDs. These designs use replication, withdrawal of treatment, reversal of treatment, reinstatement, criterion-referenced change, rapid alternations, baselines, and simultaneous multibaselines to control for extraneous variable. A collection of SSEDs is available to evaluate single treatments, multiple treatments, and interaction between different treatments. Table 9–1 summarizes information on the major SSEDs along with the kinds of questions they can answer.

Table 9–1. Summary of Major Single-Subject Designs and Their Applications

Design	Research Questions	Strengths and Limitations
AB design (case studies)	Is there an apparent change due to treatment?	Clinically useful; results only suggestive; lacks internal validity
ABA design	Is a treatment effective? Is there a cause-effect relation?	Controlled experimental design; can assess treatment effects and isolate cause-effect relations; not for producing lasting treatment effects
BAB design	Is a treatment effective? Is there a cause-effect relation?	Controlled experimental design; can assess treatment effects and isolate cause-effect relations; may produce lasting treatment effects
ABAB design	Is a treatment effective? Is there a cause-effect relation?	Controlled experimental design; can assess treatment effects and isolate cause-effect relations; may produce lasting treatment effects
Multiple baseline across behaviors	Is a treatment effective? Do only treated behaviors change? Do untreated behaviors remain at baseline?	Fairly well controlled; clinically useful; may produce lasting treatment effects; problems of repeated measurement
Multiple baseline across participants	Is a treatment effective? Do only treated participants change? Do untreated participants remain at baseline?	Fairly well controlled; clinically useful; may produce lasting treatment effects; problems of repeated measurement
Multiple baseline across settings	Is a treatment effective? Does the behavior change only in the treatment setting? Does the behavior remain at baseline in untreated settings?	Fairly well controlled; clinically useful; may produce lasting treatment effects; problems of repeated measurement
ABACA/ACABA design	Are two or more treatments effective? Is one treatment more effective than the other?	Well-controlled design; can assess the independent and relative effects of two treatments; need to use counterbalancing
Alternating treatments designs	What are the relative effects of two or more treatments?	Somewhat weak control; can identify effective and ineffective treatments; may produce lasting treatment effects

continues

Table 9–1. *continued*

Design	Research Questions	Strengths and Limitations
Interactional design	Is there an interaction between two or more treatments? What are the relative effects of different treatment variables?	Fairly well-controlled design; clinically useful; can show interactive effects; can separate ineffective treatment components from effective ones
Changing criterion design	Is a treatment effective? Do behaviors approximate changing treatment criteria?	Somewhat weak control; useful only for certain kinds of behaviors

References

Baer, D. M., Wolf, M. M., & Risley, T. R. (1968). Some current dimensions of applied behavior analysis. *Journal of Applied Behavior Analysis, 10,* 117–119.

Bailey, J. S., & Burch, M. R. (2017). *Research methods in applied behavior analysis* (2nd ed.). Thousand Oaks, CA: Sage

Barlow, D. H., Nock, M. K., & Hersen, M. (2009). *Single-case experimental designs: Strategies for studying behavior* (3rd ed.). Boston, MA: Pearson.

Boring, E. (1950). *A history of experimental psychology* (2nd ed.). New York, NY: Appleton-Century-Crofts.

Brown, R. (1973). *A first language: The early stages.* Cambridge, MA: Harvard University Press.

Browning, R. M. (1967). A same-subject design for simultaneous comparison of three reinforcement contingencies. *Behavior Research and Therapy, 5,* 237–243.

Cozby, P. C., & Bates, S. C. (2018). *Methods in behavioral research* (13th ed.). New York, NY: McGraw-Hill.

Freud, S. (1944). *New introductory lectures on psychoanalysis.* New York, NY: Norton.

Galton, F. (1880). I. Statistics of mental imagery. *Mind, 19,* 301–318. [May be found at dalton.org]

Guyatt, G., Keller, J. L., Jaeschke, R., Rosenbloom, D., Adachi, J., & Newhouse, M. T. (1990). The *n*-of-1 randomized controlled trial: Clinical usefulness. Our three-year experience. *Academia and Clinic, 112,* 293–299.

Guyatt, G., Sackett, D., Adachi, J., Roberts, R., Chong, J., Rosenbloom, D., & Keller, J. L. (1988). A clinician's guide for conducting randomized trials in individual patients. *Clinical Epidemiology, 139,* 497–503.

Hartman, D. P., & Hall, R. V. (1976). The changing criterion design. *Journal of Applied Behavior Analysis, 9,* 537–532.

Hegde, M. N. (1980). An experimental-clinical analysis of grammatical and behavioral distinctions between verbal auxiliary and copula. *Journal of Speech and Hearing Research, 23,* 864–877.

Hegde, M. N. (1998). *Treatment procedures in communicative disorders* (3rd ed.). Austin, TX: Pro-Ed.

Hegde, M. N. (2007). A methodological review of randomized clinical trials. *Communication Disorders Review, 1*(1), 17–38.

Hegde, M. N. (2018). *A coursebook on aphasia and other neurogenic language disorders* (4th ed.). San Diego, CA: Plural.

Hegde, M. N., Noll, M. J., & Pecora, R. (1978). A study of some factors affecting generalization of language training. *Journal of Speech and Hearing Disorders, 44,* 301–320.

Horner, R. D., & Baer, D. M. (1978). Multiple probe technique: A variation of the multiple baseline. *Journal of Applied Behavior Analysis, 11*, 189–196.

Janosky, J. E. (2005). Use of the single subject design for practice-based primary care research. *Postgraduate Medical Journal, 81*, 549–551.

Janosky, J. E., Leininger, S. L., Hoerger, M. P., & Libkuman, T. l. (2009). *Single subject designs in biomedicine*. New York, NY: Springer.

Johnston, J. M., & Pennypacker, H. S. (2009). *Strategies and tactics of behavioral research* (3rd ed.). London, UK: Routledge.

Kazdin, A. E. (2010). *Single-case experimental designs: Methods for clinical and applied settings* (2nd ed.). New York, NY: Oxford University Press.

Kratochwill, T. R., Hitchcock, J., Horner, R. H., Levin, J. R., Odom, S. L., Rindskopf, D. M., & Shadish, W. R. (2010). Single-case designs technical documentation. Retrieved from http://ies.ed.gov/ncee/wwc/pdf/wwc_scd .pdf

Lane, J. D., & Gast, D. L. (2014). Visual analysis in single case experimental design studies: Brief review and guidelines. *Neuropsychological Rehabilitation, 24*(3–4), 445–463.

Logan, L. R., Hickman, R. H., Harrris, S. R., & Heriza, C. B. (2008). Single-subject design: Recommendations for levels of evidence and quality rating. *Developmental Medicine & Child Neurology, 50*, 99–103.

McReynolds, L. V., & Engmann, D. L. (1974). An experimental analysis of the relationship between subject noun and object noun phrases. In L. V. McReynolds (Ed.), *Developing systematic procedures for training children's language* (pp. 30–46). Rockville Pike, MD: Asha Monographs No. 18.

Morgan, D. L., & Morgan, R. K. (2009). *Single-case research methods for the behavioral and health sciences*. Thousand Oaks, CA: Sage.

OCEBM Levels of Evidence Working Group. (2011). *The Oxford 2011 levels of evidence*. Oxford Center for Evidence-Based Medicine. Retrieved from http:www.cebm.net/ index.aspx?o=5653

Piaget, J. (1959). *The language and thought of the child*. London, UK: Routledge & Kegan Paul.

Punja, S., Schmid, C. H., Hartiling, L., Urichuk, L., Nickes C. J., & Vohra, S. (2016). To meta-analyze or not to meta-analyze? A combined meta-analysis of N-of-1 trial data with RCT data on amphetamines and methylphenidate for pediatric ADHD. *Journal of Clinical Epidemiology, 76*, 76–81.

Schlosser, R. W. (2009). *The role of single-subject experimental designs in evidence-based practice times* (Technical Brief No. 22). Washington, DC: National Center for the Dissemination of Disability Research.

Sidman, M. (1960). *Tactics of scientific research*. New York, NY: Basic Books.

Skinner, B. F. (1953). *Science and human behavior*. New York, NY: Free Press.

Skinner, B. F. (1966). Operant behavior. In W. K. Honig (Ed.), *Operant behavior: Areas of research and application* (pp. 12–32). New York, NY: Appleton-Century-Crofts.

Tucker, D. J., & Berry, G. (1980). Teaching severely multihandicapped students to put on their own hearing aids. *Journal of Applied Behavior Analysis, 13*, 65–75.

Vohra, S. (2016). N of 1 trials to enhance patient outcomes: Identifying effective therapies and reducing harms, one patient at a time. *Journal of Clinical Epidemiology, 76*, 6–8.

Watson, J. B., & Rayner, R. (1920). Conditioned emotional reactions. *Journal of Experimental Psychology, 3*, 1–14.

Yin, R. K. (2017). *Case study research: Design and methods* (6th ed.). Los Angeles, CA: Sage.

Study Guide

1. Distinguish between case studies and single-subject experimental design studies.

2. In the single-subject strategy, what kinds of measures are substituted for the pre- and post-tests of the group design strategy?

3. Describe the six control mechanisms used within the single-subject strategy.

4. Distinguish intrasubject replication from intersubject replication.

5. Distinguish between reversal and withdrawal of treatment.

6. What are the limitations of withdrawal and reversal when used in clinical treatment research?

7. Design a study in which you would use the reversal procedure to demonstrate the effects of a speech sound treatment program.

8. How many times is a treatment effect demonstrated when that treatment is reversed and reinstated once? Illustrate with an example.

9. Why is criterion-referenced change the weaker of the control strategies?

10. Describe how rapid alternations can demonstrate the controlling effects of an independent variable.

11. Define baselines. Discuss the baseline criteria.

12. Describe how a good potential for contrast can make it possible to use a variable baseline in evaluating treatment effects.

13. In an *ABA* design, what conditions are not supposed to show contrast?

14. How do simultaneous multi-baselines help rule out the influence of extraneous variables? Discuss all three varieties of the design.

15. Describe the *ABAB* design and point out its advantages and disadvantages from the clinical research standpoint.

16. Describe the three variations of the multiple baseline design.

17. What problems do you face when the multiple behaviors used in a multiple baseline design are not independent of each other?

18. Suppose you wish to evaluate two methods of teaching basic vocabulary to individuals with language disorders. What design would you use? Justify your answer.

19. Compare and contrast the *ABACA/ACABA* design with the alternating treatments design.

20. Why do you need both the *ABACA* and *ACABA* sequences?

21. What kinds of questions are answered by the alternating treatments design?

22. Describe the carryover and contrast effects.

23. What is an interaction? How do you study it within the single-subject strategy?

24. Reviewing the literature, find two methods of prompting naming responses to individuals with aphasia. Then design a study to evaluate the independent and interactive effects of the two methods with a single-subject interactional design. Use both the sequences described in the text.

25. Describe the difference between the *A-B-BC-B-BC* design and the *A-BC-B-BC-B* design.

26. Describe the changing criterion design. Illustrate the design with a hypothetical study.

27. What kinds of behaviors are especially suited for the changing criterion design?

28. Suppose you wish to study whether clients prefer one treatment over the other, assuming that both are equally effective. What design would you use?

29. What are *N*-of-1 clinical trials? How are they different from randomized clinical trials using group designs?

30. Summarize the advantages of SSEDs in clinical research.

10

Statistical Analysis of Research Data

Chapter Outline

- ◆ Historical Introduction to Statistical Analysis of Research Data
- ◆ Statistical Significance
- ◆ Hypothesis Testing
- ◆ Statistical Analysis of Group Design Data
- ◆ Systematic Reviews and Meta-Analyses
- ◆ Visual Analysis of Single-Subject Data
- ◆ Statistical Analysis of Single-Subject Data
- ◆ Statistical Significance Versus Clinical Significance
- ◆ Summary
- ◆ References
- ◆ Study Guide

Research data generated from group designs and single-subject designs are analyzed differently. Statistical analysis is imperative for group design studies. Historically, behavioral researchers using single-subject designs have relied on non-statistical methods of data analysis. However, there are statistical procedures for analyzing single-subject research data. In this chapter, we will address the various methods of analysis of research data generated from both the research traditions.

Although group designs are statistical in nature, it should be clear that research designs and statistics are not the same. Unfortunately, many books that purportedly deal with research designs do not describe experimental designs to any significant extent. Instead, they describe statistical analyses of data generated by group designs. It is not uncommon for statistical texts to promote the ubiquitous analysis of variance as a research method or design. This practice promotes the mistaken notion that research designs and statistics are the same.

One should remember that statistics is neither research nor research design but rather a method of analyzing certain kinds of data. McCall (1923) cogently stated that "there are excellent books and courses of instruction dealing with the statistical manipulation of experimental data, but there is little help to be found on the *methods of securing adequate and proper data* to which to apply statistical procedures" (p. 23; italics added). It is unfortunate that a statement McCall made nearly a century ago still needs to be reiterated. Designs are methods of collecting adequate data, group designs are only one set of methods, and statistics are but one method of analyzing research data.

Historical Introduction to Statistical Analysis of Research Data

The group design strategy is a method in which statistical means derived from the performances of individuals in two or more groups on one or more dependent variables are compared. The method is now extensively used in experimentally evaluating the effects of new medical and surgical treatment procedures in what are more popularly known as **randomized clinical trials**, described in Chapter 4.

The group design strategy has its roots in biopsychological measurement, development of statistics, and agricultural research. In fact, the development of statistics is intricately associated with the measurement of human variation—both physical and psychological. Statistical concepts that are fundamental to the group design strategy include the theory of probability and the normal probability curve, random sampling, inferential statistics, statistical significance, and inferential generality. In this chapter, we do not go deeper into generality because it is addressed in greater detail in the next chapter.

Theory of Probability and Normal Probability Curve

The mathematical theory of probability deals with potential occurrences of events versus their actual occurrences. Consequently, probability is expressed in terms of a ratio between possibilities and actualities. In other words, the likelihood of something happening is dependent on all possible occurrences of that event; a single occurrence of an event is a fraction of all such occurrences. The early development of this mathematical theory was rooted in gambling that was popular with the 17th- and 18th-century European aristocrats, especially the French. Known as the *game theory,* it tried to predict certain outcomes given all the possible outcomes according to the rules of a game. Subsequently, mathematicians and statisticians took the concept of probability and developed it further (Hacking, 1975; Hald, 1998).

The basic concept of the **theory of probability** is typically described with examples of a coin toss. A toss of a coin has two possible outcomes: one head or one tails. An actual outcome of a single toss of a coin may be either heads or tails. Statistically, the probability between these two outcomes is the same: There is a 50% chance that it will be tails and an equal chance that it will be heads. This probability is expressed as 1 of 2, ½, or .5, which is typically expressed as $p = .5$ (in which the p stands for probability).

The relevance of the probability theory to any kind of experimentation is simple: What is the probability that the results of an experiment will be the same or similar if the same experiment were to be repeated one or more times? Obviously, one cannot trust a study's results if they are unlikely to be replicated. The goal of all experimentation is to produce results that have a high probability of being replicated or, in other terms, a high probability of being true. Therefore, group experimental treatment researchers estimate the probability of obtaining the same or similar results when the experiment is repeated. We will return to this point when we consider the concept of statistical significance of experimental data.

The development of the concept of the **normal probability curve** has had a significant effect on the eventual group comparison approach in experimental research, including controlled research in medicine, psychology, and education. The credit for developing the concept of the normal curve has been given to the French mathematician and astronomer Pierre Simon Laplace (1749–1827). The normal curve came to be known as the *Gaussian distribution* or the *Gaussian curve* mainly because it was Karl Fredrick Gauss (1777–1855), the German mathematician and astronomer, who described how errors in repeated observations of a phenomenon may be symmetrically distributed around a mean or average value. In the bell-shaped normal curve, deviation from the mean value suggests variability in the occurrence of a phenomenon.

Soon the significance of the normal distribution became evident in the works of Adolphe Quetelet (1796–1874), the Belgian astronomer and statistician who is often considered the founder of modern statistics (Boring, 1950). Quetelet claimed that data obtained on variations in human characteristics (e.g., height or weight) are normally distributed. Quetelet was probably the first statistician to exalt the mean or the average to the level of an ideal that nature strives and sometimes fails to achieve. His doctrine, *l'homme moyen* (the average man), stated that the *average* is what nature intends to create, and all deviations from the average, including those on the positive side of the mean, are nature's errors.

When psychological testing of human skills and characteristics, especially intelligence, became well established in Britain and the United States after World War II, all individual performances began to be evaluated against the average, giving rise to the notion of the statistical **norm**. Subsequent developments in agricultural research included the techniques of random sampling and inferential statistics, which led to the group comparison approach in human experimental research.

Early Statistical Concepts

Historically, the group design strategy is based on the works of a few individuals who were simultaneously mathematical statisticians, philosophers, psychologists, and biologists of the 19th century. An important event in the development of statistical methods took place in 1901 when Sir Francis Galton (1822–1911) and Karl Pearson (1857–1936) led a few interested persons in establishing a journal called *Biometrika* to publish mathematical and statistical research in psychology and biology. The same year, Pearson established a biometric laboratory at the University College, London (Boring, 1950; Hill, Forbes, Kozak, & McNeill, 2000). Although Galton's main interest was mental (intellectual) inheritance, he offered one of the earliest views of what statistics ought to do: reduce the immense or even infinite variability in everything we measure to a compact form. Even today, statistics is considered a group of *data reduction* methods.

Pearson's interest was mathematical statistics. Galton had already worked out the basic method of a **correlation** by way of studying **regression to the mean** ("regression toward mediocrity" in Galton's words) in physical and mental characteristics across successive generations. Later, Pearson worked out the mathematical details of the *correlation index* as he called it. It was the Irish statistician Fran-

cis Edgeworth (1845–1926), who in 1892, renamed it the **coefficient of correlation**. It still is abbreviated as *r,* which stands for Galton's term, *regression.*

Pearson was an avid promoter of the use of statistics in biology and psychology. He was even accused of the belief that statistics can help draw valid conclusions from invalid data, a view repugnant to scientists (Boring, 1950). Fortunately, his systematic work was more influential than his controversial belief in the power of statistics. His contributions firmly established the statistical approach to research in biology, psychology, most social sciences, and eventually medicine.

Randomization and Inferential Statistics

It was the work of Sir Ronald A. Fisher (1890–1962) that firmly established the practice of group experimental designs based on statistical analyses (Fisher, 1925, 1942, 1951, 1956). His writings are a classic within this philosophy of research. Fisher believed that statistical techniques and research designs are two aspects of the same whole (Fisher, 1951). A brilliant British statistician and a geneticist, Fisher had an unsatisfactory career for a few years as a teacher in schools and colleges. When, in 1919, the famous statistician and geneticist Karl Pearson offered him a job at the prestigious biometrics laboratory named after Galton at London's University College, he rejected it in favor of a statistician's job at an agricultural research station, known as the Rothamsted Experimental Station, situated some 25 miles north of London (Box, 1978).

From 1919 to 1933, Fisher's job was to analyze archival data on agricultural experimentation that had been collected over a period of 67 years. As he studied old data, he began to formulate new and better methods of data analysis, including analysis of variance and analysis of covariance. Even more important, as he critically evaluated the results of old experiments, he began to think of new methods of data collection—experimental designs. He first developed **nonrandomized blocks designs** (described in Chapter 8) to compare multiple treatments applied systematically (nonrandomly). Soon he realized, however, that systematic application of treatments confounds their effects. To reduce such errors, Fisher introduced the concept of **randomization** of treatments. He would thus let chance decide which plot of land received what kind of seed, how much water, what kind of fertilizer, and so forth, with a condition that all treatment permutations and combinations have an equal chance of appearing in the experimental arrangement. Subsequently, he developed factorial designs (described in Chapter 8). Fisher's first *randomized experimental research study* was laid out in 1926 in an agricultural plot at Rothamsted. He then went on to design many agricultural experiments to study the interaction between various soil conditions, seed quality, fertilizer, weather, watering practices, and so forth (Box, 1978).

Fisher's method of randomization also was a means to go beyond the actual observations (experimental results) and thus to make his enterprise worthwhile as well as efficient. For Fisher, it was not sufficient to find out that under given conditions a plot of agricultural land yielded more than another. He needed to *predict* that given the same or similar conditions, other plots in other parts of the country could realize the same or similar crop

output. Fisher considered all experimental results based on sample observations as an estimation of **parameters**, aspects of the population (Box, 1978). The values of variables actually observed and transformed into a statistic such as a mean in a study sample are estimates of population parameters. This means that Fisher needed to *generalize* from what he studied (a small set of observations) to what he did not (a large set of potential observations). As noted in Chapters 4, 7, and 8, to extend the conclusions of a study based on a random sample to a population is to achieve **inferential generality**. Fisher's mathematical analysis convinced him that a random selection of units for observation from a population of potential observations was the initial step in extending the conclusions from a sample of observations to all potential observations. In other words, what can be observed is a sample, but useful conclusions must apply to the population. Moreover, to make that extension possible, the sample must represent the population. The only way to make a small sample represent the much larger population is to draw the sample randomly.

Although random selection theoretically helped reduce errors of observation, Fisher still needed tools of analysis that, when applied to the results, would essentially support or refute the hypothesis that a treatment was or was not effective. He reasoned that a treatment is effective if the obtained results, especially the difference in yield between the treated and untreated plots, could not be due to chance. The same reasoning is used in current group treatment research in all clinical disciplines. A treatment or a teaching method is effective only when the observed differences in performance of participants in the experimental (treated) and control (untreated) groups exceed chance occurrences.

How can a researcher determine whether the differences in the treated and untreated groups are not due to chance but only to treatment? Fisher's answer was a series of statistical techniques, such as the **analysis of variance**, to estimate the probability of the results of an experiment being due to chance alone. It may be noted parenthetically that it is in Fisher's honor that the statistical outcome of analysis of variance is called the *F* ratio (Kerlinger, 1986), although the original set of ratios was calculated by an Indian statistician named Mahalanobis (Box, 1978). Such techniques of quantitative analyses are known **as inferential statistics** because they help infer the probability of obtaining the same or similar results when the experiment is repeated with samples drawn from the same population.

Research methods Fisher developed in his agricultural fields were later extended to educational, social, psychological, and medical research, underscoring the fact that apparently very different disciplines can use the same set of research designs. It became clear that, just as with agriculture, multiple variables affect human behavior, including response to clinical and educational treatments. The results of all controlled group design studies, including randomized clinical trials in medicine and other health professions described in Chapter 4, are analyzed with techniques of **inferential statistics** that help generalize the conclusions of a sample study to the population from which that sample was drawn.

The main concern in the group design strategy is the mean or average outcome of experimental manipulation. The mean is the basic ingredient of all inferential statistical analyses. For Fisher, it was the average yield of a plot treated in some manner that mattered. An individual plant's yield was not of much concern. The same is true of the modern-day group treatment researcher. Unlike in the single-subject design, it is the mean group performance that matters, not how an individual in a group performed or reacted to the treatment.

Statistical Significance

When a statistical analysis is performed on group experimental data, the meaning of the resulting outcome (such as the *F* ratio of analysis of variance) may not be clear. Correct interpretation of inferential statistics required an additional development: the concept of statistical significance. For example, does a given *F* ratio suggest that treatment indeed was effective in the sense that the results could not have been due to chance variations? Significance tests help answer that question and thus help interpret the meaning of statistical tests. Therefore, **statistical significance** is present when the observed differences in the performances of the experimental and control groups are *probably* due to treatment (systematic variance) and not chance (random variance). To put it differently, statistical significance of observations based on a sample suggests that the probability of sample statistics being a true estimation of the population parameters is high. Note that the statements of significance are expressed in terms of probability, not certainty.

Statistical significance is typically expressed in levels, which suggest different probabilities. Statisticians have adopted two levels of significance: .05 or .01; Fisher was the first to suggest the .05

level (Cochran, 1980). The significance levels are also known as **p** values (probability values). Investigators generally choose one of the two p levels, although other levels may be chosen as well. Each statistic is reported as being significant at the chosen level. For instance, when a statistical test is said to be significant at the .05 level, it means that there is a 5% chance that the results of the experiment are due to chance and not treatment. Alternatively, it means that there is a 95% chance that results are due to treatment. Note that such statements are based on hypothetical replications and repeated sampling from the same population. In other words, it means that if the study were to be repeated 100 times, each time drawing a different random sample from the same population, the probability of obtaining similar results is 95% in the case of a .05 significance level. A more stringent .01 level of significance means that the results are likely to be obtained on 99% of replications.

The adopted level of significance helps evaluate the researcher's hypothesis about cause-effect relations among variables or the effects of treatment or teaching methods. Unlike in the single-subject research strategy, the group design strategy typically involves testing a hypothesis about the nature of the relationship being investigated.

Hypothesis Testing

Consistent with Fisher's advocacy, most group design researchers test hypotheses about the cause-effect relations being investigated in experiments. The statistical analyses and the levels of significance described so far are all designed to test hypotheses about the nature of relationship between events examined. When an experiment is performed with two groups, and the posttest means of the experimental and control groups differ by some value, two potential explanations may be offered. One is that the observed difference (usually a degree of improvement in the treatment group) may entirely be due to chance and sampling errors. This would then mean that the treatment had no effect. This potential outcome is anticipated in all experiments and expressed in the form of a null hypothesis at the outset. A **null hypothesis**, or the statistical hypothesis, is a statement that asserts that the manipulated independent variable will have no effect on the dependent variable.

An alternative outcome of an experiment—actually a hoped-for outcome—is that the treatment, and no other variable, produced the difference between the two groups: The treatment indeed was effective. This is the **research hypothesis**, which asserts that the planned treatment will be effective. The investigator hopes to sustain the research hypothesis and reject the null via the evidence collected by the planned experiment. Fisher (1951) asserted that "every experiment may be said to exist only in order to give the facts a chance of disproving the null hypothesis" (p. 16). Although this is a questionable assertion because it can be countered that experiments exist to reveal functional relations between phenomena, the idea that experiments are designed to reject the null is now an established practice in group treatment research (see Chapter 3 for an opposing view).

Acceptance of the null hypothesis (the treatment was ineffective) obviously implies that the research hypothesis is false, that is, treatment was ineffective and will be ineffective for the population as well. Rejection of the null hypothesis (the treatment was ineffective) means that the treatment indeed had an effect in the sample and is likely to have the same or similar effect in the population as well. Because nothing is certain in science, there is always a chance that the researcher could commit an error in either accepting or rejecting the null.

Type I error occurs when the treatment was indeed ineffective, the null was true, but the researcher concluded that the treatment was effective and thus erroneously rejected the null hypothesis. In Type I error, observed differences between the experimental and control groups are really due to chance, not to treatment.

Type II error occurs when the treatment was indeed effective, but the researcher concluded that it was not. In this case, the researcher accepted the null hypothesis when it should have been rejected. In essence, mistaken rejection of the null is Type I error and mistaken acceptance of the null is Type II error. Type I error is avoided when a valid null is accepted, and Type II error is avoided when an invalid null is rejected. Levels of significance described previously help avoid these errors.

Statistical Analysis of Group Design Data

Group research designs produce data on a large number of individuals that are not easily interpreted without some help from statistical techniques. When the researcher faces 30 or more scores for the individuals in the control group and another 30 or more scores for the individuals in the experimental group, it is difficult to determine whether the differences found between the two groups are real (stable) or due to chance fluctuations.

Statistical techniques were invented to reduce large amounts of data to a manageable size. When data are reduced to a more practical size, such as a mean and a standard deviation, more sophisticated statistical tests may be calculated. We will briefly review two categories of statistical tests: *the parametric* and the *nonparametric*.

Parametric Tests of Significance

Parametric tests are based upon a mathematical model that assumes that the variables being measured are drawn from a population and that the variables conform to a normal distribution in the population. The measures of variables must be either ratio or interval data (see Chapter 6). The variance of these variables, as measured by **standard deviation**, is also assumed to be normally distributed. In addition, the sample is assumed to be randomly selected from the population it theoretically represents and is randomly assigned to the experimental and control groups. Furthermore, all parametric test calculations need a statistical mean and its standard deviations. If the study data do not meet these conditions, then a parametric test cannot be performed on them.

The *t* **test**, also known as *t* **ratio**, is the simplest parametric test. Although a *t* test for a single sample (group) is available, the most frequently used are the two varieties that apply to two groups. A *t* test is a ratio calculated by dividing the difference between two group means by the standard error of the difference between the means. It is designed to compare two group means to determine if differences in performance of the two groups are due to the treatment or chance. There are two kinds of *t* tests: one for independent samples and the other for dependent (correlated) samples. An independent sample *t* test is used when the group means are independent, as in a control group–experimental group design. The dependent *t* test is used when the same subjects are treated under different conditions, as in within-subjects or repeated-measures design. Significance of a calculated *t* value is determined by consulting an available probability table.

A more complex and powerful statistic that can handle multiple dependent variable measures is the **analysis of variance** (ANOVA), the result of which is called the *F*. A *one-way analysis of variance* involves a single treatment, although it may have different levels (e.g., different intensities). A *two-way analysis variance* involves two or more treatments, each with levels. Multigroup treatment designs, designs that test interactions between treatments and that between treatment and personal characteristics, require a complex technique such as the ANOVA, especially two-way ANOVA. We describe them as *factorial designs* in Chapter 8. ANOVA is a test of differences between two or more means in determining whether any difference between them is due to chance or to the independent variable applied to the experimental group. If a significant difference is found between the means of two or more groups, then the next step is to determine which two of the multiple mean pairs are significantly different. For that purpose, one can carry out multiple-comparison procedures on two or more group means. Such tests as the Sheffé, Tukey, and Neuman-Keuls tests help make pairwise comparisons to determine

statistical significance (see Box, Hunter, & Hunter, 2005).

One variant of the ANOVA, the **analysis of covariance** (ANCOVA), is a combination of ANOVA and linear regression. The technique statistically controls a confounding variable, called a **covariate**, that is likely to have an effect on the dependent variable but, for practical reasons, was not experimentally controlled. For instance, in evaluating two treatment procedures for apraxia of speech in adults, two experimental groups may be formed, but the researcher might suspect that the premorbid educational level of the participants, not controlled for in the study design, may affect the two treatment outcomes. In cases such as this, ANCOVA statistically calculates the effects of the uncontrolled variable, partitions it out, and removes it from the analysis of variance. The method actually adjusts the two group means on the covariate and equates those two means for analysis of variance. If a significant difference is found after the removal of the covariate's effects, then a researcher can conclude that the treatments were effective and the effects were not confounded by the uncontrolled variable.

A researcher interested in the question of whether two or more groups differ on more than one dependent variable may use a **multivariate analysis of variance** (MANOVA). For instance, two treatment methods for a particular disorder may be evaluated with participants from three socioeconomic levels. Responses of the three groups constitute multiple dependent variable measures. Instead of separately analyzing the three group responses with separate statistical tests (such as a *t* test), the investigator may perform a single MANOVA. Although this test may evaluate the significance of difference between two or more dependent variables, it does not identify the variable upon which the groups differ. This MANOVA is then followed by doing a post hoc repeated-measure ANOVA to identify the effects of the dependent variables (e.g., the three socioeconomic levels) responsible for the significant difference between the groups.

Parametric statistical techniques based upon the types of measurement and the number and characteristics of the groups used to make an inferential analysis are listed in Table 10–1.

In treatment research, the first critical question is whether the treatment had an effect that is beyond chance. Parametric statistical techniques help answer that question. A reliable change in the behavior or health status of participants that is unambiguously due to the treatment in the experimental group is deemed **statistically significant**. As noted, this significance is expressed as a probability value (**p value**). It is the probability of occurrence of the reliable change observed in the experimental group.

But there is a second critical question of the **magnitude** of the treatment effect. Experimental and control groups may differ significantly, but the effect may be relatively small or large. Therefore, significant or p value testing is followed by a calculation of the **effect size**, a *power test*. For statistics such as a t test or F (analysis of variance), effect size may be calculated for most statistics, including the t test and various forms of analysis of variance. We will see in a later section that the effect size calculations are possible for single-subject design data. There are two types of parametric effect sizes: r and d (Martella, Nelson, Morgan, & Manchand-Martella, 2013). Calculated differently for different statistics, effect sizes may be small (.2), medium (.5), or large (.8). The numbers in parentheses suggest that the experimental and control groups differ by either .2, .5, or .8 standard deviations. The larger the deviation, the greater the effect. All effect sizes are detected statistically, but the medium and larger sizes may be evident to everyone. There are different ways of

Table 10–1. Parametric Statistical Techniques Based on the Assumption That Interval or Ratio Data Are Normally Distributed and Variances of the Variables Are Equal

Types of Data	Number of Groups	Group Characteristics	Statistic
Interval/ratio data	One group	Dependent/independent	t test single group
Interval/ratio data	Two groups	Independent groups initially equivalent	t test independent groups
Interval/ratio data	Two groups	Matched groups	t test correlated groups
Interval/ratio data	Two groups	Independent nonequivalent groups	ANCOVA
Interval/ratio data	Two groups	Independent/repeated measures	ANOVA
Interval/ratio data	Two groups	Independent/repeated measures	MANOVA

calculating the effect size, but in the basic method, the difference between the two means is divided by the averaged standard deviations between the groups. Finally, effect sizes are essential to conduct meta-analysis, as described in a later section.

Nonparametric Tests of Statistical Significance

Nonparametric tests make no assumptions about the distribution of the sample or the variables in the population. Therefore, nonparametric tests are said to be *distribution free* (Box et al., 2005). Nonparametric tests of significance are appropriate for nominal or ordinal data. Such tests are calculated based upon the median of the sample data. For example, chi-square test, goodness-of-fit test, Mann-Whitney *U* test, and Kruskal-Wallis ANOVA are recommended when the underlying assumptions of parametric statistical analysis, including random selection of participants, random assignment of participants to the experimental or control groups, are invalid. Also, when the dependent variables are not measured on nominal or ordinal scales, or when a researcher is interested in comparing two proportions, two sets of frequency counts, or two sets of measures of medians, nonparametric tests are appropriate.

The **chi-square test** (χ^2) for association between variables is used to compare the number of observations, scores, participants, and objects that make up two or more categories or groups to determine if they are truly different or they differ by chance. For example, for a survey result that shows that 55% of clinicians believe that a diagnosis of childhood apraxia of speech (CAS) is valid and 45% do not, we cannot calculate means or standard devia-

tions. When those values are unavailable and have only percentages and proportions, the chi-square test is appropriate. This test does not permit the use of directional hypotheses. A directional hypothesis (one-tail hypothesis) is one in which the researcher not only predicts a difference between two groups but also predicts the direction of the difference. The directional hypothesis, for example, specifies at which end of the sampling distribution the calculated value of the statistical significance will fall positively or negatively. If the differences between observed and expected frequencies are large, then the difference may not be attributed to chance.

A second chi-square test is the **goodness-of-fit test**, also known as one-way chi-square test because the research participants are classified in only one way (e.g., either Democrats or Republicans or those clinicians who believe in childhood apraxia of speech [CAS] and those who do not). Goodness-of-fit test is used to determine whether there is a significant association between a set of observations and a hypothetical set of observations. The test is based on the assumptions that the sample size is sufficiently large, measured categories are mutually exclusive, and the observational sets are independent of each other. This analysis is made with the realization that any cause-effect relationship between the two sets of measurements cannot be determined.

If instead of two, multiple categories are observed, then a *two-way chi-square* may be used. For example, those who believe in CAS may be subdivided into male and female clinicians. Democrats and Republicans may be subdivided into rural and urban. Note that even then, the categories are independent of each other.

The **Mann-Whitney *U* test,** also known as Wilcoxon rank-sum test, is designed to determine the statistical significance between two independent, distribution-free medians, rather than means derived from ordinal scale data. This test is an alternative to the parametric t test when the samples to be compared do not meet the assumptions of the parametric test or when comparing ordinal data. For example, a clinical researcher may treat speech production to a group of persons with apraxia of speech and have a control group that receives no treatment. The participants in both the groups may be rated for their speech intelligibility and the ratings may then be ranked. Such ranked values are used to calculate the Mann-Whitney U test values to reject or accept the null hypothesis. There are two calculations possible, one for a small sample size and one for a large sample size. In both cases, the rankings are compared, and the number of times a score differs from a score in the second group determines the U. This test permits the use of one- or two-tailed hypotheses.

The **Wilcoxon matched-pair signed-rank test** is used to compare either two matched groups or two measures obtained for the same individuals. The latter case is realized, for example, when after experi-

mental treatment, the groups are measured in two follow-ups, once after 3 months posttreatment, and once after 6 months. The two sets of measures for the same individuals are not independent; they are correlated. Results of studies like this may be analyzed with the nonparametric Wilcoxon matched-pair signed-rank test. The test is based on the difference between pairs of scores and a ranking of the difference. This test is an alternative to the parametric t test for correlated means. A related test is called the **Kruskal-Wallis ANOVA**, an alternative to the parametric ANOVA, which also uses ranked scores instead of raw scores or means. Ranks for each group are summed; if the sums are similar, then there is no significant difference between the groups.

Table 10–2 provides a summary of selected nonparametric statistical tests. The table specifies the types of data and the number of groups for which the tests are applicable.

Correlational Analysis

The primary goal of correlational analysis is to explore relationships among vari-

Table 10–2. Selected Nonparametric Tests and Their Applications

Types of Data	Number of Groups	Appropriate Test
Nominal	1	Goodness-of-fit test
	2	Chi-square test
	3	No test available
Ordinal	1	One sample test
	2 independent groups 2 matched groups	Mann-Whitney U Wilcoxon
	3 or more groups	Kruskal-Wallis ANOVA

ables, but not to establish cause-effect relationships between the dependent and independent variables. Correlational procedures do not manipulate an independent variable but examine the existing relationship between variables. Group experimental designs examine differences between group means. In addition to determining the relationship between variables, correlational research may also predict the occurrence of variables. This form of analysis determines how two sets of measures may vary together or not. If two variables are highly correlated, the researcher may be able to predict one variable from the other. Thus, relational analysis shows whether a variable or variables covary with each other, while the predictive method shows whether a set of scores can predict performance on two or more measures.

Correlation coefficients are used to measure how strong a relationship exists between two variables. The **Pearson Product Moment Correlation** (PPMC) is one of several correlational coefficient measures. This measure shows the linear relationship between two sets of data. For example, one might investigate the relationship between the total frequency of words spoken by a sample of 3-year-old boys on a daily basis and the total frequency of words spoken by an age-matched group of girls. A positive relationship would suggest that 3-year-old boys produce as many words as the age-matched group of girls. A negative relationship would suggest that the two matched groups differ in the number words spoken. The PPMC calculation generates a value of between −1 and +1. The −1 means there is a strong negative correlation, while a +1 means there is a strong positive correlation, and a 0 means there is no or a zero correlation.

While the Pearson's correlation helps assess linear relationships, the Spearman correlation helps assess the relationship between rankings of two different sets of ordinal variables or different rankings of the same variable. The measure reflects the degree of similarity between two rankings. Measures of correlation do not address whether a relationship is significant. The statistical significance of rank correlations is addressed by the Mann-Whitney U test and the Wilcoxon matched-pair signed-rank test.

Systematic Reviews and Meta-Analyses

A problem practicing clinicians face is the vast number of articles published on a given topic. Finding the gist of research that may help them select treatment procedures can be a daunting task for clinicians. For researchers, too, evaluating the vast body of research to understand status of current knowledge and theory at any particular time can be a slow process.

To ease the burden of reading and critically evaluating extensive research on a given topic, experts have devised two methods to review and synthesize available evidence, offer treatment suggestions, and identify research needs. *Reviews, systematic reviews,* and *meta-analyses* are the three such methods of evaluating studies published in different national and international journals on a specific topic.

Reviews and Systematic Reviews

Reviews are traditional ways of examining a body of published scientific or clinical literature to take stock of accumulated knowledge. They may also be called **narrative reviews**. The reviewers may hand-select the studies for review and may use only a few specific criteria for study selection. Reviewers then critically examine the methods, design, results, and implications of the reviewed studies. Validity and reliability of the results, clinical implications, and future research needs may all be described in a traditional review. The traditional narrative reviewer makes no statistical analysis of published results. Such reviews are useful to students and researchers to gain a general understanding of research conducted in a particular field of study. A potential limitation of a traditional review is that the selection and evaluation of the studies and the conclusions of the reviewer may be subjective and biased.

Systematic reviews are also narrative and qualitative evaluations of research findings on a given topic, issue, or treatment procedure. Compared to the traditional reviews, they are more systematic in searching and selecting studies for review. Systematic reviewers ask specific questions, specify the study selection procedures and criteria, make a systematic search of the published literature to select studies for evaluation, make a critical evaluation of selected studies, and write a review. The organized method of selecting studies for review may help minimize selection biases (Crowther, Lim, & Crowther, 2010).

Reviews of studies that are more or less systematic are found in the introductory part of most research articles. Dissertations and theses have more extensive reviews of research done to date. However, a formal systematic review is an article by itself, published in a peer-reviewed journal.

Systematic reviews do critically evaluate studies and arrive at conclusions about the state of research on the selected topic. They suggest valid conclusions from the reviewed studies and identify research needs, unanswered questions, and needed methodological improvements. Systematic reviews do not make additional statistical analyses of published studies. (If they did, they would be called *meta-analyses*.) Considering their limitations, systematic reviews are helpful to clinicians, and perhaps more so to the researchers.

Meta-Analysis

A quantitative method of analysis and synthesis of data reported in multiple studies is **meta-analysis**, which is a statistical analysis of statistical results published in studies on a given topic. In clinical disciplines, meta-analysis is a quantitative method of combining the results of studies scattered in various national and international publications on diagnosis and treatment of diseases and disorders. These types of quantitative analyses are made to provide summative guidelines to the practitioner (Cooper, Hedges, & Valentine, 2009; Kennedy et al., 2008; Robey, 1998). Meta-analysis has been adopted by medical and health sciences, communication disorders, education, psychology, and other disciplines to document and promote evidence-based practices.

Individual studies, to be included in a meta-analysis, must have reported statistical values for their results. Effects sizes described earlier are especially important. Purely qualitative studies with no statistical analysis of results are excluded from meta-analysis. Meta-analysis of randomized group design data is different from that of single-subject design data. Meta-analytical studies are now found for both group design data and SSED data.

The meta-analyst begins by **specifying the research question**, just like an empirical investigator does. In communication disorders treatment research, one might, for example, ask what is the effect of behavioral treatment for stuttering, parent-administered language therapy for children, or clinical outcomes of therapy for aphasia. The terms in the research question must be defined precisely. What is behavioral treatment? Language treatment administered by parents? What are clinical outcomes in the treatment of aphasia? The more precise the definition of the problem, the better focused the literature search.

Once the research question has been clarified, the meta-analyst begins a systematic **search of the published literature** on the topic to retrieve the relevant studies. The analyst may use one of the several **search resources** that will facilitate the search for common conceptual terms. These include the *Thesaurus of ERTIC Descriptors, Thesaurus of Sociological Indexing,* and *Thesaurus of Psychological Index Terms*. Most informational sources use the *and/or* arrangement of terms to search. For example, a search of the aphasia treatment data might be arranged in an *and* link: Broca aphasia *and* agrammatism *and* female *and* ages 40 to 70 years. Or the search may be done with an *or* link: Broca's aphasia *or* agrammatism. Such major databases as the PubMed, PsycInfo, ScienceDirect, and ERIC, and others may be searched with several key terms that are likely to bring up the papers on the topic. Initially retrieved studies may be systematically filtered and organized on the basis of the type of design used, independent variables, dependent variables, effect size, p value, participant age, gender, and so forth.

Retrieved, filtered, and selected studies are then subjected to a statistical analysis. Many retrieved studies may be discarded because they do not meet the criteria for analysis. For example, if the purpose is to make a meta-analysis of randomized clinical trials, case studies, nonrandomized group design studies, or single-subject experimental studies may be excluded.

To evaluate the studies and to answer the research question (e.g., "Is Treatment X effective?"), the researcher conducts a statistical analysis of significance tests reported in individual studies. The most common method is to calculate an **average effect size** and its confidence interval across the selected studies that report individual effect sizes (Robey, 1998). There are published computer software to complete a meta-analysis of randomized clinical trials in medicine (Crowther et al., 2010).

In a rough and basic sense, meta-analysis gives an average of the reported effects of a treatment procedure. In clinical sciences, the traditional and systematic reviews make qualitative judgments about a treatment method, but the meta-analysis quantifies the effect of a procedure reported in multiple individual studies.

Meta-analysis is not limited to an average effect size calculated for a set of individual studies. More complex and more specific analyses may be made to answer narrowly defined questions about treatment effects. For example, if there is not much heterogeneity in the results of selected studies, a **fixed-effect analysis** may be performed. On the other hand, if there is much heterogeneity, a **random-effects analysis** may be made. Furthermore, meta-analysis may include subgroup analysis (Crowther et al., 2010). For example, in communication disorders meta-analytic studies, one might make an analysis of responses to treatment by male or female participants, individuals with more severe or less severe disorders, and so forth. *Meta-regression* is one of the subgroup of analytical methods.

There are publication standards for reporting systematic reviews and meta-analyses. Reviewers and meta-analysts are expected to follow selected guidelines in writing their reports. Moher, Liberati, Tetzlaff, and Altman (2009) describe a set of guidelines for reporting systematic reviews and randomized clinical trials in medicine. Levitt et al. (2018) describe the American Psychological Association's guidelines for reporting qualitative reviews and meta-analysis.

Meta-analyses carry their own limitations. A statistical *average effect* calculated from the average effects reported in individual studies may or may not be empirically robust. The criticism that applies to statistical significance (versus clinical significance described later) applies even more forcefully to meta-analysis. If the statistically significant results (e.g., the *p* values) reported in the original studies are limited in their clinical significance, a meta-analysis will not improve upon that. It is true that meta-analysts explicitly state their study inclusion and exclusion criteria. But explicitness of criteria is not the same as objectivity. Furthermore, although there are statistical ways of estimating it, the publication bias is not entirely removed from meta-analysis. **Publication bias** is the tendency for studies that report positive treatment effects to get published and those that obtained negative or no effects to not get published. Estimating this bias statistically may not be satisfactory. Journal editors should encourage publication of negative findings.

Visual Analysis of Single-Subject Data

Traditional researchers in experimental and applied behavior analysis who use single-subject experimental designs (SSEDs) have primarily used visual inspection (analysis) of the effects of the intervention variable(s) on the dependent variable. The **visual analysis** is an evaluation to determine the presence or absence of a treatment effect by examining the contrast between the baseline, experimental, reversal, or withdrawal conditions.

After the data are graphed, the researcher visually examines the level, slope, and trend of the baseline data compared to the treatment data points. Note is also made of the variability of changes within and between baseline, treatment, and control phases. The analysis is done to see whether there is a change in the treatment variable and, if so, whether the change may be attributed to the strength of the independent variable (treatment).

Quality Indicators

A traditional criticism against pure visual analysis is that it can be subjective and biased. Although single-subject research tends to produce large effects that convince not only the investigators but also the participants and any other observers, an element of subjectivism is a part of visual analysis. Even more important, if the effects are not as great as hoped for, and there is much variability within and across conditions, visual analysis may be difficult to make.

As we will see in a later section, statistical analysis of SSED data is one option or an addition to visual analysis. Even with that option, however, visual analysis needs some objective criteria that all investigators could apply. To help make a more uniform interpretation of treatment effects in SSEDs, Horner et al. (2005) recommend a set of **quality indicators** to enhance visual analysis. These indicators are consistent with the basic principles of SSEDs.

The first principle is the fidelity of the treatment protocol. **Fidelity** is the consistency with which the planned treatment was offered to all the participants. Was the treatment presented exactly as planned and described? The second principle is the reliability of the measures of the dependent variable. **Reliability**, as discussed in Chapter 6, is consistency of measurements and agreement among different observers. Treatment effects are measured not only by the investigator but also by external observers. Measures by two or more observers should agree. This is the **interobserver agreement**. Was there at least an 80% agreement between observers? Were there at least three to five data points per condition? Baseline, treatment, withdrawal, and reinstatements should contain sufficient data points. The third principle is the number of replications of the treatment effect across the experimental conditions. Were there at least three or more replications of the treatment effect? These quality indicators help determine the strength of the treatment variable via visual analysis.

Guidelines for Conducting Visual Analysis

A technical document, prepared by Kratochwill et al. (2010), sponsored by What Works Clearinghouse (U.S. Department of Education), specifies basic rules to be followed in conducting a valid and reliable visual analysis of SSED results. These rules, when combined with the quality indicators specified before, help make a thorough and convincing visual analysis. Additional guidelines, though more quantitative, are given in Gast and Spriggs (2010) and Lane and Gast (2013).

Kratochwill et al. (2010) recommend that to assess the effects of interventions in SSED studies, it is necessary to make a visual analysis of both within- and between-phase data. They recommend six factors to consider in visual analysis: (1) level, (2), trend, (3) variability, (4) immediacy of the effect, (5) overlap, and (6) consistency of data patterns across similar phases.

Level is the magnitude of the data (Lane & Gast, 2013) or as the mean score for a phase (e.g., baseline, treatment). The baseline data may be relatively high or low, but a sufficiently high base rate of the problem behavior will justify treatment and provide good contrast to the treatment condition in which the behavior is expected to decrease.

Trend is the direction of change in the data pattern; it is the direction in which the data have moved. The trend may be increasing or decreasing. Repeated measures in the baseline phase may show that the problem behavior is increasing, decreasing, or without a trend (stable). Increasing trend will provide a good contrast with the experimental condition and, incidentally, will require immediate intervention. Decreasing trend will show spurious effects of treatment and hence not acceptable; prudent SSED researchers will not introduce treatment. The ideal trend in the treatment phase is a decrease in the frequency of problem behavior and an increase in the withdrawal condition. If these trends are not evident in visual analysis, treatment effects are questionable.

Variability is the ups and downs in the measured values. If baseline, treatment, or withdrawal measures show alternating highs and lows, then there is too much variability that could mask or cancel out the treatment effects. Variability is the opposite of stability, which is that the measures of the dependent variables differ by a narrow margin. When the range of variability is narrow, the behavior is more stable. However, visual analysis should detect stability in the baselines taken just before treatment (no trend) but decreasing trend in the problem behavior during treatment. If the response rates vary too much in the treatment phase, then the treatment effects are questionable or uninterpretable.

Immediacy of the effect is the temporal duration between the introduction of treatment and the effects that are clear in visual inspection. It is assessed by comparing the last three data points in one phase (e.g., baseline) with the first three data points in the next phase (e.g., treatment). If the visual inspection detects changes in the target behavior soon after the introduction of treatment, the probability of a real treatment effect increases. Delayed effects may also be due to treatment, but they may be due to other variables as well. If it is known that a certain dependent variable changes slowly or gradually, then this should be considered in visual analysis.

Overlap is the degree to which measures in contrasting phases are similar. For example, the measures of the dependent variable (the target behavior) across baseline and treatment condition should not overlap (should be different). Similarly, treatment measures should not overlap with the measures for withdrawal or repeated baselines in multiple baseline studies. Overlap reduces contrast and separation increases it. Overlap and lack of contrast reduce the probability of a strong treatment effect.

Consistency is the similarity of measures across similar phases. In an *ABAB* design, the measures for the baseline (the first *A*) and treatment withdrawal condition (the second *A*) should be similar. Measures for the two treatment conditions (the first and the second *B*) should be consistent with each other.

Systematic visual analysis that includes the quality indicators and the rules to determine the treatment effects (level, trend, variability, immediacy, overlap, and consistency) will be more convincing than an unsystematic visual analysis. Good training and experience in the analysis and interpretation of SSED data will help. Statistical analysis of SSED data may supplement and enhance visual analysis. We review a few of the several statistical options available to the SSED researchers.

Statistical Analysis of Single-Subject Data

Various statistical techniques, especially designed for SSED data, are now available to supplement or enhance visual analysis. Generally speaking, SSED data do not conform to the assumptions of parametric statistical tests. Therefore, most of the available statistical tests for SSED studies are nonparametric. We give a brief overview of only a few of the recommended tests. Interested readers should consult other sources for more information and test calculations (Satake, Jagaroo, & Maxwell, 2008).

Although there are various statistical approaches to analyzing SSED data, we describe only a few effect size calculations. **Randomization test** is a widely promoted but infrequently used method by behavioral researchers. The analysis requires a priori modifications of SSEDs that violate some of their basic principles. For example, randomization test requires random assignment of treatments in SSEDs. Such randomization introduces changes in the SSEDs that are unacceptable. Even in alternative treatments design (see Chapter 9), which requires some randomization, only semi-randomization works. We concur with Haardorfer and Gagne (2010), who reviewed randomization tests and concluded that they are "an awkward fit to single-subject designs, and they are found to have low statistical power in single-subject contexts" (p. 1).

Effect Size of Single-Subject Treatment Studies

As noted before, **effect size** is a measure of the magnitude of change from baseline to treatment phases. Effect size quantifies the size of the difference between conditions. Effects sizes are routinely reported for group design treatment data. They are now becoming more common than before in the analysis of SSED studies.

Some of the technical difficulties involved in effect size calculation of SSED data include the autocorrelation of those data. When the same individuals are observed repeatedly, as they are done in SSED studies, then the measures are not independent of each other (autocorrelated). Also, the population distribution of measures may not be known. These two factors rule out the use of many parametric statistical techniques.

Effect sizes are still important for those who consider statistical analysis is more objective than visual analysis. Also, effect size calculations are essential to conduct meta-analysis of SSED data that help compare treatment effects across studies to presents a synthesis of research evidence that will be helpful to practicing clinicians.

Beeson and Robey (2006) suggest a few basic criteria necessary to calculate an effect size for SSED data. They suggest that a minimum of three baseline measures and three posttreatment probes are essential for an effect size calculation. Separate effect sizes may be calculated when multiple treatments are evaluated. The authors rule out effect size calculations for uncontrolled *AB* case studies and state further that the response rates on untreated stimulus items do not contribute to the effect size. Probe data obtained infrequently or irregularly should not enter the effect size calculation, although follow-up data may be.

Nonoverlap Effect Size Calculations for Single-Subject Experimental Studies

A group of techniques designed to calculate an effect size of SSED data is described as *nonoverlap methods*. **Nonoverlap methods** assume that if the treatment is effective, measures of control and treatment conditions are separate and distinct; they do not overlap. If there is overlap, then the treatment is ineffective because the data across those conditions are more similar than different. Parker, Vannest, and Davis (2011) describe several nonoverlap techniques that they consider blend well with visual analysis of SSED data. In visual analysis, treatment effect is inferred when the baseline and treatment data are distinct and nonoverlapping.

The nonoverlap methods are distribution free and are relatively easy to calculate. Furthermore, nonoverlap methods do not need the statistical mean or the median, which typically does not well represent SSED data. We will highlight a selected few, but to better understand all nonoverlap methods, the readers may consult Parker et al. (2011).

Percentage of nonoverlapping data (PND) is a nonoverlap method in which the highest baseline data point is identified first, and then the treatment data points that exceed the highest baseline data point are counted. Then the number of treatment data points that exceed the baseline data point is divided by the total number of treatment data points. Suppose, for instance, that a child's correct production of a speech sound varied during the six base rate sessions, but the highest recorded was 20%. During the next treatment condition, the correction production was higher than 20% in 10 out of 12 sessions. In this study, there was an 80% nonoverlapping data (8/10 = 80%). Generally, 70% or more is interpreted as a significant effect. This easy effect size has been used frequently, although the method uses a single Phase A data point—a significant loss of observational power. Its sampling distribution is unknown, so inference to population is unwarranted.

Percentage of all nonoverlapping data (PAND). In this method, fewest data points in the treatment condition that overlap with data points in the base rate condition are eliminated from analysis. Only those data points in the treatment condition that are above the highest baseline measure are counted. Taking the previous example given for PND, the highest recorded for the six baseline condition

was 20%. Assuming now that out of 12 treatment sessions, 16% and 18% correct sound productions were recorded for two sessions. Those two treatment measures that are below the highest baseline measure (20%) are removed to arrive at the number of nonoverlapping measures. Now all data across the remaining 16 sessions (6 base rate and 10 treatment) are nonoverlapping. The PAND is calculated by dividing the total nonoverlapping number by the total number of measures for all conditions, including the two removed (16/18 = 88%). The treatment effect is 88%. The PAND calculation may be supplemented with an additional statistic called the "robust Phi," a well-known effect size measure (Parker et al., 2011). The problem with PAND from a behavioral science standpoint is the removal of data for the convenience of calculating a statistic.

Percentage of data points exceeding the median. In this index, the researcher calculates the percentage of treatment data points that exceed the median of baseline data. First a median straight line is drawn across the graph, extending the line into the treatment condition. An equal number of data points fall above and below the median (line). All treatment data points that fall above the median base rate line are counted. In our continued example, assuming that all 12 treatment data points exceeded the baseline median, the treatment would be 100% effective (12/12 = 100%).

Kendall's tau (simply, tau) is an effect size measure of nonoverlap between baseline and treatment. It is a nonparametric measure of correlation between two variables that have been ranked. A modified form of tau, called tau-U, is a test designed to compare pairs of measures recorded for such adjacent phases as baseline and treatment or treatment and withdrawal or withdrawal and reinstatement in an *ABAB* design. In addition, tau-*U* can assess trend within treatment phases and control undesirable trend in baseline phases (Parker et al., 2011). Thus, calculated tau serves as an estimate of treatment effect (effect size). The significance of tau effect sizes may be tested with Kruskal-Wallis one-way analysis or Dunn post hoc analysis. Tau values calculated for different studies may be used to synthesize treatment effects across studies in a meta-analysis.

The main advantage of nonoverlapping indexes is that they all yield an effect size that can be averaged across different studies to conduct a meta-analysis of SSED studies. The methods have a serious disadvantage, however. Among those just described, only tau-*U* can control for trend in the data. Most methods, therefore, will be insensitive to an improving baseline or a deteriorating response rate under treatment. If the treatment were to be mistakenly introduced when the baseline was improving and the treatment had a negative effect, most of the nonoverlapping methods would lead to erroneous conclusions about the treatment. Furthermore, as Parker et al.'s (2011) hypothetical data illustrate, different nonoverlapping methods lead to different effect sizes for the same data set.

Variations of *d* Statistics

The ***d* statistic** is one of the effect size calculations that has received much attention. There are various forms of this test. One form of *d*, which is thought to be similar to Cohen's *d* used in analyzing group design data, is also known as the **standard mean difference test** (Busk & Serlin, 2005). In the Busk and Serlin

formula, the effect size (ES) is calculated by deducting the mean for the treatment condition from the mean for the baseline condition, divided by the standard deviation of the baseline condition. The method, however, has been criticized as not being equivalent to the *d* of group design statistics (Shadish, Hedges, Pustejovsky, Boyajian, et al., 2014). As such, it may serve better to understand the effect size of SSED studies, but may not be good to compare it with Cohen's *d* meant for group designs. Consequently, it may not be a good choice for meta-analyses in which SSED study results and group design effect sizes are averaged.

To provide for ES calculation that is comparable to that used in group design analysis, Hedges, Pustejovsky, and Shadish (HPS) (2013) have proposed a different type of *d* statistic. It is calculated by subtracting the mean outcome under treatment from the baseline outcome divided by the standard deviation. This **HPS *d*** may be used to calculate the effect size of both SSED data with at least three participants and the group design data. The HPS *d* takes into account the total variance across participants (not just the intraparticipant variation) and autocorrelations (correlated repeated measures of the same persons) of SSED data. The HPS *d* also has a correction factor for small sample size, called Hedge's *g*. Different formula for calculating HPS *d* for *AB*, *ABAB*, and multiple baseline designs have been suggested (see Shadish et al., 2014, for details). This type of *d* may be used to compare effects sizes across studies to make a meta-analysis of SSED data.

The PHS *d* assumes that the outcome measures are normally distributed and that there is no trend in the data. Neither of these assumptions may hold good for SSED data, a weakness of PHS *d*.

Meta-Analysis of Single-Subject Data

Although meta-analysis is more commonly done with group design studies, SSED data, too, may be subjected to that kind of analysis. In the more recent decades, there has been a steady increase in the publication of meta-analytical studies of SSED data, although their quality has been questionable (Jamshidi et al., 2018). Properly done meta-analysis of SSED treatment research data may help improve their generality or external validity.

The general method of performing a meta-analysis of SSED data is the same as that for group design studies described earlier. The author of a meta-analysis formulates a research question, specifies the study search methods, describes the study inclusion and exclusion criteria, completes the study search, selects the studies according to the set criteria, performs the statistical analysis, and writes up a report. Of the several statistical methods that are used in meta-analysis of SSED data, we highlight a few and give only a conceptual overview. For the actual statistical test calculations, the reader is referred to the relevant articles.

Van den Noortgate and Onghena (2008) believe that the SSED researcher's tendency to provide raw individual data for each participant has a clear advantage in making meta-analysis of similar studies. Several kinds of statistical tests necessary for a meta-analysis may be performed on the raw data provided in each study for each participant. Similar statistical tests done across SSED studies will help complete a meta-analysis.

Theoretically, all SSED studies that report one or the other form of statistical effect size can be subjected to meta-analysis. We have described several of them in the previous section. For the studies that do not report an effect size statistic, a suitable one may be calculated from the raw data for each participant in each study and for participants across studies.

There is a **multilevel meta-analysis** of SSED data (Van den Noortgate & Onghena, 2008). We know that the SSED investigators record multiple measures (observations) for each individual participant in a study. These multiple measures for the same participant tend to vary from one measurement occasion to the other. These *within-individual* variations are treated as Level 1. Measurement values vary *across participants* in the same study, and this creates Level 2. Level 3 is created by the measured values that *vary across studies* that are considered for meta-analysis. Van den Noortgate and Onghena (2008) describe several regression equation tests to compare variations in baseline condition with those of the treatment condition, variations across participants in the same study, and variations across studies, resulting in a multilevel meta-analysis. As all meta-analyses seek to do, this type of analysis can determine whether the analyzed treatment was effective within and across studies, providing a research synthesis for the practitioner.

Even though meta-analyses of SSED studies have been on the increase as noted, it is not clear that all single-subject researchers accept their value. Certain subcommunities of SSED researchers are unimpressed by statistical and meta-analytical approaches to evaluate the treatment effects of their studies. They believe that the distinction between statistical analysis, including the effect size estimates on the one hand, and clinical significance on the other, is still valid. SSED researchers also believe that because of the large effects SSED studies tend to produce, they are less likely to make the Type I error than the group design researchers. That is, because of the clinically significant effects that are clear in visual analysis, the SSED researchers are unlikely to conclude that treatment was effective when it was not.

Other subcommunities of SSED researchers are open to statistical analyses and meta-analyses of SSED data. They believe that statistical analysis meaningfully supplements visual analysis and minimizes the subjective element involved in the latter. Furthermore, meta-analysis of SSED data helps practitioners to select effective procedures, and such meta-analyses are more readily entered into evidence-based practice databases. Because of lack of statistical significance analysis, the evidence generated by SSED data has not received the attention they deserve. Increasingly greater number of statistical tools are being made available to SSED researchers and many are taking advantage of them (Shadish, Hedges, & Pustejovsky, 2014; Shadish et al., 2014).

Statistical Significance Versus Clinical Significance

Statistical techniques are well established in the analysis of group design studies and are being increasingly advocated for single-subject design studies. The parametric and nonparametric tests of significance all generate a probability (p) value to help conclude that the results were or were not due to chance. An acceptable p value may suggest that the treatment had a statistically significant effect, but it may not mean that the treatment effect was large enough to affect the lives of the individual participants in the experiment

(McClellan, 2017). The larger the sample, the greater the chance that the p value will be significant. The larger the sample, the smaller the treatment effects need to be to reach statistical significance. In most large group studies that include randomized clinical trials, significant p values may only mean small treatment effects. Such small treatment effects may or may not make a difference in the lives of the individuals who participated in the experiment. And to the contrary, in some randomized clinical trials in medicine, large treatment effects were associated with smaller p values (van Rijn, Bech, Bouyer, & van den Brand, 2017).

Two other problems are associated with large samples and small treatment effects despite significant p values. First, and as noted throughout this book, the larger the sample, the greater the difficulty in generalizing the treatment to the individual clients or patients. Second, the typical assumption that statistically significant results are robust enough to be replicated is not supported by recent evidence; many such studies have failed at replications (Ioannidis, 2014; Nuzzo, 2014). Typically recommended solution is to report 95% confidence limits and effect sizes along with a p value. These recommendations may reinforce an already strong tendency to resort to traditional statistical analysis, but they may not speak to the functional outcomes of treatment research. In the current context, however, we will set aside these two major problems and address only the issue of statistical significance not ensuring clinical significance.

What is a clinically significant treatment effect? It is a term that is also related to *personally significant, socially significant*, or *socially valid* treatment research results. The better-known *functional outcomes of treatments* roughly imply the same. *Meaningful change* in treated persons is yet another related concept. All these terms imply that successful treatment should be **clinically significant** in that it makes a noticeable difference in the lives of the individuals who receive it. Possibly, a clinically significant result is always statistically significant as well, but a statistically significant result may fall short of clinical significance. Treatment should induce **meaningful changes**, and such changes are not always guaranteed by a significant *p* value. Meaningful changes have to be large enough to reduce or eliminate the undesirable health status or the maladaptive behaviors of the individuals. Treatment should substantially reduce the negative effects of a disease or disorder so that the persons' quality of life improves. Positive changes due to treatment should be easily recognizable by those who receive treatment and those surrounding them. S. S. Stevens, the famed psychologist and a pioneer in psychoacoustics, author of the classic work, *Hearing, Its Psychology and Physiology*, had wondered, "Can no one recognize a decisive result without a significance test?" (Stevens, 1968, p. 853). Treated individuals should be able to return to their typical living habits. If the normative view is found applicable, treatment should restore the individuals to within the normative range. These are all the meanings of clinical significance.

Being concerned with the limitations of statistical significance, applied behavioral scientists, research psychotherapists and psychiatrists, and medical treatment researchers have been researching ways in which clinical significance of treatment research evidence may be documented (Jacobson, Roberts, Berns, & McGlinchey, 1999; Kazdin, 1999; Kendall, Marrs-Garcia,

Nath, & Sheldrick, 1999; McClellan, 2017; Mellis, 2018; Ogles, Lunnen, & Bonesteel, 2001). Both qualitative and quantitative methods have been proposed. The distinction should not be taken too literally because it is possible to combine elements of qualitative and quantitative (statistical) approaches to determining clinical significance. Some qualitative measure may be more quantitative than other qualitative measures.

Qualitative Measures of Clinical Significance

Early measures of clinical significance were qualitative. Such measures continue to be used, however, because the statistical measures do not capture all the different dimensions of clinical significance. A comprehensive assessment of clinical significance may need multiple, preferably both the qualitative and quantitative measures.

Social validity, which is treatment considered valid from the standpoint of society and the treated individual, has been one of the early qualitative measure of clinical significance advocated by applied behavior researchers (Wolfe, 1978). Social validity is multifaceted and may involve subjective evaluation of treatment by the treated individuals, their family members, and other people in their lives (teachers, friends, colleagues). It might also include experts who were not involved in the treatment study. Interviews and questionnaires may be used to evoke responses from the selected individuals. Treated individuals may comment on whether their quality of life has improved and if so, to what extent. Family members and significant others may support, expand, or moderate the treated individual's claims.

To further substantiate the changes of clinical significance, the investigators also may have experts rate the degree of improvement seen the treated individuals. Such ratings, somewhat quantitative, will add to the qualitative statements of treated persons and their acquaintances.

Social validity data must be interpreted with caution. Treated individuals and others in their living environment may be prone to distort the treatment outcomes. A significant change may be missed by some of all questioned or the treatment effects may be exaggerated. Some extraneous variables may come to play. For example, the spouse who is asked to judge the changes in the general or communicative behavior of an individual treated for traumatic brain injury might be influenced by marital status factors, economic factors, and child custody issues, among others.

Quality of life assessment, although not always considered a measure of clinical significance, may be useful in documenting meaningful changes that follow experimental or routine treatment. The method is similar to social validity assessment. Clinicians may interview and administer specifically designed quality of life questionnaires to clients and others in their lives to assess whether the treatment has made a difference in the client's educational, social, family, and occupational life. In communication disorders, functional communication may be the target of assessment in cases of severe speech, language, and voice disorders.

Quality of life assessment is both qualitative and quantitative. Interview data from the clients and people in their lives may be analyzed qualitatively. Questionnaires and tests may be more quantitative than the interview data. Problems with the quality of life assessment include potential subjective biases on the part of those who report. Clients and people associated may under- or overestimate the effects as well as the clinical significance of the treatment outcome. When the quality of life assessment data are used in conjunction with other measures of treatment effects (visual analysis, significance tests, effect size, etc.), a more reliable and comprehensive picture of clinal significance might emerge.

Diagnostic criterion also may be used as a qualitative method of determining clinical significance. A diagnostic interview or assessment may be conducted for each treated individual to see if the person still meets the diagnostic criterion for the disease or the disorder that received the experimental treatment. All treated individuals who no longer have the disorder (do not meet the diagnostic criterion) will have experienced clinically significant benefit from the treatment. This is similar to a related criterion used in medicine: **cure**. Obviously, cured individuals will have derived the maximum benefit from the treatment.

Some qualitative diagnostic criterion may include a quantitative criterion as well. For instance, in diagnosing stuttering, not only the presence of stuttering, but their frequency and percentage, based on the number of spoken words, may be calculated. In this case, the diagnostic criterion is both qualitative and quantitative.

Clinical significance based on a failure to meet the diagnostic criterion after treatment, if achieved, is a high level of clinical significance that all can appreciate. It is, however, difficult to achieve in most cases with communication disorders, as well as many physical diseases (cancer, neurodegenerative diseases) and social problems (e.g., crime and delinquency). Treated children with a few speech sound errors may no longer be diagnosed with a speech sound disorder, but language disorders associated with intellectual disabilities and other more permanent associated problems may make clinically significant improvements but may still qualify for the diagnosis. Similarly, persons with aphasia, dementia, traumatic brain injury, apraxia of speech, dementia, hearing loss, and those with minimal verbal skills needing augmentative or alternative methods may also achieve clinically significant improvements in their communication skills due to treatment, but they still may retain their diagnoses. This only goes to show that in many cases, clinically significant change can be achieved without eliminating the diagnosis.

Quantitative Measures of Clinical Significance

Those who advocate quantitative measures of clinical significance believe that they overcome some of the subjective aspects of qualitative measures. Of the several quantitative measures of clinical significance, we highlight a few. Readers should consult other sources for additional methods as well as methods of calculating them (Bauer, Lambert, & Nielsen, 2004; Johnson, Dow, Lynch, & Hermann, 2006; Kendall et al., 1999; Ogles et al., 2001, among others).

Previously discussed effect size, in addition to the p value, helps avoid the mistake of concluding that the treatment made a difference in those who received it when in fact it produced only a small, clinically insignificant, albeit statistically significant, effect. Large effect sizes are sometimes promoted as an index of clinical significance. Effect sizes, however, are not a convincing measure of clinical significance in individuals. Even large effects do not necessarily mean that the individuals who received treatment are now better

off in their daily living. As Kazdin (1999) has argued, a large effect sometimes may mean little or no clinical significance, and a small effect may make a big difference in some cases. It is also likely that a large effect in a group may or may not mean a significant change in all or most individual participants.

Reliable change index (RCI) is a quantitative measure of clinical significance. When the concept of reliable change is coupled with changes that are large enough to be noticed by others, clinical significance may be enhanced. Of the several statistical RCIs that are available, the one developed by Jacobsen and Truax (JT) (1991) has been used the most frequently. The JT RCI defines clinical significance as a change in the study participants with diseases or disorders (the *dysfunctional group*) that brings them closer to the *normal* or *functional group*. The method specifies three cutoff points or scores, labeled A, B, and C, that suggest clinical significance. In cutoff point A, the posttreatment score of the experimental group should be two *standard deviations away* from the mean for the dysfunctional group. In cutoff point B, the posttreatment score should lie *within two standard deviations* of the mean for the functional group. In cutoff point C, the posttreatment score lies away from the mean for the dysfunctional group and closer to the mean for the functional group. The RCI calculation for each participant is based on the pretreatment score, the posttreatment score, and the standard error for the difference between the two sets of scores. If the resulting index is greater than 1.96, the change is considered reliable, which means that the change is not likely the product of measurement error.

A potential problem with the JT RCI is that the researcher may not know the mean for the functional group on skills targeted in treatment research. For instance, to apply this method to a study of treatment effects on naming skills in individuals with aphasia, one needs normative information. What is the mean for the nonaphasic (functional) group's naming skills? The answer may be unclear. The method also requires a knowledge of the mean performance of the dysfunctional group. What is the mean performance of individuals with aphasia on a naming task? There may be no available data to answer this question.

Percentage of improvement is another quantitative measure of clinical significance. Applied behavior analysts and single-subject researchers in communication disorders routinely report percentage of improvement. Percentage of improvement over the baselines in the behaviors taught might be reported in single-subject studies. In the group designs, this indicator is calculated by subtracting posttreatment performance from pretreatment performance, divided by pretreatment performance, and multiplied by 100. The method requires a criterion percentage (of improvement) that is deemed clinically significant. Researchers might choose a relatively low (such as 50%) or high (90%) improvement as the criterion to judge that the treatment was clinically significant. To be clinically significant, the percentage of improvement should be high.

Percentage of improvement that meets a high criterion (such as 90% or better) is a relatively straightforward calculation. Its meaning is clear to the treated persons and their families. But to be clinically significant, the high percentage of improvement should be demonstrated in skills that matter. This is the issue of target behavior selection, particularly important in communication disorders. Target behaviors

should be functional to the individual in that they should enhance social and personal communication. For example, in the case of children with extremely limited language skills, the researchers can teach the names of colors and geometric shapes and show 95% or even 100% improvement in producing those words. Such an outcome would be clinically less significant than the same level of improvement in making basic requests (mands). Even a lower level of improvements in requests might be considered clinically significant.

Normative comparison, another quantitative method of evaluating clinical significance, compares the treated individuals with comparable healthy individuals or individuals with no disorder that was treated (Kendall et al., 1999). For example, children who have been treated for speech sound disorders (SSDs) with noticeable or statistically significant treatment effects may then be compared to children who are comparable in age but were not diagnosed with SSDs (the *normative* group). In essence, the method seeks to find out if treated individuals have been returned to within the normal range for health, behavior, or specific skills that were taught. If they have, then the treatment is considered clinically significant. Normative comparison is similar to the *diagnostic* or the *cure* criteria mentioned earlier. Under all three criteria, a disorder or disease is eliminated, and the individuals return to their membership in the typical (normal, normative) group.

Normative comparison presents two practical problems. First, many clinical populations under treatment may make meaningful (clinically significant) changes but may remain outside the realm of normal distribution. To return to the membership in the normal population, treated clinical populations must be effectively "cured," a condition not attained in many cases. We pointed this out in the context of the *diagnostic criterion* discussed earlier. Second, the method requires reliable and extensive norms for all skills and behaviors so as to evaluate the treated groups' skills against those norms. Such norms are especially lacking in the case of adult communication disorders, including dysarthria, aphasia, apraxia of speech, dementia, traumatic brain injury, nonverbal and minimally verbal skills, and language disorders in older students and adolescents. And many individuals, including those with severe dysarthria, apraxia of speech, or those with minimal verbal skills, may attain clinically significant improvements without gaining membership in normative groups.

Social evaluation (Kazdin, 1999) is similar to normative comparison. In this procedure, treated individuals' pre- and posttest scores may be compared with the relevant scores of a reference group of individuals who had not had the disease or disorder. If the posttest scores of treated individuals on the relevant dependent variables are similar to the scores of the reference group, then the treatment was both effective and clinically significant. It also means that practically, the individuals no longer meet the diagnostic criterion and thus are "cured." The same limitations and difficulties of the normative comparison and diagnostic criterion apply to social validation as well.

Clinical Significance in Group Versus Single-Subject Research

Frequently used quantitative measures assess clinical significance at the group level. Both the reliable change index and the normative comparison assess clinical significance of group treatment research. Researchers using single-subject designs have relied on visual inspection and percent change across control and experimental conditions to assess clinical significance. They may also use such other measures as the diagnostic criteria. Some effectively treated individuals may no longer meet qualitative and quantitative diagnostic criteria. For instance, dysfluency rates in people who stutter may fall at or below a percentage judged normal. Hoarseness of voice may be judged eliminated. Speech sound errors may be fully corrected.

Even in group design studies, individuals need to be assessed to determine clinical significance of change. To use the diagnostic criterion, for example, each research participant must be interviewed and assessed. Analysis of individual performance is typically done in single-subject designs and may be feasible in small sample group experiments. Such an analysis is rarely, if ever, done in large sample randomized clinical trials because it is not practical. It is for this reason that clinical significance of changes reported in RCTs is generally suspect or unknown.

Finally, there is no single measure of clinical significance that adequately determines meaningful change. Whenever feasible, multiple measures may be used. For instance, percentage of change across control and experimental conditions may be combined with the diagnostic criterion. And both may be reported along with quality of life assessment.

Summary

- Statistical analysis of group research data is rooted in the theory of probability and the concept of the normal distribution of variables in the population.

- Statistical significance tests help determine that the observed differences in the performances of the experimental and control groups are *probably* due to treatment (systematic variance) and not chance (random variance).

- A null hypothesis (statistical hypothesis) is a statement that asserts that the treatment will have no effect. Rejecting the null hypothesis and asserting that treatment had an effect when in fact treatment had no significant effect is Type I error; accepting the null hypothesis of no effect when there was a significant effect is a Type II error.

- Parametric statistical tests are based upon the assumption that the variables being measured are distributed normally in the population and include the t test, analysis of variance (ANOVA), the analysis of covariance (ANCOVA), and multivariate analysis of variance (MANOVA).

- Nonparametric tests make no assumptions about the distribution of the sample or the variables in the population and include the chi-square test (χ^2), the goodness-of-fit test, and the Mann-Whitney U test (Wilcoxon rank-sum test).

- Meta-analysis is a statistical method of taking stock of evidence on a treatment procedure with a goal of making summative evaluation and providing guidelines to the practitioner.

- In the visual analysis of single-subject data, the presence or absence of a treatment effect is determined by examining the contrast between the baseline, experimental, and reversal or withdrawal conditions.

- Various nonoverlapping methods and d statistics are meant for single-subject designs.

- Statistical analysis may not ensure clinical significance (functional outcomes) of treatment research.

- Measures of clinical significance include social validity, quality of life assessment, diagnostic criterion, reliable change index, percentage of improvement, normative comparison, and social evaluation.

References

Bauer, S., Lambert, M. J., & Nielsen, S. L. (2004). Clinical significance models: A comparison of statistical techniques. *Journal of Personality Assessment, 82*(1), 60–70.

Beeson, P. M., & Robey, R. R. (2006). Evaluating single-subject treatment research: Lessons learned from the aphasia literature. *Neuropsychology Review, 16*(4), 161–169.

Boring, E. (1950). *A history of experimental psychology* (2nd ed.). New York, NY: Appleton-Century-Crofts.

Box, G. E. P., Hunter, J. S., & Hunter, W. G. (2005). *Statistics for experimenters: Design, innovation and discovery* (2nd ed.) Hoboken, NJ: Wiley.

Box, J. F. (1978). *R. A. Fisher: The life of a scientist.* New York, NY: Wiley.

Busk, P. L., & Serlin, R. C. (2005). Meta-analysis of single-case research. In T. R. Kratochwill & J. R. Levin (Eds.), *Single-case research designs and analysis: New directions for psychology and education* (pp. 187–212). Hillsdale, NJ: Erlbaum.

Cochran, W. C. (1980). Fisher and the analysis of variance. In S. Fienberg, J. Gani, J. Kiefer, & K. Krickberg (Eds.), *R. A. Fisher: An appreciation* (pp. 17–34). New York, NY: Springer-Verlag.

Cooper, L., Hedges, L., & Valentine, J. (Eds.). (2009). *The handbook of research synthesis and meta-analysis.* New York, NY: Russell Sage Foundation.

Crowther, M., Lim, W., & Crowther, M. A. (2010). Systematic review and meta-analysis methodology. *Blood, 116*(17), 3140–3146.

Fisher, R. A. (1925). *Statistical methods for research workers.* London, UK: Oliver & Boyd.

Fisher, R. A. (1942). *Design of experiments.* London, UK: Oliver & Boyd.

Fisher, R. A. (1951). *The design of experiments* (6th ed.). New York, NY: Hefner.

Fisher, R. A. (1956). *Statistical methods and scientific inference.* London, UK: Oliver & Boyd.

Gast, D. L., & Spriggs, A. D. (2010). Visual analysis of graphic data. In D. L. Gast (Ed.), *Single-subject research methodology in behavioral sciences* (pp. 199–275). New York, NY: Routledge.

Haardorfer, R., & Gagne, P. (2010). The use of randomization tests in single-subject research. *Focus on Autism and Other Developmental Disorders, 25*(1), 47–54.

Hacking, I. (1975). *The emergence of probability.* New York, NY: Cambridge University Press.

Hald, A. (1998). *A history of mathematical statistics from 1750 to 1930.* New York, NY: Wiley.

Hedges, L. V., Pustejovsky, J. E., & Shadish, W. R. (2013). A standardized mean difference effect size for multiple baseline designs across individuals. *Research Synthesis Methods, 4,* 324–341.

Heyvaert, M., & Onghena, P. (2014). Analysis of single-case data: Randomization test for measures of effect size. *Neuropsychology Rehabilitation, 24*(3–4), 507–527.

Hill, G., Forbes, W., Kozak, J., & McNeill, I. (2000). Likelihood and clinical trials. *Journal of Clinical Epidemiology, 53*(3), 223–227.

Hong, E. R., Ganz, J. B., Mason, R., Morin, K., Davis, J. L., Ninci, J., . . .Gilliand, W. D. (2016). The effects of video-modeling in teaching functional living skills to persons with ASD: A meta-analysis of single-case studies. *Research in Developmental Studies, 57,* 158–169.

Horner, R. H., Carr, E. G., Halle, J., McGee, G., Odom, S., & Wolery, M. (2005). The use of single subject research to identify evidence-based practice in special education. *Exceptional Children, 71*(2), 165–179.

Ioannidis, J. P. A. (2014). How to make more published research true. *PLoS Medicine, 11*(10), e1001747.

Jacobson, N. S., Roberts, L. J., Berns, S. B., & McGlinchey, J. B. (1999). Methods for defining and determining the clinical significance of treatment effects: Description, application, and alternatives. *Journal of Consulting and Clinical Psychology, 67*(3), 300–307.

Jacobson, N. S., & Truax, P. (1991). Clinical Significance: A statistical approach to defining meaningful change in psychotherapy research. *Journal of Consulting and Clinical Psychology, 59*(1), 12–19.

Jamshidi, L., Heyvaert, M., Declercq, L., Fernadez-Castilla, B., Ferron, J. M., Moeyaert, M., . . . Van den Noortgate, W. (2018). Methodological quality of meta-analysis of single-case experimental studies. *Research in Developmental Studies, 79,* 97–115.

Johnson, E. K., Dow, C., Lynch, R. T., & Hermann, B. P. (2006). Measuring clinical significance in rehabilitation research. *Rehabilitation Counseling Bulletin, 50*(1), 35–45.

Kazdin, A. E. (1999). The meanings and measurement of clinical significance. *Journal Consulting and Clinical Psychology, 67*(3), 332–339.

Kendall, P. C., Marrs-Garcia, Nath, R., & Sheldrick, R. C. (1999). Normative comparison for the evaluation of clinical significance. *Journal of Counseling and Clinical Psychology, 67*(3), 285–299.

Kennedy, M. R. T., Coelho, C., Turkstra, L., Ylvisaker, M., Sohlberg, M. M., Yorkston, K., . . . Kan, P. F. (2008). Intervention for executive functions after traumatic brain injury: A systematic review, meta-analysis and clinical recommendations. *Neuropsychological Rehabilitation, 18*(3), 257–299.

Kerlinger, F. N. (1986). *Foundations of behavioral research* (3rd ed.). New York, NY: Holt Reinhart & Winston.

Kratochwill, T. R., Hitchcock, J., Horner, R. H., Levin, J. R., Odom, S. L., Rindskopf, D. M., & Shadish, W. R. (2010). *What Works Clearinghouse: Single-case designs technical documentation*. Retrieved from http://ies.ed.gov/ncee/wwc/pd/wwc_scd.pdf

Lane, J. D., & Gast, D. L. (2013). Visual analysis in single case experimental design studies: Brief review and guidelines. *Neuropsychological Rehabilitation, 24*(3-4), 445–463.

Levitt, H. M., Bamberg, M., Creswell, J. W., Frost, D. M., Josselson, R., & Suárez-Orozco, C. (2018). Journal article reporting standards for qualitative primary, qualitative meta-analytic, and mixed methods research in psychology: The APA Publications and Communications Board Task Force report. *American Psychologist, 73*, 26–46.

Martella, R. C., Nelson, J. R., Morgan, R. L., & Marchand-Martella, N. E. (2013). *Understanding and interpreting educational research*. New York, NY: Guilford Press.

McCall, W. A. (1923). *How to experiment in education*. New York, NY: McMillan.

McClellan, J. (2017). Clinical relevance versus statistical significance [Editorial]. *Journal of the American Academy of Child and Adolescent Psychiatry, 56*(12), 1008–1109.

Mellis, C. (2018). Lies, damned lies and statistics: Clinical importance versus statistical significance in research. *Paediatric Respiratory Reviews, 25*, 88–93.

Moher, D., Liberati, A., Tetzlaff, J., & Altman, D. G. (2009). Preferred Reporting Items for Systematic Reviews and Meta-Analyses: The PRISMA statement. *PLos Medicine, 6*(7), e1000097.

Nuzzo, R. (2014). P values, the "gold standard" of statistical validity, are not as reliable as many scientists assume. *Nature, 506*, 150–152.

Ogles, B. M., Lunnen, K. M., & Bonesteel, K. (2001). Clinical significance: History, application, and current practice. *Clinical Psychology Review, 21*(3), 421–446.

Parker, R. I., Vannest, K. J., & Davis, J. L. (2011). Effect-size in single-case research: A review of nine nonoverlap techniques. *Behavior Modification, 35*(4), 303–322.

Robey, R. R. (1998). A meta-analysis of clinical outcomes in the treatment of aphasia. *Journal of Speech-Language-Hearing Research, 41*, 172–187.

Satake, E., Jagaroo, V., & Maxwell, D. L. (2008). *Handbook of statistical methods: Single-subject designs*. San Diego, CA: Plural.

Shadish, W. R., Hedges, L. V., & Pustejovsky, J. V. (2014). Analysis and meta-analysis of single-case designs with a standardized mean difference statistic: A primer and applications. *Journal of School Psychology, 52*, 123–147.

Shadish, W. R., Hedges, L. V., Pustejovsky, J. V., Boyajian, J. G., Sullivan, K. J., Andrade, A., & Barriento, J. L. (2014). A *d*-statistic for single-case designs that is equivalent to the usual between groups *d*-statistic. *Neuropsychological Rehabilitation, 24*(3–4), 528–553.

Stevens, S. S. (1968). Measurement, statistics, and the schemapiric view. *Science, 161*(3844), 849–856.

Van den Noortgate, W., & Onghena, P. (2008). A multilevel meta-analysis of single-subject experimental design studies. *Evidence-Based Communication Assessment and Intervention, 2*(3), 142–151.

van Rijn, Bech, A., Bouyer, J., & van den Brand, J. A. J. G. (2017). Statistical significance versus clinical relevance. *Nephrology, Dialysis, and Transplantation, 1*(32 Suppl.), i6–ii12.

Wolfe, M. (1978). Social validity: The case for subjective measurement or how applied behavior analysis is finding its heart. *Journal of Applied Behavior Analysis, 11*(2), 203–214.

Study Guide

1. Research designs and statistics are not the same. Explain why.

2. Justify the statement that statistics is neither research nor research design but rather a variety of methods of analyses. Explain.

3. Describe the relation between agricultural research and randomized clinical trials.

4. What is the theory of probability? How is it used in group design research?

5. Fisher considered all experimental results based on sample observations as an estimation of what happens in the population. How does this idea apply in group experimental design and statistical generalization?

6. What is statistical significance? How is it used in group designs of research?

7. What is a *p* value? What is its role in interpreting the results of a group design study?

8. Compare and contrast the role of a hypothesis in-group design research versus single-subject design research.

9. Describe and distinguish Type I versus Type II errors.

10. What assumptions underlie parametric statistical techniques? Give some examples of parametric tests.

11. A researcher interested in the question of whether two or more groups differ on more than one dependent variable may use what test of significance? Justify your answer.

12. Nonparametric tests are said to be *distribution free*. Explain the statement.

13. Correlation does not mean causation. Explain why this statement is correct.

14. Describe the purposes and procedures of a meta-analysis.

15. What are the advantages and disadvantages of visual analysis of single-subject research data?

16. What are nonoverlap measures? Describe two of them.

17. What statistical tests might a researcher consider in analyzing single-subject data?

18. What is clinical significance? How does it differ from statistical significance?

11

Generality Through Replications

Chapter Outline

- Direct Replication
- Systematic Replication
- Sample Size and Generality
- Failed Replications: Sources of Treatment Modifications
- Homogeneity and Heterogeneity of Participants
- Summary
- References
- Study Guide

The various group and single-subject designs described in the previous chapters help establish cause-effect relations between independent and dependent variables. Necessarily, any experimental study is done in a given setting, by a single or a few investigators, and with selected participants. A laboratory study may isolate a cause-effect relation between two variables. A clinical study may show that a treatment technique was effective in a few individuals, as in single-subject design studies, or a larger number of individuals, as in randomized clinical trials. Such experimental treatment studies also demonstrate a cause-effect relation. When cause-effect relations are demonstrated under well-controlled conditions, internal validity (described in Chapter 7) is ensured. Once a cause-effect relation emerges within a single study, the next question to be asked is whether the same relation holds good when other investigators in other settings and with other participants investigate the same variables. As noted in Chapter 7, this is the question of generality of research findings.

Generality is the extent to which conclusions of a research study can be extended to persons who have not been included in the study; like reliability, generality is quantitative. There is more or less generality for otherwise valid and reliable data. In this chapter, we shall be concerned with the *procedures* used to establish generality of research data. The emphasis will be on the generality of data relative to clinical treatment research.

The clinical importance of the question of generality is obvious. Clinicians wish to know whether a given procedure, demonstrated to be effective in a particular study, will be equally effective when other clinicians in other settings use it to treat their clients. The question of generality is related both to reliability and to the range of conditions under which a demonstrated cause-effect relation holds good.

Replication is the repetition of a study with or without variations. It is the method of establishing generality of research findings. A single study, no matter how well done or how large the sample, cannot establish generality. A study must be repeated to find out if the evidence holds under different circumstances. A study can be replicated in different ways, and different replication strategies are used in different stages of research. The questions and strategies of replication have received much attention from behavioral scientists, who have described two major kinds of replications: direct and systematic (Barlow, Nock, & Hersen, 2009; Sidman, 1960).

In Chapter 9, it was pointed out that single-subject designs replicate the treatment effects within the same study; this is known as **intrasubject replication**. Such replications help increase the confidence one can place in the experimental findings, but they may not suggest generality. Both *direct* and *systematic* replications are necessary to establish generality.

Direct Replication

In **direct replication**, the same researcher repeats the same experiment in the same physical setting. Only the participants are new, though they are similar to those in the original study. Because different but similar participants are used, direct replication is **homogeneous intersubject replication** by the same investigator in the same setting.

When a treatment is found to be effective with a set of participants with a particular disorder, direct replication is attempted. It does not matter whether the single-subject or group design strategy was used in the original study because generality is not a matter of design; it is a matter of repeating the experiment with some variation, minimally with new participants. Therefore, the investigator finds new participants who are similar to the original participants and repeats the experiment. If the treatment shows similar effects with new participants, generality of findings begins to emerge.

In clinical research, there is no 100% replication of an experiment. Even if the same original participants are used in the first replication, the experiment is not a 100% replication because of the prior exposure to the treatment variable. Therefore, direct replication of treatment effects requires that the treatment procedure be the same as in the original experiment. The treatment, the client disorder or behaviors, the physical setting, and the clinician-experimenter all stay constant through the direct replication series. Generally, the experimental design is also the same, although variations in design are possible.

The new participants used in a direct replication must be similar to those in the original study. The clients selected for replication of a treatment method should have the same disorder and be similar on relevant assigned variables. For example, when a language treatment procedure is found to be effective with four to six persons with aphasia, the research clinician may find other persons who are similar to the original ones and repeat the experimental treatment program.

Homogeneous intersubject replication is a safer initial strategy than the **heterogeneous intersubject replication** in which different kinds of participants are used in replication. If the method does not work with a heterogeneous set of participants, it is difficult to say why. Continuing our example of treatment evaluation involving persons with aphasia, it

is possible that compared with those in the original study, a replication study may have persons who differed on the kind of aphasia, health status, premorbid educational and intellectual levels, postonset duration before therapy is introduced, ages, socioeconomic status, and so forth. In this case, if the investigator fails to replicate the original effects of the treatment procedure, it is difficult to know whether the failure was due to differences in one, some, or all of the variables that were different in the second set of participants. To avoid this problem, the initial replication of a study should use participants who are similar to those in the original study.

Problem of Finding Homogeneous Participants

Homogeneous participants are similar on measured variables; **heterogeneous participants** are different. The requirement that direct replication involve participants who are similar to those used in the original investigation can pose a difficult problem for the clinician researcher.

Ideally, the investigator has either strictly homogeneous or strictly heterogeneous participants in the original investigation. In practice, participants in most experiments are more or less homogeneous. In the single-subject strategy, the participants are expected to be homogeneous; in the group strategy, they are expected to be heterogeneous. When the participants in the original study were homogeneous, the participants in direct replication are expected to be similar to those in the original study and homogeneous among themselves. When the participants in the original study were heterogeneous, the participants in the direct replication are expected to be similarly heterogeneous.

It is somewhat easy to find homogeneous or heterogeneous animal subjects for research. The investigator can control the animal subjects' genetic and environmental history to produce similar or different animals that can then be used in the original, direct, and systematic series of experiments. In human research, especially in human clinical research, this ideal sequence of original, direct, and systematic research is difficult to achieve. Therefore, those sequences are not as well distinguished in human clinical research as they are in animal research. Practical exigencies of direct and systematic human clinical research replications create an interwoven sequence.

In practice, neither a single-subject design study nor a group design study is likely to have the kinds of participants they are supposed to have. The participants in a single-subject design study, though few, may be more heterogeneous than expected. The participants in a group clinical study, though many and randomly selected, may be less heterogeneous than expected. In essence, participants in clinical research are neither ideally homogeneous nor ideally heterogeneous. If the target is a heterogeneous sample, the clinician does his or her best to increase the diversity of participants. If the target is a homogeneous sample, the investigator tries to minimize differences in participant characteristics. In either case, the eventual participant sample is not likely to be ideally homogeneous or heterogeneous.

Another difficulty with participant selection for either an original or a replicative study is that the researcher who can strive for an ideal sample may not *know* what an ideal sample is. Homogeneity or heterogeneity of participants is a matter of judgment based on past research and clinical experience. Investigators judge the similarities and differences between individuals on known variables, but unknown variables may make participants either similar to, or different from, each other. Assume, for example, that the age at which schooling is started affects the outcome of aphasia treatment but no researcher is aware of this. Therefore, researchers will not consider that variable in judging homogeneity and heterogeneity of participants for a study on aphasia treatment. Consequently, participants who are similar on this variable may be considered different, and vice versa.

Practical difficulties in obtaining participants for a study often lead to compromises in the application of adopted participant selection criteria. Age ranges may be extended or restricted to accommodate available participants. Differences in health history may be ignored. Although the initial plan may be to have participants of only one gender, the eventual sample may contain females and males. Most investigators make these and other compromises sooner or later. Though justified on practical grounds, such compromises may create difficulties for interpreting data and for planning replications.

When the participants in the original study were about as homogeneous as expected, and all of them reacted the same to the treatment variable, the investigator may search for similar participants for a direct replication. There is no guarantee, however, that the participants selected for the direct replication will be similar to those in the original study. They are likely to be more or less homogeneous among themselves and more or less similar to the participants in the original study. If the participants selected for direct replication are about as similar to those in the original study, another replication may be attempted. In some cases, the investigator may decide that it is time to initiate systematic replications, which involve participants who differ from those in the original, as well as direct replication studies.

To a certain extent, an original study that contains heterogeneous clients and produces consistent data is already a systematic replication. In other words, an initial study may have produced data showing effectiveness for a procedure despite failed attempts to obtain homogeneous participants. For example, the investigator wishing to evaluate the effects of a new treatment for individuals with apraxia of speech (AOS) may not have been able to select persons of the same age, health history, and severity of AOS. Instead of not doing a study because it may be imperfect, the investigator, trying his or her best to minimize the differences between participants, may go ahead with the study. If the results are consistent across those somewhat different participants, the original study itself can be considered a systematic replication. Such a study will have demonstrated that different participants react the same to the same treatment. In effect, a risky original treatment evaluation involving heterogeneous participants may produce the same results as a subsequent systematic replication.

Research philosophies generally discourage such studies in the initial step because when the results are not uniformly good or bad, an unambiguous interpretation of results is not possible, although researchers who use the group designs are generally not as concerned about individual variability in response to treatment as are those who use single-subject designs. However, when practical considerations force the selection of available clients for an initial study, the next attempt often depends upon the judg-

ment of the investigator. If the sample is thought to be relatively heterogeneous and the results are consistent, replications may be either direct or systematic. However, when the results are inconsistent across clients while there is reason to believe that the sample was heterogeneous in some respects, then the investigator will have learned a lesson. He or she will not try too hard to interpret the data in any global manner and instead will look at individual differences that might have accounted for divergent data. In further studies, a more serious attempt may be made to obtain homogeneous sets of participants. In essence, there are very few rigid rules that an investigator can follow in determining the exact nature and sequence of replication.

Direct replication need not be an endless series of studies. When the effect of an independent variable is replicated across a few participants, systematic replication may be initiated. Within the philosophy of single-subject designs, Barlow et al. (2009) recommend that when a procedure has been directly replicated in four participants or clients, systematic replication should be started. Continued direct replication may not be productive beyond that point. This recommendation is especially acceptable when the demonstrated treatment effects are strong and individual variability has been minimum.

Systematic Replication

Direct replication can demonstrate only that the causal relation found in the original study may have some homogeneous subject generality. That is, a treatment was effective in similar participants when the same investigator applied it in the same setting with different but similar clients. However, direct replication does not tell whether the treatment will be equally effective when different investigators apply it to different clients, in different settings, and perhaps with different response classes. In essence, to establish all the different kinds of clinical generality described in Chapter 7, one needs systematic replication.

In systematic replication, one or more variables or aspects of procedures are varied at a time to see if the results of the direct replication series can still be duplicated. For the sake of clear interpretations, it is necessary to vary only one or two variables at a time. If too many factors are varied simultaneously, a failure to replicate the findings of the direct replication series is difficult to understand, although success in such cases results in significant economy of effort.

It is possible that the same investigator makes the initial systematic replication. Once it has been determined that a given functional relation is reliable and that it has some degree of participant generality, the investigator may wish to find out if the same relation can be found in participants who are in some specific ways different from those in the earlier studies. A clinician who has found that a given treatment procedure is effective with several clients showing a particular disorder may ask the following kinds of questions:

1. Is the treatment effective in the same setting, but with participants who show a variation of the same disorder (e.g., more or less severe)?
2. Is the treatment effective in the same setting with participants who have the same disorder but are different in other respects (e.g., of different socioeconomic status)?

3. Is the treatment effective in the same setting, with individuals who have an altogether different disorder?
4. Is the treatment effective in a different setting, involving similar individuals?
5. Is the treatment effective in a different setting, also involving individuals who show a variation of the same disorder?
6. Is the treatment effective in a different setting, also with individuals who show a different disorder?

Those are not the only questions the clinician could ask. However, they illustrate the basic nature of systematic replication, which investigates the effects of one variable (treatment) when other variables come to play.

Systematic replication of clinical treatment effects is a time-consuming process because the diagnostic categories are not strictly homogeneous. There usually is notable intersubject variability among such clinical groups as persons who stutter, children who have hearing loss or language disorder, and persons who have aphasia or dysarthria. The variability in such background variables as age, gender, education, premorbid health status, and socioeconomic status of clients within diagnostic categories is well known. Besides, clients within and across diagnostic categories vary in the severity of the disorder, subtypes within the disorder, the degree and types of prior treatment experiences, and so forth. A treatment procedure that works well with young individuals with language problems may or may not work with older persons having the same disorder. Clients with multiple misarticulations may not react as favorably to a treatment procedure as those with single-phoneme misarticulations. A procedure that is effective with persons who have mild stutterings may not be equally effective with those who have severe stuttering.

On the other hand, certain treatment techniques may be effective within and across diagnostic categories. Obvious differences between clients in age, gender, and diagnostic categories and subcategories do not necessarily mean that they will react differently to the same treatment procedure. Such behavioral treatment procedures as modeling, differential reinforcement, and corrective feedback work well across people with varied types of disorders, including communicative disorders (Hegde, 1998).

Systematic replications help establish that a given treatment procedure works when other clinicians implement it. When other clinicians are equally capable of administering the treatment procedure, the results must be comparable to those of the original investigator. If other clinicians cannot replicate some dramatic results of a study, then those results must be attributed to some extraneous factors. Those extraneous factors may include such variables as the personality or the special interpersonal skills of the original clinician. What is more important is the possibility that the original investigator may not have described all aspects of the treatment procedure. Certain critical elements of the procedure may not have been included in the description, and hence those who try to replicate the study may not do precisely what the original clinician did.

It is likely that other clinicians will replicate a treatment procedure in a setting different from that of the original setting. In this case, successful replicative attempts demonstrate generality not only

across participants and clinicians, but also across settings.

Successful replication across clients, clinicians, and settings is essential to a widespread practice of therapeutic techniques. A treatment procedure can be recommended for general application only when it is shown that a variety of clients can benefit from it. In speech-language pathology, however, many therapeutic practices are neither experimentally evaluated nor replicated.

When the treatment of a given disorder is effective and replicated, the question that arises is whether the technique can be equally effective with different disorders. A successful language treatment technique or components of the technique may be useful in treating speech sound or voice disorders. We know, for example, that modeling, shaping, and differential reinforcement are useful components of therapy for many kinds of verbal and nonverbal behavior disorders.

The fixed notions of nosology—the science of classifying disorders—discourage replication of a technique across disorders. There is an implicit assumption that different diagnostic categories necessarily require treatment techniques that are independent of each other. This assumption may not be valid in speech-language pathology, in which diagnostic categories are not strictly etiologic but often are descriptive. As a result, topographically different behaviors such as high vocal pitch or dysfluency may be susceptible to the same treatment variables. Furthermore, there is no compelling reason to believe that different instigating causes of communicative disorders necessarily dictate totally different treatment variables. For example, whether a language disorder is thought to be due to genetically determined intellectual disability or some unexplained environmental events may not be critical in shaping specific verbal responses in a group of clients.

It is clear that systematic replication across clients and disorders will help reduce unnecessary diversity in treatment techniques. If there are a few core techniques whose limited variations can help treat a variety of communicative disorders, so much the better. Economy in treatment procedures that does not do any injustice to individual differences may be a desirable outcome of systematic replication.

Conditions Necessary for Systematic Replications

Systematic replications of research data are possible when the treatment techniques are specified and well researched through experimental methods and direct replications. Procedures for measuring dependent as well as independent variables should be objective and standard. The dependent variables should be conceptualized on empirical (not just logical or theoretical) grounds and should be defined in such a way that reliable observations can be made. In addition, the treatment outcome criteria must be measurement oriented. To realize these conditions, the discipline should have a long and strong experimental history.

Carefully planned and extensively conducted systematic replications are rare in speech-language pathology. As noted before, direct replication follows experimental analysis of treatment procedures, which in turn leads to systematic replication. Many treatment techniques in speech-language pathology are yet to be subjected to experimental analysis. Treatment procedures often are vague and riddled with controversies. For the most part, treatment techniques are justified on the basis of clinical judgment; speculative theories and presumptions; liberal recommendations coming from such nonclinical disciplines as linguistics, well-recognized authorities, and subjective preferences; tradition; dated training; and personal experience not supported by objective evaluations.

There is little agreement on the dependent variables and their measurement procedures. As we shall see in Chapter 13, most of the dependent variables are conceptualized on logical, topographical, theoretical, and speculative grounds. For example, what are the dependent variables in the case of speech and language behaviors? Phonological knowledge and mental representations? Knowledge of grammatical rules? Semantic notions? Pragmatic rules? Response classes? In literacy, is it phonemic awareness or observable reading and writing? What are the dependent variables in stuttering treatment? Stuttering events? Dysfluency rates? Molar moments? Negative attitudes? And how can any one of these be measured? When there is much controversy about the dependent variables (compounded by disagreement on treatment—independent variables) and the controversies are debated by speculative opinions, experimental analysis becomes difficult.

In the experimental evaluation of treatment, outcome must be specified in terms that different investigators can use. If the few treatment evaluation studies that are done do not report their treatment evaluation procedures in objective terms, other investigators cannot replicate those studies. The questions are these: How did the clinician determine the effectiveness of a treatment procedure? What magnitude of change in the clients' problem behaviors did the clinician require before concluding that the treatment was effective? Was it a statistical or clinical criterion? Did the investigator adopt generalization or maintenance of the target behaviors as the criterion, or both? Answers to questions such as these are important in treatment evaluations and their replications.

One may think that different clinicians should agree upon the evaluative criteria so that investigators can use the same criteria. However, agreement among investigators is not the issue. Whether some specified criterion is described in operational terms at all is the issue. Such a criterion can be used in evaluating treatment effectiveness regardless of agreement among investigators.

Systematic replications are a sure sign of the advanced scientific status of a clinical profession. However, to achieve such a status, experimental evaluation of treatment procedures is essential. Although a general agreement upon the dependent and independent variables and their measurement procedures is likely to cause more rapid progress, diversity of approaches, by itself, is not a hindrance to scientific progress. The hindrance is a lack of appreciation of the philosophy and methodology of science. What is crucially needed to achieve scientific progress is a commitment on the part of investigators to the experimental methodology of natural sciences. Because science is a self-corrective method, things will be sorted out in the process of experimental research.

Sample Size and Generality

The size of a sample used in a study is a significant issue in generality. There are two views on the relation between sample size and generality. The first view is

that only large sample studies can hope to claim generality. Historically, group design advocates have argued that generality is possible only when the sample is large enough to represent the population. To represent a population, the sample must not only be large, but it also should be drawn randomly from that population. This argument is presented especially in the context of statistical (inferential) generality. Randomized clinical trials, described in Chapter 4, are based on this argument. Those who advocate the use of randomized clinical trials in medicine insist that there is no generality without large numbers of participants, in most cases, several thousand persons.

The second view is that large samples are unnecessary to claim generality and that a single study, no matter how large its sample, cannot demonstrate generality. Advocates of single-subject designs have argued that generality is achieved only by replication. They further argue that strong experimental effects produced in a few individuals under well-controlled conditions are more likely to be replicated than are weak effects demonstrated in large groups summed across individuals for statistical analysis. Indeed, these two differing views on generality are at the heart of the skepticism typically expressed by group design advocates about the usefulness of single-subject designs. Skepticism turns into outright rejection when single-subject experimental designs are confused with uncontrolled case studies.

There is a long history of scholarly debate on the importance of the individual and the group in philosophy and subsequently, in such sciences as biology, psychology, sociology, and medicine (Allport, 1962; Barlow et al., 2009; Dukes, 1965; Skinner, 1953, 1956; Valsiner, 1986a, 1986b). The perspectives in psychology and historical developments in the design of experiments in agriculture have greatly influenced this debate. In psychology, studying groups of individuals was seen as a method of understanding the individual as well. The counterargument has been that group averages do not teach us anything significant about the individual.

Rational arguments aside, behavioral scientists have provided plenty of experimental evidence that strong effects produced under tightly controlled conditions in just a handful of participants may be replicable. As pointed out elsewhere in the book, Skinner's (1953) principles of operant behavior and Pavlov's principles of classical conditioning have been initially formulated with a few animal participants but later replicated in many human experiments. Behavioral treatment studies also have demonstrated that most treatment effects demonstrated in single-subject studies have been replicated (Barlow et al., 2009; Kazdin, 2010). One of the early advocates of single-subject designs in clinical psychology, Shapiro (1961) demonstrated through his experiments that data supporting a scientific law discovered in the context of one or two participants are replicable across many participants. Other historically significant advocates of research with a small number of participants have documented much systematic and replicated knowledge stemming initially from one or few participants (Bolgar, 1965; Dukes, 1965). Dukes has pointed out that if the objective is to study an individual's uniqueness, a single participant exhausts the population. He has further pointed out that when data generated from a single-subject study contradict previously established data with large numbers of participants, the negative evidence is useful because it shows the limits of generality. In treatment research, it is important to understand individual response to treatment so that practitioners can make meaningful judgments about treatment application to their individual clients.

Large samples, while not so critical for establishing generality of treatment effects, may be necessary to predict group actions or opinions. Statistical generality is useful in such studies as sample surveys whose goal is to predict what a majority of people will do or say. Being nonexperimental, sample surveys do not try to change something, as experiments seek to do. Therefore, in sample surveys, the action of an individual does not matter. What matters is the action of a defined population. Therefore, a large number of heterogeneous participants who represent that population must be studied to achieve generality. Large samples may also be needed in clinical sciences to predict the average number of people who will benefit from a treatment. Finally, large samples are typically needed in nonexperimental epidemiological studies.

To establish generality of treatment effects, it is clear that the traditional argument for large samples is highly questionable. Beside the criticism that they may be unnecessary, large samples have other limitations that render them especially troublesome to clinicians who wish to generalize the data to particular patients or clients they serve. Both the treatment researcher and the practicing clinician wish to apply the results of a treatment study to individual clients. But this is exactly where the randomized large sample clinical trials fail. Not only single-subject design experts (Barlow et al., 2009; Johnston & Pennypacker, 2009; Kazdin, 2010) but also psychologists (Valsiner, 1986b) and several medical statisticians and treatment research experts (Dekkers & Boer, 2001; Feinstein, 1970, 1995; Kaptchuk, 2001; Pringle & Churchill, 1995, among others) have pointed out serious limitations of randomized large group medical treatment research. The group averages reported in randomized control trials may predict the parameter (average value) of the population, but they do not predict an individual's reaction or performance under the same treatment. Valsiner (1986b) has stated that "group data, statistically aggregated, may allow us to make generalizations about populations. . . . However, inference from the population system to its parts (individual persons in the sample) is epistemologically questionable" (p. 394). Feinstein (1970), a medical expert in statistics and treatment research, has stated that a problem with randomized clinical trials in medicine "is the frequent claim that a large heterogeneous population gives the results 'wider applicability.' . . . The scientific effect of a diverse poorly identified mixture is to produce imprecision, confusion, and perhaps delusion, not generalizability" (p. 76). He further pointed out that the results of randomized clinical trials "will be meaningless because a clinician will not know how to apply them in the future; he cannot determine whether 'good risk' and 'poor risk' patients responded the same way to each therapeutic agent" (p. 289). Consequently, Feinstein has suggested that small group treatment research will produce more meaningful data than large randomized clinical trials. Furthermore, a significant number of medical researchers have been advocating for single-subject designs in medical treatment evaluations and N-of-1 clinical trials in which one or more patients participate (Gabler, Duan, Vohra, & Kravitz,

2011; Guyatt et al., 1990; Janosky, 2005; Logan, Slaughter, & Hickman, 2017; see Chapter 8 for more). Arguments presented by such medical researchers are consistent with those of single-subject researchers who seek to produce logical generality on the basis of which clinicians can select researched treatment procedures for their individual clients.

Failed Replications: Sources of Treatment Modifications

Whether in basic research or treatment research—a functional relation found in experimental research—may or may not be replicated. Several reasons may account for failed replications. As we will see in Chapter 17, fabricated research is one of the main reasons why replications, especially by other investigators, fail. Disregarding this unethical research practice for the moment, we discuss the reasons for and the meaning of failed replications.

When an investigator fails to replicate his or her own previous findings, the first consideration is the *reliability* of the original findings. It is possible that the functional relation found in the original study was mistaken in that extraneous variables, not the manipulated independent variables, were responsible for changes in the dependent variables. This is the question of inadequate experimental control and limited or no internal validity. Findings of questionable internal validity are not replicable, but the researcher does not know this until an effort to replicate has failed.

On the other hand, a study may have had good internal validity in that the external variables were ruled out and the results obtained were valid in the case of the original participants. Direct replication of such a study with new participants might still fail. Such a failure suggests a more complex situation than those involving questionable internal validity. Failed direct replications of valid data are both challenging and interesting. In clinical treatment research, those failures can be a valuable source of treatment modifications that suit individual clients.

When a well-researched treatment procedure cannot be replicated across clients, several possibilities must be considered. Perhaps the participants used in the original and replicated experiments differed and this made a difference in treatment effects. The clients in the replication series may be thought of as belonging to the same diagnostic category as those in the original study, but in reality, they may form a subcategory. For example, *children with language disabilities* may not be a homogeneous group despite commonly observed language problems. Past learning experiences, intelligence, or other important variables that differ across children who show the same type of language disorder may produce divergent data. The importance of some of these variables may not have been apparent to the investigator. In essence, all clients with language disorders may not benefit from the same treatment procedure. Similarly, all persons with stuttering or aphasia may not react the same way to a treatment procedure known to be effective with some of them.

In systematic replication, the investigator takes careful note of client differences, because establishing generality across different kinds of clients is the goal in this type of replication. In direct replication, on the other hand, the investigator tries to have clients who are similar to those in the original study, but this objective may not have been realized in a particular replication. When the replication fails, one must look for possible differences in clients' background variables or the special characteristics of the disorder some of them exhibited. In such cases, a modification in the technique or a totally different technique may be necessary. Persons with dysarthria in a replication study may have additional health problems that were not present in the participants of the original study. Persons with stuttering in the replication series may have had marked breathing abnormalities associated with their stutterings, and this may render a pure syllable prolongation approach less useful compared with its use for those without such abnormalities. A modified breathing component may prove effective either alone or in combination with syllable prolongation. The researcher may then pursue this question and eventually offer suggestions on differentially treating persons with unique characteristics.

Sources of failure to systematically replicate the results of a study may be more transparent than those in a direct replication series. The investigator knows the differences between the participants in the original study and those in the replication because such differences are built into a replicative study. A treatment procedure known to be effective with children exhibiting a speech sound disorder may be evaluated with adults who have the same disorder. Or a technique known to be effective with children who have language disorders may be tried with those who have a speech sound disorder. There is no guarantee, however, that the known difference is the source of failure when it occurs; for example, failure with adults treated with a procedure known to be effective with children does not necessarily mean that age is the critical variable. Some unknown variable or variables may be responsible for the failure.

The influence of unknown variables can be suspected when replicative efforts are continued despite an initial failure and suddenly a success emerges, even though the participants showed the same difference as in the earlier series. For instance, following a failure to replicate a study with clients older than those in the original study, an investigator may replicate the results in a subsequent effort, also involving older participants. This would then suggest that age may not have been the reason for the initial failure and that there were other, unsuspected variables. An unsuspected difference in the family background of participants or hereditary differences may account for the initial failure.

Generally speaking, it is the success that must be replicated, but a single failure may also be replicated when there is reason to believe that the original findings were strong and reliable and that the initial replication may have failed because of some flaw in the study. A second failure, however, may convince the investigator that additional efforts are not worthwhile. In fact, in clinical treatment evaluations, repeated attempts to replicate failed treatments may be unethical.

What is done when a failure is considered genuine may depend on the investigator's dispositions and personal beliefs. The investigator who still believes that the overall approach evaluated in the original study is valid may proceed to modify the procedure. This modified technique then goes through the initial experimental evaluations, followed by its own direct and systematic replications. However, the investigator who has second thoughts about the effectiveness of the technique is unlikely to replicate it with or without modifications. Replications are done to support as well as refute certain existing practices. When replications done to refute a given approach succeed in the refutation, the investigator is likely to stop, although those who believe in its success may redouble their efforts.

In essence, failed replications are full of good lessons. They point out possible exceptions to a general rule. Clinically, failed replications suggest limitations of generally effective treatment procedures. Such exceptions are important in science because the scientist is interested in identifying the limits of known functional relations. Exceptions are equally important for clinicians because their philosophy and methodology are based upon individual uniqueness as well as human generalities. The instant a generally effective treatment procedure fails with a given client, the clinician has made an empirical contact with individual uniqueness. A responsible clinician may then think that the best course of action is to modify the procedure to suit the individual or to evaluate a totally new approach that may prove more successful. In this way, when the message of failed replications is heeded, a clinical science moves ahead.

Homogeneity and Heterogeneity of Participants

That people are similar and yet unique is a fundamental behavioral principle that, while advancing science, creates problems as well. This is the issue of homogeneity and heterogeneity of participants. The issue is relevant to animal as well as human research and to basic as well as clinical research. Within a single study, whether the participants were homogeneous or heterogeneous can make a difference in internal validity and generality. Depending on the research design philosophy and the purposes of the experiment, investigators strive to have either homogeneous or heterogeneous participants.

For group designs, heterogeneous samples are considered ideal because such samples are expected to represent the necessarily heterogeneous population. Only when this is not practical would an investigator think of using homogeneous participants, hoping to show that a given variable has an effect in the case of individuals with known (and homogeneous) characteristics. For single-subject designs, investigators usually try to select homogeneous participants, but heterogeneous participants pose no serious problems because the data analysis is participant specific. In all research strategies, success with diverse participants is a cause *célèbre* for the researcher. However, if the results are different across heterogenous participants, the investigator does not know why.

When the purpose of an experiment is systematic replication across participants, one would, of course, select participants who are in some specified way different from those in the original study. The tactic is to select homogeneous participants who are heterogeneous relative to those in the original study.

As noted earlier, homogeneity is more easily achieved in laboratory experiments involving animal participants. We also noted that in human research, especially in clinical research, homogeneity of participants is a strongly wished for but rarely achieved goal. In this section, we shall take a critical look at this concept, because so many clinical researchers agonize over it.

There is no doubt that homogeneity of participants would make the life of the clinical researcher much easier. If all children with language disorders were the same, the problem of replication would be a minor one. If all persons who stuttered were the same, a single effective treatment would be sufficient, and the burden of replication would be pleasantly light. However, people are just not as homogeneous as the methodology of research requires them to be. People are different, and they do not seem to care about the clinical researchers' pressing problem! Therefore, instead of searching for homogeneous participants that may not exist, it may be prudent to consider heterogeneity as a fact of life and design studies accordingly. In essence, people cannot be changed but research tactics can be.

The basic problem is that the concept of homogeneity is difficult to define and perhaps naïve or even invalid. When are clients homogeneous? Is it when they are of the same age? (Do all children of the same age behave the same?) When they are of the same social status? (Do people within the same social status necessarily behave the same?) When they come from similar family background? (Do the members of a family always behave the same?) When they have similar intelligence? (Do people with similar IQs behave the same?) When they have the same educational background? (Does a 4-year college education create similar individuals?) When they all have suffered the disorder for the same duration? (Does 2 years of stuttering make some individuals the same compared with those who have stuttered for 4 years?)

A set of converse questions can also be asked: Are there no behavioral patterns that are similar across age groups? Do people with different social strata ever share common behavioral patterns? Do the members of the same family—let alone those with similar family backgrounds—behave differently? Do people with different levels of intelligence ever behave similarly? Do people with the same level of education behave differently? Do clients with the same disorder, the same level of severity, and the same duration of history ever behave differently?

The questions raised here are not just rhetorical. The point is that there are no fixed answers to those questions. A bias one way or the other is not implied. In case of given individuals, the answer to any one question may be positive or negative. What is suggested here is that the goal of homogeneity, either in an original series of experimental evaluation or in direct and systematic replications, should not stultify research. If the available clients are somewhat different, then the investigator should carefully describe the differences among them and offer results separately for the individuals. When the group means do not mask the individual differences, there is no major problem with variability in treatment reactivity. An ensuing analysis of reasons for variability may be required, but the data generated by the study will be valuable. It is better to do research with differing clients than to wait for homogeneous clients that may never be found.

The foregoing discussion suggests that there are significant participant selection problems in conducting direct and systematic replications. Besides, research strategies themselves make replications more or less difficult. Generally speaking, the group design strategy, which is difficult to employ in many kinds of clinical treatment research, also is difficult to use in replication studies. The required number of participants may not be available for a series of direct and systematic replications. The single-subject strategy, on the other hand, encourages replications of treatment techniques. In the treatment of language, speech sound, and fluency disorders, the single-subject studies of behavioral treatment techniques have provided impressive and replicated evidence. Comparable evidence has not emerged from the group design strategy. Every time a clinician uses a treatment procedure under controlled conditions with one or few clients, the cause of replication is advanced. This is made possible by the clinically practical single-subject strategy.

Summary

- **Generality**, a matter of replication, refers to the extent to which the conclusions of a research study may be extended beyond the limits of that original study.
- **Replication** may be direct or systematic.
  - **Direct replication**, done by the same investigator, duplicates the same procedure with different participants who are similar to those in the original study, resulting in **homogeneous intersubject replication**.
  - **Systematic replication** extends the results of a study to heterogeneous participants, different settings, and researchers, resulting in **heterogeneous intersubject replication**.
- Some claim that only large samples can demonstrate generality. Others claim that single-subject data are replicable and hence can establish generality.

- Failed replications suggest that the original data may have been unreliable or that the replication was not methodologically sound.
- **Homogeneity** and **heterogeneity** are relative concepts. There are similarities and differences among individuals.

References

Allport, G. D. (1962). The general and the unique in the psychological sciences. *Journal of Personality, 30*, 405–422.

Barlow, D. H., Nock, M. K., & Hersen, M. (2009). *Single-case experimental designs: Strategies for studying behavior* (3rd ed.). Boston, MA: Pearson.

Bolgar, H. (1965). The case study method. In B. B. Wolman (Ed.), *Handbook of clinical psychology* (pp. 28–39). New York, NY: McGraw-Hill.

Dekkers, W., & Boer, G. (2001). Sham neurosurgery in patients with Parkinson's disease: Is it morally acceptable? *Journal of Medical Ethics, 27*(3), 151–156.

Dukes, W. F. (1965). *N* = 1. *Psychological Bulletin, 64*, 74–79.

Feinstein, A. R. (1970). Statistics versus science in the design of experiments. *Clinical Pharmacology and Therapeutics, 11*, 282–292.

Feinstein, A. R. (1995). Meta-analysis: Statistical alchemy for the 21st century. *Journal of Clinical Epidemiology, 48*, 71–97.

Gabler, N. B., Duan, N., Vohra, S., & Kravitz, R. L (2011). N-of-1 trials in medical literature: A systematic review. *Medical Care, 49*(8), 761–768.

Guyatt, G., Keller, J. L., Jaeschke, R., Rosenbloom, D., Adachi, J., & Newhouse, M. T. (1990). The n-of-1 randomized controlled trial: Clinical usefulness. Our three-year experience. *Academia and Clinic, 112*, 293–299.

Hegde, M. N. (1998). *Treatment procedures in communicative disorders* (3rd ed.). Austin, TX: Pro-Ed.

Janosky, J. E. (2005). Use of the single subject design for practice-based primary care research. *Postgraduate Medical Journal, 81*, 549–551.

Johnston, J. M., & Pennypacker, H. S. (2009). *Strategies and tactics of human behavioral research.* (3rd ed.). Hillsdale, NJ: Erlbaum.

Kaptchuk, T. (2001). The double-blind, randomized placebo-controlled trial: Gold standard or golden calf? *Journal of Clinical Epidemiology, 54*, 541–549.

Kazdin, A. E. (2010). *Single-case research designs: Methods for clinical and applied settings* (2nd ed.). New York, NY: Oxford University.

Logan, L. R., Slaughter, R., & Hickman, R. (2017). Single-subject research designs in pediatric rehabilitation: A valuable step towards knowledge translation. *Developmental Medicine and Child Neurology, 59*, 574–580.

Pringle, M., & Churchill, R. (1995). Randomized controlled trials in general practice: Gold standard or fool's gold? *British Medical Journal, 311*, 1382–1383.

Shapiro, M. B. (1961). The single case in fundamental clinical psychological research. *British Journal of Medical Psychology, 34*, 255–262.

Sidman, M. (1960). *Tactics of scientific research.* New York, NY: Basic Books.

Skinner, B. F. (1953). *Science and human behavior.* New York, NY: Free Press.

Skinner, B. F. (1956). A case history in scientific method. *American Psychologist, 11*(22), 1–233.

Valsiner, J. (Ed.). (1986a). *The individual subject and scientific psychology.* New York, NY: Plenum Press.

Valsiner, J. (1986b). Different perspectives on individual-based generalizations in psychology. In J. Valsiner (Ed.), *The individual subject and scientific psychology* (pp. 391–404). New York, NY: Plenum Press.

Study Guide

1. Why should a clinician be concerned with the generality of clinical and experimental data?

2. What kinds of generality are not established by a group design study even when the investigator has drawn and assigned participants randomly?

3. What is the method of establishing generality of research findings?

4. What is direct replication?

5. Suppose that you have just completed a study in which you evaluated a particular method of teaching correct production of speech sounds to 5-year-old children who exhibit speech sound disorders in the absence of any other communicative disorders. Now you wish to do a direct replication study. How would you do it? (You may make up whatever information you need to answer this question.)

6. What is considered to be the safest initial direct replication strategy? Why?

7. Define *systematic replication*.

8. Suppose you have completed a study in which you experimentally evaluated the effects of a treatment program designed to teach morphological features to 5-year-old children with intellectual disabilities. Now you plan to do a systematic replication study. How would you do it? Specify the variables that will be the same as in the original study as well as those that will be different. Use hypothetical information.

9. What are the different parameters of systematic replication in clinical research?

10. What conditions are necessary for conducting systematic replication?

11. Summarize the two arguments on the relation between sample size and generality of research findings.

12. What is the value of failed replications? Give a hypothetical example from clinical research.

13. Assuming it is practical, what is gained by having homogeneous participants in clinical research?

14. Critically evaluate the concepts of homogeneity and heterogeneity of human research participants.

12

Comparative Evaluation of Design Strategies

Chapter Outline

- Research Questions and Investigative Strategies
- Advantages and Disadvantages of Design Strategies
- Problems Common to Design Strategies
- Philosophical Considerations in Evaluation
- The Investigator in Design Selection
- The Final Criterion: Soundness of Data
- Summary
- References
- Study Guide

In Chapters 8 and 9, we described two major approaches to designing experimental research: the group strategy and the single-subject strategy. In this chapter, we discuss the strengths and weaknesses of the two approaches. The purpose of this chapter is to help researchers select appropriate methodological strategies for investigating a variety of research questions.

A research strategy is appropriate or inappropriate only for a particular investigation. Every design with a sound structure has its place in scientific research. However, a design that is perfectly suited to one kind of investigation may be somewhat inappropriate to another kind; it may be totally wrong for yet another kind. Therefore, the appropriateness of a design is judged in relation to the research question or questions the investigator seeks to answer.

Many research questions can be answered by two or more methods. In such cases, selection depends mostly on the training, experience, and philosophy of the investigator. An investigator tends to use either the group or the single-subject strategy partly because of training and research philosophy. When an investigator is inclined to use either of those strategies, the selection may depend upon practical considerations. For example, the number of participants available for a study may determine whether one selects a single-subject interactional design or a factorial group design. If many participants are available, the factorial design may be used. If only a few individuals are willing to participate, the single-subject interactional design may be selected.

Research Questions and Investigative Strategies

Though we pay much attention to them, research *methods* are subservient to research questions. An investigator may find a method fascinating and try to find a problem that can be investigated with it. Such a search for a problem can be intolerably long. More typically, scientists first have research questions and then look for methods to answer them.

Problems or research questions fall into different types of investigations, which were considered in Chapter 4. Taken together, the kind of question and the type of research determine the strategy selected for the study. We shall review several kinds of research questions and suggest more or less appropriate design strategies to answer them. Because it is not possible to describe all kinds of research questions one can investigate, suggestions will be generic. Therefore, this discussion will be illustrative only; no attempt is made to list every correct design one could use in answering particular types of questions. The reader may think of other types of research questions and appropriate strategies to answer them.

What Are the Dependent Variables?

This question is about the existence or description of variables. The investigator may ask, "Does it exist? If so, what are its characteristics?" The investigator may suspect a new disorder, a new disease, or a new effect, and proceed to find out if it exists.

The dependent variable suspected to exist is investigated mostly through descriptive research or case study methods. Once it is found out that a hitherto unknown dependent variable (effect) exists, causal variables may be investigated. Most pilot studies and descriptive studies of new phenomena fall into this category. For example, an investigator may research the communicative effects of a new genetic syndrome or a new disease that affects children's development.

How Are the Dependent Variables Distributed in the Population?

This type of question is the heart of normative research. The investigator is interested in finding out the distribution of certain dependent variables in selected populations. For example, what are the language characteristics of 3- and 4-year-old children? How many phonemes can children at different age levels produce correctly? Do 5-year-old children produce more dysfluencies than 3-year-old children? Any kind of research that attempts to establish norms would ask questions of this kind.

Studies designed to answer this kind of question are descriptive, not experimental. The group design strategy is appropriate because a large number of participants, selected randomly, is needed to answer such questions. Participants are selected from different age levels and are observed for somewhat brief periods with limited response sampling. The observed characteristics of participants of different ages are described. These studies seek inferential generality; therefore, the method includes statistical analyses of data. See the section covering *normative research* in Chapter 5 for details.

How Are the Variables *Differentially* Distributed in a Population?

Questions concerning the *differential* distribution of a variable are researched in clinical sciences. The research involved

is a combination of three types: ex post facto, normative, and standard-group comparison. Investigators typically ask such questions as whether people who stutter and people who do not stutter differ in their personality, or whether persons with and without laryngectomy differ in their smoking histories. Investigations into such questions seek to determine the differential distribution of certain variables in contrasting populations. Whenever clinical and nonclinical groups are compared on some variable that is not manipulated, the question is one of differential distribution of variables.

Studies investigating differential distribution of variables use the group methodology. No experimental designs are needed because the studies are descriptive. The selected dependent variable is measured in groups that are different on some criterion, which is often a clinical diagnosis. The different values of the dependent variables in the two groups are statistically evaluated and reported. For example, it may be found that the scores on a test of intelligence are differentially distributed in misarticulating and typically speaking children. Children with and without language disorders may score differently on a test of narrative skills.

What Factors May Have Contributed to This Effect?

This type of question is asked when the event under investigation has a history and the causes of the event have occurred in the past. The ex post facto method of research is used to answer this kind of question. Most case studies are of this type. The effect is directly observable, but the causes are not. The experimenter cannot manipulate the causes. The investigator makes a search of the factors that may have, in the past, contributed to the effect under study. See ex post facto research in Chapter 5 for details.

Factors that may have contributed to an effect are widely investigated in clinical sciences. Questions about the causes of most disorders in human beings often fall into this category. These questions can be researched with either the group strategy or the single-subject strategy. Often, the history of a small number of clients or of a single client is investigated to find out if potential causal factors were or are evident. Whether it is a group or a single-subject study, this type of research is best described as a case study and does not have an experimental design in the technical sense of that term.

What Are the Effects of an Independent Variable?

An investigator may simply ask, what happens when I manipulate this variable? What effects follow when a factor is introduced, removed, or reinstated? Questions of this kind attempt to find out the unknown, or not well-understood, effects of independent variables. For example, one may ask several questions: What happens when the auditory feedback for speech is presented to the speaker with a delay? What happens to the electroencephalographic patterns when meaningful linguistic stimuli are introduced? What are the effects on children's language of training mothers to read stories aloud? What are the effects of reducing the rate of speech in persons who stutter? Questions such as these concern the effects of selected independent variables. Evaluation of clinical treatment procedures involves these kinds of questions.

Finding the effects of independent variables requires the experimental method.

Group designs or single-subject designs may be used. To control for potential extraneous variables, the investigator must select one of the true experimental designs. Within the group strategy, the pretest-posttest control group design or the posttest-only control group design may be selected to investigate the effects of independent variables. Among the within-subjects group designs, the two-group single-treatment counterbalanced design is appropriate. Among the time-series designs, a nonequivalent two-group design may be used with the understanding that there is no sampling equivalence of the groups. Within the single-subject strategy, an *ABA, ABAB* reversal or withdrawal designs, and multiple baseline designs may be selected.

Is a Treatment Associated With Improvement?

A clinician may try a new procedure by carefully measuring the behaviors before and after treatment. If systematic changes are seen after treatment, it is considered possible that the treatment worked. The method used is that of a case study.

Obviously, case studies lack appropriate controls. Therefore, the studies lack internal validity, and the clinician cannot assert that the treatment was indeed effective. Improvement may be claimed with a successful case study. Nevertheless, research of this type is useful because improvement in client behaviors, when documented systematically, may suggest that it is worthwhile to design a more controlled study to evaluate the treatment procedure.

Repeated and reliable pretreatment measures, measurement during treatment sessions, and posttreatment measures that show a convincing change in client behaviors help establish the value of case studies. Missing pretreatment measures, lack of measures during treatment, and small changes after treatment invalidate most studies of this kind.

Uncontrolled treatment studies can use either a single-subject or a group design. The one-group pretest-posttest design of the group strategy, or the *AB* design of the single-subject strategy, would be appropriate for this kind of research.

Is a Treatment Effective?

Questions of the effectiveness of clinical treatment procedures are similar to those concerning the effects of independent variables because both are experimental. However, questions of treatment effects are a part of clinical research. Therefore, in answering such questions, some investigators avoid certain designs that are appropriate to investigate the effects of independent variables within basic research.

Effects of treatment procedures can be assessed with either an experimental group design or a single-subject experimental design. The pretest-posttest control-group design or the posttest-only control group design can help evaluate the effects of single treatment variables. Among the within-subjects designs, the two-group single-treatment counterbalanced design can be used. One of the quasi-experimental designs, such as the nonequivalent two-group time-series design, also can be used, but with some loss of rigor because of the lack of randomization.

Among the single-subject designs, the *ABAB* reversal or withdrawal designs; the multiple baseline design across subjects, settings, or behaviors design; and the changing criterion design may all be appropriate.

Is One Treatment More Effective Than the Other?

The relative effects of two (or more) treatments become an issue when it is known that, compared with no treatment, all of them are effective to some degree. Is reinforcing fluency more or less effective than counseling people who stutter for their emotional problems? In teaching language response classes, is modeling without client imitation more or less effective than modeling that requires client imitation? Is informative feedback on performance accuracy in therapy for childhood apraxia of speech more or less effective than reinforcement in the absence of feedback? Questions such as these attempt to find out if one treatment is better than the other.

Evaluation of the relative effects of treatment requires the experimental method. Within the group design strategy, the multigroup pretest-posttest design may be used. The number of groups is the same as the number of treatments that are evaluated. An extra group that does not receive treatment is needed if the absolute treatment effect also is of concern. Factorial designs such as the randomized blocks design and the completely randomized factorial design also are excellent means of evaluating the effects of multiple treatments.

The single-group time-series design with multiple treatments can also be used to determine if one treatment is more effective than the other. The within-subjects crossover design can answer the same kind of questions.

The *ABACA/ACABA* single-subject design may be used to evaluate the relative effects of two or more treatments. Also appropriate is the alternating treatments design, which may be the most frequently used single-subject strategy in assessing multiple treatment effects.

Is There an Interaction Between Treatment Components?

Many treatment procedures contain different elements that may interact with each other. Does muscular relaxation and reinforcement for correct pitch interact in the treatment of a voice disorder? Does reinforcement for correct production and corrective feedback for incorrect production of phonemes in articulation therapy produce an interactive effect? Is it more effective to combine stimulus pictures and objects in language therapy? Such questions about interaction may be investigated through an experimental design. Selected elements of a treatment program are typically applied in isolation and in certain combinations to assess the independent and interactive effects of those elements.

Within the group design strategy, the factorial designs are excellent to analyze interaction of treatment elements. The completely randomized factorial design is best suited for an analysis of interaction between two or more treatment elements

In the single-subject strategy, the interactional design can help answer the same question. Nonetheless, the factorial (group) interactional designs are better than the single-subject interactional design. In a factorial design, multiple treatments are not confounded because different treatments are applied to different groups of participants. But the possibility of confounding effects exists in the single-subject interactional design because it evaluates the effects of multiple treatments in the same clients.

Do Participant Variables Interact With Treatment Variables?

Interaction can exist not only between treatment variables but also between treatment and participant characteristics. The same treatment may have different effects in male and female participants, high school and college graduates, and urban and rural clients. A treatment may be more or less effective depending on the severity of the disorder treated. Such *assigned variables* (see Chapter 3) interact with treatment. Therefore, to establish the generality of findings, one must know who reacts in what way to the same treatment procedure. This type of research is experimental, because the treatment is always an active variable.

The randomized blocks design of the group (factorial) design strategy is best for analyzing the interaction between the participant variables and treatment. Within the single-subject approach, a particular design that can help answer this kind of question is lacking; the question must be addressed through replications. In a series of single-subject designs, the investigator may study participants of different characteristics and note possible differences in the effects of treatment. Eventually through this approach, data on interactions between participant variables and treatment may be accumulated. This approach is less precise and less efficient than that of the factorial design.

Is One Treatment Preferred Over the Other?

Two or more treatments may be equally effective in treating a disorder, but clients may prefer one over the other. As long as the preferred method is effective, it may be better to select it over the other, less preferred, method. A knowledge of client preference as well as objective effects of treatment can be useful in clinical practice. This kind of research requires experimental methods.

There is no specific group design to study client preference of treatment. Client preferences can be assessed indirectly by differential dropout rates when different treatments are offered and by post hoc analysis in which the participants are questioned about their preferences. However, these procedures do not permit an experimental analysis of client preferences. Within the single-subject strategy, the simultaneous treatments design offers a direct method for analyzing the client preferences. When different treatments are offered simultaneously to the same client who is then free to choose, the client may seek one treatment more frequently than the other. This then suggests client preference. However, a preferred treatment may or may not be the most effective technique, as noted in Chapter 8.

What Components of a Treatment Package Are Most Effective?

When several treatment components are included in a package, one may wish to know which ones are more effective. This question concerns an experimental analysis of existing packages whose development has not been based on systematic research. In this case, the package is broken down into its components to find out which ones are more or less effective. Two or more components may then be evaluated in a particular study. This question is of interest regardless of

potential interaction, although it is better analyzed in an interactional design. As already noted, many treatments of communication disorders are packages of different treatment components. What is needed is a strategy to discard elements that are ineffective, improve those that are somewhat effective, and describe those that are most effective.

The factorial design of the group strategy is useful in determining the relative efficacy of treatment components. The completely randomized factorial design is especially useful. Different components are applied to different participants in a factorial arrangement. In the same process, one can also analyze the interaction between the applied components. Of the single-subject designs, the interactional design can be used for the same purposes. The design can help determine the relative and interactive effects of treatment components. Other factors being equal, the group factorial designs are a better alternative to single-subject interactional design.

What Is the Optimal Level of Treatment?

This question concerns the mechanics of arranging treatment sessions or the intensity of treatment. The question can be asked even about the most effective treatments. For example, assuming that a given treatment is effective, one can ask whether a 50-minute treatment session is more effective than a 30-minute session. Is therapy two times a week just as effective as therapy four times a week? The answers to such questions help arrange effective and economical schedules of treatment.

Questions about the optimal level of treatment are better answered within the single-subject strategy. Single-subject designs that permit parametric variations of treatment are best suited for answering questions of this kind. The same participants may be exposed to the same treatment but with variations in the durations of sessions or the weekly frequency. Such variations are counterbalanced across participants. A second choice would be the single-group time-series design with multiple temporary treatments. The multiple temporary treatments would consist of variations designed to determine the optimal level of treatment.

Can We Predict the Group Behavior?

Although we have emphasized the importance of studying individual participants in a clinical science, it is sometimes necessary to ignore the behaviors of individual participants and ask questions about behaviors of groups. For example, a classroom teacher may wish to keep a group of children relatively quiet although every child may not necessarily be quiet all the time. Small variations in individual behaviors are ignored as long as the collective behavior of the group is acceptable. The speech and language clinician treating a group of children may face a similar situation.

Analysis and prediction of group behaviors is better accomplished by the group design strategy. Most group prediction studies are not experimental, however. A pollster who predicts the winner of an election is simply measuring and predicting group behavior without trying to change that behavior. On the other hand, some questions of group behaviors involve experimentation. Scientific or professional organizations may wish not only to find out about some particular behaviors of a group of people but also to change some of those behaviors. A speech and hearing organization, for example, may attempt to first find out how much people know about its services and then design an experimental publicity campaign to increase the amount of information people have. Of the group designs, the time-series designs with repeated measures before and after the experimental manipulations are especially helpful. Single-subject designs are not efficient in predicting group behaviors.

How Effective Is the Treatment Across Individuals?

Clients or their families often wish to know the overall success rate of treatments they seek. They ask questions such as these: How many people who stutter generally improve under treatment? What is the success rate of therapy for childhood apraxia of speech? Can persons with aphasia be helped? What percentage of the children who receive language therapy improve? How many children with early language intervention can attend regular educational programs? Such questions attempt to predict treatment effects across large numbers of participants. Differential predictions may be attempted on the basis of diagnostic categories, age levels, and such other variables. These questions are important because clinical services are supported by those who ask them. They are important for scientific reasons, too.

The overall effectiveness of treatment procedures is best evaluated with group designs. Group designs with a relatively large number of treated and untreated individuals can answer these questions more effectively than single-subject designs. However, with accumulated evidence, single-subject designs can eventually answer such questions as well. A review of replicated single-subject studies can help determine the percentages of clients who improve with treatment. Nevertheless, a well-conducted group design study with a large sample can provide that information more expeditiously.

The types of questions described so far are by no means exhaustive, but they do illustrate the relation between research questions and designs. Each question is answered by a different kind of data, and each design generates its own kind of data. After having asked a question, the investigator must determine what kind of data will answer it and what kind of design will generate those data.

Advantages and Disadvantages of Design Strategies

Throughout the book, the various advantages and disadvantages of the group and single-subject design strategies have been discussed in several contexts. Therefore, what follows is a summative evaluation of both the group and single-subject design strategies. Listed are the major advantages and disadvantages of each of these approaches.

Advantages of Group Designs

Group designs have the following advantages over single-subject designs:

1. Group designs are generally effective in assessing the distribution of dependent variables in a population.

2. Group designs offer a means of evaluating the *differential* distribution of variables in defined populations (normal vs. clinical groups).
3. Small sample group designs are more efficient than large sample group designs in analyzing single treatment effects.
4. Group designs are effective in the analysis of the relative effects of multiple treatments.
5. The group strategy offers useful methods for assessing the interaction between two or more treatment variables.
6. Group designs are the most effective in assessing the interaction between treatment and client characteristics.
7. The group strategy is especially useful in determining and predicting group behaviors.
8. The group strategy is effective in predicting treatment effects based on diagnostic categories.
9. Because group designs have well-defined structures, the investigator need not make too many decisions while implementing a study.

Some of the advantages just listed may be hard to realize in practice. However, the advantages relative to group behaviors and predictions often are realized. The designs are best suited for investigating nonclinical and nontreatment-related issues in which the behavior of individual participants is not of particular interest.

Disadvantages of Group Designs

Generally, group designs with small samples fare better than those that draw large samples. Because of their reliance on group performance differences, the group design strategy has the following disadvantages:

1. The large sample group designs are generally not practical in clinical sciences that emphasize experimental treatment evaluation.
2. The large sample group designs are weak in evaluating treatment effects on individual participants; clinicians cannot extend the conclusions of a group study to individual clients.
3. Large sample group designs are weak in empirical manipulations because of the excessive reliance on statistically significant changes in dependent variables. Instead of producing larger effects of the independent variables, the group approach seeks more powerful statistical techniques that show that smaller effects are significant.
4. The group strategy is generally inadequate in measuring dependent variables. The pretests and posttests are a poor substitute for reliable and continuous measurement of dependent variables.
5. The group strategy is weak in the analysis of individual behaviors and their controlling variables.
6. The group strategy is not suited for evaluating the optimal level of treatment.
7. The group strategy is not effective in assessing the individual preference of treatment procedures.
8. Group designs are not flexible. They must usually be carried to their conclusion even when things go wrong during a study.
9. The large sample group designs are not conducive to replication.

Advantages of Single-Subject Designs

Single-subject designs have the following advantages over group designs:

1. Single-subject designs are better than group designs in the analysis of individual behaviors and their controlling variables.
2. Single-subject designs are more effective than group designs in the experimental assessment of the effects of single treatment variables on the behaviors of individual participants.
3. Single-subject designs can produce data that are especially applicable to individual clients (high on logical generality).
4. Single-subject designs are generally more practical than group designs. They have the potential of being replicated more easily than the group designs.
5. Single-subject designs can help determine the client preferences of treatment procedures when multiple treatments are equally effective.
6. Single-subject designs are effective in determining the optimal level of treatment.
7. Independent variables in single-subject designs typically produce larger effects on independent variables than group designs.
8. Single-subject designs offer more reliable and extensive measurement of the dependent variables than group designs offer because in single-subject designs, the measurement is continuous.
9. Single-subject designs are more flexible and allow modifications during the course of investigations.

Disadvantages of Single-Subject Designs

Compared with group designs, single-subject designs have the following disadvantages:

1. The single-subject strategy is much less effective than the group strategy in predicting group behaviors.
2. The single-subject strategy cannot efficiently study the distribution of variables in the population.
3. The single-subject strategy is inefficient in finding the differential distribution of variables in the population.
4. The single-subject strategy cannot make statistical statements regarding the overall effectiveness of treatment programs across large numbers of clients.
5. Single-subject designs are not efficient in evaluating the interaction between treatment variables and client characteristics.
6. Single-subject designs are not efficient in assessing the effects of multiple treatments without interference among treatments.
7. The single-subject approach is weak in its assessment of interaction between different treatment variables.
8. Single-subject designs require on-the-spot decisions at various stages of a study.

The advantages and disadvantages of all designs should be placed in a philosophical perspective, which will be done later in this chapter. Also, the advantages should be weighed against the disadvantages in the context of a particular study and its purpose.

Problems Common to Design Strategies

Some problems are common to both the group and the single-subject strategies. It is necessary to note the common problems because they may sometimes be blamed on one or the other design strategy. Many problems are simply a part of the research process.

Intersubject and Intrasubject Variability

All research designs must handle variability in the phenomenon they observe. Generally, variability is not a creation of research strategies but a creation of the nature itself. A participant's behavior varies because the factors that affect that behavior naturally vary. Different individuals vary because they are exposed to different factors or independent variables.

However, as we know, design strategies handle this variability in different ways. In the group design strategy, this variability is handled statistically; in single-subject strategy, it is handled experimentally.

Unexpected Change in the Control Mechanisms

Though the control condition, participants, or behaviors should not change in either strategy, they sometimes do. Participants in a control group may improve without treatment. In a single-subject design, the behavior under a control condition may change; for example, a behavior in a multiple baseline may change before the treatment is applied to it.

Problems of change in the control mechanism suggest that either the conditions were not well controlled or the behaviors were correlated (i.e., the behaviors were not independent response classes). Other independent variables may have been active, or the treated and as-yet-untreated behaviors may be responses of a single class.

Generality

Generality is a common problem of research, but the proponents of group designs usually make it appear to be predominantly a problem of single-subject designs. As noted before, random selection of participants from a population usually does not materialize in group designs, and hence, inferential generality is rarely achieved. If a random sample *is* drawn, inferential generality to the population may be achieved, but clinician generality and setting generality would not be established.

Generality is not a problem of research designs; rather, all designs have to face this problem. No strategy offers it automatically. To achieve generality, both group design studies and single-subject design studies must be replicated. In fact, the group strategy lacks logical generality by design and inferential generality by default. The single-subject strategy lacks inferential generality by design, but it does provide logical generality. Both strategies can demonstrate other kinds of generality only through replications.

Problems of Implementation

Many problems of research are not problems of design strategies but simply problems of implementation. Research is a complex task, the implementation of which can go wrong at any time. Participants may be hard to find and, once found, hard to retain until the end of the study. Needed instruments may be expensive, and once they are acquired, they do not seem to give notice before they break down. These and many other problems of implementing research studies are common features of research.

Philosophical Considerations in Evaluation

In the comparative evaluation of design strategies, one cannot ignore the philosophical considerations that created some of the differences between the group and the single-subject approaches. Many of the procedural differences grew out of different conceptual bases.

As noted elsewhere, the group design strategy is heavily influenced by the logic and procedures of statistics (Fisher, 1925; Cook & Campbell, 1979; Shadish, Cook, & Campbell, 2002). Statistical reasoning treats individual variability as controllable mostly through methods of statistical analysis, not through methods of experimentation. The behavior of the individual is of interest only as it contributes to the statistically stable measure, such as the mean. Theoretically, the group design approach tries to build a science of behavior by observing many participants in single studies.

The single-subject strategy, on the other hand, was influenced heavily by the tradition of experimentation, not by the statistical analysis of data (Johnston & Pennypacker, 2009; Sidman, 1960; Skinner, 1953). It treats individual differences and variability as experimentally controllable phenomena. The behavior of the individual is of primary concern. The approach considers the statistically stable mean a creation of methods of analysis; therefore, the mean is not considered an empirical value. Theoretically and practically, the single-subject approach starts with one or a few individuals, studies them, draws conclusions, and extends those conclusions only to similar individuals—if at all. This approach also tries to build a science of behavior by intensively observing many individuals across studies, but few in given studies.

The Investigator in Design Selection

A theme of this book is that science is both a public and a personal matter. Many scientific decisions are made for objective reasons, and many others are made for personal reasons. Still others are made for practical reasons. There is nothing good or bad about these reasons; that is simply the way it is. Also, there is no other way because scientists are people and science is what these *people* do.

All responsible scientists first consider what they think are the objective bases of selecting a design. The investigators first determine the nature of the question asked and what kind of data will answer it. Then a design that will produce relevant data in as clear and as practical a manner possible is selected. Once the method has been selected, scientists try to use it as precisely and thoroughly as they can.

Objective reasons are not entirely free from personal reasons, however. Personal reasons are nothing but the past training and experience of the investigator. As such, they are not necessarily subjective in the prejudicial sense of the word. An excellent design choice is as subjective as

a poor choice; both are partly determined by the scientist's training and experience. Generally speaking, those who are trained in a particular tradition of research try to make the best possible decision within that tradition. Sometimes, scientists reject the tradition of research in which they were trained; in such cases, the scientists are said to "adopt a different tradition." This happens because their experience has taught them a different lesson. When scientific behavior itself becomes the subject matter of scientific analysis, these reasons will be objective in the same sense that any other behavioral phenomenon is objective.

Finally, the selection of a design is partly a matter of practical exigencies. The investigator may know very well that an elegant factorial design with multiple cells is the best design to analyze the interaction between treatment variables, but not having enough clients, he or she may settle for the less efficient single-subject interactional design. Another investigator may select a single-group treatment design because of a preference for avoiding a control group that must be denied treatment or given deferred treatment. Practical exigencies seem to play a greater role in clinical treatment research than in basic laboratory research. Availability of clients, the need to offer treatment as promptly as possible, and other ethical considerations create a host of exigencies for the clinical investigator.

The Final Criterion: Soundness of Data

In the evaluation and selection of a design, it is better to keep in perspective that, after all, a design is only a means of producing data. A method is as good as the data it generates. As pointed out by Sidman (1960), though the type and the quality of data depend upon the method used, sound data can stand by themselves. Bad methods may not produce sound data, but sound data must be accepted regardless of methodological biases one may hold.

The soundness of data must be judged in a broad context, and no objective rules are available to make this judgment. Even the original investigator's judgment regarding the importance of his or her data cannot always be trusted (Sidman, 1960). Data rejected by the investigator may be important or may prove to be important in light of evidence that comes later. Data hailed as important may be worthless or may prove to be irrelevant later. Methodological or theoretical faddishness may make poor data look good as long as that faddishness lasts. Relevant data that contradict faddish trends of the times may be considered irrelevant.

The value of given data can and must be judged regardless of the hypothesis they are supposed to support or repudiate. A set of data may not serve the purposes of an investigator, but it may still be sound. The data generated by a particular study may fail to confirm a pet hypothesis or may force the acceptance of an unfavored one. Data not sought in a study may emerge accidentally, and those sought may not emerge. None of these contingencies are important in evaluating the soundness of data.

Another consideration in the evaluation of data is the methodological soundness of studies, which can be determined regardless of theoretical or personal biases (Sidman, 1960). Data that are generated by acceptable methods of observation and experimentation must be welcomed even if the data contradict the investigator's preconceptions. Strong and unambiguous effects of independent variables demonstrated under controlled conditions must be accepted regardless of theoretical or personal points of view. Data that resolve contradictions, shed light on poorly understood phenomena, clarify relations between events, and show patterns in seemingly chaotic happenings are always important. Similarly, data that show effective treatment of disorders, methods of solving practical problems, and effective ways of studying a difficult phenomenon are valuable. As Sidman (1960) has pointed out, it is the cumulative development of a science that eventually determines the importance and soundness of data.

Summary

- In evaluating designs and design strategies, the clinician should consider the type of research question, applicability to clinical science, and soundness of data. Table 12–1 summarizes the major research questions and design options.
- Group designs are more effective than single-subject designs in determining the distribution of dependent variables in samples of participants, group trends and characteristics, the differences between clinical and nonclinical groups, interaction between treatment variables, interaction between treatment and participant variables, and in predicting treatment effects based on diagnostic categories.

Table 12–1. Comparative Summary of Design Options

Research Question	Design Options		Comments
	Group	**Single Subject**	
What are the dependent variables?	Case study	Case study	Descriptive studies
How are the variables distributed in a population?	Uses the group method; no particular design; descriptive studies	None available; unattractive because it is nonexperimental	Descriptive and normative studies
How are the variables differentially distributed in a population?	Uses the group method; no particular design; descriptive studies	None available; unattractive because it is nonexperimental	Normal versus clinical group comparisons use this approach
What factors may have caused this effect?	Case study	Case study	Not experimental; no controls
What are the effects of an independent variable?	Pretest-posttest control group design; posttest-only control group design; within-subjects and time-series designs	*ABA* reversal or withdrawal design; *BAB* design; *ABAB* multiple baseline and changing criterion design	Controlled design is needed; both the strategies offer designs; consider the strategic and design-specific limitations
Is a treatment associated with improvement?	One-group pretest-posttest design	*AB* design	Uncontrolled treatment evaluations
Is a treatment effective?	Pretest-posttest control group design; posttest-only group design; within-subjects and time-series designs	*ABA* reversal or withdrawal design; *BAB* design; *ABAB* multiple baseline and changing criterion design	Controlled design is needed; both the strategies offer designs; consider the strategic and design-specific limitations
Is one treatment more effective than the other?	Multigroup pretest-posttest design; factorial designs; crossover designs; time-series designs	*ABACA/ACABA* design; alternating treatments design	Only relative effects are frequently assessed; control groups may be added; group designs are somewhat better

continues

Table 12–1. *continued*

Research Question	Design Options Group	Design Options Single Subject	Comments
Is there an interaction between treatment components?	Completely randomized factorial design	Interactional design	Group strategy is better; multiple treatments interference in the single-subject design
Do some clients benefit more than other clients from the same treatment?	Randomized blocks design	An efficient design is not available	Group strategy can isolate an interaction between assigned variables and treatment
Do clients prefer one treatment over the other?	An efficient design is not available	Simultaneous treatments design	Preference, not necessarily effectiveness, is analyzed
What are the most effective components of a treatment package?	Completely randomized factorial design	Interactional design	Relative as well as interactive effects are analyzed
Can an effective treatment package be developed?	Any controlled design to begin with and then a factorial design	Any controlled design to begin with and then the interactional design	Requires a two-stage evaluation of independent components and their interactions
What is the optimal level of treatment?	An efficient design is not available except for the single-group time-series design with multiple temporary treatments	Most single-subject designs; parametric variations of treatment may be introduced in successive stages of treatment	Single-subject approach is preferable because of its flexibility
How do certain groups behave?	Time-series designs with repeated measures before and after treatment	An efficient design is not available; handled through replications	Group strategy is efficient in describing and predicting group behaviors

- The disadvantages of group designs include limited applications in clinical treatment evaluation, lack of logical generality, weak treatment effects, inadequate measurement of dependent variables, insensitivity to individual uniqueness, and inability to evaluate client preferences for treatment.
- The advantages of single-subject designs include their sensitivity to individual behaviors and uniqueness, appropriateness to treatment evaluations, high logical generality, practicality, replicability, reliable measurement of dependent variables, large magnitude of treatment effects, and usefulness in determining client preferences for treatment procedures.
- The disadvantages of single-subject designs include their limited usefulness in predicting group behaviors, group performance under given treatments, establishing group- or age-based norms, and evaluating the interaction between multiple treatments or between treatment and client characteristics.

- The final criterion in the selection of design strategies is the soundness of data. Procedures that produce sound data are always acceptable.

References

Cook, T. D., & Campbell, D. T. (1979). *Quasi-experimental design: Design and analysis issues for field settings.* Chicago, IL: Rand McNally.

Fisher, R. A. (1925). *Statistical methods for research workers.* London, UK: Oliver & Boyd.

Johnston, J. M., & Pennypacker, H. S. (2009*). Strategies and tactics of behavioral research* (3rd ed.). London, UK: Routledge.

Shadish, W. R., Cook, T. D., & Campbell, D. T. (2002). *Experimental and quasi-experimental designs for generalized causal inference* (2nd ed.). Boston, MA: Houghton, Mifflin, and Company.

Sidman, M. (1960). *Tactics of scientific research.* New York, NY: Basic Books.

Skinner, B. F. (1953). *Science and human behavior.* New York, NY: Free Press.

Study Guide

In answering Questions 1 through 11, make sure you (a) identify the type of research, (b) specify the type of design (group or single subject), (c) describe the basic elements of the procedure, and (d) justify the selection of the design. You must make up such needed information as the age of the participants, the kind and the severity of a disorder, and sample size.

1. Design a study in which you would investigate the potential independent variables of conductive hearing loss in a group of school-age children.

2. Suppose you wish to find out the stages in which children acquire the passive sentence forms. Design a study that would have a local but adequate sample. Use hypothetical information regarding the size of the population.

3. Compared with normally hearing persons, how frequently do children and adults with hearing loss initiate conversation in a group? Design a study to answer this question.

4. Design two studies in which the effects of an independent variable are evaluated under controlled conditions. In the first study, the temporary effect of a variable on some aspect of speech, language, or hearing will be evaluated. For example, the effects of white noise or delayed auditory feedback on speech may be temporary. In the other study, the relatively permanent effect on some aspect of speech-language behavior will be evaluated. The effects of treatment or teaching procedures are of this kind.

5. You wish to find out if one teaching or treatment method is more effective than another. From your study of your specialty, select two potential treatment procedures and design a study to evaluate their relative effects to determine if one of them is more effective than the other.

6. Find a treatment procedure that contains at least two dissimilar elements. Then design a study in which you would determine the interactive effects of the two selected components. Design both a single-subject study and a group design study.

7. You suspect that the social class of your clients influences the outcome of language treatment. Design a study to investigate this possibility.

8. Find two equally effective treatment procedures for a given disorder. Then design a study in which you would determine if selected clients prefer one procedure over the other.

9. Suppose you have repeatedly faced parents of children with language disabilities who ask you whether language therapy for these children will increase their chances of completing high school. How would you design a study to answer that question?

10. Summarize the advantages and disadvantages of the group design strategy.

11. Summarize the advantages and disadvantages of the single-subject strategy.

12. What kinds of problems are common to different design strategies?

13. Specify why the soundness of data is an important criterion in the evaluation of design strategies.

13

Designs Versus Paradigms in Research

Chapter Outline

◆ Limitations of Exclusively Methodological Approaches

◆ Research Methods and Subject Matters

◆ Philosophy as Methodology

◆ Philosophy of Subject Matters

◆ Philosophy of the Science of Speech and Language

◆ Philosophical Ways of Handling Methodological Problems

◆ The Interplay Between Philosophy and Methodology

◆ Summary

◆ References

◆ Study Guide

Most books and graduate courses on research concentrate on research methods. Methods, however, are only a part of research. Two other parts of research are equally important: knowledge of the subject matter and knowledge of its philosophy. It is necessary to understand what to investigate and why it is important to investigate it, as well as how to investigate it. It is not clear why, in discussions of research, the knowledge and philosophy of subject matters do not receive much, if any, attention. Many writers pay exclusive attention to the methods of research and ignore the questions of the conceptual and philosophical bases of research.

Limitations of Exclusively Methodological Approaches

Methodology is the study of how to do research and includes a discussion of the following: how to observe, measure, and record a phenomenon; how to fit research questions to research methods; how to set up conditions in such a way that a cause-effect relation is revealed; how to manipulate independent variables; and how to make sure that unwanted variables do not influence the results. Methodology tells a researcher *how* to investigate when he or she knows *what* to investigate.

However, methodology does not tell what to investigate. A thorough study of the methods of research may still leave the investigator with nothing to investigate. Knowledge of the group and single-subject designs or of the various statistical techniques will not necessarily suggest research questions. The knowledge of research designs is useless without a worthwhile question that needs to be answered.

An important point about research methods is that they are secondary to the subject matter and its philosophy. In many ways, the nature of a subject matter and its philosophy shape methodologies. Meaningful studies can be designed only when an investigator has a critical understanding of the subject matter, its philosophy, and the concepts and methods of science and research.

Research Methods and Subject Matters

It was pointed out in Chapter 3 that the basic methods of science are independent of any subject matter. Investigators in any discipline may borrow applicable methods from science. A subject matter that successfully applies the methods of science is a branch of science. However, the methods of science are not a closed set. The set is open and dynamic, and it is shaped by the nature of different disciplines that have used the scientific approach in studying common and unique problems. New methods are added to the set by different disciplines. Such additions conform to the basic logic of science and enrich scientific methodology.

The independence of most methods of science and subject matters suggest that an understanding of the methods alone will not lead to significant research in given subject matters. A thorough knowledge of the subject matter is necessary before the application of research methods in answering important research questions. Theoretically, students can learn how to do research independently of their subject matters. They can later combine this information on research methods with their independently acquired knowledge of the subject matter. In practice, however, this may not be the best strategy for learning how to do research.

The way many graduate students are asked to study research methods suggests that it may not be important to understand *what* to investigate and *how* to investigate in the same context. Graduate courses on research methods, often taken in departments outside students' major discipline, offer methods independent not only of the subject matter of research but also of all philosophical concerns. Because of the highly prevalent notion that statistics and research designs are the same thing, more and more students in a variety of social, behavioral, and health-related disciplines are asked to take courses on statistics that count as courses on research designs. Students from different disciplines take these courses with the implied assumption that information on research can be acquired with no philosophical concerns relative to their subject matter. Many students, however, cannot integrate the subject matter with research methods that are offered in a content-neutral manner. They do not appreciate the philosophical issues relative to their subject matter. Knowledge of analysis of variance or of research designs does not necessarily make a student a competent researcher.

An exclusive concern with methodology leaves the student with no philosophical sophistication needed to do research. Therefore, in this chapter, we address some of the philosophical issues that play a major role in the research process.

At the very outset, a few points must be made clear. An examination of philosophical issues inevitably raises questions about personal biases and views. Also, such an examination raises the question of what kinds of research (unrelated to methodology) are more or less valuable. The discussion can raise unsettling questions about a person's philosophy, which is an inclination to investigate certain kinds of questions with certain methods. Perhaps partly because of this reason, authors typically shy away from more personally colored philosophical issues and stay close to more objective methodology.

Methodological questions have relatively straightforward answers. Although different tactics can be used to investigate a certain problem, some are clearly more appropriate than others, and some are undoubtedly wrong. However, philosophical issues are not as easily resolved. Therefore, *the philosophical questions to be discussed in this chapter do not have right or wrong answers.* The sole purpose of this chapter is to draw attention to a neglected aspect of research. We take certain philosophical positions, as everyone else does, and surely (and we believe appropriately) our positions will be clear in the following discussion as one of the different views.

Another point that must be made at the very beginning is that both methodology and philosophy are important. There is no suggestion here that philosophical considerations should supersede methodological considerations. The main emphasis here is on giving philosophical issues the attention they deserve. In the best tradition of research, both methodology and philosophy play a significant role. They influence each other and help each other evolve. At a more advanced stage, there is a productive interplay between the philosophy and methodology of a subject matter. We return to this point later.

Philosophy as Methodology

It is appropriate to contrast philosophy with methodology, but probably a more significant factor about philosophy is that it can have very direct consequences for methodology. In many respects, the philosophy of a subject matter is also its methodology. In this section, we shall explore this idea and then return to the question of interplay between philosophy and methodology.

Very few, if any, disciplines have a single philosophy. Different philosophical approaches coexist in many disciplines. Therefore, disciplines are likely to have different *paradigms*. **Paradigms** are conceptual frameworks that include certain basic assumptions about a discipline. Such assumptions dictate the nature of questions asked and the methods used to answer them. Philosophical or paradigmatic variations within a discipline create several methodological issues. This discussion is concerned with: (a) the philosophy of subject matters, (b) the philosophy of the science of speech and language, (c) the philosophical ways of handling methodological problems, and (d) the interplay between philosophy and methodology.

Philosophy of Subject Matters

The philosophy of a subject matter is different from the accumulated knowledge and methods of that subject matter. However, an overall **philosophy** of a subject matter is a broader view of what that subject matter has been and what it ought to be; the philosophy of a subject matter is a conceptual evaluation of the methods, questions, theories, social applications, and overall implications of that subject matter. Such a philosophy does not necessarily evaluate the empirical findings of a discipline; that is the stuff the subject matter is made of. It does not directly evaluate particular designs, methods, or modes of data analysis. Instead, the philosophy concerns itself with the way the subject matter and its methods have been conceptualized, the approaches taken to the issues of methodology, the strengths and the limitations of those concepts and methods, and the overall significance of the knowledge generated within the discipline.

When a discipline is also an applied profession, additional philosophical considerations emerge. Among the questions a clinical profession attempts to answer are these: Can the discipline solve its problems? Does it address the concerns philosophically as well as methodologically? Does the profession have a philosophy that moves it forward? Are the methods used consistent with the profession's applied objectives? Does it promote a discussion of ethical issues? In essence, the philosophy of an applied discipline asks and evaluates a generic question: Is the profession able to meet its scientific and social challenges in an efficient and responsible manner?

The philosophical concerns of the kind described here are not totally independent of the subject matter and its methodology. In fact, questions of philosophy can be answered only in the context of a particular discipline, its methods, and their outcome.

The philosophy of a subject matter is not a discussion of vague and irrelevant issues. Contrary to the popular notion, **philosophy** is a dialogue on conceptual as well as practical and ethical issues. There is nothing more practical than an evaluation of the degree to which a profession has achieved its scientific and applied objectives. Such an evaluation is a philosophical venture. A serious examination of the philosophy of a subject matter and its conceptual frameworks can suggest better ways of reconceptualizing the issues or even the entire subject matter. This may help meet the practical challenges of the profession.

When a discipline reaches a certain stage of sophistication and advanced knowledge, philosophical issues become clear and often pressing. For example, the question of life and death, certainly one of the most profound of the philosophical issues, became pressing when medical technology advanced to the stage where life (as defined in a technical and legal sense) could be sustained through artificial means. On the other hand, if individuals belonging to a discipline are sensitive to philosophical issues from the beginning, then it is possible that certain faulty concepts and methods can be avoided.

Different traditions of research within disciplines often are a product of divergent philosophical positions. Whether philosophical assumptions are made explicit or not, they have a profound influence on what sorts of phenomena are researched and how. Natural sciences are bound by some common assumptions about natural phenomena. As we noted in Chapter 3, natural scientists believe that events are caused and that causal relations between events can be discovered (**determinism**). Scientists also believe that some form of sensory observation is necessary for a thorough study of a phenomenon (**empiricism**). Also, natural sciences have certain common philosophical

assumptions about their methods. Most natural sciences have a commitment to experimental methodology. They have a strong tradition of experimental research. As a result, there is a large body of replicated knowledge. Natural scientists also believe that variability is mostly **extrinsic** and therefore subject to experimental control. This philosophical assumption may have done more than anything else to successfully control and alter the variables dealt with in natural sciences. It also shows how a philosophical assumption dictates a certain methodology.

In natural sciences, there is a long tradition of empirical research as opposed to logical speculation. This may be partly due to the philosophy of natural sciences, which drives the scientists out of their armchairs and into their laboratories. The philosophy of natural sciences insists that empirical investigation is the best method of producing knowledge: One must find out through experimentation; speculation can serve a purpose only when it leads to experimental verification.

The philosophy of science makes a distinction between scholarship and scholasticism. **Scholarship** is the product of informed, authoritative, and evaluative awareness of the existing knowledge in a given subject matter. Scholarship is needed and valued in sciences, art, literature, and the professions. **Scholasticism**, on the other hand, is a *method* of generating knowledge that does not necessarily use observational and experimental methods; instead, it relies on authorities, traditions, ancient and sacred sources, and logic. Natural sciences have moved away from scholasticism, which is good at generating controversies but inefficient in producing empirically validated knowledge. Unfortunately, some of the lesser developed sciences have not been especially successful in rejecting scholasticism and moving on to the realm of empirically verified knowledge based on observation and experimentation.

Philosophy of the Science of Speech and Language

A philosophy of the *science* of speech and language should have emerged before a methodology of clinical intervention in speech and language disorders. However, the sequence of development within communication disorders has been the other way around. The field started as a profession and then slowly began to move in the direction of a science. Failures and inadequacies in the practice of the profession have prompted practitioners to become more and more scientific. Therefore, it is not clear whether we have a dominant philosophy of the science of speech and language and, if we do, what it is.

When a subject matter starts as a profession, it is very likely to borrow philosophies from relevant disciplines. Probably three major sources influenced speech-language pathology: medicine, education, and behavioral and social sciences. Most of the early clinical conceptual models were influenced by medicine. Medical concepts such as symptomatology, pathology, diagnosis and differential diagnosis, etiology, prognosis, and functional-organic distinction were and still are influential in speech-language pathology. The very name of the profession proclaims all of them.

Schools of education influenced much of the training and practice model of speech-language pathologists. Largely because the public schools provided most of the jobs, the philosophy of education has had a large influence on the way the profession was conceptualized and the way clinicians were educated. Most speech-language pathologists were asked to take several courses in the department of education with the idea that both the science and the profession of speech and language have something to gain from such courses. Possibly, this approach had some negative impact on the development of speech and language as a science.

Among the behavioral and social sciences, psychology and linguistics have had the greatest influence on speech-language pathology. The early influence was from psychology, which probably had a more favorable impact on audiology than it did on speech pathology. Experiments in sensory psychology, especially auditory sensations and perceptions, had a tremendous effect on the new science of audiology. Initially, the branch of psychology that tended to influence speech pathology was not experimental but clinical. The clinical psychology of the time was mostly Freudian in its orientation. Psychodynamics and psychodiagnosis were the dominant themes of clinical psychology. These themes blended well with the medical philosophy of finding an internal cause and treating it; the only difference was that the cause in clinical psychology happened to be in the mind of the client (such as the bad self-image of a person who stutters).

Subsequently, applied behavior analysis, another kind of psychology, began to influence speech-language pathology (Fisher, Piazza, & Roane, 2011). Techniques of behavior change began to be used in the modification of speech, language, fluency, and voice disorders. However, this influence, even today, is strictly methodological. Radical behaviorism

(Skinner, 1953)—the philosophical parent of applied behavior analysis—has had very little effect on the way the behavioral principles are applied in speech-language pathology. In other words, there is some appreciation of methodology of behavior change but not of the philosophy of that change (behaviorism). Consequently, the application of behavioral technology within the field of speech and language pathology has been devoid of philosophical strengths. Behavioral methodology is often grafted onto the incongruent philosophies of cognitivism and nativism, whose major sources of influence have been mentalistic linguistics and psycholinguistics.

Linguistics did not exert much influence until the entry of speech-language pathologists into the realm of language and its disorders. At the time when language clinicians began to assess and treat language disorders in children, Chomsky's (1957) generative transformational grammar dominated linguistics. Speech-language pathologists borrowed the same philosophical approach, with its purely structural orientation and a tendency toward nativism. This philosophical approach encouraged speculative and mentalistic writing, which has been flourishing ever since. Ironically, speech-language pathologists did not lead the experimental research on the treatment of child language disorders. Behavioral psychologists who did not share Chomsky's philosophy of nativism, rationalism, and mentalism led that research.

The observation that a philosophy either encourages or discourages certain kinds of research is clearly demonstrated in the case of language. Structurally oriented linguistics encourages normative, descriptive, and rationally theoretical research. The presumed independent vari-

ables are often not susceptible to experimental manipulations. Innate structures, cognitive notions, knowledge of the universal grammar, mental representations, and grammatical competence are not experimentally manipulable independent variables, though they figure importantly in linguistic theories of language. On the other hand, environmental contingencies that are supposed to control language within the behavioral philosophy encourage or even require experimental methodology. Experimental research on language and language treatment has typically been the product of behaviorism, whereas descriptive, normative, and predominantly theoretical writings of a mentalistic nature have been the product of the linguistically oriented approach.

If communication sciences and disorders does not permit definitive statements about a philosophy, that is probably because we have not been philosophically aware as a discipline. There have been no systematic attempts at creating a unifying philosophy of speech-language research and clinical practice. The *science* in the profession has followed a certain subject-matters-are-science approach. Anatomy, physiology, and acoustics are typically considered under *speech science,* whereas the study of speech sound articulation or fluency disorders is *clinical.* Offended by this approach, some who studied language simply renamed their subject matter *language science,* with few, if any, meaningful consequences.

In treatment and applied research, **eclecticism**, if that could be described as a philosophical position, has prevailed. Within the best tradition of eclecticism, one is supposed to select what is valid from different approaches. Validity is determined on the basis of controlled, replicated evidence. In practice, however, eclecticism has meant borrowing from different sources with no regard for philosophical differences or experimental evidence. Such borrowings have been based on subjective opinions and feelings.

When the basic study of a subject matter and its clinical activities are influenced by contradictory philosophies, that subject not only lacks a unifying philosophy but is also riddled with controversies. This has been a major problem in the study of language and its disorders and phonological study of speech sound disorders. While the basic analyses of language and phonological aspects of language have been based mostly on structural properties, remedial approaches have necessarily looked elsewhere for help. Behavioral approaches that are not necessarily congruent with purely structural approaches have influenced remedial efforts and research. Consequently, conceptual inconsistencies and philosophical problems have resulted.

In its efforts to establish a philosophical base, a new discipline must consider several factors. Some of these factors will now be addressed.

Philosophical Aspects of Dependent Variables

Researchers, knowing the effects but not the cause, start an investigation. Therefore, much scientific discussion centers on independent variables (causes), not dependent variables (effects). Nonetheless, the neglected question of the dependent variables is important.

The question of the dependent variables is none other than the all-important question of what it is that we are trying to study. A scientific study starts with an observed effect, but the scientist may

face two problems to begin with. The first problem, which is generally appreciated, is that the effect may not have been understood fully. For example, in the study of stuttering, the analogy of the six blind men trying to explore an elephant was often used to describe the problem of each investigator seeing only a part of a large effect. When the totality of an effect is not understood, descriptions, explanations, and theories of that effect will be inadequate. In the course of a causal search, more may be understood about the effect itself. Descriptions and explanations of the effect will be modified as more is learned about the nature of the effect.

The second problem is not as well appreciated as the first. A serious problem with the dependent variable can arise when its conceptualization is inadequate, is mistaken, or does not allow experimentation. It is known that a science makes progress when its dependent variables are firmly and clearly established. This means that when we are sure of what we are studying, we may be better able to explain it through experimental research. Obviously, experiments on vague effects may not isolate specific causes. Physical sciences have made great strides partly because of their definitive dependent variables.

The problem with the dependent variables used in speech-language sciences and pathology is basically conceptual and philosophical. We face methodological problems largely because of ignored conceptual and philosophical issues. Whether the dependent variables we study are inadequate or mistaken depends upon particular points of view, but whether the variables are experimentally accessible can be better argued or illustrated.

Many controversies about language have resulted from the confusion regarding the dependent variables themselves. The grammatical, semantic, and pragmatic so-called revolutions in linguistics that have affected speech-language pathologists are mostly a debate about the dependent variables. The single most critical question for these controversies is this: What is language? As the answers have differed, so have the dependent variables. Is language the innate knowledge of the rules of universal grammar, as Chomsky claimed? Is language simply grammar, as is also claimed by the generative linguists? Is language semantic notions, as is claimed by generative semanticists? Is language pragmatic structures or notions or rules? Is language the use of those pragmatic rules? Is language cognitive structures, as is claimed by other scientists? Is language an unobservable mental system, or is it the observable production of whatever it is supposed to be? Is language a type of behavior? Is it similar to other kinds of behaviors, or is it special? These are only a sampling of questions asked in the study of language, and as can be seen, they are not about the *causes* of language but the *effects* being studied. In essence, speech-language pathologists have been wondering about the dependent variables themselves.

The way a dependent variable is conceptualized can make it more or less susceptible to an analysis of cause-effect relations. The philosophy of the dependent variable will determine to a large extent what kinds of methods will be used to study it and, in turn, what kinds of knowledge this study will generate.

When the effects are supposed to lie in a realm not accessible to observation, the causes also tend to be hypothesized to exist within that unobservable realm. If the dependent variable is a mental system, then its independent variable is thought to exist within the same mental domain. It need not necessarily be that way, but those who postulate internal effects also tend to explain them on the basis of internal causes; unfortunately, neither internal effects nor internal causes are observable, and science requires that both the effect and the cause be observable. However, on a temporary basis, scientists can tolerate the idea of causes that have been postulated but not yet demonstrated. There is then an expectation that such a demonstration is forthcoming. On the other hand, scientists may not have much patience with effects that are not observed and that perhaps cannot be observed. In such cases, scientists do not see anything to be explained. Mental rules and representations, cognitive structures, innate systems, and such other internal dependent (or independent) variables fall into this category.

The same situation exists in phonology. The real dependent variables, it is argued, are not the production of particular phonemes, but the knowledge of the speech sound system. Phonological rules, which are extracted from behavioral regularities, are considered the essence of phonological behaviors. The dependent variables are once again unobservable.

The question of the dependent variable also has plagued the study of stuttering. The multitudinous definitions of stuttering reflect nothing but a controversy (or confusion) about the dependent variable. Stuttering is variously defined as role conflict, avoidance behavior, prosodic defect, phonatory problem, laryngeal aberration, incoordination between neuromotor systems, auditory perceptual defect, production of certain kinds of dysfluencies, or production of all kinds of dysfluencies at a certain frequency level, just to name a few. The more serious problem is that some of these conceptualizations are unobservable. When investigators within a discipline do not agree on the nature of the effect, there can be little agreement on its causes. When there is no agreement on the nature of the effect, there is no reliable measurement of it.

In a clinical discipline, controversies concerning the dependent variables are carried into treatment. Such controversies make it difficult to conduct research on treatment effects. When certain treatment effects on controversial dependent variables are evaluated, the clinician does not know which dependent variables change under what treatment conditions. Such treatment evaluation studies also are not easily replicated.

For different clinicians to treat a disorder successfully, empirical specification of that disorder (the dependent variable) is essential. If clinicians are researching and treating different dependent variables, there can be very little unambiguous communication between them. In the case of stuttering, for example, the clinician who corrects the prosodic defect may not be doing the same thing as the one who reduces the avoidance behaviors. Success rates of treatment procedures also vary tremendously, not necessarily because people who stutter are heterogeneous, but simply because different dependent variables are targeted.

From the standpoint of the philosophy of science (not that of a subject matter), the dependent variables must at least be observable in some empirical sense. Effects that do not generate empirical consequences cannot be observed or explained. Scientists, like everyone else, do not try to solve problems that do not exist. Unobservable dependent variables are a handicapping luxury for the clinician who must stay close to empirical data. Dependent variables in language, speech, fluency, and voice must be empirically real. There is no assurance that such variables as the rules of universal grammar and knowledge of phonological systems are not simply inferred entities. There is not even assurance that grammatical categories, semantic notions, and pragmatic rules are separate and independent behaviors in the sense that they are empirically real.

Questionable dependent variables pose another danger to the researcher and the clinician. It is easy to confuse those dependent variables with independent variables. Is knowledge of the rules of universal grammar a dependent variable or an independent variable? In other words, is it part of the language or is it the cause of language? It can be either, depending on whose work one is reading. In the Chomsky-type theory, knowledge of the rules is sometimes the dependent variable and at other times the independent variable. Similar confusion exists in phonological and pragmatic analyses of language.

Sometimes dependent and independent variables may be confused even when a given variable is clearly dependent. This problem exists in stuttering research concerned with various neurophysiological activities of people who stutter. For example, is the slow phonatory reaction time in people who stutter a dependent variable or an independent variable? In other words, when people who stutter take more time to say what they are asked to say, do we observe a part of stuttering or do we observe a cause of stuttering? Is the observed excessive tension in the laryngeal muscle during stuttering a part of stuttering, an effect of stuttering, or the cause of stuttering?

It is not suggested here that all researchers should agree on their dependent variables, so they can make collective progress. Such a prescriptive suggestion is not acceptable to scientists because it is likely to inhibit creativity. What is suggested here is that speech-language pathologists pay attention to some fundamental philosophical issues when considering, advocating, and researching certain dependent variables. At the least, investigators, in formulating their dependent variables, must address questions such as these: Are the dependent variables observable? Do they have empirical validity? Do they have more than speculative substance to them? Do they encourage experimental research? Clearly, these questions do not stem from a particular view of the subject matter, or from personal biases, but rather from the philosophy of science itself.

The Philosophy of Measurement

It was noted briefly in Chapter 6 that measurement philosophies are a part of the subject matter. Such philosophies influence the kinds of research done in a discipline. The point is that the philosophy of measurement is itself a part of methodology used in many investigations and that those philosophies are intricately connected with the conceptualizations of the dependent as well as the independent variables.

The two interrelated issues relative to the philosophy of measurement are *what is measured* and *how it is measured*. Both dependent and independent variables are measured in research, but it is the measurement of the dependent variable that can pose significant problems. It is obvious that the measurement of any variable depends on the way it is conceptualized.

In communication disorders, some dependent variables can be measured directly, others only indirectly, and some not at all.

Social and psychological sciences have devised a variety of indirect measures of their dependent variables, largely because of the prevailing tendency to hypothesize dependent variables that are not directly observable and hence not measurable. Elaborately developed rating scales; personality inventories; and interest, attitude, feelings, and opinion questionnaires illustrate a complex set of measures analyzed through an equally complex set of statistical techniques. Unfortunately, the scientific return on such complex activities is usually poor because the nature of the dependent variable thus measured is not at all clear. It is one thing to measure the number of times a college student visits the library over a period of time and an entirely different thing to measure what the student says or rates on a questionnaire about the same behavior. The dependent variable, in this case the frequency with which he or she visits the library, is perfectly observable, although not without some inconvenience on the part of the researcher. The shortcut often taken is to simply ask persons about a particular behavior and treat their verbal statements as the measure of the dependent variable.

In communication disorders, indirect measures have been used frequently. Instead of measuring stuttering directly, it may be measured through a rating scale. Experts may be asked to judge whether a person's stuttering is a mild, moderate, or severe. Different judges' ratings may be averaged to derive a single rating on a given client. The rate of speech has sometimes been used as a measure, not of rate itself but of stuttering, on the assumption that slower rate is indicative of stuttering. If one wonders why stuttering could not be measured directly, the answer lies in the way stuttering was conceptualized. Evidently, to some investigators, stuttering is not a dependent variable that can be observed and measured in *real numbers*. When stuttering is conceptualized in terms of bad self-image, it is difficult to count it in mathematical units. Some indirect number systems that give the impression it is being measured will have to be devised.

It is probably better to have dependent variables that permit at least indirect measures than to have those that do not permit any measurement at all. Many of the variables that figure in the linguistic analysis of language and phonology can hardly be measured. It is not clear how one measures the knowledge of the grammatical or phonological rule system. In such cases, observable behaviors are measured, and their patterns established. Patterns of correct and incorrect responses are thought to reflect the underlying knowledge systems. Such knowledge systems are then thought to have been measured indirectly. In this case, measurement is by inference, which is a highly questionable scientific practice indeed.

It appears as though the philosophy of the subject matter of speech and language pathology considers direct measures of behaviors either inadequate or invalid. The prevailing practice of measurement by inference in communication disorders suggests that somehow counting the production of various verbal behaviors in numbers and percentages is either unimportant, invalid, or both. There is probably a prevailing opinion that directly observable dependent variables are superficial and that in-the-head, inferred variables are complex and scientifically more valuable.

In summary, one measures only what one thinks is important to measure, and what one thinks is important is a matter of one's philosophy of the subject matter. Once again, it is possible to think of some conditions of measurement purely from the philosophy of science. It is preferable to measure the dependent variable as directly as possible. It is also preferable to measure the variable in mathematically valid units (numbers) and not with a simulated system of numbers with nonmathematical definitions (see Chapter 6 for details). It is certainly best to avoid measurement by inference when the inevitable effect is unchecked speculation.

The Locus of the Independent Variables

How independent variables are conceptualized is another philosophical matter that profoundly affects the methods of research and research reporting. It may be recalled that to establish cause-effect relations, the experimenter manipulates independent variables under controlled conditions. The cause of a certain event may be discovered accidentally, in which case the influence of prior conceptualization may not have played a critical role. In fact, prior conceptualization can sometimes delay accidental discoveries by making the scientist less observant of unsuspected relations. In any case, we will consider the following two questions in this section: What are independent variables? Where are they located within the operating philosophy of a given discipline?

Systematic thinking about the nature of causes and the philosophy of causation has a long history because this is the stuff science is made of. As we noted in Chapter 3, most dependent variables have a chain of causes, which can be analyzed at different levels. A person's aphasic speech problem may have been caused by brain damage, but the brain damage also is an effect of some other cause such as a head injury or a stroke. The head injury and stroke have their respective causes, and so forth. In this chain of events, a particular event and its cause may be the focus of analysis at a given time, but there often is a larger picture of multiple events that are interrelated.

In the case of communicative behaviors and their disorders, causes are complex and perhaps involve multiple chains of events. But more important, the causes are often historical. By the time a clinician sees a child who has a language disorder or any other disorder of communication, the independent variables will already have occurred. That is why a retrospective search for causes through the method of case history is commonly employed in clinical sciences. As we noted in Chapter 5, such ex post facto studies are done with the hope of uncovering past causes of current effects.

Uncovering the past causes of current effects has many pitfalls. We can never be sure that the event identified as the cause in a historical record was indeed the cause of the effect under study. Because the experimenter is not able to manipulate the suspected independent variable under controlled conditions, the cause-effect relation remains correlative and speculative.

The search for a cause that is still in the system has been prompted by the medical model. A virus or a bacterium or a lesion may be found in the body while the disease is still current. In this sense, the past cause is still active and observable, and in many cases, that cause can be removed, killed, or neutralized. In the case of communication and other behavior disorders, causes that are in the sys-

tem are not encountered frequently. Even when they are, they are confounded with events in the life of the client. Such factors as a cleft palate, intellectual disability, and brain damage are often suggested as the causes of certain communication disorders. These causes are comparable to the causes found in medical diagnoses. While this may be true to a certain extent, the resulting effect is not entirely the product of those causes. In most cases, environmental events interact with those causes and produce a more complex effect on communication. This point is illustrated by the intact need for speech modification even when a cleft is surgically repaired. People with similar organic conditions may have vastly different behaviors or behavior potentials.

The nature of the independent variables we deal with in communication disorders is complex because some of them are **relations between events**. Such relations are transitory. They have occurred in the past, and they often produce effects that accumulate over time. In this process, many variables come together to produce the eventual, magnified effect (called a disorder) that the clinician sees all at once and often after a lapse of time. If one suspects a certain pattern of parent-child interaction as the cause of stuttering in young children, then those interactions are simultaneously transitory, historical, cumulative, and interactive. Tracking such cause-effect relations is one of the most challenging tasks scientists face.

The **locus of the independent variables** is an issue that has not received much direct attention, but it has been debated in an indirect manner. The questions, phrased in nontechnical terms, are these: Where are the independent variables located? Where do we look for them? Some look for them in the genetic mechanism of individuals, others in the dynamics of the neurophysiological systems of speech production. Still other investigators look for the causes in the environmental events that may have produced the effects under study. At a more complex level of analysis, interaction between some of these variables may be the target of study.

The philosophy of the locus of the independent variable that one adopts significantly affects his or her methods of research. Of course, the philosophy has an initial impact on the kinds of causes looked for: genetic, neurophysiological, environmental, interactive, and so on. The kinds of causes thought of will influence the methods used to track them down.

If the causes looked for are within the *genetic* and *neurophysiological mechanisms,* then the methods are mostly nonexperimental. Genetic studies of human behaviors and disorders are retrospective, and they make the best effort at reconstructing the events so that a pattern emerges. The patterns may suggest different possibilities of inheritance or potential genetic mechanisms at work. Investigations of neurophysiological mechanisms examine existing structural variables and functional (working) dynamics. Such investigations compare the structures and dynamics found in individuals with a given effect against those without the effect. In other words, the method is mostly that of standard-group comparison. Observed structural and dynamic differences may then be related to the existing effect in one population and its absence in the other. People who stutter, for example, may be found to be slower than people who do not in their muscular or vocal reaction times. The two groups may be different in their reactions to certain central auditory stimulus materials.

When independent variables have an *internal locus,* what happens internally when an observable response is made becomes a subject of speculation. For example, when a child with speech sound disorders is thought to lack a *mental representation* of phonemes, the independent variable of speech sound disorders has an internal locus. The independent (causal) variable will have been inferred from a dependent variable (speech sound disorders). When the correct production of phonemes is taught, another inference follows: The child now has a mental representation of phonemes. When the observed, measured, and manipulated single independent variable was treatment, unobserved, unmeasured, and unmanipulated mental representation gives an air of importance to the study. Similar problems exist with such proposed independent variables as grammatical competence, knowledge of the rules of grammar or phonology, cognitive structures, and internalized pragmatic rules or notions. These independent variables do not allow direct experimentation, and, therefore, they have to be inferred from dependent variables (client responses of one kind or another). This comment does not necessarily question the validity of those inferred independent variables. A knowledge of phonological rules may indeed underlie speech sound productions, both normal and deviant. But neither the child nor the expert knows that for sure. Other than the speech sound disorders (dependent variables) and the manipulated treatment (independent variables), nothing else has been observed, measured, or manipulated.

Independent variables that have external loci can be controlled and investigated with experimental methods. Opportunities for direct experimentation in themselves do not validate the proposed independent variables, but they are opportunities for self-correction. Positive reinforcement, differential reinforcement, corrective feedback, and other kinds of environmental contingencies are more susceptible to experimental analysis than are genetic or neurophysiological independent variables. Indeed, most of the experimental research in speech-language pathology consists of independent variables of external locus. Controlled treatment research on disorders of speech sound production, language, fluency, and voice have necessarily manipulated independent variables in the form of various stimuli and response consequences.

The question of the locus of the independent variables is also related to the issue of variability discussed in Chapter 7. The assumption of intrinsic variability is the same as the assumption of internal locus of independent variables, and the assumption of extrinsic variability is the same as that of the external locus of independent variables. These philosophical positions have similar methodological implications. The concepts of intrinsic variability and internal locus of independent variables are hard to adapt to the experimental methodology.

Philosophical Ways of Handling Methodological Problems

Generally, and often appropriately, investigators think of methodological solutions to methodological problems. However, there are philosophical solutions to methodological problems. An investigator should at least be aware of such solutions, even if he or she rejects them

after due consideration. Methodological problems can be handled philosophically. A few illustrations will serve to make this point.

When we say that a methodological problem is handled philosophically, we do not mean that somehow the need to design a procedure is bypassed. We mean only that the problem is approached from a different philosophical, rather than methodological, perspective. Instead of adding another procedural component to the methodology, the investigator reconceptualizes either the dependent or the independent variable or some aspect of the experimental control. The new perspective may lead to new methods.

Intersubject Variability

As we noted in Chapter 7, intersubject variability poses a significant methodological problem in most animal and human research. This problem is handled with relative ease in animals by controlling their genetic history as well as current environmental conditions. Obviously, such tight control cannot be achieved with human participants. Therefore, human intersubject variability must be handled differently.

Intersubject variability can be handled either methodologically or philosophically. Statisticians have historically offered methodological solutions to the problem of intersubject variability. When a given sample of participants shows unacceptable amounts of intersubject variability, the investigator is advised to increase the sample size. The assumption is that the greater the number of participants, the higher the chances of neutralizing the effects of variability, because the opposing directions of variability within large groups may cancel each other. In this approach, there is no real reduction in variability, however.

A related methodological solution to intersubject variability is the use of statistical procedures of analysis. Bypassing the variability within the group, one can analyze the results through such techniques as the analysis of variance and still be able to draw some conclusions regarding the effect of independent variables on dependent variables. To be sure, within-group variability affects the analysis, but having more participants will make it possible to tease out the effects despite background variability. Once again, variability remains untouched.

There are two philosophical ways of handling intersubject variability. First, variability is not treated as an unwanted or interfering problem. Within this philosophy, intersubject variability does not need bypassing techniques. This position also holds that statistical methods of handling variability are not effective. Those methods either leave variability at their usual level or magnify it by increased sample size. Variability, on the other hand, is thought of as a matter of exerting greater control over the extraneous variables that are responsible for that variability. Instead of leaving the variability intact and finding methods of analysis that would still show the effects of independent variables, the investigator may take extra steps to better control the conditions of the experiment so that the variability within (and across) participants is reduced. Behavioral research has shown that variability is often the result of poorly controlled experimental conditions or weak independent variables.

Second, variability itself may be the subject of experimental analysis. Within

this philosophical view, questions about why individuals differ are considered worthy of research. This approach may need new methods, but only after such a philosophical shift.

Integrity of Dependent Variables

As we know, the kinds of dependent variables selected for study are often a matter of the philosophy of a given subject matter. A problem that has plagued investigators in psychological and social research is the reactivity of the dependent variable (see Chapter 7). **Reactive dependent variables** are those that change simply because they are measured. Attitudes, feelings, and opinions are on the top of the reactive variables list. Such changes then confound the effects of the independent variables. Because the dependent variables must be measured before the independent variable is introduced, reactivity can pose significant problems.

We noted in Chapter 8 that Solomon (1949) had devised a methodological solution to the methodological problem of measurement effects on dependent variables. His four-group design, considered one of the most complex and ideal of the group designs, makes it possible to identify the presence and the magnitude of reactivity. He simply increased the number of groups in a design so that the effect of the independent variable could be tested with and without pretesting. This is an excellent illustration of methodological handling of a methodological problem.

A philosophical approach to the same problem would prompt serious thinking about the integrity of the dependent variable under study. Perhaps the dependent variables must be reconceptualized. Possibly, attitudes and opinions that are notoriously reactive are not solid dependent variables. Such unctuous dependent variables may suggest that at best they are indirect measures of whatever is measured. Perhaps there is a more direct way of measuring what the reactive variable is supposed to measure. Such a philosophical approach asks some basic questions: What is it that we wish to change? What is the true dependent variable? Is it a person's response to a questionnaire, or is it the actual behavior under some specified conditions? Can we measure the behavior more directly than by accepting an indirect measure of it from what the person says about it?

A reconceptualization of *attitudes,* for example, would show that they are a surrogate for real behaviors and that the only practical reason to measure them is that they are more easily measured than the real behaviors. However, it is not impossible to measure the real behaviors for which the attitudes are a surrogate. A philosophical shift, then, would suggest that instead of a four-group design to handle reactivity, one might measure dependent variables that have a greater degree of integrity.

Reconceptualization of dependent variables is perhaps the most important philosophical method of handling a methodological problem. The very first question an investigator should ask about a research problem is the integrity of the dependent variable. It should be reliably and validly measurable. When there is no reasonable assurance of this, the investigator must consider other dependent variables. Generally speaking, if a dependent variable has to be measured only indirectly and without its actual occur-

rence, then a reconceptualization should be considered. Indirectly measured dependent variables are abundant in speech-language pathology. Rules of universal grammar, phonological knowledge and rules, phonemic awareness, alphabet knowledge, print awareness, self-confidence, and negative attitudes are but a few of the many variables that are surrogates for real behaviors. Real behaviors they stand for are all measurable, and in fact many are routinely measured, but not directly named.

The Magnitude of Change in the Dependent Variable

How much of an effect the independent variable should produce to suggest a cause-effect relation is a significant problem in research. The problem is compounded by intersubject and intrasubject variability. Under an experimental condition, the dependent variable must change more than it typically does on its own. How much more should it change has always been a difficult question, for which the traditional answer has been methodological.

The methodological approach is to use statistical methods of analysis that, depending upon the sample size, require relatively small amounts of change in the dependent variable. **Statistical significance** is a measure of the effect of the independent variable over and beyond chance variations in the dependent variable. An important factor related to statistical significance is the sample size. When the other variables are held constant, the larger the sample size, the smaller the magnitude of change (in the dependent variable) needed to conclude that the manipulated variable was indeed responsible for the change. In essence, to show an effect, the methodological approach recommends that a large number of participants be used. Taking this recommendation seriously, medical and social scientists have produced increasingly smaller effects in their experiments with increasingly larger numbers of participants.

A philosophical approach may not accept a methodological shortcut to this problem. Accordingly, there is no substitute for producing a large enough change needed to show that the independent variable did produce a change (and that the change was meaningful). Therefore, the only acceptable solution is to make the changes large enough to convince an observer without help from levels of statistical significance. This philosophy has gained additional strength in clinical sciences, where the effect of treatment procedures must be large enough to make a difference in the life of the clients. Statistical significance may or may not imply clinical significance, as discussed in Chapters 7 and 10. So the philosophical solution, which of course is no solution at all from the critics' standpoint, is to produce large effects after all.

The Interplay Between Philosophy and Methodology

We have so far considered how philosophical positions can influence methodological problems. However, methodology also has philosophical implications. Different methods shape different philosophies. Methods limited to naturalistic observations lead to different philosophies than do those that involve experimentation. For example, pure normative research is likely to shape a philosophy of language

that is very different from the philosophy that would emerge from experimental analysis of language learning and teaching. Investigators who merely observe language and those who affect it by experimentation give different answers to questions regarding what language is, and how and why is it learned. In a more advanced stage of scientific research, there is a lively interplay between philosophy and methodology.

Although it was suggested earlier that philosophy can help resolve some of the methodological problems, it is not necessary to have a firm philosophy of the subject matter before one ventures into research. Also, in the beginning stage of a discipline, a commitment to a philosophy of a subject matter can be premature and can limit the kinds of questions asked or methods tried. In the absence of a philosophy of the subject matter, empirical scientists should adopt the philosophy of science. The basic philosophy of science can often be a better guide than premature philosophies of a subject matter. The philosophy of science also can suggest more fruitful questions for research than can existing nonexperimental data, speculative theories, untested clinical procedures, or personal philosophies, which are often no more than pet notions.

In the context of behavior science, Skinner (1956) has stated that when he started his research career, he had no particular physiological, mentalistic, or conceptual model of behavior. He was committed to the methods and philosophy of the natural sciences. Behaviorism, which is the philosophy of his kind of behavior science, evolved as data evolved. As the philosophy evolved and began to be applied to various behavior disorders, new methods evolved. Some of the experimental designs, including the multiple baseline design and the changing criterion design, were developed or modified in the applied contexts. However, in this endeavor, the applied researchers were guided by the philosophy of behaviorism.

A long tradition of research helps accumulate replicated data on the important questions pertaining to a given field of study. Whether this research is done with the philosophy of the subject matter or within the philosophy of science may not be crucial. Once an experimentally valid database is created, philosophical implications begin to emerge. Those implications then guide further research. From this point on, methodology and philosophy influence each other.

When a given philosophy is not yet capable of suggesting appropriate methods, one should again follow the lead of the basic methods of science. Whenever possible, the experimental methodology should be preferred, since this method can pay larger dividends than any other. Cumulative experimental research can help shape a more useful philosophy of the subject matter and take both the subject matter and its philosophy to a level of development where new methods can be derived from that philosophy. Perhaps speech-language sciences and disorders will soon reach this level.

Summary

- A philosophy of a subject matter is at least as important as its methods.
- A philosophy of a subject matter is an enquiry into the value, usefulness, practicality, and overall implication of a subject matter and its methods; it can suggest new methods for study.
- The philosophy of speech and language should consider the definition of dependent variables, methods of measurement, and the locus of the independent variables.
- There are philosophical ways of handling such methodological problems as intersubject variability, integrity of dependent variables, and the magnitude of change in the dependent variables.
- A discipline makes progress because of an interplay between philosophy and methodology.

References

Chomsky, N. (1957). *Syntactic structures.* The Hague, the Netherlands: Mouton.

Fisher, W. W., Piazza, C. C., & Roane, H. S. (Eds.). (2011). *Handbook of applied behavior analysis.* New York: NY: Guilford Press.

Skinner, B. F. (1953). *Science and human behavior.* New York, NY: Free Press.

Skinner, B. F. (1956). A case study in scientific method. *American Psychologist, 11,* 221–233.

Solomon, R. L. (1949). An extension of control group design. *Psychological Bulletin, 46,* 137–150.

Study Guide

1. In addition to a knowledge of methodology, what are the two other parts of research that an investigator must be familiar with?

2. What are the limitations of a pure methodological approach to research?

3. Why should you be concerned with the philosophical issues relative to research?

4. How is a philosophy of a subject matter different from its accumulated knowledge and methods?

5. What are some of the philosophical concerns of an applied (clinical) discipline?

6. What discipline seems to have had an early influence on the training of speech-language pathologists?

7. What are the two behavioral and social sciences that had an influence on the development of communicative disorders?

8. Specify the importance of dependent variables in developing a philosophical base for research.

9. What are some of the problems associated with many of the dependent variables used in speech-language pathology? Give examples.

10. Specify the relation between the way a dependent variable is conceptualized and the method of measurement used to measure that variable. Give an example.

11. What is meant by the *locus* of independent variables? How are the loci of such variables related to research methodology?

12. Which kind of locus is more susceptible to experimental methodology? Why? Illustrate your answer.

13. How is intersubject variability handled methodologically? How is it handled philosophically?

14. What is meant by "integrity of dependent variables"?

15. What is a methodological approach to handling the issue of the magnitude of the effects of independent variables? What is a philosophical approach?

PART III

Doing, Reporting, and Evaluating Research

14

How to Formulate Research Questions

Chapter Outline

◆ How to Formulate Research Questions

◆ Preparation of Theses and Dissertations

◆ Summary

◆ Reference

◆ Study Guide

One would think that it should be possible to tell a beginning graduate student how to do research and the student in turn follows the suggestions and completes a study. Unfortunately, telling someone how to do research is not easy and the effects are not always predictable. Therefore, the authors realize the potential pitfalls in writing this and the other chapters in this final section of the book. Nonetheless, it is possible to offer a few suggestions that may help in the pursuit of knowledge.

Most graduate seminars on research methods and designs require the students to write a research proposal. Students are typically expected to suggest a research question and describe an appropriate method for investigating it. A majority of students find this a difficult assignment. The very first question they face is simple but often debilitating: Where do I start? Students will also quickly find out that answering one question will only make them qualified to face other questions.

As described in Chapter 2, research generally does not follow a fixed pattern that can be described. The formative process of research is a set of ever-changing contingencies. Therefore, the researchers should train themselves to become more sensitive to the changing contingencies in the process of research and keep learning in that process. In the beginning, this learning is difficult and full of uncertainties. Therefore, the problems graduate students face in writing a research proposal are both natural and inevitable.

Uncertainties in the research process are never totally resolved, no matter how experienced the investigator. Therefore, students should hope to do their best, start the work as early as possible, and believe that research can be fun.

In this chapter, the emphasis will be on formulating research questions. Once a research question is formulated, the investigator thinks of the best method of studying it. The information on methods of study is the essence of many previous chapters. Therefore, the issue of selecting methods will be addressed only briefly in this chapter.

How to Formulate Research Questions

The first problem the student faces is how to find a **topic of research**. This is essentially the problem of finding research questions. Research questions are sometimes literally found in some sources, and at other times they are formulated. On the one hand, a research paper, a textbook, a review article, or another researcher may suggest a problem that needs to be investigated. In this case, the student finds a research question. On the other hand, the student's own scholarship may prompt a new question that needs to be answered. In this case, the student will have thought of an original idea, and the resulting question is a self-formulated one.

Either a found or a formulated research question, if it is worthy of investigation, is acceptable. Nevertheless, it is best for students to learn the process of formulating research questions. The best way to learn to be independent researchers is to know how to formulate research questions based on critical scholarship.

Research questions identify gaps in our knowledge about a phenomenon. When those questions are validly answered with methods of science, the gaps in our knowledge are narrowed or filled. Research questions, when researched, may produce new information or verify the reliability and validity of known information. Research that produces new information is *original,* and that which verifies the results of earlier studies is *replicative.* Both kinds of research are valuable. However, to learn more about the research process, the student should think of a question that either has not been answered or not been answered appropriately. An exercise of this kind will teach the student more about research than will an attempt to replicate a well-done study. In any case, the student needs to start looking for a problem to investigate, and there are several places to look.

Formulating research questions may be relatively easy or difficult depending on the student's degree of knowledge and scholarship. Knowledge itself does not guarantee that research questions will be found, however. The student should read the literature critically, taking note of the kinds of research done and the methods used. The student should judge how well the research has been done and come to understand what is still not known.

At this point, it may be appropriate to give the student the bad news: No amount of "how to" suggestions will replace careful and scholarly review of the literature. But even before doing that, there are a few things the student should do. What follows is a series of interrelated steps the student should take to formulate a research problem and plan for an investigation.

Identify a Broad Area of Research

The first thing to do is find a broad area of investigation or a general topic that is of interest. In communication disorders, the student may consider such areas as cleft palate, dysarthria, language acquisi-

tion, speech sound disorders, treatment of stuttering, types of aphasia, or maintenance of clinically learned behaviors. It is better to select an area that is personally interesting; after all, the student will be living with it for a while.

Once an area or topic has been selected, the student should read or reread the basic information on it. It is often useful to read what is written on that topic in a recently published standard textbook. Even research that produces advanced information requires a command of the elementary information. For example, a student wishing to do a piece of research on children's language learning should have a good grasp of the basic textbook information on this subject. A student who goes directly to theoretical writings, more advanced books, or journal articles without a good grasp of the basic information will waste time.

Identify the Current Trends

The researcher should then proceed to find the current trends on the topic. The research done in recent years must be carefully reviewed. There are no specific guidelines on what is recent and what is not; it depends upon the amount and the chronology of research on a given topic of investigation. Some topics have both a long history and a high level of current research activity. Other topics have a long history but a low level of current research activity. Still other topics have a recent history with a high density of studies. Finally, there are recent topics with few studies. No recent trend can be fully understood without a historical background, however. Therefore, it is essential to know the classic studies and theories before reading recent research papers. Students should not refrain from reading sources that may be hundreds of years old with the fear that the sources may be dated. Classic, scholarly information is never dated, even when the information is controversial.

Generally speaking, in most empirical research with no compelling reason to go back, 7 to 10 years of research may be considered current or recent. This guideline, however, may be more often violated than followed, and for good reasons. For instance, to gain a good historical understanding of a specific topic, one may need to go back more than 10 years. Other topics may be of very recent origin. In any case, there are many ways of finding the current trends, and the student must use most if not all of them. Research begins with a search—search of the published research literature. A thorough and systematic literature search is essential in finding possible topics for research.

Several sources help identify the current trends in research. Most likely, scientific and professional journals are a good starting point.

Study Journal Articles

The student must find the major journals that publish research articles on the selected topic. Journals published by one's own professional organization (such as the American Speech-Language-Hearing Association) are usually excellent sources as the articles in them will be of immediate relevance. To achieve a broader understanding of the context and issues involved, the student may expand the search and read articles in national and international journals, related professional organizations, research institutes, and private publishing houses. For instance, journals published in many branches of medicine, psychology, linguistics, education,

special education, audiology and hearing science, education of the deaf, biology, and acoustics may provide information from different perspectives that might suggest research questions.

Depending on the general area of investigation being considered, the student will have to concentrate upon certain kinds of journals. In the case of most topics in communication disorders, various national and international journals in the discipline will be the primary source of information. If the general area of investigation is the typical learning of speech and language, journals in linguistics, psychology, and communication disorders are likely to have relevant articles. If the research topic is treatment of various behavioral disorders including communication disorders, various journals of speech-language pathology, applied behavior analysis, and psychology may be searched. Researching diagnosis and treatment of communication disorders may require a search of medical and educational journals.

University students may access journal abstracts, and in many cases full texts of published papers, through their university libraries that subscribe to databases. Student members of their professional organizations (e.g., ASHA, the American Speech-Language-Hearing Association) may be able to access research papers published by their organizations. Journals that ASHA publishes are abstracted by databases, including MEDLINE.

Research the Databases

An efficient method of information retrieval is to use one of the several digitized data search services available on the Internet. There are dozens of scientific databases. Students and faculty may gain access to database services free of charge if they go through their university library's website. University libraries subscribe to many database services and offer the information free of charge to students and faculty.

Most database services provide only abstracts of articles, but they may provide a bibliography of published research. The general public may access several databases for full texts of some, not all, articles. Practically all databases are interactive; that is, a student can first ask the system to list articles on a general topic and then narrow the field down to a specific area of investigation. Most entries may be printed outright. Students can request the library for full text of articles that are not readily available through the database service. Within a few days, the library will obtain a digital copy of the article and send it via e-mail to the student.

Most students now have the skill to navigate through the Internet and the specific databases to get the information they need. University libraries offer workshops and other forms of assistance to students who need to learn the basics of database search. Information specialists in the library may also offer individual assistance upon request. It is best for the student to learn advanced database search skills as early as possible.

Most computerized services save time, although the specificity of information on speech and hearing publications may be variable. Students with Internet connections can search the databases of the world from their own home. Nonetheless, the student must plan the search well and make sure the terms to be used in the search are specific and are known to be a part of the database. A random search may yield a few good results but may also frustrate the student with a vast amount of irrelevant information. Also, because

it takes time to obtain articles through interlibrary loan program, it is important for the student to submit requests for full texts of articles as soon as possible.

Among the several databases, those that are especially useful to students in communication sciences and disorders include the following:

● American Speech-Language-Hearing Association's journal database includes all articles published in its own journals. Abstracts are free, but full- and student-members of the association may access full texts.
● MEDLINE/PubMed is a massive database of journal articles published in biomedical journals around the world. MEDLINE abstracts are free for all, but full texts of articles may be restricted.
● PsycInfo is a large database of psychological and related research published worldwide. It is maintained by EBSCO for the American Psychological Association.
● ScienceDirect is yet another large database of abstracts of medical, health, and scientific articles and, in some cases, full texts.
● ERIC (Educational Resources Information Center) is a vast computerized database service devoted to research in education and related fields. It is managed by EBSCO for the U.S. Department of Education.
● ProQuest Dissertation and Theses Global is the world's largest database of its kind. A repository for the U.S. Library of Congress, ProQuest contains abstracts and some full texts of doctoral dissertations and master's theses from universities in 88 countries.

- Linguistics and Language Behavior Abstracts, another online database managed by ProQuest, can be useful in searching literature on a variety of subjects, including audiology, speech pathology, laryngology, neurology, otology, linguistics, and applied linguistics.
- SAGE Research Methods and SAGE Research Methods Datasets include papers and other publications on research methods and data sets to teach and learn about research methods.

Computerized data search is efficient because the student need not worry about targeting specific journals. Instead, the student can search by key terms (topics) to find articles published in various sources and countries. In some cases, the number of available articles may be few, but in many cases, the number may be overwhelming. Therefore, the student must narrow the search, be more selective, obtain the most essential articles, and read them thoroughly and critically.

In reading journal articles on the topic, the student should take note of the kinds of studies that are repeated. In a given period of time, several persons may have published on a particular topic, and the questions researched may be the same or similar. Should the student find this to have happened during the last few years, a recent trend may have been identified. In such cases, it is also necessary to find out why similar studies were repeated. It is possible that a controversy about the first one or two studies stimulated people with different views. This may have led to studies designed to produce contrary evidence. If this is the case, the research information will be controversial, and the student may find it relatively easy to find a problem, because controversies are an excellent source of research questions.

Consult Other Sources

Review articles are especially good sources for research questions. In a review article, the author will have surveyed most of the published information on the topic and made a critical analysis of what is known and with what degree of generality, and what kinds of research needs to be done. The reference list attached to a review article can direct the student to most relevant articles. The author will have pointed out the good and the bad about the research attempts in a particular area of investigation. A good review article points out both the methodological strengths and weaknesses of the past studies. Frequently, a well-written review article identifies research questions for future investigations. One of those questions may be quite appropriately selected.

Studies that are described as *exploratory* or *preliminary* may also be a source of research questions. These labels are sometimes an excuse for poorly designed studies, but when they are not, they may contain seeds of new studies. Even when they are methodologically inadequate, the student with a good knowledge of designs can improve upon them if the basic idea is sound. Good exploratory studies suggest emerging trends in the field. They often suggest the topics of the future.

Descriptive studies can also be a source of new experimental investigations. Some of the original investigators of descriptive studies suggest further experimental studies on the issue. Many descriptive studies, however, do not have any hints of experimental studies. In such cases, the student is alone in going beyond the investigator's descriptions to think of experimental questions.

The student should not ignore *scholarly exchanges* between authors as a source of research questions. Some journals publish such exchanges, often called *Letters to the Editor,* which typically are critical responses to published research followed by the author's rebuttal. Some of these exchanges can fail to illuminate the issues at hand because of a personal and subjective tone, but several of them can suggest questions for further research. Journals also may publish critical commentaries on previously published articles as regular papers. Some journals publish *special issues* devoted to scholarly articles on a given topic and include exchanges between experts.

Additional sources of information can be found in *books*. After having reviewed the basic information and some journal articles, the student may be ready to read some specialized books. Books on recent advances are occasionally published in every field, and most contain critical reviews and summaries of recent research information. Such books can serve the student well by giving both a current overview and suggestions on potential research questions.

Edited books on controversies in selected clinical or theoretical issues can be helpful to students and more advanced researchers. Books on controversies are edited by an expert, and the chapter authors are experts who are generally known for their contrasting views. Students should not shy away from controversial issues because, as suggested earlier, they are a good source of research problems.

Finally, the *workshops, symposia, seminars*, and *presentations* at professional meetings and conventions may give the most recent information on a variety of topics and issues. The quality of presentations at such gatherings varies tremendously, however. With a critical approach, the student can find many research questions in good presentations. A significant advantage of professional meetings is the opportunity to meet researchers who have researched the selected area. Through these meetings, the student researcher can often get expert advice. Such advice, however, can be sought at any time during the planning and implementation of a study by contacting experts, who are usually happy to advise interested students.

Identify the Classic Questions

Many graduate students and professionals find it attractive to do research on topics of recent interest, often resulting in an overemphasis on identifying current trends in the search for a research question. Furthermore, research on current topics is generally more easily published than research exploring unknown, unappreciated, or unpopular areas and views.

Nothing is wrong with researching currently popular topics, but a potential problem must be avoided: Current trends of research are not necessarily the most creative or worthwhile. Research and theory also have their fashionable trends, which are called, in a more obscure way, *zeitgeist.* For instance, the semantic analysis of language, the distinctive feature analysis of speech sound production, the phonatory reaction time of people who stutter have had their heyday, only to be overshadowed by newer trends. Therefore, one should be aware that some highly regarded current trends may be nothing more than a passing fancy, and such trends are not the only ones that generate original research. Indeed, researchers should not be discouraged from asking old, unusual, novel, or unpopular questions. All problems without solutions are of current interest. Any question whose answer has a potential for producing new knowledge or replicating old knowledge is worthy of investigation.

A significant question, posed long ago, may be still unanswered, perhaps because past methods were inadequate and unproductive. Therefore, investigations on that question may have dwindled; a student could investigate with new and more productive methods to study the old but unresolved question. In some cases, theoretical or conceptual advances in the field may suggest new ways of looking at old problems. In such cases, it is appropriate to renew an old line of investigation.

The basic experimental questions of causality are timeless. For example, clinical research questions concerning the effects of treatment procedures and refinement of those procedures are never out of date. In fact, new trends tend to emerge in the *theoretical* explanation of phenomena; some of these theoretical trends may prove unproductive. In the basic experimental and empirical analysis of phenomena, most of the procedures are well established, and the questions are classic, simplifying the selection of a topic and methods for studying that topic.

Concentrate on a Specific Area of Research

After the preliminary information-related research on a general topic, such as language acquisition or the treatment of phonological disorders, the student should narrow the problem down to a more spe-cific area of investigation. In children's language learning, for example, one might think of morphological mastery or discourse learning. Even more specifically, the student might concentrate on irregular morphemes, adjectives, or some specific sets of grammatic features. The student might start with a topic of social communication skills and narrow it down to story narration or discourse on a topic. The research done so far should guide the student in this regard; obviously, the student would not select a research question that has been overly and perhaps quite adequately researched. The initial survey of the literature should have indicated that the selected problem or some aspect of it still needs to be investigated.

When the student has selected a specific area, more reading is needed. The student must go back to the journals and carefully read reports of major studies on the specific area being considered. This reading is more critical and analytical than the first pass. The student should make a critical analysis of theoretical and conceptual information, paying particular attention to research methods. Indeed, detailed notes should be taken of the methods and procedures of the studies because the student may use some of those methods and because the student may wish to avoid the methodological deficiencies of past studies.

Formulate a Specific Research Question

A critical reading of a particular area should lead to a more specific research problem. The student should know that the journey from a general topic to a particular research problem can be long and frustrating. One may have a desire to do some research on treatment of childhood apraxia of speech, but a specific research question may not emerge for some time.

At this point, it may be useful to write a general description of the research problem. Once again, the student should recheck the major sources to make sure that the problem either (a) has not been researched, (b) has not been researched in the manner being considered, or (c) has been researched but with room for significant methodological improvement. A difficult problem a majority of students face at this point is confirming that the study as planned has not been done. Students often find themselves discarding their pet ideas one by one because previous investigators were ahead of them.

Writing research questions takes some skill and practice. Research questions should be as direct as possible and as technical as necessary. Furthermore, they are typically about some objective phenomenon, perhaps asking whether the phenomenon exists and, if so, investigating its descriptors. Research questions can also ask whether a certain variable (such as a treatment) has an effect and whether two or more variables interact. Purely descriptive research involves somewhat simpler questions than experimental research. For example, "How many phonemes are produced by 2-year-old children?" is a relatively simple descriptive question. On the other hand, the question of whether two or more phonological treatment components have certain independent and interactive effects, and if so to what extent, is experimental in nature and, therefore, more complex.

A variety of research questions were described in Chapter 12. The kind of research question formulated for a particular investigation depends on the type of research contemplated. Normative and standard-group comparison research mostly involve questions that evoke descriptions. Ex post facto, experimental, and correlative research ask questions of a relation between two or more variables. In fact, specifying the variables of a study is probably the most crucial step involved in planning the study.

Specify the Variables in Technical Language

The student will find that a serious attempt to specify the variables to be investigated will force clearer thinking about the entire research plan. The student must try to answer several questions: What are my dependent variables? How many dependent variables do I have? What are my independent variables? How do I control my independent variables? What kind of relation is to be studied: cause-effect relations, correlative relations, or additive and interactive relations? Direct answers to questions such as these will help the student to clarify the research problem and design appropriate methods.

The dependent and independent variables must be clearly separated in studies that include both of them. The typical dependent variables in communication disorders include various kinds of speech, language, and hearing behaviors and their disorders. In a particular study, a specific aspect of these behaviors constitutes a dependent variable. In other words, although *language* may be a dependent variable, one needs to specify a particular aspect of it, for example, the production of the plural morpheme at the word level. Stuttering can be a dependent variable, but it is better to specify what exactly will be measured to document the occurrence of that disorder. In essence, the dependent variable must be described in specific, unambiguous, *measurable* terms.

An independent variable, being the manipulated or suspected cause of the dependent variable, should be described in equally specific language; after all, this is the variable whose effects are measured in experimental studies. While reading the literature, the student should pay particular attention to the way different investigators have described and measured dependent and independent variables. Often, students will find themselves confused about the status of the variables in their study. The student should know the definitions and characteristics of different kinds of variables (see Chapter 3).

The operational specification of variables also involves considerations of measurement. As we know from Chapter 6, variables can be measured in different ways, some more suitable to given problems than others. The student should always think in terms of more objective, more direct, and more discrete types of measures of the behaviors under study. Sometimes, it may be found that the problem is very intriguing, but the variables involved cannot be measured easily.

After specifying their variables, some investigators formulate their hypotheses. A research investigation does not require a hypothesis, but if one is preferred, it must be written clearly so that it specifies the variables to be investigated. See Chapter 3 for additional information on hypotheses.

Talk to Someone

Talking to someone about a research problem can be a great help. The person the student talks to need not be an expert on the subject. In the process of talking,

the student may find that he or she has not thought through the research question or a methodological aspect of the contemplated research. The student may also find gaps in his or her understanding of theoretical concepts involved in the study. Such deficiencies in the understanding of the research topic or the procedure will force more homework or clearer thinking. This step can be taken at the very beginning and repeated at every stage of the investigation.

Talking to an expert, however, can have additional advantages. The expert can help the student avoid false starts or dead-end projects. In talking with the expert, the student may find out that a particular study has or has not been done. The expert may also pose gentle and supportive challenges so that the student attains greater clarity in thinking. The student may gain more confidence in the idea being considered, and under the best possible conditions, the exchange may inspire and motivate the student to go ahead with the project.

Evaluate the Significance of the Research Questions

In the process of selecting a research problem, the student must judge whether it will be a valuable study. The question to be researched must be of some scientific, theoretical, or applied significance. Some of the most common questions asked in evaluating the significance of research questions include the following: Is the research meaningful? Is it likely to contribute new knowledge or to expand upon the existing knowledge? Does it help solve a problem? Does it have the potential to explain an event hitherto unexplained? Does the research show a new method of studying a difficult problem? Does it improve clinical techniques? Does it produce an effect unobserved so far? Does it help detect an effect that has been suspected but not observed? These are some of the many questions one can ask in evaluating the significance of research questions.

To judge that a given piece of research is valuable, one need not seek an affirmative answer to all the questions just posed. A single affirmative answer may be sufficient to justify a study. Evaluation of the significance of research problems and questions is one of the most difficult tasks in the research process. We shall return to this important issue in Chapter 16.

Think of the Methods

It is generally assumed that the researcher thinks of the methods only after having decided upon the problem. In practice, however, such a sequence is seldom realized. Methods must be considered even during the process of selecting a problem or rejecting others. If the investigator cannot think of a procedure for researching a particular question, that question may have to be rejected or postponed for future consideration. In fact, one way to screen out poor research ideas is to realize their methodological impracticality.

Other practical considerations assume importance in the process of problem selection. The student must consider the availability of participants, special equipment, and laboratory facilities that are accessible. For example, if it is known that laryngectomy patients are not being served in a particular clinic, questions of the effectiveness of a certain laryngectomy treatment procedure may not be practical unless the student is willing to

go elsewhere. If a particular research idea needs expensive biofeedback equipment that the department does not have, perhaps some other problem must be found. Similarly, if the research idea requires a specially constructed acoustic laboratory that does not exist, then that idea may have to be rejected.

When a research question is sound, a lack of available methods (not physical instruments) should only signal a challenge to one's scientific ingenuity. The idea need not be rejected, but it may not be implemented immediately. It may take some time before an appropriate method is devised to study the problem. Meanwhile the graduate student needs a practical problem for the thesis or some specific assignment so that he or she can graduate within a reasonable period of time. Sometimes, a seasoned researcher is likely to move on to something that can be done more easily than the project that takes extra time, effort, and thinking.

Questions that are too broad (e.g., what causes language disorders?) or too vague (e.g., how do children learn language?) do not lend themselves to methodological planning. As soon as the student begins to consider how a piece of research can be implemented, the problem itself begins to be seen in a different light. In essence, methodological considerations force problem specificity. Therefore, it is a good idea to think about the problem and the methods in an interwoven fashion. However, once a specific problem has been found, the investigator can spend more time on working out details of methods.

One of the first methodological considerations is the *participants of a study*. The student must decide upon the number of participants and their characteristics. Clinical or nonclinical participants and their social, personal, health, and other relevant characteristics must be considered. The age and gender of the participants should also be decided upon. The clinical and nonclinical participants must be described in terms of the criteria used in separating them. If patients with aphasia are going to be used in the study, how are they going to be diagnosed? Who are not aphasic? Who will make the judgments? By what means? How and where are they going to be found? By what criteria are they finally going to be included in the study? These are the questions of participant selection procedures or criteria. There are both inclusion and exclusion criteria—they specify the characteristics that will admit individuals to the study as well as those that will exclude individuals from it.

Whether one wishes to use a *large random sample* or a *small group of relatively homogeneous participants* is also an important question. In most clinical studies, available participants are recruited with a few restrictions. For example, an investigation concerned with language disorders may exclude those with neurological handicaps or hearing impairment. Certain syndromes or special conditions that complicate language problems may be excluded. A relatively narrow age range may be specified as acceptable. With some such restrictions, the participants may be selected on the basis of availability.

A difficult aspect of planning for a study is determining the kinds of instruments that will be used in it. The term *instruments* includes all the kinds of equipment or apparatus that will be used in the study. The type of instruments needed for a study depends mostly upon the nature of the dependent variables and the kind of measures selected for the study (see Chapter 6 for details).

The stimulus materials to be used in the study also are part of the instruments. Questions designed to evoke responses, modeling, and the specific target behaviors, and instructions to be given the participants, also should be prepared beforehand.

Another important aspect of the procedure is the overall plan and the specific design of the study. The selected design may be of the single-subject or group variety. The design typically dictates the number and sequence of the conditions of the study. These conditions, such as the pretest, experiment, and posttest, must be specified. As we noted in Chapter 11, the selection of a design depends upon the nature of the research question asked.

Finally, the student must have some idea of the kinds of data the study will generate and how they will be analyzed. The method of analysis is mostly determined by the design and the kinds of data. Studies of group designs generate data that are appropriately handled by statistical methods of analysis, whereas single-subject design studies generate data that can be evaluated visually and quantitatively, although statistical methods of analysis also are available. See Chapter 10 for details.

When statistical methods of data analysis are used, the student must understand the limitations and appropriateness of the tests to be used. As described in Chapter 10, each statistic is based on certain assumptions, such as the normal or nonnormal distribution of the dependent variable being measured and the methods of measurements used (continuous, categorical, and so on). The data for which the selected statistic is applied should not violate those assumptions. Most students need to consult an expert in statistics before selecting statistical techniques of analysis.

The foregoing is by no means an exhaustive survey of questions that must be addressed in planning a research study. The list can, however, promote the understanding of some major steps that must be taken in developing a research study.

Preparation of Theses and Dissertations

In a majority of graduate programs in communicative disorders, a master's thesis is optional; however, a few programs may require a thesis from all candidates for the master's degree. A dissertation is always required of doctoral candidates. The graduate schools of all universities and the academic departments have printed guidelines on thesis and dissertation preparation. The student should follow these guidelines. In addition, there are many published guides on thesis and dissertation preparation. Consult your advisor for a recommended book.

In formulating questions for a thesis or dissertation, the student follows the same steps as described earlier. However, theses and dissertations require a more careful and thorough literature search than that needed for a class paper. It is expected that a student planning a thesis or dissertation has a good background in the field, and therefore the search can be more specific and goal directed from the beginning.

An initial step in the preparation of a thesis, however, is to find a faculty advisor who is willing to direct the research. Unlike class projects and research assignments, theses and dissertations need close supervision from the advisor. In completing an original study for a thesis or dissertation, the student works closely with the faculty advisor.

It is in the best interest of the student to find a faculty advisor who is an expert in the particular area selected for investigation. In this way, the student can be sure of getting technical advice and help in the conduct of the research study. Generally speaking, the student and the advisor will spend much time discussing potential research problems. When a problem is finally selected, it is the student's responsibility to make sure that current information on the topic has been thoroughly researched. The design and the procedures of the study are then discussed with the advisor and finalized.

Most theses and dissertations are evaluated by a committee of three to five members. The advisor serves as chair of the committee. The student, in consultation with the advisor, selects members for the committee. Depending on the research problem being investigated, the student may select a committee member from outside the department. Psychologists, statisticians, linguists, and medical and other professionals may be selected.

Once the committee is formed, the student must write a detailed proposal of the study and submit it for approval. Usually, an oral presentation is also made. During this oral presentation, the student briefly reviews the literature and justifies the study and its procedures. The committee's task is to ensure that the student understands all aspects of the proposed research and that the methods and procedures are appropriate. If necessary, the committee may suggest changes in the methods of the proposed study.

After obtaining the approval of the committee, the student must submit the proposal to an institutional review board (IRB), which reviews the proposal from the standpoint of human participant or animal subject protection. An IRB's task is to determine whether the study poses any risks to the participants and, if so, what steps must be taken to minimize them. Chapter 17 offers discussion of the ethical issues involved in the conduct of research, along with human participant and animal subject protection procedures.

The student can begin the actual investigation only after the thesis or dissertation committee and the IRB approve the study. When the study is completed, it is written according to the guidelines established by the student's department and the graduate school of the university (Hegde, 2018). Most departments of communicative disorders use the guidelines of the *Publication Manual of the American Psychological Association* (APA, 2010). The student should consult the most recent edition of the APA *Manual* or other accepted sources.

Once again, the student works very closely with the advisor (the committee chair) in writing the thesis or dissertation. Most students revise the thesis or dissertation several times before the advisor accepts it tentatively. Finally, when the advisor considers it appropriate, an oral examination is scheduled. The entire committee once again meets to judge the appropriateness of the thesis or dissertation for the degree being sought.

During the oral examination, the student describes the study and its results and conclusions and also relates the findings to previous research and theories. In essence, the student defends his or her work during this oral examination. Approval is granted when the committee is satisfied with the thesis or dissertation and its defense. Following this approval, any changes and corrections the committee suggests are incorporated, and the final copy of the thesis or dissertation is submitted to the graduate school. If it is deemed appropriate, the graduate school then accepts the document on behalf of the university.

Completing a thesis or dissertation can be extremely time-consuming. It takes hard work and typically involves extra expense. However, it is a worthwhile aspect of graduate education. It is the only opportunity for students to do a piece of original research evaluated and approved by a team of experts in the field. There is no better way to learn about research than completing a thesis or dissertation. Well-planned and well-conducted theses or dissertations meet standards of publication.

Summary

Research questions are those that, when answered, fill gaps in knowledge. The first step in conducting research is to formulate a research question by taking the following steps:

- Identify a broad area or topic of research that interests you.
- Identify the current trends of research on the selected topic by searching:
  - Printed journals in the major field and in related fields
  - Digitized research database services
  - Books
  - Symposia, seminars, conventions, and other presentations
- Identify the classic questions that still need to be answered.
- Concentrate on a specific area of research.
- Formulate a specific research question.

- Specify the variables in technical language.
- Talk to people.
- Evaluate the significance of the research questions.
- Think of the methods.
- In preparing theses and dissertations, follow the guidelines of your department and the instructions of your advisor.

References

American Psychological Association. (2010). *Publication manual of the American Psychological Association* (6th ed.). Washington, DC: Author.

Hegde, M. N. (2018). *A coursebook on scientific and professional writing for speech-language pathology* (5th ed.). San Diego, CA: Plural.

Study Guide

1. What are research questions? Where do you find them?

2. What are the nine steps you should take to formulate research questions?

3. Describe how the process of formulating a research question proceeds from a review of a broad area of research to a narrowly specified research question.

4. Describe the usefulness of a published review article in your search for a research question.

5. What are the main sources of information on the current trends?

6. What is meant by "classic research questions"? Why are they important?

7. Why is it necessary to specify the variables of a research question in technical language? Give an illustration by writing a research question that specifies its variables in technical language.

8. What are the advantages and disadvantages of talking to experts and laypersons?

9. What are some of the questions you would ask in determining the significance of research questions? Are the answers to those questions always clear and objective? Why or why not?

10. Specify why methodological impracticality is one of the early considerations in the selection of research problems.

11. Formulate a research question that would be considered "classic" in its import. Specify the variables in technical language. Write a brief justification of the research the question would lead to.

12. Formulate a research question that would reflect a recent trend in your subject matter. What makes it recent? What are your variables? Justify your study.

15

How to Write
Research Reports

Chapter Outline

- General Format of Scientific Reports
- Structure and Content of Research Papers
- Writing Without Bias
- Good Writing: Some Principles
- Writing Style
- Writing and Revising
- Summary
- References
- Study Guide

Writing a research report and submitting it for publication are the two final steps in doing research. Besides research articles, scientists and professionals also write integrative articles, critical reviews, philosophical essays, books, manuals, many types of clinical reports, and a variety of other kinds of reports.

Most universities require adequate writing skills of their graduate as well as undergraduate students. Students who wish to complete a thesis as part of the requirement for graduate degrees are especially concerned with writing skills.

This chapter covers writing in general and writing research reports in particular. We describe five aspects of scientific and professional writing: (a) the format of a research article, (b) writing without bias, (c) principles of good writing, (d) conceptual considerations, and (e) style.

General Format of Scientific Reports

Each professional and scientific community has an accepted and relatively uniform format for reporting research findings. Editors of journals and books and professional organizations impose such formats. Standardized writing formats make the editorial process manageable. Printing in a single format is more efficient than printing in varied formats. Readers find it easy to understand research reports written in a standard format.

The prescriptive formats are especially required of articles submitted for publication in scientific and professional journals. Books, manuals, and other kinds of written materials are not as strictly controlled by such formats. Therefore, we shall be mostly concerned with journal article formats in this section.

A widely used format for journal articles is that of the American Psychological Association (APA). As early as 1929, a group of anthropological and psychological journal editors was concerned about lack of a standard format of reporting scientific studies. The first APA publication guide was published in 1944 and became known as the *Publication Manual*. The current version as of this writing, the sixth edition published in 2010, has gained wide acceptance (American Psychological Association, 2010). The reader should check the APA website for the latest edition.

Some kinds of research speech-language pathologist do may be published in medical journals. In that case, they need to follow the guidelines of the American Medical Association (2007). Researchers should consult the publication policy of a journal to which they submit their articles. We review the APA style, sixth edition, because ASHA has adopted it for all its journal publications.

The most common forms of journal articles include research reports or articles, review articles, and theoretical articles. Journals also may publish book reviews, commentaries, and other forms of papers.

An **article** or a **research report** describes an original or replicated research study. Articles have sections arranged in a fairly rigid format: *introduction, method, results, discussion,* and *references.*

A **review article** makes a critical assessment of published research in an area of investigation. Being integrative and evaluative, review articles point out research advances and summarize the state of the art. They highlight methodological and conceptual problems of past investigations and suggest questions for future research. The format of a review article is more flexible than that of a report because the article is organized according to the issues raised and data evaluated.

A **theoretical article** either presents a new theory or critically examines existing theories in an area of investigation. Theoretical articles, too, have flexible formats dictated by the nature and number of issues and theories reviewed in them.

Many journals also publish scholarly exchanges between authors. In some journals, such exchanges are published in the form of **letters to the editor**. The letters often are critical evaluations of articles published in recent issues of the same journal. The author of the original article usually writes a rebuttal. These exchanges do not have a fixed format, and they generally do not have subheadings.

Theses, **projects**, and **dissertations** have a fixed format, but academic departments and universities often have their own variations of a general format. The formats of these documents contain certain unique aspects, such as an approval page, a table of contents, and a copyright authorization page. However, the body of the text, references, figures, tables, and appendixes may be prepared according to one of the widely accepted publication styles, such as that of the APA.

A **research proposal** typically is not published. Research proposals are made to various government and private agencies that financially support research. Each agency has its own guidelines and formats within which the proposals should be prepared. Those who seek funds should strictly follow these formats and guidelines. To demonstrate their knowledge of research methods and scientific writing styles, graduate students taking seminars on research methods may be required to write a research proposal.

Authors in communicative disorders, including student writers in most educational and clinical programs, are expected to follow the APA format. The American Speech-Language-Hearing Association (ASHA) uses the APA format for its journals. Therefore, the *Manual* should be studied carefully in preparing manuscripts. To begin with, the *Manual* gives a brief description of the content and organization of manuscripts. In subsequent chapters, it gives comprehensive guidelines on the format of research articles. There are guidelines on punctuation; spelling; capitalization; use of italics; abbreviations; the arrangement of headings and subheadings; quotations; the use of numbers; the metric system; preparation of tables and figures; the reporting of statistical and mathematical formulas; footnotes and notes; citations of printed, digital, and other kinds of publications; and the reference list. In addition, the manual also gives detailed instructions on how to prepare a manuscript.

Structure and Content of Research Papers

Writing an article to describe a piece of empirical research is the prototype of scientific writing. An investigator who can write an acceptable report generally can write other kinds of articles and proposals, with necessary modifications. Sections such as *introduction, review of literature,* and *discussion* are common to most types of scientific writing.

Various scientific and professional organizations also have published the journal article reporting standards that must be followed. These standards specify the kinds of information that must be included within the accepted format of research papers. The American Psychological Association has published the *Journal Article Reporting Standards for Quantitative Research* regardless of research designs used (Appelbaum et al., 2018) and *Qualitative Primary, Qualitative Meta-Analytic, and Mixed Methods of Research* (Levitt et al., 2018). There are several other reporting guidelines. For example, the *Consolidated Standards of Reporting Trials* (CONSORT) (Schulz, Altman, & Moher, 2010) applies particularly to randomized clinical trials (RCTs) in medicine. It includes 25 items an author is to consider in writing an RCT report for publication. PRISMA, the *Preferred Reporting Items for Systematic Review and Meta-Analyses* (Moher, Liberati, Tetzlaff, & Altman, 2009), has 27 specifications the author should consider.

It is not our goal to reiterate all that is published in various reporting standards. We highlight some major aspects of both the structure and content of research articles. Before preparing their reports, authors should consult the reporting standard that apply to the article they plan to write. For most authors, the APA reporting standards may be appropriate. Those who conduct randomized clinical trials may wish to consult the APA standards and one of the other standards published in medical journals (e.g., the CONSORT or the PRISMA).

Title Page

The title page contains the **title of the article**, the **author's name** and **institutional affiliation**, and a **running head**. The title of an article should be brief and to the point. Long and wordy titles conceal the essence of a paper and thus may fail to draw reader attention. It is best for the title to specify the experimental variables that were investigated. For example, the title *The Effect of Time-Out on Stutter-*

ing specifies both the dependent and the independent variable studied. The title is also direct, brief, and self-explanatory. The APA *Manual* limits the title to 12 words.

The author's name is written on a separate line, starting with the first name, the middle initial, and last name. Words such as *by* or *from* are not added to the author's name. Titles and degrees also are omitted. The name of the institution and the city where the study was conducted is written on a separate line below the author's name. If there is no institutional affiliation, only the name of the city is written.

An **author note** is typed below the author/affiliation lines, centered on the title page. Below the "Author Note" are the: (1) address of the department; (2) changes, if any, in affiliation since the research was completed; (3) acknowledgments and any special circumstances including conflicts of interest; and (4) mailing address and the e-mail of the contact author. Each of these elements takes a separate paragraph.

An abbreviated version of the title is typed flush left at the top of each page, preceded by the term *running head*. The running head is printed flush left on all pages of the published article. Using the automatic function of *headers* in the word processor, the page numbers are typed right-justified on the top of each page, including the first page.

Abstract

Scientific articles require an abstract, which is written on a separate page. A good abstract will attract the reader to the whole article, whereas a bad one may turn the reader away. Therefore, it is important to write an abstract with an attractive style. The APA *Manual* requires the abstract to be accurate, concise and specific, nonevaluative, and coherent and readable. It should highlight the problem investigated, the methods, the procedures, the results, and the main conclusions. An abstract may contain abbreviations with explanations (except in the case of standard, literal abbreviations such as *vs.*). To save space, it is written in active voice (but without the personal pronouns *I* or *we*). All numbers except those that start a sentence should be written in digits. Quotations are typically avoided in abstracts. The APA *Manual* suggests a range of 150 to 250 words for abstracts, but each journal may have a specific limit. Scientists follow the journal policy in preparing their abstracts.

Introduction

The text of the paper starts with an introductory section without a heading. This initial section of a paper introduces the reader to: (a) the general area of investigation, (b) the general findings of past investigations, (c) the specific topic of the current investigation, (d) selected studies that have dealt with the topic in the past, (e) the problems and limitations of past studies, (f) some of the questions that remain to be answered, and (g) the specific problem or research questions investigated in the present study.

The opening sentence introduces the reader to the broad area of which the present investigation is a part. In most cases, the problem of the study is not stated at the outset. The reader is prepared for the problem by an initial description of the general area and the findings of the past studies. For example, if the investigation to be reported is about a particular language treatment procedure designed to teach specific morphological features,

the introductory section may first make a few statements about research on language treatment in general, and some of the relevant studies and their results may be summarized or cited. The writer then introduces the specific topic that helps focus on the investigation. In our example, the research on teaching morphological features would be highlighted. Past studies that are especially relevant to the topic investigated may then be reviewed in some detail. Methods and procedures of selected studies on teaching morphological features would be reviewed. Finally, the author brings the problem investigated into sharper focus. The introduction may end with a formal statement of the research problem or problems.

A well-written introduction moves from the general to the particular. The initial general framework helps the reader place the investigation in a proper theoretical, conceptual, and methodological perspective. With each additional paragraph, the writer takes the reader closer to the particular research question investigated. A smoothly written introduction does not need a separate section called *rationale* or *justification*. The entire introductory section should make clear to the reader the need for the study and the reasoning behind it.

A critical part of the introduction is the review of the past studies. A well-written review justifies the study and sets the stage for it. The review summarizes the major findings of past research. It may be critical, because in many cases, a study is undertaken because of the limitations of past studies. In some cases, the same question may have been researched, but inadequately. In other cases, a new method the author has used may be expected to prove more effective than previous methods in studying a phenomenon. In still other instances, the problem may not have been conceptualized at all in the manner of the investigation to be reported. Therefore, a critical analysis of the past research often justifies an investigation.

The critical review should be fair and objective. Its tone should not be judgmental, emotional, or polemical. Nevertheless, it should be direct. The limitations of past studies should be stated honestly and unambiguously; that is, the literature review should not be an exercise in diplomacy. Some investigators can write critical reviews more tactfully than others, but tact should never conceal valid criticisms that help advance the cause of knowledge.

The introduction to a direct or systematic replicative study does not involve much critical assessment of past studies and their methodologies. Direct replication studies need very brief introductions, mainly to justify the need for replication. Systematic replication studies do this and also describe the specific ways in which the present study is different from the original study.

The review of literature should point out the logical or empirical relation between the past studies and the present research. It should show how the study is built upon the past evidence and methodology. It is good to remember that a vast majority of research questions are hinted at or directly suggested by past studies. Knowledge is both continuous and evolving; utterly original studies are often the stuff the junior scientist's dreams are made of. Therefore, the past studies are not criticized to show that the present study is so original that it bears no relation to other studies or present knowledge. Instead, the review should show how the present study is conceptually and methodologically related to the past

research while also pointing out its innovative aspects.

Toward the end of the introduction, the research question is formally stated. Hypotheses, if proposed, may be stated at this point. The research questions and hypotheses should be written in direct, clear, and terse language.

Method

The second section of a research article describes the method of the study. How the study was conducted is described in detail so that a reader can evaluate its appropriateness to investigate the research questions. The description should be specific enough to permit a replication of the study by other investigators.

At the outset, the approval of the institutional review board (IRB or the Human Participants Protection Committee) may be stated. In randomized clinical trials in medicine, an additional board, called the Data and Safety Monitoring Board (DSMB), is formed and described in the report. While the IRBs review the study and approve the procedures before the study is begun, DSMBs monitor safety of drugs being evaluated and the integrity of data being collected throughout the course of the study. The DSMB may make recommendations to the principal investigators any time during that course.

The method section of an empirical study has at least three subsections: *participants,* the *apparatus* or *materials,* and the *procedure.* Additional headings may be used when necessary. For example, clinical treatment studies may describe the *pretreatment measures* or *baselines, treatment procedures,* and *probe* or other *posttreatment* procedures under separate headings.

Reports of multiple experiments are also likely to have additional subsections.

Participants

The participant characteristics, number, and selection procedures are described in this subsection. Studies in communicative disorders describe the participants' age, gender, health, geographical location, family background, and communicative behaviors. In most cases, studies provide detailed information on the participants' speech, language, voice, fluency, and hearing. Other relevant characteristics may be described.

The number of participants who were initially selected and who eventually completed the study should be specified. In a group design, the number of participants assigned to different groups also should be described.

The participant selection procedure should be described in detail. What was the sampling procedure? Was it a random sample? Were the participants randomly assigned to the different groups? Were the participants selected because of easy access? Was the investigator trying to achieve a sample representative of the population? Were they clinical participants who were seeking professional services? Were there criteria by which potential participants were excluded from the study? How were the participants screened? Were the individuals paid for their participation? Were the participants aware of their group membership in treatment studies or were they blinded (unaware of their own treatment or control group membership)? These are some of the questions that are answered in describing the participant selection procedure. Study approval of the IRB should also be mentioned in this section.

Measures and Measurement Instruments

In this section, the physical setting in which the study was carried out and the equipment and materials used are described. Institutions or places where the data were collected are described. In a treatment study, the clinic name and the room dimensions where the sessions were held also are described.

In treatment research studies, whether those who measured the dependent variables for treatment effects were masked (blinded) or not must be specified. Masked investigators are unaware of the experimental or control group membership of participants they evaluate for changes in the dependent variable. In most speech and language treatment studies, it is not possible to mask the investigators who measure treatment effects because the effects are readily seen, but masking is critical in medical treatment research.

Instruments and materials used in measuring the dependent variables of the study are described fully. How the variables were measured and the kinds of measures obtained are clearly specified. The name, model number, and the manufacturer of the instruments used should be specified, however. Instruments include standardized tests whose full names are given with references. Custom-made or rarely used instruments should be described in detail. If needed, drawings, photographs, and additional descriptions may be given in an appendix.

Research Design

Whether the study was observational, correlational, longitudinal, normative, survey, or experimental is specified in the method section. Whether group or single-subject design, the more commonly used designs may be simply mentioned by name and referenced, but an uncommon design may be described in greater detail.

The different experimental conditions of the single-subject design or the different groups of the group design used in the study must be described in detail. How groups of participants were treated differently or how the separate conditions of an experiment differed from each other should be specified. Finally, how the reliability of the data was established should be described.

Experimental Manipulations and Treatment

In experimental studies, how the independent variable (treatment) was manipulated and measured should be described in detail. The duration of each treatment session and the frequency of those sessions should be specified. The intervention technique should be described in sufficient detail to permit replication by other investigators.

Instructions given to the participants, if they are unusual, may be described verbatim. The setting in which the treatment was delivered should be clear to the reader. Who treated the participants, what were their qualifications, and what level of study-specific training was given to them need to be described. If language other than English was used in treatment sessions, that should be specified.

Results

This section opens with a brief statement of the problem investigated and the general findings of the study. An overview of the results is followed by a detailed presentation of quantitative, qualitative, graphic, and tabular presentation of the findings.

In the results section, the findings are reported without interpretations and evaluations. Quantitative data may be presented concisely in tables. Baseline or pretest data may be compared and contrasted with the results for experimental sessions or durations. The changes noted in the dependent variables across baseline and experimental conditions are better represented graphically. Group design studies do not report individual data, but single-subject designs do. Tables and graphs should supplement, not duplicate, the text.

The kinds of statistical analysis performed on the data should be described. In randomized clinical trials, data missing for various reasons (e.g., participant dropout, control participants crossing over to treatment) may be analyzed with the **intention-to-treat** method in which missing data are estimated ("imputed") and included in the final analysis (Fisher et al., 1990). In this method, all randomized persons are included in the analysis even when there are no observed data for them. Analyzing data from those who received the treatment and stayed until the end of the study is called the **as-treated analysis** or **per-protocol analysis**. In either case, the number of participants dropped out or (in medical research) died must be reported. The reasons for dropout and missing data must be described.

The traditional inferential statistical tests are typically reported in terms of their value, the probability level (the p value or significance level), and degrees of freedom when appropriate. The meaning of the obtained statistical value is also briefly stated. **Effect size** estimates and confidence intervals for those estimates may be reported (see Chapter 10 for statistical analysis of experimental data).

In all treatment research reports, treatment fidelity should be evaluated and reported. *Treatment fidelity* refers to the adequacy of treatment delivery as described in the method section. The researcher should present evidence that the treatment was indeed delivered as planned and that the clients or patients adhered to the treatment protocols. External observers may be employed to evaluate whether the treatment protocols were strictly followed. Negative side effects, if observed, should be carefully described.

The results section may have subheadings (e.g., *Experiment 1, Experiment 2*). It may also have subsections in which different kinds of data are reported (e.g., *Treatment 1, Treatment 2*). In organizing the results of a study, the student should consult the APA *Manual* and the manuscript submission guidelines of the journal to which the author plans to submit the paper for publication.

Discussion

In the discussion section, the author points out the meaning and significance of the results. The section opens with a brief statement of the problem and the results of the study and proceeds to discuss the theoretical and applied implications of the findings. The results of the study are related to the findings of previous investigations. In this section, the problems and limitations of the study also may be pointed out, along with suggestions for further research.

A well-written discussion places the results of the study in the larger context of past research on the issue at hand. Ide-

ally, a discussion is an integrative essay on the topic investigated, but it is written in light of the data generated by the study. The similarities between present and past findings are highlighted, as are the differences. When the results are consistent with past findings, the discussion will give a coherent, possibly advanced, picture of the phenomenon investigated. When the results contradict previous findings, the author may discuss possible reasons. Methodological problems and differences typically explain such contradictions.

The discussion should answer the research questions posed in the introductory section. The author should try to answer them as directly as possible. The answers may be positive or negative, but they should be stated clearly. Possibly, the author may say that the results failed to answer the questions. In any case, vagueness and hedging should be avoided. It is possible, though, that the results of a study do not support a strong and direct answer. In such cases, some authors prefer to be vague and tentative. Even then, a direct statement that the results were ambiguous is preferable to vagueness that leaves the reader confused.

Null or alternative hypotheses, when proposed by the author, are supported or refuted in the discussion section. Clarity and directness are important here, too. Some authors may be reluctant to admit that their hypotheses were not supported by data, and the discussion may therefore be vague or distorted. There may be reasons to suspect the results, however. If so, the reasons may be clearly stated, along with better tests of the hypotheses. Even then, the author should state unambiguously that the results obtained did not support the hypotheses.

A common problem in many discussions is a labored effort to explain the results, especially when the results are unexpected from a particular viewpoint. Excessive speculation results. Such speculations are typically so far removed from the results that the discussion and the results seem disconnected. Why the results were the way they were is an interesting question, but it should not lead to unnecessary speculation. The best approach is to describe implications that are close to data. Obviously, data that cannot be explained need further study. Speculation will not explain them unless it is verified by additional experiments.

Discussion of Single-Subject Studies and Multiple Experiments

Discussion of single-subject studies and those of multiple experiments is handled differently. In a single-subject study, a common discussion section is appropriate as long as the research questions and methods were common across the participants. However, sometimes a single-subject study may involve more than one experiment, each with single or multiple participants. The questions researched with various participants may be different though closely related. Such may be the case within a group study as well, and then it is better to write the discussion separately for the experiments. In this case, brief discussion follows the results of each experiment. However, at the end, a general discussion of the experiments taken as a whole is also needed. Different experiments are a part of a single study mainly because they are related in some conceptual and methodological manner; therefore, a common discussion is needed to suggest the significance of the results and their interrelations.

Discussion of Treatment Effects

Discussion guidelines described so far apply to treatment research studies as well. However, there are some special considerations in discussing the results of treatment research investigations.

Obviously, the main point of discussion of treatment research results is to state whether the intervention was found to be effective or not. An unambiguous conclusion may or may not be supported by the data; therefore, it is necessary to discuss the limitations of the results obtained. It is important to discuss the internal validity of the results reported. If the experimental controls were good and the treatment was found to be effective, discussion might suggest acceptable internal validity of the results.

Another significant point of discussion is external validity or generality. The extent to which the results may be generalized should be made clear. The limits of such generalization should be pointed out. The researched treatment may be applicable only to a narrowly defined group of individuals, or it may have wider applicability. The technique also may be inappropriate to clients of certain characteristics. Furthermore, clinical significance, practicality of the technique, its efficiency, and cost-effectiveness also may be discussed. Additional variables to discuss include measured treatment outcomes and extent of follow-up. Finally, limitations of the technique and the future research needs may be mentioned.

References

Within the body of a paper, references support statements the author makes about past investigations and the views of other authors. The authors and their works cited in the text are listed in the reference list and placed after the discussion section.

The citations in the text and the reference list should match perfectly. There should be no citation in the text that is omitted from the reference list, and there should be no reference that is not cited in the text.

A reference list should not be confused with a bibliography. A reference list contains only those studies that are cited in an article. Studies not mentioned in the text, no matter how relevant, are not included in a reference list. A bibliography, on the other hand, is a comprehensive list of published studies on a particular topic or area of investigation. One can prepare a bibliography without writing an article, but a reference list is always a part of an article.

All professional and scientific journals specify the reference list format for authors. As noted earlier, ASHA journals use the APA style, but other journals may have their own styles. Authors should prepare the reference list according to the accepted format of a journal to which they plan to submit their articles.

Appendix

Appendixes provide information that cannot be integrated with the text. For example, a new test protocol, detailed description of a new equipment, and drawings of certain stimulus materials may be provided in an appendix.

Appendixes are used more frequently in dissertations, theses, and projects than in research articles. Raw data on individu-

als or groups of participants, instructions, papers relative to human participant protection, and details of statistical analyses may be placed in appendixes.

Writing Without Bias

Scientific writing is objective in that it is free from bias. It avoids words and expressions that unfavorably reflect upon individuals and groups. Stereotypic and prejudicial expressions about genders, individuals with disabilities, minority and ethnic groups, and differing sexual orientations and gender identity may be found in some everyday expressions. Persons who do not necessarily share the implied sexism or racism may utter them. Nevertheless, such expressions are offensive and inappropriate in everyday usage as well as in scientific writing. In their pursuit of knowledge, scientists are committed to fair treatment of individuals and groups of persons and must not use language that implies bias.

Among the biases that can creep into writing, racism and sexism are probably the most common. Racist expressions in describing participants and in exploring the meaning of research findings should be avoided. If it is necessary to identify participants as belonging to particular ethnic or cultural groups, terms that are nonevaluative should be used. The best practice is to select the terms the groups use to refer to themselves in formal writings and discussions. Such expressions as *culturally deprived* or *disadvantaged* have a pseudoscientific connotation, but they are also biased. They imply that one culture is the standard against which other cultures are evaluated. For example, in communication disorders, the expression *Standard English,* more preferably described as the *Mainstream English*, is often contrasted with *Black English* or forms of English influenced by a primary language. Standard English implies that the language spoken by one group is the standard by which the language spoken by the other group is judged. (This is the reason why the term *Mainstream English* is preferred.) Another mistake made by many writers is to describe foreign languages they know very little about as *dialects.*

Many expressions that imply sexism are a part of long-established traditions of language usage, and therefore, they may not be easily recognized as sexist. One of the most inappropriately used personal pronouns is *he.* It is often used to refer to any child, student, customer, or client. Indiscriminate use of male personal pronouns may imply that all executives, doctors, nurses, firefighters, engineers, supervisors, department heads, garbage collectors, or professors are male. A frequently misused noun that implies sexism is *man.* It is the *man* who searches for knowledge, achieves great things, and provides the workforce. It is *mankind* that experiences great problems or solves those problems. In cases such as these, other terms, including *human beings, people, persons, humanity,* and *humankind,* are appropriate. (See Hegde, 2018, for additional examples.)

Besides implying bias, indiscriminate use of certain words may create ambiguity. The word *men* in a given context may refer to people of both sexes or only to male persons. Therefore, words should be chosen for their particular relevance, not because of their habitual usage. This will help avoid both bias and ambiguity.

The APA *Manual* suggests that in describing clinical populations, it is the person, not the disability, that should come first. For example, the term *a person who stutters* is preferable to *a stutterer.* In reporting empirical studies, the classic term *subject* should be replaced with *participants* because the individuals who participate in research studies play an active role.

The APA *Manual* contains additional guidelines on writing without bias and ambiguity. The American Speech-Language-Hearing Association has adopted similar guidelines. Multiple exemplars of bias-free writing may be found in Hegde (2018).

Good Writing: Some Principles

A format of research articles, such as the one discussed earlier, may not necessarily ensure good writing. While adhering to an accepted format, scientific writing should be good writing. Good writing involves an understanding of both structural principles and conceptual considerations.

Structural Principles

Grammar specifies the structural principles of language. The term *grammar* includes the morphological as well as the syntactical aspects of language. In addition, one also should consider punctuation. Minimally, good writing is grammatically correct. Many books on writing include basic information on rules of grammar and correct contemporary usage of language (Bates, 2000; Butterfield, 2015; Hegde, 2018; Kirszner & Mandell, 2002; Morris & Morris, 1992; Strunk & White, 1999; Thomas & Turner, 1994).

Though it is not the purpose here to review rules of grammar, it is necessary to point out a few common problems that should be avoided in writing research papers. There also are some guidelines that are not a matter of correct or incorrect grammar but rather of preference.

Sentence Structure

By definition, a sentence is grammatical: It is correct and complete. Therefore, the writer should avoid sentence fragments that result from a lack of certain grammatical features or inappropriate punctuation.

Missing grammatical features create sentence fragments of the following kind:

✗ **Incorrect:** The group was scheduled to come to the laboratory on Monday. *But got there on Tuesday.* (The subject is missing in the second sentence, making it a fragment.)

✓ **Revised:** The group was scheduled to come to the laboratory on Monday but got there on Tuesday.

✗ **Incorrect:** The author finally found the participants. *In the Psychology 10 class.* (The fragment has no verb.)

✓ **Revised:** The author finally found the participants in the Psychology 10 class.

Many problems arise when punctuation marks are used to break strings of words at inappropriate junctures. For example, a subordinate clause, which needs an independent clause, should not be punctuated as a sentence:

✗ **Incorrect:** The testing was completed in two sessions. *Because the instrument broke down.* (The

subordinate clause is punctuated as a sentence.)

✓ **Revised:** The testing was completed in two sessions because the instrument broke down.

Similar problems arise when a prepositional phrase, a verbal phrase, an absolute phrase, an appositive, a compound sentence, or an incomplete clause is punctuated as a sentence. None of these can stand alone as sentences. An example of each illustrates these problems:

✗ **Incorrect:** The dysfluency rate of person who stutters decreased dramatically. *In the final two sessions.* (The prepositional phrase is punctuated as a sentence.)

✓ **Revised:** The dysfluency rate of person who stutters decreased dramatically in the final two sessions.

✗ **Incorrect:** The experiment had 50 participants. *Divided into two groups.* (The participial phrase, a type of verbal phrase, is punctuated as a sentence.)

✓ **Revised:** The experiment had 50 participants. They were divided into two groups.

✗ **Incorrect:** The participants were eight men. Their speech characterizing severe stuttering. (An absolute phrase is punctuated as a sentence.)

✓ **Revised:** The participants were eight men. Their speech was characterized by severe stuttering.

✗ **Incorrect:** The participants were tested in a sound-treated room.

A room that was especially built for the experiment. (The appositive is punctuated as a sentence.)

✓ *Revised:* The participants were tested in a sound-treated room, a room that was especially built for the experiment.

✗ **Incorrect:** Many persons with aphasia have word-finding problems. *And may also find it difficult to remember names.* (The second part of the compound sentence is punctuated as a separate sentence.)

✓ *Revised:* Many persons with aphasia have word-finding problems and may also find it difficult to remember names.

✗ **Incorrect:** Regulated breathing, a highly researched technique known for its effectiveness with young children who stutter, which is developed by Azrin and associates. (The subject *Regulated breathing* has no predicate.)

✓ *Revised:* Regulated breathing, a highly researched technique known for its effectiveness with young children who stutter, was developed by Azrin and associates. (Relative pronoun *which* was deleted; the predicate *was developed* was added.)

Many grammatically incorrect sentences can be rewritten in different ways because the same idea can be expressed in different forms. Therefore, the revised versions of incorrect sentences are only illustrative.

Generally, the longer the sentence, the easier it is to make a mistake in its structure and the harder it is to find the miss-ing element or confusing feature. Shorter, simpler sentences are preferable because they reveal their problems somewhat easily. Such sentences also are easy to understand. However, many times transition words (such as *but, so, or*, etc.) that show relations between thoughts and sentences prevent ambiguity and keep the text from seeming fragmented.

Verbs

It is preferable to use verbs in their *active voice*. Active voice is more direct and emphatic than the passive voice. Active voice is also brief.

✗ **Passive:** The children were brought to the clinic by their mothers.

✓ *Revised:* The mothers brought their children to the clinic.

However, *passive voice* may be preferable when the agent of an action is unimportant or unknown:

✓ **Correct:** An increased prevalence of stuttering in the female population *was reported* in the literature.

Most scientific papers are written in the *past tense*. Reports of empirical studies review past studies and describe a completed study. Therefore, the *review,* the *methods,* and the *results* are reported in the past tense.

✓ **Correct:** Smith (2015) reported similar findings.

✓ **Correct:** Ten adults who stutter were selected.

✓ **Correct:** The scores of male and female participants were the same.

When reporting something that began in the past and continues into the present, the present perfect tense is used:

- ✗ **Incorrect:** Since the invention of the audiometer, all audiologists used it.
- ✓ *Revised:* Since the invention of the audiometer, all audiologists *have used* it.

- ✗ **Incorrect:** Over the years, behavioral scientists replicated Skinner's findings.
- ✓ *Revised:* Over the years, scientists *have replicated* Skinner's findings.

It is preferable to write the discussion section in the present tense:

- ✓ **Correct:** The data suggest a need for further research.
- ✓ **Correct:** The result shows that it is better to use both the treatment procedures.
- ✓ **Correct:** One conclusion of the study is that reduced rate of speech affects the frequency of dysfluencies.

Agreement

Agreement between various elements of a sentence is one of the critical tests of grammatically correct sentences. Mistakes often are made in this case. Participants and verbs must agree in number and person, whereas pronouns and their antecedents must agree in number, person, and gender. See Hegde (2018) for more examples.

Singular subjects take singular verbs and plural subjects take plural verbs:

- ✓ **Correct:** The *result is* questionable.
- ✓ **Correct:** The *results are* reliable.

In simple and direct sentences, it is easy to see a mistake in subject-verb agreement that may be less conspicuous in complex sentences. Mistakes are likely when intervening phrases are included in a sentence. For example:

- ✗ **Incorrect:** This *result,* also reported by many past investigators, *are* not consistent with the theory.
- ✓ *Revised:* This *result,* also reported by many past investigators, *is* not consistent with the theory.

- ✗ **Incorrect:** These *techniques,* when used appropriately by a competent clinician, *is* known to be effective.
- ✓ *Revised:* These *techniques,* when used appropriately by a competent clinician, *are* known to be effective.

Intervening phrases that include *as well as, along with, in addition to, including,* and *together with* do not change the number of the subject:

- ✗ **Incorrect:** The *accuracy* of phoneme productions as well as the rate of correct responses *increase* during treatment.
- ✓ *Revised:* The *accuracy* of phoneme productions as well as the rate of correct responses *increases* during treatment.

- ✗ **Incorrect:** Error *scores,* along with the correct sore, *was* used in the analysis.

✓ *Revised:* Error *scores,* along with the correct score, *were* used in the analysis.

Generally, compound participants joined by *and* have plural verbs (e.g., Mother *and* child *were* interviewed together). Exceptions are when an expression, though containing *and,* suggests a single concept or individual:

✓ **Correct:** Who says country *and* western *is* dead?

✓ **Correct:** The president *and* chief executive officer *is* Mr. Smith.

Additionally, a singular verb is used when *each* or *every* precedes a compound subject joined by *and:*

✓ **Correct:** *Each* test and measurement procedure *was* pilot-tested.

✓ **Correct:** Every *child* and adult *goes* through the same procedure.

When two subjects are linked by *or,* *either/or,* or *neither/nor,* the verb should be plural if both the subjects are plural and singular if both subjects are singular:

✓ **Correct:** *Either* verbal praise or informative feedback *is* combined with modeling.

✓ **Correct:** *Either* verbal reinforcers or tokens *are* combined with modeling.

However, when a singular and a plural subject are linked by *neither/nor,* *either/or,* or *not only/but also,* the verb form is determined by the subject that is nearer to it:

✗ **Incorrect:** Neither the treatments nor the *result are* replicable.

✓ *Revised:* Neither the treatments nor the *result is* replicable.

✓ *Revised:* Neither the treatment nor the *results are* replicable.

✗ **Incorrect:** Not only the instruments but also the *procedure are* described.

✓ *Revised:* Not only the instruments but also the *procedure is* described.

✓ *Revised:* Not only the instrument but also the *procedures are* described.

A few indefinite pronouns (*both, many, several, few, others*) are always plural and therefore take plural verbs. Most others (*another, anyone, everyone, each, either, neither, anything, everything, something,* and *somebody*) are singular and therefore take a singular verb:

✓ **Correct:** Both of us are busy.

✓ **Correct:** Only a few were interested.

✓ **Correct:** Anyone is acceptable, providing the subject selection criteria are met.

✓ **Correct:** Something was missing in that procedure.

✓ **Correct:** Everything is fine.

✓ **Correct:** Either of them is acceptable.

However, some indefinite pronouns such as *some, all, none, any, more,* and *most* can be singular or plural. The verb form is singular or plural depending upon the noun the pronoun refers to:

✓ **Correct:** None of the *participants were* pretested.

✓ **Correct:** None of the *techniques was* correct.

✓ **Correct:** Some of this *effect is* understandable.

✓ **Correct:** Some of the *techniques are* useless.

Collective nouns also take singular or plural verbs. A collective noun that refers to a single unit takes a singular verb; one that refers to individuals or elements of that unit takes a plural verb:

Singular: The *group* was tested in a single session.

Singular: The *number* of participants was small.

Plural: The *members* of the control group were tested separately.

Plural: A number of *participants* were absent.

As a general rule, *the number* is singular, and *a number* is plural. But phrases that refer to fixed quantities (*majority, three-quarters*) are collective nouns:

Singular: *The majority* was against the idea.

Plural: *A majority* of people were against the idea.

Singular: *Three-quarters* of the amount is withheld.

Plural: *Three-quarters of those* completing the treatment improved significantly.

Some subjects that are typically in the plural form still take singular verbs:

✓ **Correct:** The *news is* bad.

✓ **Correct:** *Statistics is* but one method of data analysis.

✓ **Correct:** *Economics is* not an exact science.

✓ **Correct:** *Politics* does not thrill me.

However, when words like *statistics* refer not to a *set* of techniques but to certain *data,* a plural verb is appropriate:

✓ **Correct:** The *statistics show* that the treatment of aphasia is successful.

Certain nouns have unusual plural forms and should not be used with singular verbs:

Plural: The baseline *data were* recorded on a separate sheet.

Singular: The *datum is* as solid as it can be.

Plural: Such *phenomena were* not observed.

Singular: The same *phenomenon was* not reported.

Plural: The *loci* of stuttering *were* highly varied.

Singular: The *locus* of response control *was* shifted.

Plural: The *theses were* too long.

Singular: The *thesis was* completed on time.

In popular writing and newspaper articles, *data* may be treated as singular. The singular form, *datum,* is rarely used for this reason. In scientific writing, however, *data* is always plural. A few other words have dual plural forms, though one of them may be preferred. For example, *appendices* and *appendixes* are the two plural forms of *appendix,* but *appendixes* is the preferred form in scientific writing. Similarly, both *indices* and *indexes* are acceptable plural forms of *index,* but *indexes* is preferred.

In using a linking verb, it is important to make sure that the verb agrees with its subject. A typical mistake is to make the verbs agree with the subject complement.

✗ **Incorrect:** The *problem were* the instruments.

✓ **Revised:** The problem was the instruments.

Correct Use of Modifiers

Modifiers connect ideas while adding information. In a sentence, the word or phrase to which a modifier refers should be clear. A *misplaced* modifier (an adjective or an adverb) refers to a wrong word or phrase in a sentence. A *dangling* modifier does not modify any word or phrase in a sentence.

Misplaced modifiers confuse the reader by not specifying which word or group of words is being modified (Hegde, 2018). This is more likely to happen when the words that are modified and the modifiers are too far apart.

✗ **Incorrect:** The author and her assistants tested the hearing of all participants using the procedure described earlier. (Who used the procedure is not clear.)

✓ **Revised:** The author and her assistants, using the procedure described earlier, tested the hearing of all participants.

✓ **Revised:** Using the procedure described earlier, the author and her assistants tested the hearing of all participants.

✗ **Incorrect:** Distant and mysterious, he stared at the sky. (Who or what is distant and mysterious?)

✓ **Revised:** He stared at the sky, distant and mysterious. (The sky is distant and mysterious.)

Generally, it is better to place modifiers immediately before or after the words or phrases that are modified. Certain modifiers (*only, hardly, simply*) should be placed before the words they modify. Different placements will change the meaning of sentences:

✗ **Incorrect:** The past studies *only offer* limited solutions to this problem.

✓ **Revised:** The past studies *offer only* limited solutions to this problem.

✗ **Incorrect:** The participants in Group 1 scored a mean of 23.9 but the participants in Group 2 scored *only a mean* of 14.6.

✓ **Revised:** The Group 1 participants scored a mean of 23.9 but the Group 2 participants scored a *mean of only* 14.6.

✗ **Incorrect:** The implications *are simply* not clear.

✓ **Revised:** The implications *simply are* not clear.

✗ **Incorrect:** The results *hardly are* impressive.

✓ **Revised:** The results *are hardly* impressive.

Sentences with *dangling modifiers* should be rewritten to include words or phrases that are indeed modified:

✗ **Incorrect:** Several additional effects are observed *using this technique.* (The modifier has no reference in the sentence.)

✓ *Revised:* Several additional effects are observed in *clients* using this technique.

✓ *Revised:* Several additional effects are observed when *therapists* use this technique.

✗ **Incorrect:** Using the standard procedure, the participants were screened for hearing problems by the experimenter.

✓ *Revised:* Using the standard procedure, the experimenter screened the participants for hearing problems. (The experimenter, not the participants, used the standard procedure.)

✗ **Incorrect:** Consistent with past studies, Johnson and Williams (1985) found that their female participants performed better than the male participants.

✓ *Revised:* Johnson and Williams (2018) found that their female participants performed better than the male participants. This result is consistent with that of past studies. (The result, not Johnson and Williams, is consistent with past studies.)

Parallel Forms

Sentences expressing parallel ideas can be especially troublesome. Parallel ideas should be expressed in the same grammatical form: words, phrases, clauses, or sentences (Hegde, 2018). Parallel forms are used for emphasis, clarity, and variety. Such forms help maintain continuity of ideas. When used judiciously, parallel forms add force to writing. They also facilitate conciseness. Many parallel forms require a careful use of coordinating conjunctions: *and, but, or,* and *nor.*

✓ **Correct::** The author studied books, charts, and tables.

✓ **Correct:** The clients found the procedure complex but useful.

✓ **Correct:** The experimental participants were either adults or children.

✓ **Correct:** The responses were neither correct nor adequate.

Parallel forms are necessary in expressing paired ideas:

✓ **Correct:** His comment was brief but forceful.

✓ **Correct:** Stuttering is aversive, but silence is painful.

✓ **Correct:** We analyzed immediate generalization and subsequent maintenance.

✓ **Correct:** The more clients you treat, the more you learn.

✓ **Correct:** The treatment phase was over; the maintenance phase was beginning.

Parallel forms also can help highlight contrast or opposition between paired elements in a sentence:

✓ **Correct:** It is better to directly treat stuttering in children than to merely counsel their parents.

✓ **Correct:** Establishing target behaviors is easier than making them last.

Several mistakes result in faulty parallelism. A common mistake is to write the different terms of a parallel construction in different terms:

✗ **Incorrect:** In the past, many people who stutter had received inadequate treatment because the therapists lacked adequate training, supervised experience, and *the therapists' knowledge of stuttering has been limited.* (The final element in the list is nonparallel.)

✓ **Revised:** In the past, many people who stutter had received inadequate treatment because the therapists lacked adequate training, supervised experience, and *scientific knowledge of stuttering.* (Parallelism is restored.)

Another mistake is a failure to repeat a parallel element in a series that signals the parallelism. The result is a broken pattern. Such sentences should be revised to restore parallelism:

✗ **Incorrect:** Persons with communication disorders have difficulty talking, reading, and *self-confidence.* (The final element is not parallel with the previous elements.)

✓ **Revised:** Persons with communication disorders have difficulty *talking, reading,* and *maintaining* self-confidence. (All three elements are parallel.)

✗ **Incorrect:** Some of the side effects of punishment are aggression, emotionality, and the *client may*

also learn to punish others. (Mixed constructions.)

✓ **Revised:** Some of the side effects of punishment are *aggression, emotionality,* and *imitative punishment.* (Parallelism is restored.)

✗ **Incorrect:** Differential reinforcement helps maintenance by *not* allowing a rapid extinction, increasing the response strength, and improving the chances for generalization. (*Not* does not apply to all the elements in the series.)

✓ **Revised:** Differential reinforcement helps maintenance by not allowing a rapid extinction, by increasing the response strength, *and* by improving the chances of generalization. (The preposition *by* is repeated to prevent confusion between the elements in the series.)

Shifts Within and Between Sentences

Sentences and paragraphs must be consistent in tense, voice, mood, person, and number. Wrong or unnecessary shifts in them confuse the reader:

✗ **Incorrect:** The therapist *told* the client that she would not take him to outside situations unless he *maintains* fluency in the clinic. (There is a shift in the tense.)

✓ **Revised:** The therapist *told* the client that she would not take him to outside situations unless he *maintained* fluency in the clinic.

✗ **Incorrect:** The clinician *was* well trained. She *knows* how to treat a variety of communication disorders. Nevertheless, she *had* difficulty treating this particular client. (There is a shift in tense between the sentences.)

✓ *Revised:* The clinician *was* well *trained*. She *knew* how to treat a variety of communication disorders. Nevertheless, she *had* difficulty in treating this particular client.

✗ **Incorrect:** Van Riper first *developed* cancellation and later pull-outs *were also* developed. (There is a shift from the active to the passive voice; who developed pull-outs is not clear.)

✓ *Revised:* Van Riper first *developed* cancellation and later developed pull-outs.

✗ **Incorrect:** It is important that a client *possess* a digital recorder and *uses* it regularly to record his speech. (There is a shift from subjunctive to indicative mood.)

✓ *Revised:* It is important that a client *possess* a digital recorder and *use* it regularly to record speech.

✗ **Incorrect:** When *one* is reviewing the literature, *you* find that not many studies have been done on the issue. (There is a shift from second to third person.)

✓ *Revised:* When *one* is reviewing the literature, *one* finds that not many studies have been done on the issue.

("A review of the literature shows that not many studies have been done on the issue" is probably preferable to either of those sentences.)

✗ **Incorrect:** If a *client* does not attend at least 90% of the treatment sessions, *they* will not show signifi-

cant improvement. (There is a shift in number.)

✓ *Revised:* If a *client* does not attend at least 90% of the treatment sessions, *he* or *she* will not show significant improvement.

Punctuation

The student writer should consult other sources (Hegde, 2018; Kirszner & Mandell, 2002; Strunk & White, 1999) for a complete discussion of punctuation and mechanics. The APA *Manual* also covers the basic information on the correct use of the period, the comma, the semicolon, the colon, the dash, quotation marks, parentheses, and brackets. The student should learn to correctly use these elements of punctuation.

Other Structural Matters

The student should be familiar with other structural matters important in writing clearly and correctly. Such features as spacing, capitalization, italics, abbreviations, colon, comma, period, slash, titles and levels of headings, quotations, parentheses, numbers, metrication, tables, figures, reference citation, reference lists, and so on must be used correctly. The APA *Manual* has detailed information. Hegde (2018) has multiple exemplars of correct and incorrect usages relevant to scientific and professional writing in speech-language pathology.

Conceptual Considerations

A mastery of the principles of grammar, punctuation, and related matters will help the writer organize a piece of writing. Those principles are matters of structure necessary for correct and acceptable expressions. However, a mastery of those principles may not necessarily ensure concise, adequate, clear, and coherent writing. Despite a good command of the structural principles, a writer may find it difficult to write well. Such a difficulty typically is the result of conceptual, rather than structural, problems.

While most principles that govern matters of structure may be specified, conceptual matters can be discussed only in general terms. There are no finite and explicit rules that dictate conciseness, comprehensiveness, clarity, coherence, and an engaging style. These parameters of writing are often judged by a reader's response to a piece of writing. The writing is not concise if unnecessary words and expressions distract readers. The writing is not adequate if readers think that some information is missing. The writing is not clear if readers are not sure what is said. The writing is not coherent if readers become confused. The writing is not engaging if the reader stops reading. Good writing is effective. Therefore, good writing is often judged by its effects on the reader.

Knowledge of the Readership

A knowledge of the readership can help one write effectively. A main difficulty of writing is that the author knows what he or she wishes to say even without writing it out, but the reader does not know. The author will have no difficulty understanding his or her own deficient writing. Unfortunately, what is perfectly clear to the author may be ambiguous to the reader.

The writer should read his or her writing from the viewpoint of the reader. The writer should judge whether a reader *without* the knowledge of what is being said can understand the material. This

skill in reading one's own writing from the viewpoint of a naive reader is important for all writers.

The author should know the educational level of the readership. The extent of a readership's technical sophistication will determine the overall writing style, the number of examples given, and the amount of elaboration. Successful writers always know who their audience is and adjust their writing styles accordingly.

Concise Writing

Many first drafts are too long. Therefore, conciseness should be the main target for the second draft. If new sentences should be added, the writer should see whether a comparable number of sentences can be deleted. Long papers tend to be wordy, clumsy, redundant, and indirect. The writer can usually cut the number of words, phrases, and sentences to make a piece more readable. It is best to read what you have written with the assumption that the length as well as the number of sentences can be cut.

The writer should examine every sentence and judge whether it is necessary and whether it can be shortened. The meaning of a sentence should be understood by the reader at the first reading. A sentence that must be reread to be understood is probably too long, clumsy, or ambiguous. Shortening it may help achieve effective as well as concise communication. Most readers prefer shorter to longer sentences. Therefore, other factors being equal, the author is more likely to hold the reader's attention with shorter sentences than with longer ones.

Neither the sentence length nor the type should be monotonously uniform, however. There should be a balance between shorter and longer sentences.

Also, not all long sentences are necessarily difficult to understand; some longer sentences can be made more readable by breaking them up with chunking devices such as semicolons and dashes. Other longer sentences can be clear and direct without such devices. Longer sentences are sometimes necessary to express a complex concept. Also, when longer sentences are used sparingly and mixed with shorter ones, the reading becomes less monotonous.

Simple, active, declarative sentences are typically short and direct, but they can be dull, too. Therefore, an interesting piece of writing usually has a mixture of different types of sentences. Some sentence types, such as those using the passive voice, generally tend to be longer than other types. A shorter sentence type should be preferred as long as it is just as effective as the longer type.

Writing is not concise when it is redundant and wordy. Saying the same thing in different ways is sometimes necessary in teaching a difficult concept. However, when it seems necessary, the writer should check whether the clarity of the first statement can be improved. If a statement can be tightened up, a subsequent redundant statement can be avoided.

A typical redundancy is a result of saying the same thing in both positive and negative ways:

The female participants generally performed better than the males on the experimental task and the male participants' performance was inferior to that of the female participants.

The second clause says in negative terms what the first clause says in positive terms. One of them is unnecessary, and most experts prefer the positive sentence forms.

Some of the warning signs of potentially redundant statements are phrases such as *in other words, to put it differently, to repeat,* and *to reiterate.* What follows such phrases or clauses can be redundant, although in some kinds of writing (such as in textbooks), such repetitions serve a teaching purpose.

Some redundancy in talking and writing is necessary to facilitate a proper understanding of complex materials. In scientific articles and books, summaries and abstracts repeat what has been elaborated in the body of the text. Readers are better able to focus on the text when they are given the gist of the material at the very beginning. A summary at the end may help readers remember the main points of the text; such devices that reinforce a reader's understanding are not redundant.

Wordiness results when words that do not add any meaning at all are added to sentences (Hegde, 2018). Needless words and phrases and circumlocution cause wordiness. The result is an unnecessarily long sentence:

✗ **Wordy:** It seemed to the author that it is important to consider many factors in selecting a specific design for the study.

✓ *Revised:* Many factors were considered in selecting a design for the study.

In many cases, phrases such as *who were (are), which were (are), that is,* and *there were (are)* can be eliminated:

✗ **Wordy:** Eighteen persons who were living in rural areas were participants.

✓ **Revis**ed: Eighteen persons living in rural areas were participants.

✗ **Wordy:** Two instruments, which were in good calibration, were used in the study.

✓ *Revised:* Two instruments in good calibration were used in the study.

✗ **Wordy:** The study that is well known was done by Smith (2015).

✓ *Revised:* The Smith (2015) study is well known. Or, Smith's 2015 study is well known.

✗ **Wordy:** There were several factors that prompted the selection of only the male participants.

✓ *Revised:* Several factors prompted the selection of only the male participants.

Many standard phrases often used to initiate sentences can also be eliminated:

✗ **Wordy:** As far as the results are concerned, they appear reliable.

✓ *Revised:* The results appear reliable.

✗ **Wordy:** For all intents and purposes, the two treatment techniques are similar.

✓ *Revised:* The two treatment techniques are similar.

✗ **Wordy:** With reference to the Smith (2019) study, the methods were appropriate.

✓ *Revised:* The methods of the Smith (2019) study were appropriate.

Or, Smith's (2019) methods were appropriate.

✗ **Wordy:** In terms of its effects, the treatment was good.

✓ *Revised:* The treatment was effective.

Many words used as fillers are known as *utility* words (Kirszner & Mandell, 2002). Often, they are unnecessary:

✗ **Wordy:** It was actually a good study, but it did not produce worthwhile data.

✓ *Revised:* It was a good study, but it did not produce worthwhile data.

✗ **Wordy:** The deteriorating response situation was a problem.

✓ *Revised:* Response deterioration was a problem.

Certain needlessly wordy, though popular, phrases should be replaced with single words or shorter phrases:

due to the fact that	because
in spite of the fact that	though
on account of the fact that	because
at the present time	now
at this point in time	now
until such time as	until
used for the purposes of	used to (for)
the question as to whether	whether
have the ability to	be able to
hands on experience	experience

| in the event that | if |
| by means of | by |

See Hegde (2018) for additional examples of wordiness and means of revising them.

Certain other, longer, phrases include words with overlapping meanings. Such phrases can be reduced to single words or shorter phrases:

future prospects	prospects
advance planning	planning
absolutely incomplete	incomplete
exactly identical	identical
repeat again	repeat
each and every	each *or* every
totally unique	unique
uniquely one of a kind	one of a kind *(or* unique)
reality as it is	reality
solid (or actual or true) facts	facts
famous and well known	*either* famous *or* well known
three different kinds	three kinds

See Hegde (2018) for additional examples of redundant writing and means of correcting them.

Although concise writing is a virtue, writing that is too concise can pose problems for the reader. Depending upon the readership, some elaboration is necessary; that is, sometimes the same thing needs to be said differently. Examples duplicate what is said otherwise, but they are essential in any kind of writing. Therefore, conciseness should not supersede the purpose of effective communication. The final criterion is economical as well as effective communication.

Conciseness is an issue of degree, and different types of writing require various degrees of conciseness. Journal articles are written for specialists with technical knowledge and therefore are concise. Books are written for readers with different levels of formal and informal education, and therefore, have a greater range of style than journal articles. Theses, dissertations, term papers, and other pieces of writing that are expected to demonstrate a writer's knowledge of an area are more comprehensive than concise. Details are expected in these writings so that the knowledge of the writer can be evaluated. Though the instructor who evaluates the writing "knows what the student is talking about," the student should still furnish the details necessary for an evaluation.

Adequate Writing

Most books on writing do not emphasize adequacy. The typical mistake made by an established writer is to write too much rather than too little; therefore, books on writing tend to emphasize conciseness. On the other hand, beginning writers, especially student writers, tend to write too little rather than too much. Essay answers at the undergraduate and graduate may be overly restricted, and important information may often be missing in such restricted writings. The first drafts of theses and projects tend to omit necessary details, so many graduate students are asked to expand their first drafts to include missing details.

442 CLINICAL RESEARCH IN COMMUNICATION DISORDERS

Inadequate writing is as problematic as excessive writing. In scientific reports, theses, and essay examinations, the writing should be adequate. These pieces of writing are evaluated by other individuals. Those who read essay answers should judge whether the student knows the information requested. Inadequate answers are taken to represent inadequate knowledge. Students often complain that although they knew the material, they still got a poor grade; however, it is the students' *writing,* not their knowledge, that the instructor has access to. Therefore, answers should be adequate.

Scientific reports, including theses and dissertations, also are evaluated by other individuals. This evaluation is done to find out, among other things, if the procedures used were appropriate to answer the research questions and whether the results were reliable. To make this evaluation, the reader should have sufficient details about the procedures, results, and methods of analysis. The reader also should be given enough background information. An adequate overview of past research should be available in a report. Omission of significant details makes it difficult to evaluate the significance of a study.

Inadequate writing is one of the main reasons why certain scientific reports cannot be replicated. Insufficient information on the types of participants used, experimental manipulations, independent and dependent variables, and control procedures can make replication difficult for other investigators.

Clear Writing

Clear writing is important in both science and everyday life. When there is no clarity, there is no communication. Much worse, there may be serious misunderstand-

ing. Clear writing cannot be achieved by doing just one thing right. Several factors contribute to clarity. To write clearly, the author should avoid ambiguity, euphemism, jargon, clichés, colloquial expressions, and dead metaphors and similes. At the same time, the author should use the right words and exercise care in the use of abstract versus concrete words and figures of speech.

Ambiguity results from many structural problems of the kind discussed in some of the previous sections. For example, misplaced and dangling modifiers, faulty parallelism, inappropriate shifts within and between sentences, and wrong punctuation can make the meaning of sentences unclear. Structural accuracy, combined with directness and simplicity, will reduce ambiguity.

Unclear writing also may result from words and phrases that, for many reasons, do not convey the precise meaning to the reader. Euphemisms, clichés, colloquial expressions, and ineffective figures of speech are some the reasons for this lack of precision.

Avoid Euphemisms. Euphemisms are neutral or positive-sounding expressions that replace expressions with negative connotations. Several euphemistic expressions have become a part of everyday language. Homeless people are *residentially challenged,* poor people are *disadvantaged,* and older persons are *senior citizens.* Failing students are not dismissed but *counseled out,* and a student is not asked to retake an examination but is *given another opportunity to demonstrate knowledge.* Such euphemistic expressions hamper clarity.

Technical-sounding euphemisms can distort meaning in scientific reports. Instead of saying that some speech clinicians do not like to treat people who stutter because of lack of training, one may say that the treatment of stuttering is negatively affected by some clinicians' unfavorable attitude toward people who stutter. It is difficult to determine the meaning of this sentence, but it could possibly be that *the negatively affected treatment* is ineffective treatment, and *the clinicians' unfavorable attitude* may be a euphemistic reference to clinicians' inadequate training or incompetence. Intellectual honesty is an important aspect of scientific writing. Euphemism is anything but intellectual honesty and therefore has no place in scientific writing.

Avoid Jargon. Jargon is defined as the technical or specialized terms of a particular discipline as well as useless and incomprehensible vocabulary. Scientific reports cannot be written without technical terms. Technical terms are often preferable to lay terms because of the latter's imprecise and varied connotations. Therefore, jargon, in the sense of technical and specialized terms, cannot be altogether avoided in scientific writing. However, when a scientist or a professional person writes for the general public, extra care should be taken in the selection of words. Technical words should be used most sparingly and with enough explanations in everyday language.

Technical words should be used only when necessary, however. A nontechnical word may be preferred to a technical word if it conveys the same meaning with the same precision. For example, if the word *language* will do, there is no sense in using *linguistic competence*. Of course, there may be a reason to prefer *linguistic competence* over *language*, particularly when describing a certain theory. In essence, the use of every technical word should be justified.

The most debilitating form of jargon is pseudotechnical gibberish. Its sole purpose is to obscure the message and presumably impress the naive audience. Careful writers avoid this kind of jargon. Sometimes, acceptable jargon in one field may be befuddling nonsense that gives an air of pseudotechnicality in a different field. Speech-language pathology is full of this kind of borrowed and grafted jargon: *input, output, end gate, information processing, governor, filter, comparator,* and so on. Most of it is borrowed from engineering and computer science. The relevance of such jargon for speech-language pathology is mostly presumed and theoretical. In fact, unless there is a scientific justification, jargon borrowed from other disciplines is better avoided. It makes very little technical sense to say, *"The child seems to have processed the linguistic input as a single unit,"* when all that the child did was to point to the right picture when requested to do so.

Avoid Clichés. Standard phrases give brevity and clarity to writing. Minimal use of phrases such as *wear and tear* and *at its best* is acceptable. However, overuse of clichés (standard expressions that have become dull because of overuse) obscures writing. A piece of writing filled with standard phrases betrays the author's lack of creativity. Besides, many overused standard phrases have lost their precise meaning. As a result, the writing becomes vague. For example, a clinician who writes, "This technique is not my cup of tea," is not saying anything clearly. The statement means, among other things, that the technique is ineffective or that the clinician simply does not know how to use it. Or, when a clinician writes about the *dashed hopes and aspirations of parents of children with language disorders,* we do not know whom to blame for dashed hopes and aspirations.

Avoid Colloquial Expressions. With few exceptions, technical writing should not contain colloquial expressions. Colloquial expressions may not be appropriate in formal writing of any kind. In a scientific report, *the author feels that* is too loose and colloquial. The author's feelings are probably irrelevant in the context. *Feels that* should be replaced by *thinks that* or *believes that.* Similarly, *language* should be preferred to *tongue* and *stomach* to *tummy.* Other kinds of colloquialism to be avoided include contractions (*isn't, won't*); abbreviations such as *TV, phone,* and *exam;* and phrases such as *sort of, you know, get across,* and *come up with.*

An extreme form of colloquialism is called *slang* (e.g., *spaced out, uptight, for sure, rad*). They have no place in scientific writing unless this form of speech is itself the matter of investigation.

Avoid Dead Metaphors and Similes. These are expressions that were once colorful and effective but now are cliché. Expressions such as *dead as a door nail, a shot in the arm, off the beaten path, sit on the fence,* and *beyond a shadow of doubt* are best avoided in scientific writing. They are probably not useful in any kind of writing. In exploring the meaning and implications of scientific data, direct and nonmetaphorical use of language is essential.

Use the Right Words. Words with exact meaning should be selected over those that are too broad or vague in their meaning. In scientific writing, technical words offer more precise meaning than their counterparts used in everyday language. For example, in the behavioral science literature, *reinforcer* is a technical term, which should not be used interchangeably with *reward* or *award.*

Sometimes, when none of the everyday words serve the scientific purpose, a scientist may create new words to suggest a specific event or process. Such neologism is acceptable in scientific writing. However, neologisms of bureaucracy (including educational, scientific, and professional bureaucracy), the advertising industry, and business can only obscure the meaning of a message. Many neologistic verbs have been created by adding *-wise* and *-ize* to nouns, although many such expressions eventually become standard usage. A careful writer will not rush to use them. For instance, words such as *inferiorize, therapize, rigidize, gradewise, economywise,* and *timewise,* even if they are commonly used, are better avoided.

The careful writer should be aware of subtle distinctions in meaning of words. Many pairs of words are mistakenly used interchangeably. For example, in the following pairs of words, the meaning of each word is different: *disinterested* and *uninterested, alternate* and *alternative, anticipate* and *expect, continual* and *continuous, farther* and *further, imply* and *infer, stationary* and *stationery, economic* and *economical, historic* and *historical, affect* and *effect.* A dictionary or a thesaurus can help distinguish the meanings of these and other commonly confused words (see Hegde, 2018, for additional examples of commonly confused or misused words).

Select Abstract and Concrete Words Carefully. Abstract words refer to concepts and relations between concepts. Most abstract words may not stimulate the senses because they do not always refer to sensory experiences. Concrete words refer to things and events that may stimulate the senses. Such words help recall sensory images of all kinds. Therefore, concrete words are more direct and easier to understand. To be understood, abstract words require a certain level of conceptual understanding of the subject matter.

A general rule is that concrete words are preferable to abstract words. By generating sensory images, concrete words help the reader understand experiences the author has written about. Concrete words are especially useful in literary essays, journalistic reports, stories, and novels. These kinds of writings conjure up vivid images and sensations. Poetry, on the other hand, consists of many abstract words. That is why a serious poem is more difficult to understand than a novel or a short story: Undefined, abstract words lead to different interpretations. By not defining the abstract words used, the poet creates multiple meanings, which make a small poem a complex piece of writing.

Abstract words are useful in scientific writing. Scientific reports are typically about events and their relations, and many of these relations are abstract. However, unlike the poet, the scientist defines the abstract words precisely so that multiple meanings are not suggested. Many abstract words are found in the literature review and discussion sections of a scientific report. However, even in scientific reports, concrete words should be used in describing persons, things, and events. Participants should be described in specific terms (*12-year-old boys*) rather than in general terms (*young people*). Similarly, instruments, procedures, and results should be described in concrete terms.

Use Figures of Speech Sparingly. Figures of speech, including similes and metaphors, also help make the writing vivid to the reader. Similes suggest a similarity between two essentially unlike items (a

new house is *like* a black hole; it sucks in all your money). Metaphors equate two dissimilar things (*all the world's a stage*). Analogies describe a new concept in terms of a familiar concept (*the nervous system is like a telephone network*). Personification attributes human qualities to inanimate entities (*the dark clouds were looking mean and ferocious*).

Overuse of figures of speech can hinder direct and technical communication. Once again, they are more appropriately used in literary writings than in scientific reports. An exception is scientific writing meant for the general public, in which figures of speech can help readers understand complex ideas.

Some forms of figures of speech extend beyond single sentences. For example, *analogical reasoning* can be considered a figurative way of thinking about one subject matter in terms of another subject matter. Descriptions of the nervous system and its functioning in terms of computer networks (e.g., *inputs and outputs*) or the language of industry (e.g., *auditory signal processing*) illustrate this approach.

Coherent Writing

One writing problem often shown by student writers is incoherent writing. An essay or a review paper may lack a structure, an orderly progression of ideas and concepts, or smooth transitions from sentence to sentence, paragraph to paragraph, and section to section.

Some planning and thinking can improve the coherence of writing. The different sections of a paper and the contents of each section or topic should be determined first. Next, the sequence of these sections should be determined. Even though sections and contents of most scientific reports are relatively fixed, subheadings under these major sections vary. Therefore, some planning is needed to make scientific reports coherent and easy to understand. The sequences of sections, headings, and subheadings of articles with more flexible formats should be carefully thought out.

When sections and their contents are planned, an orderly progression of ideas can be achieved by using transitions between units of writing. The paragraph is the most important of these units. Each section or topic contains several paragraphs, and smooth transitions between them are essential to achieve coherent writing.

A single concept or a brief topic gives a paragraph its unity. For example, the age, socioeconomic status, and the occupational level of the participants used in a study may be described in a single paragraph. How the participants were selected may be described in a different paragraph because of a change in the idea or topic. If the selection criterion can be expressed in a single sentence, it may be a part of a larger paragraph. The basic rule is that a paragraph should have conceptual unity. Therefore, the beginning of a new paragraph suggests a transition to a new idea, topic, or subtopic.

Paragraphs should not be too long, nor should they (except rarely) consist of single sentences. Readers find lengthy paragraphs formidable, but a succession of very brief paragraphs can make the writing fragmented. A single-sentence paragraph is generally inappropriate, but it is acceptable on occasion; for example, single-sentence paragraphs can make a point emphatically or can highlight a transition to a new topic.

The first sentence in a paragraph usually suggests the topic or concept to be described in it (Hegde, 2018). If the paragraph continues with the same idea described in the previous paragraph, then a transitional sentence, which makes a reference to the previous paragraph, is needed. To achieve a smooth transition, a paragraph should begin as well as end appropriately. If the same general idea is to be discussed in several paragraphs, the end of each paragraph should be linked to the beginning of the next paragraph. Such linking can often be achieved by a common word or a phrase that is repeated in the final sentence of the previous paragraph and the first sentence of the new paragraph.

There are also many kinds of paragraphs; perhaps the most important are those that introduce or conclude a section or topic. Some topics should be introduced slowly, preparing the reader with a few sentences; other topics can be introduced without much background information. Each section or topic should begin with an introductory paragraph. The need for paragraphs that suggest conclusion is somewhat varied; they are needed at the end of major sections and topics but may not be needed at the end of subtopics. Complex and lengthy discussions almost always need paragraphs that give a summary.

So far, we have discussed concise, adequate, clear, and coherent writing. These qualities of writing require a competent conceptual handling of the subject of writing. The final point we need to discuss briefly is the matter of *style*.

Writing Style

A format is not the same as a *style* of writing. Organization and mechanics of writing is its **format**. Formats make writings of different authors more similar than different. But a style of writing makes writing unique and dissimilar. **Style** is the most individualistic of the aspects of writing. It is the style, not an adherence to the rules of grammar and other writing principles, that distinguishes one great writer from another. The style, among other qualities, separates Walt Whitman from Robert Frost, James Joyce from J. D. Salinger, and Maya Angelou from Arundhathi Roy. There are good styles and bad styles, but more important, each outstanding writer has his or her own unique style.

Grammatical correctness does not necessarily ensure a unique style. A piece of writing may be structurally flawless but boring because of a lack of style. A style is a writer's creative use of language. It is the distinguishing pattern of words that a writer creates to produce a unique effect upon the reader. Literary writers pay close attention to style. How a story is told is at least as important as what that story is. Scientific writers, on the other hand, generally tend to pay less attention to style. They concentrate more on technical, correct, clear, concise, and adequate writing. The meaning of a poem can be intentionally obscure, but the poem may still be hailed as important; obscure scientific articles generally remain obscure. Scientific writers restrict the reader response to particular meanings of words, whereas a poet or a novelist, as noted earlier, intentionally broadens the reader response by using words with multiple meanings and then by not defining them. Nevertheless, style is important in scientific writing. There is nothing wrong with the creative use of language in scientific writing when the author does not violate the principles of effective and accurate communication. In fact, a creative writing style can enhance scientific communication.

Some unreadable scientific writing may be so because of the authors' dull style.

Bold and novel use of language within the limits of scientific communication can improve the readability of most research papers. An excessive concern with structure and format makes scientific papers extremely formal and boring to read. Surely, a breezy and informal style is not appropriate for scientific discussions, but within the limits of seriousness, one can write with lucidity, style, and beauty.

Writing with a creative style that conforms to the rules of scientific and technical communication is one of the most difficult challenges writers in sciences and professions face. A lack of serious interest in good literature among many scientists and professionals may be one reason why most scientific writing lacks unique style; a study of good literature, ideally started early in life, would help scientists improve their writing style. Such a study should focus upon great writers of contrasting styles.

Writing and Revising

Writing correctly and with a good style is a matter of writing frequently and revising as often as necessary. Like any other skill, writing will not improve unless one writes. Good writing requires practice; very few writers manage to write very little yet extremely well. Most writers have to write, write, and write before they achieve a certain ease and style of writing.

The art of revising is very important for a writer. The writer is the first reader of what he or she writes and, therefore, should be the first critic of writing. The writer also begins as a mild critic of his or her own writing but should learn to be a stronger critic of that writing, at least privately and while revising.

Revisions and self-editing eventually refine a piece of writing. Self-editing requires a critical reading of one's own writing. Most writers, especially student writers, make the mistake of not having enough time to revise a piece before it is submitted for publication or evaluation, yet many problems of writing can be avoided simply by allowing enough time to make revisions of the first draft.

Even the most established writers revise their manuscripts several times. In fact, better writers revise more often than the mediocre. The final manuscript is vastly different from the original draft. It is best to wait few days after the original writing before attempting revision. A few good books on writing and comments from friends and colleagues can usually help in the revision process. Suggestions from persons not familiar with the subject matter can help improve the readability and clarity of technical papers, and suggestions from colleagues and experts can help improve scientific accuracy.

Summary

- Scientific and professional writers should follow an accepted format of writing. The format of the American Psychological Association is widely used and is accepted by the American Speech-Language-Hearing Association.
- Most scientific reports use the following structure:
  ○ Title page
  ○ Abstract
  ○ Untitled Introduction
  ○ Method
  ○ Results
  ○ Discussion
  ○ References
  ○ Appendix
- All writing should be free from gender, sexual orientation, racial, ethnic, cultural, and other kinds of biases. The writers should follow established guidelines on writing without bias.
- In reporting research articles of both qualitative and quantitative research, the author should use the published reporting standards, such as those by the American Psychological Association.
- Good writing requires that the author follow established structural principles.
- Good writing also requires:
  ○ Knowledge of the readership
  ○ Concise writing
  ○ Adequate writing
  ○ Clear writing
  ○ Coherent writing
- Authors should develop a unique writing style and reserve time to rewrite and revise everything they write.

References

American Medical Association. (2007). *American Medical Association manual of style* (10th ed.). Baltimore, MD: Williams & Wilkins.

American Psychological Association. (2010). *Publication manual of the American Psychological Association* (6th ed.). Washington, DC: Author.

Appelbaum, M., Cooper, H., Kline, R. B., Mayo-Wilson, E., Nezu, A. M., & Rao, S. M. (2018). Journal article reporting standards for quantitative research in psychology: The APA Publications and Communications Board Task Force report. *American Psychologist, 73*, 3–25.

Bates, J. D. (2000). *Writing with precision*. New York, NY: Penguin Books.

Butterfield, J. (2015). *Fowler's dictionary of modern English usage* (4th ed.). New York, NY: Oxford University Press.

Fisher, L. D., Dixon, D. O., Herson, J., Frankowski, R. K., Hearron, M. S., & Peace, K. E. (1990). Intention to treat in clinical trials. In K. E. Peace (Ed.), *Statistical issues in drug research and development* (pp. 331–350). New York, NY: Marcel Dekker.

Hegde, M. N. (2018). *A coursebook on scientific and professional writing for speech-language pathology* (5th ed.). San Diego, CA: Plural.

Kirszner, L. G., & Mandell, S. R. (2002). *The Holt handbook* (6th ed.). New York, NY: Harcourt College.

Levitt, H. M., Bamberg, M., Creswell, J. W., Frost, D. M., Josselson, R., & Suárez-Orozco, C. (2018). Journal article reporting standards for qualitative primary, qualitative meta-analytic, and mixed methods research in psychology: The APA Publications and Communications Board Task Force report. *American Psychologist, 73,* 26–46.

Moher, D., Liberati, A., Tetzlaff, J., & Altman, D. G. (2009). Preferred Reporting Items for Systematic Reviews and Meta-Analyses: The PRISMA statement. *PLoS Medicine, 6*(7), e1000097.

Morris, W., & Morris, M. (1992). *Harper dictionary of contemporary usage* (2nd ed.). New York, NY: Harper.

Schulz, K. A., Altman, D. G., & Moher, D. (2010). CONSORT 2010 statement: Updated guidelines for reporting parallel group randomized trials. *Annals of Internal Medicine, 152*(11), 726–732.

Strunk, W., Jr., & White, E. B. (1999). *The elements of style* (3rd ed.). Boston, MA: Pearson.

Thomas, F., & Turner, M. (1994). *Clear and simple as the truth: Writing classic prose*. Princeton, NJ: Princeton University Press.

Study Guide

1. Go to your department or university library and select a thesis prepared in your subject matter. Make a complete outline of the format of that thesis. Note the differences between the format of a research article published in a journal and the thesis.

2. Surveying a few journals in your subject matter, select (a) an article, (b) a report of an empirical study, and (c) a set of exchanges between two or more authors. Make an outline of these publications, retaining only the major headings. Note the similarities and differences in the formats of those three types of publications.

3. What are the characteristics of a good abstract? What is its usefulness in published papers?

4. Select a report of an empirical study from one of the journals you normally read. After having read the article, write an abstract of that report. Do not use the author's abstract. Later, compare your abstract with that of the author. Can you improve your version or the author's? If so, rewrite one or both.

5. Describe the seven factors that a well-written *introduction*

addresses. Find a published article whose introduction is well written because it includes those seven factors. Also, find an introduction that you think is not as well written. Justify your selection.

6. What are the standard subheadings of the Method section of a published empirical report prepared according to the APA *Manual*?

7. What does the discussion section of a technical paper contain?

8. Select: (a) two journal articles, one written by a single author and the other written by three or more authors; (b) one book edited by a single author; (c) one book written by a single author; (d) one book written by three authors; (e) a chapter published in an edited book; and (f) a thesis. Following the APA guidelines, prepare a *reference* list of these publications.

9. Distinguish between a reference list and a bibliography.

10. Select a paper you have written and critically evaluate the writing in terms of the common structural mistakes. Make sure the paper selected was not edited by someone else. Can you find faults with your own writing? Rewrite your paper to make it more effective and readable.

11. What are the conceptual considerations of good writing? What aspect of good writing seems to give you the most difficulty? How can you gain control over that aspect of your writing?

12. Give an example of the following: (a) euphemism, (b) jargon, (c) cliché, (d) colloquial expression, and (e) dead metaphor and simile.

13. What are figures of speech? Give examples. What is their place in scientific writing?

14. What is meant by the "style" of writing? Should scientific writings have a style? Justify your answer.

15. Write a two-page essay on your professional objectives. Put it aside for several days or a week. Then reread it and critically evaluate your writing. Rewrite your essay to make it more attractive. Have someone read and criticize it for you.

16. Identify two or three outstanding contemporary American writers of fiction, poetry, or essays. Select those known to have received critical acclaim (not necessarily those on the best-seller list). Read at least one book by each of the selected authors.

16

How to Evaluate Research Reports

Chapter Outline

◆ Professionals as Consumers of Research

◆ Understanding and Evaluating Research

◆ Evaluation of Research

◆ Evaluation of Research Reports: An Outline

◆ A Hierarchy of Treatment Research Evidence

◆ Evaluation and Appreciation of Research

◆ Summary

◆ References

◆ Study Guide

Research evaluation is an important task of scientists and professionals. Sometimes it is assumed that professionals who do not do research need not be concerned with its evaluation. This is a mistake because professionals, as consumers of research, need to determine the usefulness of research information they wish to use in their clinical practice. Because not all research studies are equally valid or reliable, clinicians should be critical consumers of research.

Professionals as Consumers of Research

Clinical practice and research can influence each other when clinicians understand and evaluate research and when researchers understand and investigate clinical issues. The clinicians must understand and evaluate clinically relevant research. Clinicians who can do this have a good chance of influencing the course of research so that the researchers will generate clinically useful data.

Clinicians who are not in touch with research are likely to perpetuate the use of less effective or ineffective assessment and treatment procedures. Such clinicians may also be the permanent victims of faddish changes in theory and practice. Acceptance of new research and theories regardless of their scientific merit can lead to an abandonment of proven procedures. A questionable promise of a "new and revolutionary" approach may discourage attempts at refining existing, satisfactory techniques. Such efforts are more economical than those needed to develop new techniques.

Uncritical clinicians are more likely to accept only the popular or forcefully promoted techniques. Those clinicians may fail to take note of the subtle, significant, and cumulative scientific progress in their subject matter. Clinicians who cannot appreciate research may be unable to contribute to their body of knowledge.

Understanding and Evaluating Research

To evaluate research, one must first understand it. Many students who read research reports find it difficult to understand them; there are many sources of this difficulty, and different students may find certain sources especially debilitating.

The first source of difficulty is lack of knowledge of the subject matter or the particular issue of a report. A grasp of the technical vocabulary and the necessary theoretical concepts is essential for understanding research. A piece of research can be evaluated only in the broader conceptual and empirical context in which it was done.

The second source of difficulty is lack of knowledge of the methods of investigation. The student needs to be familiar with the basic concepts of science, such as control, causality, and causal and other kinds of analysis. The student should understand the logic and the conditions of experimental manipulations. Knowledge of the methods of analysis, especially those of statistics, is essential in understanding many research reports.

The third source of difficulty may be lack of technical understanding of various aspects of research. Journal articles are typically written for technically competent readers. Because of space limitations and production costs, journal articles are rarely self-explanatory. Many concepts, procedures, design aspects, and theoretical backgrounds are mentioned only briefly on the assumption that readers are familiar with them. If the student is not already familiar with such elements, other sources should be consulted.

The fourth source of difficulty is lack of experience in reading research articles. Like doing good research, evaluating research takes experience. Students usually find that as they read more reports, the reports are easier to understand.

Students who understand research reports cannot necessarily evaluate them, however. Students may make satisfactory reports on journal articles; summarize the studies adequately; and understand the rationale, methods, results, and conclusions of particular studies. Nevertheless, students may find it difficult to evaluate the *reliability* and *validity* of the studies they seem to understand.

Students may uncritically accept the conclusions of methodologically defective studies, perhaps because they do not detect logical inconsistencies, faulty designs, questionable methods of analysis, and conclusions that the data do not warrant. Many instructors find that students need instruction and practice in evaluating research reports, and often students benefit from instructors' modeled evaluations. Some clinicians who try to read, understand, and evaluate research studies also experience similar problems.

Evaluation of Research

As pointed out by Sidman (1960), research studies are evaluated for the: (1) scientific importance of the data, (2) their reliability, and (3) their generality. These three evaluation objectives can be accomplished by a critical analysis of the conceptual background of a study, the research questions asked, the methods used, the procedures of analysis, and the manner in which the conclusions were drawn. This critical analysis also tries to place the study in the overall context of its subject matter.

Scientific studies can be subjected to two kinds of evaluation. We call the first the *internal consistency evaluation,* and the second, *the external relevance evaluation.* After describing these two types of evaluations in the form of an outline, we offer specific suggestions for evaluating research studies.

Internal Consistency Evaluation

The internal consistency evaluation is done within the confines of the study itself. The external relevance evaluation, on the other hand, is done to judge a study's importance in enhancing the knowledge within the subject matter. Before a study's relevance to the subject matter is determined, an internal consistency evaluation should be completed.

The **internal consistency evaluation** is concerned with the integrity of the structure of the study. This evaluation judges the study on its own terms. It is concerned with consistency in its purpose, methods, results, and conclusions. An important task in this evaluation is to determine whether the effects produced in a study were indeed due to the experimental manipulations (internal validity). Reliability of the results is also considered in the internal consistency evaluation.

The purpose of an investigation is an important criterion of internal consistency evaluation. A study is internally consistent only in relation to its purpose, including the questions asked and the methods needed to answer them. In judging the adequacy of the methods used, one cannot use absolute criteria. The methods of a study are adequate or inadequate to answer the particular questions of that study. As we have noted elsewhere, a design may be adequate to answer one type of question but inadequate to answer another type. A method of analysis may be correct for one kind of data but incorrect for another kind. Therefore, what the experimenter tried to accomplish in the study is an important basis for judging its internal consistency.

The type of question asked determines the experimental design. If the question is one of interaction between two or more variables, a factorial group or a single-subject interactional design should be used. A simple two-group design or an *ABA* design will not answer that question. When the purpose is to find a causal relation between two variables, a correlational method is not appropriate, but when the purpose is to find out if two variables covary, that correlational method is appropriate.

In most cases, methodological errors threaten the internal consistency of a study. In addition to selecting a wrong design to answer the research questions, the investigator can make other mistakes; for example, the participant selection procedure may be inappropriate. When a heterogeneous set of participants is needed or intended, the investigator may select a small number of available subjects. When homogeneous participants are needed, the selected participants may be heterogeneous. Participants may be matched only on some of the relevant variables. The selection criteria may be too stringent or too lenient. As a result, participants who are appropriate for the study may

be rejected and those who are not may be selected.

Mistakes in measuring the dependent variables, choosing instrumentation, arranging the experimental conditions, manipulating the independent variables, and building effective control procedures into the experiment can also hamper internal consistency. The pretest measures or the baselines of the dependent variables may not be reliable. The method of measurement may not be accurate. When a direct measure (frequency) of the response is required to answer the questions, only indirect measures (questionnaire responses) may have been obtained. The reliability of the instruments used in measurement may have been questionable or unknown.

Experimental conditions are a part of the design. Once the right design is selected, the required conditions should be arranged accordingly. Unfortunately, even after the right design has been selected, mistakes may be made in arranging the experimental conditions. For example, in a single-subject interactional design, more than one treatment variable may be changed across experimental conditions. The results then cannot be interpreted because of the confounding effects of multiple treatments.

Effective manipulation of the independent variables is necessary to achieve the goals of most experimental studies. Weak manipulation of the selected independent variable may fail to produce an appreciable effect. For example, a treatment variable applied only briefly may not provide an answer if the question is concerned with long-term effects. When an everyday experimental schedule is required, a twice-weekly schedule may be ineffective. The intensity of the independent variable may also be weak. The verbal *no,* for example, may be delivered in a weak, unsure, soft voice. An investigation on the effects of masking noise on stuttering may use only a 30-dB masking noise, which may be less than what is required to produce an effect.

The reader may recall from Chapter 7 that appropriate controls are necessary to establish the internal validity of an experiment. Internal validity ensures that the changes observed in the dependent variable are indeed due to the manipulations of the independent variables. In a treatment research study, the investigator must show that the treatment was better than no treatment. Internal validity can be achieved by various means, including a no-treatment control group, multiple baselines, reversal of treatment, and withdrawal of treatment. In the group design studies, mistakes in achieving equivalent groups are common. Was a population accessible for sampling? Were both random selection and random assignment of participants used? Was the matching done on all relevant variables? When answers to questions such as these are negative or doubtful, control procedures of a study will be judged inadequate.

In single-subject designs, the baselines may be too brief, unstable, or improving. Some of the baselines in a multiple baseline design may show changes without treatment. When the treatment is withdrawn in an *ABA* design, the effects observed earlier may not dissipate. These and other problems question the adequacy of control procedures and hence the internal consistency of a single-subject study.

Faulty analysis of results is another problem that thwarts the internal consistency of research studies. In group design studies, inappropriate statistics may be used in data analysis. For example, parametric statistical techniques may be used when the data warrant nonparametric statistics. In case of a pretest-posttest control group design, the pretest and posttest means of the experimental group may be compared with a *t* test and the corresponding means of the control group may be tested with another *t* test. Chapter 8 points out that this is an incorrect method of analysis.

In single-subject design studies, comparisons of nonadjacent experimental conditions may be made to demonstrate experimental effects. For example, an investigator who administers reinforcement for a desirable behavior in one condition may compare reinforcement and punishment for an undesirable behavior administered in another condition when these two conditions are separated by a baseline. This is a wrong procedure because in the evaluation of multiple treatment effects, only adjacent conditions can be compared.

Finally, mistakes are made in drawing conclusions from research studies. When faulty methods of analysis are used, wrong conclusions are inevitable. The most common of these mistakes is to draw conclusions that are not consistent with the results. The results may show weak experimental effects, but the author may conclude that the effects were strong. Much worse, experimental effects may be inferred when there were none. In the statistical approach, this mistake is known as a *Type I error* in which a null hypothesis is rejected when it should have been retained; in other words, a nonexistent treatment effect is asserted. On the other hand, an effect may be denied when there was one. In statistical analysis, this is known as a *Type II* error in which the null is retained when it should have been rejected; to put it differently, treatment was judged to be ineffective when in fact it was effective.

Many other mistakes are possible in the interpretation of data. Subtle distortions in data are thought to result from author's convictions that are not supported by the data. Some investigators have greater faith in their own convictions than in demonstrated empirical relations. In such cases, authors may try too hard to explain away conflicting results.

The effects of wrong statistical analyses and misinterpretations of results need not totally invalidate a study, however. As long as the report describes the results separately and completely, the methods of analyses and the author's conclusions can be separated from those results. The evaluator can come to his or her independent conclusions. A clear separation between the results and the author's conclusions is an important aspect of internal consistency evaluation. Beginning students often cannot make this distinction. They tend to equate "the study showed that" with "the author concluded that." Obviously, those who cannot distinguish the results from the wrong conclusions of a study will be misled by the author.

The reliability of the results of a study is often judged on the basis of the internal consistency evaluation. Though the author has reported acceptable intersubject and intrasubject reliability measures, serious mistakes in the implementation of a study are grounds for questioning the reliability of the results. There will be no assurance that if the procedures are properly implemented, the same results would be observed.

When internal consistency questions have been satisfactorily answered, external relevance evaluation becomes important. However, should the internal consistency evaluation reveal serious problems with the study, the external relevance evaluation is a moot issue. Unreliable results of invalid experimental operations never have external relevance.

External Relevance Evaluation

The **external relevance evaluation** determines the data's importance to the subject matter. The experimental data of a given study may be reliable and internally consistent, but their significance to the subject matter may still be limited. Do the data advance the cause of understanding the phenomenon? This is the question of external relevance evaluation.

Compared with the internal consistency evaluation, the external relevance evaluation is more *global*. This global evaluation is done at different levels or within different contexts. The importance of data is evaluated by placing them in the larger context of research on the phenomenon addressed by the study. In turn, the particular phenomenon is also placed in the context of the larger subject matter of which it is a part. The contexts in which the data are placed for evaluation may be multiple and ever increasing in scope. Data are placed first in the smaller context of the research questions asked by the study, then in the larger context of the topic of investigation, then in the still larger context of the subject, and finally in the context of the total subject matter. The number of contexts in which the data are evaluated depends on the scope of the questions investigated and the scope of the subject matter.

The multiple contexts of ever-increasing scope that are used in evaluating the importance of a research study can be illustrated with an example. Suppose that a study asks whether experimental teaching can alter the known normative sequence of morphological acquisition. Taking young children, the investigator teaches selected grammatical morphemes ahead of the developmental schedule and in a reversed order. The author concludes that it is possible to teach morphemes ahead of, and in a sequence other than, the normative sequence.

In making the external relevance evaluation of this study, the student first places the data in the context of studies on language acquisition. What kinds of studies have been done in the past? What is the significance of this study? Does this study use an approach that is different from the approaches of the past studies? Does it say anything new about the language acquisition process?

The significance of the study is evaluated next in the larger context of the analysis of language, not just language development. Does it offer a way of analyzing language behavior? Does the experimental method contribute anything new toward an understanding of language behavior in general? What kinds of theoretical statements do the results support?

In the third and still larger context, the significance of the data can be evaluated by judging their relevance to the treatment of language disorders. Are the data related to the clinical treatment of language disorders? Do they shed light on the selection of target behaviors? Do the results have implications for sequencing target behaviors in clinical treatment?

Finally, the study may be placed in the context of speech-language behaviors and disorders in general. Does it have implications for studying normal communication? Does it suggest that similar methods of analysis can be used in studying speech sound production or other norm-based behaviors? Possibly, the study can be placed in the still broader context of analysis of developmentally based behaviors of all kinds.

Another concern of external relevance evaluation is the *generality* of data. An internally consistent study may or may not have external generality. However, as noted in Chapter 6, no single study can ensure all kinds of generality because generality is a function of replication. Therefore, an evaluation of generality attempts to determine the potential for replication. The main question to be answered is whether the study is described in sufficient detail to make replications possible. The research questions, procedures, designs, and experimental variables should be described operationally. The study then can be replicated by other investigators in other settings using different participants. A report that does not describe its procedures (including the dependent and independent variables) in sufficient detail is evaluated negatively from the standpoint of replication and generality.

The external relevance evaluation is the more difficult of the two evaluations because it involves a value judgment. This evaluation asks simple questions that are difficult to answer: Is this study important, valuable, and relevant to the field of investigation? Does it make a significant contribution to the subject matter? These questions are difficult to answer for several reasons. First, students need to have broad scholarship in the subject matter to judge the overall significance of a study. Second, individual evaluators almost always judge the importance of scientific data from the standpoint of their personal perspectives. This is necessarily so because scientists who evaluate the scientific significance of their colleagues' data do not have a common set of criteria. What is an important criterion for one evaluator may be trivial to another evaluator. After a thorough discussion of the evaluation of scientific importance of data, Sidman (1960) said,

> If science is to use the importance of data as a criterion for accepting or rejecting an experiment, it should have a set of rules within which the scientist can operate when he has to make his evaluation. Do such rules actually exist? The answer is no. (p. 41)

Lack of objective rules and the subjective nature of evaluation of the external relevance of data suggest that we should be careful in rejecting any experimental data as unimportant. Negative evaluation of the external relevance of a study often is made on the basis of one's own theoretical biases and convictions arising from personal experiences. If the results are not consistent with such biases and convictions, a negative judgment may be rendered. However, this can be a bad practice because the value of certain experimental data can be independent of theoretical viewpoints and personal biases. This is true of the biases and convictions of both the evaluator and the original investigator. If it appears that the methods and procedures of a study were appropriate, the data whose significance is not clear should be afforded the benefit of doubt. The original investigator may have rejected such data because they did not support his or her preconceived ideas. An evaluator may think that the data are trivial because of narrow views. In such cases, the best course of action is to reserve judgment. Sound experimental data survive negative judgments of fellow scientists.

The difficulties involved in making external evaluation should not discourage us from trying, however. For both scientific and professional reasons, we should judge the importance of the studies we read. One should try to make the best possible judgment yet remain open to a different judgment. An uncritical acceptance of everything—perhaps desirable for personal reasons—is not helpful in advancing the science of a subject matter. Uncritical acceptance of scientific literature can be detrimental to the professional's integrity and to the progress of clients under treatment.

What follows is an integrated outline for making a summative evaluation of research studies. It includes questions of both internal consistency evaluation and external relevance evaluation.

Evaluation of Research Reports: An Outline

Before using this outline, the student should make sure that he or she is familiar with the subject matter and the concepts that serve as background to the study being evaluated. Also, the student should understand the general methods of the study, its research design, the concept of experimental control, internal and external validity, methods of statistical analysis, and statistical significance.

In evaluating a published research study, the student may first check to see if the report meets the journal article reporting standards described in Chapter 15. The American Psychological Association has published a set of standards (Appelbaum et al., 2018; Levitt et al., 2018). Published reports that do not meet the publication standards are hard to evaluate because critical information about some or all aspects of the methods, data, and data analysis may be missing. The following outline consists of a series of questions the student might answer in evaluating published research reports. The outline includes most of the critical questions the APA publication standards specify. By answering following questions, a student may take note of the deficiencies in reporting as well as problems in the study methods, execution, data analysis, and data interpretation:

I. Significance of the Problem Investigated (External Relevance)
   A. Was the problem investigated significant?
   B. Does the problem concern an important area of investigation?
   C. Does the problem, when answered, advance understanding of the relevant issues?
   D. Does the problem have basic (theoretical) implications, applied implications, or both?

II. Introduction and Literature Review (Internal Consistency)
   A. Was the introduction section clear and complete?
   B. Did the introduction help focus on the problem investigated?
   C. Does the literature review justify the study?
   D. Was the review objective, impartial, and appropriately critical?
   E. Did the review give a historical perspective if one was required to understand the investigation?
   F. Did the review point out the strengths and limitations of previous studies?
   G. Did the introduction place the research questions in the context of previous investigations?
   H. Overall, did this section make it clear why the study was made?

III. Statement of the Problem
   A. Was the problem stated clearly?
   B. Did the problem statement specify the variables in operational terms?
   C. Was the problem statement clear enough to permit a replication?
   D. If hypotheses were made, were they stated clearly?
   E. If there were no hypotheses, did the author specify the research questions?

IV. Methods
   A. Were the methods described clearly and adequately?
   B. Could one replicate the methods?
   C. What type of study was it? (See Chapters 4 and 5)
      1. A normative study?
      2. A standard group comparison study?
      3. An epidemiological study?
      4. A sample survey?
      5. An uncontrolled unreplicated case study?
      6. An uncontrolled directly replicated case study?
      7. An uncontrolled systematically replicated case study?
      8. A controlled unreplicated study?
      9. A controlled directly replicated study?
      10. A controlled systematically replicated study?

D. What was the design of the study?
 1. A single-subject case study or group case study?
 2. A nonrandomized group design?
 3. A randomized two-group design? If so, what kind?
 4. A randomized multigroup design? If so, what kind?
 5. A factorial design? If so, what kind?
 6. A time-series design? If so, what kind?
 7. Any other kind of group design? If so, what kind?
 8. An *ABA* or *ABAB* design? If so, what kind?
 9. A multiple baseline design? If so, what kind?
 10. The interactional design?
 11. The alternating treatments design?
 12. The changing criterion design?
 13. Any other kind of single-subject design? If so, what kind?
 14. Was the design appropriate for answering the research questions?
 15. Was the selected design used correctly?
 16. Were the experimental conditions arranged logically?
 17. Did the design include adequate controls?
 18. Did the control procedures rule out the sources of internal invalidity to a satisfactory degree?
E. Who were the participants?
 1. Did the author specify the number of participants and their selection and exclusion criteria?
 2. Did the author give a full description of the participants?
 3. Was the selection procedure adequate for the purpose and design of the study?
 4. How were the participants divided into experimental and control groups?
 5. Were the participants matched and, if so, on what variables?
 6. In a group design study, did the author use both random selection and random assignment?
 7. In a single-subject or small group study, were the participants homogeneous or heterogeneous? In either case, were the individual participants described in sufficient detail?
 8. In a clinical study, did the author describe the disorder, its history, and measured severity of the selected participants?
F. What kinds of instruments did the author use?
 1. Did the author describe the instruments and give their make and model numbers?
 2. Was information provided on reliability of the instruments used?
 3. Were there sufficient descriptions of the functioning of complex and new instruments used in the study?

4. Were the instruments selected appropriate for the purposes of the study?

G. Were the procedures described adequately?

1. What was the study location?

2. In a treatment study, did the author describe all the treatment steps (independent variables)?

3. Is the description of treatment detailed enough to permit replication?

4. How were the independent variables manipulated?

5. What was the frequency and duration of treatment sessions?

6. Did the author measure treatment fidelity? How?

7. What kind of probes or follow-ups were conducted?

8. What was the involvement of the family members, teachers, and others?

9. Was the treatment or teaching extended to nonclinical settings? If so, how?

H. What were the dependent variables?

1. Were the variables described in operational terms?

2. How were the variables measured?

3. How were the pretests and baselines established?

4. Were the pretreatment measures reliable?

5. Did the experimenter establish reliability and validity of the dependent variable measures? By what procedures?

6. Were the reliability indexes satisfactory?

I. Did the author describe the instructions given to the participants?

J. What were the stimulus materials?

V. Results

A. What were the results of the study? Were they described objectively and without evaluations and interpretations?

B. In a single-subject design study, did the author describe the results of individual participants separately?

1. Were the single-subject results visually represented?

2. Were the baseline data stable or otherwise acceptable?

3. Do the results show convincing contrast across the baseline, experimental, and other conditions?

4. Did the author describe data both qualitatively and quantitatively?

5. Did the author use statistical techniques in data analysis? Were they appropriate for single-subject designs?

6. Were the results clinically significant? Did the author report a clinical significance test appropriate for study design?

C. In a group design study, were the group performances clearly distinguished?
   1. In small group studies, did the author summarize individual differences in results?
   2. Did the author describe the group data qualitatively and quantitatively?
   3. What were the methods of analysis and were they appropriate?
   4. Did the author give descriptive statistics in sufficient detail?
   5. Did the author use the correct inferential statistical procedures?
   6. Did the author report the value of inferential statistical tests and their probability (p) levels?
   7. Were the results clinically significant? Did the author report a clinical significance statistic appropriate for the study design?
D. Were the figures, tables, and appendixes used effectively?
E. Was the overall data presentation orderly and logical?

VI. Discussion
A. Did the author discuss the results adequately? Did the discussion section examine the meaning and implications of the results?
B. Did the author try to answer the research questions in light of the data?
C. Did the author clearly state whether the hypotheses were supported or not supported by the data?
D. Did the author relate the observations to previous findings?
E. Did the discussion examine the theoretical implications of the results?
F. Did the discussion suggest applied implications? Were the applied implications specific enough? Can a clinician implement these suggestions in clinical practice?
G. Did the discussion suggest additional research questions?
H. Did the discussion summarize the problems and limitations of the study?
I. Did the author avoid excessive speculation, fruitless debates, and questionable attempts to explain the results?
J. Did the author accept negative findings?
K. Did the author suggest questions for future research?

VII. Reference List
A. Did the author follow the selected format in arranging the references? Was the reference list accurate?
B. Did the author list all references cited in the text and only those cited in the text?

VIII. Appendix
A. Did the author provide needed additional materials in the appendix?
B. Was the appendix section used prudently?
C. Was the appendix necessary and sufficient?

D. Did the author put additional material necessary to understand the study on the journal's website if one is made available?

The outline just given is not meant to be comprehensive. It is meant to alert the student to some important questions that should be answered in evaluating a research study.

Some evaluative questions, such as those concerned with the scientific importance of an investigation, are harder than others to answer. Also, it is better to do this evaluation after all other questions have been answered. If the study design is problematic and the procedures inadequate, then the larger questions of meaning and significance of the results may be irrelevant. Evaluating the introduction, literature review, and procedures requires conceptual as well as technical knowledge. Evaluating the discussion section also demands broad scholarship in the subject matter. Evaluation of data presentation, reference, and appendixes requires knowledge of the accepted format, such as that of the American Psychological Association.

As noted before, to evaluate is to judge. Though it may be difficult, the student should not hesitate in making judgments and checking them with those of others who are more knowledgeable.

A Hierarchy of Treatment Research Evidence

Evaluation of treatment research is a special concern for all practitioners. The outline of evaluation given in the previous section applies to all research, including treatment research. Nonetheless, a more succinct method of evaluating and classifying treatment research evidence is helpful. The clinician needs to make a quick judgment regarding whether the evidence offered in favor of a treatment procedure is acceptable and whether the evidence has any generality.

Often called the **levels of evidence**, there are several recommended ways of classifying treatment research evidence (some of them summarized at http://www.asha.org/Research/EBP/Assessing-the-evidence). The Oxford Center for Evidence-Based Medicine's levels of evidence is commonly cited and generally accepted (OCEBM Levels of Evidence Working Group, 2011). To help busy practitioners to make a "fast and frugal judgement" about treatment procedures, the OCEBM suggests the following five levels of treatment research evidence:

Level 1: Systematic review of randomized trials or N-of-1 trials

Level 2: Randomized trial or observational study with dramatic effects

Level 3: Nonrandomized controlled cohort/follow-up study

Level 4: Case series, case-control studies, or historically controlled study

Level 5: Mechanism-based reasoning

The inclusion of N-of-1 trials is a welcome change from the previous document because they are essentially single-subject design studies. Nonetheless, single-subject design research that is more common in communication disorders than in medicine is not explicitly included. In the

OCEBM terminology, cohort/follow-up studies track patients and healthy individuals for long durations. Case series are multiple case studies on the same topic, and case-control studies compare treated individuals with existing nontreated individuals (not to be confused with control groups in experimental studies). Historically controlled studies are case studies with an archival comparison group. Mechanism-based reasoning is nothing more than expert opinion.

There are also evidence levels that apply specifically to single-subject designs (Logan, Hickman, Harris, & Heriza, 2008). In the Logan et al. hierarchy, randomization is considered to provide better evidence even with N-of-1 and single-subject designs. Good quality results from randomized N-of-1 trials, single-subject alternating treatments designs, and multiple baseline designs are placed at Level 1 evidence. Nonrandomized *ABAB* design studies are not included in Level 1. They are placed at Level IV. *AB* case studies are at the lowest level. Logan et al. (2008) suggest that if the results in a single-subject design are replicated across three or more participants, settings, or behaviors, generalizability may be ensured. A limitation of this hierarchy is that it places too much emphasis on randomization, which is not a typical feature of all single-subject designs. Treatment may be randomized or semi-randomized only in multiple treatment evaluations.

As reported in the context of N-of-1 trials in medicine in Chapter 9, many researchers have repeatedly stated that clinicians cannot use the results of randomized clinical trials in treating their individual patients (Guyatt, Drummond, Maureen, Mead, & Cook, 2015). On the other hand, the results of single-subject experiments are applicable to individuals.

Nonetheless, the currently available levels of evidence have a randomized group design bias and a statistical significance bias, and they tend to exclude or downgrade evidence the single-subject designs generate (O'Donohue & Ferguson, 2006). Furthermore, current levels of evidence, including the well-known Oxford levels, are insensitive to replications—a critical variable in generalizable evidence. Even a single large sample randomized clinical trial may be at or near the top level. This is not acceptable. Therefore, clinicians urgently need new levels of evidence that are design neutral and include valid and replicated evidence generated by sound experimental methods regardless of research traditions. We describe Hegde's (2004, 2010) treatment evidence hierarchy that is design neutral and emphasizes experimental control and generality. Clinicians may conveniently use these levels to evaluate treatment research and select treatment procedures. This evidential hierarchy is based on the classification of treatment research described in Chapter 4: (a) uncontrolled unreplicated, (b) uncontrolled directly replicated, (c) uncontrolled systematically replicated, (d) controlled unreplicated, (e) controlled directly replicated, and (f) controlled systematically replicated. Each of these six types of treatment research produces a level or hierarchy of evidence for efficacy, generality, or both.

A clinician who comes across a treatment research study may classify it into one of these six types of research. The clinician can then determine the hierarchical level of evidence, the degree of efficacy demonstrated, and the extent of generality that may be claimed. However, if an article or an oral presentation on a treatment procedure was not based on any kind of empirical research, then it is best described as *expert advocacy*, not treatment research. Treatment procedures that are based on expert advocacy, not empirical research, should be greeted with cool skepticism until some kind of empirical evidence is marshaled in their favor.

Techniques based on expert advocacy should not be used in routine practice unless no technique has evidence in its favor. This is certainly not the case with most adult and child language disorders, speech sound disorders, stuttering, aphasia, and autism spectrum disorder. Treatment research evidence is emerging on other disorders (e.g., voice disorders, apraxia of speech, dysarthria, and traumatic brain injury). The clinician should deem it unethical to select a procedure based exclusively on expert advocacy when techniques with research evidence are available.

When a treatment procedure has undergone some level of empirical investigation, the clinician can apply the following hierarchy to classify the level of evidence and the extent of generality. In most cases, the clinician can find that evidence in favor of certain treatment procedures has reached a fairly high level in the hierarchy. Generally speaking, the clinician might also prefer a technique that has reached a higher level of evidential hierarchy compared to one that is placed at a lower level.

Level 1. Uncontrolled Unreplicated Evidence

A case study produced the initial level of evidence for a treatment procedure. There were not controls to show that the method, not something else, produced the changes in the clients who received a treatment.

- **Evidence.** Documented *improvement* in routine treatment or teaching; children have learned skills under this method; clients have improved with the technique.
- **Design Strategy.** Preexperimental: group designs (e.g., one-shot group, one-group pretest-posttest); single-subject designs (*AB* design).
- **Replication.** None (good potential).
- **Evaluation.** Improvement may be claimed but not effectiveness. Evidence is correlational but better than expert advocacy.
- **Recommendation.** The technique may be used with caution, claiming only improvement and keeping an eye for replications and controlled evaluations.

Level 2. Uncontrolled Directly Replicated Evidence

This second level of evidence is produced by an investigator who repeated his or her own case study. The same improvement has been documented a second time.

- **Evidence.** Uncontrolled treatment; improvement obtained by the same clinician with different clients.
- **Design Strategy.** Preexperimental.
- **Replication.** Direct; no change in methods, settings, or clinicians.
- **Evaluation.** Replicated improvement; still no evidence of effectiveness; good candidate for experimentation.
- **Recommendation.** Use the technique with caution, claiming only improvement and watching for systematic replications and controlled research.

Level 3. Uncontrolled Systematically Replicated Evidence

This level of evidence is produced by other investigators who applied a technique in different settings with different clients, possibly with some procedural modifications, obtaining a similar degree of improvement.

- **Evidence.** Improvement documented by other clinicians in other settings, possibly with methodological changes.
- **Design Strategy.** Preexperimental.
- **Replication.** Systematic; varied settings, clinicians, and clients.
- **Evaluation.** Still, only improvement is demonstrated; however, an excellent candidate for experimentation.
- **Recommendation.** Use it with caution, claiming only improvement and watching for further replications and controlled evaluations.

Level 4. Controlled Unreplicated Evidence

This is the beginning of controlled evidence for a treatment method. An experimental design has been used to rule out extraneous variables, thus establishing a cause-effect relation between the treatment and the changes it produced.

- **Evidence.** Treatment is demonstrated to be effective.
- **Design Strategy.** Group (e.g., pretest-posttest control group; posttest-only control group); single-subject (e.g., *ABA, ABAB,* multiple baseline designs).
- **Replication.** None (good potential).

- **Evaluation.** Cause-effect relation has been demonstrated; treatment is shown to be effective; however, generality has not been established yet.
- **Recommendation.** Use the technique with a greater degree of confidence; still be cautious because the effects have not been replicated; watch for replications.

Level 5. Controlled Directly Replicated Evidence

At this level, data for generality of a treatment procedure begin to emerge because the same investigator has repeated an experimental study on a treatment procedure.

- **Evidence.** Treatment effects demonstrated when the method is repeated under the original conditions.
- **Design Strategy.** Group and single-subject experimental designs.
- **Replication.** Direct; replicated by the same investigator in the same setting without procedural modifications.
- **Evaluation.** Treatment is not only effective but seems to have some generality as shown by the successful replication.
- **Recommendation.** Use the technique with a greater degree of confidence, watching for systematic replications that may produce supportive or contradictory evidence.

Level 6. Controlled Systematically Replicated Evidence

This is the highest level of evidence for effectiveness of a technique. Repeated studies have shown that the method (with or without modifications) is effective and that different clinicians in different settings can get the same or similar results.

- **Evidence.** Effectiveness as well as generality across settings, clients, and settings has been demonstrated.
- **Design Strategy.** Experimental group and single-subject designs.
- **Replication.** Replicated by different investigators in different settings with methodologic modifications.
- **Evaluation.** Replicated cause-effect relations; good generality.
- **Recommendation.** Select this technique as the best of the available alternatives that have not reached this level of evidence. If multiple techniques have reached this level of evidence, select the one that is easier to use, socially more acceptable, or more efficient (takes less time to produce the same level of effect).

To achieve a more thorough evaluation of treatment research, the clinician should combine the outline of evaluation given in the previous section with this treatment research evidence hierarchy. In combination, the two sets of guidelines will provide a comprehensive method of evaluating treatment research evidence.

Evaluation and Appreciation of Research

Clearly, the theme of this chapter is critical evaluation of research reports. Without counteracting that theme, we would also like to state that we should learn to appreciate research. A critical consumer of research is not necessarily the one who is always looking for the perfect study, or the one to condemn. Students working on research projects often think that their studies should be perfect in all respects. It is good to remember that a perfect study is more easily designed than conducted. Studies designed by even the best researchers are not likely to be perfect.

Because all studies tend to have some limitations, it is necessary to weigh those limitations against the strengths of a given study. In some cases, the conceptual or methodological limitations of a study can be so serious as to render the data worthless. A student should recognize such limitations. On the other hand, the limitations of other studies may be such that the results are still meaningful within those limitations. A student should recognize this as well.

The results of scientific studies on given issues can be arranged on a hierarchy of broad patterns and rough stages of progression. Some studies are uncontrolled, some have a certain degree of control, and others are more tightly controlled. The results of each of those studies should be evaluated in light of their limitations. For example, the results of a one-group pretest-posttest study or an *AB* single-subject study may indicate that a given treatment produced notable changes in certain client behaviors. That there was no control in the study is certainly a serious limitation, but the results may still be considered worthwhile. A conclusion that the treatment is worthy of further experimental manipulation is favorable as well as acceptable. On the other hand, an evaluation that the treatment and the changes in the client behaviors were causally related is favorable but not acceptable. The judgment that the results do not mean anything is unfavorable as well as questionable.

It may be helpful to distinguish serious *errors* in the design and implementation of a study from design *limitations* and acceptable *compromises* that are a part of any research study. Only serious errors in the design of a study (e.g., a wrong experimental design) invalidate the results. Design limitations and acceptable compromises, on the other hand, set limits within which meaningfulness of results can be interpreted.

It is possible to retain a critical outlook on research while maintaining enthusiasm for research. A critical outlook is not the same as a cynical outlook. After all, one who reads and evaluates research regularly should find some research interesting and stimulating. If not, there is no guarantee that that person will continue to read and evaluate research reports.

Summary

- Professionals are consumers of research. To provide good service, professionals should be knowledgeable and critical consumers of research.
- Technical knowledge of the field, the methods of research, and experience in reading and evaluating research reports are all necessary to evaluate research.
- Research evaluation is of two kinds:
  - Internal consistency evaluation: This is a critical analysis of the methods and procedures of the study and whether they were appropriate to answer the question investigated.
  - External relevance evaluation: This is a critical examination of the importance of the study and its implications for the discipline.

The overall significance of the study and the generality of the results are assessed in external relevance evaluation.

- It is best to use a prepared outline in evaluating research studies.
- Treatment research may be evaluated for the following six levels of evidential hierarchy:
  1. Uncontrolled unreplicated
  2. Uncontrolled directly replicated
  3. Uncontrolled systematically replicated
  4. Controlled unreplicated
  5. Controlled directly replicated
  6. Controlled systematically replicated
- It is important to evaluate as well as appreciate research.

References

Appelbaum, M., Cooper, H., Kline, R. B., Mayo-Wilson, E., Nezu, A. M., & Rao, S. M. (2018). Journal article reporting standards for quantitative research in psychology: The APA Publications and Communications Board Task Force report. *American Psychologist, 73*, 3–25.

Guyatt, G., Drummond, R., Maureen, O., Mead, M. O., & Cook, D. J. (2015). *User's guide to the medical literature: A manual for evidence-based clinical practice* (3rd ed.). New York, NY: McGraw-Hill Education/American Medical Association.

Hegde, M. N. (2004, July). *Levels of evidence: A design-neutral hierarchy.* Paper presented at the ASHA SID4 Leadership Conference, Portland, OR.

Hegde, M. N. (2010). New levels of treatment research evidence. *Journal of the Indian Speech and Hearing Association, 24*(2), 73–83.

Levitt, H. M., Bamberg, M., Creswell, J. W., Frost, D. M., Josselson, R., & Suárez-Orozco, C. (2018). Journal article reporting standards for qualitative primary, qualitative meta-analytic, and mixed methods research in psychology: The APA Publications and Communications Board Task Force report. *American Psychologist, 73,* 26–46.

Logan, L. R., Hickman, R. R., Harris, S. R., & Heriza, C. B. (2008). Single-subject research design recommendations for levels of evidence and quality rating. *Developmental Medicine and Child Neurology, 50,* 99–103.

OCEBM Levels of Evidence Working Group. (2011). *The Oxford 2011 Levels of Evidence.* Oxford, UK: Oxford Center for Evidence-Based Medicine.

O'Donohue, W., & Ferguson, K. E. (2006). Evidence-based practice in psychology and behavior analysis. *The Behavior Analyst Today, 7*(3), 335–338.

Sidman, M. (1960). *Tactics of scientific research.* New York, NY: Basic Books.

Study Guide

1. What is the difference between *understanding* and *evaluating* scientific reports?

2. Why should clinicians who are not expected to do research understand the research methods and concepts of science?

3. What kinds of difficulties do you, as a graduate student, face in understanding research articles? What can you do to overcome those difficulties?

4. What are Sidman's three criteria by which scientific studies are evaluated?

5. What is internal consistency evaluation? How is it done?

6. What is external relevance evaluation? How is it done?

7. Are there objective rules by which scientists can determine the scientific importance of data?

8. What is a treatment research evidence hierarchy? Describe it.

9. Select a journal report that you understand well. Make sure the report is of an empirical investigation (not a review or theoretical article). Using the outline of evaluation given in this chapter, evaluate the report. Have your instructor or someone knowledgeable take a look at your evaluation.

10. Select an article that reports on a treatment or teaching method. Evaluate it according to the guidelines given, combined with a treatment levels hierarchy, and determine the level of evidence it offers. Make your recommendation about the use of the method and justify your recommendation.

17

Ethics of Research

Chapter Outline

◆ Fraud in Scientific Research

◆ Ethical Justification of Treatment Evaluation

◆ The Protection of Human Participants in Research

◆ Ethical Issues With Treatment Research

◆ Consequences of Ethical Constraints

◆ Protection of Animal Subjects

◆ Dissemination of Research Findings

◆ Summary

◆ References

◆ Study Guide

The practice of science raises many ethical issues because science is both a personal and a social activity. Science is powerful: It can produce beneficial as well as harmful effects for people. It can improve lives and living conditions and cure diseases. Science can also create devastating effects on lives, as do weapons of mass destruction. The products of science can be beneficial when responsible individuals and agencies use them. But science can be dangerous in the hands of wrong people. Therefore, it is no surprise that such a powerful enterprise should operate under ethical constraints. Such constraints are welcomed by both scientists and nonscientists so that the practice of science does not adversely affect individuals and society.

Research is an ethical activity. Scientists seek knowledge, try to solve practical problems, design new methods of treating diseases and disorders, and try to develop new technological solutions that benefit humankind. But they also have the responsibility of doing all of this in an honest, responsible, open, and ethically justifiable manner.

Clinical research in medicine and human service professions raises some additional ethical issues. Treatment-related research can sometimes pose a dilemma concerning the client's right to receive prompt and appropriate treatment and the profession's need to evaluate effectiveness of new treatment procedures. Our discussion of ethical issues will consider the problems involved in clinical as well as nonclinical research.

In this chapter, we address seven fundamental ethical issues that affect research: (1) fraud in scientific research, (2) the ethics of treatment evaluation, (3) the protection of human participants, (4) the consequence of ethical constraints, (5) ethical issues with treatment research, (6) the ethical issues relative to animal subjects, and (7) the dissemination of research findings.

Fraud in Scientific Research

Scientists produce data and evidence about the behavior of natural phenomena. These data and evidence constitute our knowledge of those phenomena. Normally, the reliability and validity of this knowledge are judged on methodological grounds. The results of scientific observation and experimentation are tentatively accepted when the methods and procedures were appropriate and used correctly. Typically, faulty methods and procedures of research studies are the main source of questionable data. Data produced by defective methods may reflect on the competence of scientists who produce it but not their ethical conduct.

There is another source of questionable data, which is more difficult to determine—the personal conduct of scientists themselves. Both the scientific and the general community believe, most appropriately, that scientists are people with integrity. The observations scientists report are normally not suspected on personal grounds because it is believed that: (a) the data and evidence scientists report are a product of honest work, (b) the methods and procedures were indeed implemented the way they were described in the report, and (c) the reported quantitative values were observed and recorded during the study, as described procedurally.

A majority of scientists report only the findings of work they have done. Studies may have methodological limitations, but scientists try to implement the selected procedures in the best possible manner.

They record the quantitative values of the studied variables as truthfully as they can. Scientific misconduct and fraudulent research lack these qualities. A panel on scientific responsibility and the conduct of research formed by the National Academy of Sciences, National Academy of Engineering, and the Institute of Medicine defined misconduct in science as "fabrication, falsification, or plagiarism, in proposing, performing, or reporting research. Misconduct in science does not include errors of judgment; errors in the recording, selection, or analysis of data; differences in opinions involving the interpretation of data; or misconduct unrelated to the research process" (Panel on Scientific Responsibility and the Conduct of Research, 1992, p. 5). Fabrication is cooking up data and falsification is data distortion.

The history of science has documented several instances of fraudulent conduct by scientists in almost all disciplines. It is known that in 1912, an archaeologist reported the discovery of a human skull and jaw bone so different from the known forms of historic and prehistoric skulls that it forced scientists to think of a different evolutionary sequence. The skull came to be known as the "Piltdown man" because it was discovered in Piltdown Common, England (Campbell, 1976). However, during the 1950s, it became clear that a human skull and an ape jaw were used to construct the new find.

One of the better-known cases of possible fraud is that of the famous British psychologist Cyril Burt, who claimed that intelligence is mostly inherited. His evidence was that identical twins reared in different environments are still very similar in their intelligence as measured by standardized tests (Burt, 1972). His work had a significant effect on the prac-

tice of education and the study of intelligence and inheritance of behavioral traits. Because of his published contributions to science, Burt was widely recognized as an international authority on the genetics of intelligence. He received numerous prestigious awards and was knighted by the British government.

A shocked scientific community learned in 1976, mainly through popular press, that Burt may have falsified much of his data on identical twins and heritability of intelligence (Devlin, 1976; Gillie, 1976). The number of identical twin pairs he actually studied became questionable. The existence of several sets of identical twins Burt is supposed to have studied could not be documented. Whether he indeed had some of the research assistants mentioned in his publications also was questioned (Kamin, 1974). Because of these accusations, Burt's data have generally been excluded from any scientific discussion of heritability of intelligence. Nonetheless, experts believe that although Burt was somewhat careless in reporting empirical data, the accusations against him may be false and may have been engineered by overzealous environmentalists who believe that intelligence is largely determined by environmental influences; those who defend Burt and others with similar publications generally believe that intelligence is inherited, and some groups or races are more intelligent than others (Jensen, 1992).

A series of more recent publications that have been extremely influential on both sides of the Atlantic is that of British biomedical researcher Wakefield. In 1998, Wakefield and his colleagues reported a study in which they linked disintegrative psychosis, gastrointestinal diseases, and autism spectrum disorder to measles, mumps, and rubella vaccine (Wakefield et al., 1998). Several more publications linking the vaccine to autism spectrum followed. Many parents in the United Kingdom and United States took Wakefield's research as proof that vaccines were dangerous. A few years later, the venerable medical journal *Lancet* that had published his articles retracted them as being fraudulent or untrustworthy. Nonetheless, many parents in many countries still believe in a connection between vaccines and autism spectrum and refuse to get their children vaccinated. Retracted articles continue to be cited by others, reinforcing the use of discredited data (Granter & Papke, 2018). Unfortunately, once published, invalid studies have a long shelf life.

Plagiaristic practice of scientists is another serious problem. A review of misconduct in science conducted by the National Science Foundation found 20 allegations of plagiarism and 9 allegations of data fabrication in a total of 41 allegations (Panel on Scientific Responsibility and the Conduct of Research, 1992). Some scientists and professionals who plagiarize others' writings and publish them in their own name seem to survive surprisingly well. For instance, a medical scientist named Elias A. K. Alsabti had plagiarized already published articles and republished them under his own name. Nonetheless, he was successful in obtaining positions in at least seven universities and hospitals, although at each institution his actions were either suspicious or were documented to be plagiaristic. When he was asked to leave one institution, he easily and quickly found a position in another (Miller, 1992). A more recent and ironic instance of plagiarism was that a scientist had published a paper on plagiarism that was itself plagiarized! There have been instances when graduate students had submitted plagiarized papers written on *research ethics and integrity* (for these and other examples, visit retractionwatch.com).

How common are outright fraud in which data are completely cooked up and more subtle distortions, partial fabrications of evidence, selective suppression or deletion of data, deceptive data analysis, deceptive reporting of data, and such other forms of research misconduct? They are more common than thought. One way to find out is to track the number of retractions of previously published papers. Journal editors retract previously published papers when they determine that the papers contained fraudulent, fabricated, or otherwise untrustworthy data. A trustworthy website funded by respectable private foundations lists retracted papers and periodically updates the list (visit retractionwatch.com).

In their analysis of the number of retracted published papers, Azoulay, Bonatti, and Krieger (2017) found that 23,620 papers from 376 scientists published in journals between 1977 and 2007 were later retracted for researcher fraud or other kinds of misconduct. During the same period, 46,538 papers published by 759 scientists were never retracted. These are alarming figures. About 38% of papers published in peer-reviewed biomedical journals were later judged fraudulent and retracted by the journal editors. The true extent of fraud in research may still be unknown (Miller & Hersen, 1992; Ranstam et al., 2000).

In addition, inappropriate protection offered to human participants, inhumane treatment of animal subjects, and misuse of research funds also are parts of unacceptable research practices (Miers, 1998). In a survey of medical fraud, 51% of reporting biostatisticians closely associated with medical treatment evaluation studies in multiple countries knew of at least one fraudulent research study (Ranstam et al., 2000). It has been suggested that the incidence of fraud may be higher in epidemiological research (Ranstam et al., 2000). Fraudulent research is generally high in biomedical research. In another survey, 32% of scientists suspected fraudulent practices by their colleagues (Tangney, 1987).

Institutional procedures to deal with research fraud did not exist prior to 1980s (Miller & Hersen, 1992; Miers, 1998). Since then, there has been an increase in the number of reported scientific misconduct. One paper cites an average of two reports per month of potential misconduct received by a large federal agency that supports biomedical and behavioral research: National Institutes of Health (Miers, 1998). Various procedures to deal with research fraud now exist in most if not all universities, research institutions, and government agencies that support research (Panel on Scientific Responsibility and the Conduct of Research, 1992). Of lately, research institutions have required all researchers to take the Collaborative Institutional Training Initiative (CITI) online training modules, which review scientific ethics and procedure of institutional review boards (citiprogram.org). This training provides uniformity of experience in these important areas of responsible research.

There may be actual or felt pressure to produce certain kinds of data. Some scientists who are well known for their theories may be especially under this kind of pressure. It is not uncommon that a particular laboratory typically produces data that are consistent with one view, whereas another laboratory equally typically produces contradictory data on the same issue. It is believed that some hired research assistants are prone to distort the data they collect on behalf of professors and scientists whose theories are widely accepted (Diener & Crandall, 1978; Shaughnessy & Zechmeister, 1985).

As we discussed in Chapter 3, a scientist's public position in the form of theories and hypotheses can create pressure to uphold those positions regardless of the actual data. Instead of contradicting his or her previously stated positions, the scientist may resort to distortions in observations and interpretations of data. One way of avoiding the personally troublesome situation of having to contradict oneself is to refrain from prematurely committing oneself to a particular view.

Many scientists, however, will not hesitate to reverse themselves or modify their positions in light of new data. Scientists are expected to say only what their data suggest, and those who do so are the exemplary and should be emulated by students and other scientists.

A commitment to a view or a philosophy cannot be avoided forever, however. Accumulated experimental data have theoretical as well as philosophical implications that cannot and should not be ignored. Commitment to a particular view only after replicated experimental data have accumulated can reduce the chances of having to contradict oneself.

Particular viewpoints and experimental data can be questioned inappropriately. In such cases, defense of those viewpoints and data is appropriate. A scientist has every right to defend his or her position and point out the inappropriateness of apparently contradictory positions.

As we noted in Chapter 3, the tendency to value data and evidence more than a particular point of view is a characteristic of all good scientists. Within the best traditions of science, scientists do not try to *prove* or *disprove* any particular view. Instead, they seek truth. It is only as a by-product of this search that a particular view gets either supported or rejected.

Ethical Justification for Treatment Evaluation

A special concern of clinical researchers is the effects of experimentation on individuals who seek professional services. The concern is serious in the evaluation of treatment; the ethical dilemma is real. An ethical dilemma is whether to experiment or not experiment with different treatment procedures. It is sometimes suggested that clients should be treated—not experimented upon. This suggestion implies that experimental treatments are somehow more detrimental to clients than nonexperimental treatments.

A closer examination of the issue reveals that the distinction between experimental and nonexperimental treatments may be less meaningful than that between effective and ineffective (or dangerous) treatments. It is the ineffective or dangerous treatment that is detrimental to clients regardless of whether it is considered experimental or routine. It is the practice of ineffective or dangerous treatment procedures that is unethical.

When is a treatment experimental? This question is easily answered when a clinician calls a treatment experimental. The clinician then systematically collects data, uses certain control procedures, and thus tries to evaluate the effects of a particular treatment procedure. The effects may be positive, and the clients may have benefited just as much as those under an

equally effective but routine treatment procedure. Nonetheless, what about the use of a treatment procedure whose effects have never been experimentally evaluated but, regardless, routinely used? Is this an experiment? Most people tend to think that as long as a procedure is more or less routine—and is not called "experimental" by the clinicians who use it—it is not experimental. Even more important, when the treatment procedure is not clearly defined, the goals are subjectively stated, and the improvement criteria are not specified, most people do not consider that treatment experimental. This assumption has created a false issue of ethics in treatment research.

In speech-language pathology, many treatment procedures are based not on experimental evidence but on clinical traditions and experiences. The trial-and-error approach of many clinicians may constitute an endless series of errors. When a clinical hunch is wrong, nothing better may be available, and therefore, the same ineffective practice may be perpetuated. Presumably, ineffective procedures continue to be used because the clinician either does not know that the technique is ineffective or cannot implement a better procedure. Oddly enough, not many ethical concerns are raised about this kind of clinical practice.

Another kind of clinical practice is also oblivious of ethical concerns—a practice based on complex, impressive, but nevertheless speculative theories. *Theory-based treatment* is currently a trending term in speech-language pathology. Unfortunately, most theories are a collection of unverified hypotheses but are not recognized as such. Theories of this kind are sometimes so prestigious that in the judgment of many clinicians, a treatment procedure that is supported by a theory *ought* to work, even though there is no controlled evidence in its favor. Conversely, clinicians may believe that a treatment procedure that works well but is not a part of an accepted theory should be discarded. Unfortunately, this practice jeopardizes both service and knowledge.

It is when clinicians wish to determine the effects of treatment objectively that ethical concerns seem to be pressing. Addressing this issue, Barlow, Hayes and Nelson (1984) stated that "if the intervention is poorly specified; goals are unclear; and if measures are weak, infrequent, or nonexistent, then there is *less* of an ethical worry. Our own cultural ambivalence about science has turned vice into virtue, sloppiness into safety" (p. 285).

The ethics of treatment evaluation involve at least three related issues. The first is whether treatment evaluation is necessary. The second is whether treatment evaluation is ethically justified. The third is whether treatment and treatment research are different kinds of activities. We shall briefly address these three issues.

Is Treatment Evaluation Necessary?

Whether treatment evaluation is necessary may not sound like an ethical issue, but it is at the heart of ethical controversy. Those who question the ethics of treatment evaluation imply that it is not necessary. When the necessity of researching treatment of a disorder is questioned, three assumptions may be implied. The first assumption is that an effective procedure to treat that disorder already exists and that the effects are objectively documented. The second assumption is that there is no room to improve the efficacy of the proven procedure. The third assump-

tion is that there is no need to find a more effective procedure. In many cases, these assumptions may be wrong.

First, many diseases and disorders do not have treatments demonstrated to be effective. Second, the efficacy of effective treatments that do exist for certain disorders can perhaps be improved by controlled research. In the case of communication disorders, few people assert that we have perfectly effective treatment procedures that cannot be improved upon. Third, even if there are effective procedures, it is possible to develop more effective procedures because no treatment research has reached its pinnacle. In the end, we have no choice but to experiment because we need: (a) to have effective procedures, (b) to know that the procedures we are using are effective, (c) to improve the efficacy of effective procedures, and (d) to develop more effective procedures.

Is Treatment Evaluation Ethically Justified?

If it is concluded that treatment evaluation is necessary and that such treatment evaluation is no more harmful to clients than unverified procedures (which might actually be ineffective or dangerous), the second issue—whether treatment evaluation is ethically justified—appears in a different light. Obviously, treatment evaluation is justified. Indeed, systematic and objective evaluation of treatment procedures is one of the ethical responsibilities of clinical professions. Continued practice of treatment procedures whose effects are not objectively documented is unethical. Whether a treatment is old or new and whether it is practiced by a few or many are irrelevant. Procedures that have been used widely and for a long time may still be ineffective and hence detrimental to clients. Therefore, it is a pseudo-question to ask whether clinicians should experiment with their treatment procedures.

Some scientists assume that experiments that produce no effects or negative effects are of greater ethical concern than those that produce positive effects. Therefore, when treatment research on a given procedure produces no effect or negative effect, the clients may be said to have been used as "guinea pigs." However, it is ironic that the same procedure, used routinely, may not raise the same ethical question. Experiments showing that certain procedures are not useful or even harmful may prevent the widespread use of such procedures. Because negative evidence prevents continued damage to clients, studies that produce it should be welcome. It may be recalled that the Phase I clinical trials in medicine test the safety of new drugs, some of which may turn out to be unsafe. Therefore, the outcome of an experimental treatment is never a basis on which to judge the ethics of clinical experimentation. Efforts at empirical determination of effectiveness, ineffectiveness, or negative effects of treatment procedures are necessary and ethical. We know the effectiveness of a technique only when we evaluate that technique. As pointed out by Barlow et al. (1984), systematic "evaluation [of a treatment] is not what makes it experimental. It just keeps us from fooling ourselves when it is" (p. 287).

Are Controlled Evaluations Different From Routine Treatment?

The third issue, whether routine treatment and controlled treatment evaluations are different kinds of activities, has been discussed occasionally (Siegel & Spradlin, 1985). If treatment evaluation is inherently different from treatment, then is there a justification for subjecting clients who need treatment to something other than treatment?

There is no question that in some specific respects, controlled evaluation of treatment is different from routine treatment. The crucial difference is that routine treatment does not use control procedures whereas treatment evaluation does (e.g., control groups or such controlled conditions as baselines and reversals). Nonetheless, the difference between controlled treatment evaluations and routine treatments does not lead to the conclusion that treatment evaluation is unjustified. Before a procedure is used as routine treatment, it should undergo treatment evaluation so that people are not routinely offered an ineffective or harmful treatment. Therefore, treatment and treatment evaluation ought to be different, and both are necessary.

The discussion so far is not intended to suggest that there are no ethical problems in conducting treatment research. There are several problems, but they arise only because of the necessity of experimental treatment evaluations. In other words, whether clinicians should experimentally evaluate their procedures is not an ethically or otherwise valid question. The answer to that question is *yes*, and therefore we have ethical concerns. Several of these ethical concerns associated with treatment research are addressed in the remainder of this chapter.

In evaluating treatment effects, the researcher should take precautions to reduce the risk, if any, to the participants. In fact, steps to reduce the risks to human participants should be taken in all kinds of research, not just clinical treatment research. We shall now turn to this important ethical issue.

The Protection of Human Participants in Research

Responsible scientists have always been concerned with the welfare of individuals who serve as participants in various medical, biological, behavioral, and other kinds of experiments. Scientists have known that the need to produce knowledge that will benefit humankind should be balanced with the risks that such an enterprise might pose to the human participants.

Human subject protection policies were not widely enforced until the U.S. Congress passed the National Research Act, which was signed into law in 1974, although several ethical guidelines were published much earlier. An early set of ethical guidelines for research is known as The Nuremberg Code published in 1949 (see Brody, 1998, for a reprint) after the famous Nuremberg trial in which it was revealed that Nazi physicians had conducted unconscionable and incredibly cruel experiments on Jewish people in concentration camps. The Nuremberg Code recognized for the first time that human participation in experiments should be voluntary and that the risks should be minimal (Brody, 1998). Then in 1964, the World Medial Association adopted what is known as *The Helsinki Declaration on Research Ethics*. The Helsinki Declaration was based on the Nuremberg Code, but it further elaborated on the risks and benefits of human participation in clinical research as well as basic biomedical research. The World Medical Association (2013) has periodically revised the original declaration.

It soon became evident that abuse of human participants was not limited to an aberrant era of the Nazis. In 1966, Beecher published an article in which he made reference to 50 unethical experiments performed on human beings in the post–World War II United States. He gave details on 22 of them. He cited a placebo-controlled trial that evaluated the effects of the drug chloramphenicol against a placebo in patients who had typhoid fever. In this study, even beyond the point where the effectiveness of the drug was clear in the experimental group, the patients in the placebo-controlled group continued to receive placebo, leading to a very high death rate among them.

Testing potential toxicity of new drugs on institutionalized people has been an especially alarming abuse of research participants. In one experiment, toxicity of a drug on the liver was tested with healthy institutionalized people without their consent. When the participants developed hepatic dysfunction because of toxicity, their livers were biopsied to confirm the damage. Incredibly, when they got better, a few of them were given the same drug again to replicate the toxicity effects. In another experiment, institutionalized children with intellectual disabilities were injected with isolated strains of hepatitis virus to understand the course of the disease (Beecher, 1966; Brody, 1998). Such instances as injecting cancer cells to unsuspecting patients hospitalized for various diseases also have been documented (Katz, 1972).

Unethical experiments on minority groups constitute another group of abusive studies. In one such experiment, known as the Tuskegee Syphilis Study, poor rural African Americans who had syphilis were initially enrolled in an observational study that began in 1930s to understand the natural course of the disease (Jones, 1981). The study was continued until the early 1970s, although by that time penicillin was well established as the most effective treatment for syphilis. No informed consent was obtained from the patients, and they were strongly persuaded from seeking treatment that had become available. Similar abuse of human participants has been documented in most other countries (Brody, 1998). Even in the era of post–human protection laws, U.S. government-supported medical research teams have been conducting unethical drug experiments on unsuspecting patients in Africa and other countries (Angell, 1997). Several websites, including those of the Alliance for Human Research Protection (ahrp.org) and the Public Citizen (citizen.org), routinely report on currently conducted abusive research studies.

The National Research Act of 1974 has significantly reduced abusive experiments in the United States. The act established the National Commission for the Protection of Human Subjects of Biomedical and Behavioral Research, which in 1979 issued general guidelines on human participant protection in a document known as the *Belmont Report*. Since then, the human subject protection in research has been federally mandated. A federal office within the Department of Health and Human Services (DHHS) (http://www.hhs.gov/ohrp/) issues guidelines and periodic updates (Office for Protection from Research Risks, 1991, 1993). All researchers are expected to follow the latest set of federal guidelines and guidelines at their research facility.

Most scientific and professional organizations such as the American Speech-Language-Hearing Association (2016) and the American Psychological Association (2002) have published guidelines on research ethics and human participant and animal subject protection. Furthermore, almost all universities, hospitals, schools, and research organizations have their own additional guidelines. All of these guidelines are consistent with those issued by the federal agencies. Once again, researchers are expected to follow the current guidelines in their institution.

The most salient feature of the human participant protection procedures is the review of research proposals by an institutional review board (IRB). These boards are federally mandated but locally formed and administered. Most colleges and universities have multiple IRBs functioning at the level of the department and at level of the school (or college) in which the department is housed. Usually, there is also a university-wide IRB that receives reports from IRBs at the lower levels.

It is mandatory to submit all research procedures to one of these IRBs, known as human participants committees. These committees or boards review proposals to determine whether proposed studies pose any risk to the participants and, if so, what steps should be taken to reduce that risk. The human participants committee may also deny approval to carry out a study on the basis of unacceptable risks to the participants, but this is rare.

Because human participant protection procedures apply only to individuals who participate in research and not to routine clinical or educational procedures, a clear understanding of the legal concept of research is necessary. According to the regulations, **research** is any systematic investigation designed to develop or contribute to generalizable knowledge. The clinician who treats a client without an attempt to contribute knowledge is not doing research. In such cases, application of new treatment procedures does not require institutional review. However, if the clinician plans to publish the outcomes of a treatment procedure under controlled or uncontrolled conditions, then the study is research and an IRB should review the proposal.

All theses and dissertation proposals are routinely submitted to an IRB. A clinician who is not sure whether an undertaking contains an element of research or is simply a routine clinical procedure should submit a written description of the activities to an IRB for review and advice.

Institutional review boards should have at least five individuals. The DHHS regulations also stipulate that IRBs should contain at least one person who is not a scientist and one person who is not affiliated with the institution where the research will be conducted. (One person can satisfy both requirements.) Most college and university IRBs that review in-house proposals that do not receive funds from federal agencies do not recruit members from outside the university. Proposals that do not involve risks to participants may be reviewed only by one or two members of a university department's review committee, with a report of this action being made to a higher, fully constituted IRB. When risks are involved, such expeditious reviews are not allowed. In fact, studies that pose risks may be reviewed by multiple IRBs within an institution. The author of a research proposal may be asked to speak to the committee but does not take part in the review process. The major concerns of an IRB in reviewing research proposals include the risk-benefit ratio, informed consent, and the privacy of the participants.

The Risk-Benefit Ratio

It is assumed that participation in any kind of research may involve risk to participants. Some of the risks may be psychological. For example, research involving the experimental evaluation of the effects of shock or white noise on stuttering may create emotional stress or anxiety in stut-terers. The procedures also may create physical harm or injury. For example, in medical research, new medical or surgical treatment procedures may pose significant risks to the lives of the patients. Certain other procedures may cause social embarrassment; for example, a study may be designed to evaluate the maintenance of target behaviors in natural settings. A person who stutters may have his or her treated fluency monitored in a supermarket, where the client may be forced into speaking in difficult situations.

In this case, the IRB's tasks are to determine: (a) whether the study poses risks to participants and, if so, (b) whether it is minimal and, if not, (c) how to handle the unacceptable level of risk. Risks are judged to be minimal when the expected level of risk does not exceed the level experienced in daily life situations. As a rough guideline, the amount of risk (stress) experienced while taking ordinary psychological or physical tests is considered minimal. In the case of research that poses minimal risk, an IRB may quickly approve the study.

When the risk is judged to be more than minimal, the IRB does not necessarily deny permission to conduct the study. Instead, it reviews the procedures set forth by the investigator to handle that risk. The IRB may suggest modifications in the procedure. The intensity of potentially damaging experimental stimuli such as shock and noise may be limited. The participants may be allowed to determine the intensity levels presented to them. People who stutter may not be taken to social situations to test their fluency until after they have demonstrated fluency in more controlled, less embarrassing situations.

Potential risks to certain populations, such as children, are usually viewed conservatively. Whether the participants are children or adults, an IRB may suggest less stressful methods of data collection or, when this is not possible, require constant and professional monitoring of the participants' reactions to the experimental procedures. For example, the IRB may require the presence of a physician or a clinical psychologist if the experimental procedures are thought to cause physical or psychological stress. The IRB may also require that the experiment be terminated if participants show unacceptable levels of emotional reactions.

The IRBs evaluate not only the potential risks but also the potential scientific benefits. It is important to realize that the scientific benefit, not the benefit to the participant, is what is evaluated. Other factors being equal, a research study that provides no benefits to participants may be approved when the study is expected to generate scientific information. However, in this context, IRBs face a difficult task because they are generally not expected to evaluate the methodological or theoretical soundness of the studies they review. When it is considered appropriate, an IRB may seek an independent evaluation of the proposal's scientific merits from qualified scientists.

The federal regulations and the guidelines of professional organizations and universities are not designed to prevent all research studies that pose risks to human participants. Rather, they are intended to make sure that adequate protective measures are taken when there is risk. Many research studies that do pose various levels of risk to the participants may be valuable because they produce scientific knowledge and eventual benefit to people. It may be noted that many people volunteer for risky experiments that may eventually benefit society. Those who volunteer for experimental medical or surgical treatments such as new drug evaluations, organ transplants, and artificial heart surgeries do so because they wish to advance knowledge that might benefit others.

Most research studies in speech-language pathology and audiology involve only a minimal risk to participants, and many clinical treatment studies actually improve the client's clinical conditions. Experimental studies on treatment of dysphagia, however, may pose aspiration and other kinds of risks to patients. Regardless, it is important to test established procedures for their experimentally demonstrated effects. Also, as new treatment procedures are developed, a cautious approach is needed. New procedures should be put to experimental tests with appropriate safeguards for the participants.

Informed Consent

A person's informed consent to participate voluntarily in research is one of the most important ethical principles of research. Informed consent involves three components. First, the participants should fully understand the procedures of the study. Second, they should freely and voluntarily consent to participate in the study. Third, the participants should be free to withdraw from the study at any time with no negative consequence to them.

Potential participants should not be contacted until after the approval of the IRB. This is because the method of subject contact itself may involve some coercion, and no person should be recruited by even the subtlest forms of coercion. For example, an instructor may ask his or her students to participate in an experiment in such a way as to imply that a lack of participation may have punitive consequences. A clinician may ask clients to participate in an experimental treatment while giving the impression that no other treatment is available. Therefore, an IRB screens the proposed method of contacting and recruiting participants.

In obtaining informed consent from potential participants, the researcher should fully describe the procedures and purposes of the study. The individuals should know what is expected of them, what kinds of stimulus conditions they will be exposed to, what kinds of responses they will be asked to make, and how long they need to participate in the study. They should understand the risks and benefits of participation. In clinical treatment research, they should fully understand the procedure of the treatment being evaluated. Availability of alternative treatment procedures should be specified to the participants. When the risk is more than minimal, the possibilities of compensation also should be described. The potential participants should be informed of the names of persons (other than the investigator) they may contact about the research. The potential participants should understand that participation is entirely voluntary and that they are free to withdraw from the study at any stage with no penalty or prejudice. Furthermore, the researcher should take into consideration the cultural and linguistic diversity of each participant. Finally, the individuals contacted should be told whether and to what extent their anonymity will be protected during and after the study.

The potential participants should have all the information in writing, usually called the *informed consent form*. They usually sign their name on the same document to indicate their full understanding of the procedures, risks, and benefits and to indicate their willingness to participate in the study. The writing should be simple and nontechnical so that the individuals can understand the full implications of their participation. When the participants are children, parents give informed consent. Children ages 7 to 18 years may also sign the informed consent form along with their parents. The children should be informed at a level appropriate for them to understand the procedures. Children under the age of 7 years may be asked to sign an *assent form* cosigned by the parent/guardian. Special efforts are needed to make sure that communicatively disabled individuals understand the procedures of a study before deciding to participate.

Investigators in some studies, especially in neuroscience and psychology, may deceive participants about the purpose of their studies. The justification is that knowledge of the purpose of the study will affect the results. Giving placebo in medical trials to the control group participants is considered *concealment* but not deception, but this is arguable. In psychological research, telling participants that the purpose of the study is to analyze racial prejudices may result in invalid data. In such cases, the IRBs may approve deception, sometimes euphemistically described as *incomplete disclosure*. A variation of deception is called **authorized deception**, in which the potential participants may be told that deception is a part of the study procedure or that some part of information supplied to them may be inaccurate. Individuals may then decline participation. In either case, the participants are debriefed (told of the real purpose of the experiment and why they were misled) at the conclusion of the study. In authorized deception, debriefed participants have a right to withdraw their results from the study. Any form of deception is controversial, and critics assail it as unethical because it compromises informed consent. Several investigators who deceived their subjects have further misled the readers of their published reports by omitting this part of the procedure or saying that the standard informed consent was obtained (Miller & Kaptchuk, 2008).

The Privacy of the Participants

The privacy of the participants of research studies is another important ethical issue. Clinicians know that the privacy or confidentiality of clients is an important professional consideration regardless of research concerns; likewise, research investigators should take every possible step to protect the privacy of their research participants.

Most research studies are published in one form or another. Publication will include descriptions of participants. Therefore, the participants should give informed consent to such publication. The typical procedure is to inform the participants that their confidentiality will be protected when the studies are published. In most cases, the participants' names and other identifying data will not be published.

Participant identity may be revealed in certain kinds of publications. For example, the picture of a client may be a part of a research article showing various physical characteristics of a genetic syndrome. In such cases, the clients, their guardians, or both should give explicit written permission to publish pictures. Similar permission should be obtained when audio or video recordings are expected to be published in some form. Most speech and hearing centers routinely obtain such permission from the clients, their guardians, or both. This procedure facilitates the future research use of client information.

Throughout the study, information obtained about individuals, their families, institutions, and organizations should be kept strictly confidential. The participants should be informed of the procedures by which the confidentiality of the participants and institutions will be maintained. An investigator may propose, for example, that the individuals will be coded, and the names of the participants will not be used in any stage of data analysis. Access to confidential information about individuals may be restricted. Only the principal investigator may know the names of the participants. However, student clinicians who take part in clinical treatment research may know the names, because in essence, they are part of the research team. In such cases, the student clinicians are advised to strictly follow the study protocol of confidentiality. An IRB may find that the safeguards need improvements and make suggestions to that effect. Eventually, the potential participants or their guardians judge for themselves whether the proposed methods of protecting confidentiality are acceptable.

The ethical issues discussed in this chapter are not always amenable to objective and unambiguous resolution. The regulations and guidelines recognize the difficulty involved in assessing the risk-benefit ratio, the need for deception, and the possibilities of the invasion of privacy of research participants. The investigator and the IRB make the best possible judgments, taking all of the important factors into consideration.

As we have noted, IRBs are responsible for making sure that individuals who serve as participants in research studies are treated fairly and honestly. However, the presence of such boards and committees does not reduce the responsibility of the investigator. It is the investigator who is ultimately responsible for his or her conduct in the course of research investigations, and the IRBs have to trust the authors in following the approved procedures. When violations occur, the IRB does not have the power to take punitive steps against investigators, but the authorities of the institution will investigate violations and take appropriate actions.

Ethical Issues With Treatment Research

The ethical restraints imposed on the research community have produced many beneficial effects for individuals who participate in experiments as well as society at large. Such restraints may have prevented many abusive research efforts. Nonetheless, there still are some ethical problems with certain accepted research practices. Some of these problems may be inevitable and an acceptable price to pay for scientific knowledge; others may be solved, or their effects reduced by making methodological changes in investigation.

We shall consider a few current research practices that do *not* violate existing laws and guidelines on human biomedical and behavioral research but nonetheless raise certain ethical issues. The major research practices that raise ethical concerns include the no-treatment control group, placebo-control group, randomization, blinding, treatment reversal or withdrawal, and general methods of subject recruitment.

Ethical Concerns With Informed Consent Procedures

As noted in this chapter, human participant protection is a phenomenon of the latter half of the 20th century. It is now a standard research practice to obtain *informed consent* from participants who agree to participate in a research study. The participants' signature on the informed consent form fulfills the legal obligation of this aspect of human participant protection procedure.

In recent years, questions have been raised about the effectiveness and empirical validity of most informed consent procedures used in medical treatment research. There is evidence that many patients may not fully understand the nature of randomized clinical trials (RCTs). People whose educational level is low may find the informed consent procedure, sometimes running into a hundred pages, written by pharmaceutical company lawyers, especially daunting (Hegde, 2007). The concept of randomization has been especially difficult for many people to grasp; for example, sometimes even after giving informed consent to participate in RCTs, participants still expect to receive the treatment they want. In some cases, less than half the participants may grasp the concept of randomization of treatment allocation (Snowdon, Garcia, & Elbourne, 1997).

Conditions under which informed consent is sometimes sought also bring into question the degree to which consent is truly informed and voluntary. In some studies, an informed consent is sought from people who are distressed about their own or their family member's acute and rapidly deteriorating disease. Family members who face a life-or-death situation may be asked to give informed consent for a new treatment study. The validity of informed consent sought from parents for entering their newborn baby into RCTs has come under heavy criticism. Emotionally distraught parents, having just learned that their newborn has a serious health problem that may threaten the baby's life, may be asked to make certain quick judgments about entering or not entering an RCT. Most parents of sick children, it has been observed, will give consent to any kind of procedure that may offer even a faint chance or hope for their children's survival (McIntosh, 1993; Snowdon et al., 1997). Validity of informed consent obtained under stressful conditions from people with limited education may be highly questionable. In fact, an editorial in *Lancet,* one of the world's leading medical journals, has concluded that "informed consent from poorly educated parents entering a complex trial in stressful conditions is a sham" ("Your Baby Is in a Trial," 1995, p. 806). For these and other reasons, some investigators wonder whether informed consent is just a myth (Silverman, 1989).

Besides raising ethical concerns, informed consent has permanently changed the nature of data collected in RCTs. We will address this issue of the effects of informed consent on data and their interpretation in a later section.

Ethical Concerns With No-Treatment Control Groups

As described in Chapters 4 and 8, the RCTs and any kind of treatment research that uses a group design for treatment evaluation may use a control group that receives no treatment until the end of the study. Some studies have long durations, months or even several years. Therefore, participants in the no-treatment control group may go without a much-needed treatment for a long time. Provided the participants understand that they may not receive treatment when they agree to participate, the use of such no-treatment control groups is acceptable under most governmental and institutional research guidelines, although some international guidelines are more restrictive than those in the United States (Brody, 1998). Nonetheless, many medical researchers have raised valid ethical issues with this accepted research practice.

Most RCTs in medicine employ multiple physicians as principal investigators who are responsible to recruit patients to the trial. In recent years, there has been significant difficulty in recruiting patients to RCTs in medicine. Many eligible patients, especially those who understand randomization, are unwilling to participate in clinical trials because they know that they only have a 50% chance of receiving treatment for their disease. Opting out of the trial, they seek immediate treatment outside the scope of the study. Those who do not fully understand randomization may agree to participate, thinking that they might get the real treatment.

Even those patients who agree to participate in a study involving a no-treatment control group may drop out of the study as their clinical condition worsens or when they find out that those in the experimental group are getting better with treatment. In one study in speech-language pathology, parents of control group children who stutter demanded treatment for their children when they learned that fluency of children in the experimental group had improved (Onslow, Andrews, & Lincoln, 1994). When control group participants demand the experimental or some other treatment, the investigators are legally bound to offer it.

Those who stay with the study and receive no treatment may be frustrated with their participation or distressed about not getting treatment. From a legal standpoint, the investigators may not be concerned because the participants have agreed to participate on their own accord (we will have more about the validity of this claim in a later section). From an ethical standpoint, the matter may be serious. For example, a postrandomization study of patient reactions to random assignment has revealed that patients may be "heartbroken" to find that they are not allocated to the treatment group (Snowdon et al., 1997). Significant dropout is a likely consequence.

There is evidence that many physicians and surgeons are reluctant to enter their patients into RCTs because of the uncertainty involved in the trials, that is, the possibility that treatment will be denied to their sick patients. Many practitioners think that their primary responsibility is to their individual patients, not to the aggregate of patients the trials are concerned with (Taylor, 1985). Pediatricians may be especially reluctant to enter sick children under their care into randomized experiments (Morris, Zaritsky, & LeFever, 2000). Generally, physicians who do not enter their eligible patients into randomized trials cite their ethical commitment to providing the best possible care for their patients. They see a conflict between this commitment and the denial of treatment to control groups in clinical trials.

Treatment denial to a control group is acceptable when no treatment for a disorder or disease is available and the treatment being evaluated is the only *potential* recourse. Recognizing this, many RCTs in medicine use control groups that receive an existing or standard treatment while the experimental group receives the new treatment under investigation. From a scientific standpoint, it is better to compare a new treatment with no treatment; however, comparing the effects of a new treatment against those of an existing treatment is an ethically justified compromise.

In most experiments, control conditions used with the single-subject designs are just as effective as control groups, without the ethical issues associated with those groups. An ethical guideline all researchers must follow is that a risky procedure is justified only when there are no safer alternatives of securing valid data. Single-subject designs offer alternative procedures that avoid control groups who do not receive treatment for extended durations.

Ethical Concerns With Placebo-Control Group

In RCTs, a control group may receive a placebo, described in Chapter 4. The placebo-control groups were designed when it was found that many patients feel better when they take something that is thought to be medicine, even though it has no medicinal properties (such as a sugar or lactose pill). It became evident that some of the effects of a new medication (actually, any medication) may be due to this placebo effect. In experiments on medical treatment effects, investigators believe that they have to demonstrate that the effects of a medicine exceeded that of the presumed placebo effect.

As pointed out in Chapter 4, the presence and the extent of the placebo effect have been debated in medical literature. Our concern here is not whether the placebo effect is real but what ethical problems the widely used placebo control groups pose for both the investigators and participants.

Participants who are members of a placebo-control group in RCTs receive an inert material or a lactose tablet that looks exactly like the drug whose effect is under investigation. In a single-blind study, the participants who receive a placebo do not know that fact. In a double-blind study, neither the participants nor the immediate investigators who administer the placebo (as well as the medicine) and then measure the effects know that fact.

Patients who receive a placebo, like those who receive no treatment, go without much needed treatment. Beyond that, those who receive a placebo in a single- or double-blind study tend to believe that they are being treated, for that is the essence of the placebo concept. That they have given informed consent does not affect this hope or expectation. As noted before, patients in a no-treatment control group may be heartbroken to know that they are not getting treatment in an RCT; this applies to placebo-control group participants as well, except that for a while, they are fooled into thinking that they are getting real medicine. Consequently, patients may think that RCTs that involve either no treatment or placebo are a gamble, and many who participate in such experiments have much uneasiness about them (Madden, 1994).

In surgical treatment evaluation, placebo is less commonly used, but when it is used, it raises the most serious ethical concerns. Placebo in surgical treatment studies involves performing sham surgical procedures to make the patients think that they have been operated on to treat a condition. For instance, in a randomized placebo-controlled evaluation of the effects of intracerebral transplantations of fetal mesencephalic tissue in patients with Parkinson's disease, a hole was drilled into the skull of the placebo-control group patients to simulate the surgical treatment procedure (Dekkers & Boer, 2001). Patients randomly assigned to placebo-control groups in all surgical treatment evaluation studies undergo such sham surgery, which exposes them to unnecessary risks of injury, infection, surgical accidents, and other unexpected negative consequences.

From an ethical standpoint, one could argue that the administration of a placebo is a misleading aspect of RCTs. It is especially so in studies in which the participants are blinded; in such cases, the participants are given a worthless treatment, and to compound the ethical problems, this fact is concealed from them. In light of the controversy about its very existence, the ethical problems of placebo administration may outweigh its presumed advantages. That the patients have given informed consent to be randomized in a study that uses a control group does not remove these ethical concerns (Rothman & Michels, 1994). In fact, the revised Declaration of Helsinki issued by World Medical Association (2013) states that placebo-controlled clinical trials may be conducted only when there is no standard treatment against which the new treatment may be compared. Furthermore, when an untested treatment is offered because no other treatment is available for a disease or disorder, experimental evaluation of that treatment should begin as soon as possible.

Ethically, no-treatment control groups may fare slightly better than placebo-control groups. Minimally, patients participating in no-treatment control groups are not fooled into thinking that they are receiving treatment. Patients in both the types of control groups may suffer serious physical consequences of denied treatment, including deterioration in symptoms, reduced effectiveness of subsequent treatment because of more advanced disease, and, possibly, death. Participants in placebo-controlled experiments involving medicine may fare slightly better than those in experiments involving surgical treatment. Setting aside the serious consequences of not treating a disease, placebo in medical research is at least a harmless lactose tablet; placebo in surgical treatment research is a sham and a dangerously invasive procedure.

Ethical Concerns With Randomization

Theoretically, randomization, as described in Chapter 4, should be done at two levels to ensure group equivalency and statistical generality: random selection from the population and random assignment to the groups. In practice, though, participants are rarely drawn randomly from a population. Only those who give consent to participate in a study are randomly assigned to treatment and experimental groups.

Statisticians and others argue that randomization is the essential element of objective treatment evaluation—an argument rejected by those who advocate the single-subject approach. The central ethical issue with randomization is that people are assigned to one of the several groups, including one that receives a less effective treatment, a more effective treatment, no treatment, or a placebo treatment. As discussed before, informed consent may or may not be truly informed and valid in the case of all participants, and even when it is, sick patients volunteer in the hopes of beating the odds of randomization in favor of receiving a beneficial treatment. But when they find out that they have been assigned to a less effective treatment or a placebo, many refuse further participation; those who continue their participation resent randomization. A study of the reactions of parents who had entered their babies into

a randomized clinical trial showed that most parents had strong negative reactions to the random method of allocating treatment. The parents thought that was against the basic tenet of making treatment decisions based on the clinical condition of a patient (Snowdon et al., 1997).

Many practicing physicians and surgeons are reluctant to enter their eligible patients to RCTs because they believe that random allocation of treatment is inherently against their ethical responsibility of treating their patients with the best possible care (Taylor, 1985; Verdu-Pascal & Castello-Ponce, 2001). Research scientists, however, argue that when we do not know what is the best possible treatment, we need to find out by experimentation. When, in their judgment, randomization is the only way to generate valid scientific data on different treatment options, they see no compelling ethical dilemmas. No one, of course, would argue against the ethical need for treatment evaluation. However, arguments can be made that randomization is neither needed nor justified in all cases of treatment evaluation. Even more critically, randomization does not work as supposed; there is no random selection from the population and the recruited (self-selected, not randomly selected) participants, randomized to treatment and control groups, do not stay randomized. Called the **N-of-1 trials** in medicine, single-subject design studies may replace randomized group designs in most cases. (See Chapter 9 for N-of-1 clinical trials.) Instead of one large-scale study, many small-scale studies may be conducted. These studies can generate scientifically valid data to help choose the best possible treatment without the ethical concerns of ineffective randomization of treatment allocation.

Ethical Concerns With Treatment Withdrawal or Reversal

Concerns raised so far apply to group designs with random selection and assignment of participants to different treatments, placebo treatment, or no treatment. Most single-subject designs avoid those procedures and thus the ethical concerns associated with them. The *ABA* and *ABAB* designs, however, do pose ethical concerns because of treatment withdrawal and reversal associated with them. These concerns were discussed in detail in Chapter 9 and are only briefly reviewed in this chapter.

In the *ABA* design, the participants derive only a temporary benefit. If the treatment is effective, it will be evident in the experimental (*B*) condition. Whether effective or not, the treatment is withdrawn in the final *A* condition. In the case where the treatment has been effective, the clinical problem is allowed to return to its baseline level in the withdrawal condition: This return to baseline creates ethical problems. For the clients and the family, it is illogical to reverse the beneficial effects of a treatment. Although the clients and their families will have given informed consent, anecdotally, some fail to appreciate the need. And they may be correct because there are alternatives —such as multiple baseline designs.

Treatment reversal, which is essentially the same as withdrawal in its final effect (which is to recover the baseline), also can cause ethical problems and participant rejection, as does randomization. In some cases, reversal may be more distressing than withdrawal. In behavioral treatment research, when the treatment is withdrawn, the client is simply engaged in conversation, play, and such other activities. Therefore, withdrawal looks natural to consumers. The reversal, however, does not look natural to them. In reversal, an incompatible behavior may be taught, and in many cases, the incompatible behavior is the very undesirable behavior that was reduced under treatment. For instance, differential reinforcement may reduce errors of articulation in the *B* condition and the same differential reinforcement technique may be used to increase the errors in the reversal condition.

As pointed out in Chapter 9, some research questions are best served by the reversal design. In all other cases, it may be preferable to avoid the reversal as a control mechanism.

The *ABAB* design also may contain either a reversal or withdrawal condition and would pose similar ethical problems. These problems are somewhat muted because those conditions are temporary, the effective treatment is reinstated, and the participants end the experiment with accrued benefit from the experiment. One might still consider multiple baseline designs as ethically more attractive alternatives, because these designs do not involve treatment withdrawal or reversal. The reason to use the *ABAB* design is that it is more powerful in demonstrating the cause-effect relationship than the multiple baseline design.

Ethical Concerns With Participant Recruitment

Subject recruitment procedures, even when they do not explicitly violate existing ethical guidelines on research, can still pose ethical problems. Subject recruitment is typically difficult for treatment research.

Most investigators try to do their best in recruiting participants who are appropriate for their studies. Investigators try to balance participants of different characteristics. Nonetheless, practical difficulties in recruiting participants with expected characteristics can create certain ethical problems.

One of the problems faced by speech-language pathologists and perhaps psychologists as well is the *repeated recruitment of the same participants* in multiple experiments. Psychology students are often recruited for participation in experimental studies that faculty members conduct, and the same students may repeatedly take part in multiple experiments. The students' experience in one experiment may influence their performance in the other. In communication disorders, the same few individuals that are seeking treatment for months and years may be the participants in multiple treatment efficacy studies. This is likely to happen in cases of aphasia, intellectual disabilities, motor speech disorders, cerebral palsy, stuttering, autism spectrum disorder, hearing loss, and other conditions that require long-term treatment. In all such cases, the results may be somewhat ambiguous because the experimental design used may make no allowance for analyzing the effects of prior participation in studies. Minimally, the investigator should give the history of study participation history of all the participants in research submitted for publication.

Another problem in participant recruitment may involve *subtle forms of coercion*. Despite an investigator's best effort to avoid any hint of coercion, people in certain positions may feel an obligation to participate in an experimental study. Students, for example, when asked to con-sider participation in an experiment, may feel obligated to participate, despite the faculty member's insistence that the participation is entirely voluntary. Clinicians who are providing treatment or those who are supervising clinical practicum in university clinics and, in turn, request participation of clients in research also may exert a subtle form of coercion.

There may be no effective solution to the problem of subtle coercion that people who are asked to participate in experimental research may feel. Recognizing this potential problem, however, is the ethical responsibility of all investigators who will then take all steps necessary to minimize such coercion. Investigators who work hard to earn a reputation for not taking punitive measures and showing subtle, unpleasant reactions to non-participants will have done their best to minimize ethical concerns of this kind.

All treatment researchers know that there are participants who are difficult to recruit. Generally, people belonging to minority groups, people who belong to lower socioeconomic classes, and people who live far away from urban research centers may be difficult to recruit for experimental studies. Medical treatment research tends to oversample men at the cost of women. People living near a university often are easily recruited by university-based researchers. These practical exigencies, however, create ethical dilemmas because they exclude a significant portion of people from participating in treatment evaluation studies. Unfortunately, the conclusions of the very studies in which they do not participate are frequently extended to them. This is unacceptable both scientifically and ethically; all investigators have an ethical responsibility to recruit a diverse set of people, representative of the group to whom the conclusions of a study are meant to be generalized.

While nonparticipation of people who are economically or otherwise disadvantaged is a serious problem, overrepresentation of disadvantaged people in certain kinds of studies is an equally serious problem. There is some evidence that in studies on new and risky treatment for serious diseases, disadvantaged people (relatively poor, less educated, and without health insurance) may be overrepresented. On the other hand, studies on disease prevention include a disproportionate number of healthy, more affluent, and educated people (Gorkin et al., 1996; McKee et al., 1999). Such imbalances in recruiting participants is an ethical issue because the burden of evaluating the unproven and potentially risky techniques may fall on the shoulders of the disadvantaged while deriving long-term benefits from disease prevention research may be the privilege of the affluent. That both the groups are biased samples that limit generality is a separate but equally troubling issue.

Consequences of Ethical Constraints

Ethical constraints on research, especially the procedures designed to protect human subjects, are necessary. No one argues that the restrictions should be relaxed to make it easier to conduct treatment and other kinds of experimental research. On the contrary, even tighter restrictions on treatment research practice may need to be imposed because of the repeated research fraud and persistent ethical concerns with currently accepted treatment evaluation procedures described previ-

ously. Nonetheless, it is necessary to discuss some unexpected or unwanted consequences that ethical restraints have on the conduct of all research, especially on treatment research.

The data that treatment research generates under current ethical guidelines are inherently different from those that could be generated under a different set of circumstances. In making appropriate interpretations of treatment data, one needs to consider the conditions under which they were collected. Failure to consider the effects of ethical restraints on data collection may lead to questionable conclusions. Even more important, in the era of informed consent and voluntary participation in treatment research, certain standard methods of treatment research may be questionable. We shall address: (a) the biasing effects of informed consent and voluntary participation and (b) the participants' autonomy in the research process. These factors have decidedly changed the nature of treatment research evidence and have serious consequences for data interpretation.

The ethical problems associated with informed consent were previously discussed. This section covers the effects that informed consent has on the nature and quality of data. The biasing effects of full disclosure and the de facto self-selection of participants are both examined.

The Biasing Effects of Informed Consent

Participation without the informed consent of individuals is a serious ethical breach that is no longer expected to happen. On the other hand, informed consent and voluntary participation have changed the workings of random selection and assignment procedures. A troubling problem is the scientific consequence of informing the participants about certain procedures and their expected effects.

When participants are given the full details regarding the purposes and procedures of certain treatment techniques, a biasing effect may be created. This effect may then confound the effects of the treatment itself. For example, if people who stutter are told that the purpose of the experiment is to decrease their stuttering with a verbal *no* every time they stutter, some participants may monitor their stuttering more carefully. Such monitoring may produce its own effect on the frequency of stuttering.

A verbal conditioning study has documented the effects of disclosing the purpose of an experiment to the participants (Resnick & Schwartz, 1973). In this study, one group of participants was told that the purpose of the study was to increase a certain class of verbal behaviors by verbal reinforcers, which was the actual purpose of the study. Another group was simply told that the purpose was to study certain aspects of communication. The group that was informed of the actual purpose of the experiment did not show an increase in behaviors that were followed by the experimenter's verbal stimuli, whereas the group that was not informed showed the typical increase.

There are also research questions that cannot be answered unless the purposes of a study are concealed. For example, if a psychologist studies anger in a contrived laboratory situation, telling the potential participants about the purpose and the procedure of the study may make it subsequently impossible to evoke anger. Similarly, if a psychologist studies the con-

ditions under which people express surprise, full disclosure of the stimuli to be used in evoking surprise will leave nothing to study.

Many researchers in the past have not fully disclosed the purpose and the procedures of their studies to the participants. This has raised the ethical question of deception (Kelman, 1972; Milgram, 1977). Deception may be mild or extreme. A general description of the purpose and procedure may be provided while some crucial information is withheld from the participants. Deception may also involve total misrepresentation of the purposes of the study. The acceptability of a certain degree of deception or misrepresentation that does not create additional risks to the participants and that is considered absolutely essential to the study is debatable. One extreme position would consider any level of deception unethical and unacceptable and the other extreme position may allow it. Generally speaking, ethical standards of research require full disclosure.

Aspects of a study may be concealed only when the study itself does not produce any negative effects for the participants and there is no other way of studying that phenomenon (such as in a study on surprising conditions or stimuli). In such cases, participants who are not informed should be debriefed as soon as their participation is over. In **debriefing**, the participants are given a full description of the actual purposes and procedures of the study with an explanation as to why the information was withheld from them until the end of their participation. This is done to avoid any potential negative effects of the experimental procedures and the deception. For example, individuals who were made to experience anxiety, anger, or some other strong emotion in front of an audience may feel better when they find out the true nature of the experiment.

Effects of Participants' Autonomy

The most serious consequence for data generation is caused by the participants' autonomy, appropriately granted under all ethical guidelines on research. Unlike in the preinformed consent era, all participants now participate on their own accord. As noted before in this chapter, the participants may withdraw from any study at any time without negative consequence to them. In treatment studies, they may demand a treatment they are not assigned to, may demand treatment when they are assigned to a no-treatment or placebo control group, may request modification in their existing treatment plan, and so forth. These requirements, whose necessity and validity are not in question, produce profound consequences for treatment research, especially for RCTs.

The inevitable consequence of participant autonomy is that in all RCTs, participants are self-selected. *Participant autonomy* and *randomization* are contradictory terms. It is well documented that potential and eligible participants freely exercise their autonomy, as they should. In fact, 50% or more of eligible patients refuse to participate in RCTs because of the fear of getting randomized no-treatment or placebo control groups (Blichert-Toft, Mouridsen, & Andersen, 1996; Snowdon et al., 1997). Generally, more patients volunteer to participate if all groups are offered treatment (Jenkins & Fallowfield, 2000). When participants retain the right

to agree or refuse to participate, when they may drop out of the study at any time, and when they are allowed to demand and get the treatment they were not assigned to, then there is essentially no random selection or random assignment of participants or treatments. Therefore, the legally guaranteed participant autonomy renders randomization of RCTs meaningless. In RCTs, randomization supposedly determines who gets into the study, who gets what treatment, who gets no treatment, and who gets the placebo. But none of this holds good in RCTs when patients "vote with their feet" (Silverman & Altman, 1996, p. 171).

Feinstein (1970), a distinguished medical researcher, is among the very few who recognize that subject autonomy negates randomization. The general problem of participant autonomy, however, has been widely recognized by medical experts who call this a *nonconsenting bias* (Marcus, 1997) or *volunteer bias* (Edlund, Craig, & Richardson, 1985). Because of participant autonomy, the participants who eventually complete an RCT may not represent the population of patients who have the same disorder or disease. Consequently, the results cannot be extended; in other words, because of participant autonomy, the RCTs cannot claim statistical generality. Unfortunately, most of them do so anyway. For example, medical researchers continue to insist on RCTs because they allow statistical generality.

What is suggested here should be clear to the reader: Informed consent of participants is more valuable than the method of randomization. If ethically justified informed consent has a negative consequence for randomization, then the researchers should reconsider the theory, method, and value of randomization. Because researchers do need to keep informed consent, they may have to give up some of the cherished, but rarely realized, benefits of randomization.

Protection of Animal Subjects

We have concentrated on the ethical treatment of human participants in this chapter because of the preponderance of research involving human participants in clinical disciplines and education. However, ethical guidelines also should be followed when animal subjects are used in research.

Animals are frequently used in laboratory and field experiments. Research studies in medicine, biology, ethology, psychology, and pharmaceutics involve animals. Most new drugs are first used with animal subjects. New surgical procedures often are experimentally performed on animals. When the effects of new chemicals (other than drugs) are studied, once again animals are the primary participants. In behavioral and psychological research, animals with normal neurophysiological structures or those with altered structures (e.g., induced brain lesions) have been subjected to various stimuli. Any new research on the brain that involves an invasive procedure is first tried out on animals. Monkeys, rats, mice, cats, dogs, and fish often are used in these experiments.

In communication disorders, the use of animal subjects is limited. However, there are special problems that are studied with animals. In the study of the evolution and functioning of phonation, various species of animals are studied. Some of these studies may involve surgi-cal procedures to analyze the structures of phonatory mechanisms. Research on subhuman language or communication systems has involved animals, especially chimpanzees that have been taught various forms of nonverbal communication.

Animals probably are more frequently used in the study of audition. Chinchillas, for example, have frequently been used in the study of hearing because their auditory mechanism is similar to that of humans. Other animals used in auditory research include gerbils, cats, monkeys, guinea pigs, rats, mice, and birds. By using animals to study the electrical responses of cochlea, scientists have helped develop and refine cochlear implants for people who are deaf. Much of our knowledge of noise-induced hearing loss is derived from experimental research with animal subjects. Research on ototoxicity frequently involves animal subjects (Folkins, Gorga, Luschei, Vetter, & Watson, 1993).

The appropriateness of using animals in potentially dangerous experiments has been an issue at all times (Folkins et al., 1993; Rosenfeld, 1981). Advocates of animal rights have argued that many scientific experiments in which animals are subjected to painful and damaging procedures are unethical and should be banned. Those who justify the use of animal experiments remind everyone that many life-saving drugs, vaccines, and surgical procedures would not have been developed without animal experimentation.

Despite the controversy, animals will continue to be used as participants in scientific experiments. Therefore, the need to follow ethical guidelines in the care of laboratory animals is clear. There are various local, state, and federal laws pertaining to the use of animals in scientific research. Among others, the American

Psychological Association (2012) and National Research Council (2011) have published guidelines on the care and use of animals in research laboratories. These guidelines are periodically revised, and new federal guidelines are published in the *Federal Register.* Researchers should consult the current guidelines and adhere to them.

The guidelines suggest that the acquisition, care, use, and disposal of animals should follow federal, state, and local laws. The guidelines specify that those who engage in animal experimentation receive special training in the care of animal subjects. The experimenters are expected to minimize discomfort, illness, deprivation, stress, and pain due to the experimental procedures. Before animals are subjected to such procedures, scientists should consider alternative methods that are less painful or stressful. Radical procedures should be justified in terms of the scientific, educational, or applied benefit. Animals should be anesthetized before they are subjected to surgical procedures. Animals should be housed in comfortable and clean settings in which they are properly fed. While in the custody of scientists, animals should receive humane care. All institutions and laboratories that use animals in research should have an Institutional Animal Care and Use Committee to review policies and procedures and to ensure that the animal subjects are used according to established guidelines (Folkins et al., 1993).

Dissemination of Research Findings

The worth of a piece of research is judged by other scientists and, when possible, by the society at large. However, people, including scientists, can make this judgment only when research findings are disseminated. Therefore, dissemination of research findings is an ethical responsibility of researchers.

One can argue that if research findings are never going to be published, any amount of risk that the participants experience is unacceptable. Even when no risk is involved, efforts are involved. As participants, individuals give their time for research. Many experience inconveniences because of their participation in research. Individuals are expected to volunteer for research on the assumption that they contribute to the advancement of scientific knowledge. Unpublished results, unfortunately, do not advance scientific knowledge.

The information generated by scientific studies should receive the widest possible dissemination and the most appropriate dissemination. A majority of scientific studies are appropriately first published in scientific journals. When certain findings are technical and subject to misunderstanding by the general public, it may not be desirable to publish those findings in popular media. When it is judged that the findings of a treatment study are highly tentative, it may not be appropriate to disseminate them to potential clients who may be candidates for that or similar treatment. Most scientists prefer that the initial findings be published in a scientific or professional journal so that other experts can evaluate those findings and, if possible, replicate them. Scientists typically react negatively to publications of "new" and "revolutionary" scientific findings and clinical treatment procedures in popular media. Scientifically well-established findings, of course, should receive the widest possible dissemination. Such findings may be published in popular sources as well as in professional journals.

In conclusion, when scientists pay due attention to the ethical principles that govern research and publication, a responsible practice of science emerges. Ethical principles are meant to reduce the undesirable side effects of scientific research and thereby increase the potential of benefit to humankind. Every researcher should be fully knowledgeable in ethical principles so that the practice of science will be as responsible as its products are enlightening.

Summary

- The practice of science is an ethical activity. It is presumed that scientists report only what they observed and studied and that no data are falsified or fabricated. However, cases of scientific fraud are periodically reported.

- Scientists seek to produce positive effects, but negative effects may be associated with many desirable effects of science. The effects of science on society is an ethical issue.

- It is the ethical responsibility of clinical researchers to evaluate the effects of their treatment procedures in an ethically justifiable manner.

- All researchers should follow established procedures of protecting human participants and animal subjects in research. The human participant protection procedures involve such issues as the risk-benefit ratio, informed consent of participants, and the protection of participants' privacy.

- There are ethical concerns with treatment research methods: Informed consent may not fully accomplish its objectives; no-treatment and placebo-control procedures pose special ethical dilemmas; randomization may be both unethical and ineffective; some participant recruitment strategies may be questionable.

- Ethical constraints, though necessary, have certain consequences for study design and data interpretation. Informed consent and participant autonomy essentially negate randomization because under these rules all participants are self-selected.

- An ethical responsibility of researchers is to disseminate research findings. Such dissemination justifies research and the acceptable risk and inconvenience the participants may have faced.

References

American Psychological Association. (2002). Ethical principles of psychologists and code of conduct. *American Psychologist, 57*(12), 1060–1073.

American Psychological Association. (2012). *Guidelines for ethical conduct in the care and use of nonhuman animals in research*. Retrieved from http://www.apa.org/science/leadership/care/guidelines.aspk

American Speech-Language-Hearing Association. (2016). *Ethics in research and professional practice*. Retrieved from http://www.asha.org/code-of-Ethics/#569.5

Angell, M. (1997). The ethics of clinical research in the Third World. *New England Journal of Medicine, 337*, 847–849.

Azoulay, P., Bonatti, A., & Krieger, J. (2017). The career effects of scandal: Evidence from scientific retractions. *Research Policy, 46*(9), 1552–1569.

Barlow, D. H., Hayes, S. C., & Nelson, R. O. (1984). *The scientist practitioner: Research and accountability in clinical and educational settings.* New York, NY: Pergamon.

Beecher, H. K. (1966). Ethics and clinical research. *New England Journal of Medicine, 274,* 1354–1360.

Blichert-Toft, M., Mouridsen, H., & Andersen, K. W. (1996). Clinical trials. *Seminar in Surgical Oncology, 12*(1), 32–38.

Brody, B. A. (1998). *The ethics of biomedical research: An international perspective.* New York, NY: Oxford University Press.

Burt, C. (1972). Inheritance of general intelligence. *American Psychologist, 27,* 175–190.

Campbell, B. G. (1976). *Humankind emerging.* Boston, MA: Little, Brown.

Dekkers, W., & Boer, G. (2001). Sham neurosurgery in patients with Parkinson's disease: Is it morally acceptable? *Journal of Medical Ethics, 27*(3), 151–156.

Devlin, T. (1976, October 25). Theories of IQ pioneer 'completely discredited.' *Times.*

Diener, E., & Crandall, R. (1978). *Ethics in social and behavioral research.* Chicago, IL: University of Chicago Press.

Edlund, M. J., Craig, T. J., & Richardson, M. A. (1985). Informed consent as a form of volunteer bias. *American Journal of Psychiatry, 142,* 624–627.

Feinstein, A. R. (1970). Statistics versus science in the design of experiments. *Clinical Pharmacology and Therapeutics, 11,* 282–292.

Folkins, J. W., Gorga, M. P., Luschei, E. S., Vetter, D. K., & Watson, C. S. (1993). The use of nonhuman animals in speech, language, and hearing research. *ASHA, 35,* 57–65.

Gillie, O. (1976, October 24). Crucial data was faked by eminent psychologist. *Sunday Times.*

Gorkin, L., Schron, E. B., Handshaw, K., Shea, S., Kinney, M. R., Branyon, M., . . . Follick, M. J. (1996). Clinical trial enrollers vs. nonenrollers: The Cardiac Arrhythmia Suppression Trial (CAST) Recruitment and Enrollment Assessment in Clinical Trials (REACT) project. *Controlled Clinical Trials, 17*(1), 46–59.

Granter, S. R., & Papke, D. J. (2018). Medical misinformation in the era of Google: Computational approach to a pervasive problem. *Proceedings of the National Academy of Science, 115*(25), 318–321.

Hegde, M. N. (2007). A methodological review of randomized clinical trials. *Communicative Disorders Review, 1*(1), 17–38.

Jenkins, V., & Fallowfield, L. (2000). Reasons for accepting or declining to participate in randomized clinical trials for cancer therapy. *British Journal of Cancer, 82*(11), 1783–1788.

Jensen, A. (1992). Scientific fraud or false accusation? The case of Cyril Burt. In D. J. Miller & M. Hersen (Eds.), *Research fraud in behavioral and biomedical sciences* (pp. 97–124). New York, NY: Wiley.

Jones, J. (1981). *Bad blood.* New York, NY: Free Press.

Kamin, L. J. (1974). *The science and politics of I.Q.* Hillsdale, NJ: Lawrence Erlbaum.

Katz, J. (1972). *Experiments with human beings.* New York, NY: Russell Sage Foundation.

Kelman, H. C. (1972). Human use of human subjects: The problem of deception in social psychological experiments. *Psychological Bulletin, 67,* 1–11.

Madden, M. (1994). What women affected by breast cancer think about research and randomization: A report of the SSRU pilot study. In P. Aldersen (Ed.), *Breast cancer, random control trials, and consent* (pp. 62–76). London, UK: SSRU.

Marcus, S. M. (1997). Assessing non-consent bias with parallel randomized and nonrandomized clinical trials. *Journal of Clinical Epidemiology, 50*(7), 823–828.

McIntosh, N. (1993). Strengthen ethical committee's role. *British Medical Journal, 307,* 1496.

McKee, M., Gritton, A., Black, N., McPherson, K., Sanderson, C., & Bain, C. (1999). Interpreting the evidence: Choosing between randomized and non-randomized studies. *British Medical Journal, 319,* 312–315.

Miers, M. (1998). Current NIH perspectives on misconduct in science. In A. E. Kazdin (Ed.), *Methodical issues and strategies in clinical research* (2nd ed., pp. 787–694). Washington, DC: American Psychological Association.

Milgram, S. (1977, October). Subject reaction: The neglected factor in the ethics of experimentation. *The Hastings Center Report*, 7(5), 19–23.

Miller, D. J. (1992). Plagiarism: The case of Elias A. K. Alsabati. In D. J. Miller & M. Hersen (Eds.), *Research fraud in the behavioral and biomedical sciences* (pp. 80–96). New York, NY: Wiley.

Miller, D. J., & Hersen, M. (Eds.). (1992). *Research fraud in the behavioral and biomedical sciences.* New York, NY: Wiley.

Miller, F. G., & Kaptchuk, T. K. (2008). Deception of subjects in neuroscience: An ethical essay. *Journal of Neuroscience*, 28(19), 4841–4843.

Morris, A. D., Zaritsky, A. L., & LeFever, G. (2000). Evaluation of ethical conflicts associated with randomized, controlled trials in critically ill children. *Critical Care Medicine*, 28(4), 1152–1156.

National Research Council. (2011). *Guide for the care and use of laboratory animals* (8th ed.) Washington, DC: National Academies Press.

Office for Protection from Research Risks. (1991). Protection of human subjects: Title 45 Code of Federal Regulations, Part 46 (GPO 1992-O-307-551). *OPRR Reports*, pp. 4–17.

Office for Protection from Research Risks. (1993). *Protecting human research subjects: Institutional review board guidebook.* Washington, DC: Government Printing Office.

Onslow, M., Andrews, C., & Lincoln, M. (1994). A control/experimental trial of an operant treatment for early stuttering. *Journal of Speech and Hearing Research*, 37, 1244–1259.

Panel on Scientific Responsibility and the Conduct of Research. (1992). *Responsible science: Ensuring the integrity of the research process* (Vol. I). Washington, DC: National Academies Press.

Ranstam, J., Buyse, M., George, S. L., Evans, S., Geller, N. L., Sherrer, B., . . . Lachenbruch, P. (2000). Fraud in medical research: An international survey of biostatisticians. *Controlled Clinical Trials*, 21(5), 415–427.

Resnick, J. H., & Schwartz, T. (1973). Ethical standards as an independent variable in psychological research. *American Psychologist*, 28, 134–139.

Rosenfeld, A. (1981). Animal rights vs. human health. *Science, 18*, 22.

Rothman, K. J., & Michels, K. B. (1994). The continued unethical use of placebo controls. *New England Journal of Medicine, 331*, 394–398.

Shaughnessy, J. J., & Zechmeister, E. B. (1985). *Research methods in psychology.* New York, NY: Knopf.

Siegel, G. M., & Spradlin, J. E. (1985). Therapy and research. *Journal of Speech and Hearing Disorders, 50*, 226–230.

Silverman, W. A. (1989). The myth of informed consent: In daily practice and in clinical trials. *Journal of Medical Ethics, 15*(1), 6–11.

Silverman, W. A., & Altman, D. G. (1996). Patients' preferences and randomized trials. *Lancet, 347*, 171–174.

Snowdon, C., Garcia, J., & Elbourne, D. (1997). Making sense of randomization: Responses of parents of critically ill babies to random allocation of treatment in a clinical trial. *Social Sciences and Medicine, 45*, 1337–1355.

Tangney, J. P. (1987). Fraud will out—or will it? *New Scientist, 115*, 6263.

Taylor, K. M. (1985). The doctor's dilemma: Physician participation in randomized clinical trials. *Cancer Treatment Report, 69*, 1095–1100.

Verdu-Pascal, F., & Castello-Ponce, A. (2001). Randomized clinical trials: A source of ethical dilemmas. *Medical Ethics, 27*(3), 177–178.

Wakefield, A. J., Murch, S. H., Anthony, A., Linnell, J., Casson, D. M., Malik, M., . . . Smith, J. A. (1998). Ileal-lymphoid-nodular hyperplasia, non-specific colitis, and pervasive developmental disorder in children. *Lancet, 351*, 637–641.

World Medical Association. (2013). World Medical Association Declaration of Helsinki: Ethical principles for medical research involving human subjects. *Journal of the American Medical Association, 310*(20), 2191–2194.

Your baby is in a trial [Editorial]. (1995). *Lancet, 345,* 805–806.

Study Guide

1. What are the sources of questionable data?

2. How are theories and hypotheses related to the questions of reliability and validity of data?

3. Describe some of the undesirable side effects of science and technology. What steps do you suggest to counteract them?

4. What is an apparent ethical dilemma of clinical experimentation?

5. When is a treatment experimental?

6. What are some of the false questions relative to the ethics of clinical experimentation?

7. Is the question, "Should we experiment with treatment procedures?" ethically or otherwise valid? Justify your answer.

8. Should one experiment with an untested treatment procedure that has been used widely over a number of years? Why or why not?

9. Does the practice of a treatment procedure, when it is not called "experimental," raise ethical questions? Under what conditions are such questions likely to be raised?

10. What is "research" according to the National Research Act?

11. What is an institutional review board? How is it constituted? What are its concerns?

12. What is a risk-benefit ratio? How is it determined? In this process, whose risk and whose benefits are evaluated?

13. Does the presence of risk to the participants automatically mean that a study cannot be conducted? Justify your answer.

14. What are the three components of informed consent?

15. You wish to evaluate a stuttering treatment program using one of the group designs. Describe the procedures for obtaining informed consent from your participants.

16. What procedures would you use in protecting the privacy of your clients who participate in research studies?

17. What are the ethical concerns with informed consent procedures?

18. Summarize the ethical concerns with no-treatment and placebo control groups. What solutions would you offer?

19. What ethical consequences does randomization have on data?

20. What are the negative consequences of treatment withdrawal or reversal? How are these consequences handled?

21. Describe the major ethical problems with participant recruitment.

22. Describe the various consequences of ethical constraints on data and their interpretation.

Index

A

AB design, described, 275

ABA design, 88
  described, 25–26
  withdrawal, 276–278

ABAB design, 88, 279–282

ABCB design, 281

Absolute effect, 117

Abstract words, writing and, 444–445

Academic discipline, communication
    disorders as, 4

Accidental
  discoveries, hypotheses and, 56
  sampling, 80

Accuracy, 176

Active variables, 48

Adequate writing, 441–442

African Americans, ethnographic research
    and, 148

Age, described, 130–131

Agreement
  of elements in sentence, 431–434
  interobserver, 327
  ratio, unit-by-unit, 176

Alliance for Human Research Protection,
    480

Alsabti, Elias A. K., 474

Alternating treatments design (ATD),
    291–296

Alternations, rapid alterations, as control
    mechanism, 97–98

Ambiguity, in writing, 442

American Medical Association, 418

American Psychological Association (APA),
    326, 420, 495–496
  Publication Manual, 414, 418

American Speech-Language-Hearing
    Association (ASHA)
  APA format used by, 418, 419, 480
  journal database, 405

Analysis of covariance (ANCOVA), 319

Analysis of variance (ANOVA), 202, 316,
    319
  main effects in, 234

Anatomists, 8

ANCOVA (Analysis of covariance), 319–320

Animal studies, ethics of, 495–496

ANOVA (Analysis of variance), 202, 316,
    319
  main effects in, 234

Antiscientific ideology, human behavior
    and, 41

APA (American Psychological Association),
    326, 420, 495–496
  Publication Manual, 414, 418

Aphasia, 70–71

Appendix, research papers and, 427

Applied
  behavior analysis, 269–270
  research, 135, 138–142
    strengths/weaknesses of, 142

Appreciation, of research, 466–467

Archival data, 243

Articles
  described, 418
  journal, identifying current trends with,
    404

Articulation, phenomenon of, 46

ASHA (American Speech-Language-
    Hearing Association)
  APA format used by, 418, 419
  journal database, 405

Assent form, 483

Assigned variables, 48–49, 366

Assignment
  random, 81
    of participants, 81–82

As-treated analysis, 424

ATD (Alternating treatments design),
    291–296

Attrition
  defined, 199
  internal validity and, 199–200

Author note, 420
Authorized deception, 483
Autonomy of participants, 494–495
Average effect, 326
  size, 325

B

Baselines, 98–106
  criteria, 99
  described, 98, 271
  deteriorating, 100
  improving, 100
  potential for contrast, 101
  simultaneous multiple, 99, 102, 104, 106
Basic research, 135
  described, 11
Behavior
  analysis
    applied, 269–270
    behavior, 268–269
  free will and, 189
  observation of, qualitative research and, 147
  as science, 41–43
Belmont Report, 480
Between-groups design, 135, 192, 218, 246
Bias
  informed consent and, 492–494
  investigator, 57
  nonconsenting, 494
  observer, 171–172
  publication, 326
  subject selection, 199
  volunteer, 494
  writing without, 427–428
Biochemists, 8
Bioengineers, 8
Biography, qualitative research and, 147
Biologists, 8
Biometrika, 314
Black English, 428
Blinding
  described, 85
  single or double, 84–87
Books, edited on controversies, as source of research, 407
The British Medical Journal, 77

Broca's
  aphasia, 267
  speech area, 267
Bureaucratic reasons, for conducting research, 21
Burt, Cyril, 473

C

Carrover effects, 252
  contrast effects and, 295–296
Case study (history) method, 124–127
  control, 141–142
  individuals, 268
  one-shot, 220
  procedures, 124–126
  qualitative research and, 147
  strengths/weaknesses of, 126–127
Casually related events, 187
  causality, 50–53, 114
  multiple, 50–52
Cause-effect relations, 59, 344
  between treatment and positive changes, 115
  conditions to be met for, 76
  consequences and treatment, 116
  controlled
    conditions and, 54
    unreplicated evidence and, 466
  correlation and, 255
  establishing, 23
  ex post facto method and, 126
  experimental research and, 138, 223
  experiments and, 134
  identification of, 125
  independent variables and, 47, 391, 395
  internal validity and, 194
  isolation of, 135, 193
  medicine vs. communication disorders and, 111
  multi-group time-series design and, 245
  research design and, 186
  single-subject approach, 87
  treatment research and, 114
Causes precede effects, 59
Ceiling effects, 252–253, 291
Change, criterion-referenced, 94–96
Chemical phenomena, 40

Chemists, 8
Child psychology, 8
Childbed fever, 35
Children, informed consent and, 483
Chi-square test, 321
Chomskyan innate hypotheses, 43
Chomsky's nativist theory, 43
Cineradiography, 175
CITI (Collaborative Institutional Training
    Initiative), 475
Classes, generality within and across,
    208–209
Clear writing, 442–445
Cleft palate, 51
Clichés, writing and, 443–444
Client-assisted measurement, 169–170
Clinical generality, 204, 214
Clinical profession, communication
    disorders as, 4
Clinical relevance, 202, 209–210
Clinical research, 10–11, 138–142
    applied, 152
    generality, across clients, 205
    group designs in, 255–259
    matching participants in, 84
    in single-subject design study, 303–304
    strengths/weaknesses of, 142
Clinical science
    communication disorders as, dependent
        variables and, 13
    educators and, 15
Clinical significance, 107, 202, 209–210
    group vs. single subject research, 338
    qualitative measures of, 334–336
    quantitative measures of, 336–338
    vs. single-subject design study, 333–338
    vs. statistically significant, 333–338
    treatments and, 70–71
Clinical trials
    described, 77
    N-of-1 randomized, 302–303
    randomized, 77–87, 140, 312
        control/experimental groups, 87
        described, 77–78
        group treatment research and, 84–87
        matching of participants, 83–84
        nonprobability sampling, 80–82
        placebo effect and, 86

probability sampling, 78–80
random assignment of participants,
    82–83
random selection of participants, 77–78
self-selection in, 107–109
single or double blinding, 84–87
vs. single-subject treatment research,
    106–113
treatment administration, 84
Clinical usefulness, of research, 10–11
Clinical validity, 202, 209–210, 214
    vs. statistical generality, 107
Clinically significant
    effects, 70–71
    treatments, 334
Cluster sampling, 79
Coefficient of correlation, 314
Coercion, ethics and, 491
Cognition, intervening variables and, 48
Coherent writing, 445–446
Cohort studies, 141
Collaborative Institutional Training
    Initiative (CITI), 475
Colloquial expressions, avoiding, 444
Communication
    disorders, 47
        as academic discipline, 4
        as clinical profession, 4
        clinical professions community and,
            concerns of, 6–7
        as clinical science, dependent
            variables and, 13
        deductive reasoning and, 61
        vs. medicine, treatment research and,
            111–113
        studies of, 44–45
        variables and, 48
    normal, variables and, 48
Communicative behavior measures,
    162–169
Community intervention, 140
Comparisons
    normative, 337
    standard-group, 131–133
        procedures, 131–133
        strengths/weaknesses of, 132–133
Completely randomized factorial design,
    234–236

Complex counterbalanced designs, 250
Components, of treatment, interaction between, 366
Concise writing, 438–441
Concrete words, writing and, 444–445
Consecutive sampling, 80
Consistency, 175
    described, 328
Consolidated Standards of Reporting Trials (CONSORT), 421
CONSORT (*Consolidated Standards of Reporting Trials*), 421
Constraints, logical, 74–77
Contextually correlated behaviors, 163
Contrast
    effects, carryover effects and, 295–296
    potential for, baselines, 101
Control
    experimental, 62
    mechanisms, unexpected change in, 371–372
Control groups, 87, 133
    ethical issues with, 110–111
        no treatment, 486–487
        placebo-control group, 487–489
    posttest-only, 225–226
    relative effects and, 229
Controlled
    conditions, 54, 56
        cause-effect relations and, 54
    data, 63
    directly replicated
        evidence, 466
        treatment research, 118
    experimental conditions, 134–135
    group designs, 219
    replicated data, 63
    research, 69
    systematically replicated
        evidence, 466–467
        treatment research, 118–119
    treatment evaluations, 140
    unreplicated treatment research, 116–118
Controlling relation, 54
Controls
    single-subject treatment research, 87–106
        baselines, 98–106

criterion-referenced change, 94–96
    rapid alterations, 97–98
    reinstatement of treatment, 93–94
    replication of, 88–89
    reversal of treatment, 91–93
    withdrawal of treatment, 89–91
Convenience sampling, 80
Conversation, qualitative research and, 147
Correlated events, 187
Correlation
    described, 254
    by regression to the mean, 314
Correlation index, 314
Correlational
    analysis, 219, 253–255, 322–323
    design, 253
Counterbalanced, 246–247
    crossover group designs, 291
    designs
        within-subject designs, limitations of, 251–253
Counterbalancing
    described, 248
    order effects and, 294–295
Covariate, 319–320
Criterion
    design change, single-subject design study, 289–290
    referenced change, 94–96, 289
Crossover designs, 246–247, 249
Current trends
    identifying, 403–406
        current trends with, databases, 404–405
        study journal articles, 404

D

d statistic, 331
Dangling modifiers, 434, 435
Data
    controlled, 63
    controlled replicated, 63
    defined, 62
    descriptive, 62
    points, percentage of exceeding median, 330
    quantitative, 62
    soundness of, 373–374

statistical analysis of, 272–274, 312–316
   probability theory and, 312–314
uncontrolled, 63
visual inspection of vs. statistical
   analysis, 272–274
Data and Safety Monitoring Board
   (DSMB), research papers and, 422
Databases, identifying current trends with,
   404–405
Debriefing, 493
Deception, authorized, 483
Deductive
   method, of research, 23
   reasoning, 59–61
      communication disorders and, 61
      inductive reasoning compared with,
         60–61
   theory, building, 59–60
Delayed consequences, of treatment, 69
Dependability, 175
Dependent variables, 13, 46–47, 76
   change in, magnitude of, 395–396
   described, 362–363
   distribution of, 363
   integrity of, 394–395
   philosophy of, 386–389
   reconceptualization of, 395
   repeated measurement of, 271–272
Descriptive
   clinical (applied) research, 139
   data, 62
   studies
      communication disorders, 44–45
      as source of research, 406–407
Design
   selection, investigator in, 373
   strategies
      advantages/disadvantages of, 369–371
      common problems of, 371–372
Deteriorating baseline, 100
Determinism, 40–41, 383
DHHS (Health and Human Services), 480
Diagnostic criterion, 335, 338
Differential distribution, of a variable, 363
Dimensional quantity, 158
Direct
   consequences of treatment, 69
   effects of treatment, 70–71
   replications, 69, 344–347

Disclosure, incomplete, 483
Discourse analysis, qualitative research
   and, 147
Discussion section, research papers and,
   425–426
Discussions, affect of, 10
Dissertations, 419
   preparation of, 413–414
Distribution free, nonparametric tests, 321
Documentation
   client, 6
   of outcomes, 72–73
   research report, 30
   systematic, 73
Double blinding, 84–87
DSMB (Data and Safety Monitoring
   Board), research papers and, 422
Durational measures, 164–165
Dyadic interaction, 168
Dysarthria, 47

E

Ebbinghaus, Hermann, 267
EBSCO, as source of research, 405
Eclecticism, 385–386
Edgeworth, Francis, 314
Education for all Handicapped Children
   Act of 1977 (P.L. 94-142), 5–6
Education programs, 11
Effect sizes, 424–425
   average, 325
   described, 329
   nonoverlap calculations, single-subject
      design study and, 329–331
   single-subject design study and, 329
Effectiveness
   defined, 73, 74
   improvement and, 69
   of treatments, 365–366
      across individuals, 368–369
   vs efficacy, 69, 73–74
Effects
   clinically significant, 70–71
   demonstrating, 26–28
Efficacy, 73
   defined, 73
   vs. effectiveness in treatments, 69, 73–74
Electroencephalography, 174

Electromyography, 174
Elements, agreement of in writing, 431–434
Empirical
  conditions, 76
    treatment research and, 74–77
  research, article, 13–16, 33
Empiricism, 41, 383
English, writing without bias, 428
Epidemics, defined, 139
Epidemiological research, 139–142
Epidemiology, defined, 139
Equivalent frequency distribution matching, 83
ERIC, 325
  as source of research, 405
Error variance, 190
Ethics
  constraints, consequences of, 492–495
  of research, 472–497
    animal studies, 495–496
    autonomy of participants, 494–495
    control groups and, 110–111
    fraud and, 472–476
    informed consent, 482–486
    participant privacy, 484–485
    placebo-control group, 487–489
    randomization and, 489
    recruitment of participants and, 490–493
    risk-benefit ratio, 481–482
    treatment evaluation, 476–478
    treatment issues and, 485–492
    treatment withdrawal, 490
Ethnocultural groups, generality across, 206–207
Ethnographic research, 147–148
Ethology, defined, 44
Euphemisms, writing and, 442–443
Evaluations
  philosophical considerations in, 372–373
  treatment evaluations, 140
Events
  casually related, 187
  correlated, 187
  explaining, 23–24
  independent, 187
Evidence
  based practice, 68

levels of, 463–467
  controlled directly replicated, 466
  controlled systematically replicated, 466–467
  controlled unreplicated, 466
  statistically significant and, 464
  uncontrolled directly replicated, 465
  uncontrolled systematically replicated, 466
  uncontrolled unreplicated
  scientific, 63
Ex post facto research, 124–127
  described, 152
  procedures, 124–126
  strengths/weaknesses of, 126–127
Experiment
  defined, 53, 133–134
  independent variable and, 77
Experimental
  clinical research, 11
  control, 62, 106–107
  data, statistically significant of, 313
  designs
    controlling variability, 192–193
    true, 223–228
  groups, 87, 133
  psychology, 8
  research, 133–138
    basic/applied, 135
    cause-effect relations and, 138, 223
    clinical, 139
    design, 186
    procedures, 134–135
    strengths/weaknesses of, 136–138
    validity of, 193–201
  validity of operations, 194
Experimenters, generality across, 207–208
Experiments, described, 44
Explanation, science and, 45
External validity, 114, 201–210, 213, 214
  across
    ethnocultural groups, 206–207
    experimenters, 207–208
    individuals, 205–206
    response classes, 208–209
    settings, 207
  described, 63, 201
  factors affecting, 210–212
  logical, 204–209

Extraneous
variables, 75–77, 134–135
variance, 190
Extrinsic, variability, 190–192, 213

F

Factor, defined, 231
Factorial designs, 231–236
Failed replications, 353–355
Faulty analysis, 171
Fechner, Gustav, 267
Federal Register, 494
Fiber-optic scope, 174
Fidelity, described, 327
Field
completely randomized factorial design,
236
experiments, 135
trials, 140
Figures of speech, writing and, 445
Fisher, Ronald A., 256, 314–315
Fixed-effect analysis, 325
Fleming, Alexander, 27, 34–35
Floor effects, 252–253
Fluency, 46
Formal view, of research, 28–30
Formative view, of research, 30–34
Formats, writing and, 447–448
Four-group experimental design, 226
Framework, of research designs, 186–187
Fraud, in research, 472–476
Free will, 189
Frequency
measures, 163–164
ratio, 178
Functional
analysis, 50–53
outcomes of treatments, 333–334

G

Galton, Francis, 160, 314
Galvanic skin reflex (GSR), 174
Game theory, 313
Gauss, Karl Fredrick, 313
Gaussian
curve, 313
distribution, 313

Generality, 114, 201–210, 213, 214
across
ethnocultural groups, 206–207
experimenters, 207–208
individuals, 205–206
response classes, 208–209
settings, 207
clinical, 204, 214
described, 63, 201, 344, 372
factors affecting, 210–212
inferential, 202–204, 218, 315
logical, 107, 204–209, 272
sample size and, 351–353
statistical, 114, 201–210, 352
types/limitations of, 201–210
Generalization, described, 213
Generalized treatment consequences,
71–72
Geneticists, 8
Goals, defined, 44
Goodness-of-fit test, 321
Grammar
correct, 447
described, 428–429
Grounded theory, 147, 148
Group behavior, predictability of behavior,
368
Group designs, 192
between, 192, 218, 246
characteristics of, 218–219
experimental
limitations of, 256–259
strength of, 256
parallel, 218, 246, 303
posttest-only control, 225–226
preexperimental designs, 219–222
pretest-posttest control, 223–225
Solomon four, 226–228
statistical analysis of data, 318–323
strategy, 372
true experimental designs, 223–228
well-controlled, 219
Group treatment research
randomized clinical trials, 77–87
matching of participants, 83–84
nonprobability sampling, 80–82
probability sampling, 78–80
random assignment of participants,
82–83

Group treatment research; randomized
clinical trials *(continued)*
    random selection of participants,
        77–78
    single or double blinding, 84–87
    treatment administration, 84
Groups
    control of, 87, 133
    experimental, 87, 133
GSR (Galvanic skin reflex), 174

H

Hawthorne effect, 211
Health and Human Services (DHHS), 480
Hearing, Its Psychology and Physiology,
    334
Helsinki Declaration on Research Ethics,
    479, 487
Heterogeneity, of participants, 355–357
Heterogeneous
    intersubject replication, 345
    participants, 345
Hill, Austin Bradford, randomized trials
    and, 77–78
Hispanic Americans, ethnographic
    research and, 148
History (participants')
    described, 195
    internal validity and, 195
Homogeneity, of participants, 355–357
Homogeneous
    intersubject replication, 344
    participants
        described, 345
        problem of finding, 345–347
HPS *d*, 331
Human behavior
    antiscientific ideology and, 41
    variability, 188
Human Participants Protection Committee,
    108
    research papers and, 422
Hypotheses
    accidental discoveries and, 56
    Chomskyan innate, 43
    described, 23, 58
    function of, 55

myopia, 37
need for, 55–57
null, 29, 56, 317–318
in research, 54–57, 317
testing, 317–318
theories and, 57–58
Hypotheses non fingo, 55
Hypothetical constructs, 48

I

Idemnotic measurements, 159
Immediacy, described, 328
Implementation
    problems of, 372
    science, 142–143
Improvement
    consequences of treatment and, 73–74
    defined, 73–74
    effectiveness and, 69
    percentage of, 337
    treatment and, 364–365
Improving baseline, 100
Inadequate writing, 442
Incidence, defined, 139
Incomplete disclosure, 483
Independent
    effect, 117
    events, 187
    variables, 47–48
        cause-effect relations and, 47, 391, 395
        described, 76–77
        effects of, 364
        locus of, 390–393
        manipulation as, 54
Indirect
    consequences of treatment, 69
    self-report measures, 170–171
Individuals
    case study method, 268
    generality across, 205–206
    importance of differences of, 270–271
    neurophysiological study of, 267–268
    profiles, logical generality and, 204
    psychological study of, 267–268
    study of, 266–268
Individuals With Disabilities Education Act
    (P.L. 101- 476), 6

Inductive
  method, of research, 23
  reasoning, 58–59, 298–299
    deductive reasoning compared with, 60–61
Inferential
  generality, 202–204, 218, 315
    group design strategy and, 312
  statistics
    randomization and, 314–316
    techniques, 202
Informed consent, 482–484
  biasing effects of, 492–494
  ethical issues of, 485–486
Informed consent form, 483
Inhouse
  knowledge, need to produce, 8–9
  problems, solving, 24
Initial cluster, 79
Instigating causes, 52
Institute of Medicine, ethics and, 473
Institutional Animal Care and Use
    Committee, 496
Institutional review boards (IRB), 108, 480–484
  informed consent and, 481–484
  research papers and, 422
  research participants privacy, 484–485
  risk-benefit ratio and, 481–482
Instrumentation, internal validity and, 197–198
Integrated moving average model, 244
Intention-to-treat method, 424
Interaction, defined, 232
Interactional
  effects, 117–118
  studies, designs for, 299–302
Interactive variables, 187–188
Interference, multiple treatment, 211–212
Internal validity, 75, 106–107, 194–201, 203, 213
  attrition and, 199–200
  cause-effect relations and, 194
  instrumentation and, 197–198
  maturation (participants') and, 195–196
  participants' history and, 195
  statistical regression and, 198–199
  subject selection bias and, 199

testing and, 196–197
  treatment diffusion and, 200–201
Interobserver
  agreement, 327
  reliability, 176–178
Interpretation, objective, 57
Interresponse time measure, 165–166
Intersubject
  replication, 89
  variability, 371, 393–394
Interval scale, 162
Intervening variables, 49–50
Intervention, community, 140
Interviews, qualitative research and, 147
Intragroup counterbalancing, 248
Intraobserver reliability, 176
Intrasubject
  counterbalancing, 248
  replication, 88–89, 344
  variability, 371
Intrinsic
  variability, 189–190
  view, of variability, 213
Introduction, to research papers, 421–422
Introspection, 267
  qualitative research and, 147
Intuition, qualitative research and, 147
Investigative strategies, 362–369
Investigators
  bias of, 57
  in design selection, 373
  qualitative research and, 147
IRB (Institutional review board), 480–484
  informed consent and, 482–484
  research papers and, 422
  research participants privacy, 484–485
  risk-benefit ratio, 481–482

J

Jargon, writing and, 443
Jefferson, Thomas, 85
*Journal Article Reporting Standards for
    Quantitative Research*, 420–421
Journal articles, identifying current trends
    with, 404
Journal of Applied Behavior Analysis, 12
Journal of Clinical Epidemiology, 259

Journal of Mixed Methods Research, 151
Journal of Neuropsychological Rehabilitation, 259
Journal of Quality and Quantity, 149
Journal of the American Medical Association, 500

K

Kendall's tau, 330–331
Knowledge
    evaluation of research and, 452
    need to produce in-house, 8–9
Kruskal-Wallis ANOVA, 321, 322
Kymograph, 174

L

Lancet, 474, 486
Language
    classifying behaviors of, 11
    phenomenon of, 46
    philosophy of science of, 384–386
    skills, improvement of, 75
    technical, specifying variables in, 409–410
Laplace, Pierre Simon, 313
Latency measures, 166
Latin square design, 250
Lectures, affect of, 10
Letters to the editor
    described, 419
    as source of research, 407
Level of data, 327
Levels of evidence, 463–467
    controlled
        directly replicated, 466
        controlled systematically replicated, 466–467
        controlled unreplicated, 466
        statistically significant and, 464
    uncontrolled
        directly replicated, 465
        systematically replicated, 466
        unreplicated, 465
Levels of measurement, 160–162
    nominal scale, 161
    ordinal scale, 161
Life
    assessment, quality of, 335

events, internal validity and, 195
Linguistics, 8, 385
Linguistics and Language Behavior
    Abstracts, as source of research, 406
Locus of the independent variables, 390–393
Logical
    constraints, treatment research and, 74–77
    generality, 107, 204–209, 272
London University College, 314

M

Mainstream English, 419–427
Maintained consequences, 71–72
Maintaining causes, 52
Manipulation
    as independent variable, 54
    systematic, 62
Mann-Whitney U test, 224, 239, 339
    static-group comparison and, 222
    statistically significant and, 321–323
MANOVA (Multivariate analysis of variance), 319–320
Market-driven outcomes, 72
Matching
    equivalent frequency distribution, 83
    participants, 83–84
Maturation (participants')
    described, 196
    internal validity and, 195–196
MBDs (Multiple baseline designs)
    single-subject design study, 282–287
        across behaviors, 282–285
        across settings, 286–287
        across subjects, 285–286
        additional control in, 288–289
        repeated baselines problem, 287–288
Meaningful changes, 334
Measured values
    validity of, 194
    variability of, 327–328
Measurement
    client-assisted, 169–170
    communicative behaviors, 162–169
    defined, 158
    described, 44
    durational, 164–165

indirect, self-reports, 170–171
instruments, research papers and, 423
latency, 166
mechanically assisted, 174–175
philosophies of, 158–160, 389–390
process, observer in, 171–174
research and, 24
of research designs, 187
scales of, 160–162
  frequency, 163–164
  interval, 162
  nominal, 161
  ordinal scale, 161
  ratio, 162
time, interresponse, 165–166
Measures
research papers and, 423
stability of, 99
Mechanical devices, described, 174
Mechanically assisted observation/
  measurement, 174–175
Medicine
vs. communication disorders, treatment
  research and, 111–113
research and, 8
MEDLINE, as source of research, 405
Mental expectation, 207
Mentalism, 41, 49
Meta-analysis
described, 324
multilevel, 332
of single-subject design study, 332–333
statistical analysis and, 324–326
Metaphors, writing and, 444
Meta-regression, 326
Methodology
approaches, limitations of exclusively,
  380
described, 380
interplay of philosophy and, 396–397
philosophy as, 382–384
problems, handling, 393–396
Methods, thinking of the, 411–413
Mind, intervening variables and, 48
Misplaced modifiers, 434
Mixed-methods research (MMR), 150–151
described, 153
strengths/weaknesses of, 151
MMR (Mixed-methods research), 150–151

described, 153
strengths/weaknesses of, 151
Models, communication disorders, 44–45
Modifiers, writing and, 434–435
Moment of observation, 167
Momentary time sampling, 167–168
Morphemes, measured production of,
  86–87
Moving average model, integrated, 244
Multigroup
posttest-only design, 230–231
pretest-posttest design, 229–230
Multilevel meta-analysis, 332
Multiple baseline designs (MBDs)
across settings, 286–287
additional control in, 288–289
repeated baselines problem, 287–288
single-subject design study, 282–287
  across behaviors, 282–285
  across subjects, 285–286
Multiple causality, 50–52
Multiple causation, 187
Multiple experiments, research papers
  and, 426
Multiple treatment
evaluation designs, 228–231
ineffective treatments in, 298–299
interference, 211–212
Multiple treatment comparison
single-subject design study for, 290–299
  ABACA/ABABA design and, 291–293
  alternating treatments design and,
    293–296
  ineffective treatments in, 298–299
  simultaneous treatments design and,
    296–297
Multiple-treatment interference, 252
Multistage sampling, 79
Multivariate analysis of variance
  (MANOVA), 319–320
Myopia, hypotheses, 37

N

Narrative reviews, 324
National Academy of Engineering, ethics
  and, 473
National Academy of Sciences, ethics and,
  473

National Commission for the Protection of Human Subjects of Biomedical and Behavioral Research, 480
National Research Council, 496
National Science Foundation, 474
Natural
    events
        control of, 45
        described, 44–45
        understanding, 45
        as variables, 46
    phenomena, curiosity about, 22–23
    rates, of responses, 98
    science, variables and, 383
Negative interaction, 232
Nervous system, intervening variables and, 48
Neuman-Keuls test, 319
Neurophysiological
    study, of individuals, 267–268
    variables, 51
No treatment control group, ethical concerns with, 486–487
N-of-1 trials, 302–303, 489
Nominal scale, 161
Nonconsenting bias, 494
Nonequivalent control group design, 236–238
Nonexperimental research, 140
Nonoverlap
    calculations, effect sizes, single-subject design study and, 329–331
        methods, 329–330
        described, 329
Nonoverlapping data, percentage of, 330
Nonparametric tests of statistically significant, 321–322
Nonprobability sampling, 80–82
Nonrandomized blocks designs, 315
Nonrepresentative sample, 145
Normal probability curve, 312–314
Normative
    comparison, 337
    research, 127–129
        described, 152
        procedures, 128–129
        strengths/weaknesses of, 129–131
Null hypotheses, 29, 56, 317–318

Nuremberg Code, 479
Nuremberg trial, 479

O

Objective
    interpretation, 57
    procedures, 43–44
Obligatory contexts, 163
Observation
    of behaviors, qualitative research and, 147
    described, 44
    mechanically assisted, 174–175
    moment of, 167
    quantified, 158
    reliability through multiple, 99
    research and, 24
Observer
    bias, 171–172
    training, 172
One-group
    pretest-posttest design, 219, 220–221
    single-treatment counterbalanced design, 247–249
One-shot case study, 219, 220
One-way analysis of variance, 319
Operant level, of responses, 98
Operational definitions, 162
Operationally, described, 47
Order effects, 251–252
    counterbalancing effects and, 294–295
Ordinal scale, 161
Original research, 403
Oscilloscopes, 175
Outcomes
    defined, 73
    documentation of, 72–73
Overlap, described, 328

P

p value, 320
Pairs of participants, matching, 83
PAND (Percentage of all nonoverlapping data), 330
Papers
    research
        abstract, 420–421

appendix to, 427
discussion section, 425–426
introduction, 421–422
measures/measurement instruments, 423
method of study section, 422–423
participants section, 423
principles for good writing of, 428–446
references section, 426–427
research design section, 423–424
results section, 424–425
structure/content of, 419–427
title page, 420
treatment section, 424
writing without bias, 427–428
structure/content of, experimental manipulations section, 424
Paradigms, 382
Paragraphs, writing and, 446
Parallel
forms, in writing, 435–436
groups strategy, 218, 246, 303
Parametric tests
described, 318
of significance, 318–321
Participant-observer, 147
Participant variables, treatment variables and, 366
Participants, 81–82
assignment of
matching, 83–84
random, 82–83
autonomy of, 494–495
heterogeneity of, 355–357
heterogeneous, 345
homogeneity of, 355–357
homogeneous, problem of finding, 345–347
intensive study and, 270
matching, 83–84
pairs of, matching, 83
privacy of, 484–485
protecting, 479–481
recruitment of, ethics of, 490–493
research papers and, 423
selection of, 272
Pearson, Karl, 314

Pearson Product Moment Correlation (PPMC), 177, 323
Penicillin, 34–35
discovery of, 27
Percentage
of all nonoverlapping data (PAND), 330
of data points exceeding the median, 330
of improvement, 337
of nonoverlapping data (PND), 330
Per-protocol analysis, 424
Personally significant, 333
Phenomena
biological, 40
controlling, 25
physical, 40
Philosophy
of dependent variables, 386–389
described, 382
empirical, 41
of handling methodological problems, 393–396
interplay of methodology and, 396–397
of measurement, 389–390
as methodology, 382–384
scholasticism, 40
science as, 40–41
determinism, 40–41
theology, 40
Phonemes, measured production of, 86–87
PHS d, 331
Physical phenomena, 40
Physiologists, 8
Piltdown man, 473
Pious fraud, 85
P.L. 93-348 (National Research Act of 1974), 107–108, 257, 480
P.L. 94-142 (Education for all Handicapped Children Act of 1977), 5–6
P.L. 101-476 (Individuals With Disabilities Education Act), 6
Placebo
control group, ethical issues with, 487–489
controlled randomized clinical trial, 230
described, 85–86
effect, 85–86, 211, 487
Plagiarism, 474

Planning, importance of, 37
A Plea for Freeing the History of Scientific Discoveries From Myth, 30
PND (Percentage of nonoverlapping data), 330
Pneumotachograph, 175
Population
    defined, 78, 202
    random sampling and, 256–257
Positive interaction, 232
Posttest, sensitization to treatment and, 210–211
Potential for contrast, baseline, 101
PPMC (Pearson Product Moment Correlation), 323
Practical problems, solving, 24–26
Practice effect, 251–252
Predictability, 175
    of group behavior, 368
Prediction, explanation and, 45
Pre-experimental designs
    group designs, 219–222
    single-subject design study, 275–276
Preferred Reporting Items for Systematic Review and Meta-Analyses, 421
Preferred treatment, 366–367
Presentations
    effect of, 10
    as source of research, 407
Pretests, 84
    sensitization to treatment and, 210–211
Prevalence, defined, 139
Privacy
    of participants, 484–485
    research participants, 484–485
Private curiosity, 22
Probability
    normal curve of, 312–314
    sampling, 78–80
        group design strategy and, 312
    theory, statistical analysis and, 312–314
    value, 320
Probes, described, 271
Problems, practical, solving, 24–26
Procedures, objective, 43–44
Proportional stratified sample, 79
Proposal, research, 419
ProQuest Dissertation and Theses Global, as source of research, 405

Prospective studies, 140–141
Psychological study, of individuals, 267–268
PsycInfo, 325
    as source of research, 405
Public Citizen, 480
Publication bias, described, 326
Publication Manual of the American Psychological Association, 414, 418
Publishing, research results, 33
PubMed, 325
    as source of research, 405
Punctuation, writing and, 437
Purposive sampling, 81–82

Q

Qualitative Primary, Qualitative Meta-Analytic, and Mixed Methods of Research, 421
Qualitative research, 146–150
    described, 153
    strengths/weaknesses of, 149–150
Quality
    indicators, visual analysis and, 326–327
    of life assessment, 335
Quantified observations, 158
Quantitative data, 62
Quantity
    dimensional, 158
    research, 149
Quasiexperimental designs, 219, 236–240
Questionnaire, validity of, 170
Questions
    relation between research types and, 151–152
    research, 362–369
        described, 402–403
        evaluating significance of, 410–411
        formulating, 402–413
        formulating specific, 408–409
        identifying classic, 407–408
Quetelet, Adolphe, 159, 313
Quota sampling, 80–81

R

Random
    assignment
        described, 81

of participants, 81–82
effects analysis, 325
sampling, 145, 203, 222
  clinical populations and, 256–257
  group design strategy and, 312
  nonequivalent control group design and, 236
  simple, 78
  SSED data and, 274, 304
  stratified, 79
selection, 81
Randomization
  blocks design, 232–234, 366
  described, 218, 314–315
  ethical concerns with, 489
  inferential statistics and, 314–316
  test, 329
Randomized clinical trials (RCTs), 140, 312
  autonomy of participants, 494–495
  described, 77–78
  ethics of randomization and, 489
  group treatment research, 77–87
    control/experimental groups, 87
    matching of participants, 83–84
    nonprobability sampling, 80–82
    probability sampling, 78–80
    random assignment of participants, 82–83
    random selection of participants, 77–78
    single or double blinding, 84–87
    treatment administration, 84
  informed consent and, 485–486
  N-of-1, 302–303
  no-treatment control group and, 486–487
  placebo
    control group, 487–489
    effect and, 86
  self-selection in, 107–109
  vs. single-subject treatment research, 106–113
Randomized factorial design, completely, 234–236
Rapid alternations, as control mechanism, 97–98
Ratio scale, 162
Rationalism, 41

RCI (Reliable change index), 336
RCTs (Randomized clinical trials), 312
  autonomy of participants, 494–495
  described, 77–78
  ethics of randomization and, 489
  group treatment research, 77–87
    control/experimental groups, 87
    matching of participants, 83–84
    nonprobability sampling, 80–82
    probability sampling, 78–80
    random assignment of participants, 82–83
    random selection of participants, 77–78
    single or double blinding, 84–87
    treatment administration, 84
  informed consent and, 485–486
  N-of-1, 302–303
  no-treatment control group and, 486–487
  placebo
    control group, 487–489
    effect and, 107–109
  self-selection in, 107–109
  vs. single-subject treatment research, 106–113
RDD (Regression discontinuity design), 239–240
Reaction time, 166
Reactive dependent variables, 394
Readership, knowledge of, 438
Reasoning
  deductive, 59–61
    communication disorders and, 61
  inductive, 58–59
Recruitment of participants, ethics of, 490–493
References, research papers and, 426–427
Regression discontinuity design (RDD), 239–240
Regression to the mean
  correlation by, 314
  internal validity and, 198–199
  pretest-posttest control, 225
  single/double binding and, 86
Reinstatement of treatment, 93–94
Relations
  controlling, 54
  between events, 391

Relative effects, 117, 228
  ABACA/ABABA design and, 291
  alternating treatments design and, 293
  carryover/contrast effects and, 295–296
  clinical trials and, 77
  control groups and, 229
  multigroup
    posttest only design, 230
    time-series designs and, 245
  nonequivalent control group design
    and, 236
  pretest-posttest designs and, 229
  simultaneous treatments design and,
    296–297
  two or more treatments, 12, 88, 97, 293,
    365
Reliability
  defined, 99, 175, 327
  failed replications and, 353
  interobserver, 176–178
  intraobserver, 176
  measurement of, 175–176
  of standardized tests, 178
  through multiple observations, 99
Reliable change index (RCI), 336
Repeated
  group, 243
  measures design, 246–247, 249
Replicated groups, 243
Replication, 63
  described, 344
  direct, 344–347
  failed, 353–355
  heterogeneous intersubject, 345
  homogeneous intersubject, 344
  intrasubject, 344
  systematic, 347–350, 354
    conditions necessary for, 350–351
  treatment research and, 69, 88–89
Replicative research, 403
Reports
  research, 30
    described, 418
    dissemination of findings, 496–497
    general format of, 418–419
    publishing, 33
  scientific, general format of, 418–419
Representative sample, 218

Reputational sampling, 81
Research
  applied, 138–142
    strengths/weaknesses of, 142
  appreciation of, 467–468
  basic, 11
  classification of, 113–119
  clinical, 138–142
    strengths/weaknesses of, 142
    usefulness of, 10–11
  concentrate on specific area, 408
  conducting, 28–34
    formal view of, 28–30
    formative view of, 30–34
  controlled, 69
    treatment, 116–118
  controlling phenomena and, 25
  deductive method of, 23
  described, 21
  dissemination of findings, 496–497
  empirical, article, 33
  epidemiological, 139–142
  ethics and, 472–497
    animal studies, 495–496
    autonomy of participants, 494–495
    fraud and, 472–476
    informed consent, 482–486
    participant privacy, 484–485
    placebo-control group, 487–489
    of randomization, 489
    recruitment of participants and,
      490–493
    risk-benefit ratio, 481–482
    treatment evaluation, 476–478
    treatment issues and, 485–492
  ethnographic, 147–148
  evaluation of, 4–5, 452, 453–463,
    467–468
    external revelance, 456–458
    internal consistency, 453–456
    outline, 458–463
  evidence-based practice and, 68
  ex post facto, 124–127
    procedures, 124–126
    strengths/weaknesses of, 126–127
  experimental, 133–138
    basic/applied, 135
    cause-effect relations and, 138, 223

clinical, 11, 139
   procedures, 134–135
   strengths/weaknesses of, 136–138
hypothesis, 54–57, 317
identifying area of, 403
inductive method of, 23
levels of evidence and, 463–467
   uncontrolled unreplicated, 465
limited by, 9–10
matching participants in clinical, 84
meta-analysis and, 325
methods, subject matters and, 380–381
mixed-methods, 150–151
   described, 153
   strengths/weaknesses of, 151
need for in-house, 8–9
nonexperimental, 140
normative, 127–131
   procedures, 128–129
   strengths/weaknesses of, 129–131
null hypotheses, 29
original, 403
participants in
   protecting, 479–481
   random selection of, 77–78
problems of, 10–13
professionals as consumers of, 450
qualitative, 146–150
   described, 153
   strengths/weaknesses of, 149–150
questions, 362–369
   identifying classic, 407–408
reasons for conducting, 21–28
   curiosity about natural phenomena,
      22–23
   demonstrate certain effects, 26–28
   explain events, 23–24
   solving inhouse problems, 24
   solving practical problems, 24–26
replicative, 403
reports, 30
   described, 418
   dissemination of findings, 496–497
   general format of, 418–419
   publishing, 33
   scientific, general format of, 418–419
results, publishing, 33
serendipity in, 34–37

single-subject, 76
   approach, multiple control conditions,
      87–106
topic of, 402
translational, 142–144
   described, 152
   strengths/weaknesses of, 142
treatment
   controlled directly replicated, 118
   controlled systematically replicated,
      118–119
   controlled unreplicated, 116–118
   uncontrolled directly replicated, 115
   uncontrolled systematically replicated,
      115–116
   uncontrolled unreplicated, 114–115
types and questions, 151–152
uncontrolled, 68–69
understanding of, 452–453
variables, 45–50
Research data
   statistical analysis of, 312–316
      probability theory and, 312–314
   statistically significant of, 316–317
Research designs
   described, 186–187
   framework of, 186–187
   research papers and, 423–424
   structure and logic of, 187–188
Research papers
   dissemination of findings, 496–497
   measures/measurement instruments,
      423
   strengths/weaknesses of, participants
      section, 423
   structure/content of, 419–427
      abstract, 420–421
      appendix to, 427
      discussion section, 425–426
      experimental manipulations section,
         424
      introduction, 421–422
      method of study section, 422–423
      references section, 426–427
      research design section, 423–424
      results section, 424–425
      title page, 420
      treatment section, 424

Research papers *(continued)*
  writing
    principles for good, 428–446
    without bias, 427–428
Research proposal, described, 419
Research questions
  described, 402–403
  evaluating significance of, 410–411
  formulating, 402–413
    specific, 408–409
Research reports
  described, 418
  evaluation outline, 458–463
  scientific, general format of, 418–419
Response
  class
    described, 208
    generality within and across, 208–209
  rate, without a trend, 99–100
Responses
  natural rates of, 98
  operant level of, 98
Retrospective studies, 140
Reversal of treatment, 91–93
  ethics of, 490
Review articles, as source of research, 406
Review articles, described, 418–419
Reviews
  described, 323
  narrative, 324
  systematic, 324
Revising, writing and, 447–448
Risk-benefit ratio, 481–482
Rosenthal effect, 207
Rotation experiments, 246–247
Rothamsted Experimental Station, 314–315
Routine treatments, treatment evaluations
    and, 478
Ruling-out extraneous variables, 75
Running head, 420

S

SAGE Research Methods, as source of
    research, 406
Sample
  in clinical trials, 78
  defined, 202

nonrepresentative, 145
random, 145
size, generality and, 351–353
surveys, 144–146, 152
  strengths/weaknesses of, 145–146
Sampling
  accidental, 80
  cluster, 79
  consecutive, 80
  convenience, 80
  equivalence
    of groups, 218
    random assignment and, 81
  interval, 79
  multistage, 79
  nonprobability, 80–82
  probability, 78–82
  purposive, 81–82
  quota, 80–81
  random, simple, 78
  reputational, 81
  self-selection, 80
  sequence, 168
  snowball, 81
  stratified
    proportional, 79
    random, 79
  systematic, 79
  time, 166–167
  verbal interaction, 168–169
Scales of measurement, 160–162
  durational, 164–165
  frequency, 163–164
  interval, 162
  nominal scale, 161
  ordinal scale, 161
  ratio, 162
Scholarly exchanges, as source of research,
    407
Scholarship, 383
Scholasticism, 40, 41, 383
Science
  as behavior, 41–43
  defined, 40
    as set of methods, 43–44
  described, 21
  as a philosophy, 40–41
    determinism, 40

empirical, 41
as a set of methods, 43–44
of speech and language, 384–386
ScienceDirect, as source of research, 405
Scientific
activity, outcome of, 44–45
curiosity, 22
data, 62
evidence, 61–62, 63
hypotheses, 55
laws
described, 61
theories and, 61–62
methods
need to study, 5–8
legal/social considerations, 5–6
observations, making, 172–173
orientation, of clinical professions
community, 6
reports, general format of, 418–419
Scientist, characteristics of, 42–43
Selection, random, 81
Self-editing, writing and, 448
Self-reports, indirect measures, 170–171
Self-selection
described, 80
in randomized clinical trials, 107–109
Seminars, as source of research, 407
Semmelweis, Ignaz, 35
Sensitization, to treatment, 210–211
Sentences
structure, writing, 429–430
writing, shifts within/between, 436–437
Separate sample pretest-posttest design, 238–239
Sequence sampling, 168
Sequential
confounding, 252
effects, 252
Serendipity, in research, 34–37
Settings, generality across, 207
Sheffé test, 319
Sidman avoidance, 36
Significance, parametric tests of, 318–321
Similes, writing and, 444
Simple random sampling, 78
Simultaneous multiple baselines, 99, 102, 104, 106

Single blinding, 84–87
Single-group time series designs, 240–245
Single-subject data
statistical analysis of, 328–333
visual analysis of, 326–328
Single-subject design study, 70, 76, 192–193
attrition and, 200
characteristics of, 270–274
clinical research in, 303–304
vs. clinical significance, 333–338
criterion design change, 289–290
disadvantages of, 371
effect size of, 329
experimental control in, 274–275
external validity and, 201
historical background of, 266–270
applied behavior analysis, 269–270
experimental analysis of behavior, 268–269
study of individual, 266–268
meta-analysis of, 332–333
multiple baseline designs (MBDs), 282–287
across behaviors, 282–285
across settings, 286–287
across subjects, 285–286
additional control in, 288–289
repeated baselines problem, 287–288
multiple treatment comparison, 290–299
ABACA/ABABA design and, 291–293
alternating treatments design and, 293–296
ineffective treatments in, 298–299
simultaneous treatments design and, 296–297
nonoverlap calculations for, 329–331
preexperimental, 275–276
research papers and, 426
small number of participants in, 270
statistical regression and, 199
treatment diffusion and, 200–201
treatment evaluation, 276–290
ABA reversal design, 278–279
ABA withdrawal design, 276–278
Single-subject strategy, 372

Single-subject treatment research
multiple control conditions, 87–106
baselines, 98–106
criterion-referenced change, 94–96
rapid alterations, 97–98
reinstatement of treatment, 93–94
replication of, 88–89
reversal of treatment, 91–93
withdrawal of treatment, 89–91
vs. randomized clinical trials, 106–113
Snowball sampling, 81
Social evaluation, 338
Social validity, 107, 202, 209–210, 334–335
Socially
significant, 333
valid, 333
Solomon four-group design, 226–228
Speech
behaviors, classifying behaviors of, 11
language pathologists, training models
for, 15
philosophy of science of, 384–386
sound disorders, 47
Spot checking, 167–168
Stability, 175
of measures, 99
Stable response rate, 99–100
Standard deviation, 318
Standard English, 428
Standard mean difference test, 331
Standard-group comparisons, 131–133
described, 152
procedures, 131–133
strengths/weaknesses of, 132–133
Standardized tests, reliability of, 178
Statistical (inferential) generality, 202–204,
213
Statistical analysis
correlational analysis and, 322–323
of data, 272–274
early concepts of, 314
of group design data, 318–323
historical introduction to, 312–316
hypothesis testing, 317–318
meta-analysis and, 324–326
of single-subject data, 328–333
statistical significance and, 316–317
systematic reviews of, 323–324

visual analysis and, guidelines for
conducting, 327–328
Statistical generality, 352
vs. clinical validity, 107
Statistical hypothesis, 56
Statistical regression, internal validity and,
198–199
Statistical significance, 71, 138, 209
vs. clinical significance, 333–338
correlational analysis and, 323
described, 395–396
of experimental data, 313
group design strategy and, 312
levels of evidence and, 464
Mann-Whitney U test and, 321–323
meta-analysis and, 326
nonparametric tests of, 321–322
of research data, 316–317
research reports evaluation and, 458
SSED data and, 333
statistical analysis and, 316–317
tests and, 319
Wilcoson rank-sum test and, 321–322
Statistic-group comparison, 219, 222
Statistics, variations of *d*, 331
Steady states. *See* Baselines
Stevens, S. S., 334
Strata, defined, 79
Strategies
design, advantages/disadvantages of,
369–371
investigative, 362–369
Stratified sampling
proportional, 79
random, 79
Stuttering, 47, 52
Style, writing and, 448
Subject
matters, research methods and, 380–381
mortality, internal validity and, 199–200
selection bias, internal validity and, 199
Surveys
purpose of, 144–145
sample, 144–146
described, 152
strengths/weaknesses of, 145–146
Switch-over designs, 246–247
Syllogism, described, 59

Symposia, as source of research, 407
Systematic
  documentation, 73
  observation, of research designs, 187
  replication, 347–350, 354
    conditions necessary for, 350–351
  reviews, 324
    of statistical analysis, 323–324
  sampling, 79
  variance, 190
Systematically manipulated, 62

T

t ratio, 318–319
t test, 318–319
Tau, 330–331
Technical language, specifying variables
    in, 409–410
Technology, described, 24
Testing, internal validity and, 196–197
Theology, 40
Theoretical article, described, 419
Theory
  defined, 57
  grounded, 147, 148
  hypotheses and, 57–58
  of probability, 313
  scientific laws and, 61–62
Theory-based treatment, 476
Thesaurus of ERTIC Descriptors, 325
Thesaurus of Psychological Index Terms,
    325
Thesaurus of Sociological Indexing, 325
Theses, 419
  preparation of, 413–414
Third-party payment, 6
The Three Princes of Serendip, 34
Time
  measures
    interresponse, 165–166
    momentary, 167–168
    sampling, 166–167
  sampling, 166–167
  series designs, 240–246
    single-group, 240–245
Title page, 420
Topic of research, 402

Training
  models
    problems associated with, 13–16
    for speech-language pathologists, 15
  observer, 172
  programs, 11
Translational research, 142–144
  described, 152
  strengths/weaknesses of, 144
Treatment
  administration, randomized clinical trials
      and, 84
  by-levels, 231
  clinical significance and, 70–71
  clinically significant effects, 70–71
  components of, interaction between, 366
  consequences of, 69–74
    generalized, 71–72
    improvement, 69–70
  diffusion, internal validity and, 200–201
  effectiveness of, 365–366
    across individuals, 368–369
  effects of, 70
    magnitude of, 320
    research papers and, 426
    size, 320
  efficacy vs. effectiveness, 73–74
  ethical issues with research and,
      485–492
  evaluations
    controlled, 140
    ethical justified, 477–478
    ethics and, 476–478
    necessity of, 477
    routine treatments and, 478
    single-subject design study, 276–290
  fidelity, 425
  improvement and, 364–365
  interference of multiple, 211–212
  maintained consequences of, 71–72
  modification sources, 353–355
  multiple, evaluation designs, 228–231
  optimal level of, 367–368
  outcomes, 72–73
  package, 367
  preferred, 366–367
  pretest/posttest sensitization to, 210–211
  reinstatement of, 93–94

Treatment *(continued)*
  research, 13
    classification of, 113–119
    controlled directly replicated, 118
    controlled systematically replicated,
      118–119
    controlled unreplicated, 116–118
    described, 68–69
    empirical conditions, 74–77
    goals of, 68
    logical constraints, 74–77
    in medicine vs. communication
      disorders, 111–113
    replications and, 69
    single-subject approach, multiple
      control conditions, 87–106
    uncontrolled directly replicated, 115
    uncontrolled systematically replicated,
      115–116
    uncontrolled unreplicated, 114–115
  reversal of, 91–93
    ethics of, 490
  techniques, independent variables and,
    48
  variables, participant variables and,
    366
  withdrawal
    ethics of, 490
    single-subject research and, 89–91
Trends
  of data, 327
  identifying current, 403–406
    study journal articles, 404
    with databases, 404–405
  response rate without a, 99–100
True experimental designs, 219
  group designs, 223–228
Tukey test, 319
Tuskegee Syphilis Study, 479–480
Two-way
  analysis of variance, 319
  chi-square test, 321
  factorial design, 233

U

Uncontrolled
  data, 63

directly replicated evidence, 465
    treatment research, 115
  group designs, 219
  research, 68–69
    systematically replicated treatment,
      115–116
    unreplicated treatment, 114–115
  systematically replicated evidence,
    466
  unreplicated evidence, 465
Unit-by-unit agreement ratio, 176
University College, London, 314

V

Vaganotic measurements, 159
Validity, 385
  clinical, 202, 209–210, 214
  experimental
    across settings, 207
    operations, 194
    research, 194–201
  external, 114, 201–210, 213, 214
    across ethnocultural groups,
      206–207
    across experimenters, 207–208
    across individuals, 204–209
    across response classes, 208–209
    described, 63, 201
    factors affecting, 210–212
    logical, 204–209
  internal, 75, 106–107, 213, 312
    attrition and, 199–200
    cause-effect relations and, 194
    instrumentation and, 197–198
    maturation (participants') and,
      195–196
    participants' history and, 195
    statistical regression and, 198–199
    subject selection bias and, 199
    testing and, 196–197
    treatment diffusion and, 200–201
  measured values, 194
  social, 107, 202, 209–210, 334–335
  statistical, vs. clinical validity, 107
Variability, 188–-192
  extrinsic, 190–192, 213
  intersubject, 393–394

intrinsic, 189–190, 213
of measured values, 327–328
Variables, 45–50
  active, 48
  assigned, 48–49, 366
  controlling, 192–193
  defined, 46
  dependent, 13, 46–47, 76, 362–363
    distribution of, 363
    integrity of, 394–395
    magnitude of change in, 395–396
    philosophy of, 386–389
    reconceptualization of, 395
  differential distribution of, 363
  extraneous, 75–77
  independent, 47–48
    cause-effect relations and, 47, 391, 395
    described, 76–77
    effects of, 364
    locus of, 390–393
    manipulation as, 54
  interactive, 187–188
  intervening, 49–50
  natural science and, 383
  neurophysiological, 51
  reactive dependent, 394
  in technical language, 409–410
Variance
  analysis of, 202, 316, 319
    main effects in, 234
  error, 190
  extraneous, 190
  systematic, 190
Verbal interaction, 168
  sampling, 168–169
Verbs
  use of, 430–431
  writing and, 430–431
Vienna General Hospital, 35
Visual
  analysis
    described, 326
    guidelines for conducting, 327–328
    of single-subject data, 326–328
  inspection, of data, 272–274
VIT (Voice initiation time), 166
Voice, 46

Voice initiation time (VIT), 166
Voice termination time (VTT), 166
Volunteer bias, 494
VTT (Voice termination time), 166

W

What Works Clearinghouse, 327
Wilcoson rank-sum test, statistically significant and, 321–322
Wilcoxon matched-pair signed-rank test, 322, 323
Withdrawal of treatment
  ethics of, 490
  single-subject research and, 89–91
Within-subjects designs, 246–247
Wordiness, 439
Workshops
  effect of, 10
  as source of research, 407
World Medical Association, 479, 487
Writing
  abstract words and, 444–445
  adequate, 441–442
  agreement between elements, 431–434
  clear, 442–445
  clichés and, 443–444
  coherent, 445–446
  colloquial expressions and, 444
  concise, 438–441
  concrete words and, 444–445
  euphemisms and, 442–443
  figures of speech and, 445
  formats and, 447–448
  jargon and, 443
  knowledge of the readership, 438
  metaphors and, 444
  paragraphs and, 446
  parallel forms, 435–436
  principles for good, 428–446
    conceptual considerations, 437–446
    structural principles, 428–437
  punctuation and, 437
  research papers, structure/content of, 419–427
  revising and, 447–448
  self-editing and, 448
  sentence structure, 429–430

Writing *(continued)*
sentences, shifts within/between, 436–437
similes and, 444
style, 446–447, 448
use of modifiers in, 434–435
verbs and, 430–431

without bias, 427–428
Wundt, Wilhelm, 267

Y

Young formula, 178